MAKING UZBEKISTAN

MAKING UZBEKISTAN

Nation, Empire, and Revolution
in the Early USSR

Adeeb Khalid

CORNELL UNIVERSITY PRESS   ITHACA AND LONDON

Cornell University Press gratefully acknowledges receipt of a subvention from the Office of the Dean of the College and the Jane and Raphael Bernstein Chair in Asian Studies at Carleton College, which assisted in the publication of this book.

First published 2015 by Cornell University Press
First paperback printing 2019

Library of Congress Cataloging-in-Publication Data

Khalid, Adeeb, author.
   Making Uzbekistan : nation, empire, and revolution in the early USSR /
Adeeb Khalid.
      pages cm
      Includes bibliographical references and
      index. ISBN 978-0-8014-5409-7 (cloth)
      ISBN 978-1-5017-3585-1 (pbk.)
   1. Uzbekistan—History—1917–1991. 2. Asia, Central—History—Revolution,
1917–1921. I. Title.
   DK948.85.K47   2015
      958.708'41—dc23   2015023300

For Haroun and Leila
—with all my love

Contents

Maps

Acknowledgments

In the decade and a half that this book has taken to research, I have accumulated many, many debts to people and institutions. I acquired that most precious commodity, time away from teaching, thanks to support from the National Endowment for the Humanities, the American Councils for International Education, the American Council of Learned Societies, the Carnegie Corporation of New York, and the John Simon Guggenheim Foundation. A Distinguished Visiting Scholar award from the John W. Kluge Center for Scholars at the Library of Congress provided six idyllic months of work in 2010–11. The book has taken longer to complete than I had led the granting agencies to believe it would. I thank them all for their patience and hope that the final product has been worth the wait.

I thank the Poullada family for the invitation to present the Leon B. Poullada Memorial Lecture Series at Princeton University in October 2010. Those lectures allowed me to think through the overall structure of the book. A brief *séjour de recherches* at the Fondation des Sciences de l'Homme in Paris in June 2010 enabled fruitful interaction with French colleagues and allowed me to work with the papers of Mustafa Cho'qoy. I am also grateful for comments and questions from the numerous audiences that have listened to presentations of material from this project. No presentation was more fruitful than the one I gave to the Berkeley Russian history *kruzhok* in March 2012. Comments from participants helped break a logjam in my thoughts and set me on the path to the final draft of this book.

Some material in chapter 4 originally appeared in "Central Asia between the Ottoman and the Soviet Worlds," *Kritika* 12, no. 2 (2011): 451–76. Chapter 12 includes material that first appeared in Russian in "Rozhdenie natsii," *Neprikos-novennyi zapas*, no. 78 (2011): 34–46.

Over the years, I have benefitted immensely from help, encouragement, advice, and support offered by many friends and colleagues. I am particularly grateful to those who shared precious and hard-to-get source materials with me. Shoshana Keller gave me her notes from the Communist Party archives in Tashkent, where she was able to work in 1991–92 and which have remained closed to foreign scholars ever since. All citations marked "AAP RUz" in chapter 11 are thanks to her. That chapter would look very different without her gift. Stéphane Dudoi-gnon, in addition to thought-provoking conversations and wonderful hospitality all along, also gave me a digitized copy of the complete set of *Shu'la-yi inqilāb*, the Persian-language journal from Samarqand. The kindnesses Sherali *aka* Turdiyev extended to me in Tashkent included providing copies of two typescripts that Laziz Azizzoda wrote "for the drawer" in his retirement. It is my great sorrow that Sherali *aka* did not live to see the completion of this book. Rinat Shigabdi-nov, Elyor Turaqulov (Musabaev), and Ergash *aka* Umarov provided help and multiple kindnesses in Uzbekistan. Akram Khabibullaev has been a friend and a guide throughout the project and helped me in numerous ways. Bruce Grant went above and beyond the call of friendship and read a penultimate draft of the whole manuscript. Shahzad Bashir listened to incessant monologues about this project and gave sage advice all the way through. This book would have been the poorer without the help and support of Sergei Abashin, Laura Adams, Mounira Azzout, Bakhtyar Babadjanov, Michael David-Fox, Cloé Drieu, Adrienne Edgar, Gero Fedtke, Vincent Fourniau, Vladimir Genis, Numanjon Ghafarov, Fran Hirsch, Peter Holquist, Marianne Kamp, Emin Lelić, Terry Martin, Chris Mur-phy, Doug Northrop, Madeleine Reeves, Jeff Sahadeo, Paolo Sartori, Paul Stron-ski, Barno *opa* Umarova, Franz Wennberg, and Tomohiko Uyama. Volker Adam, Mayhill Fowler, and Artemy Kalinovsky provided bibliographical help and copies of important materials. Colleagues at Carleton College aided and abetted me in various ways for long years; special thanks go to Scott Carpenter (who gave insightful comments on a chapter), Susannah Ottaway, and David Tompkins.

Roger Haydon shepherded the manuscript through review and production with great felicity. It was a great pleasure to work with him to turn this seem-ingly never-ending project into a book. Not the least of Roger's achievement was finding excellent readers for the manuscript, whose comments were immensely helpful in finalizing the argument. Bill Nelson drew the fine maps for this book. Susan Barnett, Karen Laun, and Emily Powers made the production process a joy to experience.

Carleton College has been a great place to work all these years. A large faculty development grant in 2000–2001 made the initial foray into the archives possible. Since then, the college has been very generous in granting leaves and supporting research travel. I am delighted to acknowledge the contribution of the Jane and Raphael Bernstein Chair in Asian Studies and History to my research. The Institute of History of the Uzbekistan Academy of Sciences hosted me in 2000–2001, and IFEAC, the French Institute of Central Asian Studies, provided a wonderfully collegial environment. I would also like to express my gratitude to the staffs of the institutions where I did the bulk my research: the Central State Archives of Uzbekistan, the Rare Books Section of the Alisher Navoiy National Library of Uzbekistan and the Beruni Institute of Oriental Studies in Tashkent; the State Archive of the Russian Federation, Russian State Archive for Sociopolitical History, and the Russian State Library in Moscow; the Library of Congress in Washington, DC; the British Library in London; and Atatürk Kitaplığı in Istanbul. The Slavic Reference Service at the University of Illinois at Urbana-Champaign provided answers to numerous questions with great effect. Many thanks also to the interlibrary loan staff at the Laurence McKinley Gould Library at Carleton College and to Brad Schaffner, the College Librarian, for their help.

The greatest debts are owed, of course, to those who suffered the most from this project, namely my immediate family. Leila was not even born when I embarked on this book, so she has never known her father not to be preoccupied with it. She is quite happy that the end is in sight. Haroun bore the rigors of silly apartment no. 4 with good grace and has come of age with this book. I am relieved that I have finished it before he finishes university. Cheryl has been the lodestar of my life since we met. Without her love and support, none of this would have taken place. My debt to her cannot be expressed in words.

Technical Note

Nomenclature

This book explores a period when ethnic and national designations and self-ascriptions were in great flux. I have tried to use, to the extent possible, the nomenclature of the period itself rather than projecting current designations back into time. Until 1917, the most common designation for the population discussed here was "Muslims of Turkestan." The adjective "Muslim" in this book pertains to the population. It does *not* indicate a particular commitment to Islamic propriety or politics. The Muslim intellectuals discussed in this book took positions that stretched from the reform of Islam to its rejection. I also use, interchangeably, the terms *indigenous* and *native* to describe the Muslim population that I discuss. The "natives" were counterpoised, most often, to "Europeans," the settlers who arrived in the wake of the Russian conquest. They were predominantly Russians (until 1917 the term included those we would call Ukrainians now), but they also included Poles, Germans, Ashkenazi Jews, and members of other nationalities from the European part of the empire. In everyday practice, these newcomers (*prishlye*) found much in common with each other and distinguished themselves clearly from the natives. I have used "Europeans" to describe the newcomers as a whole, although I also use "Russian" as a rough synonym in places. This usage is a useful reminder that "Europe" and "Europeans" are not eternally fixed signifiers, but that their meaning shifts over time and place.

Central Asia was the meeting place of two linguistic traditions, the Turkic and the Persian. Turkic was counterpoised to Persian but internally differentiated into a number of dialects that had become distinct languages by the early twentieth century. The term *Uzbek* was in common use for the contemporary literary Turkic language of Transoxiana before the revolution, and I use it so. On the contrary, as I show in chapter 9, the term *Tajik* was never used before 1924 for the Persian language spoken in Central Asia, which was referred to as Persian (*fārsī*). This is the term I use for the period before the creation of Tajikistan. Until 1925, the Russian term *Kirgiz* denoted peoples who called themselves Kazakh and Kyrgyz. Depending on the context, I have translated *Kirgiz* either as "Kazakh and Kyrgyz" or as "Kazakh." Thus the first Kazakh autonomous republic created in 1920 was called Kirgizskaia respublika (or Kirrespublika). I have translated that name as the Kazakh Republic.

For an excellent overview of the political and administrative structure of the Soviet Union in the 1920s, see Stephen Kotkin, *Magnetic Mountain: Stalinism as a Civilization* (Berkeley, 1995), xix–xxiii. Turkestan (and Uzbekistan until 1926) had a four-level administrative hierarchy that descended from oblast, through *uezd* and *volost*, to the village. The regionalization (*raionirovanie*) of 1926 brought in a three-level administrative structure consisting of *okrug*, *raion*, and village.

The Russian Empire used the Julian calendar. One of the modernizing reforms of the Bolsheviks was a switch to the Gregorian calendar on 1 February 1918. I have avoided using a double dating system and cited dates according to the calendar in use at the time of a given event or publication. For dates in early 1918, I have indicated the use of the Julian calendar by adding "o.s." (old style) in parentheses after the date.

All web sites cited in the notes were current as of 1 January 2015.

Transliteration

Turkic languages appear in the notes according to their current orthographies. I have transliterated languages written in Cyrillic (Tatar and Kazakh) and used contemporary Latin orthographies for Turkish and the few citations in Azeri. Uzbek, the language of a large portion of the sources used in this book, has been written in at least six different orthographies in three different scripts in the twentieth century. Since this is a book on history, not philology, I have used a single system for transliterating all titles, regardless of the script of the original. Although the bulk of contemporary Uzbek publishing continues in Cyrillic, a standard Latin alphabet is also in widespread use. I have used this alphabet to transliterate all Uzbek names and titles in this book (including those that were published in the Latin script used between 1928 and 1940), with the singular exception of the term *boy* (wealthy), which I have rendered as *bai* in order to avoid visual confusion with the English word of the same spelling. For Persian (and "Tajik") written in the Arabic script, I have used the *International Journal of Middle East Studies* system of transliteration, but have transliterated later Tajik texts from the Cyrillic. For Russian, I have used the Library of Congress transliteration without the diacritics, and have Anglicized a few commonly used terms by removing the terminal soft sign (for instance, for oblast or volost).

Names and Places

Surnames had just begun to appear in Central Asia in the period discussed here and not all individuals used them. Many authors were known by their pen names. I have referred to individuals as they were best known at the time (thus Munavvar qori, not Abdurashidxon o'g'li; Cho'lpon, not Sulaymon; but Behbudiy, not Mahmudxo'ja). In the 1920s, authors commonly used pseudonyms (sometimes for reasons of safety, sometimes not) or initials to sign their work. I have used the names as they appear in the byline of the work cited but added the author's name in brackets where it could be ascertained. Indispensable in this regard was a key to pseudonyms of the period published by the poet Oltoy Bois Qoriyev in his old age. Oltoy, a participant in the literary life of the 1920s, was arrested in 1930 and spent many years in the Gulag before resuming literary work in the 1960s. See Bois Qoriyev, "Adabiy taxalluslar haqida," *O'zbek tili va adabiyoti*, 1967, no. 1: 51–58. Authors' names in footnotes are transliterated according to the rules of the language of the work cited. In my own voice, however, I invariably spell names according to the rules of the language a given person identified with.

Place names all over the former Soviet Union have changed multiple times over the course of the twentieth century. I have used the names that were current in the period discussed here. Where Russian forms of place names differed from their native versions (Alma Ata for Almaty, for example), I have consistently used the local forms transliterated from local languages, and not through the Russian (thus Khujand, not Khodzhent).

Abbreviations

AAP RUz Arkhiv Apparata Prezidenta Respubliki Uzbekistan
GAFO   Gosudarstvennyi arkhiv Ferganskoi oblasti
GAgT   Gosudarstvennyi arkhiv goroda Tashkent
GARF   Gosudarstvennyi arkhiv Rossiiskoi Federatsii
GASO   Gosudarstvennyi arkhiv Samarkandskoi oblasti
IOR   India Office Records
O'zFAShI O'zbekiston Fanlar Akademiyasi Sharqshunoslik Instituti
RGASPI   Rossiiskoi gosudarstvennyi arkhiv sotsial'no-politisheskoi istorii
TNA   The National Archives (UK)
TsGARUz Tsentral'nyi Gosudarstvennyi arkhiv Respubliki Uzbekistan
f.   fond (collection)
op.   opis' (register)
d.   delo (file)
l., ll. list, listy (folio)
ob.   obratnoe (obverse)
o.s.   old style (to denote use of the Julian calendar in 1918)

MAKING UZBEKISTAN

Introduction

This book tells the story of the emergence of Uzbekistan in the turbulent era of the Russian revolution. In the decade and a half after the fall of Russian autocracy in 1917, traumatic upheavals—war, economic collapse, famine—transformed local society and brought new groups to positions of power and authority in Central Asia, just as the new revolutionary state began to create new institutions that redefined the nature of power in the region. Upheaval also produced hope and ambition, as local actors seized the opportunity presented by the revolution to reshape their society. The intertwined passions of nation and revolution reconfigured the imaginations of Central Asia's intellectuals and the political landscape of the region. The energies unleashed by the revolution also made possible the golden age of modern Uzbek literature: the modern Uzbek literary language as we know it today took shape in the period. The novel appeared as did a self-consciously modern poetics and a vibrant theater. This was the period when giant literary figures—Fitrat, Qodiriy, Cho'lpon—produced their finest work.

The creation of Uzbekistan was the triumph of a national project of Central Asian Muslim intellectuals who had come to see themselves as Uzbeks. The formation of that republic was, I argue, the fulfillment in contingent Soviet conditions of a national project that long predated the Russian revolution. The intelligentsia came to have a deep fascination with the idea of revolution as modality of change, for only revolution could deliver the nation from its backwardness. The national project therefore did not defend a pristine traditional culture but sought to revolutionize it. The revolts against convention and tradition with their

1

iconoclastic fervor defined the new culture that emerged in this period. The decade of the 1920s was one of a cultural revolution driven by the energies and passions of the Uzbek intelligentsia. The intelligentsia found much common ground with the Soviets, but ultimately, the logics of the two projects were different, as were the requirements of state power. Ultimately, the Uzbek intelligentsia, both the prerevolutionary cohort as well as the first Soviet generation of it, perished at the hands of the Soviet state. But the Uzbekistan that had emerged in 1924 was in many ways the lasting legacy of the prerevolutionary intelligentsia. More fundamentally, it was the triumph of the idea of the nation as the most logical, if not self-evident, form of political organization, both a prerequisite for and a guarantor of modernity. This idea wreaked havoc on existing notions of loyalty and solidarity, though it did not completely erase them. It also led to the disaggregation of Central Asia's sedentary Muslim population into the distinct nations of the Uzbeks and the Tajiks. This book explores the processes through which this disaggregation took place.

Uzbek intellectuals did not have the stage to themselves, however. The Bolsheviks had their own program of remaking the world. The emergence of Uzbekistan took place at the intersection of two competing projects of modernity that nevertheless shared a great deal. Both projects launched often merciless attack on traditional society during this decade, but little of it can be understood as the straightforward imposition of the Soviet regime. The revolution of 1917 had energized groups in local society to transform their own society. They seized on the opportunities presented by the revolution and the new revolutionary regime to implement, by force if necessary, their desiderata of reform. I conceive the history of this period as a struggle between two competing visions of modernity, those of Bolshevism and of Jadidism, an indigenous movement of modernist reform.[1] The Bolsheviks were motivated by a vision, utopian and brutal at the same time, of remaking the world, overcoming "backwardness" where necessary, and dragging all peoples to the brilliant future of communism. Jadidism's vision was Muslim and nationalist. After 1917, radicalized by frustration with opposition from within local society, Jadidism became fascinated by revolution as a means for bringing about the change its proponents fervently desired. If the nation did not recognize its own good, then it had to be dragged into the modern world, kicking and screaming if necessary. For different reasons both favored a cultural revolution, which included mass education, land reform, women's liberation, and perhaps paradoxically for the Bolsheviks, the creation of national identities. Yet the logics underlying the two visions were different, and

---

1. Adeeb Khalid, *The Politics of Muslim Cultural Reform: Jadidism in Central Asia* (Berkeley, 1998).

the relationship between them was always fraught. A central concern of the book is to trace the tension and contention between the two projects. This contention took place in institutions being created by the Soviet regime. For much of the 1920s, central control was tenuous enough to allow non-Bolsheviks the leeway necessary to make such contention possible.

The contention between these two visions of modernity coexisted with intense struggles within Central Asian society. Jadidism was radicalized as much by opposition from within its own society as by opposition from without (of which there was plenty). The Jadids' claim to leadership in 1917 was resisted by established elites in society; this resistance, and the need to defeat it, was what drove the Jadids to ever more radical positions, and it was opposition to their vision from their own society that underwrote the many revolts of the era. Exploring struggles within Central Asian society is a central concern of this book. The contest I describe is thus not between united indigenous society and a Bolshevik regime intent on transforming it, but between a number of actors, differently positioned, both indigenous and foreign, who struggled over the nature of the transformation and over the meanings to be attached to them. The consequences, both intended and unintended, of this contest shaped Central Asia in crucial ways.

A New History of Central Asia

The scholarly intervention I am most interested in is in the history of modern Central Asia. The opening of the archives and unprecedented access to the region for foreigners since the twilight years of the Soviet Union have transformed the historiography of the region. In addition, the passing of the Cold War has allowed scholars to ask new questions and to use new comparative and conceptual frameworks. We have very fine studies of the period of the revolution that have thoroughly discredited the Soviet narrative of the revolution. Instead of the March of History being marshaled by an omniscient and ubiquitous party, we see the contingency of the moment and its colonial context, not historical regularity (*zakonomernost'*). Marco Buttino and Jeff Sahadeo foreground ethnic conflict between Russian settlers and the indigenous population as the main feature of the years immediately following the collapse of the autocracy.[2] Vladimir Genis focuses on the foibles of various Russian figures, who with their varying degrees

---

2. Marco Buttino, *La Rivoluzione Capovolta: L'Asia centrale tra il crollo dell'impero Zarista e la formazione dell'URSS* (Naples, 2003); Jeff Sahadeo, *Russian Colonial Society in Tashkent, 1865–1923* (Bloomington, 2007); A. Khalid, "Turkestan v 1917–1922 godakh: bor'ba za vlast' na okraine Rossii," in *Tragediia velikoi derzhavy: natsional'nyi vopros i raspad Sovetskogo Soiuza* (Moscow, 2005), 189–226.

of conceit are engaged in what can only be called "revolutionary adventurism."[3] Other scholars have explored the workings of Soviet nationality policy in Central Asia, and as a result we have excellent studies of the making of Turkmenistan,[4] Kyrgyzstan,[5] and Tajikistan,[6] and of the national-territorial delimitation of Central Asia that created the current political boundaries in the region (see below). Yet others have fruitfully deployed insights from postcolonial studies to investigate Central Asia's relationship to the Soviet state.[7] We also have a number of studies of selected aspects and episodes of the history of the period, from antireligious campaigns,[8] through film,[9] to a major study of unveiling and new conceptions of women.[10]

The historiography produced in Uzbekistan itself remains, sadly, its own field with its own imperatives. The Soviet narrative has been replaced by a national one, even as methodological and institutional continuities with the Soviet past remain strong, as does the role of the state as sponsor of the work of historians. The result is often the inversion rather than the subversion or outright abandonment of Soviet categories. In Uzbekistan, the early Soviet period has come to be seen as the source of Uzbek national statehood, a period in which a national liberation movement was violently defeated by the forces of "Soviet colonialism."[11] Not surprisingly, this literature tends to underplay conflict within Muslim society.[12] The Jadids play a central role in this narrative as

---

3. V.L. Genis, "*S Bukharoi nado konchat'...*": *k istorii butaforskikh revoliutsii* (Moscow, 2001), and *Vitse-konsul Vvedenskii: Sluzhba v Persii i Bukharskom khanstve (1906–1920 gg.). Rossiiskaia diplomatiia v sud'bakh* (Moscow, 2003).

4. Adrienne Edgar, *Tribal Nation: The Making of Soviet Turkmenistan* (Princeton, 2004).

5. Benjamin Loring, "Building Socialism in Kyrgyzstan: Nation-Making, Rural Development, and Social Change, 1921–1932" (Ph.D. diss., Brandeis University, 2008). Ali İğmen, *Speaking Soviet with an Accent: Culture and Power in Kyrgyzstan* (Pittsburgh, 2012) provides a fine study of culture making in Kyrgyzstan, but it pays scant attention to the 1920s.

6. Paul Bergne, *The Birth of Tajikistan: National Identity and the Origins of the Republic* (London, 2007).

7. Douglas T. Northrop, *Veiled Empire: Gender and Power in Stalinist Central Asia* (Ithaca, 2004); Paula Michaels, *Curative Powers: Medicine and Empire in Stalin's Central Asia* (Pittsburgh, 2003); Cassandra Cavanaugh, "Backwardness and Biology: Medicine and Power in Russian and Soviet Central Asia, 1868–1934" (Ph.D. diss., Columbia University, 2001).

8. Shoshana Keller, *To Moscow, not Mecca: The Soviet Campaign against Islam in Central Asia, 1917–1941* (Westport, CT, 2001).

9. Cloé Drieu, *Fictions nationales: Cinéma, empire et nation en Ouzbékistan (1919–1937)* (Paris, 2013).

10. Marianne Kamp, *The New Woman in Uzbekistan: Islam, Modernity, and Unveiling under Communism* (Seattle, 2007).

11. See *Turkestan v nachale XX veka: K istorii istokov natsional'noi nezavisimosti* (Tashkent, 2000), and *O'zbekistonning yangi tarixi*, 3 vols. (Tashkent, 2000–2001).

12. In addition to the works cited above, see Saidakbar Agzamkhodzhaev, *Istoriia turkestanskoi avtonomii (Turkiston muxtoriyati)* (Tashkent, 2006) for this tendency.

the spiritual fathers of the nations and its martyrs. Their works have been put back into print in the Cyrillic script and select Uzbek scholars have been able to use party and secret police archives (usually closed to researchers) to produce a small corpus of biographies or biographical notices. Still, no comprehensive overview of Jadidism or the political history of the 1920s has yet seen the light of day.[13]

For all the new work that has appeared, large gaps still remain in our understanding of the early Soviet period in Central Asia and the making of Uzbekistan and Uzbekness. Of the Western scholars discussed here, only Marianne Kamp and Adrienne Edgar make substantial use of materials in Central Asian languages and place Central Asians at the center of their attention (as opposed to being concerned about the workings of the Soviet state or the Communist Party). Furthermore, we know very little about the "Turkestan period," that is, the years between the revolution and the national delimitation. Most scholars have treated this period only glancingly, as background to other concerns, but there is no connected account of these crucial years.[14] Bukhara in this period is still less known.[15] These gaps mean that we know far less about Uzbekistan and its origins than we do about the other countries of Central Asia. This is a surprising situation, for it is fair to say that the history of Uzbekistan is in some sense the history of all of Central Asia. Uzbekistan was the key Central Asian republic, heir to the Jadids' prerevolutionary concept of the "Turkestani Muslim" nation and home to most of the sedentary Muslims of Central Asia (and all of the region's major cities). It was also the center of political power in the region. The other republics were all defined against Uzbekistan, none more so than Tajikistan.

This book attempts to fill these gaps by providing the first connected account of the history of the sedentary societies of Central Asia in the immediate aftermath of the Russian revolution. It combines macrolevel questions about the nature of Central Asia's transformation with microlevel reconstruction of

---

13. The study of Jadidism and the Jadids was pioneered in the Gorbachev years by Begali Qosimov, Naim Karimov, and Sherali Turdiyev, all of them specialists in literature. Historians were late to arrive on the scene, and to this day philologists dominate the field. The following broader works are worth mentioning: D. A. Alimova, ed., *Jadidchilik: islohot, yangilanish, mustaqillik va taraqqiyot uchun kurash* (Tashkent, 1999); Begali Qosimov, *Milliy uyg'onish* (Tashkent, 2002); Naim Karimov, *XX asr adabiyoti manzaralari* (Tashkent, 2008).

14. The early work by Alexander J. Park, *Bolshevism in Turkestan, 1917–1927* (New York, 1957), was heroic in its attempt to squeeze a meaningful narrative out of the available documentation. It remains the only work explicitly devoted to that decade in Turkestan.

15. The new, post-Soviet literature has barely touched the Bukharan People's Republic. The prearchival works of Hélène Carrère d'Encausse, *Réforme et révolution chez les Musulmans de l'empire russe*, 2nd ed. (1966; reprint Paris, 1981); and Seymour Becker, *Russia's Protectorates in Central Asia: Bukhara and Khiva, 1865–1924* (Cambridge, MA, 1968) still remain unsurpassed.

historical detail that has long been obfuscated or misunderstood. It traces the emergence of the idea of Uzbekness among Muslim intellectuals and the creation of Uzbekistan during the national delimitation of Central Asia in 1924. Its focus is squarely on the prerevolutionary intelligentsia of Turkestan and Bukhara and their passage through the tumultuous years of the Russian revolution and the establishment of Soviet rule. In doing so, the book offers a new explanation of the ways in which Uzbekness was imagined and Uzbekistan realized.

Nation, Progress, and Civilization in an Age of Revolution

The revolution radicalized Jadidism and broadened its horizons, but it did not create it. Rather, the project had its roots in the aspirations of a nascent intelligentsia that had emerged in the cities of Central Asia in the decades following the Russian conquest of the 1860s and 1870s. Seeking answers to their society's predicament, the Jadids, as the proponents of Jadidism are known in the literature, had been seized by a passion for progress (*taraqqiy*) and civilization (*madaniyat*) well before the revolution. The Jadids tied their advocacy of progress and civilization to a reform of Islam. An aggressively modernist interpretation of Islam allowed the Jadids to argue that "true" Islam enjoined Muslims to seek progress and that, conversely, only progress and civilization would allow Muslims to really know Islam. Political strictures ensured, however, that the reform project remained solely within the realm of culture and directed at Central Asian society itself. The thoroughgoing critique of cultural practices and the claim to leadership implicit in it created considerable opposition from established elites that did not share this diagnosis of the ills of their society, but the reformist project and its vocabulary had become a feature of urban life in Central Asia by 1917. This vision of change was rooted in Muslim discourses of modernity that animated intellectuals across the Muslim world at the turn of the twentieth century. Progress and civilization were also intimately connected to the nation. As a node of solidarity that would supersede notions of identity and belonging based on the dynasty, lineage, or locality, the nation (*millat*) was crucial to the intelligentsia's quest for modernity. It also laid the basis for new claims to leadership in society and inaugurated a new politics within it. It was this project that was energized and radicalized by the revolution. Little about the passions and enthusiasms of the Jadids is understood if we ignore the burdens of the prerevolutionary past.

For the Jadids, the Russian revolution was the chance to put their program in action; it was not synonymous with Bolshevism. For them, the locus of the revolution was the nation, not class. Discourses of the nation had arrived in Central Asia by the turn of the twentieth century and had made the nation seem to be a prerequisite of modernity. Now, in 1917, the moment seemed to have come for the nation to take its place in the sun. The failure to seize the opportunity to act, wrote a Jadid teacher, "will be an enormous crime, a betrayal of not just ourselves, but of all Muslims."[16] However, in the open politics of 1917, they discovered that they could not convert their enthusiasm for change into political influence or votes. The nation, it turned out, did not care for their vision of change. The result was not a retreat into moderation but further radicalization. The Russian revolution and the broader geopolitical transformation of the world in its aftermath further convinced them of the futility of exhortation and gradualism as modalities of change.

Enthusiasm alone was not enough, of course. The intense state-building undertaken by the Bolsheviks provided a channel for that enthusiasm and rendered it real. Curiously for devoted materialists, the Bolsheviks too construed backwardness in cultural as much as in economic terms. For Stalin, writing in 1919 as people's commissar for nationalities affairs, the most important tasks of Soviet power in "the East" were "to raise the cultural level of [its] backward peoples, to build a broad system of schools and educational institutions, and to conduct . . . Soviet agitation, oral and printed, in the language that is native to and understood by the surrounding laboring population."[17] This was precisely the desire of the indigenous intelligentsia as well. This substantial overlap between the two visions of modernity produced both collaboration and contention. The new regime that the Bolsheviks began to put in place mobilized the population and created institutions that immensely increased the reach of the state into society. Indigenous intellectuals had a significant role in the process. They flocked to the new institutions being created by the Bolsheviks, who wanted interlocutors in local society who would, at the very least, conduct "Soviet agitation . . . in the language understood by the surrounding laboring population," but also help them govern these distant peripheries of Soviet territory. Yet there was no straight path from Jadidism to Communism.[18] Many Jadids joined the party in the first years of the revolution (1918–20); some never did, and others were expelled once the center asserted better control over the region. Those actors who entered public life after 1920 did so primarily through the party and often had a different generational identity, so that conflict between different "generations" of Uzbek

16. Muallim M.H., "Bukun qondoy kun?" *Kengash* (Kokand), 15.04.1917, 12.

17. I.V. Stalin, "Nashi zadachi na Vostoke," *Pravda*, 02.03.1919.

18. I myself had suggested such a transition in earlier work (Khalid, *Politics*, 287–301). This book complicates the picture.

intellectuals was a key feature of the period studied here. Ultimately, a new cohort of self-consciously Soviet intellectuals emerged and did much to oust the pre-revolutionary intelligentsia from public life.

Between Empire and Revolution

The Russian revolution was also a postcolonial moment. Tsarist Russia was a particularist empire that took difference for granted.[19] In few places was the distance between the indigenous population and the state greater than in Central Asia, the last major territorial acquisition of the empire. Bukhara and Khiva were protectorates and technically not part of the Russian Empire. Turkestan was governed under its own statute that defined the place of its inhabitants in the imperial order. Its native Muslim population were Russian subjects but retained Islamic courts for personal law and for commercial disputes not involving non-Muslims. They were not subject to military conscription, were not incorporated into the empirewide system of ranks and standings (*sosloviia i sostoianiia*), and were marked by their confessional status as Muslims. After the 1905 revolution, Turkestan was briefly granted (unequal) representation in the State Duma, but that was quickly revoked under Petr Stolypin's electoral reform of 1907. Locally, a two-tier system of administration took shape, in which the lowest level of administration continued to be staffed by local functionaries who worked in local languages. More broadly, the difference between "natives" and "Europeans" was inscribed into the habitus of everyday life and into space. The vast majority of Europeans lived in the "new" cities that emerged alongside existing urban centers or in European-only villages in the countryside. Central Asia had a dual society in which natives and Europeans lived side by side without interacting a great deal.[20]

This colonial difference was destroyed by the February revolution. The Provisional Government declared all subjects of the Russian Empire to be free and equal citizens, regardless of sex, religion, or ethnicity, and gave all an equal right to vote. But it was the Bolsheviks, with their relentlessly universalist project of social revolution, who set out to reintegrate Central Asia into the Russian state on a new basis. Their promise of autonomy within a universalist dispensation was the greatest part of their appeal to the non-Russian peoples of the former

---

19. Jane Burbank, "The Rights of Difference: Law and Citizenship in the Russian Empire," in *Imperial Formations*, ed. Ann Stoler, Carole McGranahan, and Peter Perdue (Santa Fe, NM, 2007), 77–111. Jane Burbank and Frederick Cooper, *Empires in World History: Power and the Politics of Difference* (Princeton, 2010), see the maintenance of difference as a key feature of empires.

20. See Khalid, *Politics*, chap. 2, for a more extended discussion of Turkestan's status in the empire.

Russian Empire. The Jadids before 1917 had hoped to overcome this difference and sought inclusion in the imperial mainstream. The promise of equality and autonomy attracted them to the new order. Yet they understood the revolution in their own way, as a modality of radical change in the service of the nation. They had little use for the language of class espoused by the Bolsheviks. The pursuit of national revolution would displace established elites and replace them with a new leadership, but it did not mean full-scale social revolution along class lines. For the Jadids, the revolution was not synonymous with Bolshevism, but rather an era of opportunity that began in February 1917. This was to lead to perpetual tension between the Jadids and the Bolsheviks, but the promise of equalization was a powerful one.

That promise was not always fulfilled. The Europeans in Central Asia, peasant settlers and urbanites alike, refused to shed their privileges and share power, resources, and jobs with the natives. Central authorities initially intervened quiet forcefully against the settlers (see chapter 3), but ultimately realized that Europeans were the main pillars of its support in Central Asia and that it could not afford to alienate them. Also, Soviet ambitions always outran resources at hand in the decades under review here. In the early 1920s, the need to reestablish state control and to institute mechanisms of revenue extraction tended to override the commitment to radical redistribution. By the end of the 1920s, this failure of the promise of equalization led to disenchantment not just among the prerevolutionary Jadids, but also among Muslim Communists, many of whom wondered out loud about "Red colonialism."

Colonialism indeed lies at the center of debate in the post-Soviet historiography of Central Asia. Many scholars have seen the Soviet Union as little different from other modern empires. In the words of Douglas Northrop, who has made the case most eloquently, "The USSR, like its Tsarist predecessor, was a colonial empire. Power in the Soviet Union was expressed across lines of hierarchy and difference that created at least theoretically distinct centers (metropoles) and peripheries (colonies). . . . [While] it may not have been a classic overseas empire like that of the British or Dutch, the USSR did have a somewhat comparable political, economic, and military structure; a parallel cultural agenda; and similarly liminal colonial elites."[21] However, as I have argued elsewhere, the comparison with other colonial empires of the twentieth century does not work.

---

21. Northrop, *Veiled Empire*, 22. For other interventions in this debate, see Laura Adams, "Modernity, Postcolonialism, and Theatrical Form in Uzbekistan," *Slavic Review* 64 (2005): 333–354; Drieu, *Fictions nationales*; and Benjamin Loring, "'Colonizers with Party Cards': Soviet Internal Colonialism in Central Asia, 1917–39," *Kritika* 15 (2014): 77–102, who makes a nuanced argument based on economic, not cultural, policy.

The Soviet Union's cultural agenda—mass education in indigenous languages, fighting illiteracy, public health, political mobilization—had more in common with those of the mobilizational states of the interwar era, while its attempts to engineer society—land reform, organization of marginal groups in society, reshaping the body social—have no parallels in the colonial empires of the era.[22] And yet the gap between ambition and achievement remained wide, and indeed, as stated above, the Soviet state made its peace with the settler population. It could not completely vanquish the habitus of empire. Central Asia in the decades under review hung between empire and revolution.

At the same time, I show that Soviet policies changed much about Central Asia, as did the violence and destruction of the years of revolution and civil war. Central Asia was a very different place in 1931 than it had been in 1917. I do not disagree with recent scholarship that argues that the Soviet state in the 1930s was weak and therefore had to resort to violence,[23] but in Central Asia, that violence destroyed alternatives. Collectivization and the expansion of cotton tied Central Asia, and Uzbekistan in particular, to the Soviet economy; the closing of the borders cut Central Asia off from the rest of the world, while the silencing of the prerevolutionary intelligentsia transformed the parameters of public discourse. Uzbekistan was on its way to becoming Soviet.

Muslim Intellectuals in Their Society

My main focus in this book is on those Muslim actors in Central Asia who shared an orientation to the future and who were at home with the ideas of progress and civilization. These modernist intellectuals were not a homogenous group. The Jadids, who had championed the new (i.e., the phonetic) method of teaching the Arabic alphabet and a whole lot of other things that came with that, had legitimated their project through an aggressively modernist interpretation of Islam. They described themselves as *ziyoli* ("enlightened"), *taraqqiyparvar* ("proponents of progress"), or simply *yoshlar* ("the youth"). After the revolution, their ranks were joined by a new cohort of activists who entered public life through party or Soviet institutions with no previous involvement in Muslim cultural reform. Those who joined the party and achieved high office in it (from October

---

22. Adeeb Khalid, "Backwardness and the Quest for Civilization: Early Soviet Central Asia in Comparative Perspective," *Slavic Review* 65 (2006): 231–251.

23. Jan Gross, *Revolution from Abroad: The Soviet Conquest of Poland's Western Ukraine and Western Belorussia* (Princeton, 1988); Lynne Viola, *The Unknown Gulag: The Lost World of Stalin's Special Settlements* (New York, 2007).

1921 on, the Communist Party of Turkestan was headed by Central Asians) had a different trajectory and a different sensibility toward the project of transforming society. A later cohort of a self-consciously Soviet intelligentsia that appeared in the middle years of the 1920s was more radical still and deeply critical of their elders. Factional struggles and intergenerational conflicts were a defining feature of the period under review here and figure large in the narrative below. Nevertheless, all cohorts shared a distance from traditionalist conservatives in their society who anchored their own authority in the past and its traditions, whose inheritors they claimed to be. In the contentious cultural politics of the period, the intelligentsia and the conservatives squared off time and time again.

In focusing on modern intellectuals, I go against recent trends in the study of the Muslim communities of the Russian Empire. Muslim intellectuals have been in bad odor with Western scholars of the Russian Empire and the USSR. The historiographical return of the Tsarist Empire has put the focus on how the empire operated rather than how it collapsed. As a result, historians of Russia have become suspicious of narratives, spun by intellectuals, of the empire's oppressiveness, and begun to look for non-elite perspectives. For Robert Crews, insight into Muslim life in the Russian Empire comes from the petitions "ordinary Muslims" wrote to the state and the correspondence between the Muslim spiritual assembly and state authorities.[24] From a different position on the scholarly map, specialists in Islamic studies also join in the suspicion of modernist intellectuals, although for them the "real" insight into Muslim society is to be gained from documents produced by Muslim jurists and ulama in a Muslim space allowed by the Tsarist and (briefly) the Soviet regimes. For one of them, concern with modernist intellectuals is "*jadīd*ophilia," a "perennial bane of contemporary studies of Islam in Central Asia." The Jadids were "a tiny minority in their societies, shaped ... by the impact of Russian rule," who used "new media afforded them by the colonial power."[25] For another, insight into Muslim society and its dynamics can be gleaned only from authentically Islamic sources, such as *waqf* documents, records of *qazi* courts, and legal disputations among the ulama—elite discourses, but properly authentic ones.[26] Modernist intellectuals are creatures of colonialism and (therefore?) unworthy of scholarly inquiry.

---

24. Robert Crews, *For Prophet and Tsar: Islam and Empire in Russia and Central Asia* (Cambridge, MA, 2006). Dealing with the Soviet period, Douglas Northrop (*Veiled Empire*, passim) dismisses "a relative handful" of intellectuals (as well as Communists and women activists) from his account of the *hujum*, the campaign against the veil, to present a picture of a conflict that pitted "Uzbeks" against "foreign Bolsheviks."

25. Devin DeWeese, review of *Islam after Communism: Religion and Politics in Central Asia*, by Adeeb Khalid, *Journal of Islamic Studies* 19 (2008): 137–138.

26. See the manifesto-like piece by Paolo Sartori, "Towards a History of the Muslims' Soviet Union: A View from Central Asia," *Die Welt des Islams* 50 (2010): 315–334.

This refusal to accord attention to modernist intellectuals renders Central Asian society synonymous with its "tradition" and flattens its contours. It deprives us of any understanding of debate or contention within that society and makes it easier to see (in the case of the Soviet period) the history of the region as a straightforward encounter between two clearly defined, distinct, and homogenous entities, "Central Asia" and the "Soviet regime." Moreover, to dismiss modernist intellectuals because they treacherously used "new media afforded them by the colonial power" is also to refuse all comprehension of how culture is produced and reproduced under colonialism, how, indeed, newness comes into this world. At root in all these critiques, ultimately, is a hankering for authenticity. Modernist urban intellectuals are dismissed from consideration because they were not just numerically unrepresentative but also because they adopted inauthentic cultural positions. In this book, I argue for the impossibility of authenticity. Rather, I see cultures as historically contingent, contested, and constantly emergent. It is precisely through the appropriation of new media and new technologies of culture that traditions are contested and reshaped. Nor, for that matter, can we take conservatives who argue in terms of "tradition" at face value, for they too were as much products of history as those who rejected "tradition."[27] The established elites of Turkestan and the emir of Bukhara were created by the Russian conquest. The modernist intelligentsia, for its part, was less directly influenced by imperial models than its counterparts in other colonial situations. Its cultural moorings were in discourses of Muslim modernism that captured the imaginations of intellectuals across the Muslim world at the turn of the twentieth century. Many of its models of change came from the Ottoman Empire or from other Muslim communities of the Russian Empire, most notably the Tatars, where contentious debates over culture and identity raged in the decades before 1917. But more important, a disinclination to take modernist intellectuals seriously prevents any serious understanding of internal dynamics of Muslim societies.

I do not claim that the modernists that I study were the embodiment or the sole voice of their society. Rather, I bring to the center of our attention the enormous amount of contention within Central Asian society in this period, which in turn forces us to abandon the dichotomy of "Muslim society" and "foreign Bolsheviks." War, famine, and insurgency ripped society apart, widening cracks that had already existed before 1917. We simply cannot speak of a single "Uzbek Muslim society" that responded to outside pressures. Rather, we need to locate

---

27. My sense of cultural change is rooted in a Bourdieusien sociology of knowledge and culture that destabilizes "rules" and focuses instead on strategies. As in much of my work, I am influenced here by Pierre Bourdieu, *The Logic of Practice*, trans. Richard Nice (Stanford, CA, 1990), and *Language and Symbolic Power*, trans. Gino Raymond and Matthew Adamson (Cambridge, MA, 1991).

different actors and examine how they mobilized resources, both symbolic and material, to achieve their goals.

Nation Making and National Projects in the Soviet Union

Few episodes in Central Asian history have been more prone to mythmaking than the so-called national-territorial delimitation of 1924 that led to the creation of ethno-territorial republics in place of the old entities of Turkestan, Bukhara, and Khiva. It is all too easy to see the process as a classic case of divide and conquer. Indeed, this judgment remains unshakably in place in Western accounts of the region and has proved immune to all evidence to the contrary.[28] This is in complete contrast to current historiography in Central Asia itself, which takes the existence of nations as axiomatic and sees in early Soviet policies a historically "normal" process of nationalization.[29] Central Asian scholars who criticize the process do so for the "mistakes," deliberate or otherwise, that gave lands belonging to one nation to another, but do not see it as a fraudulent enterprise.[30] Indeed, archivally grounded research has clearly shown that the delimitation was part of a pan-Soviet process of creating ethnically homogenous territorial entities; that local cadres played a central role in the debates over the delimitation; and that the Soviets saw the main problem in Central Asia to be its political fragmentation, rather than some overwhelming unity that

---

28. The divide-and-conquer argument is grist for the mill of general writing on Central Asia, but it persists even in the specialized literature. The generalizations are depressing. "The potential for political solidarity among Soviet Muslims was attacked by a deliberate policy of divide and rule," writes Malise Ruthven. "Central Asian states of today owe their territorial existence to Stalin. He responded to the threat of pan-Turkish [sic!] and pan-Islamic nationalism by parceling out the territories of Russian Turkestan into the five republics" (Ruthven, *Historical Atlas of Islam* [Cambridge, MA, 2004], 103). Ahmed Rashid, *Jihad: The Rise of Militant Islam in Central Asia* (New Haven, 2002), 88, opines that Stalin drew "arbitrary boundary divisions" and "created republics that had little geographic or ethnic rationale." Philip Shishkin one-ups Rashid when he writes, "Soviet dictator Joseph Stalin ... drew borders that sliced up ethnic groups and made it harder for them to mount any coherent challenge to Soviet rule. If you look at a map of the Ferghana Valley, ... the feverish lines dividing states zigzag wildly, resembling a cardiogram of a rapidly racing heart"! Shishkin, *Restless Valley: Revolution, Murder, and Intrigue in the Heart of Central Asia* (New Haven, 2013), 238.

29. To be sure, there are differences between the historiographies of the different countries today. Kyrgyz historians see the delimitation as the moment of the birth of the statehood of their nation. There is likewise no animus against the process among historians in Kazakhstan and Turkmenistan.

30. See, for example, Arslan Koichiev, *Natsional'no-territorial'noe razmezhevanie v Ferganskoi doline (1924–1927 gg.)* (Bishkek, 2001). Tajik scholars express grievances about the manner in which the delimitation robbed "the Tajik people" of their historic territory, but their animus is directed against "pan-Turkists" rather than against the Soviet state. I discuss this matter in chapter 9.

needed to be broken.[31] More generally, our understanding of Soviet nationalities policy—the assumptions behind it and the forms of its implementation—has been transformed over the last two decades. We now know that the Soviets took nations to be ontological givens and considered it a political imperative to accord administrative and national boundaries.[32] More sophisticated accounts of Central Asia's delimitation have emphasized the importance of classificatory projects of ethnographers and the Soviet state.[33] No account of the delimitation, however, has paid adequate attention to the role of Central Asia's indigenous elites in the process or placed the delimitation in context of the rise of national movements in the region. As a result, even the new work on Soviet nationalities policy has little to say about the motivation of indigenous elites. Its heroes are Soviet policymakers and ethnographers who implement a pan-Soviet policy in Central Asia. As implementers of a policy of scientific categorization, they appear in a more positive light than Stalin simply drawing lines on the map, yet they still overshadow indigenous elites, who remain largely invisible in the new literature.[34] In this book, I suggest a different genealogy of the emergence of the nations of Central Asia.

"Chaghatayism" and the Making of Uzbekistan

Uzbekistan emerged during the process of the national-territorial delimitation of Central Asia in 1924, yet it was not a product of the party or the Soviet state. Rather, as I show in chapter 8, it was the victory, in Soviet conditions, of a

---

31. The most notable work is by Arne Haugen, *The Establishment of National Republics in Soviet Central Asia* (London, 2003); see also the excellent account of the creation of Turkmenistan in Edgar, *Tribal Nation*, chap. 2; and the thoughtful appraisal of the process in Madeleine Reeves, *Border Work: Spatial Lives of the State in Rural Central Asia* (Ithaca, 2014), chap. 2

32. The major landmarks in the literature on nation making in the USSR are Ronald Grigor Suny, *The Revenge of the Past: Nationalism, Revolution, and the Collapse of the Soviet Union* (Stanford, 1993); Yuri Slezkine, "The USSR as a Communal Apartment, or How a Socialist State Promoted Ethnic Particularism," *Slavic Review* 53 (1994): 414–452; Terry Martin, *The Affirmative Action Empire: Nations and Nationalism in the Soviet Union, 1923–1939* (Ithaca: Cornell University Press, 2001); Ronald Grigor Suny and Terry Martin, eds., *A State of Nations: Empire and Nation-Making in the Age of Lenin and Stalin* (New York, 2001); and Francine Hirsch, *Empire of Nations: Ethnographic Knowledge and the Making of the Soviet Union* (Ithaca, 2005).

33. Juliette Cadiot, *Le laboratoire impérial: Russie-URSS 1860–1940* (Paris, 2007); S. N. Abashin, *Natsionalizmy v Srednei Azii: v poiskakh identichnosti* (St. Petersburg, 2007); Svetlana Gorshenina, *Asie centrale: L'invention des frontières et l'héritage russo-soviétique* (Paris, 2012); and Hirsch, *Empire of Nations*.

34. The one exception is Adrienne Edgar who in her fine book, *Tribal Nation*, sees Turkmen Communists as real actors in the making of their republic. Nevertheless, to the extent that there was no prerevolutionary intelligentsia among the Turkmens, the scope of the ambitions of the Turkmen national Communists was more strictly defined by the experience of Soviet rule than was the case in Uzbekistan.

national project of the Muslim intelligentsia of Central Asia. Muslim intellectuals, not Soviet ethnographers or party functionaries, were the true authors of Uzbekistan and the Uzbek nation.

The idea of the nation had arrived in Central Asia well before the revolution, but it was the revolution, with its boundless promise of opportunity, that planted the nation firmly at the center of the intelligentsia's passions. The revolution also reshaped the way the nation was imagined. As I have shown elsewhere in detail, before 1917 the Jadids generally saw the nation as encompassing "the Muslims of Turkestan," a territorially limited confessional nation.[35] The revolution saw a rapid ethnicization of the Jadids' political imagination, as they came to be fascinated by the idea of Turkism. A Turkestan-centered Turkism (quite distinct from "pan-Turkism" that was a constant bugbear of Soviet and Western historiography) saw the entire sedentary population of Central Asia as Uzbek. They claimed the entire tradition of Islamicate statehood and high culture in Central Asia on behalf of the Uzbek nation. The rule of the Timurids was the golden age of this nation, when a high culture flourished in the eastern Turkic Chaghatay language. I use the term *Chaghatayism* to describe this vision of the Uzbek nation.[36] The Jadids reimagined the "Muslims of Turkestan" as Uzbek, and Chaghatay language, modernized and purified of foreign words, as the Uzbek language. The Uzbek nation thus imagined has rather little to do with the Uzbek nomads under Shaybani Khan who ousted the Timurids from Transoxiana, because it claimed the mantle of the Timurids themselves.

The era of the revolution provided a number of opportunities—all eventually aborted—for realizing a Central Asian national project, from the autonomous government of Turkestan proclaimed at Kokand in November 1917 (chapter 2 below), through the renaming of Turkestan as the Turkic Soviet Republic in January 1920 (chapter 3), to the attempt at creating a national republic in Bukhara (chapter 4). The Chaghatayist idea lurked behind all those projects, but it was the national delimitation of 1924 that provided the clearest opportunity of uniting the sedentary Muslim population of Turkestan into a single political entity. The book traces this process of reimagination and the unexpected realization of this project in 1924.

The success of the Chaghatayist project also defined the way in which the Tajiks were imagined. As I show in chapter 9, most Persian-speaking intellectuals in Central Asia were also invested in the Chaghatayist project, even as the denial of the Persianate heritage of Central Asia was foundational to it. In the absence of any mobilization on behalf of a Tajik nation, the Chaghatayist project prevailed

---

35. Khalid, *Politics*, chap. 6.

36. The term was used in the 1920s in a pejorative sense by critics of the idea. Despite this baggage, I find the term quite apt for describing the fundamental claims of the Uzbek national idea as developed by the Jadids.

during the national delimitation. "Tajik" came to be defined as a residual category comprising the most rural, isolated, and unassimilable population of eastern Bukhara. It was only after the creation of Tajikistan that some Tajik-speaking intellectuals began to defect from the Chaghatayist project and a new Tajik intelligentsia began pressing for Tajik language rights and a larger national republic. The delimitation froze the identity politics of the early 1920s in time. The current shape of Tajikistan can only be understood in the context of the triumph of the Chaghatayist project in 1924.

Clearly, Central Asia of the 1920s has much to tell us about nations and nation making in general. In discussing these issues, I eschew the term *nationalism*, which I find too broad and laden with too many pejorative connotations to be of much analytical use. For the Bolsheviks and their political police, "nationalism" was a negative force that worked in the interests of the counterrevolutionary bourgeoisie. Accusations of nationalism were fatal to many of the figures encountered in this book. Much of that suspicion has remained and nationalism carries the connotations of chauvinism in the languages of the post-Soviet space. I prefer to make finer distinctions within the phenomenon of nationalism. I am interested in the national project of Central Asian intellectuals that emerged from their fascination with the nation and in their struggles for its realization. Those struggles took place within the putative nation as much as externally. The national project aimed to "awaken" the nation to consciousness, to make it think of itself as a nation—in short, to nationalize it. To this end, the national project also sought to reshape the putative nation, to educate it, to make it healthy, to rearrange family life. All national movements, it is safe to say, operate within a matrix of authenticity and modernity. The nation has to change to become modern, to acquire the tools of progress that would lead to self-strengthening and lead the nation to claim its place in the world. At the same time, that change is justified as the reclamation of a past greatness that overcomes the corruption of the present. In this book, I trace the ways in which the nation was articulated by the intelligentsia.[37] The story I tell is one of striving for the nation, not of its full realization (if such a thing is ever possible). There is no doubt that in the period covered by this book, the putative nation remained largely indifferent to the national project, or rather, beyond its reach, but that fact does not render the project of creating the nation any the less relevant or worthy of study.

If, as Partha Chatterjee has argued, the national movement has to declare the sovereignty of nationalism in native society before engaging the colonial state in a political struggle for independence, then that struggle had not been resolved in

---

37. I find particularly pertinent the work gathered in Ronald Grigor Suny and Michael D. Kennedy, eds., *Intellectuals and the Articulation of the Nation* (Ann Arbor, MI, 1999).

Central Asia by 1917.[38] Indeed, most national movements have to battle on two fronts, against the external foe (the colonizer) and against opposition in their own society, where the idea of the primacy of the nation has to triumph. Often the struggle against forces in their own society is more crucial. This was certainly the case in Central Asia. In 1917, the Jadids sought—and failed—to convince their society of the need to organize along national lines and to cede the leadership to them. In fact, the revolution appeared so attractive to the Jadids as a modality of change precisely because of their weakness in their own society. They found it difficult, however, to put Soviet institutions to their own use. Whether it was on the question of schooling or the position of women, on the place of Islam in society or the direction of the new literature, the Bolsheviks and Muslim intellectuals had different visions. For much of the first decade of Soviet rule, the party remained unable to control the personnel in its own ranks and in the institutions it built. Once it was more confident of its hold over the region, by 1926, it opened a so-called "ideological front" with the goal of stamping its authority on its institutions and assuring the ideological purity of their mission. The prerevolutionary intelligentsia began to be squeezed out. The first purge of the national intelligentsia in 1929–30, I argue, was a landmark in the exclusion of the intelligentsia from the political process, and the end of an era. The intelligentsia never became a state elite capable of nationalizing society in a way that, say, Atatürk or Reza Shah or any number of Central European regimes of the interwar period did. This peculiar location of the national intelligentsia was a specifically Soviet aspect of the Uzbek national project.

At the same time, we see the significance of the political arena in gaining recognition for a nation. Just who constitutes a nation and who remains a mere group is always a matter of recognition. An Uzbek nation emerged because there was a movement for it that pursued the project in the politically relevant venues (here, the various organs of the Soviet state). Similarly, Kyrgyz and Qaraqalpaq autonomous republics emerged because of advocacy by dedicated cadres. The Tajik case was different. Conversely, had there been a national movement on behalf of a Sart or a Qipchaq nation, the map of Central Asia would look different today. In the Soviet context—but not only in the Soviet context—gaining recognition for the existence of a nation was more important than the creation of a broad-based popular national movement; it preceded the creation of a national consciousness among members of the nation. Once a nation has been recognized and territorialized, then it could begin to blossom. It acquired state structures, a newly codified and formalized "national" language, a host of national symbols, a national historiography, all sorts of common practices of being national—all built in accordance with Soviet nationalities policies and with the resources of the Soviet state.

---

38. Partha Chatterjee, *The Nation and its Fragments* (Princeton, 1992).

And yet, the role of the Soviet state is easy to exaggerate. Scholars have rightly pointed to Soviet policies of cultural development that fought illiteracy, spread schooling in indigenous languages, and helped create new institutions for the production of culture as fundamental features of the cultural landscape that emerged in the young Soviet state.[39] This scholarship is a necessary corrective to older views that focused only on Soviet repression of non-Russian nationalities and saw the nationalities policy as a thin veil for Russification. A number of very fine works have traced the emergence of national identities in the early Soviet period as a result of Soviet nationalities policies.[40] But since much of this new scholarship focuses primarily on policy as it was debated and formulated at the center, it runs the risk of exaggerating the role of the Soviet state and rendering it more benevolent that it perhaps was. I examine Soviet nationalities policy from the vantage point of its ostensible beneficiaries. The new culture was not a creation of the Soviet state, let alone its gift to benighted peoples (as Soviet historiography asserted and contemporary Russian scholarship continues to insist). It emerged through a complex interplay between the new revolutionary state and indigenous cultural elites, which had their own understanding of what revolution and Soviet power were about. Indigenous elites were often disappointed in what they could achieve in practice, while bringing them in line (or eliminating them from the public sphere) was a basic preoccupation of the Soviet regime and its organs of political control. Soviet cultural policies were productive and destructive at the same time. The massacre of the indigenous intelligentsia with which this book closes cannot be separated from the achievements of Soviet nation and culture building.

Cultural Revolution

The idea of the nation lay at the heart of a cultural radicalism that swept the Central Asian intelligentsia in the era of the Russian revolution. The cause of the nation led the Jadids to ever more radical stances in the years after 1917. The nation had to be enlightened and modernized and internal reaction defeated. What was required was nothing short of a revolution of the mind, of instilling

---

39. The most thorough account of these policies is in Martin, *The Affirmative Action Empire*.

40. See, for instance, Edgar, *Tribal Nation*; Bruce Grant, *In the Soviet House of Culture: A Century of Perestroikas* (Princeton, 1995); İğmen, *Speaking Soviet with an Accent*; George O. Liber, *Soviet Nationality Policy, Urban Growth, and Identity Change in the Ukrainian SSR, 1923–1934* (Cambridge, 1992); Loring, "Building Socialism in Kyrgyzstan"; Brigid O'Keeffe, *New Soviet Gypsies: Nationality, Performance, and Selfhood in the Early Soviet Union* (Toronto, 2013); Yuri Slezkine, *Arctic Mirrors: Russia and the Small Peoples of the North* (Ithaca, 1994); David Shneer, *Yiddish and the Creation of Soviet Jewish Culture, 1918–1930* (Cambridge, 2004); Anna Shternshis, *Soviet and Kosher: Jewish Popular Culture in the Soviet Union, 1923–1939* (Bloomington, 2006).

among the population new ways of thinking and of seeing the world. A new culture had to rise from the ashes of the old. The cultural life of the decade after the revolution was marked by a series of revolts—against the authority of established elites in society, against the epistemological order that underpinned it, against rules of social behavior, against the conventions of the Turko-Persian literary tradition, and against Islam itself. This cultural radicalism of the period is seldom appreciated, for its evidence lies not in archival documents but in the cultural production of the period.

That production, for all its significance to modern Uzbek culture, has not received the attention it deserves. In Uzbekistan itself, its study has always been hamstrung by political considerations. The main figures of the period were all discovered to be enemies of the people and opponents of Soviet power by 1937. Although most were "rehabilitated" politically (the criminal charges against them dismissed), few were returned to their rightful place in the literary history of the republic until the very last years of the Soviet period. Most Soviet-era literary history continued to tiptoe around the complexities of the 1920s and to ignore the central place of the giants of the decade. Since the demise of the USSR, there has been a tendency to go to the other extreme, to turn the literary figures of the 1920s into national heroes, the moral and cultural leaders of the Uzbek nation. Such a posture also evades serious reckoning of their revolts against convention and of their mutual conflicts. For their part, Western scholars have all too often seen this literature only as a vehicle for political protest against Soviet rule and read it only as Aesopian fables of criticism and resistance.[41] They have been so busy reading between the lines for coded political messages that they have often missed what the lines in fact say. Often literary scholars do not appreciate the highly charged atmosphere of the era and the intense conflicts that existed within Central Asian society and mistake criticisms of Central Asian society (a fundamental trait of Jadidism since the moment of its emergence) for criticisms of the Soviet order. This insistence on reading critique directed solely outward at the "colonizer" is unwarranted when one is dealing with a time of immense internal turmoil. Indeed, the focus on decoding alleged political messages has even precluded the study of the technical aspects of the literature of the period, of its formal and morphological novelties.[42]

---

41. Edward Allworth, *Uzbek Literary Politics* (The Hague, 1964), and *Evading Reality: The Devices of 'Abdalrauf Fitrat, Modern Central Asian Reformist* (Leiden, 2002).

42. There are exceptions, of course, but they prove the rule by their paucity; see Christopher Murphy, "The Relationship of Abdulla Qodiriy's Historical Novels to the Earlier Uzbek Literary Traditions (A Comparison of Narrative Structures)" (Ph.D. diss., University of Washington, 1980); and Sigrid Kleinmichel, *Aufbruch aus orientalischen Dichtungstraditionen: Studien zur usbekischen Dramatik und Prosa zwischen 1910 und 1934* (Wiesbaden, 1993).

All of which is a shame, because the decade of the 1920s is when modern Uzbek literature took off. It was the decade when the novel made its first appearance, drama flourished, and new styles of poetry transformed the conventions hallowed by the ages. It is not too much to say that the 1920s saw a true cultural revolution in Central Asia, which forms the basis for modern Central Asian culture to this day. This cultural revolution is a central concern of this book.

It should be clear that I use the term *cultural revolution* in quite a different meaning than the English language historiography of the USSR, which following the usage coined by Sheila Fitzpatrick, uses the term for a very specific campaign by the party to seize control of cultural and scientific institutions between 1929 and 1932.[43] What I have in mind was not a "revolution from above," but a bout of creativity from below that resulted from the enthusiasms unleashed by the revolution. The new cultural field created by the Soviets was a mixed blessing. It created institutions (a relatively stable press, a publishing industry, institutions that supported historical or ethnographic research) that could support cultural production as a professional (and remunerative) enterprise, but it also brought new obligations and new means of control. In fact, as we shall see, Soviet cultural institutions barely existed before 1924 and much cultural production took place outside of or parallel with Soviet institutions. Chig'atoy Gurungi (Chaghatay Conversation), the literary circle that organized the first conference on language and orthographic reform in 1921, had no formal connection to the state, nor did the benevolent societies that sent students abroad in 1922 and 1923, or the Friends of New Life (see chapter 6). All of these organizations were shut down by the state.

The cultural production of 1920s provides an excellent window into the radicalism of the period. I introduce a number of texts not studied before. I place them in the longer term trajectories of various currents of modernism that crisscrossed the Muslim world in the decades preceding the revolution. Until 1917, Russian models were largely irrelevant to Central Asian literary production; it was only in the mid-1920s that Russian literary and cultural influences became significant in Central Asian cultural life. I take seriously what the texts themselves say. I insist on reading their criticisms of local society, its customs and traditions, and of the conservative opponents of reform literally as criticisms, rather than as coded protest against the Russians or the Soviet order. In my translations, I err on the side of literalness in an effort to convey the sense of the text. Likewise,

---

43. Sheila Fitzpatrick, "Cultural Revolution in Russia 1928–32," *Journal of Contemporary History* 9 (1974): 33–52, and "Cultural Revolution as Class War," in *Cultural Revolution in Russia, 1928–1931*, ed. Sheila Fitzpatrick (Bloomington, 1978), 8–40.

I make no claims of having produced poetic translations of the poetry that I quote. In many cases, where the poetic structure is completely lost in translation, I have provided the original text as well.

This radicalism extended to Islam itself. While we have a good sense of the Soviet campaigns against Islam,[44] we know much less about debates over Islam among Muslims in the era of the revolution. Yet Jadidism was from the beginning a movement for the reform of Islam, and Islam was under contention throughout this period. The revolution had produced, among other things, considerable religious ferment, which I discuss in chapter 7. The line between reform and revolution, I argue, could be porous indeed when it came to the critique of customary practices. Here, as in many other aspects, the Jadids and the Bolsheviks could share a great deal without seeing eye to eye on everything.

The Soviet Union from the Edge

In this book I also offer a history of the Soviet Union, but with a vantage point firmly anchored on the periphery. This reversal of the gaze presents the Soviet Union in an unaccustomed light. We see the actual implementation of policies devised at the center under local conditions that were often quite different from those of the capitals. Students of Soviet history will see how the Soviet Union appeared from Tashkent or Bukhara, and if they might find it a little unfamiliar, I will consider my job well done.

The involvement of indigenous elites with their own understandings of what the revolution was about and their own hopes shaped Soviet rule in crucial ways. Moreover, local events shaped the evolution of Soviet rule much more than pan-Soviet developments, to the point where the usual periodization of early Soviet history is of little use in understanding Central Asian developments. The transition from "war Communism" to the New Economic Policy (NEP) gutted the already tiny budgets of local institutions as central subventions disappeared, but otherwise made rather little difference. Far more important was the consolidation of Soviet rule in the region, which involved bringing the countryside under control by defeating the Basmachi and rebuilding the ruined infrastructure of the region. It was only by 1923 that Soviet authorities were confident of their control and could think of enforcing Soviet legislation and implementing pan-Soviet policies. The national delimitation was one such move, which was widely seen

---

44. Keller, *To Moscow, Not Mecca*; for an overview, see also Adeeb Khalid, *Islam after Communism: Religion and Politics in Central Asia* (Berkeley, 2007), chap. 3.

as a second revolution in Central Asia, one that would secure the foundations of Soviet rule. The establishment of national republics was followed in 1926 by the opening of the "ideological front," which aimed at asserting ideological purity in cultural production and supplanting the Jadids, who now came to labeled the "old intellectuals" (*eski ziyolilar*), from their position of prominence in the cultural field. Both the timing and main concerns of the campaign owed much more to local concerns (the party's newfound sense of political strength in the region) than to any central initiative. Likewise, the purge of Uzbekistan's Narkompros in 1929 cannot be seen as connected to the cultural revolution as defined by Fitzpatrick. Not only was the term never used, but the main concern of the purge was to "cleanse" the commissariat of nationalism, not to proletarianize it.

Nationality, in a perverse way, became all important to the Soviet state in Central Asia. Soviet nationality policy clearly was instrumental in creating national republics, but it never trumped the significance of class. The Soviets were therefore suspicious of the Jadids for their propensity to think primarily in terms of the nation. By the late 1920s, the obsession with fighting "nationalism" had led the Soviets to putting nationality at the center of their attention. The gravest political crimes with which Central Asian elites were charged in those years were those of "nationalism," of the "distortion of nationalities policy," and not those of right or left deviation or anything directly to do with class. By 1937–38, charges of nationalism spelled the demise of the Uzbek intelligentsia.

The Global and the Local

Much of what I describe about the national project in Central Asia will sound familiar to students of national phenomena around the world. In insisting that nations are not natural givens but are imagined and articulated in particular historical circumstances, I seek to put the study of Central Asia in a broad comparative perspective. My hope is to deexoticize the region and its historiography and to move discussion of Central Asian history away from a single-minded focus on its specificities and uniqueness, or of Soviet wickedness. At the same time, I recount the local to point to the many contingencies and local specificities that made Central Asia what it was. I seek to balance the local and the global in the themes that I examine.

I place developments in Central Asia against two different backdrops. The first is provided by the Soviet Union. The February revolution of 1917 set in motion numerous national movements that sought various kinds of autonomy and the creation of national cultures. The outburst of cultural creativity, the experimentation with new forms of cultural production, and the embrace of modernity by the Uzbek intelligentsia has parallels in many other parts of the

USSR.[45] In response, the Bolsheviks evolved a nationalities policy that sought to preempt nationalism by co-opting certain key cultural demands to "Soviet construction" and creating a system of national autonomy within Soviet bounds. This created the institutional landscape in which national intelligentsias could strive to implement their agendas for cultural transformation. In the chapters that follow, I draw attention to parallels in other Soviet republics, but I cannot do so in every case simply for reasons of space.

The other backdrop against which I examine Central Asian developments is provided by the broader Muslim world of the time, in particular Turkey, but also the lands directly bordering Central Asia, Afghanistan and Iran. These states also saw the implementation of national projects (of different levels of intensity), new cultural forms, and a challenge to the place of Islam and the ulama. The state was very differently positioned vis-à-vis reform in these instances, but nevertheless, the similarities are striking. Turkey in particular had long been seen as a model for emulation by Uzbek intellectuals, but the Soviet state also kept an eye on developments in these countries as it implemented its own policies in Central Asia. Central Asian developments—the insistent nationalization of elite discourse, the cultural radicalism, the new notions of the place of women in society, the displacement of Islam from public life—remain a little known part of the modern history of the Muslim world, even if they share much in common with developments elsewhere. I hope to incorporate Central Asia into that history.

At the broadest level, I wish to contribute to a more dispassionate view of the twentieth century. As the century recedes into the past, there is a tendency to see it simply as the triumph of liberalism and the free market, and to disown the passions aroused by ideas of revolution and radical change. It is important therefore to recall how many people such passions moved and the often unexpected turns their pursuit took.

A Note on Sources

I have sought in this book to use Russian and Central Asian sources contrapuntally. Uzbek and Tajik sources—the local periodical press, the new prose literature, pedagogical materials—portray the hopes and aspirations (and the concrete

---

45. Yuri Slezkine, *The Jewish Century* (Princeton, 2004); Kenneth B. Moss, *Jewish Renaissance in the Russian Revolution* (Princeton, 2009); Irena Makaryk and Virlana Tkacz, eds., *Modernism in Kyiv: Jubilant Experimentation* (Toronto, 2010); Irena Makaryk, *Shakespeare in the Undiscovered Bourn: Les Kurbas, Ukrainian Modernism, and Early Soviet Cultural Politics* (Toronto, 2004); Oleh S. Ilnytzkyj, *Ukrainian Futurism, 1914–1930: A Historical and Critical Study* (Cambridge, MA, 1997); Myroslav Shkandrij, *Modernists, Marxists and the Nation: The Ukrainian Literary Discussion of the 1920s* (Edmonton, 1992).

actions) of the Central Asian intelligentsia, many of whom entered, as noted, the Soviet apparatus. They also allow us to see how the regime wished to present itself to the indigenous population. The vast bulk of this material is in Uzbek, although important works were penned in Persian (or Tajik, as the language came to be known). The periodical press flourished after the revolution. The year 1917 saw the emergence of a prolific independent press in Central Asia. While that independence was rapidly curtailed in 1918, the "red press" that emerged the following year was a direct successor, an arena of vernacular debate about society, its present and its future, often carried out in a hybrid political language that reflected very well the ambiguities of the period. I make systematic use of the press of that time.

I juxtapose my reading of vernacular sources to documentation from official archives.[46] The archives do not contain "the truth," but they allow us to speak at a level of detail that was inconceivable before the opening of the Soviet archives around 1990. The most useful (and least problematic) are the records of the various government agencies whose work was relevant to the issues discussed in this book. Here, in the mundane records of government decisions, petitions, budget requests, and other paperwork, we see our protagonists as actors. But policy was decided by the Communist Party, which had proclaimed for itself a monopoly on political decision making in the new revolutionary state. Its archives provide candid records of how policy was debated, decreed, and implemented. The archives are much richer in minutes (*protokoly*) of meetings than in verbatim accounts (*otchety*); the former tend to be quite laconic, seldom indicating the degree of discord and or the level of rancor in the meeting. (The difference is glaringly obvious on the few occasions when one encounters both the verbatim account of a meeting and the minutes.) Nevertheless, party documents provide indispensable insight into the making of policy and the assumptions and worldviews that underpinned it.

The most problematic source used for this book is the immense mountain of paper generated by the political police, known successively in the years under review as the Cheka, the GPU, the OGPU, and the NKVD. The archives of the political police itself remain closed to scholars both in Russia and in Central Asia,[47] but duplicates of some of its documentation can be found in party and state archives, and a fair bit of it has been published since the Gorbachev years.

---

46. For a more extended examination of the issues raised in the following paragraphs, see my "Searching for Muslim Voices in Post-Soviet Archives," *Ab Imperio* 2008, no. 4: 302–312.

47. Access to the records of the ChK-GPU-OGPU-NKVD is possible under certain conditions in Russia. In Uzbekistan, the political police archives have been opened up to local researchers under highly restrictive conditions, primarily to enable a national project of commemorating national martyrs and "victims of repression." Scholars can publish quotations from the records but do not seem to be able to provide actual citations.

This material is of several kinds: digests (*svodki*) of reports from the field prepared for the eyes of policymakers; denunciations and testimonies provided by various individuals; and the indictments and "confessions" of its victims. The svodki in particular have been widely used by historians of Central Asia as transparent vehicles of rare information. Yet it is clear that there are a number of problems with treating them as forthright representations of reality. The neatly typed documents that greet researchers in the archives contain many layers of literary production and many kinds of translations. They are based on reports from the field gathered, presumably, by "native" informants who commanded local languages. They were then translated into Russian by professional translators, before being excerpted, abstracted, and classified in the course of the production of the digest in a way that was worthy of the eyes of the exalted readers. This is a complex production process about which we know very little, yet each of its stages takes us farther and farther from any access to "reality" the spy reports might have afforded in the first place. The translation involved is not just linguistic (from Uzbek or Kazakh or Tajik into Russian) but also conceptual. The svodki often have Central Asians often using a vocabulary that sounds very strange indeed—it is most likely the result of translators translating the reports from a "Muslim" political language into "Bolshevik," partly as a reflex and partly as a way of ensuring intelligibility for the anticipated readership.[48] Ultimately, the svodki are most useful as catalogues of the fears and anxieties of the regime and of the way it discerned reality. We need also to remember that the political police was *parti pris* in the politics of the era. Its members sat in on the deliberations of organs of political power, it provided advice to party authorities, and actively sought to shape official policy. Its documentary production is scarcely neutral.

The testimonies (*pokazaniia*), often detailed accounts written by those accused of serious political crimes, are even more complex texts that contain elements of self-fashioning, self-exculpation, self-explanation as well as (attempted) negotiation with the captors. As with denunciations, they have to be read as strategic texts. The confessions often published triumphantly by the regime itself (the best known example of this was the verbatim account of the final show trial of the "Trotskyite" opposition in 1938, in which the accused confessed to ludicrous charges brought against them by the NKVD, yet which were immediately published in several foreign languages) are useful only as records of the "legal" (procedural?) ploys used by the organs to frame their victims. Several of these documents have been published, and yet they provide singularly little enlightenment into the complexities of the era.

---

48. I have not found any spy reports from the field in the archives, but in many other cases, where Russian and vernacular versions of the same document are to be found in Soviet-era files, it is not at all uncommon to find wide divergences between the two.

The most significant function of this sort of documentation in my argument is, however, to indicate the position of the ChK-GPU-OGPU-NKVD on given issues. Historians have no choice but to use these documents, but they have to be read with due skepticism and at some distance.

The one thing we lack are ego documents that might give us insight into the private worlds of our protagonists. Many of them did gather private archives and wrote diaries and carried on copious correspondence with their peers. Very little of that material has survived the assault of the political police on the intelligentsia. Arrests were followed by the confiscation of private papers. What happened to those papers, whether they were destroyed or might still lie in some vault in Tashkent or Moscow, remains unknown. As a result, we know rather less about our protagonists as human beings than we would like. For all their relative chronological proximity to us, Central Asian intellectuals of the early Soviet period remain very distant. We can study their work but their lives remain only dimly visible. For this reason, I have resisted the temptation to psychologize the individuals I discuss. Nevertheless, I hope that they appear as complicated figures, whose desire to define and to lead the nation was both a responsibility and an opportunity, whose political and generational revolts were connected, and whose love for the nation and disdain for its current state were intertwined.

The chapters that follow chapter 1 fall into three groups. Chapters 2–5 trace the turbulent politics of the period up until 1924. Each chapter deals with a different political project: an autonomous Turkestan in the framework of the February revolution, an autonomous Turkestan within the Soviet order, the pursuit of a Muslim modernist republic in Bukhara, and finally, the Soviet state's project of building a Soviet Central Asia. Chapters 6–9 discuss the cultural revolution of the era. They highlight the cultural radicalism of the decade by introducing key texts and describing key debates, include those on the place of Islam in society. More than anything else, they document the triumph of the idea of the nation in Central Asia and explain the creation of Uzbekistan and Tajikistan as two distinct national republics. Chapters 10–12 document the political and cultural transformations of the period after 1926, when the party opened the "ideological front" and began asserting its monopoly over cultural policy. The main narrative extends to the purge of Narkompros and the campaign against alleged nationalist secret societies between 1929 and 1931, but of course chapter 12 extends to the final obliteration of the Uzbek intelligentsia in 1938. I have hoped to produce a connected account in a single interpretative framework of the transformation of Central Asia during the early Soviet period. The book introduces historians to cultural debates of Central Asia that have seldom been noted. It provides an account of the origins of modern nations in Central Asia, and it serves, finally, as an elegy for two lost generations of the Central Asian intelligentsia.

INTELLIGENTSIA AND REFORM IN TSARIST CENTRAL ASIA

Writing in the period of political liberalism inaugurated by the revolution of 1905, Munavvar qori Abdurashidxon o'g'li saw the situation in Turkestani society as follows:

> All our acts and actions, our ways, our words, our maktabs and madrasas and methods of teaching, and our morals are in decay. . . . If we continue in this way for another five or ten years, we are in danger of being dispersed and effaced under the oppression of developed nations. . . . O coreligionists, o compatriots! Let's be just and compare our situation to that of other, advanced nations; . . . let's secure the future of our coming generations and save them from becoming slaves and servants of others. The Europeans, taking advantage of our negligence and ignorance, took our government from our hands, and are gradually taking over our crafts and trades. If we do not quickly make an effort to reform our affairs in order to safeguard ourselves, our nation, and our children, our future will be extremely difficult.
>
> Reform begins with a rapid start in cultivating sciences conforming to our times. Becoming acquainted with the sciences of the [present] time depends upon the reform of our schools and our methods of teaching.[1]

---

1. Munavvar qori Abdurashidxon o'g'li, "Isloh ne demakdadur," *Xurshid*, 28.09.1906; this editorial is now available in my English translation as "What Is Reform?" in *Modernist Islam: A Sourcebook, 1840–1940*, ed. Charles Kurzman (New York, 2002), 227–228.

Munavvar qori's sense of crisis and impending doom, as well as his faith in the power of knowledge and education to provide the panacea for all the ills of society, were widely shared among the nascent intelligentsia of Turkestan. They saw thoroughgoing reform as the only guarantee for survival in a modern era in which sovereignty had been lost to colonial rule due to "negligence and ignorance." The cultivation by Muslim society of modern knowledge and the creation of elites capable of functioning in the modern world were the only way for Islam and Muslims to prosper, indeed to survive as a community, in the world created by colonialism. The key concepts in this cultural project were taraqqiy, progress, and madaniyat, civilization. Not qualified by any adjectives, both these concepts were taken to be universal: progress and civilization were necessary to all societies and achievable by all those who put enough effort into cultivating knowledge. An aggressively modernist interpretation of Islam rendered it entirely compatible with modern forms of knowledge and the concept of progress. In common with many other modernisms in the colonial world, then, Jadidism produced new ways of imagining the world as it wrestled with the dialectic between authenticity and modernity. The community itself was imagined anew as a nation, tied to a particular history and a particular territory. The Jadids argued this from a self-consciously Islamic position, which led them to a thoroughly modernist understanding of their religion, one that saw Islam as entirely compatible with modern civilization and with the concept of the nation.[2]

The decade and a half before 1917 saw the emergence of a project of cultural reform based on this critique. The reformist critique was directed almost entirely at indigenous society itself. Its flagship was the reform of the *maktab*, the traditional elementary school, and the introduction into it of the new (i.e., the phonetic) method of teaching the alphabet. The reformist project also entailed the creation of new forms of knowledge (about history, geography, and Islam itself), the creation of new forms of sociability (benevolent societies, theatrical groups), and new forms of public space. The main venues for the propagation of the reformist message were print and theater, new intellectual technologies introduced by the colonial power. Much of this reform revolved around the idea of the nation, which in turn brought new claims and new responsibilities. With sovereignty lost, it was up to the nation to pull itself up by the boot straps, which required leading groups within it to recognize their duty and to fulfill it. In the columns of the vernacular press, which led a fitful existence from 1906, and on the stage of the theater, reformers exhorted their society to mend its ways, to

---

2. Much of this chapter recapitulates the argument from my earlier work, *The Politics of Muslim Cultural Reform: Jadidism in Central Asia* (Berkeley, 1998). I have added citations to more recent scholarship here but otherwise kept references to a minimum.

reform the maktab and to establish new schools. They implored the ulama and the wealthy to do their duty and criticized them when they did not. The ulama were supposed to use their moral authority to return society to "true Islam" by condemning customary practices such as shrine visitation, the celebrations (to'y) associated with life-cycle events, and myriad other divergences from scripturalist understandings of Islam. The wealthy were supposed to use their wealth for the good of the nation by establishing benevolent societies and funding schools, scholarships, the publication of useful books, and theater. Reform attracted some ulama to its side, and many wealthy merchants were active proponents of it. Yet the reformist critique was also a claim to leadership that was met with opposition. The reformist project was deeply contested, and this contestation shaped the ground on which the political battles of the early Soviet period were fought in Central Asia. This project of cultural reform was transformed by the revolution of 1917. None of the characters we meet in this chapter expected to see the world turn upside down as it was in 1917—or, for that matter, to have one to day to justify their motives in the language of proletarian revolution. Nevertheless, the Central Asian intelligentsia did not enter the fray empty handed. In 1917 and in the years that followed, it sought to realize its goals, even as conditions changed rapidly and transformed those goals too.

Authority and Leadership in Muslim Society

This advocacy of reform arose in a political and cultural landscape created by the Russian conquest of Central Asia. The peculiar institutional arrangements put in place by the Russian state in its colony, with its preservation of difference and the refusal to assimilate, shaped the way the new intelligentsia saw the challenges facing their society and their responses to those challenges. Russian rule had also shaped the indigenous society in which the intelligentsia emerged, and which determined the social fortunes of the reform project.

Russia was a particularist empire, in which the tsar-emperor ruled over a vast array of regions and social groups, each with a specific legal status and specific obligations to the state. The empire existed through the maintenance of difference. Yet, within that array of difference, Turkestan occupied a unique place. It was conquered very much in the context of imperial competition with other European powers at a time when imperial rule over "uncivilized" peoples was clearly seen as a hallmark of civilization. For Russians and other contemporary observers, there was no question that the Russian advance into Central Asia was part of the European conquest of non-European lands in the age of empire. The kind of rule the Russians established in Central Asia was more similar to colonial rule in other empires of the day, with which the Russians routinely compared it, than with other non-Russian parts of the Russian Empire.[3] The Russian state did not co-opt existing elites into the Russian nobility, nor did it extend the empirewide system of ranks and standings (*sosloviia i sostoianiia*) to the region. In general, the social and political distance between the rulers and the ruled remained greater than anywhere else in empire, with the possible exception of Siberia and the north (but where the indigenous population was much smaller and did not pose a demographic threat to Russian dominance). Central Asia was different from the rest of the empire. For K. P. Kaufman, the first governor-general of Turkestan and in many ways the architect of Russian rule there, Islam was the embodiment of this difference. Kaufman thought the incorporation of the region into the mainstream of Russian political life possible, but only in the long term. In the short run, the Islamic "fanaticism" of the local population made the task impossible. The solution was to ignore rather than to suppress Islam, which, deprived of state support, would decay. For this reason, Kaufman ensured that the Orenburg Spiritual Assembly, the bureaucratic institution created by Catherine II to regulate Islamic affairs among the Tatar and Bashkir populations, did not extend its jurisdiction to Turkestan. Rather, he instituted a policy of disregarding (*ignorirovanie*) Islam that lasted, despite doubts and occasional dissent, down to 1917. Disregard meant that Islam was to have no official status, and its carriers were to receive no official recognition or appointments.[4] The state did not seek to control mosques and madrasas and it left intact Islamic courts, even as it tinkered with their competence. The Statute for the Administration of Turkestan (1886) made the office of the Islamic judge (qazi) elective and strictly limited its jurisdiction. Disregard thus did not mean that Islam and Islamic institutions continued unchanged—far from it—but it did mean a degree of legal pluralism.[5] This maintenance of difference created a dual society, in which Muslims and Russian settlers coexisted largely in parallel. Muslim society occupied a considerable autonomous space under Russian rule.

---

3. For a more expansive treatment of this subject, see my "Culture and Power in Colonial Turkestan," *Cahiers d'Asie centrale* 17–18 (2009): 403–436.

4. On the Spiritual Assembly, see D. D. Azamatov, *Orenburgskoe magometanskoe dukhovnoe sobranie v kontse XVIII–XIX vv.* (Ufa, 1999). Spiritual assemblies existed also in the Crimea and Transcaucasia; see James Meyer, "Turkic Worlds: Community Representation and Collective Identity in Russia and the Ottoman Empire, 1880–1917" (Ph.D. diss., Brown University, 2007).

5. Paolo Sartori has published a great deal on Islamic courts in the Tsarist period; his "Constructing Colonial Legality in Russian Central Asia: On Guardianship," *Comparative Studies in Society and History* 56 (2014): 419–447, is particularly significant for the question at hand here.

Disregard also did not mean disinterest. From the beginning, the Russians sought to influence Muslim opinion. The *Turkiston viloyatining gazeti* (Turkestan Gazette) established by Kaufman in 1870 was one of the earliest (and longest running) Turkic-language periodicals in the Russian Empire. From 1883, it was under the editorship on Nikolai Ostroumov (1846–1930), a graduate of the Kazan Theological Academy, where he was a student of the noted missionary Nikolai Il'minskii.[6] He came to Turkestan on Il'minskii's recommendation to Kaufman and made it his career. Ostroumov was an Orientalist of considerable accomplishment, and he used his knowledge in the service of empire. His Orientalist credentials attracted the attention of the authorities, and over the years he became the resident expert of everything connected with local life, and his opinions were routinely solicited by the authorities on all subjects having to do with Islam or Muslims. Even as he wrote polemical works against Islam, he served as director of schools in Turkestan, the principal of the teachers college, and editor of *Turkiston viloyatining gazeti*, to which he invited local authors to contribute. It was better for debates in Muslim society to take place under Ostroumov's watchful eye than on their own.

Muslim society was reshaped after the conquest in significant ways. Defeat spelled the end of the old khanly elites: some were actively dispossessed and exiled, others emigrated to Afghanistan or Chinese Central Asia, yet others sunk to the status of mere landholders. Their place was taken by the ulama and a new group of urban merchants. The ulama emerged with heightened status both because of the loss of countervailing groups and because they could now claim to be keepers of moral authority in the absence of Muslim sovereignty in the region. Kaufman's policies also ensured that the ulama survived the conquest well. The impulse to nonintervention left the madrasas largely intact, as it did the status of waqf property, for although the Russians sought to regulate it, the concept of waqf was never abolished, nor was the regulation ever very successful. Islamic courts provided another venue for the exercise of the authority of the ulama.

The ulama accommodated themselves to imperial rule. As did their counterparts across the colonized world, the ulama of Turkestan came to accept the legitimacy of Russian rule. As long as the Russians permitted the performance of Islamic ritual and left the shariat in place, the ulama were prepared to accept their rule as legitimate. The ulama of Turkestan retained their autonomy and continued to operate in the patterns of sociability to which they were accustomed,

---

6. On Ostroumov's missionary background, see Robert P. Geraci, *Window on the East: National and Imperial Identities in Late Tsarist Russia* (Ithaca, 2001), 55–56, 90.

without any form of bureaucratization or hierarchy that had become the norm among other Muslim populations of the Russian Empire. The ulama retained their source of moral and cultural authority, and became the sole bulwarks of moral authority; indeed, the elimination of tribal chiefs, who had often competed with the ulama, gave the latter a stature in society that was in many ways unprecedented.

The merchants were beneficiaries of the new colonial economy, driven by cotton, that took shape in the decades after the conquest. By the turn of the twentieth century, a number of wealthy merchants (*boylar, ag'niyo*) had emerged as new urban notables. Some of them had been decorated by the state as honorable (*pochetnye*) citizens and acted as intermediaries of sorts between the state and the indigenous population. In Tashkent, which had a municipal duma (council), they dominated the Muslim seats (limited by law to no more than one-third). These new elites reached their compromises with the new order, which in turn defined the positions they came to occupy in the new politics of culture in Turkestan. It was this conjuncture of forces that the new intelligentsia challenged with its advocacy for reform. Their call for reform was also a claim to leadership in society and a challenge to the authority of established elites. It engendered a great deal of conflict within Muslim society.

The new intelligentsia was a self-conscious group that came together around the advocacy of reform. Many of its members came from Turkestan's cultural elite and possessed substantial cultural capital. Almost all of them were very young. Their claim to know the path to salvation was subversive of the order that had emerged after the conquest, while their assurance in assigning responsibility and blame irksome to those whose authority they questioned. The intelligentsia is known in the historiography as the Jadids, from their advocacy of the *usul-i jadid*, the new method of teaching the alphabet. I use this term too, mostly for convenience, but we should note that the terms most commonly used by the reformers themselves were *taraqqiparvar*, "proponent of progress," or ziyoli (lit., "enlightened").[7] Their opponents often called them yoshlar, "the youth," or *jadidchi*, "proponents of the new," in a pejorative sense. In a society where age engendered respect, the assertion of power by the youth was deliciously subversive, but could also be turned into a handicap.

Many Jadids were ulama in their own right, but they as a group also had the support of some ulama as well as some merchants. A number of Tashkent's wealthiest citizens came together to found the Imdodiya (Assistance) benevolent

---

7. These and similar terms, such as *ravshanfikr* and *ochiqfikrli*, "of enlightened thought," were commonly used in the Turko-Persian world at this time.

society which funded schools, provided scholarships, and established a reading room. But for many if not most boylar, the claims of the Jadids remained the pretentious prattle of youth who sought to corrupt Muslim culture through mimicry of the Russians. The relationship between a new cultural elite basing its claims on the authority of progress, civilization, and the needs of the age, and the established elites possessing cultural capital rooted in the past was always tense. In Tashkent, the Jadids' advocacy of theater was a particularly sore point. According to Laziz Azizzoda, the boylar first excluded the youth from Imdodiya and then even resorted to intimidation and attempted assassination to keep the youth in their place.[8] The Jadids' position in society was precarious as they entered the age of revolution in February 1917.

The Geography of Reform

The Jadids remained very much a part of the broader Muslim world. To get a sense of their imaginative universe, we can do no better than to turn to "Dr. Muhammad-Yor," a short story, one of the first in Uzbek, that a very young Abdulhamid Sulaymon published in 1914. Under the nom de plume of Cho'lpon, Sulaymon was to revolutionize Uzbek poetry in the years after 1917, but this piece of juvenilia, written when he was sixteen, was all earnestness. That earnestness, however, reveals to us many key features of the Jadid understanding of the world. Muhammad-Yor was born in a "dark corner of Turkestan," but to a father who had seen the world in this youth, when he traveled around the Muslim world and the Russian Empire after going on the hajj. The father decided to educate his son "according to the needs of the time," and hired a Tatar graduate of the Galiye madrasa in Ufa to teach his son the basics. Muhammad-Yor could not continue his education for lack of money and could not find anyone in that dark corner to help him, even as wealthy merchants spent fortunes on feasts and celebrations. After Muhammad-Yor's father was murdered in a brawl, the result of the ignorance reigning in society, fortune (and the help of enlightened outsiders) took him to Baku, where a benevolent society established by the enlightened Muslim millionaires of the city paid for his education at a *gimnaziia*. His hard work garnered him first position in the final exams and admission to the medical faculty at the University of St. Petersburg. Having finished his education there,

---

8. Laziz Azizzoda, "Turkistonning uyg'onish tarixi" (ms., 1925/1967; O'zFAShI inv. 11895), 130–131. This manuscript is a complex text that includes several layers of recapitulation of a work first composed in 1925, but confiscated by the OGPU upon the author's arrest in 1927. It nevertheless contains information not otherwise available.

Muhammad-Yor went to Switzerland "to gain practical experience" and polish off his education. He returned, first to Baku to lecture for two years to pay back his obligations to the benevolent society that had funded much of his education, and then returned to his native Turkestan to become "a servant of the nation."[9]

Knowledge was Muhammad-Yor's salvation and his quest for it took to ever higher levels of modernity and civilization, from his "dark corner of Turkestan" to Baku, the city of Muslim millionaires and benevolent societies, to St. Petersburg, the imperial capital, and finally to Western Europe, the place where the highest forms of knowledge was to be found. Having ascended to the top in his quest, Muhammad-Yor dutifully brought his knowledge back to his homeland and put it at the service of his nation. It is this sense of duty that makes him praiseworthy for Cho'lpon, but the progression of his quest accurately describes the variety of contexts in which Turkestan existed. Turkestan was nestled in the concentric circles of a bigger Turkic Muslim world, the Russian Empire, and the modern world.

And yet Muhammad-Yor's peregrinations did not reflect reality all that accurately. Very few Central Asians studied in Russia, let alone in Europe. The Jadids of Central Asia were different from most colonial intellectuals in that the colonizer did not provide the models for political action or aesthetic judgment. Indian national elites had long been educated in English (and in England) and colonial subjects of France had been coming to Paris to study for a while. In Turkestan, however, Russian education made little headway in the half-century that Tsarist rule lasted. Kaufman's early hope that Russian educational institutions would attract Muslims and make "useful citizens" out of them came to naught, as very few Muslims enrolled in them. Fewer still attended higher educational institutions in Russia itself. The number of Turkestanis with a Russian higher education remained very small. The most significant access to Russian remained the so-called Russo-native schools that combined a Russian curriculum in the morning with traditional Muslim education in the afternoon. They had been established in 1884 when the administration began to worry about the miniscule numbers of Muslims learning Russian. After a rocky start, they had become well established as knowledge of Russian became a necessity for many people. By 1916, there were ten in Tashkent alone, where native members of the municipal duma demanded the creation of another ten schools.[10] In the end, Russian-native schools were

9. Abdulhamid Cho'lpon, "Do'xtur Muhammadyor," *Sadoi Turkiston*, 04.07.1914, 25.07.1914, 10.08.1914, 26.10.1914, 05.11.1914, 12.11.1914; see my translation, "Doctor Muhammad-Yar," in *Modernist Islam*, 264–269.

10. *Turkiston viloyatining gazeti*, 18.06.1916; on the demand for more schools, see Khalid, "Culture and Power," 426–429.

successful but not for the reasons envisioned by the authorities. They were supposed to produce interpreters and translators who might work as intermediaries between the colonial regime and the indigenous population. They might have done that, but many of their graduates later became the mainstay of the Communist Party and the Soviet administration after 1917.

Several Jadids attended Russo-native schools, and many others knew Russian to one degree or another. Yet Russian was not the predominant channel for new ideas. Far more important in shaping the worldview of the Jadids were debates in the overlapping Muslim communities of the Russian and Ottoman empires. Print, steam, and telegraph created a new transimperial community of intellectuals that could then imagine new kinds of ties among themselves, new collective affinities, and new models of action. This new public space emerged in the 1880s with the rise of a nonofficial Ottoman press and of commercial publishing in the Ottoman Empire.[11] Steamships and the modern postal system carried these publications to the turcophone communities of the Russian Empire. Turkic-language publishing had existed in the Russian Empire for over a century by then, but little of it was commercially viable and few newspapers received permission to publish. A major landmark came in 1883 with the establishment in Bağçasaray in the Crimea of the bilingual newspaper *Tercüman / Perevodchik* (Interpreter), which under the tireless editorship of Ismail Bey Gasprinskiy quickly acquired a readership that spanned the Turkic-reading communities of the Russian Empire and extended well into the Ottoman Empire and beyond. *Tercüman* remained the only major nonofficial Turkic-language periodical in the Russian Empire until the revolution of 1905 and acquired a position of great influence out of proportion to the size of the Crimea. With the political liberalization in the Russian Empire after 1905, Turkic-language newspapers emerged in large numbers in the Tatar lands and in Transcaucasia.[12] The Constitutional Revolution in the Ottoman Empire gave rise to a feisty, independent press that continued to be read in the Russian Empire. The audience of this press included many who could read Turkic, even if they did not speak it. The Turkic press was a model for the press in Iran and even Afghanistan. More significantly for our purposes, Bukhara, where the language of culture and the chancery had long been Persian, became part of this reading public. *Tercüman* as well as Ottoman newspapers (and, after 1905,

---

11. On the Ottoman press, Fuat Süreyya Oral, *Türk Basın Tarihi*, 2 vols. (Ankara, 1967–70); and Hasan Duman, *İstanbul Kütüphaneleri Arap Harflı Süreli Yayınlar Toplu Kataloğu, 1828–1938* (Istanbul, 1986), have not been superseded.

12. The best account of the Muslim press of the Russian Empire still is Alexandre Bennigsen and Chantal Lemercier-Quelquejay, *La Presse et le mouvement national chez les Musulmans de Russie avant 1920* (Paris, 1964).

Tatar ones as well) appeared as the major vehicle for modern forms of knowledge in Bukhara.[13]

Newspapers from the two empires crossed back and forth across an imperial boundary that was far from impermeable. Newspapers were read in both the empires, they quoted each other, reprinted articles or cartoons from each other, and referred to each other as "our esteemed colleague" (*mu'tabir rafiqimiz*). Writers, too, contributed to multiple newspapers throughout this public space. These overlapping readerships created a venue in which ideas from the differing political landscapes of Russia and the Ottoman Empire (and the broader world in general) offered new models for the future. It was also in this common public space that a great many new models of politics, society, and culture developed. Authors and readers were differently located, of course, on either side of the imperial border: Ottoman authors were concerned above all else by finding ways of strengthening the state, while Russian Muslim authors had different concerns in which the state did not loom large as the motor of reform. Even in the "dissi-dent" press established in Istanbul by émigrés from the Russian Empire, we find a complex stance toward Ottoman society. Writers envied the fact that the Otto-mans possessed sovereignty, but they also scolded them for not being more interested in (and solicitous of) other Turkic populations of the world.[14] Yet, for all this, Turkic-language newspapers shared a number of common themes. Their authors were familiar with common models of progress, civilization, reform, modernity, language, and identity, even as they debated them and took various positions with regard to them.

Nor were periodicals the only medium of this exchange. Belles lettres and models associated with them also circulated in this public space. The new lit-erature that emerged in Central Asia was much more indebted to developments in the Muslim world than anything going on in Russian literature. Russian and broader European influences arrived in Central Asia through Ottoman, Tatar, or Azerbaijani translation. In theater, Azerbaijani troupes that had been tour-ing Turkestan since the turn of the twentieth century were the most significant model, while much of the modern poetry that emerged in these years was influ-enced by Ottoman models.

Patterns of travel also followed the printed word. When the Jadids traveled, and many of them did, they went to other Muslim lands. Many performed

---

13. Sadriddin Ayniy, *Buxoro inqilobi tarixi uchun materiallar* (Moscow, 1926). For a reference to Istanbul newspapers being read in Bukhara in the 1890s, see Ahmad Makhdumi Donish, *Risola, yo mukhtasare az ta'rikhi saltanati khonadoni manghitiya* (ms. ca. 1895; Dushanbe, 1992), 91.

14. Volker Adam, *Rußlandmuslime in Istanbul am Vorabend des Ersten Weltkrieges: Die Berichter-stattung osmanischer Periodika über Rußland und Zentralasien* (Frankfurt am Main, 2002), chap. 5.

the hajj, which took them to India, Afghanistan, Iran, and Egypt. The most important destination, however, was Istanbul.[15] The attraction of the Ottoman Empire for Muslim reformers lay not in primordial religious or ethnic solidarities—as the much abused terms "pan-Islamism" and "pan-Turkism" imply—but rather in the fact that the Ottoman Empire was the most powerful (mostly) sovereign Muslim state left in the age of empire. The fascination with the Ottomans was politically problematic, as Russians, both in officialdom and in the intelligentsia, saw the specter of pan-Turkism and pan-Islamism behind every such move. The Okhrana, the Tsarist secret police, was convinced of "Turkish emissaries" roaming the lands of the Tsars practically at will, and Russia's Muslims felt constantly the need to affirm and reaffirm their loyalty to the Tsar.

Travel did not have to be long distance, nor personal motivations so abstract. Laziz Azzizoda, scion of a learned family and a student at Beglarbegi madrasa in Tashkent, had only to take the tramway to the new city to discover a new world. Every week in the summer, he went to the new city's park to listen to the Uspenskii symphony. The "multicolored flowerbeds, the beautifully dressed Russian women (and Tatar women with their faces wrapped in thin kerchiefs)" left a deep imprint on him. "I felt a certain freedom unique to the new city," he wrote many years later. "At such moments, the new city seemed like paradise compared to the hell of life in the old city. For the old city had neither gardens, nor green trees, nor any theaters. Dust ruled in the summer, mud in the winter."[16] The impression was deep enough that in 1913, he "introduced novelties in [his] life," when he began dining at a table with fork and knife and decorated his home in a "semi-European fashion." He also had his wife dress in European fashion and leave the house without the paranji.[17] No doubt, in writing about his motivations six traumatic decades later, Azzizoda endowed them with greater deliberation than was perhaps the case, but the challenge and the temptation that he described were no doubt there. Western dress and habits in fact became statements of cultural orientation that many Jadids made. Hamza Hakimzoda Niyoziy scandalized Kokand as much by his fondness for sharp suits as by his love of the violin. (Their opponents, of course, used "Jadid" also to mean "dandy," "fop," and worse.)

---

15. See Lâle Can, "Trans-Imperial Trajectories: Pilgrimage, Pan-Islam, and the Development of Ottoman-Central Asian Relations, 1865–1914" (Ph.D. diss., New York University, 2012); James Meyer, "Immigration, Return, and the Politics of Citizenship: Russian Muslims in the Ottoman Empire, 1870–1914," *IJMES* 39 (2007): 15–32.

16. Azizzoda, "Sarguzashtimdan bir lavha" (typescript, 1974), 20.

17. Ibid., 12–13.

Such patterns of behavior are well known to us from a variety of colonial situations, although in the Russian context, they continue to be described by the term "Russification." Azizzoda's fascination with the new city or Hamza's with the violin was part of a quest for civilization, which alone would allow their society to take its place in the world. Muslim modernists routinely used the word *civilization* (madaniyat) without quotation marks. In late Ottoman discourse, civilization was a universal. "The edifice of civilization is built on two principles, one material and the other moral," the late Ottoman court historian Ahmed Lütfi Efendi wrote in 1875. "The moral principle is devoutness. . . . The material principle comprises the rescue from idleness of the populace by the farmers, merchants, and artisans, and the restrengthening of the principles that justify the production of wealth and discipline."[18] Devoutness and hard work would lead all societies to the same destination. The Jadids' fascination with civilization was combined with the hope of acquiring it for their own society, so that it too could take its place in the world. Their "mimicry" did not turn them into Russians but rather opened new ways for thinking about identity and culture that were profoundly subversive of both the colonial order and of existing norms in local Muslim society. The present backwardness of their society was all too painfully obvious to them; the task was to overcome it by acquiring the tools that had made the great powers of the age great.

Bukharan Trajectories

A rather different situation arose in Bukhara, which the Russians did not annex, but left as a protectorate, in which the emir stayed on his throne and was free to act in internal affairs. This status was new to the Russian Empire and again pointed to the pan-European colonial context of Russian expansion in Central Asia, for the protectorate was modeled directly on the princely states of India. Muzaffar, the defeated emir, cast himself as the defender of the last bastion of Islam in the region, seeking to keep all foreign influences at bay, even as the protectorate, by giving the Russians a stake in upholding the emir against his domestic opposition, actually left him stronger in internal affairs than his predecessors had ever been.[19] The Russians even annexed to the protectorate the mountainous principalities of

---

18. Quoted in Fatma Müge Göçek, *Rise of the Bourgeoisie, Demise of Empire* (New York, 1996), 118. For an overview of Ottoman debates over the term, see Kevin Reinhart, "Civilization and its Discussants: *Medeniyet* and the Turkish Conversion to Modernism," in *Converting Cultures: Religion, Ideology, and Transformations of Modernity*, ed. Dennis Washburn and A. Kevin Reinhart (Leiden, 2007), 267–289.

19. I have dealt with these issues in greater detail in Adeeb Khalid, "Society and Politics in Bukhara, 1868–1920," *Central Asian Survey* 19 (2000): 367–396.

Darvoz and Qorategin that the emirs of Bukhara had never been able to subjugate. Russian backing gave Muzaffar unprecedented control over governors of the provinces, leaving only the ulama as potential sources of opposition. Over the next few years, he proceeded to turn the ulama into a subservient estate by creating numerous sinecures for them. He and his successors also used appointments to offices and ranks as levers to enhance their position vis-à-vis the ulama.

The fundamental fact of Bukharan politics under the protectorate was the struggle between the ulama, divided into factions, and the emirs.[20] The ulama's factions were held together by ties of mutual obligation among equals, and by patron-client relationships among those of different ranks, with the intense loyalty of current and past students a major asset for the main antagonists. The two main factions of the ulama were the Kulobi (or *kuhistānī*), grouped around ulama from Kulob in eastern Bukhara who had appeared on the scene in Muzaffar's time, and the Bukharan (or *tumānī*), comprised of local ulama whose positions the new comers had encroached. The two factions competed fiercely for appointments and the emir's patronage. All factional disputes among the ulama became imbued with a sacral tinge and were played out as debates over the proper interpretation of Islam. Generally speaking, ulama of the Bukharan faction assumed a purist posture through which they criticized the Kulobis for several practices widespread in Bukhara that they deemed contrary to the shariat. With the emirs also asserting their credentials as guardians of orthodoxy, there was little room for reform.

Yet the new economy produced new needs. The city's merchants, newly integrated into the global economy, wanted new legal structures, with guarantees for property and contracts, and opportunities for their sons to acquire a modern education. The new method of education appeared in a few schools and even a Russo-native school opened its doors in Bukhara. By the beginning of the twentieth century, these pragmatic concerns had turned into a systematic dissatisfaction with the state of affairs in Bukhara, as the merchants chafed at the arbitrary rule of the emir and his functionaries, and looked enviously at the relatively stable rule of law in Turkestan. These concerns brought Bukharan merchants together with certain ulama and a fledgling group of new intellectuals in an alliance advocating reform. The merchants included millionaires such as Muhiddin

---

20. Our best sources on factions among the ulama and the contours of this politics are Sadriddin Aynî, *Ta'rikhi amironi manghitiyai Bukhoro* (1921; reprint Dushanbe, 1987), 96–100; and Abdurauf Fitrat, "Buxoro ulamosi," *Hurriyat*, 03.11.1917; see also Stéphane A. Dudoignon, "Faction Struggles among the Bukharan Ulama during the Colonial, the Revolutionary, and the Early Soviet Periods (1868–1929): A Paradigm for History Writing?" in *Muslim Societies: Historical and Comparative Perspectives*, ed. Sato Tsugitaka (London, 2003), 62–96; and Khalid, "Society and Politics."

Mansurov and Latif Xo'jayev, men of substance who competed directly with the emir in his commercial ventures. Another major supporter of reform was Sharifjon Makhdum, a notable whose father had been *qazi kalon* (chief judge) in the 1880s, before being supplanted by Kulobis. His family controlled land in the provinces and maintained networks of patronage in the capital. Sharifjon was a leading figure in the city's literary life: he wrote under the pen name of Sadr-i Ziyo, and his house was the scene of constant literary activity.[21] The reformers organized in secret societies that both defined and limited their course of action.

Unlike in Turkestan, the state appeared as the logical locus of reform in Bukhara. Bukharan reformers hoped that the emirs would take the initiative and implement reform. Ottoman models appeared even more applicable to Bukhara than to Turkestan. While they waited, however, the merchants established a benevolent society to send Bukharan students abroad for a modern education not available to them locally. It was no coincidence that they chose not St. Petersburg or Tehran, but Istanbul as the destination. This choice was fateful, for it was through these students that not just Ottoman state models but a fascination with Turkism came to define the desiderata of Bukharan reform.

The most important Bukharan to study in Istanbul was Abdurauf Fitrat (1886–1938), one of the central characters in this book. The son of a prosperous merchant, Fitrat spent the four tumultuous years from 1909 to 1913 in Istanbul as a student. These were the years in which the hopes unleashed by the Constitutional Revolution were soured by the wars in Libya and the Balkans and debates over the future of the empire—on "how to save the state"—raged in the press. Late Ottoman Islamism (the political orientation that saw Islam as the most significant node of solidarity for saving the empire) was deeply intertwined with Turkism,[22] and Fitrat was deeply immersed in these debates. We know little about Fitrat's activities in Istanbul other than that he studied at the Medreset ül-Vâizin, a reformed madrassa with a wide-ranging curriculum that included Turkic history, taught by Yusuf Akçura, one of the most important Turkist thinkers.[23] He first appeared in print in the pages of the journal *Hikmet* and was close to other émigrés from the Russian Empire. Nevertheless, the experience was transformative for him, and it marked his thinking for the rest of his life.

---

21. Sharifjon Makhdum has elicited considerable interest from scholars in recent years and many of his works have been published. For biographical information, see Muhammadjān Shakūrī Bukhārī, *Ṣadr-i Bukhārā* (Tehran, 2002); Stéphane A. Dudoignon, "Les 'tribulations' du juge Ẕiyā: Histoire et mémoire du clientélisme politique à Boukhara (1868–1929)," *Annales: Histoire, Sciences Sociales,* 2004, no. 5–6: 1095–1135.

22. Adeeb Khalid, "Ottoman 'Islamism' between the Ümmet and the Nation," *Archivum Ottomanicum* 19 (2001): 197–211.

23. There is a passing mention of Fitrat studying at the Medreset ül-Vâizin in *Oyina* (17.05.1914), 588; on that institution, see Hüseyin Atay, *Osmanlılarda Yüksek Din Eğitimi* (Istanbul, 1983), 308–311.

Istanbul made Fitrat into a Bukharan patriot. His first book, a brief tract titled *A Debate between a Bukharan Professor and a European on the Subject of New Schools*, was an argument on the permissibility (from the point of view of Islam) and the necessity of modern education for Muslims in Bukhara. Fitrat's argument, articulated by the European, is entirely from the point of self-strengthening: "Strive until you too have that which made the Christians victorious over you."[24] This was the first of several occasions when Fitrat used a stern but sympathetic outsider as his mouthpiece to articulate his desiderata for reform. The *Debate* was popular enough in Central Asia (Mahmudxo'ja Behbudiy published a translation into Uzbek; about Behbudiy, see more later in this chapter) that the emir banned its import into his domain. A far more significant work was the *Tales of an Indian Traveler*, in which Fitrat uses an Indian visitor to articulate a critique of the current state of affairs in Bukhara. As the Indian travels through Bukhara, he notes the chaos and disorder in the streets, the lack of any measures regarding hygiene and public health, the complete lack of economic planning or public education, and the corruption of morals and improper religious practices. Government officials have no care for the good of the state; the ulama "drink the blood of the people," and ordinary people are victims of ignorance. The solution was for the emir to fulfill his duties as a Muslim sovereign and to establish order through providing modern education, public healthcare, and the establishment of economic policy.[25] The Indian traveler, of course, is a literary artifice. The solutions proposed by him have little to do with India; they all come from the hopes and desires of late Ottoman reformers and the *étatisme* of the Young Turks.

Fitrat ended his *Debate* with a passionate plea to the emir, "the kind father of the Bukharans, the king who protects his people," to act before it was too late, before "our imams are replaced by priests, our call to prayer by a bell, and our mosque by a church." It was the emir's duty as a Muslim sovereign to implement self-strengthening reform: "Give some thought to what the solution might be for us miserable ones. Who is our deliverer? Who will grasp our hand and pull us from this maelstrom? . . . Is today not our best opportunity, since we have, in your august personage, a kind father, a wise ruler, and an intelligent king?"[26] Down to 1917, Fitrat and other reformers continued to look to the emir to take the lead in the matter of reform.[27] Yet their loyalty was already conditional. The Jadids had come to see Bukhara as a transhistorical subject that existed quite apart from the emir and its dynasty. For Fitrat, Bukhara was "My homeland! The place where

---

24. Fiṭrat Bukhārāyī, *Munāẓara-yi mudarris-i bukhārāyī bā yak nafar-i Farangī dar Hindustān dar bāra-yi makātib-i jadīda* (Istanbul, 1327 m./1911), 31.

25. 'Abd ul-Ra'ūf [Fitrat], *Bayānāt-i sayyāḥ-i hindī* (Istanbul, 1330/1912).

26. Fitrat, *Munāẓara*, 65.

27. 'A. Fitrat, "Iqdāmāt-i iṣlāḥkārāna-yi hukūmat-i Bukhārā," *Oyina*, 30.01.1915, 198–200.

my body and my soul prostrate / My haven, my honor, my glory / my Ka'ba, my *qibla*, my garden."[28] And lurking in the petitions to the emir was an even more subversive concept, that of "the honorable Bukharan nation" (*millat-i najība-yi bukhārāyī*) that had a claim to Bukhara higher than that of its dynast. The emir now was the servant of the nation and held office on its sufferance. Like so many other monarchs in the modern age, the basis of the Bukharan emir's legitimacy had shifted under his throne. In 1917, the emir's refusal to act and his persecution of reformers was to delegitimize him in the eyes of the reformers.

Nation and Homeland in Turkestan

In Turkestan, too, the concepts of nation and homeland altered conceptions of community and identity in profound ways. Munavvar qori had addressed the plea with which we began this chapter to his "coreligionists and compatriots" (*vatandoshlar va dindoshlar*); the two categories of *vatan* and *din*, homeland and religion, together defined the nation on whose behalf the Jadids worried and shed tears. Theirs was a territorially defined confessional nation, most commonly called before 1917 "the Muslims of Turkestan." It included almost all the indigenous population of Turkestan, with the exception of local ("Bukharan") Jews, although in practice the latter shared much with the Muslims. It drew lines against other Muslim communities, whether inside the Russian Empire (Tatars, Azerbaijanis) or beyond. The Muslims of Turkestan were a specific group in the Muslim world at large. "Turkestan," of course, was the creation of Russian rule, but like so many other colonial entities, it had come to be meaningful as a node of identification. "Turkestan" denoted the Russian province of that name; it excluded the protectorates of Bukhara and Khiva or the lands under Chinese or Afghan control. "Muslim," on the other hand, denoted members of confessional community, not one defined by the strength of inner belief or of ritual observance. In both Russian and indigenous usage, "Muslim" was used as an adjective pertaining to the local (sedentary) population—the "Muslim part of town," "Muslim clothing," and even a "Muslim language." Such confessional uses of the term *Muslim* were quite common at the time (and have been more common since then than we often recognize), and we can see the Jadids' advocacy of "the Muslims of Turkestan" as a form of confessional nationalism. Such a view, however, has to be qualified in two important ways.

---

28. Fiṭrat Bukhārā'ī, *Sayḥa* (Istanbul, 1911), excerpted in Sadriddin 'Aynī, *Namūna-yi adabiyāt-i tājīk* (Moscow, 1926), 535.

First, discourses of ethnic belonging had already made deep inroads into Jadid thinking. The idea that the world was divided into discrete nations united by language and common descent through history was entirely new but very compelling to intellectuals in the age of empire. The corollary that national bonds were the most powerful, that knowledge of and pride in one's national origins were a necessary source of strength presented itself as natural. In Central Asia, this took the form of Turkism, the idea that the various peoples who speak Turkic languages are related and that their language, their culture, their contributions to the Islamicate past should be a point of pride. Turkism as it developed was deeply influenced by new European scholarship on history, Turcology, and anthropology, and by an enthusiasm for romantic nationalism common to the age.[29] The classificatory schemes used by anthropologists as well as states further made ethnicity seem an obvious category of identification.[30] As a cultural phenomenon, Turkism underwrote new ways of seeing the world and of imagining community that proved deeply subversive of older ways (confessional, dynastic, regional) of thinking about politics. It is unfortunate that so much scholarship conflates Turkism with *pan*-Turkism, the idea of the political unification of all Turkic peoples, and sees it only as a malign political force.[31] Pan-Turkism was one

---

29. The most concise account of the origins of Turkism in nineteenth-century discoveries in Orientalism and Turkology remains that of Ziya Gökalp, *Türkçülüğün Esasları* (Ankara, 1923), 5–10. Accounts of Turkism that trace connections across the two empires include: Akçuraoğlu Yusuf [Yusuf Akçura], "Türkçülük," in *Türk Yılı 1928*, ed. Akçuraoğlu Yusuf (Ankara, 1928), 288–459; Rafael Muhammetdin, *Türkçülüğün Doğuşu ve Gelişmesi* (Istanbul, 1998); Aybeniz Aliyeva Kengerli, *Azerbaycan'da Romantik Türkçülük*, trans. Metin Özarslan (Istanbul, 2008). In English, see David Kushner, *The Rise of Turkish Nationalism, 1876–1908* (London, 1977), which focuses only on the Ottoman Empire.

30. The state remained hesitant to recognize nationality as a category, and the 1897 census eschewed it (although the category of "native language" used by the census was widely understood to be a surrogate for it). Nationality, however, was routinely used by government statisticians and by anthropologists all through the late imperial period. That there was little agreement over ethnic categories is a different question. See S. N. Abashin, *Natsionalizmy v Srednei Azii: v poiskakh identichnosti* (St. Petersburg, 2007), 132ff.

31. In Russian and Soviet thinking, pan-Turkism was in turn rendered synonymous with pan-Islamism and associated with various regressive phenomena. This view was canonized by A. Arsharuni and Kh. Gabidullin, *Ocherki panislamizma i pantiurkizma v Rossii* (Moscow, 1931) and seldom questioned since. Post-Soviet Russian scholarship, written without recourse to work in any language other than Russian, let alone to Ottoman archival sources, effortlessly replicates the voice of Tsarist officialdom in its assessment of the two "pans." For a gratuitous example that simply replicates the voice of the Tsarist secret police and presents it as proof, see T. V. Kot′iukova, "Turetskie emissary v Rossii: dokumenty TsGA RUz 1910–1914 gg.," *Istoricheskii arkhiv*, 2004, no. 4: 85–94; for a critique and a partial corrective, see Al′fina Sibgatullina, *Kontakty tiurok-musul′man Rossiiskoi i Osmanskoi imperii na rubezhe XIX–XX vv.* (Moscow, 2010). More recent work has begun to separate Turkism from pan-Turkism, although it remains the exception rather than the rule; see O. N. Seniutkina, *Tiurkizm kak istoricheskoe iavlenie (na materialakh istorii Rossiiskoi imperii 1905–1916 gg.)* (Nizhnii Novgorod, 2007); Säbit Shïldebay, *Türïkshïldïk jäne Qazaqstandaghï ült-azattïq qozghalïs* (Almaty, 2002).

effect of the fundamental cultural shift that Turkism represented. The awareness of the Turkic origins of a community did not automatically lead to the aspiration for political unity with all other Turks. Turkism remained a polyphonic discourse in which ethnically based arguments could be deployed against other Turkists.[32] A major debate among the Tatar intelligentsia on the eve of the Russian revolution pitted "Tatarists"—those who argued that Tatars were a distinct nation, although Turkic speaking—against the "Turkists," who argued that Tatars were part of broader community of Turkic peoples. The Tatarists did not deny the Turkic origins of their community, but emphasized its uniqueness.[33] More important, as we shall in this book, the Turkestan-centered Turkism that appealed to Central Asians often took on anti-Ottoman or anti-Tatar forms.

The main currents of Turkism evolved in the Turkic-language public space described above that straddled the Ottoman and the Russian empires. In the Ottoman Empire, Turkism took the form of pride in the term *Turk* and in the contributions of the Turks to the Ottoman state. It also led to a critical attitude toward the Ottoman literary language and to a campaign of simplification that would bring the written language closer to the spoken. The rapid emergence of political Turkism after 1908, with the formation of national clubs and parties, was possible only on the basis of the long-term development of cultural Turkism. In the Russian Empire, Turkism meant the discovery of the Turkic past of various Turkic communities, a new sense of their belonging to a family, and aspirations to some sort of unity. By the turn of the twentieth century, a number of authors in both empires had written Turkist histories of their communities.[34] Turkism—and ethnic ideas in general—had in fact crept into all currents of political and social thought in large parts of the Turkic world, so that even Islamist authors were comfortable using ethnic arguments. No Central Asians contributed to the articulation of Turkism in the prewar era, but Turkism nevertheless has a serious impact on the thinking of the Jadids. It led, for instance, the Jadids to disavow the label "Sart," a generic term used by outsiders (Russians, but also Tatars and Kazakhs) to describe the sedentary population of Central Asia, and to insist that others use the "proper" national names of the peoples of Central Asia.[35] "In our

---

32. I have made this point earlier in Khalid, *Politics*, 207–208.

33. See R. F. Mukhametdinov, *Natsiia i revoliutsiia: transformatsiia natsional'noi idei v tatarskom obshchestve pervoi treti XX veka* (Kazan, 2000), 27–37.

34. In the Russian Empire, the first such histories appeared in the Volga-Ural region: Hasan Ata Mulla Muhammad oghli al-Abashi, *Mufässil tarikh-i qävm-i Türki* (Ufa, 1909); Ahmed Zeki Velidi, *Türk ve Tatar tarikhi* (Kazan, 1912); A. Battal, *Tatar tarikhi* (Kazan, 1912). These were all Turkist accounts of the history of the Muslim community of the Volga-Ural region; there was little pan-Turkist about them.

35. On the struggles around the term *Sart*, see Khalid, *Politics*, 199–209; on debates among Russian ethnographers over the definition of the term, see Abashin, *Natsionalizmy v Srednei Azii*, 95–176.

age, the 'national' [*milliyat*] question has taken precedence over the question of religion among Europeans," wrote an author, "so there is no harm if we too occasionally discuss the 'Sart' question, which is considered a national question, and thus remember our nation."[36] Turkism produced new communities and new divisions in the minds of the Jadids, so that an open letter by seven individuals to Behbudiy's magazine could state matter-of-factly that "everyone knows that the population of Turkestan is composed of Uzbek, that is Turkic; Tajik, that is, Persian [*fors xalqi*]; and Arab (Xo'ja) groups."[37] At bottom was a conviction, shared by many around the world at the time, that "religion exists only on the basis of the nation and national life. . . . A religion without a nation is destroyed."[38] Nationhood, the solidarity along lines of blood and language, was essential for survival. More important, the "Muslims of Turkestan" had come to be ethnicized.

The second thing to remember about the confessional nationalism of the Jadids is that even when they spoke of "the Muslims of Turkestan," their real constituency was much more circumscribed and encompassed only the sedentary population of the region. The Jadids came from the cities of Transoxiana and had no ties to nomadic societies, even as the distinction between nomad and sedentary had long been seen as fundamental in Central Asia. That distinction had been further heightened by the markedly different imperial policies pursued by the Russians in the nomadic parts of Turkestan. Kazakh elites in what became the Steppe *krai* had been sending their sons to Russian schools since the middle of nineteenth century. Kazakh elites in Turkestan continued the practice, so that Kazakhs from Syr Darya and Semirech'e oblasts accounted for a disproportionate part of the Russian-educated native population. More significantly, Kazakh elites from Turkestan were much more likely to participate in debates centered in the Kazakh press in the north, in Omsk, Troitsk, and Orenburg. Serali Lapin, a lawyer and an interpreter who was to play a prominent role in 1917, wrote extensively in the Russian press of Tashkent and in the Kazakh newspapers of the Steppe krai, but never in the Uzbek-language press of Turkestan. The reform of Muslim institutions played a negligible role in the thinking of the Kazakh intelligentsia, which was much more concerned with issues of Slavic settlement and loss of land by the nomads. The Kazakh intelligentsia had its own networks, its own debates, and its own passions.[39] Turkmen elites too had reached rather different

---

36. "Sort so'zi ma'lum bo'lmadi," *Oyina*, 19.07.1914, 923.

37. "Toshkanddan gila=o'pka," *Oyina*, 01.03.1914, 354.

38. A. Muzaffar, "Din millat, millat milliyat ila qoimdir," *Sadoi Turkiston*, 26.11.1914; 02.12.1914; 10.12.1914.

39. On the Kazakh intelligentsia and its articulation of a Kazakh identity, see D.A. Amanzholova, *Kazakhskii avtonomizm i Rossiia: istoriia dvizheniia Alash* (Moscow, 1994); or Steven Sabol, *Russian Colonization and the Genesis of Kazak National Consciousness* (Basingstoke, 2003).

accommodations with the Russian state (several khans had in fact been given military ranks in the Russian army), and in the absence of a tradition of book learning and city life, cultural or religious reform never emerged as a viable phenomenon in Turkmen society. One can even go so far as to argue that the term *Muslim* in the usage discussed above was restricted only to the sedentary populations of Central Asia, and that the nomads were always implicitly excluded from it. We should therefore be wary of claims of a primordial unity of the people of Turkestan that was shattered by Soviet machinations. Turkestan was quite literally a creation of the Russian conquest, and it encompassed no unity.

The Political Trajectory of Jadidism

Down to 1917, Jadidism remained primarily a cultural movement directed at the reform of Muslim society itself, rather than a discourse of political rights directed at the Russian state. To the extent that the Jadids had a political program, it was marked by a desire for inclusion into the mainstream of imperial life and the abolition of the distinctiveness of native status. Sovereignty was never an issue, not even in 1917; rather, the Jadids strived for autonomy, which, coupled with equality within an imperial framework, would produce the conditions for the flowering of the newly imagined nation of Turkestan. For obvious reasons, the nation was essential to the Jadids. As a cultural elite, they could only conceive of community as based in culture, and the only claim to leadership they could make was along cultural lines—that their possession of the cultural capital needed to navigate the modern world left them uniquely qualified to guide the nation to its salvation. A politics based on class was anathema to them. "Our present epoch is not propitious for carrying out their program," Behbudiy wrote of the Social Democrats in 1906. "Their wishes appear fantastic and joining this party is extremely dangerous for us Muslims."[40] The radical transformation of society advocated by the Social Democrats would be highly intrusive of Muslim society, its cultural practices and its solidarities, and, in the process, jeopardize the Jadids' claim to lead reform. Behbudiy need not have worried for the moment. Realities of empire ensured that Social Democratic ideas had little resonance in Muslim society until 1917. Socialism (and class-based politics) remained a European phenomenon. There were several Social Democratic circles in Turkestan (the province was a dumping ground for political exiles), but their members made

---

40. Al-Hoji Mahmudxo'ja valadi Qori Behbudxo'ja, "Khayr al-umur awsaṭihā," *Xurshid*, 11.10.1906. This suspicion marked Jadid thinkers throughout the Russian Empire; Musa Jarullah Bigi, the prominent Tatar Jadid, expressed very similar sentiments when taking stock of the Muslim political movement in 1915: *Islahat esaslari* (Petrograd, 1915), 200.

little attempt to proselytize among the natives. The urban poor of the local population used a completely different language of labor. Crafts guilds reproduced a sacralized understanding of work and a world in which neither class nor revolution figured.[41] In any case, older solidarities of craft guilds had been severely disrupted by the advent of capitalism, and already by the turn of the century, guild lodges (*takiya*) were reported to be in disuse.[42] Caught in this transformation, Muslim artisans and craftsmen did not formulate a voice of their own.

A Jadid political program could exist only in the realm of the hypothetical, because the Tsarist order afforded few opportunities for political activity. The Turkestan statute had introduced the electoral principle for lower-level administrative positions, such as volost administrators, judges, and village elders, and Tashkent received a municipal duma under the 1870 urban self-government law, but there was no space for the articulation of collective demands. Even the 1905 revolution produced minimal effect in Turkestan. The region received some representation in the State Duma, although natives and non-natives voted in separate curiae, and the elections were unequal and indirect. The First Duma was dissolved before elections could take place in Turkestan, but six deputies did participate in the short-lived Second Duma. Stolypin's revision of the electoral law in 1907 completely disenfranchised Turkestan, with even the Russian population of Turkestan left unrepresented in the Third and Fourth dumas.[43] After that, Turkestan's Muslim elites pinned their hopes on lobbying the Muslim Fraction in the Duma to work on behalf of Turkestan.[44] (The Muslim Fraction was the caucus formed by deputies from other Muslim-majority regions of the Russian Empire; it stemmed from the mobilization of a pan-Russian Muslim movement, largely at the initiative of Tatar public figures in 1905. Turkestan, with a total Muslim population equal to that of the rest of the Russian Empire, had remained marginal to the movement.) In this context, Behbudiy composed a list of his desiderata for Turkestan's position in the empire. He sent a copy to the Muslim Fraction in the hope that it would use it as a guideline in seeking new legislation for Turkestan. He also presented a copy to Count K.K. Pahlen when he led a tour of inspection of Turkestan in 1908.[45] The

---

41. Jeanine Elif Dağyeli, "*Gott liebt das Handwerk*": *Moral, Identität und religiöse Legitimierung in der mittelasiatischen Handwerks-risāla* (Wiesbaden, 2011).

42. V. P. Nalivkin et al., "Kratkii obzor sovremennogo sostoianiia i deiatel'nost musul'manskogo dukhovenstva, raznogo roda dukhovnykh uchrezhdenii i uchebnykh zavedenii tuzemnogo naseleniia Samarkandskoi oblasti s nekotorymi ukazaniiami na ikh istoricheskoe proshloe," in *Materialy po Musul'manstvu*, vyp. 1 (Tashkent, 1898), 33.

43. Khalid, *Politics*, 233–235.

44. Behbudiy, "Turkiston va dumo," *To'jjor*, 09.10.1907.

45. Pahlen's brief was to inspect institutions of imperial rule in Turkestan and to suggest ways of reforming them. His report on the tour of inspection ran to twenty volumes but produced little by way of practical results.

document had no legal standing, of course, but it provides a sense of how one important Jadid figure saw Turkestan's political future.[46]

Behbudiy envisioned Turkestan as a self-governing part of the Russian Empire, on the basis of equal and universal franchise, with control over immigration and resettlement, education, and cultural life. The central pillar of Turkestan's autonomy, however, was to be an "Administration of Spiritual and Internal Affairs" (*Idora-yi ruhoniya va doxiliya*), a combination of a spiritual assembly (which had never been introduced to Turkestan) and a ministry of internal affairs. Run by men "acquainted with the shariat and the present era," and elected for a five-year term, this administration would have jurisdiction over criminal matters and supervise the work of Muslim administrators and judges, oversee all matters of civil and personal law, supervise the functioning of mosques and madrasas, and have ultimate oversight over waqf property.[47] The purpose of the administration was not just to administer, but to reform: it would work "to bring various Sufi practices in harmony with the shariat in a manner not inconsistent with the freedom of conscience, and in this way, to protect the masses from nonsense and idle tales [*xurofot va turrahot*] and the waste of time," as well as to "attempt gradually to abolish the abominable customs practiced in the name of tradition."[48] In this modernist vision, the state would reform Islam through regulation. Behbudiy's animus toward Sufi practices, which he pejoratively referred to as a combination of *sufiylik* (literally, Sufi-ness), *xonqohdorlik* ("[Sufi] lodge-keeping"), and *muridgarlik* ("disciple-keeping"), was common to all Muslim modernists of the era, who espied in these practices a corruption of the faith and of the individuals involved. A harsh critique of customs and traditions was an integral part of the Jadid project; Behbudiy hoped that a state-funded institution would do the work of combating the evils he and other Jadids saw rampant in their society. Behbudiy's hopes for the scope of autonomy are expansive, but even more interesting is his fascination with the concept of order and regulation. The Administration of Spiritual and Internal Affairs represented uniformity, regularity, and above all, modernity to Behbudiy and Jadids like him.[49]

---

46. Behbudiy published a brief account of his proposal in the Orenburg journal *Shura* but lost his own copy of it (cf. Behbudiy, "Loyiha=proyekt," *Oyina*, 21.12.1913, 202). A copy of the document, however, ended up in the private papers of Ismail Bey Gasprinskiy and was eventually published in 2001: Necip Hablemitoğlu and Timur Kocaoğlu, "Behbudi'nin Türkistan Medeni Muhtariyeti Layıhası," in *Türkistan'da Yenilik Hareketleri ve İhtilaller, 1900–1924: Osman Hoca Anısına İncelemeler,* ed. Timur Kocaoğlu (Haarlem, 2001), 448–466 (facsimile reproduction), 438–447 (transcription in modern Turkish orthography).

47. Ibid., 453–463.

48. Ibid., 457.

49. Nor was Behbudiy alone in this. Several other mass petitions in the era of the first Russian revolution demanded the creation of a spiritual assembly for Turkestan, or the extension of the jurisdiction of the Orenburg assembly to Turkestan; see *Taraqqiy—O'rta Azyaning umr guzorlig'i,* 10.01.1906, 19.01.1906.

This logic of seeking inclusion and reform led by state institutions in the right hands defined the political aspirations of the Jadids down to the end of the old regime. They took loyalist positions when the empire went to war in 1914. In 1916, when large parts of the population rose up in revolt against the decree ending the natives' exemption from conscription, the Jadids appeared on the side of the government in support of the mobilization. The Jadids' enthusiasm for conscription is usually written out of history, but it was backed by very good logic. The exemption from conscription was a key feature of Turkestani natives' exclusion from the imperial mainstream. Anything that changed that status was welcome, and the hope remained that wartime service would lead to political concessions after the war.

If there was no likelihood of imperial authorities agreeing to such a proposal, the likelihood of the ulama of Turkestan acquiescing to it was, if anything, even smaller. It was one thing for the Jadids to wish for reform; it was quite another for them to win the agreement of other sectors of their own society. As modernist intellectuals, the Jadids were pitted as much against their own society, in whose name they professed to act, as against the colonial power. In 1917, this complex position was to be all important in determining the fate of the Jadids and their project.

The Cast of Characters

Mahmudxo'ja Behbudiy (1874–1919) of Samarqand was one of the most influential Jadids in Turkestan. He came from a family of qazis and worked as a mufti all his life. But he was also successful in trade, which made him a man of substance. He maintained houses in both the old and the new city and was a prominent public figure in Samarqand. In 1900, he had gone on the hajj and traveled in Egypt and the Ottoman Empire, from where he returned convinced of the need for reform. He became involved in a number of philanthropic efforts. He also wrote a number of primers for new-method schools as well as the play *Padarkush* (The Patricide), the first Uzbek play to be staged. In 1913, he began publishing the newspaper *Samarqand* and then the magazine *Oyina* (Mirror), the most important Jadid periodical in Turkestan.[50] Behbudiy's impeccable Islamic credentials combined with his wealth made him a prominent figure in the public of

---

50. The best accounts of Behbudiy's life appeared in the press after his death in 1919; see Mātamzada (pseud.), "Mukhtaṣar-i tarjima-yi ahvāl-i Behbūdī," *Shu'la-yi inqilāb* (08.04.1920), 4–6, or Hoji Muin, "Mahmudxo'ja Behbudiy (1874–1919)," *Zarafshon*, 25.03.1923; the most substantial modern biography is D. Alimova and D. Rashidova, *Makhmudkhodzha Bekhbudii i ego istoricheskie vozzreniia* (Tashkent, 1998).

the city and of Turkestan. In 1917, he was to play an important role in Turkestan's national movement.

Munavvar qori Abdurashidxon o'g'li (1878–1931) was the most significant Jadid figure in Tashkent, in many ways the counterpart of Behbudiy. He too came from a family of ulama and had studied at a madrasa in Bukhara before becoming convinced of the need for reform and opening a new-method school in 1902. Munavvar qori published a number of textbooks for new-method schools and was involved with several of the newspapers that appeared in Tashkent, but his real role was that of a pedagogue and an organizer. Munavvar qori sought to formalize new-method schools into a network with uniform standards and curricula. His own school, called Namuna (Model), became a model institution. Munavvar qori was also active in the city's benevolent societies. Unlike Behbudiy, however, Munavvar qori kept his distance from the Russians. He was the only Jadid figure never to publish in Ostroumov's newspaper. In 1917, he too emerged as a major political figure in Turkestan.[51]

Behbudiy and Munavvar qori were quite typical of Turkestani Jadids in having Islamic credentials. Their advocacy of reform put them on a collision course with other ulama. The poet and playwright Hamza Hakimzoda Niyoziy (1889–1929) of Kokand was, as his name indicates, the son of an apothecary who had studied in Bukhara. Hamza himself attended a madrasa in Bukhara and went on the hajj. But he also fell in love with theater and the violin and became one of the pioneers of musical theater in Turkestan.[52] Abdulla Avloniy (1878–1934) had attended both the maktab and madrasa, but around the age of fourteen, "I began reading *Tercüman* and became aware of the world."[53] In 1908, he published the short-lived newspapers *Shuhrat* and *Azya*, and subsequently authored several textbooks and collections of poetry (often for classroom use), and organized a reading room in Tashkent. He was also involved in publishing and was partner, along with ten other Tashkent Jadids, in the Maktab publishing company floated in 1914. After 1914, Avloniy also wrote a number of plays for the theater, with which he was involved also as actor, director, and manager, founding Turkestan's first regular theater troupe in 1916. Laziz Azizzoda (1895–1981), who came into

---

51. On Munavvar qori, see Sirojiddin Ahmad, "Yo'lboshchi," in Munavvar qori Abdurashidxonov, *Tanlangan asarlar* (Tashkent, 2003), 9–60.

52. As we shall see in chapter 11, Hamza's life was subject to more mythologizing than most in the Soviet era, when he was presented as "the minstrel of the revolution," a freethinker from birth. Yet, he was very much a man of his times and his education. He corresponded with his father in Arabic and Persian, and his early poetry was entirely in the Islamicate mold, as is clear from his early works finally reproduced in Hamza Hakimzoda Niyoziy, *To'la asarlar to'plami*, 5 vols. (Tashkent, 1988–89).

53. Abdulla Avloniy, "Tarjimai holim" (26.11.1932), in his *Tanlangan asarlar*, 2 vols. (Tashkent, 1998–2006), 2:288. For a biography, see Begali Qosimov, "Oq tonglarni orzulagan shoir," ibid., 1:5–80.

prominence in 1917, also came from a family of accomplishment: his paternal grandfather was a *devonbegi* in Tashkent before the Russian conquest, his maternal grandfather a scholar who traveled abroad extensively. Azizzoda's father was accomplished enough to teach his son Persian and Arabic at home.[54]

For other Jadids, commitment to reform had other sources. Obidjon Mahmudov (1871–1936) of Andijon was trained as an engineer in Russia but worked in commerce, achieving the rank of merchant of the second guild. He was deeply invested in reform, establishing a printing press and founding the newspapers *Sadoi Farg'ona* (The Voice of Ferghana) and the Russian-language *Ferganskoe ekho* (Ferghana Echo) in 1914. Saidnosir Mirjalilov (1884–1937), a cotton magnate from the town of Turkiston, similarly funded benevolent activities and the theater. He was also on friendly terms with several Jadids, whom he tided over when financial difficulties arose. Ubaydulla Xo'jayev (1886–1942) was a lawyer. Born in Tashkent, he had attended a Russo-native school, which had allowed him to find work as translator for a Russian justice of the peace. When his employer was transferred to Saratov, Xo'jayev went with him. He stayed in Saratov for several years, during which he acquired considerable legal training. He returned to Tashkent early in 1913 and set up a legal practice. At the same time, he became involved in local Jadid affairs, becoming involved in a bookshop and serving as the editor of *Sadoi Turkiston*.[55] What Mahmudov, Mirjalilov, and Xo'jayev had in common was a command of Russian and the consequent ability to function in the spheres of life that operated in that language. They emerged as major figures in the politics of 1917 and kept a semiunderground national movement going beyond the reach of the Soviet state for much of the following decade.

Two literary figures who were to reshape the Uzbek literary landscape in the decade after the revolution had made their debuts by 1917. Cho'lpon, whom we have already encountered, was born to a merchant of substance in Andijon, where he attended a Russian-native school. His father had literary tastes and Cho'lpon took to them early. As early as 1908, when he was probably only ten years old, Cho'lpon was writing public-spirited poetry. "Dr. Muhamad-Yor" was his first appearance in print (the story appeared in Mahmudov's *Sadoi Farg'ona*),

54. Laziz Azizzoda, "Sarguzashtimdan bir lavha," 2–3. Azizzoda was arrested in 1927 and spent a quarter-century in labor camps and in political disgrace, before being rehabilitated. He wrote this short memoir "for the desk drawer" in his retirement. My deepest gratitude goes to the late Sherali *aka* Turdiyev for giving me a copy of the typescript.

55. Details of Ubaydulla Xo'jayev's life remain scarce. Most of the information in this paragraph comes from the Okhrana dossier from 1916: TsGARUz, f. I-461, op. 1, d. 2263, ll. 104–108ob; see also Kh. Sadykov, "Ubaidulla Khodzhaev: shtrikhi k politicheskomu portretu," *Chelovek i politika*, 1991, no. 11: 75–82.

and Cho'lpon had established his place in the city's literary life well before the revolution. By that time, however, he had rebelled against his background. His father wanted him to study at a madrasa; to avoid this fate, Cho'lpon ran away from home and spent several years in Tashkent, which is where the revolution found him. The collapse of the autocracy enthralled him with its possibilities, and Cho'lpon was very visible in public life all through 1917. He became seriously interested in theater and wrote several pieces that were performed in the early Soviet years, but it was poetry where he really made his mark. He was the main force behind the creation of modern poetry in Uzbek. In a few short years after the revolution, he produced an oeuvre of resounding beauty and a markedly new sensibility. He was one of the main contributors to the landmark anthology *Young Uzbek Poets* that appeared in 1922 and published three volumes of his own between 1924 and 1926. He brought the language of poetry closer to everyday speech and gave it an unprecedented lyricism through his adoption of new systems of rhyme and prosody. He also translated from Russian and Persian.[56] After he ran into political trouble, he turned to writing fiction again and was able to publish his novel *Night* in 1936. For the sheer range of his contributions and for the innovations he brought to the language, Cho'lpon was one of the defining figures of the cultural revolution of the 1920s.

Abdulla Qodiriy (1894–1938) was another. Born to a family of modest means in Tashkent, Qodiriy nevertheless attended a Russian-native school, where he won a gold watch as a prize for graduating at the top of his class. Upon graduation, he took up a job as the secretary for a merchant. He first appeared in print in 1915 with a short play (on the usual theme of the destructiveness of ignorance) and a few short sketches from everyday life. After the revolution, Qodiriy became a prolific contributor in the press. While he wrote social commentary, satire was his usual mode of expression. In 1923, when *Mushtum* (The Fist) was established as Tashkent's first illustrated satirical magazine, Qodiriy was its editor. Over the years, he penned a number of memorable sketches lampooning various types in Central Asian society (but with a particular fondness for traditional mullahs and eshons as his targets). From 1920 on, however, he was at work on a novel, which began to appear in segments in 1926. *O'tkan kunlar* (Bygone Days) was

---

56. A large but scattered literature on Cho'lpon has emerged since the collapse of the Soviet Union, but we still do not have a full-length biography of him. The best is Naim Karimov, *Abdulhamid Sulaymon o'g'li Cho'lpon* (Tashkent, 1991). A short biographical notice on him by V. Ian in *Bol'shaia sovetskaia entsiklopediia*, vol. 61 (Moscow, 1934), col. 684–685, still retains significance, for the author was personally acquainted with Cho'lpon. See also Ingeborg Baldauf, "Čŭlpon," *Kindlers Neues Literatur Lexikon*, vol. 21 (Munich, 1998), 270–273, and the biographical note by Stéphane Dudoignon in his translation of Cho'lpon's *Kecha: Tchulpân, Nuit* (Paris, 2009), 420–425.

the first novel in Uzbek and did much to cement Qodiriy's place in the pantheon of Uzbek literature, which even his political difficulties could not undermine.

In Bukhara we have the contrasting figures of Sadriddin Ayni and Fayzulla Xo'jayev. Ayni (1878–1954) belonged to the last generation to receive an unreformed Bukharan madrasa education. Born to a rural family of high cultural capital, Ayni was orphaned early on. He nevertheless went to study in Bukhara, where he was able to enter the patronage network of Sharifjon Makhdum and prosper in the madrasa system, rising to become a *mudarris*, a professor, at the Mir-i Arab madrasa in Bukhara. Yet, Ayni had also become interested in reform and opened one of the first new-method schools in Bukhara. A prominent figure among the ulama, Ayni emerged as one of the main reformist figures in 1917. A victim of the emir's repression of the reformers, he was imprisoned and given seventy-five lashes. He went into exile and never returned. While he worked closely with other Bukharan reformers, Ayni remained immune to the attractions of Turkism. Although he wrote extensively in Uzbek, he emerged as the founding figure of Tajik national identity in the mid-1920s. Unusually among the Jadids, he did not fall afoul of the political police and lived out his full life. In his later years, he wrote a memoir of his times as a student in Bukhara, a text that is remarkable for its sensibility in its depiction of the life of Bukharan madrasas at the turn of the twentieth century. Ayni outlived Stalin and died as a celebrated cultural hero.[57] Fayzulla Xo'jayev (1896–1938), by contrast, was the son of one of the wealthiest merchants in Bukhara. Unusually for the time, Fayzulla was sent off to school in Moscow. He returned to Bukhara when his father died when Fayzulla was twelve. He became involved in the secret societies of Bukharan reformers and emerged as one of their main leaders in 1917. The emir's persecution drove him into exile, until he returned in 1920 as the head of government in the Bukharan People's Soviet Republic. He became a major political figure in Bukhara and then in Uzbekistan, a prominent member of the Soviet political elite, even though his position was always precarious, as we will see in this book. Fayzulla's main connection to Muslim cultural reform was through his friendship with people such as Ayni and Fitrat, while his main asset was his knowledge of Russian. Unlike most Jadids, Fayzulla wielded political power.

But I accord a central place in the narrative to Abdurauf Fitrat (1886–1938), perhaps the single most influential reformist figure of the era, both a scholar and

---

57. On Ayni, see K. S. Ayni, ed., *Kniga zhizni Sadriddina Aini* (Dushanbe, 1978), which reproduces a number of striking photographs and documents from Ayni's early years. Ayni's memoirs were published as *Yoddoshtho*, 4 vols. (Dushanbe, 1949–1953) and are available in a number of editions and translations.

a political figure, revered by his followers, and a prolific writer on most aspects of culture and nationhood examined in this book. His life spanned the enormous transformations witnessed by Central Asia. Born a decade after the final subjugation of Muslim statehood in Central Asia, he died a victim of one of the twentieth century's most repressive states. He came of age in Bukhara, the bastion of Islamic learning in the region. After a conventional madrasa education, Fitrat found himself in Istanbul for further education. The four years he spent in the Ottoman capital coincided with the tumultuous era of the constitutional revolution and the Balkan wars. There Fitrat acquired his fascination with progress and modernity, and his conviction of their grave necessity for survival in the modern world, as well as his commitment to a specific national idea. His first writings, published while he was still in Istanbul, were political tracts that emphasized the need for modern education and statecraft for the sake of self-preservation and self-strengthening. Upon his return to Bukhara, Fitrat published more reformist works that sought guidance in a scripturalist understanding of Islam. The year of the revolution brought about two stark changes in Fitrat's work. Up until the revolution, Fitrat wrote almost exclusively in Persian. In 1917, he switched to Uzbek, which he also sought to reform and reshape. He also gave up on his Islamic reformism and instead focused on an insistent Turkism, which he grounded in Central Asia itself. In the decade after 1917, Fitrat published copiously. A number of plays laid out a vision of progress that argued for struggle both against colonizers (the British as well as the Russians) and against conservative forces and habits in Muslim society itself. He was a moving force behind the reform of the language and its orthography and the creation of a literary canon. Fitrat wrote poetry according to new models he championed and produced a number of works of solid scholarship that gave shape to the Chaghatayist view of Central Asian history. For two years, Fitrat was also at the helm of affairs in the Bukharan people's republic, where he served as minister for education and head of the Council on Economic Development. Perhaps the most remarkable thing about Fitrat was that while he became a champion of European learning, he never visited Europe and did not speak any European languages (there is little reason to believe that he was functional even in Russian). His access to Europe and its modernity lay through Turkish. Fitrat's career helps us trace the many paths through which ideas of modernity and progress spread around the world and found devoted proponents in all sorts of places. Fitrat was a key figure in the articulation of the Uzbek nation as the inheritor of the Turko-Islamic tradition of statehood in Central Asia and one of the most significant creators and theorizers of the new culture that emerged in the period under review here. He will appear is every single chapter of this book.

On the Eve

As the year 1917 dawned, there was little reason to believe that tumultuous change was afoot. The big issue of the moment was the rebellion in the nomadic areas of Turkestan against an imperial decree that had revoked the native population's exemption from military service and levied Turkestani troops for service in the rear. The rebellion that broke out over the summer took aim at government functionaries and European peasant settlers. Very quickly, it escalated into nakedly ethnic warfare between Europeans (settlers armed by the state as well as military reinforcements sent from European Russia) and the nomads. In true colonial fashion, the odds were stacked against the natives, and they suffered grievously. The bloodshed continued into the new year.[58] The Jadids, however, took a dim view of the uprising. For them, conscription was the removal of a legal disability, a sign of the inclusion of Turkestanis into the imperial mainstream, and a reason to hope for political concessions after the war. They actively supported the authorities' efforts to recruit, while at the same time calling attention to the atrocities being committed by armed settlers against the native population. The rebellion of 1916 and its aftermath had also made clear that the fundamental cleavages in Central Asia involved not class but race and nationality. As the new year dawned, Turkestan was besieged in this colonial conflict. By the beginning of March, the colonial order had been turned on its head. Or so it seemed.

---

58. Surprisingly, very little has been written about this rebellion. Edward D. Sokol, *The Revolt of 1916 in Russian Central Asia* (Baltimore, 1954), remains the only narrative account of the uprising. See also Jörn Happel, *Nomadische Lebenswelten und zarische Politik: der Aufstand in Zentralasien 1916* (Stuttgart, 2010), and Daniel Brower, *Turkestan and the Fate of the Russian Empire* (London, 2003), chap. 1. There do exist a number of collections of archival documents on the subject; see, for instance, *Qaharlï 1916 jïl/Groznyi 1916-i god* (Almaty, 1998), 2 vols.

THE MOMENT OF OPPORTUNITY

The collapse of the Tsarist Autocracy in February 1917 transformed the calculus of power throughout the Russian Empire. The abdication of the tsar was universally acclaimed as the dawn of liberty, the beginning of a new era in the history of the various peoples inhabiting the empire. In a series of sweeping reforms, the Provisional Government abolished all legal distinctions between citizens on the basis of rank, religion, sex, or ethnicity, and granted every citizen over the age of twenty the right to vote. It also guaranteed the absolute freedom of the press and of assembly. Turkestanis had become citizens.

This fact placed the politics of cultural reform in Turkestan on an entirely new footing. What had been merely hypothetical had become possible, and the politics of exhortation suddenly gave way to that of mobilization. For the intelligentsia, the revolution brought immense promise. The new era would allow them to implement their vision of reform and achieve the modernity of which they dreamed for the nation. The enthusiasm that the possibilities aroused and the alacrity with which the intelligentsia jumped into action are defining features of that remarkable year. And, yet, the enthusiasm quickly ran into reality. The intelligentsia faced intense opposition from within Muslim society as its claim to leadership was rejected by large segments of the Muslim population. Meanwhile, the settler population mobilized largely along ethnic lines to preserve its privileged position. Bloodshed continued in Semirech'e, while the first intimations of famine were apparent in food shortages by the summer. As political order evaporated throughout the empire, Turkestan was largely left to its own devices. By the end of the year, European soldiers and workers had seized power in the name of the revolution, transforming yet again the landscape of Muslim cultural reform.

These complicated events hurled the Jadids onto a trajectory that took them in unexpected directions. In November, they found themselves experimenting with government, as they proclaimed Turkestan autonomous and created a provisional government in Kokand. The rapidly shifting geopolitics in the winter of 1917–18, with the Russian war effort collapsing and the Ottomans advancing into the Caucasus, presented new opportunities, as it became possible briefly to imagine politics outside the Russian orbit. Yet the overriding fact of the year was intense polarization within Muslim society and a profound ethnic conflict between European settlers and the indigenous Muslim population. Many of the enthusiasms aroused by the revolution in March 1917 had drowned in blood by the next spring as Central Asia descended into chaos. These experiences had a lasting impact on the intelligentsia, for they produced an intense cultural radicalization and a far-reaching ethnicization of the political imagination. The revolution of 1917 reshaped the worldview and the agenda of reform for the intelligentsia. This chapter explores the origins of many of these transformations.

From Exhortation to Mobilization

The Jadids acted with alacrity and sought to seize the leadership of the Muslim community at the "dawn of freedom."[1] Even before the Provisional Government in Petrograd turned all former subjects of Nicholas II into equal citizens of Russia, the Jadids had begun to mobilize the urban population in Turkestan. The epicenter of this mobilization was, of course, Tashkent, where a number of public gatherings attracted thirty thousand men each in the first weeks of March. Nothing like these crowds had ever been seen in Central Asia outside of wartime. Very quickly, these meetings adopted the revolutionary order of choosing (by acclamation) presidiums and executive committees and issuing demands and proclamations. A meeting at the Jome' mosque on 13 March voted to form a forty-eight-member committee to be called the Toshkand Shuroi Islomiyasi

---

1. This chapter presents in a highly condensed form an account of the complex politics of 1917 in Turkestan. For longer accounts from various perspectives, see Saidakbar Agzamkhodzhaev, *Istoriia Turkestanskoi avtonomii: Turkiston muxtoryiati* (Tashkent, 2006); *Turkestan v nachale XX veka: k istorii istokov natsional'noi nezavisimosti* (Tashkent, 2006), 18–112; Adeeb Khalid, *The Politics of Muslim Cultural Reform: Jadidism in Central Asia* (Berkeley, 1998), chap. 8; A. Khalid, "Turkestan v 1917–1922 godakh: bor'ba za vlast' na okraine Rossii," in *Tragediia velikoi derzhavy: natsional'nyi vopros i raspad Sovetskogo Soiuza* (Moscow, 2005), 189–226.

(Tashkent Muslim Council, henceforth Shuro) which would function as the local government of Tashkent's old city.[2] Similar meetings, if perhaps on a less spectacular scale, took place in almost every city of Turkestan, with the Tashkent Shuro sending delegations to other cities to establish local counterparts, induct new members, and raise funds.[3] The Shuro could not assume the functions of municipal self-government, but it did emerge as an umbrella for all Muslim organizations in Turkestan.

The first public meetings were organized by Munavvar qori and Ubaydulla Xo'jayev.[4] The intelligentsia had assumed that its knowledge of the modern world uniquely qualified it for leadership. That claim was instantaneously contested, however. On 6 March, Xo'jayev and Toshpo'lot Norbutabekov, another lawyer with a university education, got themselves co-opted as the only two "native" members of the executive of the Committee of Public Organizations formed around the Tashkent city duma. This was an attempt to bridge the gap between the Russian and indigenous political movements and to make use of the opportunity provided by the events. But this action was resented from the beginning, with many asking why these "youth" had got elected when no one from the ulama, functionaries, or the merchants had been asked to join.[5] The ulama and the urban notables, the established elites in society, were not willing to concede leadership so easily.

Enthusiasm carried matters forward in the first weeks and the mobilization culminated in the First Congress of the Muslims of Turkestan that opened in Tashkent on 16 April. Representatives of all currents of opinion from the indigenous Muslim population attended. The sixteen-point agenda for the congress included a wide array of questions dealing with the political future of Turkestan, ranging from the attitude toward the new government, the forms of state organization, food supply, and land and water rights to questions of the reform of education.[6] The congress elected a twelve-member delegation to attend the forthcoming All-Russian Muslim Congress organized in Moscow by the Muslim Fraction of the State Duma and decided to establish a Turkestan National Central Council (Turkiston Milliy Markaz Shurosi) as its standing executive organ.[7] It also voted in favor of Turkestan being territorially

2. *Najot*, 19.03.1917.
3. *Najot*, 26.03.1917; *Ulug' Turkiston*, 25.04.1917; *Tirik so'z* (Kokand), 02.04.1917.
4. TsGARUz, f. I-461, op. 1, d. 2263, ll. 104–108ob.
5. "Toshkandda hurriyat harakatlari," *Najot*, 23.03.1917.
6. *Ulug' Turkiston*, 25.04.1917.
7. *Kengash*, 31.08.1917.

autonomous in a democratic federative Russian republic.[8] But the euphoria of the occasion could not hide deep divisions in Muslim society. The opening up on the political realm had brought existing conflicts in society to a new level and given them new urgency. The unity represented by the April congress quickly disappeared and a fractured political landscape emerged in Turkestan's Muslim society.

On one side were the self-proclaimed proponents of progress, who sought inclusion in the universalist order proclaimed by the Provisional Government. They entered the fray with great enthusiasm, forming clubs and unions, starting newspapers, opening new schools, and organizing crash courses for training teachers to teach with the new method. These were all new sites of cultural and political action that brought a number of young men into public life for the first time. Shuroi Islomiya remained their organizational hub, where the Jadids were joined by men who commanded Russian educations but had little or no prior presence in the prerevolutionary project of cultural reform. Perhaps paradoxically, the opening up of the political arena had heightened the importance of a command of Russian, without which indigenous actors could achieve little in the new political field. In the next few years, a command of Russian became a major form of political capital. Many of those who commanded Russian were Kazakhs from Semirech'e or Syr Darya oblasts, where elites had a much longer tradition of sending their sons to Russian schools than in the rest of Turkestan. One of them, Mustafa Cho'qoy (Chokaev or Shoqay, 1890–1941), scion of an aristocratic family from Aq Masjid (now Qizilorda, in Kazakhstan) and a graduate of the law faculty of the University of St. Petersburg, was to play a central role in the drama that unfolded in 1917. And then there was the formidable figure of Ahmed Zeki Velidi (Validov, later Togan, 1890–1970), the young Bashkir historian based in Petrograd who arrived in Tashkent in the hope of organizing the local political scene on behalf of the Muslim Fraction of the former State Duma. Velidi was already a widely published historian, in both Tatar and Russian, and a major Turkist thinker.[9]

More radical than Shuro was the Turon group (to'da) that coalesced around the theater troupe of the same name. The troupe had come into existence in 1914 as a result of disagreements between merchants and the youth over, among other

8. *Najot*, 23.04.1917. The resolutions of this congress can be found most easily in Robert Paul Browder and Alexander F. Kerensky, eds., *The Russian Provisional Government, 1917: Documents*, 3 vols. (Stanford, 1961), 1:420–421; see also later accounts by important participants: Mahmudxo'ja Behbudiy, "Turkiston muxtoriyati," *Hurriyat* (Samarqand), 19.12.1917, and A. Z. V. Togan, *Hâtıralar: Türkistan ve Diğer Müslüman Doğu Türklerinin Millî Varlık ve Kültür Mücadeleleri*, 2nd ed. (Istanbul, 1999), 126–128.

9. Togan, *Hâtıralar*, 125.

things, the permissibility of theater.[10] In 1917, Turon took cultural and political positions considerably more radical than those of the Shuro. Headed by Abdulla Avloniy, Turon also included Nizomiddin Xo'jayev and Shokirjon Rahimiy, and several other figures who were to be major public figures in the years to come. The modernists grounded their claim to leadership in their knowledge of the needs of the age and their ability to function in the new order, which allowed them also to plot the path to the future. That claim also entailed criticism of other groups in society that hindered the march to progress. "Old Man Ostroumov had been sent to Turkestan to put it into the deep sleep of the Seven Sleepers," wrote Mirmuhsin Shermuhammadov. "Here, he found many associates, and called upon many national infidels [*milliy kofirlari*] who answered to the name of qazi, mudarris, or to'ra," referring to titles borne by religious dignitaries. Such "enemies of the faith" (*din dushmonlari*) and "microbes of the nation" (*millat miqrublari*) had to be cast aside in the new order.[11] Indeed, the first few weeks of the revolution saw numerous qazis removed from their posts by acclamation at public gatherings, which also demanded reelections of others.[12]

On the other side were those whose authority lay in their command of the traditions of the community, the established elites in society, men of traditional Islamic learning (the ulama) and merchants (the boylar). Apart from wanting to ward off the claim to leadership staked by the Jadids, these conservative forces in society sought to *maintain* the difference that had marked their society off from the rest of the empire. They did not perceive their society to be in a crisis and did not deem radical cultural transformation necessary. They too celebrated the revolution as the dawn of liberty, but their conception of what that liberty would be was quite different. They coalesced around the defense of "Islam"—that is, their understanding of what Islam was—and the leadership was assumed by the leading ulama of Tashkent. By May, they had seceded from the Shuro and formed the Ulamo Jamiyati (Society of Ulama). On the face of it, their rhetoric was not very different from that of the Jadids. They too celebrated the revolution. "The revolution and the transformation of the times . . . has given us the possibility of complete freedom in our religious and national affairs. Therefore, it is extremely important, necessary, and obligatory for the Islamic scholars of Tashkent, as well as for merchants and other inhabitants, to work as one body and one soul to benefit from this divine gift

---

10. Laziz Azizzoda, "Turkistonning uyg'onish tarixi" (ms., 1925/1967; O'zFAShI inv. 11895), 76–77, 97.

11. Mirmuhsin Shermuhammadov, "Hurriyatdan nechuk foydalanamiz!" *Najot*, 09.04.1917.

12. *Najot*, 26.03.1917, 09.04.1917 (demand for reelection of all qazis in Tashkent), 28.04.1917 (reelection in Andijon); *Ulug' Turkiston*, 05.05.1917 (removal of qazis in Kokand). See also Muallim Shokir ul-Muxtoriy, *Kim qazi bo'lsin* (Kokand, 1917).

of LIBERTY."[13] But their conception of that liberty was quite different. Liberty meant the possibility of the full application of Islamic law as interpreted by the ulama and without any limitations placed by Russian law. In Namangan, a local committee dominated by ulama began shutting down new-method schools and arresting and flogging those who did not pray.[14] The ulama themselves, as "heirs to the prophets" (*vursat ul-anbiyo*) and interpreters of the shariat, were the logical guides to the community's salvation. The claim to leadership was backed by acerbic attacks (or counterattacks) on the "youth" and others who challenged the ulama's authority:

> In each age ... a group of hypocrites that is both prevaricator and deluder splits off [from the Muslim community] and, heaven forefend, seeks to cut down the tree of the noble shariat and to deprive people of its fruit. In its place, it seeks to plant the tree of infidelity and error and to lure Muslims off the straight path of the shariat. Particularly in our times, [such] a tribe of innovationists has emerged and has begun to invite people to error with false claims that "the rule of the shariat should end and the service to the Qur'an be over, and in its place we should make laws according to our own intellect." May God Almighty silence the tongues and blacken the faces of this tribe of hypocrites and innovationists.[15]

This was the language of an Islam that looked to tradition to affirm itself and was untroubled by fears of the inadequacy of that tradition to meet the demands of the future.

Yet, for all that, the Ulamo Jamiyati was more than just a trade union of ulama; it represented conservative groups in Muslim society who were less enthusiastic about the promise of universalism brought by the revolution and who felt threatened by the bid for leadership made by the Jadids and men of Russian education. The base of support for the Ulamo Jamiyati was composed of merchants and urban notables. It was headed not by a religious dignitary, but by the remarkable figure of Serali Lapin. A Kazakh from an important family from Aqmasjid (now Qizilorda), Lapin possessed a Russian legal education and had spent long years in state service as an interpreter.[16] He published historical works in Russian but was also active in Muslim public life. In 1914, he was one of three Turkestani delegates to the (admittedly low-profile and largely unsuccessful) fourth All-Russian Muslim Congress,[17] where he defended the shariat against Kazakh figures such

13. Ahrorxon Maxdum, "Muhtaram musulmon birodarlar," *al-Izoh*, 16.06.1917, 3.
14. *Najot*, 09.04.1917.
15. Mullo Sho Islom Kotib, "Tanbih," *al-Izoh*, 16.06.1917, 12–13.
16. TsGARUz, f. I-47, d. 2769.
17. *Oyina*, 28.06.1914, 863.

as Älikhan Bökeykhanov who wanted to exclude the Kazakh steppe from the jurisdiction of the Orenburg Spiritual Assembly.[18] Yet Lapin's daughter studied at the Smolnyi Institute for Noble Maidens in St Petersburg, imperial Russia's foremost finishing school, and married Sanjar Asfendyarov, the Kazakh doctor, historian, and politician.[19] Lapin clearly represented a constituency broader than just the ulama in opposition to the Jadids. The Ulamo Jamiyati campaigned in the municipal elections held over the summer across Turkestan and won handy victories over the Jadids. In Tashkent in July, the Ulamo Jamiyati won 62 of the 112 seats in Tashkent's city duma while the Shuroi Islomiya managed only 11.

Nowhere was the conflict between modernists and conservatives starker than in Bukhara. Bukharan reformers hoped that the demise of the old order would lead to reform in Bukhara too. A semisecret society organized in the house of Fayzulla Xo'jayev dispatched two of its members to Samarqand to send the following telegram to the Provisional Government in Petrograd: "Great Russia, through its devoted sons, has irretrievably overthrown the old despotic regime, and founded in its place a free, democratic government. We humbly ask that the new Russian government in the near future instruct our government to change the manner of its governance to the bases of freedom and equality, so that we may [also] take pride in the fact that we are under the protection of Great Free Russia."[20] Bukharan Jadids knew full well that their main support lay outside of Bukhara. In addition to the Provisional Government, they also appealed to the Shuroi Islomiya in Samarqand and to pan-Russian Muslim organizations. The Provisional Government was well disposed toward reform but divided over how to proceed. Liberals in the Provisional Government wanted to intervene forcefully and dictate terms to Alim Khan, but more moderate opinions prevailed. A. Ia. Miller, the Russian Resident (as the Political Agent now came to be called), was convinced that reform should emanate from the emir himself and should accord with "the shariat." Reform dictated from the outside, he feared, would provoke the hostility of the ulama, who could produce a conflagration across the region that might invite intervention from Afghanistan.[21] Over the month of

18. Tomohiko Uyama, "Changing Religious Orientation among Kazakh Intellectuals in the Tsarist Period: Between Sharia, Secularism, and Philosophical Search," in *Islam, State and Society across the Qazaq Steppe (18th-Early 20th Centuries)*, eds. Niccolò Pianciola and Paolo Sartori (Vienna, 2013), 113.

19. Elmira Jarïlkasïnqïzï Eziretbergenova, *Seralï Lapin: ömïrï, qoghamdïq qïzmetï, shïgharmashïlïq mŭrasï: avtoreferatï* (Almaty, 2004).

20. Quoted by F. Kasymov and B. Ergashev, "Bukharskaia revoliutsiia: dorogu vybral kurultai," *Rodina*, 1989, no. 10: 33.

21. "Bukhara v 1917 godu," *Krasnyi arkhiv*, no. 20 (1927): 81–82. For a detailed account of the relations between the Residency and the emir in the spring of 1917, see V. L. Genis, *Vitse-konsul Vvedenskii: sluzhba v Persii i Bukharskom khanstve (1906–1920 gg.)* (Moscow, 2003), 84–106.

March, Miller and Alim Khan worked out a draft of a political manifesto. After it was approved by St Petersburg, Alim Khan proclaimed it on 7 April at an august ceremony. The manifesto promised state supervision of functionaries, the suppression of unjust taxes, and the establishment of a state exchequer and a budget. It also proclaimed the creation of an elected council in the city of Bukhara to oversee matters of public health and sanitation. Finally, the manifesto expressed Alim Khan's intention of "taking all measures to disseminate education and the sciences . . . in strict accordance with the shariat," including the establishment of Bukhara's first printing press.[22] Over the previous weeks, the emir had removed several conservative ulama opposed to reform from the capital and replaced them by reformers. Sharifjon Makhdum, who became the new *qāżī kalān* (chief judge), and who had read out the manifesto, had deep connections with the city's reformers. The manifesto outlined a minimalist program of reform, but it nevertheless seemed that reformers were in the ascendant.

That sense of success did not last long. The day after the proclamation of the manifesto, the Jadids organized a demonstration to "thank the emir," but also to assert the presence of reform in public space. They were met by a counter-demonstration organized by conservative ulama and their supporters. For many who saw Bukhara as the last redoubt of Muslim rule in Central Asia, "liberty" and "equality" carried rather different connotations than they did in Turkestan. In the words of a reformist notable of Bukhara, for the opponents of reform "the meaning of liberty was just that there would be no veil or modesty for women, [who would] walk around the streets and bazaars bareheaded like the women of the Christians and mingle with unrelated men, while the meaning of equality was that there was no difference between the ulama of Islam and Jews or Hindus, and that Jadids would remove turbans from the heads of the august ulama and replace them with the Russian *shapka* or the Jewish *telpak*."[23] In its radical eradication of difference, "liberty" was akin to "disorder," and at one point, the conservative demonstration is said to have proclaimed out loud, "We do not want our Islamic lands to be liberated and we do not want indifference to the religion of the Prophet" (*māyān . . . ba ḥurriyat shudan-i mamālik-i islāmiya-yi khvudhā rāżī nadārīm va az dīn-i muḥammadī bēzārī nakhvāhīm*).[24] The fact that the Jadid

22. The text of the manifesto may be found in Sadriddin Ayniy, *Buxoro inqilobining tarixi*, ed. Sharifa Tosheva and Shizuo Shimada (Tokyo, 2010), 186–187. (This is an edition of Ayniy's manuscript that was published in a slightly shortened form as *Buxoro inqilobi tarixi uchun materiallar* [Moscow, 1926].)

23. Sharīfjān Makhdūm Ṣadr-i Żiyā, *Rūznāma-yi Ṣadr-i Żiyā: vaqāyiʿ-nigārī-yi taḥavullāt-i siyāsī-ijtimāʿī-yi Bukhārā-yi sharīf*, ed. Muḥammadjān Shakūrī Bukhārāyī (Tehran, 1382/2004), 266.

24. Muḥammad ʿAlī ibn Muḥammad Sayyid Baljuvānī, *Tārikh-i nāfiʿī*, ed. Ahror Mukhtor (Dushanbe, 1994), 47. Baljuvānī was an eyewitness who wrote his account in the second half of the 1920s. In his own voice too Baljuvānī uses *hurriyat*, liberty, almost synonymously with *fitna*, disorder.

demonstration included members of the city's Shiʻi and Jewish communities in a prominent role seemed to confirm all the fears of the conservatives. The confrontation turned bloody and many Jadids, including Sharifjon Makhdum, were assaulted. The emir had no desire to take on the conservatives. He instead chose to ride their anger to squelch all talk of reform and thereby maximize his independence from Russian rule. His government pursued the Jadids, arresting approximately thirty of them in the next few hours. Sadriddin Ayni was arrested and imprisoned in the notorious dungeon in the palace, where he was ultimately given seventy-five lashes of the whip. Other reformers fled to Kagan, the Russian settlement outside the old city, where they sought the intercession of the Residency in negotiating an amnesty for themselves and an end to the persecution of their comrades. The emir granted them an audience on 14 April, but the occasion turned into a nightmare. The ulama in the audience were in no mood for compromise, and the emir left the room in the middle of the meeting. Meanwhile, a crowd had gathered outside the palace, seeking the Jadids' heads. The Cossack escort of the Residency held it off until reinforcements could arrive from Kagan and extricate the Jadids and the Resident from their predicament.[25] This was the end of the Jadids' experience with public life in Bukhara. From then on, they were to work to bring outside forces to bear on their struggle. Their exile began in Kagan, where they formed an organization called Shuroi Islomiya after the manner of reformist Muslim organizations all over Turkestan,[26] and led eventually to Samarqand and Tashkent, and for some, to Moscow.

Alim Khan, having burned the bridges, proceeded to appoint conservatives to high ranking positions and ignore the revolution raging beyond his domain. On 6 May, Xolmurod Toshkandiy, a leading conservative, published a fatwa proclaiming all Jadids, in Bukhara and elsewhere, to be "sinners and enemies [*osiy va yogʻiy*]," whose lives and property were fair game.[27] Antireform ulama in the city had defeated the proponents of reform and the manifesto remained a dead letter. Instead, the emir spent the rest of the year building up his army and maximizing his independence from the Russian state. Bukhara came to be the center of anti-Jadid sentiment all over Central Asia, as the conflict between reformers and their conservative opponents defined the politics of Muslim society for years to come.

---

25. There are several indigenous sources on the events of March and April 1917; see Ayniy, *Buxoro inqilobining tarixi*, 169–217; Ṣadr-i Żiyā, *Rūznāma*, 257–280; Baljuvānī, *Tārikh-i nāfiʻī*, 42–51; Mirza Salimbek, *Tarikhi salimi (istochnik po istorii Bukharskogo emirata)*, trans. N. K. Norqulov (Tashkent, 2009), 140–150. On debates within the Provisional Government, see V. L. Genis, "Borʻba vokrug reform v Bukhare: 1917 god," *Voprosy istorii*, 2001, no. 11–12: 18–37.

26. "Buxoro ahvoli," *Ulugʻ Turkiston*, 25.04.1917.

27. "Bukhara v 1917 godu," *Krasnyi arkhiv*, 109; Ayniy, *Buxoro inqilobining tarixi*, 200.

That conflict was of a fundamental nature. The Jadids were enthused by the possibility of *inclusion* in a universalist order promised by the revolution. As equal citizens of Russia, Turkestanis would be able to embark on the path to civilization. The conservatives feared the loss of distinctions that set Muslim society apart from others and maintained hierarchy in the world. If liberation meant that the ulama were to wear hats and women to go unveiled, then it was not desirable.

Contesting Islam

The political mobilization of the indigenous population began in the name of "the Muslims of Turkestan." All groups in the political leadership agreed on this combination of the territorial and confessional principles, but they nevertheless imbued them with different emphases. Throughout the year, the ulama pressed their claims in terms of their possession of Islamic knowledge. They were the true guardians of the community and its guides in this moment of transformation. They had little patience for their challengers, whom they dismissed as "inexperienced youth . . . who had received neither a complete religious, nor worldly education." In the summer, the ulama refused to field a joint slate of candidates with the Shuroi Islomiya for Tashkent's municipal elections because, they argued, they knew "which children [*bolalar*] would gain control of the public affairs of the Muslims of Tashkent" if they cooperated.[28] In September, in a congress that attracted delegates from all over Turkestan as well as from the neighboring oblasts of the Steppe krai, the ulama resolved that "the affairs of religion and of this world should not be separated, i.e., everything from schools to questions of land and justice should be solved according to the shariat," of which they were to be the sole interpreters.[29] Their argument for the authority of Islam and the shariat was an assertion of their own power and of a social order that had emerged in the previous half-century.

The ulama's opponents also spoke of Islam and the shariat, but in a rather different way. For the Jadids, "the advent of liberty" was an opportunity to reform Islam and to reawaken it. Only a thoroughgoing reform would solve the community's problems and ensure its future. At the Second Turkestan Muslim Congress in early September, the Shuro presented its plan for Turkestan's political

---

28. Ulamo Jamiyati, *Haqiqatg'a xilof torqatilgan xitobnomag'a javob va ham bayon-i ahvol* (Tashkent, 1917), 2, 5–7.

29. "Ulamo isyazdining qarorlari," *Ulug' Turkiston*, 30.09.1917.

future. Turkestan was to have its own duma with authority in all matters except external affairs, defense, posts and telegraphs, and the judiciary; all citizens of Russia were to be equal, regardless of religion, nationality, or class, and the freedoms of assembly, religion, and conversion were to be guaranteed. In terms of personal law, Muslims were to be governed by the shariat, and a resolution called for the establishment of a shariat administration (*mahkama-yi shar'iya*) in each oblast. The crucial difference with the ulama's position was the provision that the administrations be elected and that their members be "educated and aware of contemporary needs" (*zamondan xabardor, ilmlik kishilar*).[30] The debate was not one between Muslim and secular notions of politics, but over different understandings of Islam. Nor were the Jadids without support from the ulama. Some Jadids had impeccable credentials as ulama (Behbudiy being the best example), but they acquired the support of some other ulama as well. In September, such reformist ulama organized a Fuqaho Jamiyati (Society of Jurists) as a counterweight to the Ulamo Jamiyati. Headed by the mufti Sadriddin-xon Sharif-xo'ja o'g'li, it consistently supported the Jadids of the Shuroi Islomiya and provided them Islamic legitimacy.[31] Yet, for many Jadids, Islam had come to be intertwined with ethnic understandings of the nation.

The Sorrows of the Homeland

Abdurauf Fitrat fled Bukhara in April and found refuge in Samarqand, where he began writing for *Hurriyat* (Liberty), a newspaper founded by Behbudiy. In July, he published a free verse poem called "Sorrows of the Homeland" that began:

O great Turan, land of lions!
What happened to you? What state are you in? What days have fallen upon you?
O glorious cradle of Chinggises, Temurs, Oghuzes, [and] Attilas! . . . How did you fall into the pit of your slavery?[32]

---

30. *Turon*, 14.09.1917. The ulama did not participate in this congress and tried to sabotage it by describing it in a pamphlet as a conference of atheists: *Kengash*, 12.09.1917. It should be obvious that the Shuro's proposals bore striking continuities with Behbudiy's desiderata of reform from 1905 discussed in chapter 1.

31. "Toshkand Fuqaho jamiyati," *Kengash*, 08.09.1917; see also Paolo Sartori, "When a *Mufti* Turned Islamism into Political Pragmatism: Sadreddin-Khan and the Struggle for an Independent Turkestan," *Cahiers d'Asie central*, no. 15–16 (2007), 128–129.

32. Fitrat, "Yurt qayg'usi," *Hurriyat*, 28.07.1917 (also in Fitrat, *Tanlangan asarlar*, 5 vols. [Tashkent, 2000–2010], 1:31).

"Great Turan" here was the homeland of the Turks, the birthplace of world conquerors, and the center of world empires, whose recent misfortunes had to be
remedied. The "Muslims of Turkestan" had become Turks and their homeland
the cradle of a great race of heroes. The Russian revolution provided the opportunity for the Turks to take their place again in the world as Turks. In the four
years that Fitrat spent in Istanbul, he had published only in Persian. His work was
intensely patriotic, but the homeland (*vatan*) then was Bukhara, which remained
ethnically unmarked. The move from Bukhara to Turan in Fitrat's imagination
was accompanied by a thorough ethnicization of the latter. In the poem quoted
above, the pre-Islamic Attila rubbed shoulders with Oghuz Khan, the mythical
Islamizer of the Turks, Chinggis Khan, the non-Muslim conqueror who ravaged
many Muslim states, and the Muslim Temur. What they had in common was their
birth in "Turan" and their ostensibly common ethnicity.

Fitrat was far from being the only one to celebrate the Turkic heritage
of Central Asia. Temur and Turan became central features of the political
imagination of the Jadids in 1917. This sudden explosion of Turkism was
startling. The years of the war almost seem to have provided a period of incu-
bation which then produced the Turkism of 1917, when freedom of expression allowed the articulation of ideas hitherto taboo. The sense of urgency
and opportunity shared by so many in the Russian Empire during that spring
and summer of revolution also likely heightened the significance attached
to Turkism. For the Jadids, as for many modernist intellectuals around the
world, the nation was the only guarantor of success in the modern world;
national self-consciousness was a necessary form of self-awareness, without
which national solidarity was impossible. And the more the ulama captured
the market on Islam, the more their challengers leaned toward the nation as
the fundamental form of solidarity.

Turkism excited Muslim intellectuals throughout the Russian Empire, and
in the free conditions of 1917 their ideas also flowed into Turkestan. The most
strident expressions of Turkism came from Tatars, whose newspaper in Tashkent was called *Ulug' Turkiston* (Great Turkestan). In its first issue, Nushirvan
Yavushev claimed that the "thirty million Turko-Tatars in Russia" were, "from
the point of view of race, nationality, and language tied to one another like the
children of the same father and the branches of the same tree. Turkestan is the
original homeland of the Turks."[33] For Yavushev, Turkic unity extended across
the entire Eurasian steppe and encompassed the Mongols as well. He wrote a play
called *Chingiz-xon* (Chinggis Khan) that extolled the conqueror as the unifier

---

33. N. Yavushev, "Turkiston oftonumiya oluv haqinda," *Ulug' Turkiston*, 05.05.1917.

of Turks, Tatars, and Mongols.[34] Yavushev was a young Tatar scholar who had who spent several years in Turkestan and Chinese Turkestan, wrote copiously in both the Tatar and the Central Asian Jadid press about his travels as well as the history of the areas he visited.[35] Zeki Velidi similarly did much to transform the parameters of Jadid discourse in this direction. In a series of essays he wrote for a Kokand journal *Yurt* (Homeland), he laid out the Turkist case in all its clarity. Turkestan was the first land inhabited by Turks to accept Islam and was one of the centers of Islamic civilization during its heyday. But the Turks, in spite of their political and demographic superiority, became "imprisoned in the civilization of the Iranians." Turkic intellectuals wrote in Arabic or Persian and neglected their own language. The literature produced at the courts of Bukhara, Ferghana, and Khiva had not a smidgeon of Turkic element in it, but was a pale imitation of Persian culture, and even the everyday speech of the cities had become inter-mixed with Persian vocabulary. All of that needed to be reversed: a search for "our own national spiritual wealth" was necessary and possible in the new order.[36] Similarly, an Azerbaijani delegation arrived in June to organize local branches of the Turkic Federalist Party that was to seek territorial autonomy for the Turkic peoples of the Russian Empire. The delegation traveled around Turkestan and at a congress in Skobelev established a Turkestan branch of the party.[37]

Yet, in the end, the Turkism of Central Asian intellectuals was not dependent on Turkic intellectuals from other parts of the Russian Empire. Fitrat articu-lated a Turkestan-centered Turkism that celebrated Turkestan's own history and its own heroes. Of those heroes, Chinggis Khan was a complex figure. His conquests had reshaped Eurasia and he had remained a source of legitimacy across the vast region. Over the centuries his memory had been thoroughly indigenized.[38] However, considerable unease remained about him, for he was a non-Muslim who was responsible for the destruction of the caliphate, and of whole cities and countries in the Muslim world. Temur (Timur or Tamerlane,

---

34. The play has not survived, but a brief synopsis may be found in Miyon Buzruk Solihov, *O'zbek teatr tarixi uchun materiallar* (Tashkent, 1935), 126–127.

35. Typhus cut his life short in the autumn of 1917; his obituary appeared in *Hurriyat*, 17.11.1917.

36. Ahmad Zaki Validiy, "Milliy, ruhoniy boylig'imiz," *Yurt*, no. 2 (16.05.1917), 17–20.

37. *Kengash*, 28.07.1917; Khalid, *Politics*, 266–267; Agzamkhodzhaev, *Istoriia Turkestanskoi avtonomii*, 159–164. The Turkic Federalist Party (Türk Ədəmi-Mərkəziyyət firqəsi) was founded in Gəncə in May 1917 and soon merged with Müsavat (Equality), the liberal democratic party of the Azerbaijani intelligentsia. See Salavat Iskhakov, *Rossiiskie musul'mane i revoliutsiia* (Moscow, 2004), 208–209; an English translation of its program is in Hisao Komatsu, "The Program of the Turkic Federalist Party in Turkistan (1917)," in *Central Asia Reader: The Rediscovery of History*, ed. H.B. Paksoy (Armonk, NY, 1994), 117–126.

38. Michal Biran, *Chinggis Khan* (Oxford, 2007); Beatrice Forbes Manz, "Mongol History Rewrit-ten and Relived," *Revue des mondes musulmans et de la Méditérranée*, no. 89–90 (2000): 129–149.

1336–1405), who had established a world empire with his capital in Samarqand, was a much more attractive figure. He was a node where the Turco-Mongol heritage of the steppe, of Attila and Chinggis, came together with the Islamicate heritage of Central Asia. His empire was centered in Transoxiana, and his court had overseen the establishment of Eastern Turkic, or Chaghatay, as a literary language. He provided both a heritage of state building and a golden age of high culture that a modern nation could claim. Temur had long been popular with Turkist authors across the Russian and Ottoman empires,[39] but his appeal to Central Asians was all the more direct. In 1917, for many Jadids, Temur became the symbol of the nation, but also its avenger. In October, Fitrat pleaded with the great conqueror to arise from his grave and punish those who had "betrayed your legacy" and caused the sovereignty of the Turks to disappear:

> Great Sovereign! The honor of Turkdom has been pillaged
> The state you established for the Turks is gone, the sovereignty you established under the Turks has gone to the enemy.
> My Sovereign!
> To shed the blood of those who betrayed Turkdom, even if they are Turks themselves, is your sacred tradition—arise!
> Crush, beat, kill those who betrayed your legacy![40]

By the autumn, the Jadid press was routinely carrying Turkist poetry, but the language of Turkism was not limited to poetry. As conflict with the ulama heightened, Turkism became ever more central to the political message of the Jadids. The Central Council issued the following proclamation in October:

> We need to conduct our affairs speedily in unity, because we are all children of the same womb, people of one race and one nation. *Bais,* ulama, merchants, youth, and students are all brothers and Turkic sons of Turks [*turk o'g'li turkdurlar*]. . . . They are all the progeny of Turkestan, children of the homeland.
>
> Muslims! All hopes of the Turks are one: . . . to defend our faith and our nation, to be the rulers of our land and our homeland, to take autonomy, to live in liberty and happiness without oppressing others and allowing anyone to oppress us.
>
> "Turkestan belongs to the Turkestanis."[41]

39. Aybeniz Aliyeva Kengerli, *Azerbaycanda Romantik Türkçülük,* trans. Metin Özarslan (Istanbul, 2008), 331–340.

40. Fitrat, "Yurt qayg'usi (Temur oldinda)," *Hurriyat,* 31.10.1917 (Fitrat, *Tanlangan asarlar,* 1:33–35).

41. "Musulmonlar!" *Turk eli,* 15.10.1917.

"Muslims" here were automatically Turks. Islam was not questioned, but it was effortlessly ethnicized.

This Turkism should not be confused with pan-Turkism. As we shall see over and over again in this book, pan-Turkism, the attempt to unite all Turkic peoples in one political entity, was seldom mooted as a proposition, and even when it was, it was always governed by local, specific considerations. The Turkism of Central Asian intellectuals was rooted in Central Asia itself. The focus on Temur delineated its boundaries and its aspirations. It evoked a state tradition and a high culture rooted in Central Asia, in many ways an eastern rival to the Ottoman realm, and one of an equally long vintage. Nor did Temur have any resonance to the Kazakh intelligentsia, since the peoples and lands they derived their nation from had never been part of Temur's imperium.

Settler Socialism

The debates described above took place in a political situation over which Central Asians had little control. Europeans in Turkestan—both long-term settlers and the soldiers who had arrived in 1916 to quell the uprising—had assumed that the indigenous population would not be an important factor in the revolution (as indeed had been the case in 1905), and that token concessions would suffice. The European population organized on its own. Liberal Russians formed committees of public safety, while those belonging to the less fortunate classes formed soviets. Neither the committees nor the soviets included many Muslims.[42] The committees for public safety in Tashkent and Samarqand co-opted two Muslims each to represent the indigenous population but were otherwise loathe to share power.[43] On 31 March, the Tashkent Soviet of Soldiers' and Workers' Deputies placed the governor general, A. N. Kuropatkin, under arrest. Petrograd approved the action and, recalling Kuropatkin, appointed a Turkestan Committee of nine members (five Russians and four Muslims, none of them from Turkestan) to govern the region until the Constituent Assembly could meet and determine its political status. Because the committee never could project its authority, Turkestan had, for

---

42. Tellingly, the Tashkent soviet was known as "the soviet of soldiers' and workers' deputies," reversing the order of workers and soldiers, and thus highlighting for the historian the preeminence of soldiers, many of them recent arrivals in the wake of the 1916 uprising, in the socialist movement in Turkestan.

43. On the ethnic dimensions of this conflict, see Marco Buttino, *La rivoluzione capovolta: l'Asia centrale tra il crollo dell'impero zarista e la formazione dell'URSS* (Naples, 2003); Jeff Sahadeo, *Russian Colonial Society in Tashkent, 1865–1923* (Bloomington, 2007), chap. 7–8; and Khalid, *Politics*, chap. 8.

all intents and purposes, become independent of the center. Events in that pivotal year transpired with little involvement of the imperial center.

The massive mobilization of the Muslim population took the Europeans by surprise and quickly led them to think of ways to prevent being drowned in the wave of democracy unleashed by the Provisional Government. In Tashkent, Russian liberals began to argue that the old and new cities should have separate dumas with separate budgets. Muslim and Russian political mobilization also took place along parallel lines, with only a few moments of interaction. To the fear of deluge by numbers was added that of a struggle for physical survival. The winter of 1916–17 was harsh, and then the rains failed in 1917. At the same time, revolutionary turbulence curtailed grain shipments from inner Russia. The result was a devastating famine that proved to be major factor in determining the course of events in Turkestan, as the heightening food-supply crisis overshadowed all other conflicts. By September, requisitions of food by soviets and other revolutionary organs had become commonplace. Indeed, the right to requisition food supplies (and property in general) and to levy contributions on the *burzhui* (the bourgeois, elastically defined) had become the most tangible kind of revolutionary activity. These requisitions had a markedly ethnic aspect to them, with Russian soldiers and workers raiding the old city and confiscating grain from "hoarders" and "speculators." This played on images of the wealth of the old city and its merchants that had long been held by Tashkent's Russians.[44] The situation was even more serious in the countryside. Semirech'e continued to be the scene of massive bloodletting throughout the summer. By the autumn of 1917, Turkestan was the scene of full-blown ethnic violence in which the Europeans had all the guns. It was in this context that on 27 October, the ispolkom of the Tashkent (new-city) soviet, backed by several groups of soldiers, began an armed insurrection against the government, which by this time was defended only by a small number of Cossack units, a group of Junkers, and some Tatar troops. These forces proved vastly inadequate, and Tashkent's Russian soldiers took power in the name of the Soviets by 1 November.

Composed entirely of Europeans, the Tashkent soviet had become the de facto ruler of Tashkent and pretended to rule all of Turkestan. There were no Muslims at all in the sovnarkom or the ispolkom of the soviet. Colonial settlers had taken power over the natives in the name of opposing class exploitation. Yet the response of Muslim society was differentiated. The Ulamo Jamiyati hastily organized a congress in Tashkent in the second week of November which resolved that, given that "the Muslims of Turkestan . . . comprise 98 percent of

---

44. For an exploration of these images, see Sahadeo, *Russian Colonial Society*, 89–91.

the population," it was "impermissible to advocate the assumption of power in Turkestan by a handful of immigrant soldiers, workers, and peasants who are ignorant of the way of life of the Muslims of Turkestan."[45] It nevertheless proposed the creation of a coalition with the Tashkent soviet to govern Turkestan until the Constituent Assembly, the main goal of the February revolution, could be convened.[46] The Tashkent soviet curtly refused the offer: "The inclusion of Muslims in the organ of supreme regional power is unacceptable at the present time in view of both the completely indefinite attitude of the native population toward the power of the Soviets of soldiers', workers', and peasants' deputies, and the fact that there are no proletarian class organizations among the native population whose representation in the organ of supreme regional power the faction would welcome."[47] In the colonial conditions of Turkestan, the language of class could legitimize the perpetuation of national and ethnic hegemony.

The Experiment in Government

For its part, the Shuroi Islomiya began to explore the entirely new territory of government in response to the seizure of power by the Tashkent soviet. The authority of the Provisional Government had completely evaporated, and it could not serve as a rallying point for any opposition to the Tashkent soviet. Other outside sources of support had also disappeared. In April, a Tatar delegation had visited Turkestan and Bukhara to help the local population organize. Its good intentions had run into local politics, and most of the members of the delegation returned home by early summer quite disillusioned.[48] The Shuro had also participated in the all-Russian Muslim political movement, which culminated in the All-Russian Muslim Congress that met in Moscow in May. The congress failed over the question of autonomy: mainstream Tatar opinion favored national-cultural autonomy, while almost everybody else voted in favor of territorial autonomy. Although, after lengthy debate, the congress passed a compromise resolution that recognized both forms of autonomy,[49] the confrontation

---

45. "15inchi no'yobirda Toshkandda bo'lg'on musulmon kiroyevoiy siyazdining qarori," *al-Izoh*, 28.11.1917, 266–267.

46. Ibid.; "Siyazdining qarori," *Ulug' Turkiston*, 18.11.1917.

47. Quoted in *Turkestan v nachale XX veka*, 74.

48. Abdullah Battal Taymas, *Rus Ihtilâlinden Hâtıralar* (Istanbul, 1947), 39; Galimjan äl-Barudi, *Khatirä däftäre* (Kazan, 2007), 53; Iskhakov, *Rossiiskie musul'mane*, 159–160.

49. The proceedings of the Moscow congress are in *Butun Rusya Müsülmanlarïnïng 1917nchi yilda 1–11 Mayda Mäskävdä bolghan umumi isyizdining protaqollarï* (Petrograd, 1917); see also Browder and Kerensky, eds., *Russian Provisional Government*, 1:409. On the conference, see Iskhakov, *Rossiiskie musul'mane*, 168–181.

cost a de facto Tatar withdrawal from the movement. In June, a new axis linking Turkestan with Transcaucasia (Azerbaijan) had emerged. The Turkic Federalist Party looked west to Baku and Gəncə, not north to Kazan. A delegation from Ferghana visited Transcaucasia to build institutional linkages.[50] Yet, with the general collapse of transport, those links were difficult to maintain, and the Shuro faced the new political situation on its own.

Its leaders decided to appeal again to the promise of representation and autonomy enshrined in the February Revolution, but to separate them from the Provisional Government.[51] To this end, they organized another congress of the Muslims of Turkestan in Kokand on 27 November. Kokand was the most vibrant commercial center of Turkestan after Tashkent and still beyond the reach of Tashkent's settler socialists. The conference gathered almost all the major figures of Muslim politics in Turkestan, with only the ulama of the Ulamo Jamiyati absent. Seralï Lapin was there, as was mufti Sadriddin-xon, the head of the Fuqaho Jamiyati. After only brief debate, the congress passed the following resolution:

> The Fourth Extraordinary All-Muslim Regional Congress, expressing the will of the peoples inhabiting Turkestan to self-determination on the principles proclaimed by the Great Russian revolution, proclaims Turkestan territorially autonomous within a Federated Democratic Russian republic. It offers the right to establishment of the form of autonomy to the Turkestan constituent assembly, which should convene as soon as possible, and solemnly declares that the rights of national minorities inhabiting Turkestan will be protected by all means.[52]

The congress elected an eight-member "provisional government of Autonomous Turkestan," which was to be responsible to a fifty-four-member council.

---

50. "Qafqoziyaga ketgan Farg'ona hay'atindan," *Hurriyat* (15.08.1917).

51. M. Chokaev, "Natsional'noe dvizhenie v Srednei Azii," in *Grazhdanskaia voina v Rossii: Sobytiia, mneniia, otsenki* (Moscow, 2002), 666–670.

52. *Pobeda Oktiabr'skoi revoliutsii v Uzbekistane: sbornik dokumentov*, 2 vols. (Tashkent, 1972), 2:27. This government came to be known in historical literature as the "Kokand Autonomy." Today, Uzbek scholars, pointing out quite correctly that the government claimed to speak on behalf of all of Turkestan, use the term *Turkiston muxtoriyati*, Turkestan Autonomy. The literature on the subject has been quite tendentious, with Soviet historiography insisting on it being a mere adventure of the local bourgeois propped up by "foreign interventionists," and foreign scholars seeing it as an attempt at national statehood. The fact that the government left behind no records, and that even references to it in contemporary sources are very scanty, makes such tendentiousness easy. The most thorough treatment of the subject is Agzamkhodzhaev, *Istoriia Turkestanskoi avtonomii*; see also *Turkestan v nachale XX veka*, 80–112.

It elected thirty-two members from among those attending; eighteen of the remaining seats were to be filled by representatives of various non-Muslim parties and organizations while four seats were to go to representatives of municipal dumas.[53] Its membership included all the prominent Muslim figures from Turkestan, but Russian-educated Muslim intellectuals predominated. The two top posts were held by Kazakhs: Muhammedjan Tïnïshbayev, a railway engineer and prominent Kazakh politician, was named prime minister and minister for internal affairs, while Cho'qoy was minister for external affairs. Several members of the cabinet had long experience with cultural reform in Turkestan. Ubaydulla Xo'jayev was minister in charge of creating a people's militia, and Obidjon Mahmudov, the businessman from Kokand with long standing as publisher and philanthropist, became minister for food supply.[54] The thirty-two members elected to the council included Lapin and Behbudiy.[55] While the council excluded the ulama, it offered moderate Russians a disproportionate role in the proposed government in an attempt to distance them from the soviets. The congress and the government elected by it were thus a broad alliance of liberal forces of the region, with both the conservative ulama and the soviets being excluded.

If the Tashkent soviet claimed its legitimacy from the rhetoric of class struggle, the government proclaimed in Kokand pinned its hopes on the promise of the February revolution. It operated within the parameters of Russian politics, claiming autonomy, not sovereignty, and bending over backward in trying to win the support of liberal Russians by offering them one-third of the seats in its governing council. The autonomy was territorial (the congress claimed to represent the "peoples [*narodnosti*] inhabiting Turkestan") within boundaries created by the Russian conquest. The new government also sought contacts with other anti-Bolshevik movements in the Russian Empire, and after lengthy debate, it decided to join the South-Eastern Union, an organization formed in the north Caucasus in October that united Cossacks and the Mountaineers of the Caucasus. Many speakers in Kokand disputed the wisdom of an alliance with a Cossack force known for its counterrevolutionary tendencies as well as its avowed intention of "placing a cross over the Aya Sofya," but the Union controlled rail routes to Russia, the only source for importing much needed grain, and the pragmatic argument won out.[56]

Other hopes aroused by the proclamation of autonomy tended to go beyond the paradigm established by the February revolution. Fitrat had celebrated the proclamation of autonomy at Kokand thus:

---

53. *Ulug' Turkiston*, 08.12.1917.
54. "Muvaqqat Turkiston hukumatining a'zolari," *Ulug' Turkiston*, 13.12.1917.
55. *Ulug' Turkiston*, 08.12.1917.
56. *Vaqït* (Orenburg), 21.12.1917.

Autonomous Turkestan! . . . I do not believe there's a greater, more sacred, more beloved word among the true sons of the mighty Temur, the indigenous Turks of Turkestan!

If there is a force that can warm the blood of the Turks of Turkestan and heighten their faith, then it's only this word: Autonomous Turkestan.[57]

Hamza likewise invoked Genghis Khan and Temur alongside the Prophet and the Qur'an in a poem celebrating the proclamation of autonomy in a poem that ended with the hope: "Long live the united nation of Islam / Long live the eternal state of the Turks" (*Yashasun endi birlashub islom millati / Yashasun bu turk o'g'lini mangu davlati*).[58] A wall calendar for 1918 published in honor of the autonomous government celebrated Chinggis Khan, who created a "great Turkic empire" that had united together "Muslim, especially Arab, governments that had fallen into internecine struggles and corruption and depravity [*fisq-fasod*]."[59] Even more interesting is a poem by Cho'lpon that was published as a broadside and reportedly recited at the Congress itself:

Ko'z oching, boqing har yon!	Open your eyes, look around!
Qardoshlar, qanday zamon!	Brothers, look what an age has dawned!
Shodlikka to'ldi jahon!	The world is filled with happiness
Fido bu kunlarga jon!	May life be sacrificed for such days.
Naqorat:	*Refrain*:
Turkistonlik shonimiz, Turonlik unvonimiz	Turkestaniness is our pride, Turaniness is our title
Vatan bizning jonimiz, fido o'lsun qonimiz!	The Homeland is our Life, May our blood be sacrificed!
Bizlar temir jonlimiz!	We are of souls of steel
Shavkatlimiz, shonlimiz!	Valiant and glorious,
Nomusli, vijdonlimiz!	Honest and conscientious,
Qaynagan turk qonlimiz! . . .[60]	We are of warm Turkic blood!

---

57. Fitrat, "Muxtoriyat," *Hurriyat*, 05.12.1917.

58. Hamza, "Turkiston muxtoriyatina," *Ulug' Turkiston*, 11.01.1918; Hamza, *To'la asarlar to'plami*, 5 vols. (Tashkent, 1988–89), 2:155.

59. A copy of the calendar is on display at the Kokand regional museum (*o'lkashunoslik muzeyi*). For a reproduction, see Qasïmkhan Begmanov, *Mustafa Shoqay jolïmen: Tarikhi–dekretï, tanïmdïq saparnama* (Almaty, 2013), 152.

60. Cho'lpon, "Ozod turk bayrami," *Asarlar*, 3 vols. (Tashkent: G'afur G'ulom, 1994), 1:126–127.

The declaration of autonomy at Kokand was for all these authors also the reentry of the Turkestani nation on the global stage. Cho'lpon's poem also contained a strong hint of its lineage: the refrain is a calque from the *Ordu Marşı* (Military March), a patriotic Ottoman march of the Young Turk era.[61] Ottoman models were never far away from Muslim politics of 1917 in Turkestan.

In fact, the convulsions let loose by the Russian revolution were transforming the geopolitical realities of Turkestan by the day. Mustafa Cho'qoy noted that "the absence of government in Russia today . . . makes the convocation of the Constituent Assembly doubtful,"[62] implying that other options could be explored. Behbudiy stressed the necessity of having Turkestani delegates present at any peace conference in the future.[63] Circumstances had forced the Kokand government to think beyond the Russian orbit. The collapse of the Russian war effort on the Caucasus front made possible an Ottoman moment in Central Asia, but the Kokand government did not survive long enough to benefit from it. For, not surprisingly, it had found its path to be extremely difficult. Seeking to mobilize support, it organized demonstrations in its support throughout Turkestan. Demonstrations took place successfully in Andijon on 3 December and Tashkent on 6 December,[64] but a second demonstration in Tashkent the following week resulted in a bloodbath. Demonstrators attacked the prison and freed prisoners taken by the soviet during its conquest of power the previous month. Russian soldiers then fired into the crowd, killing several people, while many others were killed in the ensuing stampede.[65] The freed prisoners were recaptured and summarily executed by Soviet forces. Meanwhile in Kokand, the autonomous government was discovering that while it could bring people out into the streets, it could not govern. Its members lacked any prior experience of governing. There was no bureaucratic class in Turkestan, no indigenous cadres with any experience in administration or government beyond the grassroots level, so the government was staffed by complete amateurs who were also faced with a total lack of financial and military power. The Kokand government proved incapable of levying taxes, although it managed to raise 3 million rubles through a public loan. It also sought to raise an army, but with little success. Since the indigenous population

---

61. The refrain in the *Ordu Marşı* went: *Sancağımız şanımız / Osmanlı unvanımız / Vatan bizim canımız / Fedâ olsun kanımız* (Our banner, our pride / Ottoman is our title / The Homeland is our life / May our blood be sacrificed).

62. *Vaqït,* 17.12.1917.

63. *Vaqït,* 21.12.1917.

64. *Ulug' Turkiston,* 10.12.1917, 16.12.1917; another demonstration with twenty thousand present took place in Samarqand on 22 December: *Hurriyat,* 29.12.1917.

65. "Katta miting'," *Ulug' Turkiston,* 10.12.1917; "Fojiali voqea," *Ulug' Turkiston,* 16.12.1917; "Toshkandda muxtoriyat nimoyishi," *al-Izoh,* 25.12.1917, 277.

had not been subject to conscription, the only Muslim soldiers available were Tatar or Bashkir troops stationed in the region. Members of the Kokand government traveled around Ferghana in search of money and men. We have concrete detail of some such efforts in Andijon. Cho'qoy and Mirjalilov attended a public meeting in the offices of Shuroi Islomiya in the city on 14 January 1918 (o.s.) and asked for financial support of the government. The meeting established a commission of sixteen men (including four non-Muslims), which eventually raised 17,200 rubles over three days. The following day, another meeting held in the main mosque decided to organize a militia and offered the post of its head to Mir-Ali Umarboyev, the existing *oqsaqqol* (head of the native administration) of the old city. The task proved difficult, since many objected to the appointment, while Umarboyev himself was not happy with many of the men who volunteered.[66] The army never really materialized, although according to a contemporary press report, military units belonging to the Kokand government held a parade in the old city of Kokand on 9 January 1918 (o.s.), with one thousand armed troops participating.[67] The figure was most likely an exaggeration and served little more than to alarm the Europeans. By February, the autonomous government turned to one Ergash, the commander of the militia of the old city of Kokand, and appointed him the "commander-in-chief" of its army. The grandiose title did little to hide the fact that the army had few weapons and no officers or trained men, and that it was no match to the forces commanded by the Tashkent soviet. The end came soon. In mid-February, as soon as Tashkent could spare the men, it launched an all-out assault on Kokand. The battle was won easily through the use of ruthless force, which left much of the old city of Kokand burnt to the ground. The autonomous government of Turkestan had ceased to exist after seventy-eight days.

An Ottoman Episode

For all the brevity of its existence, the Kokand Autonomy cast a long shadow in Soviet politics and Soviet historiography, where it was associated with the machinations of bourgeois nationalism and pan-Turkism, and association with it was damning proof of one's political unreliability or worse in the years to come. Kokand had represented an alternative to Soviet rule, which for the most part was

---

66. A retroactive account (from summer 1918) of these events in Andijon can be found in TsGARUz, f. 36, op. 1, d. 12, ll. 277–278ob.

67. *Ulug' Turkiston*, 21.01.1918 (o.s.).

very much within the framework of the Russian revolution. Yet several geopolitical effects of the Russian revolution had opened up an Ottoman connection that
brought in new possibilities. For a brief moment, the Ottoman Empire appeared
on Central Asia's political horizons.

The collapse of the Russian war effort on the Caucasus front in the autumn of
1917 transformed the Ottoman fortunes in a war that had so far been a dismal
failure. Already in November 1917, the Ottomans began to contemplate an offensive in the Russian Caucasus. This would have seized the moment and provided
a geopolitical buffer between the Ottoman state and Russia. The Committee of
Union and Progress (CUP) sent out a certain Hasan Ruşenî Bey to Baku to establish a Caucasian branch of the party. Over the coming months, some Ottoman
officials were to entertain grandiose visions of annexing Turkestan to the "great
caliphate" and to forestall a British advance into Central Asia and the Caucasus.
But a lack of resources stood in the way, and the Ottomans could achieve little
in the year before their defeat. Nevertheless, the volte face in the military situation transformed the political calculus of many in Turkestan, who began to hope
that the Ottomans might be a consequential presence in the chaotic affairs of the
region.[68]

The Kokand government had dispatched Mahmudov, its minister for food
supply, to Baku ostensibly in search of grain. He no doubt made use of the links
forged over the summer by the Turkic Federalist Party to make contact with
Ruşenî Bey and to seek Ottoman help for Turkestan. "We have desperate need
of qualified men from Turkey to reform the internal affairs of Turkestan and to
form a national force [*millî bir kuvvet*]," Mahmudov wrote flatteringly. "I have
come to Baku on behalf of my Turkestani compatriots to receive instructions
and men from you."[69] Ruşenî Bey seconded a team of twenty officers under one
Yusuf Ziya Bey to Kokand to help establish "national organizations" in Turkestan.
In the event, only Ziya Bey made the journey, and he was overtaken by events. By
the time he reached Tashkent after several months of difficult travels, the Kokand
government was no more and Tashkent was under Soviet rule.[70] He nevertheless
became involved in local politics and organized a branch of the CUP in Tashkent
in which members of the Kokand government participated.[71] In June 1918, this

---

68. See, e.g., Hoji Muin, "Islom dunyosining najoti," *Hurriyat*, 10.04.1918.

69. Mahmudov to Ruşenî Bey, 09.01.1918, quoted by Akdes Nimet Kurat, *Türkiye ve Rusya: XVIII Yüzyıl Sonundan Kurtuluş Savaşına Kadar Türk-Rus İlişkileri (1798–1919)* (Ankara, 1970), 512.

70. Ibid., 511–517.

71. Yusuf Ziya Bey to Galip Kemalî Bey, 16.06.1918, in ibid., 676.

organization sent a delegation to Istanbul to seek Ottoman intervention in Central Asia. The delegation, comprised of Mahmudov, Saidnosir Mirjalilov, Ubaydulla Xo'jayev, the mufti Sadriddin-xon, and several others, traveled to Moscow armed with a letter of introduction to Galip Kemalî Bey, the Ottoman ambassador to the Soviets. Galip Bey in turn organized a trip to Istanbul, where the group met Enver and Cemal pashas and Ahmed Nesimi Bey, the foreign minister.[72] (Ubaydulla Xo'jayev and Mahmudov stayed behind in Moscow, and at least the latter seems to have met Lenin in an attempt, no doubt, to convince him of some sort of a compromise with Turkestan's national leadership.)[73] A different mission led by G'ozi Yunus also visited Istanbul in August, where it pleaded with the Ministry of War for help in seeking Turkestan's independence. As a result of six decades of Russian imperialism, Turkestan lacked the "civilizational strength" necessary to strive for independence, but given proper leadership, however, its people would be willing to shed "oceans of blood" in the cause of the liberation of Central Asia and the Muslim world.[74] Neither of these missions accomplished very much. As Michael Reynolds has argued, Ottoman interest in Central Asia was primarily geopolitical, not ethnic or confessional, and in any case hamstrung by a severe lack of resources.[75] The first mission was dispatched to Switzerland in the company of Abdürreshid Ibrahim, the Tatar activist who worked for the Ottomans, and Köprülüzade Mehmed Fuad, the Turkist historian and politician, to present its case before "Europe." The end of the war caught up with the mission, however; its steamship was refused landing in Habsburg territory and returned to Istanbul.[76] The second delegation received only expressions of good wishes.[77]

The hopes of Ottoman intervention were always unrealistic, and the Ottoman defeat in October 1918 finally put paid to them. The missions accomplished little. But the Ottoman connection worked in other ways as well, in part helped by the decision of the Bolsheviks to "liberate" all prisoners of war after the signature of the treaty of Brest-Litovsk. This meant that the approximately sixty-five thousand Ottoman prisoners of war, most of them kept in camps in

---

72. Abdullah Receb Baysun, *Türkistan Millî Hareketleri* (Istanbul, 1943), 32.

73. The movements of these two figures in 1918 are rather obscure, but Mahmudov told a public gathering in Kokand in January 1920 that he had met "comrades Lenin and Trotsky" in Moscow; *Ishtirokiyun*, 25.01.1920.

74. Quoted by Michael A. Reynolds, *Shattering Empires: The Clash and Collapse of the Ottoman and Russian Empires, 1908–1918* (New York, 2011), 242.

75. Michael A. Reynolds, "Buffers, Not Brethren: Young Turk Military Policy in the First World War and the Myth of Panturanism," *Past and Present*, no. 203 (2009): 137–179.

76. A.Z.V. Togan, *Bugünkü Türkili (Türkistan) ve Yakın Tarihi*, 2nd ed. (Istanbul, 1981), 480; Baysun, *Türkistan Millî Hareketleri*, 32–33.

77. Reynolds, *Shattering Empires*, 242–243.

provincial Russia or in Siberia, were left to fend for themselves.[78] As they made their way back home, many of them traveled through Central Asia, where they stepped into the political turmoil of the period. For two and a half years, from the spring of 1918 to late 1920, Ottoman POWs were a significant feature of life in the cities. Many of them accepted offers of employment in the new schools being opened under Soviet auspices, and they were behind the appearance of a whole array of youth political organizations of a markedly Turkist orientation. A somewhat unusual figure was Said Ahroriy, an Ottoman officer of Central Asian origin (his father had emigrated from Khujand) whom fate had returned to his ancestral homeland. Ahroriy established a branch of Türk Ocağı (Turkish Hearth, the network of nationalist clubs of the Young Turk period) in Tashkent in the spring of 1918.[79] Another organization called Turk O'rtoqlig'i (Turkic Friendship) launched the short-lived newspaper *Turk so'zi* (Turkic Word) that strived, in the words of the motto on its masthead, "To liberate the Turkic nation from slavery in the realms of politics, economics, and knowledge, and thus to bring about a true Turkic civilization" (*Turk millatini siyosiy, iqtisodiy va ilmiy asoratdan qutqorib chin bir turk madaniyati vujudga keturmak*). Among its contributors were G'ozi Yunus and Said Ahroriy.[80] The schools run by the POWs acquired a distinct martial flavor (see chapter 6). Ottoman POWs also established the first boy scout troops in Central Asia, with an emphasis of discipline and fitness, and a number of other semimilitarized youth groups (*to'dalar*) with names such as Turk Kuchi (Turkic Might), Turon Kuchi (Might of Turan), Temur, and Taraqqiy (Progress).[81] It was in this milieu that secret societies seeking to organize the national movement underground emerged.

The Ottoman episode proved short-lived, for the most of the POWs dispersed or were deported by late 1920. Few of the Ottoman POWs were zealous emissaries of Turkism. For most of them, teaching was just a job to feed themselves and pay their way home.[82] The schools and clubs they staffed presented models of

---

78. Yücel Yanıkdağ, "'Ill-Fated Sons' of the 'Nation': Ottoman Prisoners of War in Russia and Egypt, 1914–1922" (Ph.D. diss., Ohio State University, 2002), 1, 229; Cemalettin Taşkıran, *Ana Ben Ölmedim: Birinci Dünya Savaşı'nda Türk Esirleri* (Istanbul, 2001), 62–63.

79. Xolida Ahrorova, *Izlarini izlayman* (Tashkent, 1998), 12–60.

80. *Turk so'zi*, 12.05.1918.

81. We know rather little about these groups, except for what can be gleaned from the press of the time, where their names crop up frequently. The Izchilar can be found in *Ishtirokiyun*, 23.10.1918, 15.02.1919, and 04.01.1920; Turon kuchi and Turk kuchi in *Ishtirokiyun*, 25.01.1920, 21.03.1920.

82. Three different memoirs of Ottoman prisoners of war in Turkestan have seen the light of day. In each case, the author took up teaching in Tashkent because he was asked to do so by locals and because he needed the money; see Tahsin İybar, *Sibirya'dan Serendibe* (Ankara, 1950), 68–69; Râci Çakıröz and Timur Kocaoğlu, "Türkistan'da Türk Subayları," *Türk Dünyası Tarih Dergisi* (April 1987), 42–43; Ziya Yergök, *Sarıkamış'tan Esarete (1915–1920)*, ed. Sami Önal (Istanbul, 2005), 235.

activity from beyond the Russian orbit. The schools educated a number of figures who went on to be prominent in public life in the 1920s, yet they also experienced a backlash both for their military character and their use of Ottoman as the language of instruction (see chapter 6). Turkism was not synonymous with an Ottoman presence, nor dependent on it.

Other members of the defunct Kokand government tried to internationalize the issue of Turkestan by presenting it at the Paris Peace Conference, again without success. One mission composed of Behbudiy, Mirjalilov, and two others was aborted when Behbudiy and his two companions were arrested by Bukharan border guards as they traveled across the emirate and tortured to death in March 1919.[83] Mirjalilov, who was waiting for them in Baku, returned to Turkestan. A second attempt to put Turkestan's case before the Peace Conference was made by Mustafa Cho'qoy. Cho'qoy seems to have acted alone after the fall of Kokand. He fled to Tashkent where he spent two months in hiding, before attempting to go to Moscow to negotiate with the Bolsheviks. He made it only to Aqtoba in the Kazakh steppe before he was arrested by Kolchak's men as "an enemy of the Russian State." With death hanging over his head, he escaped again and made his way to Ashgabat, where Russian Mensheviks had just overthrown Soviet power and set up an autonomous government in contact with British forces in Iran.[84] In Ashgabat he was joined by Vadim Chaikin, the Socialist Revolutionary lawyer who had lived in Andijon and had been sympathetic to native aspirations, and along with him, he sent a telegram in the name of a "Committee for the Convocation of the Constituent Assembly

---

83. Behbudiy's death has remained shrouded in mystery. There is no documentary proof of his death or of his destination, but Baysun says quite unequivocally that Behbudiy was part of a mission to Versailles and that he was murdered by functionaries of the emir. Behbudiy's death was widely mourned at the time, with both Fitrat and Cho'lpon writing elegies in his honor, and the emir's connection to it was one more nail in the coffin of his legitimacy in the eyes of the reformers. In recent years, Uzbek authors have attempted to hold the Cheka responsible for murdering Behbudiy; the unconvincing case is presented by Naim Karimov, *XX asr adabiyoti manzaralari* (Tashkent, 2008), 50–55.

84. The details of Cho'qoy's movements in 1918 as well of as of his political intentions remain murky. The only sources for them are later reminiscences by himself and his wife Mariia, which give differing accounts of his intentions. In an off-the-cuff comment, his wife notes that he had initially intended to go to Moscow to meet Lenin: Maria J. Çokayeva, *Mustafa Çokay'ın Hatıraları*, ed. Erol Cihangir (Istanbul, 2000), 85. Cho'qoy himself claimed in a polemic among émigrés that at the time of his arrest by Kolchak's forces, he was on his way to Vladivostok with the aim of reaching the United States and organizing a Turkestani representation there. M. Chokaev, "Organizatsiia TMB" (n.d., 1930s), Archives Mustafa Chokay Bey, carton 3, dossier 1. On the Menshevik government in Ashgabat, see V. Zh. Tsvetkov, "Zabytyi front: Iz istorii Belogo dvizheniia v Turkestane, 1918–1920 gg.," in *Grazhdanskaia voina v Rossii: sobytiia, mneniia, otsenki* (Moscow, 2002), 569–578.

of Turkestan" to Woodrow Wilson and the Paris Peace Conference, asking the congress to guarantee the territorial unity of Turkestan and the recognition of "the right of the country (whose culture is thousands of years old) to a free and autonomous existence in fraternal friendship with the people of Russia."[85] While the telegram evoked no response at the Peace Conference, it was immediately published in Turkestan and was seen by the Bolsheviks as proof that Cho'qoy was ready "to sell Turkestan to the imperialists."[86]

The telegram was the end of the matter. Turkestan remained invisible at Versailles and quickly disappeared from the world stage. Cho'qoy eventually made his way to Paris where he became active in Russian émigré circles. He wrote in newspapers edited by Kerensky and Miliukov, although by the late 1920s, his stance on questions of nationality had distanced him from the Russian community, and his activities came to center more and more on Turkestan itself. He became part of a small community of "Turko-Tatar" émigrés based in Europe and republican Turkey that also included Velidi (Togan) and Usmon Xo'jao'g'li (Usman Kocaoğlu). Cho'qoy published *Yosh Turkistan* (Young Turkestan) from his base in Nogent-sur-Marne, a village outside Paris, lectured widely, and became the spokesman for Turkestan in Europe. This made him the archdemon in the Soviet imagination, and accusations of contacts with him and his counterrevolutionary organizations in the service of imperialism were to prove fatal to many in Central Asia itself.[87]

A Society in Turmoil

The brutal victory of the Tashkent Red Guards at Kokand plunged Turkestan into a nightmare of violence that took half a decade to subside. By spring 1918, political power had ceased to exist in Turkestan. Soviet power was based, first and foremost, on armed force, which was a monopoly of the Russian settler population of the region, and which was very useful in requisitioning and confiscating property, especially food. Indeed, "nationalization"—confiscation by force—was the first revolutionary policy to be pursued by the soviet government.

---

85. TNA, WO 106/61/25.

86. "Cho'qoyev ila Choykinning sulh majlisina yuborgon tilg'iromalari," *Ishtirokiyun*, 26.03.1919.

87. A number of biographies of Cho'qoy have appeared in recent years, none of them sufficiently rigorous; see, however, Abdulvahap Kara, *Türkistan Ateşi: Mustafa Çokay'ın Hayatı ve Mücadelesi* (Istanbul, 2002), or Bakhyt Sadykova, *Mustafa Chokai* (Almaty, 2004); Begmanov, *Müstafa Shoqay jolïmen*, is excellent for reproducing rare photographs and documents.

In February, the Tashkent soviet nationalized "all cotton in Turkestan, no matter in what form or where it is located."[88] In its first months, Soviet power, as indeed the struggle over food, had a pronounced ethnic aspect. Not only was Soviet power staffed solely by Europeans, but it was largely limited to the European spaces of the new cities. The extension of Soviet power beyond these European spaces depended on military force, as was the case with the destruction of the autonomous government in Kokand or the attempted invasion, led in person by Fedor Kolesov, the Bolshevik head of the sovnarkom, of Bukhara in early March (see chapter 4). These military campaigns directly pitted Europeans against Muslims, while in the cities, food-supply questions were resolved along ethnic lines. In Tashkent, the new-city soviet began organizing raids into the old city in December 1917 to confiscate grain from hoarders and speculators. In the countryside, Russian settlers used the revolutionary slogan "power to the localities" (*vlast' na mestakh*) to confiscate land belonging to their indigenous neighbors, especially the nomads. Already armed, Russian peasants formed bands for the defense of their property and their food supplies, and for confiscating the same from their native neighbors.

For the indigenous population, the first months of Soviet power were one of great insecurity. "There is complete devastation in the localities," Eshonxo'ja Oshurxo'jayev, the first commissar for nationalities affairs, reported to the Turkestan sovnarkom in June 1918. "The population is completely lost, it does not know where to turn and where to find protection in case of need."[89] The countryside bled for years on end. The general economic difficulties caused by the war, such as inflation and the "voluntary" contributions for the war effort exacted from the population, were exacerbated by the difficulties in the cotton economy of the region. Cotton had increasingly come to dominate local agriculture, which had rendered Turkestan dependent on outside sources for its food supply. During the war years, the price of cotton relative to grain declined sharply, leading to general impoverishment among the Muslim peasants of the region. The rising food prices hit everyone, although the resulting crisis had a pronounced ethnic dimension. The crisis was made much worse by the events of 1916, which led to a drastic decrease in land under cultivation, as well as a decline in the productivity of agriculture. The famine of 1917–18 provided the backdrop to the entire political and military conflict of the years under review

---

88. *Nasha gazeta*, 28.02.1918 (n.s.).
89. TsGARUz, f. 25, op. 1, d. 87, ll. 1–2.

here.[90] Meticulous statistical work by Marco Buttino has served to delineate the full scale of the catastrophe. Between 1915 and 1920, the amount of cultivated land in Turkestan declined by half and livestock decreased by 75 percent. Cotton production practically ceased. The losses were not uniform across social groups, of course. Russian peasants saw a decline of 28 percent in their cultivated land and lost 6.5 percent of their livestock; the figures were 39 percent and 48 percent respectively for the sedentary indigenous population, and 46 percent and 63.4 percent for the nomads.[91] The civilian population of Turkestan fell by a quarter over the same five years, from 7,148,800 in 1915 to 5,336,500 in 1920. The indigenous rural population declined by 30.5 percent.[92] Irrigation networks were in ruin and whole districts depopulated. Villages were abandoned as people fled hunger, the settlers, the Basmachi, or all of them. Many fled across the frontier to Iran, Afghanistan, and Xinjiang. The full scale of the emigration is impossible to judge, but it was by all accounts substantial.[93] The bulk of the numbers were made up of Kazakh and Turkmen nomads who fled across the Soviet frontier en masse. All through the 1920s and into the early 1930s, individuals and families from the sedentary population also continued to flee across the border. Unlike the larger flights of the nomads, these were individual acts undertaken in secret through the difficult trek across the Tien-Shan into Chinese-held territory and beyond.[94] The immense insecurity produced by years of revolution, famine, ethnic strife, and peasant insurgency shook up Muslim society in numerous ways,

90. Strangely, the famine of 1917–20 in Turkestan has largely been forgotten. Little has been written on it even in post-Soviet Uzbekistan, where the period of the revolution and civil war is generally seen in a negative light. Yet, as one of the very few Uzbekistani authors to discuss the famine writes, "in its scale, this calamity did not yield to the famine of 1920–1921 in the Volga region, except that here there was neither an organized evacuation to more prosperous parts of the country, nor the help of international organizations." V. Semeniuta, "Golod v Turkestane v 1917–1920 godakh," *Chelovek i politika,* 1991, no. 12: 72. See also *Turkestan v nachale XX veka: k istorii istokov natsional'noi nezavisimosti* (Tashkent, 2000), 269–284.

91. Marco Buttino, "Study of the Economic Crisis and Depopulation in Turkestan, 1917–1920," *Central Asian Survey* 9:4 (1990): 61–64.

92. Ibid., 64–69.

93. Kamoluddin Abdullayev cites data from Tajikistan's party archives to suggest that there might have been as many as 480,000 emigrants in Afghanistan in 1925–26; see Kamol Abdoullaev, "Central Asian Emigres in Afghanistan: First Wave, 1920–1931," *Central Asia Monitor,* 1994, no. 5: 16–27.

94. This exodus created a large Central Asian diaspora in Afghanistan and beyond. See Monica Whitlock, *Beyond the Oxus: The Central Asians* (London, 2002), chap. 2. For émigré memoirs that have appeared since the end of the Soviet period, see Zuhriddin Mirza Obid o'g'li Turkistoniy, *Onda jonim qoldi mening* (Tashkent, 1992); Yousof Mamoor, *In Quest of a Homeland: Recollections of an Emigrant* (Istanbul, 2005). See also Sayfiddin Jalilov, *Buxoriylar qissasi (muhojarat tarixidan lavhalar)* (Tashkent, 2006).

reordering authority and prestige in it and sowing seeds of discord that defined conflict throughout the coming decade.

The wealthy merchants suffered greatly as a group: the inflation, the requisitioning, the forced levies, the nationalization of private property, and the abolition of free trade (even if not entirely successful) greatly diminished their wealth and with it their status in society. The violence caught up with them in many other ways as well. The misfortunes of Mir Komilboy, the Andijon millionaire and one of the most prominent public figures in Turkestan, were probably unusual, but are well documented. He had already been in trouble with the government since 1915, which had arrested and exiled him on the basis of an anonymous denunciation for "pan-Islamism" and for raising funds for the Ottoman war effort. He was released fairly quickly and returned to Andijon, only to face the wrath of the revolution. The Andijon Union of Muslim Public Organizations exiled him in May 1917 for meddling in their work. He returned in mid-July, but only on condition that he not interfere in public affairs until the election of the Constituent Assembly.[95] Those elections were, of course, overtaken by events, and instead the Russian new-city soviet arrested and shot him in February 1918 and confiscated his property.[96] Other merchants suffered fates that were less dramatic, but nevertheless suffered a great deal. Although the early Soviet press continued to present the figure of the local bourgeoisie as powerful and dominant, the old merchant class never recovered its former clout.

Confiscations and exactions were not the work of the Europeans alone. One form of mobilization in 1917 had been the emergence of artisanal guilds and associations (*jamiyatlar*) in the old cities. As organizations of "the democracy," these associations had the right to requisition property or to levy "contributions" on the burzhui. Driven by the food supply crisis, such requisitioning became commonplace during 1918 and 1919, when such organizations in Tashkent were routinely demanding large contributions, sometimes as high as 1.5 million (inflated) rubles.[97] Similar requisitions also took place in Samarkand, where on 17 August 1918 the "executive committee of Muslim workers' and peasants' deputies" resolved to raise 241,000 rubles from the bais in seventeen days.[98] The bais' loss was more than just monetary; their prestige suffered

---

95. "Protokol zasedeniia S"ezda Andizhanskikh obshchestvennykh musul'manskikh uezdno-gorodskikh organizatsii ot 14–17oe iiulia 1917 goda," TsGARUz, f. I-1044, d. 24, ll. 26–27ob.

96. Akmal Akrom o'g'li, "Mirkomilboy qanday shaxs edi?" *Sharq yulduzi,* 1992, no. 5: 96.

97. GAgT, f. 12, d. 30.

98. GASO, f. 89, d. 1, l. 128

too. The mobilization of artisanal jamiyats in 1917 was a form of renegotiating positions in society that directly challenged the bais and on which the Bolsheviks sought to capitalize (even though they did not have anything to do with igniting it directly).

A Central Asian Civil War

The most open form of contention within Muslim society was the rural insurgency of the Basmachi, which wracked Central Asia well into the mid-1920s. It arose initially in Ferghana in the winter of 1917–18 as a response, in the words of an early Soviet historian, to "the bacchanalia of plunder, requisitions, and confiscations on the part of 'Soviet power.'"[99] The rural population mobilized in order to protect its land and food supply from the depredations of Russian settlers. In 1920, after the ouster of the emir of Bukhara, the insurgency spread to the mountainous redoubts of eastern Bukhara and later appeared in parts of Samarqand oblast. Most historians have not been able to resist the temptation to see in the Basmachi a national opposition or resistance to Soviet rule.[100] While it is tempting to see the Basmachi as a form of national resistance to the establishment of a foreign form of power, the actual dynamics of the conflict were more complex. The concerns of the Basmachi were intensely local and aimed at the defense of land and resources, as well as customary practices and power relations. The customary way of life was threatened by innovations coming from the city, the modern state, and modernizing elites. Imperial collapse brought about a recrudescence of local solidarities and forms of authority that were often deeply inimical to anything the fifty years of Russian rule had brought about. The major warlords (known as *qo'rboshi*) derived their authority from a variety of sources. Madamin-bek, the first prominent leader of the movement in Ferghana, was descended from the hereditary military elite of the

99. S. Ginzburg, "Basmachestvo v Fergane," in *Ocherki revoliutsionnogo dvizheniia v Srednei Azii: sbornik statei* (Moscow, 1926), 134.

100. The view originated with Joseph Castagné, *Les Basmatchis: le mouvement national des indigènes d'Asie Centrale depuis la Révolution d'octobre 1917 jusqu'en octobre 1924* (Paris, 1925), but was canonized by Olaf Caroe, *Soviet Empire: The Turks of Central Asia and Stalinism* (London, 1954), chap. 7. Émigré writers were also inclined to this view; the émigré position is best articulated by Baymirza Hayit, *"Basmacılar": Türkistan Millî Mücadele Tarihi (1917–1934)* (Ankara, 1997 [originally published in German in 1992]); see also Ali Bademci, *1917–1934 Türkistan Millî İstiklâl Hareketi: Korbaşilar ve Enver Paşa* (1975; reprint Istanbul, 2010). This view is also popular in Uzbekistan, where the Basmachi are seen a form of national-liberation movement. See, e.g., *O'zbekistonning yangi tarixi*, 3 vols. (Tashkent, 2000), 2:83–102.

Kokand khanate.[101] In eastern Bukhara, many qo'rboshi were hereditary rulers of distant provinces that had been subdued by the emirs of Bukhara only after the Russian conquest (and with Russian help), who now felt free to act on their own and to keep the authority of the city at bay. Sayyid Ahmad-xo'ja Ovliyo-xo'ja Eshon o'g'li came from an illustrious family of Sufi masters with reportedly twenty-five thousand disciples in the mountainous fastness of Mastchoh (Matcha) in the Ferghana Valley. Ahmadxo'ja first used his authority to be elected head of the ispolkom of Isfoniy volost in Khujand uezd in 1919. He soon fell out with the Soviets and retreated to Mastchoh, where he established a statelet for three years between 1920 and 1923, which negotiated with Tashkent as an equal.[102] Yet others were outlaws who rose up in the period of collapse to offer (or enforce) protection on the rural population. The Basmachi were a revolt against the exactions (of food and revenue) of a city-based government, and for many qo'rboshis it made little difference whether that government was staffed by Europeans or Muslims.

The Basmachi represented a completely different form of leadership than urban Muslims, Jadids and Communists alike. With the partial exception of Madaminbek, the Basmachi were a force located in entirely different sections of society and represented a completely different vision of politics than the Jadids. Few of the Basmachi leaders seem to have been motivated by the creation of new state order. To the extent they did, the model was the tradition of kingship as it had developed in post-Timurid Central Asia. This intense localism had no place for the idea of the nation in it. But if the Basmachi were not "nationalists," they also did not represent a continuation of the Ulamo Jamiyati and its politics of 1917. The Ulamo Jamiyati had taken part in pan-Russian politics, if only to stake out a particularist position. The political horizons of most Basmachi leaders were much narrower. Their activity was the expression of rural particularity, in many ways a struggle against the power cities cast over the countryside. In that sense, they represented a truly alternative vision of politics that had little in common with the cities and their politics.

Most Basmachi made no distinction between urban Muslims and the Bolsheviks. In Bukhara, where the Basmachi fought the Young Bukharans, the elision was even easier to make. Both were enemies of the traditional way of life and of

---

101. Alisher Ibodinov, *Qo'rboshi Madaminbek: hujjatli qissa* (Tashkent, 1993), 16. Post-Soviet biographies of Basmachi figures published in Uzbekistan tend to be hagiographic as they seek to undo the burden of seven decades of Soviet historiography. Nevertheless, they make use of oral history sources and bring to light important information not be found elsewhere. On Madaminbek, see also Ibrohim Karim, *Madaminbek*, 2nd ed. (Tashkent, 2000).

102. Jo'ra Zokiriy, "Macho begi va bosmochiliq," *Qizil Sharq*, no. 1 (Samarqand, 1929), 131–143.

customary understandings of Islam. The enmity of Ibrohim-bek to the Jadids is the best documented. He was leading the uprising in eastern Bukhara when Usmon-xo'ja, the head of state of the BNSR, led a Bukharan militia against the Dushanbe garrison of the Red Army. Once the action was over and the Red Army had beaten back Usmon-xo'ja's units, Ibrohim-bek wrote to the Soviets thus: "Comrades, we thank you for fighting with the Jadids. I, Ibrohim-bek, praise you for this and shake your hand, as friend and comrade, and open to you the path to all four sides. I am also able to give you forage. We have nothing against you, we will beat the Jadids, who overthrew our power."[103] Enver Pasha, who arrived in eastern Bukhara in the hope of taking command of the insurgency in the name of the emir and the caliph, was promptly imprisoned by Ibrohim-bek, who told him, "I have to make war not just on the Russians, but really against the Jadids."[104] The unwillingness to make that distinction was not unique to the Basmachi. The Bukharan conservative notable Mirza Salim Bek wrote with approval that "Ergash-bek of Kokand and Muhammad Amin of Margelan with their courage and fortitude have for some time been ... exposing and killing Jadids and Bolshe-viks."[105] Equally unsurprisingly, urban Muslims were almost entirely absent from the ranks of the Basmachi. They had no place in the networks through which the Basmachi derived their power, and their understandings of politics and religion differed markedly from those of the Basmachi. Indeed, many urban Muslims saw the actions of the Basmachi at par with those of Russian settlers, the result of the ignorance of the warlords.[106]

Much of the bloodshed that took place in Central Asia was a result of the extension to the region of the Russian civil war, in which various groups of Russians fought out their battles in Central Asia. The Basmachi insurgency was (or quickly became), however, a *Central Asian* civil war, a war fought out amongst Central Asians. Instead of being a heroic national resistance against outsiders, the Basmachi was a sign of deep divisions within Central Asian society. The conflict brutalized Central Asian society and opened up deep splits in it. As the Soviets attempted to establish a new social order, they were met not by a united, cohesive

---

103. Quoted by Kamoludin Abdullaev, *Ot Sin'tsziania do Khorasana: Iz istorii sredneaziatskoi emigratsii XX veka* (Dushanbe, 2009), 192–193.

104. Şevket Sürreya Aydemir, *Makedonya'dan Ortaasya'ya Enver Paşa*, 3 vols. (Istanbul, 1970–72), 3:619.

105. Mirza Salimbek, *Tarikh-i salimi*, 255.

106. See, for instance, a piece of reportage by Cho'lpon from 1923, republished as "Vayronalar orasidan," *Sharq yulduzi*, 1991, no. 6: 23–30. Cho'lpon also wrote a number of poems decrying the destruction visited on the land in the period since the revolution. These writings are read in post-Soviet Uzbekistan as straightforward criticisms of Soviet excesses, when a greater appreciation of the historical context would problematize such readings.

local society, but a bitterly divided one. Conflicts within Central Asian society were just as important as conflicts between Europeans and Central Asians in the early Soviet period. The national movement had not won its victory in society, nor was there any consensus on the path to the future. As historians, we should rid ourselves of the phantom of Central Asian Muslim unity and look at Central Asia as an arena of multifaceted conflict.

NATIONALIZING THE REVOLUTION

Events in Turkestan had taken their own course since March 1917, when the Tashkent soviet arrested the governor general A. N. Kuropatkin and deported him back to Russia. That soviet's seizure of power in November was driven by local considerations, and although it sent a delegate to Petrograd to announce the ascent of Soviet power in Turkestan,[1] it continued to act entirely independently of the center. This independence was facilitated by the collapse of transport networks and an incipient civil war that cut Turkestan off from inner Russia. The main challenge for the Bolshevik leadership was to reestablish central control over Turkestan and to bring proper Soviet order to it. What that order was to be in a colonial situation was an open question, however, and one that was settled mostly by trial and error over the next two years. This uncertainty was compounded by the center's tenuous control over Turkestan, for its authority had to be projected through trusted emissaries armed only with mandates and powers of exhortation. This unsettled situation created an opportunity for the Jadids to join the new organs of power and to attempt to put them to their own use. The imperatives of the center thus inaugurated a new arena of politics that existed against the backdrop of the ethnic and social conflict described in the previous chapter.

How was a revolution imagined as class conflict to work out in a colonial region where national and racial distinctions were fundamental? The Bolsheviks

---

1. RGASPI, f. 5, op. 1, d. 2920, ll. 1–2ob.

had adopted a stridently anticolonial rhetoric from the beginning, but they had no clear idea of how the categories of nation and class intersected. The Bolsheviks were to come up with a ramified nationalities policy, but that did not exist in 1917. Bolshevik actions in the period until 1920 were often reactive to the challenges of various national movements, while their thinking tended to be quite flexible in its conflation of the categories of class, nation, and confession. On 20 November 1917, the new Soviet government had issued a proclamation "To All Toiling Muslims of Russia and the East" that exhorted Muslims to support the new government: "All you, whose mosques and shrines have been destroyed, whose faith and customs have been violated by the Tsars and oppressors of Russia! Henceforward your beliefs and customs, your national and cultural institutions, are declared free and inviolable! Build your national life freely and without hindrance."[2] Not only did Lenin entangle the national question within Russia with the colonial question abroad, he also equated colonialism with class oppression. Nationality seemed to be synonymous with class in colonial situations. The practical implication of this line of thought in Turkestan was to overturn the policies of the Tashkent soviet that had used the language of class to deny the colonial population all access to power. Moscow thus forced the entry of Muslims into the new organs of power at the expense of the settlers.

Such a policy was very promising to the Jadids, to whom the revolution made sense only as an anticolonial and a national phenomenon. They had also come to acquire a sincere enthusiasm for revolution as a modality of change, an enthusiasm redoubled by the opposition they had faced from their own society in 1917. The Jadids' fascination with revolution was also shaped by the new geopolitical conjuncture produced by the end of the war that created both desperation and hope. The final collapse of the Ottoman Empire, the last sovereign Muslim state in the world, seemed to indicate an existential crisis for Islam and the Muslim world. It radicalized the Jadids' reform agenda and gave it a new urgency. The Muslim world could only be saved through progress, which was possible only through revolutionary change. The Soviet regime appeared as harbingers of a new anticolonial world order that would allow the rejuvenation of Central Asia and the Muslim world at large and make it possible for it to fight back against the "imperialists" that had triumphed in the war. The geopolitics of the time allowed the Jadids to conflate Islam, nation, and revolution into a vision of anticolonial struggle with Britain as the main enemy and the Soviet state as an ally.

This anticolonial reading effectively nationalized the revolution for those Muslims who joined the new regime once doors to it were opened under pressure

---

2. *Dekrety sovetskoi vlasti*, vol. 1 (Moscow, 1957), 113–115.

from Moscow. Between spring 1918 and summer 1920, they articulated a vision of Turkestan's future that would be Muslim, national, and revolutionary at the same time. Such a Turkestan would be free of the depredations of the settlers domestically and a conduit of revolution to the Muslim world internationally. Armed with nation and revolution, Muslims would revolutionize the colonial world and bring liberation to "the East." Ultimately, however, that vision was squashed by the Bolsheviks. They were willing to push back at the power of Turkestan's settler Communists, but they had no intention of putting in their place a different group with wide autonomy and a substantially different understanding of revolution. As the center regained political control of Turkestan, it also asserted control over the meaning of revolution in the region.

The Bolsheviks and Turkestan

Turkestan was an unlikely place to experience a proletarian revolution, and the Bolsheviks' desire to control it requires at least some explanation. The most fundamental motivation for the Bolsheviks was a desire to extend Soviet rule over all of the former Russian Empire. There were two other reasons for the center's interest in Turkestan. One was the region's strategic position for revolutionizing "the East." "Eastern policy" loomed large over all discussions of Turkestan from 1918 to 1921. "It is no exaggeration to say," Lenin wrote in an open letter to "the Communists of Turkestan" in November 1919, "that the establishment of proper relations with the peoples of Turkestan is now of immense, world-historic importance for the Russian Socialist Federated Soviet Republic. For the whole of Asia and for all the colonies of the world, for thousands and millions of people, the attitude of the Soviet worker-peasant republic to the weak and hitherto oppressed peoples is of very practical significance."[3] Lenin was to persist in this opinion to the end of his active life, although many of his comrades were much more skeptical.

The second reason for Moscow's interest in Turkestan was a more straightforward one and one that placed the Soviet regime in direct continuity with the Tsarist Empire. This was the need for the economic resources of the region, especially cotton. In the most immediate short term, central authorities wanted access to Turkestan's cotton without which Russia's textile industry could not function.

---

3. V. I. Lenin, *Polnoe sobranie sochinenii*, 5th ed., vol. 39 (Moscow, 1963), 304.

The Tashkent soviet had "nationalized" all cotton in Turkestan, but the same collapse of transport and legal order that had ushered in the famine also meant that this cotton continued to lie in factories and warehouses. Moscow began sending buying missions to the region even when it was cut off from the center by the civil war. In the longer term, Turkestan's resources were to play an important part in the Soviet state's economic calculations. Economic goals were a clear part of the mandate of the Turkestan Commission (Turkkomissiia) when it arrived to knit Turkestan into the Soviet state. Even before the commission arrived in Turkestan, L. B. Krasin, the commissar for trade and industry, was pointing out that "the recent reunion of Turkestan presents the opportunity . . . for making broad use of this region as well as of countries neighboring it . . . for the export of cotton, rice, dry fruits, and other goods necessary not only for the internal market of Russia, but also for its external trade."[4]

However, Turkestan had to be knit back into the Russian state on new terms. If Soviet rule in Turkestan were to be an example to the colonial world, and indeed if Soviet rule were to be secure in Turkestan, then it needed to be distanced from its Tsarist antecedents and based on the local population. The center's primary goal in 1918 and 1919, therefore, was to force the Tashkent soviet to abandon its policy of excluding Muslims from power. In February 1918, it appointed Petr Kobozev its "plenipotentiary commissar" for Turkestan with the task of establishing oversight over local Soviet power. He arrived in Tashkent in April with two Tatar officials from Narkomnats in tow. He was preceded by a telegram from I. V. Stalin, then commissar for nationalities affairs, which announced the kinds of compromises the center was willing to make:

> We are sending to you in Turkestan two comrades, members of the Tatar-Bashkir Committee at the People's Commissariat for Nationalities Affairs, Ibrahimov and Klebleyev. The latter is maybe already known to you as a former supporter of the autonomous group. His appointment to this new post might startle you; I ask you nevertheless to let him work, forgiving his old sins. All of us here think that now, when Soviet power is getting stronger everywhere in Russia, we shouldn't fear the shadows of the past of people who only yesterday were getting mixed up with our enemies: if these people are ready to recognize their mistakes, we should not push them away. Furthermore, we advise you to attract to [political] work [even] adherents of Kerensky from the natives if they

---

4. Krasin to Eliava, 03.11.1919, in *Ekonomicheskie otnosheniia sovetskoi Rossii s budushchimi soiuznymi respublikami, 1917–1922* (Moscow, 1996), 89.

> are ready to serve Soviet power—the latter only gains from it, and there
> is nothing to be afraid of in the shadows of the past.[5]

Arif Klebleyev, in fact, had chaired the Military Council (Harbiy Shuro, the organization of Muslim—mostly Tatar—soldiers stationed in Turkestan) in Kokand, which had under his signature sent a telegram to the new Soviet government in Petrograd, asking it to command the Tashkent soviet to recognize the autonomous government at Kokand as the legal authority in Turkestan.[6] Now, three months later, he was doing the work of the central government in Turkestan.

Kobozev and his companions set about breaking the hold of the settlers on power. They mobilized the Muslim population and inducted it in the new institutions of power. A "soviet of Muslim and peasant [*dehqon*] deputies" began functioning in the old city of Tashkent in April, and its members participated in the Fifth Congress of Soviets that convened in Tashkent on 21 April. Kobozev also proclaimed a general amnesty for those who had been involved with the autonomous government in Kokand,[7] and he forced a reelection to the Tashkent soviet before the Fifth Congress of Turkestan's soviets. "A brilliant victory of ours in the elections to Tashkent's proletarian parliament has decisively crushed the hydra of reaction," he telegraphed Moscow. "White Muslim turbans have grown noticeably in the ranks of the Tashkent parliament, attaining a third of all seats."[8] At the congress, he had himself elected chair of the presidium and forced the inclusion of several Muslims in it. The congress created the Central Executive Committee of Turkestan (TurTsIK) as the supreme organ of power in the region. Kobozev ensured that nine of its thirty-six members were Muslims and that the new sovnarkom contained four Muslims out of sixteen.[9] Kobozev also spearheaded the establishment of the Communist Party in Turkestan (KPT) for the first time. The Bolsheviks in Russia itself had finally broken from the Russian Social Democratic Labor Party only in 1917, but no such change had taken place in Turkestan. Kobozev convened a conference of all Bolshevik organizations in Turkestan in June 1918 and oversaw the formation of the KPT as a branch of the Russian Communist Party. In Turkestan, it

---

5. The Tashkent soviet did not care to make this telegram public; it was published in Russian only in September, and then in an off-the-cuff manner in connection with the obituary for Klebleyev, who died of typhus in Khujand (*Nasha gazeta*, 25.09.1918). Klebleyev and Ibrahimov, however, had ensured its publication in Uzbek right away in April: *Ulug' Turkiston*, 18.04.1918.

6. "Petrog'irodga yiborilgan teleg'irom," *Ishchilar dunyosi*, no. 2 (17.01.1918 [o.s.]), 22–23.

7. GARF, f. 1235, op. 93, d. 583a, l. 69.

8. TsGARUz, f. 25, op. 1, d. 78, ll. 5–6 (16.4.1918).

9. *Nasha gazeta*, 12.05.1918.

was the revolution that created the Communist Party and not the other way round.[10]

Muslims in the Soviet Order

The first responses of the Jadids to the Bolshevik takeover had been entirely negative. "Russia has seen disaster upon disaster since the [February] transformation," Fitrat had written in November 1917. "And now a new calamity has raised its head, that of the Bolsheviks!"[11] Few Muslim figures in Central Asia disagreed. For Hoji Muin, the Bolsheviks' demands were "unnatural" and all their promises remained on paper, which was why "no nation believed them," and they were already at war with Ukraine by the new year.[12] The conquest of power by Tashkent's settler Communists drew even harsher criticisms. "Muslims . . . have not seen a kopeck's worth of good from the Freedom [i.e., the revolution]," G'ozi Yunus noted at about the same time. "On the contrary, we are experiencing times worse than those of Nicholas," for "our *tovarishes*" had subverted the freedoms proclaimed by the revolution and brought back censorship and banned organizations. The greatest danger for G'ozi Yunus lay in the plan for the socialization of land, "which does not accord with our shariat," and which would result in the alienation of all land to European settlers.[13] The bloodbath at Kokand only confirmed these doubts.

Central intervention against the settler Communists, however, offered entirely new possibilities. For many Jadids, the new organs of power became a site for the continuation of the mobilization of 1917, both against European settlers and against "reaction" in their own society. Abdulla Avloniy, the poet and pedagogue, appeared in the Tashkent soviet as a Bolshevik while the poet Tavallo took his seat as a Left Social Revolutionary, in which party he had the company of Said Karim Said Azimboyev, scion of one of the most established families of Tsarist-era Tashkent.[14] In Samarqand, Behbudiy was a member of the

---

10. The insight that the revolution created the party in Turkestan belongs to Georgii Safarov, *Kolonial'naia revoliutsiia: opyt Turkestana* (Moscow, 1922), but it bears repeating. The first congress was shambolic, and the party did not become a functioning organization until the end of 1918; see I. Sol'ts, "K istorii KPT," in *Tri goda sovetskoi vlasti: sbornik k tretei godovshchine Oktiabr'skoi revoliutsii v Turkestane* (Tashkent, 1920), 45–53.

11. Fitrat, "Siyosiy hollar," *Hurriyat*, 07.11.1917.

12. Hoji Muin, "Bolshaviqlar va biz," *Hurriyat*, 09.01.1918 (o.s.).

13. Mullo G'ozi, "Hurriyatmi? Yoki istibdod?" *Ishchilar dunyosi*, no. 3 (01.02.1918 [o.s.]), 36–39. Later in the year, G'ozi Yunus was to travel to Istanbul and seek Ottoman intervention.

14. GAgT, f. 12, d. 6, l. 96.

old-city soviet and chaired it as well.[15] Many of the younger Jadids, those who had entered public life in 1917, were particularly prominent. Laziz Azizzoda had begun teaching only in 1916 and in 1917 had been active in the Shuroi Islomiya. He joined the Bolsheviks in 1918 and by the following year had become the head of the old-city organization of the KPT in Tashkent.[16] Sobirjon Yusupov, who had been prominent in the Shuroi Islomiya throughout 1917 and was a member of the Kokand government, and Nizomiddin Xo'jayev, also a prominent activist throughout 1917, reappeared in Tashkent, where both joined the nascent KPT. By late summer, Yusupov was TurTsIK's representative in Moscow and Xo'jayev was to become chair of the Tashkent old-city ispolkom.

This was the same time, we might recall, that other activists were traveling to the Ottoman Empire in search for support. In 1918, Soviet organs represented one more option for continuing the work of 1917. The Jadids used their access to the new institutions to continue their struggle with the ulama. One of the first acts of the newly formed old-city soviet in Tashkent was to ask the city police to arrest the "counterrevolutionary" ulama of the Ulamo Jamiyati and to requisition its property. The request was duly carried out on 21 May 1918, when the commissar of the old city of Tashkent shut down the Ulamo Jami-yati and its journal *al-Izoh*, and confiscated its property.[17] The old-city soviet also took an aggressive line against the educational establishments where the ulama were based and began questioning them on their views on social justice and economic equality.[18] Over the next two years, the soviet also requisitioned property on behalf of new-method schools and theatrical groups, thus provid-ing the main institutional support for the flagship cultural institutions of the intelligentsia.[19]

The theater that prospered in 1919 and 1920 was squarely located in con-cerns of the nation. A sampling of the theatrical repertoire captures the mood of that period. It included prerevolutionary Jadid plays such as *Zaharli hayot* (A Poisoned Life) by Hamza Hakimzoda Niyoziy and *Baxtsiz kiyov* (The Unfortu-nate Son-in-Law) by Abdulla Qodiriy that recounted the harmful consequences for individuals and society of lack of education; new plays in exactly the same mode, such as *Baxtsiz shogird* (The Unfortunate Pupil) by G'ulom Zafariy,[20] or

---

15. GASO, f. 89, d. 1, ll. 87, 95, 96.

16. *Ishtirokiyun*, 01.12.1918, 08.02.1919, 04.12.1919.

17. *Pobeda Oktiabr'skoi revoliutsii v Uzbekistane: sbornik dokumetov*, 2 vols. (Tashkent, 1963–72), 2:203–204, 265; TsGARUz, f. 36, op. 1, d. 12, ll. 38–40.

18. TsGARUz, f. 36, op. 1, d. 12, l. 182–182ob; GAgT, f. 12, d. 12, ll. 14, 21–25.

19. Traces of these requisitions are to be found in GAgT, f. 12, d. 4, ll. 107, 113ob, 141; d. 24, l. 268.

20. Mirmullo Sher-Muhammad, "Tiyotir va muziqo," *Ishtirokiyun*, 06.03.1920.

Javonbozlik qurboni (Pederasty's Victim) by Xurshid.[21] Nor were all problems the product of colonialism. In perhaps the first historical play in Uzbek, called *Turkiston xonlig'i, yoxud muhabbat natijasi* (The Khanate of Turkestan, Or, the Fruits of Love), a certain A. Romiz cast an unflattering look at Turkestan's past. A boy falls in love with the daughter of the *to'qsabo*, who does not approve of the match, and instead gives his daughter to the khan as a present. When she refuses, the girl is thrown into prison, where the jailer attempts to rape her. The play ends in tragedy, when both lovers are killed during an attempt by the boy to rescue his beloved from jail. In his review, Mirmullo Shermuhammad found much to criticize about the feebleness of the plot, but welcomed the attempt to acquaint the public with the "injustices and un-Islamic [*g'ayri mashru'*] acts … of our despotic khans and their … ignorant warlords [*johil qo'rboshilar*]."[22] The revolution was the opportunity to rectify these shortcomings.

However, the new order broadened access to public life, and the Jadids were joined by a different kind of activist—men who entered public life not through involvement in cultural reform but through politics more directly. Their intellectual trajectories differed from those of the Jadids in important ways. Some arrived at participation through the radicalization of the Muslim urban population as a result of the famine and the new political situation. Others came through the ranks via political struggles over questions of food supply and the violence against Muslim peasants and nomads, and mobilized around "concern for the poor swelling up with hunger."[23] Many of these freshly minted Communists were educated in the so-called Russo-native schools (which had, ironically enough, been established with the aim of creating a group in the indigenous population fluent in Russian and therefore capable of acting as a pillar of support for Russian rule in Turkestan). They were thus fluent in Russian, which had become indispensable for participation in the new politics inaugurated by the February revolution. Few of them had been seriously involved in the project of Islamic reform that had defined Jadidism until the revolution.

It was one of these men, Tŭrar Rïsqŭlov (1894–1938), who was to be the most significant actor in Muslim politics in Turkestan over the next several years. Born in Semirech'e to a Kazakh family of modest means but high status, Rïsqŭlov attended a Russo-native school, where he acquired good enough Russian to work for a Russian lawyer and then to attend the agriculture school in Pishpek. In October 1916, he matriculated at the Tashkent normal school, and it was here that

---

21. *Ishtirokiyun*, 27.03.1920.

22. *Ishtirokiyun*, 17.03.1919.

23. *Trudy 3-go s"ezda Kommunisticheskoi partii Turkestanskoi respubliki Rossiiskoi Sovetskoi Federatsii, 1–15 iiunia 1919 goda* (Tashkent, 1919), 109 (Rïsqŭlov's speech).

the February revolution found him. He had no previous record of public life, no contacts with the Kazakh intelligentsia in Semirech'e, and he seems to have taken no part in public life in Tashkent. His was not a Jadid trajectory. In March 1917, he returned to his home town of Merke, where he supposedly founded a Union of Revolutionary Kazakh Youth. Although no documentary record has ever emerged of the existence of this organization, we know that by the winter of 1917–18, he was active in the Avliyo Ota ispolkom. He rose rapidly in soviet institutions and returned to Tashkent in mid-1918. By that autumn, he was Turkestan's commissar for health[24] and was to rise to greater heights in 1919.

Old-city soviets could articulate and defend the interests of the population of the old cities against the settlers, but they also represented a shifting a political power within the old cities. Over the summer of 1918, the old-city soviets in Tashkent, Samarqand, and Margelan granted numerous licenses to Muslim Communists to carry guns to "protect themselves from counterrevolutionaries."[25] The power of the old elites of the ulama and the *ellikboshi* (headmen elected by property holders) was being usurped by a cohort of (generally very young) men ensconced in Soviet institutions. The transition was deeply contested and resented. On 19 January 1919, when Karl Osipov, the Turkestani commissar for war, staged an unsuccessful putsch (in which he shot fourteen of his fellow commissars dead), the old city was under the control of the insurgents for most of the day, during which time the ulama reemerged as a political force. As the old order was restored for a few hours, the ulama and their fellow conservatives pursued Jadids and Communists alike.[26]

New Languages of Politics

What did Bolshevism mean to the Jadids and the freshly minted Muslim Communists of Turkestan? Their very appearance is surprising and worthy of an explanation, for until 1917 not only was there not a native Muslim working

---

24. Xavier Hallez, "Communisme national et mouvement révolutionnaire en Orient: parcours croisés de trois leaders soviétiques orientaux (Mirsaid Sultan-Galiev, Turar Ryskulov et Elbekdorž Rinčino) dans la construction d'un nouvel espace géopolitique" (thèse de doctorat, EHESS, 2012), 64–76, 253–264. The two published biographies of Rïsqŭlov treat his early life only superficially. The better work is Ordalï Qongïratbayev, *Tŭrar Rïsqŭlov: qoghamdïq-sayasi jäne memlekettĭk qïzmetĭ* (Almaty, 1994); V. M. Ustinov, *Turar Ryskulov: ocherki politicheskoi biografii* (Almaty, 1996), writes entirely within Soviet parameters and is thus incapable of bringing out the ironies of Rïsqŭlov's remarkable career.

25. GAgT, f. 12, d. 6, ll. 122, 146, 177, 216, 217; d. 17, l. 17; GASO, f. 89, d. 1, l. 141; GAFO, f. 121, op. 1, d. 33, l. 23.

26. *Ishtirokiyun*, 19.02.1919; Iu. Ibragimov, "Ianvarskie sobytiia v Tashkente," *Zhizn' natsional'nostei*, 30.03.1919.

class in Central Asia, there was also no language to articulate politics as class conflict. While a few intellectuals with Russian educations had contacts with socialist parties, there was little comprehension, let alone sympathy, for socialism among Muslims at large. After the seizure of power by the Tashkent soviet, various Muslim figures tried to use the language of class, but only to domesticate it. The autonomous government at Kokand felt compelled to garner "proletarian" legitimacy for itself and organized a conference of Muslim workers in Kokand in January 1918. At the same time, activists established a Muslim workers' soviet in Tashkent, although the only sign of its existence was its press organ, the "national, political, economic, historical, scientific, and social journal" called *Ishchilar dunyosi* (Workers' World). Despite its name, the journal aimed "to improve the material and spiritual existence of the poor who live off their labor while holding tight to the proud shariat of our Prophet," to help workers organize, and "to put in place a Turkic-Islamic policy [*Turk-Islom siyosati*]."[27] It featured harsh critiques of Bolshevik actions *and* policies and sought to educate Muslim workers on the dangers of Bolshevism. Two months later, after the destruction of the Kokand government, a "Muslim Workers' Party" appeared in Tashkent. Its founding statute declared that "because our shariat is against capitalism and speculation . . . there is no capitalism and bourgeois-ness [*burzhuylik*] in our Turkestan, and the party stands against its spread to Turkestan."[28] The platform then went on demand extensive national and linguistic rights for Turkestan's indigenous population and connected revolution directly to national liberation. Seralï Lapin, for his part, returned from the debacle at Kokand and penned a fascinating letter to the Tashkent soviet in the name of the Ulamo Jamiyati, in which he claimed that the roots of socialism lay in Islam, whose teachings about social justice foreshadowed the Marxist critique of capitalism, and thus the ulama, as the carriers of Islam, were the real force of revolution in Muslim society and the natural partners of Soviet power (unlike the "so-called progressists" who only wanted to Europeanize Muslim society and thus to pave the way for capitalism).[29]

---

27. "Maslak va maqsad," *Ishchilar dunyosi*, no. 1 (4.1.1918 [o.s.]).

28. *Xodimi islom firqasining maromnomasi / Programma musul'manskoi trudovoi partii* (Tashkent, 1918), 1 (Uzbek pagination). The Russian and Turkic texts are quite different and use very different political vocabularies.

29. Ser Ali Lapin, "Ot Tashkentskoi organizatsii 'Ulema' Russkim Sotsialistam" (17.01.1918), TsGARUz, f. 39, op. 1, d. 11, ll. 3–10; this document has now been published by M.M. Khaidarov, "'Evropeiskii sotsializm imeet svoim pervoistochnikom tot zhe samyi Islam . . .': Pis'mo russkim sotsialistam ot tashkentskoi organizatsii 'Shuro-i-Ulema.' 1918 g.," *Istoricheskii arkhiv*, 2004, no. 2: 172–182; a shortened version of Ulamo Jamiyati's proposals appeared in "Ulamo Jamiyatining taklifi," *Ishchilar dunyosi*, no. 3 (01.02.1918 [o.s.]), 42–43.

Still, socialism remained a mystery for most Muslims, and its nature and provenance continued to be discussed in the vernacular Soviet press once it emerged in June 1918. While some authors provided a basic introduction to the concepts,[30] others sought to find some sanction or precedent in the history of Islam. They found it in the teachings of Sheikh Bedreddin Simavî (1358–1416), the Bektashi Sufi figure from the Balkans who had led a revolt against Ottoman power and advocated the redistribution of land among the peasants.[31] Bedreddin was a heretical figure, of course, who was executed for his pains. Evoking him did not constitute an attempt at the formulation of a theory of "Islamic socialism," a doctrine that might explain socialism in Islamic terms as was attempted later in the twentieth century by many in other parts of the Muslim world. Rather, it was a search for intelligibility for a concept radically new to local political discourse.

In general, the new language of politics remained poorly understood. Muslims in the party, especially those who worked in Russian, quickly learned to populate their memos with seven-headed hydras of the bourgeoisie, counterrevolutions, and toiling masses (although the meanings they attached to the new vocabulary had a disconcerting tendency to be at odds with what party authorities might have in mind). For those working in vernacular languages, the challenge was much greater. The language of class-based politics had been entirely absent from local debates until 1917, and the vocabulary needed for it simply did not exist. If *exploitation* and *oppression* were to be used, they seemed a lot more applicable to imperialism, which is why an anticolonial reading of the revolution was so attractive to Muslim actors in Central Asia. Bolshevism was connected to revolution, but not class. Here is a poem titled "Bolshevism" from the official organ of the Communist Party of Turkestan as late as 1921:

Bildim bu na maslakdir?	Now I know what this principle is!
Insonlarni birlatdi . . .	It has united all humanity . . .
Bayroqlarni parlatdi! . . .	It has made banners shine . . .
Zolimlarni titratdi! . . .	It has made tyrants tremble! . . .

---

30. "Sosiyolizm ne narsa?" *Ishtirokiyun*, 07.11.1918.

31. Abu Turg'ud (pseud.), "Islom dunyosinda so'siyolizm fikri," *Ishtirokiyun*, 12.02.1919; S.M. [Sadriddin Aynī], "Islām va qāmmūnizm (Shaykh Badruddīn Simāvī)," *Shu'la-yi inqilāb*, 10.03.1921, 2–4; M., "Mundam beshyuz yil burun o'tgan musulmon kommunist (Shayx Badriddin Simoviy)," *Mehnatkashlar tovushi*, 10.05.1921, 17.05.1921. The source for all these articles was a single piece published several years previously in the Tatar journal *Shura*. Later in the twentieth century, Sheikh Bedreddin was similarly evoked by many leftists in Turkey as an indigenous predecessor, with the great poet Nazım Hikmet making him the subject of a renowned poem ("Simavne Kadısı Oğlu Şeyh Bedreddin Destanı," 1936).

Mazlumlari uyg'otdi!?	It has awakened the oppressed!
Qardoshlig'a yo'l ochdi!	It has opened the path to brotherhood!
Har yerga ziyo sochdi.[32]	It has spread light in all directions!

Unity and struggle against oppression—this was how Bolshevism made sense to Central Asians. Exploitation, class conflict, and the dialectic were still hard to find in local rhetoric.

Liberating the East

It was perhaps the mission of liberating "the East" that provided the greatest amount of common ground between the Bolsheviks and the Muslim intelligentsia of Central Asia. "The East," and the colonial world in general, were, from the first, an object of Bolshevik interest. Lenin had argued during the war that imperialism was the highest form of capitalism in which the bourgeoisie can buy off the proletariat by exporting exploitation to the colonies.[33] Depriving the European powers of their colonies was necessary for social revolution to succeed in the metropole. The Bolsheviks had dabbled with "the East" from the moment they took power (one of their earliest decrees was addressed "To the Toiling Muslims of Russia and the East") and the revolutionary potential of "the East" had already aroused the enthusiasm of activists within and without the party,[34] but it was the failure of the proletariat in Europe itself to rise to revolution (and the defeat of revolution in Germany and Hungary in 1918) that pushed colonial revolution to the forefront of Bolshevik thinking. Unexpected events, such as the emergence of Amanullah Khan in Afghanistan, who wrested his country's independence from Britain and established relations with the Soviet state, helped this geopolitical vision. By the middle of 1919, Trotsky saw "the international situation . . . shaping up in such a way that the road to Paris and London lies through the towns of Afghanistan, Punjab, and Bengal,"[35] and "Eastern policy" (*Vostochnaia*

---

32. Yangi Ishchi (pseud.), "Bolshovizim," *Qizil bayroq*, 18.01.1921.

33. V. I. Lenin, *Imperialism, the Highest Form of Capitalism* (1916).

34. K. Troianovskii, *Vostok i revoliutsiia: Popytka postroeniia novoi politicheskoi programmy dlia tuzemnykh stran Vostoka—Indii, Persii, Kitaia* (Petrograd, 1918). Troianovskii was the moving force behind the establishment of the Union for the Liberation of the East (Soiuz Osvobozhdeniia Vostoka) in October 1918: B. Gurko-Kriazhin, "10 let vostokovednoi mysli," *Novyi Vostok*, no. 19 (1927), xli.

35. Leon Trotsky, *The Trotsky Papers, 1917–1922*, vol. 1 (The Hague, 1964), 624.

politika) became all the rage in Moscow. The "national and colonial question" was a major issue at the Second Congress of the Comintern in July 1920, which convened the First Congress of the Peoples of the East in Baku in September. In all of this, Turkestan occupied a central place as "the front door to the East," the vanguard of the revolution in India and "the Muslim East." Lenin and Trotsky both contemplated setting up a military base in Turkestan even before it was meaningfully reintegrated into Soviet rule, and in 1920 the Comintern established its own Turkestan Bureau, complete with a military school, in Tashkent.[36]

Central Asian intellectuals had their own path to the idea of anticolonial revolution. As the war effort melted away in 1917, old Russia's enemies began to appear as friends, while the Bolsheviks' anticapitalist rhetoric aimed at Russia's erstwhile allies found resonance, for slightly different reasons, with the Jadids. By autumn 1917, it was permissible to openly sympathize with the Ottomans. If capitalism, so to speak, was the highest form of imperialism, then Britain and France were the champions of imperialism; alongside the world's proletariat and the entire colonial world, the Ottoman Empire (and hence the entire Muslim world) was among the victims of imperialism. The publication by the Bolsheviks of the secret treaties signed by imperial Russia with Britain and France during the war, most of them at the expense of the Ottoman Empire, touched a raw nerve among the Jadids. Even as he bemoaned the Bolshevik seizure of power in Petrograd, Fitrat wrote that "it had now become clear who the real enemies of the Muslim, and especially the Turkic, world are."[37] The Ottoman defeat, which opened the way to unprecedented British paramountcy in the Middle East, was a turning point of sorts for the Jadids, who lost a great deal of their earlier fascination with the liberal civilization of Europe and turned to a radical anticolonial critique of the bourgeois order. The situation also led the Jadids to a reevaluation of the Bolsheviks, who now appeared as agents of a new world order, an order that contained in it the possibility of national liberation and progress, as well as a struggle against reaction. The experiences of 1917 and 1918 had radicalized both the cultural and the political horizons of the Jadids and given them a fascination with the idea of revolution as a modality for change.

Anticolonial struggle, the defense of Islam, and national revolution shared the same iconoclastic mood as the Bolsheviks, and the conflation of all these

---

36. Trotsky to CC, 20.09.1919, in *The Trotsky Papers*, 1:672; Lenin to Eliava, 16.10.1919, in Richard Pipes, ed., *The Unknown Lenin: From the Secret Archive* (New Haven, 1996), 74. On the Turkestan Bureau of the Comintern, see V. M. Gilensen, "Turkestanskoe biuro Kominterna (osen' 1920–osen' 1921)," *Vostok*, 1999, no. 1: 59–77, and M. N. Roy, *The Memoirs of M. N. Roy* (Bombay, 1964), 429–438.

37. Fitrat, "Yoshurun muohidalari," *Hurriyat*, 28.11.1917.

phenomena proved remarkably easy in the fluid ideological atmosphere of the time. Fitrat, who before the war had used an Englishman as his mouthpiece in his exhortations to reform, turned to an increasingly critical view of the British. His writings from 1919 and 1920 are intensely anticolonial and specifically anti-British. From being exemplars of progress, the British had become unmitigated villains. Imperialism, exploitation, and oppression had now become the hallmarks of Europe (and Britain in particular). In numerous works, Fitrat focused on the oppression of British rule in India and celebrated those who struggled against it. For Fitrat, driving the English out of India was "as great [a duty] as saving the pages of the Qur'an from being trampled by an animal . . . a worry as great as that of driving a pig out of a mosque."[38]

Fitrat discussed the rapidly evolving geopolitics in a series of columns in *Hurriyat* and *Ishtirokiyun*, many of which he collected in a brochure called *Sharq siyosati* (Eastern Policy), published in 1919. The following year, he wrote two plays on Indian themes that are eloquent evocations of anticolonial patriotism. In *Chin sevish* (True Love), he portrayed the love of Zulaikha for Nuruddin, a patriotic, revolutionary poet, which is foiled by Rahmatullah, an Anglophile who desires Zulaikha as he has desired many young maidens before. In the tradition of Jadid theater established before the revolution, the play ends in a bloodbath, as a secret meeting of an Indian revolutionary committee, involving both Zulaikha and Nuruddin is ambushed by the police (who are led it to it by Rahmatullah). But the linkage between love, patriotism, and revolution is firmly established. True love is inextricable from patriotism, while the failure to support patriotic revolution is synonymous with treason. In *Hind ixtilolchilari* (Indian Revolutionaries), which also portrayed the struggle of Indian patriots for independence, Fitrat repeated these themes, but in a more overtly political manner. Rahim Bakhsh is an educated young man in love with Dilnavaz, both of them afire with patriotic love. After the police arrest Dilnavaz, Rahim Bakhsh has to overcome his earlier ambivalence, and he joins a clandestine group of "revolutionaries" in a mountainous redoubt on the Afghan frontier. The plot is similar in its tragic ending, but love for the country is again equated with love for a woman and the protection of her honor. Anti-imperialism, patriotism, and revolutionary action are inextricably intertwined.

In both plays, Fitrat focuses on the oppression of colonial rule. He had come a long way from his fascination with Europe and its civilization in *A Debate*

---

38. Fitrat, *Hind ixtilolchilari* (1920), in *Tanlangan asarlar*, 5 vols. to date (Tashkent, 2000–), 3:46. For a more extended analysis of the Indian theme in Fitrat's work of the period, see Adeeb Khalid, "Visions of India in Central Asian Modernism: The Work of Abdurauf Fitrat," in *Looking at the Coloniser*, ed. Hans Herder and Beate Eschment (Würzburg, 2004), 253–274.

between a Bukharan Professor and a European on the Subject of New Schools
(1913). What had changed? Fitrat himself provides the answer in a passage
in *True Love*, which undoubtedly is autobiographical at some level but is
here put in the mouth of Karim Bakhsh in *True Love*: "It is of course necessary to learn European things. Studying in Europe is necessary not so that
we praise the Europeans for being just, but to save ourselves from them, to
become toothed-and-clawed [for the struggle]. . . . The sciences we learnt
in Europe are easy to use in the way of improving the world and peace."[39]
The basic premise about the absolute necessity of self-strengthening,
and the desirability and inevitability of progress remained unchanged from
The Debate to *Eastern Policy*. The dramatic shifts in the world order and a new
sense of desperation had transformed the diagnosis. Fitrat now proposed a strategic alliance between the Muslim world and Soviet Russia. "The government of
Soviet Russia has struggled with European imperialists. Its motto is 'Victory or
Death.' This is exactly the kind of effort, and exactly this kind of nobility required
to unite the East."[40] Fitrat noted that "Comrade Lenin, the leader of Soviet Russia, is a great man, who has already begun the attempt at awakening and uniting
the East."[41] He also noted that given that the European and American proletariat
had failed to rise to the Soviets' support, the Soviets had no choice but to form
an alliance with the East.[42] Fitrat had been less than enthusiastic about the Bolsheviks in October 1917, but things had clearly changed by 1919.

Dreams of a colonial revolution were helped along by real events. Amanullah
Khan's repudiation of British overlordship was seen by many as an anticolonial
gesture. Amanullah looked to the Soviets for support and sent a mission to Moscow that passed through Tashkent in May 1919, where it established a consulate.
The Soviets took on the task of establishing a modern army in Afghanistan, with
the hope of destabilizing British rule in India. For this, they found the cooperation of Cemal Pasha, the exiled Unionist leader, whom they deemed to "enjoy
influence" among "Muslim tribes that constitute the majority of the population
in the Indus valley and the province of Punjab."[43] At the same time, many Indian

---

39. Fitrat, *Chin sevish* (1920), in *Tanlangan asarlar*, 3:10.
40. Fitrat, *Sharq siyosati* (n.p. n.d. [Tashkent, 1919]), 40.
41. Ibid., 40–41.
42. Ibid., 43.
43. So Stalin to Trotsky, 02.11.1921, RGASPI, f. 558, op. 2, d. 21, l. 168. The dalliance of the Bolsheviks with the Ottoman triumvirs remains to be fully explored, but see Kamoludin Abdullaev, *Ot
Sin'tsziania do Khorasana: Iz istorii sredneaziatskoi emigratsii XX veka* (Dushanbe, 2009), 198–232;
V.M. Gilensen, "Sotrudnichestvo krasnoi Moskvy s Enver-Pashoi i Dzhemal'-Pashoi," *Vostok*, 1996,
no. 3: 45–63, is oblivious to Turkish sources but presents good archival evidence from Moscow.

activists began to show up in Turkestan via Afghanistan, with the hope of fighting British rule in India with the help of the regime that represented revolution. The Indian revolutionaries of whom Fitrat wrote existed in real life.[44] Tashkent, in fact, was the crossroads of world revolution in 1919 and 1920, with Ottoman subjects of various stripes (exiled Unionists, representatives of the nascent nationalist resistance in Anatolia, Communists such as Mustafa Suphi, as well as ordinary POWs), Iranian exiles, and Afghan diplomats all rubbing shoulders with Indian revolutionaries. Communism was rendered synonymous with anticolonial national revolt. In 1919, Kazım Bey, an Ottoman officer sent to Afghanistan during the war as part of a German-Ottoman mission to lure that country into war against the British, showed up in Turkestan, exhorting the locals to unite with the Soviet government to fight the British, "the enemies of the freedom and independence of all humanity and the constant enemy of Muslims."[45] In January 1920, he was joined at a meeting, hosted by the Tashkent old-city ispolkom, by Hüseyin Hilmi Bey, a representative of the Anatolian national movement, in making the same plea.[46] Not surprisingly, then, the task of liberating the East and the Muslim world from imperialism took on Turkist features. Şakirbeyzade Rahim, another Anatolian representative, asserted, "Turkestan is the path to the liberation of the East, [and] the Red Soviets are the way to our natural and human rights. From now on, Turkestan and Turan will live only under the Red Soviet banner."[47]

The Bolsheviks' Eastern policy tried to ride this sentiment, but with little success. It never amounted to a coherent set of initiatives, nor could they retain control of it. A number of organizations existed at different levels of the party-state and often found themselves in competition with each other. They were often established with open-ended goals ("preparing the toilers of the East for revolution") that were often experimental. The "Eastern" activists attracted to these organizations had their own understandings of revolution and the goals of these institutions. As we shall see in the rest of this book, this problem applied to all Soviet and party institutions in Central Asia, but it stood out in particularly

---

44. No existing work does justice to this fascinating episode; see, however, G.L. Dmitriev, *Indian Revolutionaries in Central Asia* (Gurgoan, 2002); M.A. Persits, *Revoliutsionery Indii v strane Sovetov: u istokov indiiskogo kommunisticheskogo dvizheniia, 1918–1921* (Moscow, 1973). Maia Ramnath, *Haj to Utopia: How the Ghadar Movement Charted Global Radicalism and Attempted to Overthrow the British Empire* (Berkeley, 2011), chap. 5, places the revolutionaries in the broader context of anticolonial activism in India.

45. *Ishtirokiyun*, 22.03.1919.

46. Mirmullo Shermuhammadov, "Eski shahar 'Ijroiya qo'mita'sida sharafli bir majlis," *Ishtirokiyun*, 13.01.1920. At the same meeting, Kazım Bey echoed the sentiment: "My only hope and my only motto is: 'To destroy the despotic English government in union with the Soviet government.'" *Ishtirokiyun*, 13.01.1920.

47. "Turkiston aholisina," *Ishtirokiyun*, 01.01.1920.

sharp form with the nominally independent institutions formed to serve Eastern policy. The Tashkent branch of the Union for the Liberation of the East attracted many Muslims who had been active in 1917 but marginalized after the Soviet takeover. At the Baku Congress of the Peoples of the East, Enver Pasha showed up as a revolutionary and the congress in general became a forum for the criticism of the Bolshevik record in the Muslim borderlands of the former Russian Empire. Even as the Soviets welcomed a newly assertive Afghanistan as an anticolonial ally (the Afghan mission was reciprocated by a Soviet mission to Kabul headed by Iakov Surits in September 1919), they found that the Afghan government had ambitious plans of its own to extend its influence in Central Asia.[48] The Afghan consulate became the center of Muslim public life in Tashkent, where visitors of all stripes could discuss "eastern policy" according to their own lights.[49]

Nevertheless, the sense of a global struggle against British imperialism dominated the rhetoric of Muslim Communists in Turkestan and provided them with a mission of world-historical proportions. A resolution passed by the first Turkestan Congress of Muslim Communists in May 1919 conveys a sense of this combination of self-justification and self-importance:

> To the revolutionary proletariat of the East, of Turkey, India, Persia, Afghanistan, Khiva, Bukhara, China, to all, to all, to all!
>
> We the Muslim Communists of Turkestan, gathered together at our first regional conference in Tashkent, send you our fraternal greeting, we who are free to you who are oppressed. We wait impatiently for the time when you will follow our example and take control in your own hands, in the hands of local soviets of workers' and peasants' deputies. We hope soon to come shoulder to shoulder with you in your struggle with the yoke of world capitalism, manifested in the East in the form of the English suffocation of native peoples.[50]

Nor was this enthusiasm purely altruistic. If Turkestan was to be the model of a successful anticolonial socialist revolution, then the policies pursued there were of great import. Turkestan's Muslim Communists hoped that the imperatives of "revolutionizing the East" would shape Soviet policies in Turkestan. An anticolonial reading of the revolution was absolutely central to the worldview of the first

---

48. For an account of Soviet-Afghan relations in this period that emphasizes their dissonance, see S. B. Panin, *Sovetskaia Rossiia i Afganistan: 1919–1929* (Irkutsk, 1998).

49. Joseph Castagné, "Notes sur la politique extérieur de l'Afghanistan depuis 1919," *Revue du monde musulman* 48 (1921): 6–7.

50. GARF, f. 1318, op. 1, d. 441, l. 29. British intelligence picked this resolution up; a partial English translation is to be found in TNA, FO 608/209, f. 7 (29.05.1919).

Muslim Communists in Turkestan, and nowhere is it better reflected than in the political trajectory of Tŭrar Rïsqŭlov.

The Musburo and the Imagining of a Revolutionary Turkestan

The forced entry of Muslims into the organs of revolutionary power encountered the implacable opposition of the European Communists of Turkestan. Therefore Kobozev pushed for the formation of a Central Bureau of Muslim Communist organizations of Turkestan (Musburo) in March 1919, with the task of propagating the ideas of Soviet power among the indigenous population and of establishing party organizations among it. The Musburo created a network of organizations across Turkestan, recruited among the Muslim populations, and held three conferences between May 1919 and January 1920. The Musburo was granted the right to communicate directly with Moscow and the newspaper *Ishtirokiyun* was placed at its disposal.[51] It became Kobozev's main base of support in his struggles with local Russian leaders and—even more important for our purposes—an institutional framework for the assertion of Muslim power within the new institutions.

The Musburo's cause was helped by a bombshell dropped by the Central Committee on the political situation in Tashkent in July 1919. Via radiogram, it instructed local organs of power that "in the interests of the policies of worker-peasant power in the East, the broad inclusion, proportional to the population, of the native Turkestani population in State activity is necessary, without the requirement of belonging to the party, as long their candidatures are put forward by Muslim worker organizations."[52] If carried out, this directive would have utterly transformed the political situation in Turkestan. Dismayed, TurTsIK sought to conceal the news from the population. Proportional representation, it argued, would lead to a return of the nonclass principles of representative politics embodied by the Constituent Assembly in 1917, and the undoing of the "revolution" in Turkestan. The Musburo, however, swung into action. It organized a public meeting in the old city of Tashkent to publicize the contents of the radiogram, and published the text in *Ishtirokiyun*.[53] By September, with Kobozev's backing, Muslim Communists had acquired a majority in TurTsIK.

51. AAP RUz, f. 60, op. 1, d. 65, l. 20 (Kraikom KPT minutes, 18.04.1919).
52. RGASPI, f. 122, op. 1, d. 47, l. 7.
53. *Ishtirokiyun*, 10.08.1919.

The defense of the indigenous population against the depredations of European settlers, the struggle for food and against the self-proclaimed monopoly declared by the Europeans over the revolution all provided Muslim Communists the cause around which to mobilize. Thus we find Tŭrar Rïsqŭlov in November 1918 reporting to the Turkestan sovnarkom on the situation in Avilyo Ota uezd, where half the Kazakh population of 300,000 had perished from the famine but the settler-dominated uezd soviet had nevertheless levied an additional tax of 5 million rubles on the survivors.[54] For Rïsqŭlov, this was a straightforward form of colonial exploitation or, in the terminology of the day, *kolonizatorstvo*, which rapidly became the key concept for Turkestan's Communists. A term of recent vintage, it was derived from *kolonizator*, which until the revolution had the neutral meaning of "colonist" or "settler," but which had now acquired the connotation of colonial exploitation.[55] It referred to the actions of colonists, not to the system of colonialism as a whole, and as such, kolonizatorstvo was not synonymous with colonialism, nor was a critique of it necessarily a critique of all Russians or of the Russian state. Nevertheless, it was foremost a kind of inequity and exploitation that the revolution was supposed to undo. For Rïsqŭlov, this was the central issue in the revolution, and he went on to derive a theory of anticolonial revolution from this basic fact.

The fundamental fact of life in the colonial world was the opposition of colonists and the colonized and that the fact of ethnic difference between them overshadowed all else. "In Turkestan," he was to write to Lenin in May 1920, "as in the entire colonial East, two dominant groups have existed and [continue to] exist in the social struggle: the oppressed, exploited colonial natives, and European capital."[56] Colonial difference overrode class, for even workers were party to colonial exploitation. Imperial powers sent "their best exploiters and functionaries" to the colonies, people who liked to think that "even a worker is a representative of a higher culture than the natives, a so-called Kulturträger."[57] The situation had not changed after 1917. "In Turkestan," he stated at a gathering of Communists from various Muslim parts of the former Russian Empire in June 1920, "there was no October revolution. The Russians took power and that was the end of it; in the place of some governor

54. TsGARUz, f. 25, op. 1, d. 31, ll. 100–101.

55. The terms *kolonizator* and *kolonizatorstvo* do not appear in prerevolutionary dictionaries, although the former did appear in print. In any case, the usual term used for Russians who settled in non-Russian parts of the Russian Empire was *pereselentsy*, "re-settlers," and not *kolonizatory*. The use of the term *kolonizator* for Russian settlers in Turkestan, and its use to connote exploitation, was a double move of the revolutionary era. The use of the term thus explicitly foregrounded the colonial nature of Turkestan's relationship to Russia.

56. T.R. Ryskulov, "Doklad polnomochnoi delegatsii Turkestanskoi respubliki V.I. Leninu," *Sobranie sochinenii v trekh tomakh* (Almaty, 1997), 3:175.

57. GARF, f. 1318, op. 1, d. 441, l. 79 (speech at the 4th congress of KPT, Sept. 1919).

sits a worker, and that's all."[58] Undoing this ought to have been the goal of the revolution in the colonial peripheries of the empire; again, as he wrote to Lenin, "the October revolution in Turkestan should have been accomplished not only under the slogans of the overthrow of the existing bourgeois power, *but also of the final destruction of all traces of the legacy of all possible colonialist efforts on the part of Tsarist officialdom and kulaks.*"[59] The new Soviet state should be based on "the broad, active participation in state activity" of the native population led by indigenous Communists, who should enjoy complete trust and be allowed to set policy—in short, they should be able to define what the revolution was.

The relationship between the Musburo and the many national organizations operating in the old city remains difficult to trace. In December 1917, when the Kokand government organized a demonstration in its favor in Tashkent, the new-city soviet granted permission as long as demonstrators did not enter the new city. It was an open admission that Soviet power was confined to European spaces and exercised elsewhere only through the barrel of Red Guard guns. After Kobozev's intervention, the old cities continued to function in parallel with European spaces, with their soviets enjoying a great degree of de facto independence. Moreover, Muslim cells in the KPT seem to have their own rules of recruitment. G'ozi Yunus, for instance, traveled to Istanbul in August 1918 to petition the Ottoman Ministry of War for help in seeking Turkestan's independence. By October, he was back in Tashkent as a Bolshevik activist.[60] He was to be a prominent figure in the KPT during this period. Memoirs of Ottoman POWs present a picture of the old city functioning on its own, with new arrivals being offered jobs in schools that were run by other Ottoman officers, who also presided over a number of youth groups.[61] The key figure in this regard was Munavvar qori, who worked in the waqf department of Turkompros, but whose real activity seems to have been behind the scenes. He seems to have coordinated the activity of the Ottoman POWs and was so well known among them that when Cemal Pasha passed through Tashkent in August 1920, he could mention Munavvar qori by name in a letter to his fellow exiled triumvir Talât Pasha.[62] It was a sign of how things stood that Cemal also received

58. Dina Amanzholova, ed., *Rossiia i Tsentral'naia Aziia, 1905–1925 gg.: sbornik dokumentov* (Karaganda, 2005), 281.

59. Ryskulov, "Doklad polnomochnoi delegatsii," 175–176 (emphasis in the original).

60. On 8 October 1918 he received a mandate from the "Party of Muslim Bolsheviks" (*Musulmon bolsheviklar firqasi*) to establish a Bolshevik committee in Fo'lod volost in Tashkent uezd; GAgT, f. 12, d. 26, l. 14.

61. Râci Çakıröz, "Türkistan'da Türk Subayları," *Türk Dünyası Tarih Dergisi* (April 1987), 42–43; Ziya Yergök, *Sarıkamış'tan Esarete (1915–1920)*, ed. Sami Önal (Istanbul, 2005), 230–240.

62. Cemal Pasha to Talât Pasha (01.08.1920), in Hüseyin Cahit Yalçın, *İttihatçı Liderlerin Gizli Mektupları* (Istanbul, 2002), 252. See also the remarkable photographs of Munavvar qori with groups of Ottoman officers in A. Ahad Andican, *Cedidizm'den Bağımsızlığa Hariçte Türkistan Mücadelesi* (Istanbul, 2003), 106, 108.

a guard of honor from the marching bands of all the new-method schools of the city.[63] Clearly, the Soviet order in the old cities of Turkestan had own meaning.

Rïsqŭlov was an outsider to this scene, so he must have forged alliances with local actors. One of the few extant publications of the Musburo, other than the newspaper *Ishtirokiyun*, was a pamphlet titled *Navoiy's Thoughts about Human-ity*, which drew a sharp contrast between ulama who sold Islam to power (and authorized rulers' views of themselves as the shadow of God on earth) and great thinkers such as Ibn 'Arabi, Jami, Bedil, Rumi, and Navoiy, who held on to truth and rightness (*haq va haqiqat*) and promised a struggle against corrupt power.[64] The pamphlet was published without a byline, but there is good reason to believe that the author was Fitrat.[65] Clearly, there was cooperation between the Jadids and Muslim Communists such as Rïsqŭlov. In general, however, while Rïsqŭlov and his followers used the nation as a fundamental category, they did not use the language of Turkism and did not invoke Temur. And yet, at their moment of triumph, short lived though it proved to be, they pushed through a number of remarkable resolutions in a Turkist vein. In January 1920, the Fifth Congress of the KPT met with a Muslim majority and renamed Turkestan the Turkic Soviet Republic and KPT the Turkic Communist Party, and claimed that "the Turkic Soviet Republic should fully answer to the customary, historical, and economic needs of the core population [of the region]."[66] This remarkable document repays closer examination.

Rïsqŭlov arrived at the idea of a national anticolonial revolution using con-temporary Bolshevik political language. "One of the most important conditions for the achievement of the goal [of Communism] advanced by the Communist Party is the self-determination of oppressed . . . peoples," for it "unmask[s] the falsity of the policies of capitalist powers [in this regard]." The liberation of "the oppressed East, . . . the vanguard of world revolution," was another impor-tant side of the class struggle that was fundamental to revolution. With the approaching collapse of capitalism, the East was to be an indispensable ally of the Western proletariat. Turkestan, being an integral part of the East and a place where all sorts of lessons could be learned for political work in the rest of the East, was of crucial importance. "If Soviet Russia needs to show the working class of Western capitalist countries the correctness of its system, then it needs

---

63. Râci Çakıröz, "Türkistan'da Türk Subayları," *Türk Dünyası Tarih Dergisi* (July 1987), 44.

64. *Insoniyat haqinda Navoiyning fikri* (Tashkent, 1919), 2.

65. On Fitrat's authorship, see Hamidulla Boltaboyev, "Professor A. Fitratning nazariy qo'llanmasi," preface to Fitrat, *Adabiyot qoidalari*, ed. H. Boltaboyev (Tashkent, 1995), 6.

66. RGASPI, f. 5, op. 1, d. 2920, ll. 61ob-63; the document has now been published by Amanzho-lova, ed., *Rossiia i Tsentral'naia Aziia*, 223–229.

even more to show the oppressed East the proper restructuring of the social life of Muslim society in Turkestan and elsewhere." Soviet policy in Turkestan therefore had a global significance. "The crude colonialism of Tsarism produced hate and distrust toward the ruling nation. If the proletariat of the ruling nation now scorns the proletariat of the oppressed nations, it will only produce more distrust." Yet this was what had been happening since 1917. The solution, therefore, was to establish Soviet power in Turkestan in a way that would recognize both its importance to world revolution and the specificity of its colonial situation. The Musburo resolution declared, "Turkestan is the land of Turkic nationalities [*narodnosti*] . . . while the remaining population of Russians, Jews, Armenians, and others represent a newly arrived [*prishlyi*] element." Turkestan should be reestablished (in conformity with the constitution of the RSFSR) as the Turkic Soviet Republic, a national republic for its indigenous nationalities. The territorial basis of Turkestan should be replaced by the national one. This "Turkic Soviet Republic should fully answer to the customary, historical, and economic demands of the life of the [region's] core population." Finally, "in the interests of the international unification of toiling and oppressed peoples," the conference called on other Turkic republics already existing in Soviet Russia to unite with this Turkic republic, and it held out the hope that future republics in neighboring lands (Bukhara, Khiva, Afghanistan, Iran) would also join. For all these reasons, the resolution called for wide ranging autonomy for Turkestan.

Rïsqŭlov had thus connected colonial oppression to class struggle and rendered national self-determination an integral part of it. More than that, he had put Turkestan at the very center of the geopolitical aims of the Soviet regime and its Eastern policy, the interests of which required giving Turkestan wide autonomy. This anticolonial rhetorical move was coupled with a sweeping national one, which turned Turkestan into the national republic of Turkic peoples, whose unity was seen as a crucial aspect of internationalism, just as it turned Russian settlers into immigrants (*prishlye*). Colonial oppression had a class dimension to it, to be sure, but nation here trumped class. The whole "East" was oppressed and functioned as the "vanguard of world revolution." In the colonial periphery of the Russian Empire, revolution made sense only as a national enterprise.

What Rïsqŭlov and the Musburo argued here was argued by many other Muslim Communists during the Russian revolution: that in the non-Russian colonial peripheries of the empire, revolution made sense only as a national anticolonial struggle; that the colonial world was oppressed as a whole; that the duty of the Russian revolution was to undo colonial oppression at home and to liberate the colonial world abroad; and that Muslim Communists from the Soviet state had a special place in this enterprise. Revolution was a means of national liberation and modernization. This was, in Alexandre Bennigsen's apt phrase, "Muslim

National Communism,"[67] and best known to us through the figure of Mirsayät Soltangaliyev (Sultan-Galiev), the Tatar Communist who rose to be a member of the collegium of Narkomnats and who was accused in 1923 of masterminding a nationalist "antiparty" faction. Yet Muslim national Communism was neither a unified theory (or "deviation"), nor was it embodied by a single organization headed by Soltangaliyev. Rather, different activists arrived at Muslim national Communism independently. In Azerbaijan, Nəriman Nərimanov articulated remarkably similar views on nation, Islam, and revolution as did Rïsqŭlov in Turekstan.[68] Nor was the Musburo part of a wider network of organizations, but specific to Turkestan. Organizations of Muslim Communists had existed in European Russia since the first months of the revolution. An All-Russian Congress of Muslim Communists convened in Moscow in November 1918 and elected a Central Bureau of Muslim Communist Organizations of the Russian Communist Party, but its name was misleading, for it was largely a Tatar affair. Turkestan was cut off and much too far away, its problems too different from those of the Volga-Urals region, for there to be any common cause.[69] A second congress, now called the Congress of Muslim Communist Organizations of the Peoples of the East, met in November 1919, but again without any significant Turkestani participation.[70] Although the Musburo conducted some correspondence with the Central Bureau of Muslim Communist Organizations, it was not a major axis of its organizational or political activity.[71] Rïsqŭlov had little direct contact with Muslim Communists from outside Turkestan during 1919. It was only in May 1920, when he traveled to Moscow (see below) that he met his counterparts from other regions of the Soviet state. His national communism was an independent invention. The Russian revolution was a postcolonial moment and national liberation and anticolonialism inhered in the revolution itself.

---

67. Alexandre Bennigsen and S. Enders Wimbush, *Muslim National Communism in the Soviet Union: A Revolutionary Strategy for the Colonial World* (Chicago, 1979).

68. See Jörg Baberowski, *Der Feind ist überall: Stalinismus im Kaukasus* (Munich, 2003), 225–313. Unlike both Rïsqŭlov and Soltangaliyev, Nêrimanov (1870–1925) had been an established cultural and political figure in Transcaucasia before 1917, with numerous plays to his credit. For a literary biography, see Teymur Əhmədov, *Nəriman Nərimanov: Yaradacılıq yolu* (Baku, 2005).

69. RGASPI, f. 583, d. 1.

70. RGASPI, f. 583, d. 4. The best account of these conferences is to be found in A. I. Ishanov, *Rol' Kompartii i Sovetskogo pravitel'stva v sozdanii natsional'noi gosudarstvennosti uzbekskogo naroda* (Tashkent, 1978), chap. 1.

71. The Central Bureau could be used as yet another channel of communication to the center, as when Rïsqŭlov asked it in September 1919 to inform Stalin of the "abnormal situation" prevailing in Turkestan and to ask central organs of the government and the party not to take any decisions on the basis of "one-sided reports and statements" that Tashkent's "old Bolsheviks" might send in. RGASPI, f. 122, op. 1, d. 30, ll. 33–33ob. However, surviving records show no evidence of systematic interaction between Musburo and the Central Bureau.

The Turkkomissiia and the Assertion of Central Control

The Musburo's moment of triumph also proved to be its undoing. In October 1919, the Red Army was able to break the Orenburg blockade and restore a direct rail link between Moscow and Turkestan. Central authorities were finally able to assert direct control on Turkestan. Units of the Red Army arrived in significant numbers just as the Central Committee appointed a Turkestan Commission (Turkkomissiia) as its plenipotentiary organ to govern the region. Headed by Shalva Eliava, the commission included Gleb Bokii, Mikhail Frunze, Filipp Goloshchekin, Valerian Kuibyshev, and Jānis Rudzutaks. Its arrival altered the political landscape in Turkestan quite drastically and put an end to the period of quasi-independence from the center that the region had enjoyed since March 1917.[72]

The Musburo hoped that the commission would support it against the settlers. Rïsqŭlov led a crowd of five hundred Muslims in welcoming the first members of the commission when they arrived in Tashkent on 4 November.[73] The first speeches of members of the commission indeed struck the right tone. Eliava was reported to have said that Soviet Russia did not demand a social revolution from the East, and that it was sufficient to bring about national independence.[74] In December, visiting Russian enclaves in Bukhara, he told a gathering of Russians that as a result of the "incorrect policies of 1918 ... the Soviet government came to be seen as worse than the former Nicholas government by the Muslim masses."[75] Indeed, kolonizatorstvo became the political sin of the moment, and the Turkkomissiia supported the ouster of many Russian figures. The Musburo rode this wave and even resolved to raise a 200,000-strong Muslim Red Army. TurTsIK approved the resolution and sent it, along with a request for money and command staff, to the All-Russian Central Executive Committee and to Lenin personally.[76] Members of the Turkkomissiia had no objection to this request, nor did they have a definite opinion on the January resolutions that renamed Turkestan and the KPT.[77]

72. On the Turkkomissiia, see A. Khalid, "Turkestan v 1917–1922 godakh: bor'ba za vlast' na okraine Rossii," in *Tragediia velikoi derzhavy: natsional'nyi vopros i raspad Sovetskogo Soiuza* (Moscow, 2005), 214–222; V.L. Genis, "*S Bukharoi nado konchat'. . .*": *k istorii butaforskikh revoliutsii* (Moscow, 2001); B.A. Koshchanov, *Pravo na vtorzhenie* (Nukus, 1993); for a late Soviet account, see A. Akramov and K. Avliiakulov, *V.I. Lenin, Turkkomissiia i ukreplenie sovetskoi vlasti v Srednei Azii* (Tashkent, 1991).

73. *Ishtirokiyun*, 12.11.1919.

74. *Ishtirokiyun*, 24.12.1919.

75. "Turkiston komisiyasi Yongo Buxoroda," *Ishtirokiyun*, 04.01.1920.

76. GARF, f. 1235, op. 93, d. 582, l. 152.

77. As Eliava reported to Moscow on 23 January, he and Kuibyshev were inclined to approve the resolutions, while Rudzutaks was opposed and Goloshchekin uncommitted. Frunze had still not arrived in Tashkent. GARF, f. 130, op. 4, d. 786, l. 4.

Yet there were problems from the outset. The Turkkomissiia had come to establish central control over Turkestan, not to empower the Musburo, and even its actions against Turkestan's settler Communists were strategic rather than punitive. The Musburo was therefore unable to establish the same cordial relations with the Turkkomissiia that it had with Kobozev. Things came to a head with the belated arrival in February 1920 of Mikhail Frunze, the commander of the Turkestan Front of the Red Army and a member of the Turkkomissiia. Having been born in Pishpek (now Bishkek, the city bore his name for much of the Soviet period), he considered himself a "Turkestani," even though for local Communists, this only meant that he was one of the settlers. Frunze took on Rïsqŭlov and the Musburo most aggressively, harshly criticizing their stance as "narrow petty bourgeois nationalism," and forcing the Turkkomissiia to annul the resolutions of the Musburo on renaming Turkestan and the KPT. Consequently an intense struggle between Turkkomissiia and Turkestan's Muslim Communists, who now controlled both the KPT Central Committee and TurTsIK, erupted in spring 1920. Muslim Communists went on the offensive. They dragged their feet in implementing decisions of the Turkkomissiia and incessantly complained to the center about its conduct. At stake were issues both of tactics and of principle. Muslim Communists made the struggle against kolonizatorstvo the central pillar of their program. They tied the actions of European settlers in an indictment of all policies pursued until then by the Tashkent government. G'ozi Yunus toured Shïmkent uezd in Syr Darya oblast and reported that all the trees in orchards and farmland belonging to Muslims had been cut down, but the settler village of Kazanskii had a completely different look. "This is inhabited by Turkestan's fake masters, the Russian Ukes [*Rus xoxo'llari*]. . . . A group of narrow nationalists, having washed their hands with the blood of the people, put on the mask of Bolsheviks or Left SRs, and cleansed the uezd of its Muslims." Having usurped the land of Kazakh and Kyrgyz nomads in 1916, they established "the dictatorship of landlords and kulaks in the Russian settlements." The party and state institutions contained "many thieves under the mask of Bolsheviks," but "naturally, given that the Soviet government established in 1918 was headed by narrow nationalist comrades, complaints about such behavior were ineffective."[78] In expressing the hope that the Turkkomissiia would set things right, G'ozi Yunus positioned Muslim Communists as the logical bearers of Soviet rule in Turkestan.

Frunze, however, stood firm and led the Turkkomissiia to take a hard line against national Communism. In April, he even suggested abolishing the KPT

---

78. G'ozi Yunus, "Chimkand va Sayrom ahvoli," *Ishtirokiyun*, 02.03.1920. For other accounts of kolonizatorstvo, see *Ishtirokiyun*, 17.02.1920, 27.02.1920, 03.03.1920.

and beginning anew.[79] Eventually, in May, Muslim Communists circumvented the Turkkomissiia entirely and decided to put their case directly before Lenin and the Central Committee through an "extraordinary delegation" headed by Rïsqŭlov. Members of the Turkkomissiia also headed to Moscow to fight out the case. Lenin was personally involved in the deliberations, which took place just as the party was preparing to host the Second Congress of the Comintern, where the national and colonial questions were high on the agenda. Rïsqŭlov again argued on the basis of the significance of Turkestan to Soviet Eastern policy and of the colonial nature of national relations existing there to claim that Turkestan should be a national republic enjoying wide ranging autonomy, including the right to conduct its own foreign policy and to print its own money (both of which had in fact been the practice in the period since 1917).[80]

The gambit did not succeed and the delegation was overruled. Lenin was serious about Turkestan being treated gently, but there were limits to what he deemed permissible, and the Muslim Communists' demands had clearly crossed those limits. On 22 June, the Politburo passed a resolution that defined Turkestan's position in the Soviet state. External relations, external trade, and military affairs were to be the exclusive domain of the center and Turkestan's economic and food-supply policies were to operate within the framework of plans established by the government of the RSFSR. "Recognizing the Kazakhs, Uzbeks, and Turkmens as the indigenous peoples of Turkestan," the decree proclaimed "the Turkestan Soviet Socialist Republic . . . as an autonomous part of the RSFSR."[81] The Politburo granted that Turkestan had an indigenous population, but it refused to accord it the kind of autonomy that various actors, whether in the autonomous government in Kokand or in the Musburo, had demanded. At the same time, the Politburo transformed the Turkkomissiia into the Turkestan Bureau (Turkburo) as the standing plenipotentiary agent of central power. The Turkburo, which became the Central Asia Bureau, or Sredazburo, in 1922 when its jurisdiction was extended to Bukhara and Khiva as well, was expected to be the political mechanism for the assertion of central power. The Politburo also ordered the reelection of all party and soviet committees in Turkestan, in which Rïsqŭlov and his followers were ousted from office. This process was accompanied by a wave of arrests of "nationalists" as well as the deportations of many Europeans for kolonizatorstvo. Nearly two thousand European functionaries were deported

---

79. Turkkomissiia, *protokol* no. 24 (30.04.1920), RGASPI, f. 5, op. 1, d. 2920, ll. 64–64ob.

80. "Proekt Polozheniia Turkestanskoi avtonomnoi sovetskoi respubliki Ross. Sots. Federatsii" (May 1920), RGASPI, f. 5, op. 1, d. 2920, ll. 53–56. The debates of 1920 are described in detail in Hallez, "Communisme national," 380–436.

81. GARF, f. 1235, op. 93, d. 582, ll. 173–173ob; *Izvestiia* (Moscow), 27.08.1920.

from Turkestan in the autumn and winter of 1920–21, although the number of those arrested for "nationalism" remains unknown.[82] Rïsqŭlov himself was sent off to a desk job in Narkomnats, first in Moscow and then in Baku.[83]

The summer of 1920 thus marked a turning point in the establishment of Soviet rule in Turkestan. The previous two years had been a period of flux, both because of the absence of central control and of uncertainty over the limits of the permissible in terms of autonomy. This uncertainty had allowed Rïsqŭlov to theorize about anticolonial revolution rooted in the nation. That period was now over. By imposing a certain degree of control over its institutions in Turkestan, the center had curtailed the horizons of the national Communists' ambitions. From now on, national Communists were to work under closer scrutiny of the center and within more circumscribed ideological bounds. It was also a turning point in the fortunes of national organizations outside the Soviet framework. Most of the youth groups were either abolished or brought under Soviet control and the Ottoman POWs began to depart the scene. The national movement was now pushed underground. However, at the same moment as Turkestan was being domesticated, the Bolshevik conquest of Bukhara opened up entirely new avenues of hope for the national movement. Faced with the necessity of installing a government composed of Bukharans, the Soviets had little choice but to turn to Bukharan Jadids who had been radicalized by their persecution by the emir. Bukhara became a national project of a different sort.

---

82. R. Aripov and N. Mil'shtein, *Iz istorii organov gosbezopasnosti Uzbekistana* (Tashkent, 1967), 101.

83. The suggestion to remove Rïsqŭlov from the scene had come from the Turkkomissiia. "Given his present state of mind," wrote V. V. Kuibyshev, "Rïsqŭlov is somewhat dangerous for our line in the East. We therefore suggest his transfer to Moscow under the direction of the Central Committee." Kuibyshev to CC, 09.08.1920, in Amanzholova, ed., *Rossiia i Tsentral'naia Aziia*, 286–287.

THE MUSLIM REPUBLIC OF BUKHARA

By the summer of 1920, Mikhail Frunze had grown increasingly impatient with the continued existence of the emirate of Bukhara. Despite misgivings in Moscow, he opted for a military solution, and at the end of August led the Red Army to an invasion of the khanate that toppled the emir from his throne. Afraid that outright annexation would antagonize Britain, Moscow chose to install a "people's soviet republic" in Bukhara with a Bukharan Communist Party (BKP) at its head. The BKP had been re-formed for the occasion with the forced merger of an older BKP, founded in 1918 and consisting mostly of Turkestanis and Tatars with only tenuous connections to Bukhara, and the more numerous party of the Young Bukharans. Thus it was that the Young Bukharans found themselves in control of a republic established in the maelstrom of the Russian Revolution. The People's Soviet Republic of Bukhara (BNSR) proved short lived and occupies a nebulous place in the history of modern Central Asia. Soviet historiography created a general picture of the republic as a transitional entity, a stepping stone from a "popular" to a "socialist" stage in the development of the revolution, in which the Communist Party guided the people to a greater level of ideological certainty and political mobilization, saving them from the clutches of leaders of inadequate or deviant political consciousness. It thus rendered the history of the Bukharan republic into a narrative of transition, incompleteness, and deviation, and one housed entirely in Soviet categories.[1] Western accounts of the republic also depict it as transitional from protectorate to full incorporation into the Russian state.[2] Yet, seen in the context of the age and with recourse to Bukharan sources, the BNSR appears in a very different light. Bukhara was where circumstances put the Jadids in political power.[3] The BNSR was their attempt, under often hopeless conditions, to implement the agenda of Muslim reform, radicalized by the revolution, and to establish a national republic. The BNSR was rooted in discourses of Muslim modernism much more than those of Marxism or Leninism; it was a Muslim republic.

The intellectual lineage of the BNSR went back to the debates of the late Ottoman Empire. As I have noted earlier, Ottoman models had held a particular salience for Bukharan reformers since the turn of the century. The fateful decision of Bukhara's philanthropists to send young men to study in Istanbul had opened new paths of cultural influence and created in Bukhara a distant corner of the Ottoman political world. Now the Russian revolution had unexpectedly provided the reformers an opportunity to put their agenda in action. Viewed in this light, the experience of the BNSR provides us with a rare window into the political implications of Muslim modernism in the immediate aftermath of the Great War, with its interplay of reform and revolution, Islam and nation. Nor was the BNSR simply a historical curiosity. It had a significant role in the triumph of Turkism in Central Asia. It was in the BNSR that the notion of Bukhara as a Turkic state crystallized. The Young Bukharans made Uzbek the official language of state and instituted policies that reshaped the national landscape of Central Asia.

---

1. The only monograph devoted to the republic is A. I. Ishanov, *Bukharskaia narodnaia sovetskaia respublika* (Tashkent, 1969). In post-Soviet Uzbekistan, the BNSR is rendered part of a general narrative of Uzbek national history, but the volume of research has been disappointingly small. The most extended treatment is in *Turkestan v nachale XX veka: k istorii istokov natsional'noi nezavisimosti* (Tashkent, 2000), chap. 6. See also Q. Rajabov, "Buxoro xalq respublikasi: monarxiyadan demokratiya sari dastlabki qadamlar (1920–1924 yillar)," in *O'zbekiston tarixining dolzarb muammalariga yangi chizgilar: davriy to'plam,* 2 vols. (Tashkent, 1999), 2:149–158, and idem., *Buxoroga Qizil Armiya bosqini va unga qarshi kurash* (Tashkent, 2002).

2. Hélène Carrère d'Encausse, *Réforme et révolution chez les Musulmans de l'empire russe* (Paris, 1966); Seymour Becker, *Russia's Protectorates in Central Asia: Bukhara and Khiva, 1865–1924* (Cambridge, MA, 1968).

3. The short-lived Democratic Republic of Azerbaijan, proclaimed in 1918, was the first republic in the Muslim world. It too was dominated by a Muslim modernist elite. It was followed in 1920 by Soviet republics proclaimed in Khiva and Gilan. The Republic of Turkey, by contrast, was established only in 1923, after prolonged debate over the fate of the sultanate.

The Young Bukharans in Exile

The three and a half years between the February revolution and the Red Army invasion of Bukhara were a period of rapid and radical change in the worldview of Bukhara's reformers. The fiasco of April 1917 (see chapter 2) led to an exodus, first to the Russian enclave of Kagan, and then in most cases to Turkestan. Ayni was evacuated to Kagan, where he was hospitalized. He left for Samarqand later in the year and made it his home until almost the end of his life. Fitrat was in Samarqand by August, where he took up the editorship of the newspaper *Hurriyat* (Liberty) founded by Behbudiy. While the reformers—who now took to calling themselves Young Bukharans (Uzb., *Yosh Buxorolilar*, Russ., *Mlado-bukhartsy*)—attempted to involve outside forces in Bukharan affairs, the emir found in the revolutionary chaos the opportunity to maximize his independence from Russia. For the rest of 1917, he built up his support among conservative ulama and completely marginalized the Jadids, confiscating the property of those who fled, and persecuting those who remained.

The Young Bukharans hoped that the Tashkent soviet would act against the emir in a way that the Provisional Government had been unwilling to. In the event, their hand was forced by Tashkent. In March 1918, in the hubris caused by the destruction of Kokand, F. I. Kolesov, the chairman of the Tashkent sovnarkom, showed up in Kagan and announced to the Young Bukharans that he was going to invade Bukhara in five days. The Young Bukharans hastily formed a "revolutionary committee" on 17 March that formulated an ultimatum that Kolesov was to deliver to the emir. For all its daring (the emir was given twenty-four hours to agree to its terms or face an invasion), the ultimatum was remarkable for the modesty of its political aims: "Bukhara should have the constitutional form of government, and a national assembly [*milliy majlis*] should be formed, with authority over the appointments and dismissals of all qazis and functionaries other than the emir, and over the treasury and the armed forces. Until the assembly convenes, such authority should be exercised by the Young Bukharans. The emir will be retained as a constitutional monarch, answerable to the national assembly."[4] After months of social upheaval and political radicalism throughout the Russian Empire, the Young Bukharans were still aiming for constitutional monarchy.

The ultimatum failed and Kolesov's military adventure ended in utter disaster. Alim Khan played for time; after some hesitation, he promised to disarm his troops

---

4. "Buxoro inqilob oldinda," *Hurriyat*, 08.03.1918.

and invited a delegation to supervise the disarmament. The twenty-five-member delegation was massacred at night, while reinforcements destroyed railway and telegraph links to Turkestan. Kolesov's troops shelled Bukhara, unsuccessfully, until their ammunition gave out, and then retreated in much disarray. On 19 March, Kolesov sued for peace, which was signed on 25 March at Qizil Tepa.[5] Although the treaty favored the Soviet regime, it nevertheless spelled the end, for the time being, of active Soviet threats against the emir. Over the next two years, he acted as a sovereign ruler, issuing paper money for the first time, initiating diplomatic contact with Afghanistan and the British in Iran and Transcaspia, and heightening the persecution of all opposition. For the Young Bukharans, Kolesov's adventure was utterly disastrous, for the episode allowed the emir to direct the wrath of his subjects onto the reformers, whom he tarred as being traitors and apostates and no different from the Bolsheviks. In the words of a courtier, "After the end of the war with the Bolsheviks and the conclusion of peace, [we] declared war on the internal enemy, the Jadids. They were arrested on the streets, in bazaars, and in their own houses, taken to the Ark and killed without any questions ... and their property was confiscated. There were cases when a man could not intercede on behalf of another and prove that he was not a Jadid. If someone accidently said, 'I know this man, he is not a Jadid,' then, even though he spoke on the basis of conduct, deeds, and Muslim customs, he too was killed along with [the one he was defending]."[6] Kagan was too close for comfort to Bukhara and many Young Bukharans fled to Tashkent, which by May 1918 had become the main center of their activity. The exile was to reshape the political horizons of the Young Bukharans, giving them an abiding hatred of the emir and a fascination with revolution as a modality of change.

The Young Bukharans arrived in Tashkent just as Kobozev was opening the door to Muslim participation in the new organs of power. The émigrés found support from various quarters. Tashkent's old-city ispolkom and Turkomnats issued papers to a number of Young Bukharans, allowing them to travel throughout Soviet Russia,[7] while the People's Commissariat of Labor provided material support (a group of forty-seven émigrés received three Singer sewing machines to allow them to establish a tailors' "labor commune").[8] The life of exile was, of

---

5. On Kolesov's adventure in Bukhara, see V. L. Genis, *Vitse-konsul Vvedenskii. Sluzhba v Persii i Bukharskom khanstve (1906–1920 gg.)* (Moscow, 2003), 132–140.

6. Mirza Salimbek, *Tarikhi salimi (istochnik po istorii Bukharaskogo emirata)*, trans. N.K. Norqulov (Tashkent, 2009), 209. The accusation of being a Jadid came to underwrite all manner of persecution and exaction; Sayyid Mir Akram Khan, an uncle of the emir and the governor of Shahr-i Sabz, began a reign of terror in his domain in the spring of 1919 by executing a number of traders for being Jadids and confiscating their property (ibid., 245).

7. GAgT, f. 12, d. 5, ll. 72–72ob; d. 6, ll. 56, 68, 78, 215; TsGARUz, f. 36, d. 12, l. 118.

8. TsGARUz, f. 35, d. 70, l. 20.

course, beset with mutual conflict and incrimination, and the émigré community split into several groups. Fitrat, who arrived sometime in the spring, and Usmon Xo'jao'g'li styled themselves as "representatives of the Bukharan people" (*Buxoro xalqining vakillari/Predstaviteli Bukharskogo naroda*).[9] Another group headed by Usmon-xo'ja's brother Atovulla Xo'ja constituted itself as the Bukharan Social Revolutionary Party (Buxoro Ijtimoiyun-Inqilobiyun portiyasi) in May,[10] while yet another group under Fayzulla Xo'jayev came to call itself the Revolutionary Young Bukharans (Inqilobchi Yosh Buxorolilar). The two groups merged under the latter name at some point in 1919. No faction of the émigrés showed much affinity for Tashkent's Bolsheviks, although the main actors quickly moved to cultivate connections in Moscow. By October, Fayzulla Xo'jayev, Muhiddin Mansurov, and his son Abduqodir Muhiddinov were all in Moscow as representatives of the "Young Bukharan Committee," their revolutionary credentials attested to by Tashkent's Soviet organizations. In Moscow, their main point of contact was the representation of the Turkestan republic, which established a Section for Bukharan Affairs, but the Bukharans also quickly established contact with the party hierarchy and various commissariats, including that for foreign affairs.[11] Anticolonialism provided the necessary vocabulary for cooperation between the Soviet regime and the Young Bukharans, as the Moscow committee averred that "only the Russian Socialist Revolution, the vanguard warrior with world imperialism, can liberate Bukhara from the slavery into which imperialists of all countries have led it, supporting Bukharan reaction in their own interests."[12] This was a major shift in their rhetoric since March, when they had still spoken of a constitutional monarchy. Over the next two years, the Young Bukharans came to tie their vision of the future intimately to the project of "liberating the East." They received funds for publication and propaganda from the Central Bureau of Muslim Communist Organizations in Moscow and the Council for International Propaganda (Sovinterprop) in Tashkent.[13]

Young Bukharan politics shifted markedly during this time. The greatest change was in the reformers' view of the emir. In April 1917, they had appealed to Alim Khan to enact reform; in December 1917, Fitrat was describing the

---

9. For a reproduction of their letterhead, see Timur Kocaoğlu, ed., *Türkistan'da Yenilik Hareketleri ve İhtilaller, 1900–1924: Osman Hoca Anısına İncelemeler* (Haarlem, 2001), 54; the original is in TsGARUz, f. 36, d. 12, l. 95ob.

10. TsGARUz, f. 36, d. 12, l. 194.

11. Majid Hasanov, *Fayzulla Xo'jayev* (Tashkent, 1990), 31–35.

12. "Instruktsiia otdelu po Bukharskim delam" (16.11.1918), RGASPI, f. 5, op. 1, d. 2921, ll. 5–5ob.

13. RGASPI, f. 583, d. 69, l. 37; A. I. Ishanov, *Rol' Kompartii i Sovetskogo pravitel'stva v sozdanii natsional'noi gosudarstvennosti Uzbekskogo naroda* (Tashkent, 1978), 27, 34–35.

emir as a "monument of oppression" who had betrayed his people.[14] A year later, Young Bukharans in Moscow spoke of "an uprising of the people against the power of the Emir and beks" as the only solution to Bukhara's problems. In Young Bukharan manifestoes, the emir appears not as the last surviving Muslim monarch in Central Asia, as Bukharan Jadids had seen him before 1917, but as a corrupt, bloodthirsty despot who lived off the toil of the peasants in his realm: "All his thoughts are of living in luxury, and it is none of his business even if the poor and the peasants like us die of starvation. 'His highness' is a man concerned only with eating the best *pulov*, wearing robes of the best brocade, drinking good wines, and having a good time with young and good looking boys and girls."[15] This was in part related to a longer-term shift in the political views of Bukharan reformers that had disassociated the state from the ruler and rendered his legitimacy contingent on his service to the nation.[16] Thus Fitrat could state in 1919 that the emir had sold the honor of Bukhara to the English through his opposition to reform.[17] Young Bukharans came to see revolutionizing the East and liberating Muslims from imperialism as integrally connected to their own quest. The contents of *Tong* (Dawn) and *Uchqun* (Spark), the two short-lived journals published by them in Tashkent in 1920, are revealing in this regard, for rather little in their pages concerned Bukhara itself. The bulk of the attention was devoted to decrying British imperialism and discussing questions of cultural revolution.

Anticolonial revolution had little to do with class, which seldom shows up in the writings of Young Bukharans. Oppression and exploitation were national, not class, phenomena, and political liberation and cultural revolution the solution. A play by Usmon Xo'ja with the fashionable revolutionary title of *Boy birlan kambag'al* (Master and Man) did speak of the exploitation of the poor by their "bloodsucking" (*qonxo'r*) oppressors. Yet the cause of the exploitation lay in the "lack of awareness and education" (*ongsizlik, bilimsizlik*) that reigned in society as whole.[18] The masthead of *Uchqun*, edited by Fayzulla Xo'jayev, carried the statement, *Sharqni ozod qiluv, Sharq xalqining o'z ishidir* ("The Liberation of the East is the Business of the People of East"), and the journal took as its task, "To Establish Unity against Oppression" (*Zulmga qorshi ittifoq*

14. Fitrat, "Buxoroning holi," *Hurriyat*, 29.12.1917.

15. Abdulla Badriy, *Yosh Buxolilar bechora xalq va dehqonlar uchun yaxshimi, yamonmi?* (Moscow, 1919), 4–5.

16. I have explored this point further in "From Noble City to People's Republic: Re-Imagining Bukhara, 1900–1924," in *Historical Dimensions of Islam: Essays in Honor of R. Stephen Humphreys*, ed. James E. Lindsay and Jon Armajani (Princeton, 2009), 201–216.

17. Fitrat, *Sharq siyosati* (n.p., 1919), 34.

18. Usmon Xo'ja-o'g'li, *Boy birlan kambag'al: Buxoro turmushi* (Khorezm, 1920).

yasamoq). The absence of class in Young Bukharan thinking should not be surprising in the least. The Young Bukharans included not just intellectuals such as Ayni and Fitrat, but also men of substance such as Muhiddin Mansurov and his sons, Mirzo Abduqodir Muhiddinov and Mirzo Isom Muhiddinov, or Fayzulla Xo'jayev and his cousins Atovulla Xo'ja and Usmon Xo'ja. These wealthy merchant families traded in cotton and karakul and found themselves in direct competition with the emir, who had been only too happy to confiscate their property. Unsympathetic Bolshevik observers made much of this connection. In the words of G. I. Broido, "all of [Mansurov's] politics has been reduced to returning to Old Bukhara on our bayonets to reclaim his millions, and if possible, to grab some extra."[19] Put more neutrally, these men had a stake in the affairs of Bukhara and felt that they could do a better job of running the country than the emir. Their personal and altruistic motives were inextricably intertwined.

All of this made for difficult relations with Soviet authorities. To complicate things further for the Young Bukharans, in September 1918 a small group of Muslims living in the Russian enclaves in Bukhara organized their own political party "that will follow the Bolshevik program in all respects."[20] This was the Bukharan Communist Party (BKP). As a Communist party, it had the sympathy, if not always the support, of Tashkent's Soviet government, while its relations with the Young Bukharans were almost invariably hostile. Most members of the BKP were Turkestanis or Tatars with few connections to Bukhara itself, but their communism provided them with the vocabulary to heap criticism on the Young Bukharans for being part of the national bourgeoisie whose interest in politics was purely personal. The Young Bukharans, by contrast, considered the BKP mere interlopers, with a political program not applicable to Bukhara. The bitter hostility between the two groups of revolutionaries was to cast a long shadow on the course of events in Soviet Bukhara.

The Bolsheviks had contradictory feelings toward the Young Bukharans. On the one hand, they gave help to the Young Bukharans as part of their Eastern Policy and support for revolution in the colonies. The assassination of Habibullah Khan of Afghanistan rendered the idea of Bukhara serving as a potential vanguard of revolution more attractive. But the Bolsheviks also needed Bukhara as a supplier of cotton and grain during the civil war, and in November 1919 the Turkkomissiia had no qualms about appointing the Bukharan Jewish millionaire Nataniel Potelyakhov as its commercial agent in Bukhara in order to supervise

---

19. Quoted by Genis, *Vitse-konsul Vvedenskii*, 313.
20. "Yongo Buxorodan," *Ishtirokiyun*, 30.10.1918.

large-scale purchases of the crop.[21] At the same time, the Bolsheviks remained deeply suspicious of the ideological inclinations of the Young Bukharans and doubtful of the possibility of a movement against the emir gaining any traction in Bukhara.

The Young Bukharans received some support for organizing a resistance movement in Bukhara itself, although their success was limited. Their impact on Bukhara between 1918 and 1920 was minimal. A report by the Muslim secretary of the Russian Residency to the Young Bukharan Central Committee in Moscow claimed in April 1919 that many government functionaries were sympathetic to the progressives and there was considerable disaffection amongst the population as a result of heightening extraction by the state to support its military buildup.[22] But in terms of actual numbers, the situation was woeful. At the end of the drama, in August 1920, the secret organization in Bukhara claimed to have an armed unit (*druzhina*) with fifty members, but no arms to train with and no one to train them.[23] Activists conducted attacks on soldiers, assassinations, and robberies—tactics the Bolsheviks would have recognized from their own history, but which they felt were insufficient and even counterproductive in Bukhara's conditions. Most Bolshevik observers judged the Young Bukharans harshly. "The Decembrists of Asia, the Young Bukharans . . . have learnt nothing from history," wrote a commentator in Tashkent in August 1919. "They argue that the oppressed people of . . . Bukhara have to be 'liberated' from outside, with the force of the bayonets of the proletarian Red Army of Turkestan. That the 'liberated' exploited masses could, through their ignorance, see their liberators as foreign oppressors does not concern them."[24] V. V. Kuibyshev of the Turkkomissiia visited Bukhara in November 1919 and gave an equally negative assessment of the Young Bukharans, "who use our protection to act in a puerile, hooligan fashion to no end and [thus] exacerbate our relations with Bukhara. . . . The activities of the Young Bukharans," he continued, "should either be harmonized with our policies, or we should proclaim *urbi et orbi* our negative attitude toward their actions, which often have a purely

---

21. Genis, *Vitse-konsul Vvedenskii*, 194. Potelyakhov had been in a Cheka prison in Moscow, but was released at the request of Eliava, who thought that Potelyakhov's contacts at the Bukharan court would be helpful in acquiring cotton.

22. Akbar-xo'ja Islomov to Young Bukharan CC, 27.04.1919, TsGARUz, f. 17, op. 1, d. 1208, ll. 60–60ob.

23. "Doklad o deiatel'nosti Novo-Bukharskogo Otdeleniia [Tsentral'nogo Biuro Mladobukhartsev Revoliutsionerov] za period vremeni ot 10 iiulia po 19 avgusta 1920 goda" (19.08.1920), TsGARUz, f. 48, op. 1, d. 66, ll. 39–41.

24. I. B., "Khiva, Bukhara i sovetskii Turkestan," *Izvestiia Tsentral'nogo ispolnitel'nogo komiteta Turkestanskoi Respubliki RSF i Tashkentskogo soveta rabochikh, soldatskikh i dekhkanskikh deputatov*, 05.08.1919.

predatory character."[25] By the spring of 1920, with the eclipse of the Musburo, the Young Bukharans' main support in Tashkent came from Sovinterprop, while their relations with the Turkkomissiia were frigid.

In Bukhara itself, the emir strengthened his rule internally and tried to prepare for war, making considerable effort to strengthen and modernize his army. While there was no shortage of manpower, training and ammunition were a different matter. The Bukharan army reportedly had thirty thousand regular troops, but they were poorly equipped and had almost no training. The officer corps comprised a variety of men: Ottoman and Austrian prisoners of war, deserters from the British Indian army in Mesopotamia, and a few anti-Bolshevik Russian officers and Cossacks.[26] In October 1918, Alim Khan dispatched an embassy to Afghanistan that resulted in Habibullah Khan sending two hundred troops and six elephants to Bukhara.[27] Nevertheless, Alim Khan remained cautious in his dealings with anti-Soviet forces in the Russian civil war, for he wanted to give the Soviet government no reason to attack him. He obviously had no fondness for the constitutionalists in the Kokand Autonomy, but he also had nothing to do with the Basmachi and provided no help to those fleeing Turkestan. Even with the British he was careful. When the British agent F. M. Bailey showed up in Bukhara in late 1919, he was not received by any official of the government. "Have so far seen no member of Bokharan govt. who are suspicious and are afraid to have anything to do with me," he reported. "Our troops are far off and Bolsheviks are near and I suppose they are afraid of consequences if Bolsheviks hear they are helping me."[28] While the emir sat on his throne, he kept his contacts with the British limited and received little aid from them—perhaps no more than five hundred rifles supplied from Iran along with two noncommissioned officers.[29] That did not prevent him from gaining the reputation of a British stooge both in the eyes of the Bolsheviks and the Young Bukharans.

The emir's caution seemed to work and in the autumn of 1919, his relations with the Soviet government were almost warm. A. E. Aksel'rod, Soviet Russia's Resident in Bukhara, argued for a long-term solution in which a revolutionary

25. V.V. Kuibyshev to Turkomissiia, 30.11.1919, RGASPI, f. 122, op. 1, d. 45, ll. 1–1ob.

26. Estimates of the strength of the emir's army varied widely, and all numbers should be treated with caution. The figure of thirty thousand was reported (from Soviet sources) by the British agent F.M. Bailey in June 1919; TNA, WO 106/61/34 (unnumbered). Austrian POWs are mentioned in a number of sources: TsGARUz, f. 17, op. 1, d. 784, l. 1 (30.11.1918); Muḥammad 'Alī ibn Muḥammad Sa'īd Baljuvānī, Tārīkh-i nāfi'ī, ed. Mukhtor Ahror (Dushanbe, 1994), 54; Genis, Vitse-konsul Vvedenskii, 168–171 (quoting a report by P. P. Vvedenskii).

27. Mirza Salimbek, Tarikhi salimi, 235; Baljuvānī, Tārīkh-i Nāfi'ī, 54.

28. TNA, WO 106/61/34.

29. F.M. Bailey, Diary, IOR, Mss Eur F157/283, f. 201. In his published account of his adventures (Mission to Tashkent [London, 1946], 237–239), Bailey suppressed any mention of the rifles.

movement and a Muslim army raised from defectors from the emir's army would eventually lead the charge in Bukhara. An immediate military solution, he argued, would create immense problems: "Destroying the Bukharan army is very easy, but dealing with a two-and-a-half million strong population, located in mountains, would be completely impossible."[30] Aksel'rod had a sympathetic audience in Moscow in the person of G.V. Chicherin, who as commissar for foreign affairs wanted full control over Soviet actions in Central Asia in order to avoid difficulties with foreign powers, especially Britain. Lenin was also in favor of a gradual approach based on local work in cooperation with local noncommunist actors with the aim of creating a local uprising.

It was Frunze's impatience and persistence (and distance from Moscow) that led to a dramatic change in policy. For Frunze, Bukhara's status as a source of grain was trumped by its position as a haven for counterrevolutionaries and a hotbed of imperialist (British) intervention. At the same time, he saw no likelihood of an indigenous revolutionary movement: "In order to form a revolutionary upsurge in Bukhara, it is necessary to wait not months, but years."[31] Such waiting was pointless, and Frunze pushed through with the invasion, winning Moscow's consent under various pretexts.[32] As relations between Tashkent and Bukhara deteriorated over the summer of 1920, Moscow insisted Frunze work with local forces to give the invasion a veneer of revolutionary legitimacy. (Both Trotsky and Chicherin had misgivings about the effect the conquest of Bukhara might produce on Soviet Russia's rocky relations with Britain.) This insistence brought the Young Bukharans back into favor. On 3 August, Frunze forced a merger the Young Bukharans and the BKP, even though both parties were unhappy about it.[33] There was no love lost between the two parties: two weeks after the forced merger, Fayzulla Xo'jayev was complaining that "in the current situation, when I am not guaranteed against attempts at my life, there can no talk of fruitful work" together with members of BKP.[34] But Frunze's plans could not wait, and the invasion duly took place on 28 August and forced the marriage of the two parties. The new party was called BKP, but Young Bukharans had a dominant role in it.

---

30. Quoted in V.L. Genis, "*S Bukharoi nado konchat' . . .*": *k istorii butaforskikh revoliutsii* (Moscow, 2001), 4.

31. Quoted in ibid., 27.

32. In ibid., Genis provides an excellent account of the debates within the Bolshevik leadership on the fate of Bukhara.

33. RGASPI, f. 122, op. 1, d. 10, l. 62 (03.08.1920); see also A.K. Akchurin, "Vospominaniia o dvadtsatom gode v Khive i v Bukhare," in *Sbornik statei k desiatletiiu Bukharskoi i Khorezmskoi revoliutsii* (*vospominaniia uchastnikov Bukharskoi i Khorezmskoi revoliutsii*) (Tashkent, 1930), 46–49.

34. Fayzulla Xo'jayev to Turkkomissiia, 17.08.1920, RGASPI, f. 544, op. 4, d. 16, l. 48.

The Young Bukharans in Power

Thus it was that the Young Bukharans came to power as Communists. The Revolutionary Committee (Revkom), established even as the invasion took its course, included Young Bukharans, members of the old BKP, and two representatives (Sobirjon Yusupov and Nizomiddin Xo'jayev) of the KPT. Mirzo Abduqodir Muhiddinov soon emerged as its chair, and hence the head of state. The Council of Ministers (Xalq nozirlar sho'rosi) featured members of some of the city's wealthiest merchant families as well as Jadid intellectuals. Fayzulla Xo'jayev was chair; his cousin Usmonxo'ja Po'lotxo'ja-o'g'li, minister of finance;[35] Muhiddinov was minister for agriculture; and Mukammiliddin Maxdum, minister of justice.[36] Unlike in Turkestan, where the Jadids never took political power, in Bukhara Soviet tactics had placed Muslim modernist reformers in control of the state.

The forced merger with the BKP had not made the Young Bukharans convinced Communists overnight, nor had it changed the way they thought about politics. The need to placate the Soviets drove the BNSR government into an ideological bilingualism, whereby they "spoke Bolshevik" in their communications with Soviet authorities but conducted the internal business of state in the very different conceptual categories of national sovereignty and independence.[37] The situation was inherently unstable and the Soviets were able to turn the screws and bring the government into line (which was accomplished by the summer of 1923). Yet this was not the tale of a transition. Young Bukharan policies are best understood as an attempt to put into practice a set of ideas that had much more to do with statist reform on late Ottoman models than with Marx or the Bolsheviks. The evidence lies in the internal documentation of the republic, which provides insight into the political outlook of the Young Bukharans, of their hopes and desires, but which has never before been systematically analyzed.[38]

---

35. Usmonxo'ja had studied in Istanbul in the same years as Fitrat, whom he knew very well. Upon his return to Bukhara, Usmonxo'ja had established a well-equipped new-method school in his own house. His credentials as a cultural reformer were therefore impeccable. See Adeeb Khalid, "Osman Khoja and the Origins of Jadidism in Bukhara," in Kocaoğlu, ed. *Türkistan'da Yenilik Hareketleri*, 287–296.

36. The initial composition of both the Revkom and the cabinet were approved by the Turkkomissiia; see RGASPI, f. 122, op. 1, d. 10, l. 72.

37. Correspondence with Soviet or party authorities in Moscow or Tashkent or their plenipotentiary representatives in Bukhara was in Russian, but the internal republic's internal documentation—minutes of the executive branch of the government, memoranda and position papers circulated within ministries and within the council of ministers, departmental correspondence, and so forth—as well as its proclamations to its own population were overwhelmingly in Uzbek.

38. For a fuller examination of the nature of this documentation, see Adeeb Khalid, "The Bukharan People's Soviet Republic in the Light of Muslim Sources," *Die Welt des Islams* 50 (2010): 335-361.

The Tales of the Indian Traveler, Fitrat's 1912 critique of the state of Bukhara (see chapter 1), provides a roadmap of what the Young Bukharans sought to accomplish. Revolution for the Young Bukharans was a modality of change to be put in the service of the nation, not of a class. They sought to establish a centralized, modern nation-state with full sovereignty and membership in the then nascent world order of nation-states. A major goal of the state was to ensure economic development by marshaling the country's resources. It also had a clear mission to civilize its citizens, and fighting ignorance and fanaticism set the agenda for the Ministry of Education. The government also sought to reform Islam by bringing Muslim institutions and large swathes of Islamic activity under the state's bureaucratic control. Ottoman traces can be found in Young Bukharan discourses and practices at many levels. The Uzbek used in Young Bukharan proclamations and in internal bureaucratic correspondence was often heavily Ottomanate, as were the republic's chancery styles and practices. The visual evidence of the vernacular documents, as well as their tone and general sensibility, are striking in this regard. None of this is surprising. Several leading figures among the Young Bukharans had studied in Istanbul. Fitrat is the most important example, but Usmonxo'ja had also spent four years in Istanbul. A number of other students who had been sent to Istanbul before the war played significant roles in Bukhara after 1920. On the other hand, Rahmat Rafiq (1884–?) first went to Istanbul only in 1918 after being exiled from Bukhara. He spent over a year in Anatolia with the resistance before returning to Bukhara in 1921.[39]

Fitrat played major roles in the republic in a number of capacities. He first returned to Bukhara in December 1920 with an "Uzbek scientific expedition" to survey the manuscript collections to be found in the city,[40] and the goal of collecting and studying—and thereby shaping—the cultural legacy of Bukhara remained central to his work. He organized a historical society and a School of Eastern Music to which he invited the composer Viktor Uspenskii to notate traditional Bukharan music in European form.[41] But Fitrat was also involved directly in government. Between the late spring of 1921 and the summer of 1923, he occupied a number of cabinet posts, including the posts of the minister for foreign affairs (until February 1923) and for education (February to June 1923).[42]

39. Rahmat Rafiq, "Biograficheskii ocherk" (*ca.* 1924), RGASPI, f. 62, op. 4, d. 633, l. 293.

40. "Buxorog'o yuborilg'on o'zbek bilim hay'atining ishlagan ishlari," *Qizil bayroq*, 23.02.1921.

41. On the School of Eastern Music, see Aleksandr Dzhumaev, "Otkryvaia 'chernyi iashchik' pro-shlogo," *Muzykal'naia akademiia*, 2000, no. 1: 89–103; the contract with Uspenskii is in TsGARUz, f. 56, op. 1, d. 124, l. 12 (January 1923).

42. It is not possible to establish the exact sequence of Fitrat's appointments, but judging by his signatures in documents of the Ministry of Education, he became minister on 12 February 1923 and remained in that post until 24 June: TsGARUz, f. 56, op. 1, d. 222.

In 1922, he was chair of the National Economic Council, in which capacity his signature appeared on banknotes of the republic. Perhaps the most tangible result of Fitrat's influence was the Turkification of Bukhara. The language of the chancery in Bukhara had always been Persian, but the Young Bukharans hurried to proclaim Uzbek as the state language. This was the practical implementation of the Chaghatayist vision that Fitrat had done more than anyone else to articulate. As we shall see in chapters 8 and 9, the cultural politics of the Bukharan republic had a great impact on how Uzbek and Tajik identities came to be imagined in this decade.

Among the first actions of the Revkom was a series of moves to create uniform, regularized forms of administration and the establishment of centralized institutions. A decree created a uniform administrative division of the republic into provinces (*viloyat*), districts (*tumon*), and towns (*kent*), each with its own soviet apparatus.[43] Other decrees established ministries, each to be headed by a "people's minister" (*xalq noziri*) and with a presence throughout the territory of the republic. The new government also sought to bring various institutional aspects of Islamic practices under the regulatory regime of the modern state: it regularized the working of qazi courts, put education (maktabs and madrasas) under the oversight of the Ministry of Education (and nationalized their property), and brought mosques under the jurisdiction of a Waqf Administration (Avqof Idorasi).[44] The new government also made a valiant attempt to regulate waqf properties and put waqf income to public use.[45] The following year, the Central Executive Committee of the republic, as successor to the Revkom, was discussing the necessity of creating a modern prison to be housed "in a building specially designated for the purpose by the government, as in civilized states."[46] Interest in sport and physical culture also clearly marked a modern sensibility toward citizenship.[47]

The fundamental fact for the Young Bukharans was the backwardness of their country. In September 1921, the Council of Ministers sent out a circular to all

---

43. TsGARUz, f. 46, op. 1, d. 117, ll. 45ob-46.

44. Ibid., l. 49ob, 60ob, 60.

45. The regulation of waqf was easier said than done. The collection and disposal of waqf income were rooted in customary practices that were often beyond the ken of members of the new regime. The earliest correspondence within the new waqf administration related to delineating these practices before they could be regulated. TsGARUz, f. 48, op. 1, d. 64, ll. 15–17 (18.10.1920).

46. TsGARUz, f. 47, op. 1, d. 150, l. 12ob.

47. TsGARUz, f. 47, op. 1, d. 595. May Day in 1923 was marked by a sports meet held between visiting teams from the Russian Red Army in the Registan, now renamed Independence Square. Sport, the comment in the official newspaper stated, is "very important for a healthy, strong, and powerful youth . . . an important part of our new revolutionary way of life." See "Ispurt o'yunlari," *Buxoro axbori*, 10.05.1923.

local authorities, exhorting them to follow proper procedure in all respects, to keep good accounts, and to collect taxes efficiently. These tasks were important because

> the incorrect policies of the emir had left our state among the most backward in the world in terms of science and technology, industry, agriculture, or commerce. As a result, today two percent of our people can read and write, and the remaining 98 percent cannot, and as a result are completely ignorant of the world. Because our commerce was based on old principles, there is no real commerce in our state. Instead, our merchants have become middlemen between Russian merchants and our peasants, i.e., our commerce sells the wealth of the peasant to other countries . . . [and] all the profits from the commerce go to other countries. . . . It is well known that a state that is unable to find the proper path of commerce cannot have industry either.[48]

Another position paper, also from 1921 (but unfortunately unsigned), suggested that economic development could be achieved by pooling the resources of the rich. "It was this joint effort of thought and of wealth that ensured the development of commerce and industry in Europe, but since the creation of joint stock companies is not possible in the Soviet conditions in which we live, this role has to be played by the state."[49]

As we have seen, the Young Bukharans had seen the state as the leading agent of reform well before the revolution. The statist economic policy now envisioned had no place in it for the acknowledgement of class conflict, let alone any impulse to rectify class exploitation. Land reform never went beyond the expropriation of the property of the emir's family and of those who fled into exile with him, and the properties of the wealthy merchants were left largely untouched. The government did bring waqf property under its own control and granted relief to the peasants who worked waqf land by establishing a uniform tax, but otherwise it did not intervene massively in the economy.

One of the first acts of the new government was the establishment of a newspaper. This was an act of great symbolic import (since the emirs had been implacably opposed to the introduction of the press to Bukhara),[50] but the content of the newspaper was more interesting still. The first issue carried the banner headline, "Bukharan Compatriots! May your Freedom and Equality Be Blessed!" (*Buxoroli vatandoshlar! Ozodliq va tenglikingiz muborik bo'lsun!*) Underneath

---

48. TsGARUz, f. 48, op. 1, d. 5, ll. 32ob-32.
49. "Bukunki iqtisodiy holatimiz," TsGARUz, f. 46, op. 1, d. 170, ll. 19–20.
50. Sadriddin Ayniy, *Buxoro inqilobi tarixi uchun materiallar* (Moscow, 1926), 94–101.

was a diatribe against the emir by Fayzulla Xo'jayev, accusing the deposed monarch of exploitation, corruption, and heedlessness to the needs of "our sacred
home Bukhara" (*muqaddas yurtimiz bo'lgan Buxoro*). Xo'jayev also sketched out
a lineage of the new regime he represented: the new government was rooted
in the efforts of "some people who began to worry about reform ten or fifteen
years ago," only to meet the resolute opposition and persecution of the emir.
Xo'jayev made no mention of Communism, Russia, or of 1917.[51] This narrative
of the Jadids' struggle against despotism, for rights and equality of the people,
and the independence of the state was the dominant representation of the Young
Bukharan government in the months that followed.

The same rhetoric was seen in the proceedings of the First Bukharan Congress
of People's Deputies that the government hurried to convene. The congress met
in the emir's summer residence outside the city as early as 6 October and heard
speakers emphasize the end of despotism and the fact that "the [new] government is just and is the supporter of the people."[52] The beneficiaries of this end to
despotism and the proclamation of freedom and equality were the people (*xalq,
millat*) and the homeland (*yurt, vatan*), both new categories in the political life
of Bukhara but central to the thinking of the Young Bukharans. The complete
absence of a Marxist frame of reference and of class is striking in these formulations. Rather, the revolution was located in a trajectory of overcoming ignorance and achieving progress. "Brothers!" exhorted one activist, "the old regime
oppressed you because of your ignorance. Brothers, come, join the Communist
Party and become the masters of your own rights. Give your children the benefit of knowledge and education [*ilm maorifdan behramand qilib*], open schools
where such have not been opened, [and] eliminate the immoralities that had
taken root under the old government."[53] This reading of the revolution continued to dominate the press well into 1923, by which time Soviet pressure had
begun to build on the Young Bukharans. In January 1923, Fayzulla Xo'jayev could
still describe the main enemies of the republic as the ignorance of the people
(*xalqning ilmsizligi . . . ya'ni jaholat*), economic difficulties, and the destruction
of cities and villages in the course of the wars for the liberation of the people
(*xalqning ozodlik urushlari*).[54]

The Young Bukharans' domestic policies were geared at establishing a modern
centralized state with a uniform administrative structure to replace the largely

---

51. Fayzulla Xo'ja, "Kun to'g'di," *Buxoro axbori*, 09.09.1920.

52. "Buxoroning ilk quriltoyi," *Buxoro axbori*, 11.10.1920; TsGARUz, f. 47, op. 1, d. 8, l. 47 (from
a felicitationary speech by Domla Ikrom, a leading mudarris of Bukhara and an early supporter of
reform).

53. Muhammad Said, "Xitobnoma," *Buxoro axbori*, 26.11.1920.

54. Fayzulla Xo'ja, "Uch dushmon," *Buxoro axbori*, 04.01.1923.

personal power wielded by governors (*voli, hokim*) in the provinces. They also paid attention to establishing institutions of coercion to secure the power of the new regime. Even before the fighting was concluded, the Revkom had established an Extraordinary Commission for Struggle with Counterrevolution (Bukh-Cheka) on 31 August 1920.[55] It was soon followed by a separate Commission for the Defense of the Revolution, established in October,[56] and the Bukharan Red Army founded in February 1921. The local Red Army was seen as a national army. As late as the summer of 1923, when Soviet control was much greater, a Komsomol brochure argued that it was the duty (*vazifa*) of the youth of Bukhara to raise money to educate and train soldiers, for "a state without strength cannot secure its own rights."[57]

The new government made early attempts to create a narrative of national revolution and sacrifice on behalf of the nation. At its very first meeting, the Ministry of Education resolved to commission a history of the Bukharan revolution.[58] Ultimately, Sadriddin Ayni was given the contract to write the book, which appeared in Uzbek as *Materials for the History of the Bukharan Revolution*. The book is remarkable for its sensibility, which remains firmly grounded in Muslim discourses, and makes no mention of class or any materialist argument. Ayni's account retained organic links with the Islamicate historiographical tradition of Bukhara, but it provided a coherent narrative of the struggles of the Jadids against the tyranny of the emir. Ayni returned to Bukhara for the first time since 1917 and on 22 November 1920 was one of a number of Young Bukharan activists who gathered to discuss measures to memorialize those of their comrades who had been killed by the emir. The gathering resolved to strike a commission to compile a list of all those who had perished, to learn their biographies, and to commit them to writing. The meeting also resolved to turn the place where many of the "martyrs" had been buried into a park and to work toward establishing monuments to them in the city of Bukhara and the provinces. Finally, the gathering asked the Council of Ministers for funds to provide material support to the families of the "martyrs."[59] The intent clearly was to create a narrative of sacrifice at the altar of the nation by heroes seeking its liberation from a despot. Here too, the rhetoric of class was conspicuous by its absence.

---

55. TsGARUz, f. 46, op. 1, d. 115, l. 106.

56. Buxoro Shurolar Jumhuriyatining Markaziy Inqilob Qo'mitasi, Protokol/zabtnoma no. 14 (24.10.1920), TsGARUz, f. 46, op. 1, d. 115, l. 53.

57. Z. Yo'ldoshboyev, *Ishchi Buxoro xalqi o'zining milliy Buxoro qizil askaringizni tashkil qilingiz* (Bukhara, 1923); a copy of this brochure is to be found in TsGARUz, f. 47, op. 1, d. 196, ll. 68–74ob.

58. TsGARUz, f. 56, op. 1, d. 10a, l. 27.

59. TsGARUz, f. 48, op. 1, d. 17, l. 23.

Crucially, the nation was imagined to be ethnically Turkic. The Turkism of the Young Bukharans is evident in their use of Uzbek as the language of the chancery and of schooling. It was also clearly articulated by a diplomatic mission sent to the Turkish resistance movement in Anatolia. The mission arrived in Ankara in December 1921, where it addressed the Great National Assembly and was received by Mustafa Kemal Pasha himself. "The Bukharans," the delegates told the Grand National Assembly, "in addition to being citizens of the East [sharqli], are of Turkic descent. Because Bukhara is a Muslim state, it has many spiritual relations with the Turks, who have of old been the defenders of Islam. These brothers, like the various other citizens of the East, could not stretch out their hands to one another despite being one by virtue of race [ırk] and religion, because of the known policies of the imperialists, who wanted to keep the nations of the East divided in order to keep them under control and to oppress them." Islam and revolution coexist here with a national unity rooted in race or common descent. Even more interesting was the way the mission narrated the genesis of the Bukharan republic:

> The heroic defense during the Gallipoli war inspired dread in the West and made the sun of revolution rise in the East. The trustworthy liberating hands of Russian revolutionaries, who raised the banner of humanity, were united with [those of] the oppressed of the East. . . . The enlightened youth of Bukhara, who had worked continuously for 15–20 years, overthrew the cruel and despotic government [of the emir] with the help of Eastern revolutionaries.[60]

The roots of Bukharan revolution allegedly lie in the heroism of Gallipoli, which awakened the Muslim world, and in the efforts of the Bukharan intelligentsia, while the Russian revolution is only of marginal importance. The Bukharan republic is the product of Islamic renewal, national liberation, and anticolonial revolution, not of Communism or the Russian revolution.

The Bukharan government also began sending students abroad to acquire modern technical education. This placed it in a long tradition of modernizing regimes sending students abroad to acquire state-of-the-art education (Russia, Japan, Egypt, Iran, the Ottomans). The destinations chosen for the students were significant. Turkey was the first, partly because many Bukharans were already there. In late 1921, the Ministry of Education sent five hundred Ottoman liras to Bukharan students in Istanbul through the Bukharan consul in Baku.[61] Turkey

---

60. "Buhara Heyet-i Murahhasasının Kabul Merasiminde İrad olunan Mühim ve Tarihî Nutukları," *Sebilürreşad* (Ankara) 19, no. 492 (16.01.1922): 261–262.

61. TsGARUz, f. 56, op. 1, d. 25, ll. 19, 20ob.

was also the source of pedagogical materials. The same year, the Council of Ministers agreed to a request for fifty thousand gold rubles from the Ministry of Education to send an academic delegation to Turkey to acquire books and other pedagogical materials.[62] In 1922, the government decided to send a group of students to Germany.[63] A total of forty-seven students, including four girls, arrived in Berlin and were placed in various institutions of middle and higher learning.[64] A formal office, the education representation of the BNSR in Germany (Buxoro Xalq Shurolar Jumhuriyatining Olmoniyodag'i Maorif Vakolati/Delegation der Bucharishchen Republik in Kultursangelegenheiten, Deutschland), was established. Through it, the government searched for a modern printing press for Arabic script and had several books printed in Germany.[65] Finally, in March 1923, the Ministry of Education established a Bukharan House of Learning (Buxoro Bilim Yurti) in Moscow where Bukharan students, including children, could stay and do preparatory work (especially language training) for admission to *rabfak*s ("workers' faculties," institutions set up to prepare workers for admission into higher education) or other Soviet institutions.[66] In May 1924, they numbered 174 (including 35 girls).[67]

The Bukharan delegation to Germany was headed by Alimjan Idrisi, a Tatar philologist and old Jadid who had spent several years in Istanbul before the war and had been active in the same circles as Fitrat and other Bukharans in that city. Unlike Fitrat, Idrisi had stayed behind in Istanbul and spent the war working for the Ottomans, including two years as an imam at a camp for Muslim (mostly Tatar) prisoners of war in Germany. He returned to Russia after the revolution, but was promptly arrested by the Cheka. In January 1922, the Institute for Living Oriental Languages sought, through Narkomnats, his release for, it argued, he could serve the state better by using his expert knowledge.[68] By the summer of that year, Idrisi was back in Germany as director of the Bukharan delegation. In 1924, when Soviet government inspected the Bukharan student delegation, Idrisi held Turkish citizenship.[69] The Young Bukharans were mobilizing their resources outside Soviet parameters.

62. TsGARUz, f. 48, op. 1, d. 20, l. 41–40ob.

63. On this episode, see Sherali Turdiyev, *Ular Germaniyada o'qigan edilar* (Tashkent, 2006); A. Ahat Andican, *Cedidizm'den Bağımsızlığa Hariçte Türkistan Mücadelesi* (Istanbul, 2003), 261–288.

64. BXShJning Olmoniyodagi Maorif Vakolati, "Girmoniyadagi Buxoro shogirdlari" (05.12.1923), TsGARUz, f. 56, op. 1, d. 174, ll. 53–54.

65. TsGARUz, f. 56, op. 1, d. 224, ll. 94–95.

66. TsGARUz, f. 56, op. 1, d. 52, ll. 15–15ob, 28.

67. *Iubilennyi sbornik Bukharskogo Doma Prosveshcheniia imeni I. V. Stalina v Moskve / Moskovda Istolin ismida bo'lg'on Buxoro Bilim Yurti yubeley majmuasi, moy 1923–1924* (Moscow, 1924).

68. GARF, f. 1318, op. 1, d. 10, l.156.

69. RGASPI, f. 62, op. 2, d. 88, l. 111; on the fascinating life of Idrisi, see I. Giliiazov, "Sud'ba Alimdzhana Idrisi," *Ekho vekov* 3–4 (1999); available at http://www.archive.gov.tatarstan.ru/magazine/go/anonymous/main/?path=mg:/numbers/1999_3_4/05/05_3/.

In short, the Young Bukharans hoped to make Bukhara into a sovereign, modernizing nation-state with its own economic and foreign policies. They had established a Ministry of Foreign Affairs (Xorijiya nazorati) and proceeded to establish consular representations in several neighboring countries. The representatives to Kabul and Moscow bore the title of ambassador (*safīr*), while those appointed to Petrograd, Tashkent, Baku, and Tbilisi were consuls. They also hoped that the BKP would enter the Comintern as an independent party ("like the Germans"), rather than as a satellite of the Russian Communist Party (RKP[b]).[70] All such hopes were squashed by the Soviets in quick order, but they are a good indication of how the Young Bukharans imagined politics.

The Demise of the Old Culture in Bukhara

The flight of the emir and the installation of the Young Bukharans sealed the fate of the city's traditional Persian-writing cultural elite and the court-centered culture it reproduced. Although some of the notables did support the Young Bukharans, the overthrow of the old order irrevocably changed the parameters of cultural and political life in Bukhara. Some of the old notables fled with the emir, while others suffered the wrath of the Young Bukharans. The new government acted swiftly against those who had led the persecution of the Jadids since April 1917: Burhoniddin the qazi kalān, Usmonbek the qushbegi, Izomiddin Sadr the ra'is, Qutbiddin Sudur the mufti, and many others were arrested and put to work cleaning toilets and sweeping the streets. This was a very brutal turning of the tables and the ultimate insult to those whose dignity resided in the sanctity of their person and in carefully cultivated habits of gravity. After several days of this work, they were made to dig their own graves and then executed on 18 October.[71] The new government also confiscated the properties of the emir, his family, and those who fled with him. Sharifjon Makhdum, on the other hand, made his way back to Bukhara from his administrative exile in Qarshi and was appointed to a position in the waqf administration established by the new government. He also had his property, confiscated by the emir in 1917, returned to him.[72] Domla

70. RGASPI, f. 61, op. 1, d. 33, l. 1.

71. Sharīfjān Makhdūm Ṣadr-i Żiyā, *Rūznāma-yi Ṣadr-i Żiyā: vaqāyiʿ-nigārī-yi taḥavullāt-i siyāsī-ijtimāʿī-yi Bukhārā-yi sharīf*, ed. Muḥammadjān Shakūrī Bukhārāyī (Tehran, 1382/2004), 290. The records of the Bukharan revolutionary tribunal (TsGARUz, f. 1713) remain classified to this day, but notices of the executions were published in the press: "Otiluvg'a mahkum bo'lg'onlar," *Buxoro axbori*, 29.09.1920; "Oliy inqilob mahkamasining qaror va pro'toqo'li," *Buxoro axbori*, 21.11.1920; "Dar jumhūriyat-i Bukhārā," *Shuʿla-yi inqilāb*, 25.10.1920, 6.

72. Ṣadr-i Żiyā, *Rūznāma*, 289–291.

Ikrom, another old supporter of reform exiled to Ghuzor, also hastened back to Bukhara.[73] In terms of Bukharan elite politics, this meant the eclipse of the Kuhistānī faction of Bukhara's ulama and the ascendancy of the Bukharan (or *tumanī*) faction.

Initially, some of the old literary elite found a niche in the new order. The History and Archaeology Society (Tarix va osor-i atiqa anjumani) organized by the Ministry of Education in July 1921, with the aim of studying the history and historical monuments of Bukhara, included Fitrat and Sharifjon Makhdum, but also Mirza Salim Bek, whose distaste for the Jadids drips from every page of his *Ta'rikh-i salīmī*, the history of Bukhara that he was still finishing.[74] The waqf administration continued to employ members of the old fiscal administration, but now they were salaried employees, divested of their old ranks, and living in penury.[75] In other ways, too, the sun set on the old culture. The invasion of Bukhara caused immense damage to the city's heritage. The libraries of the emir and his bookish uncle Nosir-xon To'ra were destroyed in the bombing and the fires that ensued, while books from many other personal libraries were confiscated and transferred to a new national library.[76] Other libraries were culled of "glosses and [other] useless books."[77] Many madrasas emptied out, as students fled the disorder. The Ministry of Education paid considerable attention to historical and ethnographic research, but such was to be in the service of the nation, something in which the older literati had no investment. Representative of this new historical sensibility was a catalogue of Bukhara's antiquities compiled by Muso Saidjonov,[78] or the translations of European works on Central Asia by scholars such as Vámbéry and Barthold commissioned by the ministry. These translations, moreover, were not in Persian, but in Uzbek, which the Young Bukharans declared to be the state language of the new republic. While the old literati continued to compose literature and historiography along conventional lines, their epoch had passed. They had been marginalized socially, linguistically, and epistemologically.

---

73. "73 sāla javān bukhārāyī," *Shu'la-yi inqilāb*, 27.09.1920, 8.

74. TsGARUz, f. 56, op. 1, d. 10a, l. 6ob.

75. Franz Wennberg, *An Inquiry into Bukharan Qadīmism—Mīrzā Salīm-bīk* (Berlin, 2002), 26–27. Even those notables who supported the Young Bukharans did not thrive. Sharifjon retired in 1924, on the eve of the dissolution of the BNSR, and lived out a quiet life. He nevertheless died in 1932 in prison (which occupied the building of a madrasa where his father had taught and in which Sharifjon had owned a cell), having been arrested on nonpolitical charges. Muḥammad Jān Shakūrī Bukhārī, *Ṣadr-i Bukhārā* (Tehran, 1380/2002), 24–25.

76. A. Semenov, "Litsevye rukopisi Bukharskoi tsentral'noi biblioteki," *Iran*, vyp. 2 (Leningrad, 1928), 89–92.

77. TsGARUz, f. 56, op. 1, d. 83, l. 88 (1924).

78. The catalogue is now available as Muso Saidjonov, *Buxoro shahri va uning eski binolari*, ed. H. To'rayev (Tashkent, 2005). On Saidjonov, see Svetlana Gorshenina, "Musa Saidzhanov—istorik, arkheolog, iskusstvoved," *Obshchestvennye nauki v Uzbekistane*, 1995, no. 1–3: 26–29.

State and Islam in Bukhara

The Young Bukharans sought to modernize, that is, bureaucratize and regulate, Islam and to put it to their use, rather than trying to eliminate it from the public space. This caused them problems with their Soviet handlers, of course, but as long as the republic lasted, it did not lose its Islamic legitimacy. The Young Bukharans had emerged in a political landscape defined by factional struggles among ulama. While opposition to the Young Bukharans was driven by conservative ulama, they had several prominent Bukharan ulama on their side, and it is to them that they turned upon finding themselves in power. Immediately upon its formation, the new government had obtained a fatwa declaring the ouster of the emir to be in accord with the shariat.[79] The Young Bukharan government called on reformist ulama on numerous occasions to lend their authority to the government. A Society of Jurists (Fuqaho Jamiyati), established around 1922, issued proclamations to the population on behalf of the Young Bukharans and their revolution.[80] In January 1924, the government organized a conference of "enlightened ulama" that issued resolutions for the reform of madrasas, against the elaborate celebration of life-cycle feasts, and—in a sign of the times—against British imperialism in "the East."[81]

One of the earliest decrees of the new government put all qazi courts under the supervision of the Ministry of Justice. The government also established a Waqf Administration to oversee the collection of all waqf revenues as well as their expenditure. Subsequent laws abolished waqfs endowed for the use of the benefactors' descendants (*vaqfi avlod*) and transferred the endowed funds to use for cultural and educational purposes.[82] The waqf law was revised in March 1922 by a commission headed by Fitrat, which replaced the Waqf Administration with a Directorate of Waqf Affairs in the Ministry of Education. All waqf property remained exempt from taxation. Waqfs benefitting mosques were to be retained by mosques, but spent under the directorate's supervision. All other waqfs were to be put at the disposal of the waqf directorate and spent on running or building new-method schools, madrasas, and orphanages, and for publishing newspapers, magazines, and useful books—in short, for implementing the Jadid program of

---

79. GARF, f. 1235, op. 96, d. 749, l. 1 (20.12.1920).

80. Such proclamations were duly reported to state and party authorities, whose archives yield them to us; "Nāma-yi 'ulamā-yi Bukhārā" (1921), TsGARUz, f. 47, d. 26, ll. 83ob-82; "Mamlakat xalqiga ulamo xitobnomasi," RGASPI, f. 62, op. 2, d. 40, l. 180; for a printed proclamation, see the pamphlet *Khiṭāb-i Jam'iyyat-i fuqahā* (Bukhara, n.d.).

81. "Buxoro Shurolar Jumhuriyatining munavvar ul-afkor ulamolar birinchi quriltoyi," TsGARUz, f. 57, d. 27.

82. TsGARUz, f. 47, d. 70, ll. 4–5 (16.02.1921).

cultural reform.[83] Already in March 1921, the Waqf Administration was using its funds (and asking for more) to carry out repairs on historical buildings (including the Minor-i Kalon) damaged in the invasion of Bukhara,[84] and over the years it repaired several madrasas and reestablished them on a reformed curriculum.[85] Control of waqf revenues gave the state the ability to demand changes in the curriculum and a say in the hiring and firing of instructors in the madrasas of the capital. In July 1922, the waqf directorate resolved to reopen ten madrasas whose students had fled in the chaos of the revolution. These were to have approved instructors, curricula, and lesson plans.[86] Not all was so straightforward, of course. Waqf was embedded in so many layers of custom that its bureaucratization was easier said than done. Trustees leased waqf lands out to middlemen (*ijorador*), who then sublet smaller plots to individual peasants, from whom they collected the rent. Forgiving payments as a way of easing the burden on the peasants benefited the middlemen more than peasants.[87] In any case, the ability of the Waqf Administration to fully control waqf affairs, especially those outside the capital, remained limited, and many properties passed into the hands of their trustees or were confiscated by local ispolkoms.[88]

The first two sets of waqf-related legislation in Bukhara had been products of a Muslim reformist project. As Soviet control tightened on the Bukharan government after the purge of the cabinet in June 1923, the situation with waqfs also changed. In fact, as the bastion of Muslim activists, the waqf directorate bore a greater burden of Soviet suspicion than almost any other Bukharan institution. In October 1923, the government staged a conference of peasants working waqf land which issued a set of demands—that rent on waqf lands should be set by tax authorities and not by the middlemen or the Waqf Administration and that it should be limited to a maximum of 10 percent of the crop; waqfs should be divided between religious (*diniy*) and cultural and educational (*madaniy va ilmiy*) uses and should be spent for clearly (and narrowly) defined purposes; and the finances of the Waqf Administration be investigated.[89] This last demand was promptly fulfilled, as the GPU raided the offices of the Waqf Administration and confiscated its papers. The new law that followed crystallized the distinction between religious and cultural-educational waqfs, with the latter to be used for

---

83. "Buxoro Xalq Shuro Jumhuriyatining avqof ishlari haqinda Loyihasi," TsGARUz, f. 47, d. 26, ll. 75–74.
84. TsGARUz, f. 56, op. 1, d. 42, l. 14 (18.09.1922).
85. TsGARUz, f. 48, op. 1, d. 20, l. 39 (March 1921).
86. TsGARUz, f. 48, op. 1, d. 20, l. 154 (08.07.1922).
87. TsGARUz, f. 48, op. 1, d. 64, ll. 15–17 (18.10.1920).
88. TsGARUz, f. 47, d. 83, ll. 11–10ob (29.03.1922).
89. "Vaqfkor dehqonlar quriltoyi," TsGARUz, f. 57, d. 2, ll. 8ob-7 (08.10.1923).

reforming old-method schools and madrasas, appointing suitable instructors, commissioning textbooks, and publishing newspapers and magazines in order "to struggle with bigotry and ignorance."[90] The continuities with the 1922 legislation were clear, but the context was clearly different.

Consolidating the Republic

What the Young Bukharans hoped to achieve was one thing. What they could accomplish was quite another, for there were no two ways about the fact that it was the Red Army that had put them in power. Acquiring legitimacy in the eyes of their own population and consolidating power, especially outside the city of Bukhara, proved immensely difficult. For all the persecution and the exactions the emir had imposed on his population since 1917, his legitimacy had not suffered greatly. The political language favored by the Young Bukharans remained largely alien to the population. The massive destruction that accompanied the Red Army's invasion of the city did further damage to the Young Bukharans' claims to be liberators and led many to believe that the revolutionaries "had despoiled their own sacred homeland."[91] The following year, the Council of Ministers needed to exhort local authorities to show through their probity the falsity of the idea common among the people that "Bolsheviks are bandits and that our government is a similar thing."[92] Rumors circulated that the emir was about to return to reclaim the throne of his ancestors and to mete out punishment to those who had rebelled against him.[93] More real was the insurgency that gripped the republic throughout its existence. It was sparked off by a revolt of local rulers, particularly in the mountain fastnesses of eastern Bukhara. The region had never been fully controlled by the emirs in Bukhara; it was also the bastion of the conservative Kuhistani faction of Bukhara's ulama who had been the most implacably opposed to reform. The ouster of the emir led to the assertion of power by local rulers and warlords. This was the so-called Bukharan Basmachi insurgency that lasted practically the entire life of the BNSR. Elsewhere too central control was difficult to establish. Throughout the period of the insurgency, BNSR materials described the situation as a civil war, borrowing categories from the Russian civil war to cast the Basmachi as "White bandits" and agents of counterrevolution.

---

90. "Markaz avqof idorasi uchun nizomnoma," TsGARUz, f. 56, op. 1, d. 83, l. 75ob.

91. Baljuvānī, *Tārīkh-i nāfiʿī*, 71–72.

92. TsGARUz, f. 48, op. 1, d. 5, l. 30.

93. This was mentioned by Fayzulla Xoʻjayev in his official report to the Third Congress of People's Representatives, August 1922, TsGARUz, f. 47, d. 343a, l. 10, and it crops up repeatedly elsewhere in the archives as well.

Civil war is, indeed, an apt characterization of what took place in Bukhara and beyond in these years.

The government's response was to establish a Plenipotentiary Commission for Eastern Bukhara (Muxtor komisiya in Uzbek, Diktatorskaia komissiia in Russian) with wide-ranging powers to assert central control, but which achieved little success.[94] The fundamental problem was that central control could only be established through the Red Army staffed almost entirely by Europeans, which therefore looked and felt like an army of occupation. The fact that Red Army soldiers had to live off the land they controlled gave rise to all sorts of exactions, thefts, rape, and pillage that did not endear the central government to the population. The Young Bukharans could not exist without the Red Army but also resented it deeply. The distrust was mutual and its arc short and steep.

There were other issues too. From the beginning, members of the old BKP criticized the Young Bukharans for their ideological laxity. They presented themselves as a left opposition and showered the Sredazburo and the Central Committee with critiques and denunciations. Stalin was disgruntled enough with them to organize a purge of the "Leftists" and to have them exiled from Bukhara in 1922. More fundamental to the Young Bukharans was the bitter rivalry between Fayzulla Xo'jayev and Abduqodir Muhiddinov that had nothing to do with ideological stances and everything to do with personalities and a long history of commercial competition between the two wealthy families.[95] From the outset, this rivalry led to a struggle for power. The Bukharan Cheka picked up reports of a secret meeting in the house of Abduqodir Muhiddinov's brother Isomiddin in April 1921 to plot against Xo'jayev and his supporters, using tactics such as assassinations and the planting of incriminating evidence on them.[96] In August, handbills in the name of a "Committee for Truth and Justice" appeared all over the city, proclaiming that the Bukharan revolution had fallen into the hands of "a 'company' of thieves and traitors" addicted to prostitution and alcohol, and asking "sons of the sacred homeland [to] unite in order to quickly liberate the homeland from the hands of these tyrants and traitors."[97] The situation worsened and culminated in a putsch attempted by a detachment loyal to Muhiddinov that briefly placed several individuals close to Xo'jayev (including Fitrat) under arrest. Xo'jayev fled to the Soviet representative in Kagan, who sent armored cars into the old city and thwarted the uprising, and the rebels fled to Samarqand.

94. TsGARUz, f. 48, d. 17, ll. 187–188 (01.05.1921).

95. Gero Fedtke, "How Bukharans Turned into Uzbeks and Tajiks: Soviet Nationalities Policy in the Light of a Personal Rivalry," in *Patterns of Transformation in and around Uzbekistan*, ed. Paolo Sartori and Tommaso Trevisani (Reggio Emilia, 2007), 19–50.

96. RGASPI, f. 544, op. 4, d. 27, l. 149.

97. A Russian translation made by the Cheka is in RGASPI, f. 122, op. 2, d. 142, ll. 3–3ob.

Ministers loyal to Xo'jayev then tried to oust Muhiddinov from the presidency of the Revkom, but were apparently talked out of it by the Soviet plenipotentiary Iurenev.[98] This moment of support for Muhiddinov aside, Iurenev and his successors tended to favor Xo'jayev, who they felt had more support locally but also because they considered him more businesslike (and a Russophile). Muhiddinov, on the other hand, was perceived to be politically weak and more difficult to deal with. Soviet representatives were wary of "his 'Italian' moods," even as they deemed him to be an "nationalist, pan-Islamist, and a manifest Russophobe."[99] By 1922, when Stalin himself declared him "dangerous,"[100] Muhiddinov had largely lost out to Xo'jayev. But the rivalry was to fester, and as we shall in chapter 9, it was to have significant consequences for the definition of the Uzbek and Tajik nations and their mutual relations.

Yet, for all his debt to the Soviets, Xo'jayev sought consistently to maximize his (and his government's) autonomy. His strongest argument was based on the peculiar conditions of Bukhara. "While it is impossible, of course, to deny that the work of our organization has many defects," he wrote to M. P. Tomskii, the head of the Turkkomissiia, in 1921, "we should not be judged too harshly for them. Soviet Russia, having far greater forces at its command, is also not in a position to organize everything all at once. . . . We know very well that any obstinacy on our part or coercive measures on yours [to force the pace of change in Bukhara] will be fraught with pernicious consequences" that could derail the cause of the revolution in the East.[101] Indeed, the reason for the weakness of his government was Bukhara's lack of complete sovereignty. "In order to strengthen a sense among the masses of the independence and the complete liberation of Bukhara," he wrote to L. M. Karakhan, the head of the Eastern Section of the Commissariat of Foreign Affairs, in April 1922, "it is necessary for the Russian Government to broadly demonstrate its attitude in Bukhara, proclaiming publicly Bukhara's complete independence and the inviolability of its sovereign rights."[102] In 1923, when the Sredazburo moved to harmonize the economies and currencies of the three republics in Central Asia, Xo'jayev tried his best to resist it. The

---

98. The details of this episode remain murky, and Soviet officials themselves were confused about the course of events. My main source are telegrams and conversations on telex between Soviet officials during and immediately after these events: RGASPI, f. 122, op. 2, d. 142 (Fitrat's arrest is mentioned on l. 73ob).

99. Muhiddinov's "'Italian' moods" were mentioned by Pozdnyshev in RGASPI, f. 62, op. 2, d. 88, l. 14; the comment about his Russophobia comes from Iurenev and is quoted by Genis, *Vitse-konsul Vvedenskii*, 317.

100. Stalin to Orjonikidze, 14.05.1922, in *Bol'shevistskoe rukovodstvo. Perepiska, 1912–1927* (Moscow, 1996), 251.

101. Xo'jayev to Tomskii (28.08.1921), RGASPI, f. 122, op. 2, d. 142, ll. 13, 14.

102. *Bol'shevistskoe rukovodstvo*, 254.

unification of the economies of the three republics, Xo'jayev argued, would turn Bukhara into a Russian province and rob it of its sovereignty. "We are against one principle—that of the unification of the Central Asian republics. If you take that off the table, we will go along with your proposition."[103] Xo'jayev also insisted on Bukhara's right to issue its own money and complained bitterly when Soviet border guards, who patrolled Bukhara's border with Afghanistan, exceeded their authority and arrested a Bukharan customs official.[104] None of it was of much avail, but the attempts nevertheless speak much about what Xo'jayev hoped to achieve.

His cousin Usmon-xo'ja followed a different path. Elected head of the Central Executive Committee of the republic in September 1921, he defected three months later. On a tour of eastern Bukhara in the company of the minister of war Arifov, he led Bukharan units in Dushanbe in an assault on the Soviet garrison in the town that resulted in several high-level Soviets commanders being taken hostage. Usmon-xo'ja went on to proclaim a general war on all Russian troops in the republic, calling on "all those who have arms at hand" to join the struggle for "getting rid of the aggression of the enemy" that had been going on for a half-century. Although the Red Army was able to break the siege, it could not capture Usmon-xo'ja who then sought to work with Enver Pasha before going over in April 1922 to Afghanistan to seek assistance from Amanullah as well as the British.[105] He was never to return. Instead, he ended up in Turkey, where under the name Osman Kocaoğlu he formed the nucleus of a Central Asian émigré community.

Secret Societies

Many Young Bukharans were said to have been shocked by the scale of the destruction wrought on the city during the invasion,[106] and at least some of them began exploring avenues of action beyond the Soviet orbit even as they sought to maximize the independence of the republic within it. Bukhara thus became the center of a bewildering array of political machinations, cynical and utopian in equal measure, but underpinned by a sense of national liberation.

---

103. The quite remarkable transcript of this meeting is to be found in RGASPI, f. 62, op. 1, d. 6, ll. 50–59ob.

104. Letter to Znamenskii, Soviet plenipotentiary (08.01.1924), RGASPI, f. 62, op. 2, d. 88, l. 2.

105. Abdullah Recep Baysun, *Türkistan Millî Hareketeleri* (Istanbul, 1943), 65; Timur Kocaoğlu, "Osman Khoja (Kocaoğlu) Between Reform Movements and Revolutions," in *Türkistan'da Yenilik Hareketleri*, ed. Kocaoğlu, 42; RGASPI, f. 62, op. 2, d. 5, l. 231.

106. Baljuvānī, *Tārīkh-i nāfi'ī*, 70.

The arrival of Ahmed Zeki Velidi in Bukhara on 31 December 1920 seems to have been the catalyst for the formation of a formal secret organization. Velidi, whom we met in chapter 2, had followed a complex path in his pursuit of Bashkir autonomy, first siding with the Whites, then working with the Bolsheviks. By summer 1920, it was clear to him that Soviet-style autonomy was not what he wanted. He was invited to Moscow for talks with the Bolshevik leadership in June 1920, where he met several other Turkic leaders, including Soltangaliyev and Rïsqŭlov. In his memoirs, he recalls that it was then in Moscow that disgruntled national Communists from various Muslim communities decided to organize outside the party to achieve national goals to which the party was not sympathetic.[107] Nevertheless, he did not openly break with the Bolsheviks but instead went on a leave of absence.[108] He attended the Baku Congress of the Peoples of the East without being invited or elected to attend. From there, he sent a long letter to Lenin and Stalin denouncing their "colonial" policies toward "the East." His main grievance was the way the national intelligentsia had been "turned into an easily defeatable class enemy." He made a series of demands: that the center cease its persecution of national intellectuals, "consider us candidates for responsible Soviet positions," and "allow us to participate, if possible, in the organization of Soviet power and party in the new Bukharan Soviet Republic."[109] Velidi ended his letter in good party style "with Communist greetings," but Lenin and Stalin were receptive to neither the criticism, nor the demands. The lack of response caused Velidi's final break with the Bolsheviks. He made his way to Bukhara, where he stayed in hiding and undertook the organization of a secret organization to fight for national liberation.[110] In this he had the support, if not the active help, of a number of high-ranking members of the Bukharan government.

In April 1921, several figures—Bukharans, Turkestanis, a few Kazakhs—formed the Union of National Popular Muslim Organizations of Central Asia (O'rta Osiyo Milliy Avomiy Musulmon Jamiyatlari Ittihodi), or Milliy Ittihod, with a common program.[111] In 1922, the name of the organization was changed

107. A. Z. V. Togan, *Hâtıralar. Türkistan ve Diğer Müslüman Doğu Türklerinin Millî Varlık ve Kültür Mücadeleleri*, 2nd ed. (Ankara, 1999), 275.

108. S. M. Iskhakov, "A.-Z. Validov: prebyvanie u vlasti," *Otechestvennaia istoriia*, 1997, no. 6: 63.

109. A.-Z. Validov to V. I. Lenin and I. V. Stalin, 12.09.1920, in Amanzholova, ed., *Rossiia i Tsentral'naia Aziia*, 289–192. Velidi recalled the letter slightly differently in exile: A. Z. V. Togan, *Bugünkü Türkili (Türkistan) ve Yakın Tarihi*, 2nd ed. (Istanbul, 1981), 403–404.

110. Togan, *Hâtıralar*, 309.

111. Typically, there is conflicting information even about the full name of this organization. Zeki Velidi, in his first account of the formation of the organization (Togan, *Bugünkü Türkili*, 408), called the organization the Union of Central Asian Muslim National Popular *Revolutionary* Organizations (*O'rta Osiyo Musulmon Milliy Avomiy Ixtilol Jamiyatlarining Ittihodi*), but left out the "revolutionary" in his account in his later memoirs (Togan, *Hâtıralar*, 321), where he also reproduced the seal of the organization, which clearly shows the formulation I use here.

to Turkiston Milliy Birligi (Turkestan National Unity). Its initial goals, as Velidi relates them, were to secure the independence of "Turkestan" and to ensure that its destiny was in the hands of "Turkestanis." This Turkestan was to be a "democratic republic" with complete freedom in matters of religion and the separation of the affairs of state and religion. Turkestan was to have its own national army and economic independence, and it was to strive to develop contemporary education and science, with direct access to European civilization (and not through Russian). Access to the country's natural resources was to be in proportion to each nationality's share of the population.[112] In later versions of the program, both the territorial limits and the basic claims were spelt out more explicitly. "Turkestan" was used expansively to mean all of Russian Central Asia—the Tsarist province of Turkestan, Bukhara, Khiva, the Kazakh republic (i.e., the former Steppe krai), and areas of Bashkir population.[113] The claim to independence was based on the principle of national self-determination and was directed against Russian settlers and the Russian state. "Turkestan" clearly was envisioned as a Turkic homeland, and yet the program made no mention of Turkic territories under Chinese or Afghan rule. The Russian political context was all important to Milliy Ittihod.

A GPU report from 1922, based on the interrogation of one of Velidi's secretaries, gives a slightly different formulation of the goals of the organization, which here included the "achievement of full autonomy of the Eastern Soviet republics"; uniting them in a federation; the acquisition of "broad national rights"; the withdrawal of all Russian troops and the formation of national armies, with the provision that Russian troops could still guard the external borders of the federation; and the formation of a new government led by Milliy Ittihod.[114] Such a formulation, in its choice of language, is much closer to the vocabulary of Soviet debates and points to a marked continuity with the vision of the Musburo in 1920 or with the aspirations of national Communists who unlike Velidi chose to remain in the party (Rïsqŭlov, Soltangaliyev). Such a vision required revolution, but a revolution on the terms of Muslim intellectuals. Such a vision, therefore, was not necessarily anti-Soviet at its inception, although in exile it certainly became so. In other ways too, mimicry of Russian revolutionary norms marked the practice of national secret societies. Milliy Ittihod had a Central Committee and held periodic "congresses" that tackled questions of practice and policy in

---

112. Togan, *Bugünkü Türkili*, 408–409.

113. A later, much longer, version of the statutes (*nizomnoma*) of the organization, undated but written in exile in Turkey in the late 1920s, is reproduced in Andican, *Cedidizm'den Bağımsızlığa*, 761–765; see also a map of the area claimed for this "Turkestan" in Togan, *Hâtıralar*, 542.

114. RGASPI, f. 62, op. 1, d. 4, l. 30 (21.10.1922).

the same way as all Russian parties had done since 1917. The existence of secret societies no doubt worried Soviet security organs (who saw in them a doppel-ganger of the Bolsheviks themselves) and accusations of belonging to them were used as cudgels to send many men to their deaths, but these societies were less alien to the Soviet order than the Bolsheviks imagined. The mimicry and the geographical scope of Milliy Ittihod's ambitions were both proof that the orga-nization was as much a product of the Russian political scene as the Bolsheviks.

The fact that Velidi could travel throughout Central Asia incognito and evade the Cheka by staying in safe houses does indicate a level of organization and some sort of infiltration of the Soviet apparatus. Nevertheless, it is easy to exag-gerate the significance of Milliy Ittihod as a political force. Velidi himself admits that there were many axes of disagreement among the founders. The Bukharans wanted to use the secret organization primarily to maximize their independence from Soviet control, while the Turkestanis sought a broader pan–Central Asian platform to accomplish what they had not been able to achieve in Turkestan.[115] In addition, we have very few concrete indications of what the organization actually did. Indicative, perhaps, was an episode that put the notion of secret counter-revolutionary societies firmly on the Cheka's agenda. In March 1921, Chekists in Avliyo Ota arrested two men on their way to Chinese Turkestan carrying letters addressed to the consuls of Japan and Britain in Ghulja and Kashgar respec-tively. The letters, which bore the signatures of an array of impressive figures (the commander in chief of the National Army of Ferghana, the heads of the "Independence Committees" (*istiqloliyat qo'mitasi*) of Bukhara and Khiva, and the head of the Central Committee of Milliy Ittihod), asked the two governments for help in terms of "money, arms and other necessary means" for Turkestan's struggle against the "despotic aggression and unrestrained violence" of the Bol-sheviks.[116] The person who claimed to be the head of Milliy Ittihod was Mufti Sadriddin-xon, the member of the Kokand Autonomy who had gone to Istanbul on one of the missions in 1918. He had been active in underground organizations since then and was supposedly head of the Tashkent branch of Milliy Ittihod. Yet the letter was written by him at his own initiative, his title to be chair of Milliy Ittihod entirely self-proclaimed, and the Bukharan and Khivan "independence committees" figments of his imagination. Milliy Ittihod obviously had no way to control the activity of the sprawling network of contacts that constituted it. More

115. Togan, *Bugünkü Türkili*, 406–421; Togan, *Hâtıralar*, 312–313, 320–321; Munavvar qori Abdurashidxonov, *Xotiralar*, in *Tanlangan asarlar* (Tashkent, 2001), 194.

116. These letters have been reproduced and translated by Paolo Sartori, "When a *Mufti* Turned Islamism into Political Pragmatism: Sadreddin-Khan and the Struggle for an Independent Turke-stan," *Cahiers d'Asie central*, no. 15–16 (2007): 118–139.

significantly, if these two letters were the extent of the activity of secret society, then it clearly did not amount to very much.

The likelihood of letters in ornate Uzbek addressed to distant outposts of imperial diplomacy producing any result was less than negligible. Nevertheless, the letters were proof enough for the Cheka of the existence of a vast counterrevolutionary conspiracy with ties to foreign powers. Cheka agents arrested a number of men in Tashkent, including Sadriddin-xon and Munavvar qori. The latter sat in jail until December, when he was released; the other accused were tried and sentenced to death. Sadriddin-xon's sentence was, however, commuted (possibly at the behest of Cemal Pasha) to five years' imprisonment, from which he escaped to Afghanistan.[117] He was to spend the rest of his life in exile, first in Iran and then in Afghanistan, a figure of some authority among Turkestani exiles, but living in dire poverty and under the suspicion of the Afghan state.[118] Ultimately, there were severe limits to what secret societies could achieve in Central Asia. Too much of the government (and all of the army) was in European hands for a secret society to infiltrate structures of power, and without any contacts with foreign powers the likelihood of underground organization bringing about significant change was negligible. The secret societies were important for the political police, however, which could see in them an unlimited source of opposition to Soviet rule. Milliy Ittihod had a more significant presence in the imaginations of the Cheka and the OGPU than it ever did on the ground.

Less sinister, but perhaps more pertinent, was the continued existence in Turkestan of some sort of sentiment for autonomy in the style of 1917. In April 1922, with the Basmachi going strong and Enver Pasha having entered the fray, the Politburo had a moment of doubt. It sent Sergo Orjonikidze, then head of the Caucasus Bureau of the RKP(b), on a tour of inspection of Central Asia, with the specific task of ascertaining "how great is the danger of [losing] Bukhara and Ferghana."[119] Orjonikidze visited Central Asia in the company of Shalva Eliava, who two years previously had chaired the Turkkomissiia. They found the situation quite disturbing. Bukhara was in a state of "nearly universal revolt,"[120] and the situation not much better elsewhere. In Tashkent, the two Georgians sought out a meeting with Obidjon Mahmudov, Saidnosir Mirjalilov, and Munavvar

---

117. "Inqilobiy surog'," *Qizil bayroq*, 23.12.1921, 31.12.1921, 03.01.1922, 06.01.1922; "Turkistonda," *Kambag'allar tovushi*, 17.01.1922. Cemal Pasha's intercession was mentioned by Sadriddin-xon himself: Baysun, *Türkistan Millî Hareketleri*, 33–34.

118. On Sadriddin-xon's life in exile, see Andican, *Cedidizm'den Bağımsızlığa*, passim.

119. Stalin to Orjonikidze, 21.04.1922, in *Bol'shevistskoe rukovodstvo*, 247.

120. Orjonikidze to Stalin, 12.05.1922, RGASPI, f. 85, op. 23, d. 46, ll. 1–6 (also in *Bol'shevistskoe rukovodstvo*, 250).

qori, whom they recognized as leaders of a "nonparty national group." These figures, connected with the Kokand Autonomy, do not appear in accounts of Milliy Ittihod, but they had apparently continued to have some influence in Tashkent. Orjonikidze and Eliava had a pleasant lunch with them, where they were presented with surprisingly expansive demands in the name of a "national-progressive Muslim group."[121] The group demanded the abolition of "the dictatorship of the party" and the introduction of "universal equal franchise of the toilers." Turkestan was to be part of a Soviet federation, but "completely autonomous and independent in its internal administration . . . like Ukraine," with control over internal security and its own currency. The republic was also to control its own financial policy and external trade, and have the right to establish relations with other members of the federation as well as with neighboring states. All migration of settlers from "internal parts of the Federation" was to be abolished and those settlers who had arrived "because of the famine or other reasons were to be gradually evacuated back." Land confiscated or forcibly alienated in the chaos of the revolution was to be returned, the right to property recognized, and all action injurious to the religious sensibilities and institutions of the Muslim population was to be abolished. The federation was to be responsible for external relations, external defense, and the organization of posts and transport and other residual realms of administration.[122] Four years after the destruction of Kokand, these demands showed remarkable continuity with the hopes and promises of 1917. The Soviet order was clearly not irreversible in the eyes of the national movement.[123] Whether the national movement would have been able to dominate such an autonomous republic, or whether they would have lost it to conservative ulama or the Basmachi, was another question, one that the authors of these demands chose not to pose.

The visit was eye-opening for Orjonikidze, who suggested a series of major concessions—the establishment of a "national-democratic" republic in Bukhara and the re-creation from scratch of the BKP, as well as a "gradual shift in Turkestan to a form of administration [based on] people's soviets, as was the case in

---

121. Orjonikidze to Stalin, 15.05.1922, RGASPI, f. 85, op. 23, d. 53, l. 4; Munavvar qori, *Xotiralar*, 191–193.

122. "Tezisy k dokladu Natsional'no-progressivnoi Musul'manskoi gruppy Turkestana," RGASPI, f. 85, op. 23, d. 108, ll. 1–1ob.

123. The idea that "fundamental reform" was necessary to overcome "the complete alienation of the toiling masses from Soviet Power and the complete incapability of the Soviet apparat [to govern]" was also raised by Sa'dulla Tursunxo'jayev, a key member of the Musburo, who also demanded in the name of Muslim Communists complete internal autonomy for Turkestan, the establishment of economic relations with the center on the basis of treaties and agreements, and the restructuring of local soviets with the admission into them of nonparty figures. RGASPI, f. 85, op. 23, d. 69, ll. 1–2ob (20.05.1922).

north Caucasus." Orjonikidze's report is worth quoting at length, for it was the only serious argument ever made in the party for abandoning the hard line of "proletarian" power in Central Asia:

> The uninfluential group of our Communists cannot bring Turkestan politically under complete control. To hold it only with Red Army bayonets is fraught with massive problems. . . . The bitterness here against us is devilishly strong. . . . The songs of the Basmachi about the defense of religion and Muslims against the Russians no doubt give rise to many rumors. In my opinion, we should have put on something of the sort of a people's congress, having tried it out first at the level of individual nationalities and districts. [We should] allow into central power [in Turkestan] a few influential nonparty [individuals], perhaps [even] if they don't have a brilliant past, proclaim amnesty, etc. In a word, begin a "new era of Soviet Turkestan."[124]

The new era never began. Stalin, who was very much the Central Committee's point man for Central Asia, nixed these radical ideas, arguing that popular soviets would work only after a decisive military victory, "otherwise agents of Enver would end up in the popular soviets."[125] Instead, Stalin shepherded through the Politburo a resolution that granted a number of concessions in Turkestan and Bukhara.[126] It called for the return of all waqf property to local control and the legalization of qazi and *biy* courts. The resolution ushered in a short-lived period of toleration of Islamic institutions in Turkestan (see chapter 7). It also initiated a brief period of tolerance for educational activities beyond the ambit of the Soviet institutions. The main focus of this activity were two benevolent societies organized by the men who had met Orjonikidze and Eliava. Ko'mak (Aid), organized in 1922, had the aim of raising funds to send students abroad (the destination, in most cases, was Germany) for higher education. Ko'mak sought donations from various economic enterprises (cooperatives, trusts, factories, military organizations), seeking a percentage of receipts from Uzbek theatrical performances and from such traditional pastimes as *uloq* and wrestling, as well as from waqf revenues.[127] The end of the year saw the emergence of another society called Nashri Maorif (Propagation of Knowledge), with the aim of supporting education and publishing in Turkestan. As with Ko'mak, Nashri Maorif was

---

124. Orjonikidze to Stalin, 18.05.1922, RGASPI, f. 85, op. 23, d. 55, ll. 1–2 (also in *Bol'shevistskoe rukovodstvo*, 255).

125. Stalin to Orjonikidze, 19.05.1922, quoted in *Bol'shevistskoe rukovodstvo*, 256n2.

126. RGASPI, f. 17, op. 3, d. 293, ll. 9–10 (18.05.1922).

127. "Ustav kruzhka 'Kumak' uzbekskikh uchashikhsia, zhelaiushchikh otpravit'sia za predely RSFSR dlia prodolzheniia obrazovaniia" (1922), TsGARUz, f. 34, op. 1, d. 1332, ll. 16–17ob.

clearly a continuation of older Jadid patterns of action: education had, of course, always been central to the Jadid project, but in Soviet conditions it had taken on a new meaning. Budgetary outlays for education in Turkestan plummeted after the advent of NEP in 1921, while the inability or unwillingness of Turkompros to fund schools for the indigenous population was a major cause of disgruntlement. Nashri Maorif therefore sought to fill the gap through private contributions. From laconic reports in newspapers, we know that in Tashkent, Nashri Maorif had ambitions of establishing four sections, dealing with lectures, language and orthography, new terminology, and financial aid for students respectively. Its biggest success came in July 1922 when the Central Committee of the KPT "found it politically expedient to send students from the indigenous population abroad for education."[128] It even promised to support the students financially, spreading the financial burden on several local enterprises. Tŭrar Rïsqŭlov, back in Turkestan as head of the sovnarkom, played a central role in this venture, having TurTsIK establish hard currency stipends for the eleven Turkestani students. The official public rhetoric about the student missions was strikingly similar to that in Bukhara, with Rïsqŭlov arguing that the students would bring great benefit to their land [yurt] when they return with their knowledge.[129]

Yet the express purpose of the May 1922 Politburo resolution had always been "to create a shift [perelom] in the mood of the broad popular masses in favor of Soviet power and the military operations against the Basmachi started by it," and it also included a directive to the central committees of the three republics to launch a political campaign "to cleanse Turkestan, Bukhara, and Khiva of anti-Soviet Turko-Afghan elements."[130] Enver's death in battle in August allowed Moscow to breathe more easily and thoughts of concessions receded to the background. The legislation on waqfs and the courts of qazis and biys was amended and greatly tightened by December. Ko'mak and Nashri Maorif had constantly been the object of suspicion and barely tolerated even at the best of times. They were both shut down by 1923, and the students eventually recalled.

It was on this stage that Enver Pasha made the last dramatic entry of his life, when he attempted, with the help of the Basmachi, to drive the Russians out of Central Asia and to establish a sultanate in its place. The attempt was utterly misconceived from the beginning and proved short lived, as Enver was killed in action within months. Nevertheless, the episode has been mythologized ever

---

128. TsGARUz, f. 34, op. 1, d. 1588, l. 2 (31.07.1922).

129. "Germaniyadagi o'quvchilarimiz," Turkiston, 19.12.1923. Eventually, eleven Turkestani students were sent to Germany, where they joined forty-three Bukharans. Ko'mak and Nashri Maorif also sent students to Moscow, although their numbers are difficult to determine.

130. RGASPI, f. 17, op. 3, d. 293, ll. 9–10 (18.05.1922).

since, either as a gallant attempt for an Ottoman Turk to help his Muslim or Turkic "brethren," or a last hurrah of pan-Islamism or pan-Turkism in the service
of counterrevolution. In its proper context, however, Enver's last hurrah appears
much less glamorous and much less premeditated than the mythology would
allow. Enver's actions were directly connected to the geopolitical chaos of the
period, to his own frustrations in not being able to play a role in Anatolia, and to
the misfiring of Bolsheviks' own adventure in "Eastern policy." Enver had come
to Soviet Russia in search of resurrecting his power in Anatolia. For fourteen
months, he engaged in an uneasy collaboration with the Soviets. By the autumn
of 1921, however, Mustafa Kemal Pasha had emerged as the unquestioned leader
of the resistance in Anatolia and the Soviets decided to deal with him only.[131]
Feeling that the end of the road was near, Enver made his way to Bukhara, where
after a few days of enjoying official hospitality, he decided to take up arms against
the Soviets. With a small entourage, he made his way to Basmachi country, where
he expected to be received with great honor. Instead, the local qo'rboshi Ibrohim-
bek imprisoned him, releasing him after several weeks of captivity only at the
intercession of the emir of Bukhara from his Kabul exile. Enver was able to
launch organized resistance to the Red Army in the spring of 1922, but was killed
in an ambush in early August.

Enver himself seemed to have realized that "it is a big illusion if foreigners like
us think they can work with people here."[132] Enver had launched into his adventure with remarkably little knowledge of the region. Zeki Velidi felt that Enver
and Cemal thought about Central Asia only in "wholesale terms," tying it to a
broader anti-British vision and having little patience for local details.[133] Mustafa
Cho'qoy was more blunt: "Enver, like all Turks in general, knew nothing of Turkestan and Bukhara, he had no understanding of the character of their internal
events."[134] What motivated Enver was not any realistic knowledge of local politics, but personal vanity and a conceit, shared by many Ottomans, that Central
Asians would automatically look to them for leadership. This was, in truth, only
the flip side of the Soviets' own notions of Enver's "prestige" in the Muslim world
and their hopes of using it to their own ends. The reality of Central Asia proved
them both wrong.

---

131. Şuhnaz Yılmaz, "An Ottoman Warrior Abroad: Enver Paşa as an Expatriate," *Middle Eastern Studies* 35:4 (1999): 40–69.

132. Şevket Süreyya Aydemir, *Makedonya'dan Ortaasya'ya Enver Paşa*, 3 vols. (Istanbul, 1970–72), 3:624.

133. Togan, *Hâtıralar*, 323.

134. M. Chokaev, "V Turkestane," ms., ca. 1935, Archives Mustafa Chokay Bey, carton 1, dossier 8, 69.

Between a Rock and a Hard Place

The Soviets, for their part, had no interest in supporting a Muslim modernist national state in Central Asia. They acted to incorporate Bukhara into mainstream Soviet life as quickly as possible and to subjugate it to the commands of the central government.[135] The suspicions harbored by the Soviet leadership never disappeared, and attitudes within the party hierarchy toward the Young Bukharans ranged from impatience to open contempt. The years of revolution and civil war had reoriented Bukhara's foreign trade. Few Bukharan merchants accepted Russian currency issued by the Provisional Government, let alone the Soviets, and as exports to Russia fell precipitously, many began to look to markets in Afghanistan and India. Trade with Afghanistan had always been robust, but the historical Indian trade had declined after the Russian conquest, so the turn to India was a sign of Bukharan independence, even if the infrastructure for that trade had to be rebuilt. The Soviets sought to undo this development as soon as possible, both because they wanted Bukharan goods (especially cotton and grain) without having to pay world prices, and because they were suspicious of the political consequences of this redirection of trade. They had purchased grain and cotton with Bukhara throughout the three years of the emir's independence; now they expected to receive shipments for barter or in return for the financial aid they offered the new government. The first trade agreement signed between the republics in 1921 obligated Bukhara to supply 500,000 poods (8,200 tons) of grain and 160,000 poods (2,600 tons) of fodder to Russia as an expression of its support for the Bolshevik regime.[136] Moscow's interest in these materials was often nakedly selfish. In 1921, with Russia in the grip of a famine, Central Asia's supplies of food and other raw materials were irresistible. Extracting resources from Bukhara became an important part of the Turkburo's duties and Tomskii, its chair in 1921, took them seriously. "I dare say that another 500 wagonloads of grain can be squeezed out of Bukhara, even if I have to pay it another visit," he wrote to Lenin in July. "If they give me half a million poods of grain for each visit, I'll make a habit of going there, even if the trips and the Bukharan banquets destroy my stomach."[137] More generally, European party leaders found Bukharan

---

135. Bukhara thus was no exception to Soviet policy in regard to the various republics that had emerged on the territory of the former Russian Empire in the years of the civil war. However, unlike the other nominally independent states of the period, such as Ukraine or the Far Eastern Republic, which had served the Soviet state as buffers against hostile neighbors, Bukhara was seen as a revolutionary outpost in "the East."

136. RGASPI, f. 122, op. 2, d. 142, ll. 16, 32ob.

137. M. P. Tomskii to V. I. Lenin (23.07.1921), in D. A. Amanzholova and O. I. Gorelov, "'Peresmotrite delo s baranami': Pis'ma M. P. Tomskogo V. I. Leninu. 1921 g.," *Istoricheskii arkhiv*, 2000, no. 4: 8.

attempts at asserting independence treasonous and a sign of the Bukharans' bourgeois nationalism. They assumed that the BNSR would subordinate its economic policies to the interests of the Soviet state and that Bukhara would supply goods (most importantly, food and cotton) to the RSFSR and trade primarily with it. The BNSR government's attempts at running its own policy provoked hostility. Immediately after the revolution, the Bukharan government refused to put all of its supplies of grain, cotton, and astrakhan wool up for barter trade with the RSFSR. "During my stay in Bukhara I found a completely unexpected situation," wrote the representative of the People's Commissariat for Foreign Trade to Moscow. "I had expected that they will speak to me in a Communist manner [*po-kommunisticheski*], from the commonality of the interests of the two republics, but that there is not much in common is clear from the fact that the Bukharan republic has 'declared private property sacred.' Apparently, it is not easy to disavow the 'sacred' even for a Communist government if that government is headed by Mansurovs. . . . In a word, the Bukharan revkom wants to conduct its own foreign trade."[138] This hostility was also replicated among functionaries in modest positions, such as one D. G. Rozhanskii, the acting director of the Turkestan Agency for External Trade, who wrote to A. M. Lezhava, the RSFSR commissar for external trade:

> From the attached minutes of my meetings with the Bukharan government you will see their position on the question of barter. The position is such that were it not necessary for considerations of a political and diplomatic character, I would bank on the complete (temporary) curtailment of all allocations from our side, in order to confront Messrs. Muhitdinovs and Xo'jayevs with the consequences of their real policy of petty shopkeepers. You will see that under the noble screen of accountability to the people, Bukharan authorities follow the principle of the primitive Uke [*pervobyt-nogo khokhla*]: "Cough up the money and take away the goods."[139]

Bukharan attempts to trade directly with Afghanistan or Germany were met with even deeper hostility, while hesitations in carrying out Moscow's directives added fuel to the fire. In Tomskii's tart phrase, "As before, [Bukharan leaders] continue to sabotage us with bread and to beg for money. The more one finds out about the political lines of the various 'Communist' groups here, the worse it gets. They try to outdo each other in their Russophobia. They make very good use of their own position and godlessly swindle us both politically and economically."[140] The way

---

138. Vladimirov to L. B. Krasin, 09.12.1920, in *Ekonomicheskie otnosheniia sovetskoi Rossii s budushchimi soiuznymi respublikami, 1917–1922* (Moscow, 1996), 187.

139. Rozhanskii to Lezhava, 14.2.21, in *Ekonomicheskie otnosheniia*, 197.

140. Tomskii to Lenin, Sept. 1921, in Amanzholova and Gorelov, "'Peresmotrite delo s baranami,'" 11.

to bring Bukhara to heel was to insist on the economic and monetary unification of the three republics of Central Asia. In May 1922, the Bolsheviks had decided to bring Bukhara under firmer control. The Central Committee created a Central Asian Economic Council with this aim and over the next two years the Sredazburo forced the Bukharan and Khivan leaderships to accept the new conditions.[141]

The BKP's attempt to join the Comintern as an independent party also encountered resolute opposition from the RKP(b), and the BKP was admitted to the Comintern in April 1921 only as a "sympathetic organization," and then quickly merged into the RKP(b) on 1 February 1922. Similarly, Moscow had little patience with the Young Bukharans' attempt at establishing their own foreign relations. In 1922, Soviet authorities used various pretexts to prevent a Turkish diplomatic mission, sent to reciprocate a visit by the Bukharan mission of the previous autumn, from traveling beyond Batumi.[142] More interesting was an episode in 1923 when a certain Abu'l Fath Khan Mu'azzam ul-Mamalik showed up in Bukhara as the Iranian consul. The Soviet Commissariat of Foreign Affairs considered it "premature," and the BKP instructed the government to have him recalled.[143] Mu'azzam ul-Mamalik refused to take no for an answer, however, and kept issuing visas and passports from his offices in Kagan well into 1924, when the Soviet embassy in Tehran asked the Iranian foreign ministry for his recall.[144] But the biggest tussle was over the Bukharan embassy in Kabul. Established in March 1921, it coexisted uneasily with a Soviet embassy across town. The Soviets were loathe to allow the Bukharan embassy to operate independently and interfered in its communications with Bukhara. In December 1922, under Soviet pressure, the embassy was downgraded into an agency. Hoshim Shoiq, the Bukharan ambassador to Kabul, resigned in protest. He was replaced briefly by Mirza Muhammad Sharif-xo'ja, until he was recalled in May 1923 when the embassy was closed for good and the Bukharan Ministry of Foreign Affairs abolished. Sharif-xo'ja and his deputy, Mirza Isomiddin refused to return to Bukhara. Instead, they both resigned and delivered copies of their letter of resignation to the Afghan government as well as the entire foreign community in Kabul.[145]

May 1923 was a turning point. The Soviets had chipped away at the Bukharan government pretentions to independence in many different ways. In 1921,

141. RGASPI, f. 62, op. 1, d. 1, l. 1 (19.05.1922).
142. RGASPI, f. 17, op. 84, d. 413, l. 11.
143. RGASPI, f. 62, op. 1, d. 7, l. 63 (resolution by the Commissariat of Foreign Affairs); TsGARUz, f. 48, d. 236, l. 46.
144. TsGARUz, f. 48, d. 289, l. 13.
145. The GPU's Russian translation of the letter (29.05.1923) is in RGASPI, f. 17, op. 84, d. 507, ll. 25–26ob; an English translation in IOR L/P&S/10/950, ff. 440–441. Sharif-xo'ja also delivered a copy of Hoshim Shoiq's letter of resignation to the British embassy; for a translation, see TNA, FO 371/9281, ff. 112–118.

twenty-one Ottoman officers, former prisoners of war, working in Bukhara were arrested and sent off to Tashkent to be deported to Anatolia.[146] In 1922, the BNSR government fired all Ottoman prisoners of war working in Bukhara as teachers, ostensibly for provoking factionalism in the country and supporting Enver's misdeeds.[147] The following March, the Sredazburo resolved to have all remaining Ottoman officers exiled.[148] The trade delegation in Berlin was abolished and the education representation put under the control of the Soviet embassy. The Bukharan government tried to stave off the end by transferring the funds from both institutions into the personal account of Alimjan Idrisi, who in turn sought to convince German universities to sign long-term contracts to educate the Bukharan students as a way of preventing their return to the Soviet Union.[149] It did not work, and in November 1925 most of the students were recalled.

The end of the Young Bukharans' autonomy came in June 1923 when Pozdnyshev, the Soviet plenipotentiary in Bukhara, forced a purge of the Bukharan cabinet itself. The Bukharan Central Executive Committee removed four ministers from their posts and exiled them from Bukhara. The four included Fitrat (education), Atovulla Xo'jayev (Usmon-xo'ja's brother and minister of internal affairs), Sattor-xo'ja (finance), and Muinjon Aminov (economic affairs).[150] The four were accused of a similar range of crimes and sins: the abuse of power (including the use of torture during interrogation of those accused of malfeasance), corruption, incompetence, public drunkenness, and pederasty.[151] (The accusers knew how to turn the knife, for a critique of drunkenness and pederasty had been a key feature of Fitrat's reformist message.) The axe had fallen suddenly. The month before his ouster, Fitrat had been elected to a commission for "struggle with the provocations and counterrevolutionary activities of the emir's agents," which was to arrange the arrests of all former functionaries and members of the emir's family still in Bukhara.[152] The GPU and the Sredazburo considered arresting the four to be inadvisable and contented themselves with exiling them to Moscow. And they contented themselves with only four victims, although there

146. RGASPI, f. 122, op. 2, d. 165, l. 51ob.

147. TsGARUz, f. 48, d. 103, l. 28ob.

148. RGASPI, f. 62, op. 1, d. 7, l. 71 (19.03.1923).

149. RGASPI, f. 62, op. 2, d. 88, l. 111–111ob; on Idrisi's approach to the German Ministry of Education, see Dov B. Yaroshevski, "Bukharan Students in Germany, 1922–1925," in *Bamberger Zentralasienstudien: Konferenzakten ESCAS IV, Bamberg 8.-12. Oktober 1991*, ed. Ingeborg Baldauf and Michael Friederich (Berlin, 1994), 273–274; Turdiyev, *Ular*, 18.

150. TsGARUz, f. 47, op. 1, d. 198, l. 64.

151. RGASPI, f. 62, op. 2, d. 51, ll. 155ob-156. The accusations were made public at the Fourth All-Bukharan Congress in October 1923; see *Ozod Buxoro*, 16.10.1923.

152. Protokol zakrytogo zasedaniia ispolbiuro TsK BKP (19.05.1923), TsGARUz, f. 48, d. 236, l. 45.

was no shortage of denunciations of the rest. A certain Narziqul Ibrohimov, chair of the Jizzakh revkom, had denounced "the whole ruling clique" for having "assimilated itself to nationalism" and for corruption and malfeasance, with Fayzulla Xo'jayev being no different from Muhiddinov. There was obviously a lot of anti–Young Bukharan sentiment around and many of the charges that were to destroy Xo'jayev in 1938 were being bandied about in 1923.[153] But Xo'jayev was too big an asset for the Soviets to squander. Rather, the ouster of the four ministers chastened the rest of the government and brought home to it the fact of the stranglehold that the Soviets had on it. After this purge, the tone of the Bukharan government's pronouncements and activities changed dramatically. Gone were the attempts to maximize its scope of action; gone too were illusions to national independence and the use of Islamic rhetoric. Bukhara had been Sovietized.

More generally, 1923 was a turning point in the political history of Central Asia. By that autumn, the Red Army had turned the tide decisively against the Basmachi. With Bukhara under control, the Bolsheviks felt much more in control of the situation. Matters of state-building could take center stage. For the Central Asian intelligentsia, too, 1923 was a decisive point. Three different national projects—those of the Kokand Autonomy, the Musburo, and the BNSR—had failed. From now on, national projects were to work within Soviet parameters and be defined by them. As we shall see, this still left a lot of scope. But we now turn to the Soviet project of mobilization and institution building in Turkestan.

---

153. Ibrohimov's denunciation may be found in RGASPI, f. 17, op. 86, d. 133, ll. 12–14. Other denunciations of Fitrat are in RGASPI, f. 121, op. 1, d. 630, ll. 13–23.

THE LONG ROAD TO SOVIET POWER

Once they had ousted the Muslim Communists headed by Rïsqŭlov in the summer of 1920, central authorities began the process of strengthening their control over Soviet and party institutions in Turkestan. The ambitions of the Soviet state were nothing short of utopian: to remake the world, to banish "exploitation" from it, to put power in the hands of the oppressed by enabling them to take on their tormentors. This required organizing society along class lines, enforcing the dictatorship of the proletariat and its allies the poor peasants, and breaking the power of the "exploiting classes." It also meant making the beneficiaries see the world in the way the Soviets saw it—to see inequality as exploitation, class as fundamental, revolutionary struggle as the path to salvation. The establishment of Soviet institutions—"Soviet construction" in the engineering metaphor favored by the Bolsheviks—was an exercise in mass mobilization that involved bringing an ever greater number of people into the ambit of politics. Soviet construction included the organization of peasants, artisans, and women, and the youth; the creation of newspapers and schools; campaigns against illiteracy; and the establishment of a new administrative structure much denser than in the Tsarist era. This in turn required political education (*politprosvet*) or at least political literacy (*politgramota*, or *siyosiy savod*, as it was calqued into Uzbek). Social transformation was to be accompanied by cultural transformation on the terms of the revolutionary state. The self-proclaimed guide to this salvation was to be the Communist Party, the seer of the future and the monopolistic purveyor of policy and advice.

Social transformation also had a clear pragmatic purpose for the new regime. It needed a constituency in local society that would support it. The new institutions were meant to shake up existing solidarities and to challenge the authority of established groups. In attracting recruits for the new institutions, the Soviets attempted to exploit cleavages in society, of which there were many, and to mobilize support at the margins of society. They found willing recruits among the youth, impatient to challenge the authority of their elders and to remake the world in their own fashion. They found supporters among women who had fled abusive marriages or the oppression of their families. Quite a few members of the new institutions were orphans who had grown up outside the strictures of traditional family life. Indeed, an activist in Bukhara argued that orphanages were "student factories" (*talaba fabrikasi kabidir*)—they produced students for the new educational institutions being established to which parents were often reluctant to send their children.[1] Soviet institutions provided the new arena in which contests over authority in local society were to be played out. And yet those who entered new institutions often saw their goals through the prisms of their own interests. Party authorities and even more so the political police therefore constantly worried about the infiltration and clogging (*zasorenie*) of Soviet and party institutions by "alien elements" and sought perpetually to cleanse (or purge) them. The party's perpetual mistrust of native cadres was to prove fatal to many in the longer term.

All of this took place against a backdrop of economic devastation. After the years of war and civil war, cotton cultivation had collapsed, irrigation networks were in ruin, and whole districts depopulated. The ruination continued past 1920, and it took several more years of military action before Soviet control would extend over all of Central Asia. "Soviet construction" was, in effect, state building from scratch, and it had to be accompanied by economic reconstruction. The center's ability to provide help was compromised by the devastation in Russia itself. With material resources scarce and funding problematic, the tasks of political mobilization and economic reconstruction often came into conflict. The task of extracting resources and productivizing the land often overshadowed the hope of redistribution.

Similarly, the legacies of empire could not be vanquished easily. Shaking up local society was one thing; changing the balance of power and privilege between natives and Europeans was quite another. Moscow's first intervention in Turkestan in 1918 had been directed at curbing the power of the European-dominated Tashkent soviet. The Bolsheviks' use of anticolonial rhetoric and their promises

---

1. O'rtoq, "Qizlar sag'irxonasi kerak," *Buxoro axbori*, 18.04.1923.

of national autonomy gave Muslim activists hope that they would act against kolonizatorstvo and, in effect, decolonize Central Asia. This hope was given new life in 1923, when the party launched the countrywide policy of *korenizatsiia* (indigenization) that promised a form of affirmative action in the non-Russian parts of the USSR. Little came of this hope. The logics of economic productivity and political mobilization clashed, but the policy also ran into resolute opposition from Central Asia's European settlers (whose numbers were augmented by new arrivals after the revolution). Eventually, the main impact of korenizatsiia was to provide hope to national cadres; its lack of fulfillment produced discontent that was seen by party authorities and the political police as a sign of disloyalty and "nationalism." Central Asia changed enormously in the years after 1917, but it saw little of the equalization the revolution had seemed to promise. The habitus of empire survived the revolution.

Between Empire and Revolution

Central Asia was tied back to the Russian state under Soviet conditions over several years after 1920. The Politburo decrees of that summer (see chapter 3) defined Turkestan's position in the Soviet state as an autonomous republic. The Politburo abolished the Central Committee of the KPT and convened new party and soviet congresses in September to elect a new leadership. At the same time, the Turkkomissiia was turned into a standing Turkestan Bureau (Turkburo), which continued to act as the plenipotentiary organ of central control. In April 1922, it was renamed the Central Asia Bureau (Sredazburo) and its authority extended to people's republics of Bukhara and Khorezm. In 1922, authorities established the Central Asian Economic Council (SredazEkoso) with the goal of harmonizing the economies of the three republics and making them amenable to central control and planning. The Soviet intent was to normalize the situation in Central Asia by extending to it pan-Soviet institutions of power. Building institutions of central oversight was one thing, controlling the land quite another. The Basmachi insurgency was subdued only in late 1923, and the Turkestan Front of the Red Army, established in 1919, was active until 1926. The army and the political police continued to have a significant role in maintaining Soviet order in Central Asia.

The new regime made a sustained effort to mobilize the population and to productivize the land from the outset. The political and economic imperatives were completely intertwined. Economic rehabilitation would create a constituency for the new regime in a region where industry barely existed and the "proletariat" was overwhelmingly European. Besides, the center desperately needed

Turkestan's economic resources. The region supplied foodstuffs to Russia in the years of the civil war, its own famine notwithstanding, but it was cotton that took center stage. The cotton economy had suffered grievously since 1917. The collapse of credit arrangements, the disappearance of the buyers, the destruction of irrigation networks, and the nationalization of all cotton by the Tashkent soviet in February 1918 had combined to reduce drastically both the area under cotton cultivation and the average yield.[2] The dislocations of the war and civil war had brought a reversion to a barter economy and the rise of artisanal labor as imports of manufactured goods from Russia faltered. Local bazaar trade had been hit hard by the Tashkent soviet's radical nationalization of property and the (attempted) banning of private trade. The Turkkomissiia eased some of the restrictions on bazaar trade imposed by the Tashkent soviet in 1918, and the advent of the New Economic Policy (NEP) in 1921 eased the situation further. But it was the agricultural sector that predominated in Turkestan, and the government gave particular attention to the rehabilitation of agriculture and irrigation. Much of the repair of the irrigation system was done through a labor tax (*trudovaia povinnost'*) imposed by local soviets. In 1921, this amounted to 2 million man-hours of work that cleared 25,893 versts (27,623 km) of irrigation channels.[3] The government also moved to lessen the burden on the peasantry. The requisitioning that had been the norm since the Soviet takeover was replaced by a tax in kind in 1921 and eventually by a cash tax in 1924.[4] NEP had a peculiar trajectory in Central Asia. Its advent saw the shrinking of funding and the transfer of many institutions to local budgets, often with serious consequences for nascent institutions. Yet the state was seldom absent from the economy. Even as the leadership worried over the continuing strength of the "national bourgeoisie,"[5] it had begun to reshape the economy in significant ways, especially in its imposition of the centrality of cotton.

In September 1921, the Council of Labor and Defense, the organization charged with coordinating the economy of the country, established the Main Cotton Committee (Glavkhlopkom) with the charge of buying up the entire cotton harvest in the USSR, supplying it to textile mills (mostly in Russia), organizing credit for the growers, and looking after irrigation networks.[6] In practice,

---

2. V. I. Iuferev, *Khlopkovodstvo v Turkestane* (Leningrad, 1925), 111.

3. *Turkestan v nachale XX veka: k istorii istokov natsional'noi nezavisimosti* (Tashkent, 2000), 440.

4. Ibid., 451.

5. See, e.g., Kleiner, "Chastnyi kapital i nashi zadachi," *Za Partiiu*, 1927, no. 1: 38–42, who noted that 61 percent of trade remained in private hands in the tenth year of the revolution.

6. *Turkestan v nachale XX veka*, 461.

Glavkhlopkom found itself also dealing in grain, which it used to pay the peasants who grew cotton. It also attempted to fill the gap created by the demise
of the banks and the systems of credit that had earlier been available to cotton
producers. The state monopoly on the purchase of cotton was half-heartedly
revoked in 1923, but the power of Glavkhlopkom remained hegemonic. At times,
it found itself locked in conflict even with the Sredazburo, for, as Beatrice Penati
has argued, its economic logic often ran against the political considerations of
the party.[7] The state's goal was to maximize the production of cotton in Central
Asia. In 1923, the Sredazburo expressed the intention of bringing in grain to
Central Asia from elsewhere "to make room for cotton" in the fields of Central
Asia. Economic plans drawn up by the Sredazburo in 1925 asserted the centrality of cotton to Central Asia's economy.[8] By 1929, when the Soviet government
declared "cotton independence" as a major policy goal, the message was insistent:
Central Asia's primary contribution to the Soviet economy was to take the form
of producing as much cotton as possible.

National Communists often had misgivings about policy set by state organs.
The price of cotton set by Glavkhlopkom was a major issue. It was indexed to the
price of grain (so that one pood of cotton would buy 2.5 poods of grain),[9] but it
seldom covered even the costs of production.[10] In 1923, Rïsqŭlov, then head of
TurTsIK, argued that the center should pay Turkestan world prices for its cotton,
but such arguments served only to raise the center's suspicions about local Communists' loyalty and political reliability.[11] Similarly, many national Communists
had hoped that Soviet rule will bring industrialization to the region. In 1925,
Fayzulla Xo'jayev had announced that "our current policy . . . is that we will
establish new factories only in places that produce raw material for the industry,
i.e., we want to avoid the economic awkwardness of sending cotton thousands
of miles away at great expense to have it processed in Moscow, and then to have
the finished product brought back here."[12] Yet it was already becoming obvious
that the Soviet economy was to be autarkic and based on regional specialization.

---

7. Beatrice Pénati, "Le Comité du coton et les autres: Secteur cotonnier et pouvoir économique
en Ouzbékistan, 1922–1927," *Cahiers du monde russe* 52 (2011) : 555–589.

8. "Osnovnye cherty khoziaistvennykh planov Sredne-Aziatskikh respublik na 1925–26 god,"
RGASPI, f. 62, op. 2, d. 212, ll. 11–84.

9. *Turkestan v nachale XX veka*, 461.

10. Iuferev, *Khlopkovodstvo v Turkestane*, 116.

11. Rykunov to Kaganovich, 11.10.1923, in *Rossiia i Tsentral'naia Aziia, 1905–1925 gg.: Sbornik
dokumentov*, ed. D.A. Amanzholova (Qaraghandï, 2005), 397. Rykunov, the head of Turkestan's water
administration, saw in Rïsqŭlov's demands a disloyal wish for "the complete independence of Turkestan." Earlier that year, Azerbaijan and Armenia had indeed briefly ordered the payment of world
price to cotton growers, but they were overruled; see Pénati, "Le Comité du coton," 558.

12. Fayzulla Xo'jayev, *O'zbekistonning iqtisodiy tuzilishida kelgusi amallar* (Samarqand, 1926), 46.

The position outlined by Xo'jayev quickly vanished, and by 1927 economic logic had come to dictate the opposite, that industrial production be consolidated in Russia and Ukraine.[13] This confirmed Central Asia's status as the provider of raw materials for industries elsewhere. The revolution's promise of radical equalization had evaporated. As we shall, this was to create a great deal of disenchantment among Central Asian Communists.

Sovietizing Central Asia

The most important institution in the land of Soviets was the Communist Party, which was supposed to be the vanguard of the revolution and the repository of political wisdom. We will examine it separately below. There were other arenas of mobilization, too. The soviets, in urban neighborhoods and in villages and their executive committees (ispolkoms), became the basic form of administration and a new form of participation in politics that had no equivalent in the Tsarist period. They were supposed to represent the revolution in the village by placing leadership in the hands of the poor. In practice, the turnover seems to have been rather modest in the early years. The party began organizing poor and landless peasants in 1920, when it established Qo'shchi (Plowman), a union of poor and landless peasants, as a way of intervening in the life of the village. Poor and landless peasants had less invested in the status quo than their more prosperous neighbors and were seen by the regime as a key pillar of support. Over time, the union evolved into something of a parallel administrative structure to rural soviets. Yet, Qo'shchi never fulfilled its promise. The party and the political police remained suspicious of its leadership. It was mobilized to carry out the land-and-water reform of 1925–27 (see below) but was dissolved soon after.[14]

Women were another constituency to which the party looked to break the hegemony of the established order. The party established a women's section (Zhenotdel) in 1919, which made modest headway in reaching out to women. As we shall see in greater detail in chapter 6, its main constituency was women in trouble: widows, women disowned by their husbands, those escaping abusive marriages, or simply those who lived in dire poverty. After years of dislocation,

---

13. Uraz Isaev, "O natsional'nostiakh i burzhuaznykh natsionalakh," *Za Partiiu*, 1928, no. 3: 13–16.

14. We still lack an adequate study of this organization, whose documentary traces in the archives are quite elusive, consisting of formulaic minutes produced by various meetings of the organization (of questionable value for an organization the vast bulk of whose members were illiterate) in the one hand and litanies of OGPU suspicion on the other.

the number of such women was considerable. Zhenotdel provided such women employment through labor cooperatives (*arteli*) and offered legal rights that had not existed before. Urban youth, organized in the Komsomol (Communist Youth League), were perhaps the most successful of all these organizations, since it produced both political and cultural radicals who will figure large in the rest of this book.

The state also organized labor and consumers' cooperatives as a way of bringing artisans into the socialist sector of the economy and of countering the influence of the market (and of "bais and kulaks") in the economic life of the region. Cooperative credit societies provided help to peasants, although the interest rates tended to be very high.[15] These measures were combined with more active persecution of bais and kulaks. Although full-blown campaigns of deprivation of rights and elimination of whole social groups were to come later, smaller campaigns of cleansing and purging were not uncommon in the early 1920s. In 1924, merchants were being banished from Tashkent, their properties confiscated, for the sins of their social origins.[16] The full effect of the cooperative movement is difficult to judge, but it certainly contributed to a realignment of the forces in Turkestani society, as merchants lost a great deal of their economic power and their cultural and social authority.

The national-territorial delimitation of Central Asia in 1924 (see chapter 8) was a landmark in the process of Soviet construction. It was touted at the time as Central Asia's "second revolution," one that would consolidate the tasks the October revolution was supposed to have begun. With the establishment of Uzbekistan, the party began to contemplate more substantial intervention in society. One of its first moves was a reform of land and water relations in the countryside in which land was nationalized and redistributed to those who worked it. There had been one earlier attempt at land reform in 1921–22, when several thousand Slavic settlers had been deported back to Russia and their lands given back to Kazakh nomads.[17] That episode was one of restorative justice in the aftermath of the bloodletting of 1916 and the land seizures by the settlers since then. The campaign proved short lived and had not been repeated since then. The land-and-water reform of 1925–27 was the first effort at redistribution of land among the sedentary Muslim population of Central Asia. The redistribution of land was

15. *Turkestan v nachale XX veka*, 455–457.

16. *Turkiston*, 17.03.1924, 29.03.1924.

17. On this episode, see Niccolò Pianciola, "Décoloniser l'Asie centrale? Bolcheviks et colons au Semireč'e (1920–1922)," *Cahiers du monde russe* 49 (2008) : 101–144, and V. L. Genis, "Deportatsiia russkikh iz Turkestana v 1921 godu ('Delo Safarova')," *Voprosy istorii*, 1998, no. 1: 44–58.

supposed to increase economic productivity, but the main goals of the reform were political, namely, to isolate and dispossess the upper strata in the countryside, deemed to be inimical to the regime, and instead to create a constituency for the regime among landless and land-poor peasants. "There is no doubt," noted an official report in 1928, "that smaller farms are economically less strong and socially tightly connected to the Soviet system; they submit much more easily than stronger farms to interaction with the planned [sector of the] economy."[18] The program, was launched first in the three "advanced" oblasts of Samarqand, Ferghana, and Tashkent—lands which had been part of Turkestan, rather than Bukhara or Khiva, before the delimitation—and involved giving land to sharecroppers as well as land-poor and landless peasants. The full scale of the reform is difficult to ascertain with the current state of research, but it seems safe to say that the process gave the party renewed confidence in its ability to ring in major changes in Uzbekistan and thus paved the way for the campaigns of 1927 discussed in chapter 11.[19]

The land reform was accompanied by a program of "regionalization" (*raionirovanie*) that transformed the republic's administrative structure. Regionalization was to serve the multiple purposes of economic rationalization, of assimilating the administrative structures of the former Bukharan and Khorezmian territories with the rest, and of bringing Soviet power "closer to the masses."[20] Not all of these goals were achieved outright, of course, but regionalization along with the land reform produced a lot of work in surveying and gathering information about the countryside that had never been done before.[21] SredazEkoso also established a Commission for the Study of the Village, staffed by European ethnographers and economists, which produced a series of detailed case studies of villages from different parts of Central Asia.[22]

18. *Dopolnitel'nye materialy k Otchetu po provedeniiu zemel'no-vodnoi reformy v Samarkandskoi, Ferganskoi i Tashkentskoi oblastiakh UzSSR: Ekonomicheskie rezul'taty zemreformy i dannye revizii Gosfinkontrolia* (Tashkent, 1928), 100.

19. For a preliminary study, see Beatrice Penati, "Adapting Russian Technologies of Power: Land-and-Water Reform in the Uzbek SSR (1924–1928)," *Revolutionary Russia* 25 (2012): 187–217.

20. The main rationales were set out by Akmal Ikromov in a report to the Central Committee in Moscow: "Dokladnaia zapiska o raionirovanii Uzbekistana" (Aug. 1926), in *TsK RKP(b)–VKP(b) i natsional'nyi vopros*, vol. 1 (Moscow, 2005), 442–445. See also Komissiia TsIK UzSSR po Raionirovaniiu, *Materialy po raionirovaniiu Uzbekistana*, vyp. 1 (Samarqand, 1926); [Yo'ldosh] Oxunboboyev, *Royo'nlashdirishdan dehqon xo'jalig'ig'a keladurgan foydalar* (Samarqand, 1926).

21. Penati, "Adapting Russian Technologies of Power," 193–195.

22. See, e.g., B. B. Karp and I. E. Suslov, eds., *Sovremennyi kishlak Srednei Azii (sotsial'no-ekonomicheskii ocherk)* vyp. 5, *Balykchinskaia volost'* (Tashkent, 1927).

Political Literacy

Yet each of this initiatives produced expressions of dissatisfaction among the authorities and the political police. Village soviets were where the new state met rural society. They had indeed been assimilated into rural society, but alarmed Soviet officials saw them as tribunes of counterrevolution. M. S. Epshtein, the secretary of the Central Committee of the KPT, bemoaned the "extraordinary clogging of the state apparatus by elements socially alien to us."[23] Similarly, Qo'shchi was under constant suspicion of the party and the OGPU, who were convinced that it had been infiltrated by relatively prosperous landholders, merchants, or mullahs.[24] The land reform did not always go smoothly. It involved the breach of all sorts of customary practices, most sanctified by appeal to the shariat, and many peasants quailed at the prospect of committing infractions against them. The party even resorted to seeking fatwas from willing ulama to legitimize the land reform.[25]

But fatwas were not the optimal ideological tool for Bolsheviks. Their hope was to educate the masses to "think Bolshevik," so to say. To this end, they fostered a program of political education (*politprosvet*). Outside of urban Russia, the goal was nothing less than that of entrenching new habits of thought in the minds of the population, so that it would see politics in the categories and the vocabulary of the new regime. Politprosvet required "mass work" throughout the country, but with a focus on the groups that were supposed to be the main constituency of the party. With the civil war still raging, the Soviets had sent out agitational trains and river boats into lands newly won by the Red Army. The train *Krasnyi Vostok* (Red East) spent several months in Central Asia in 1920. It carried broadsheets and pamphlets, showed brief films, and staged plays.[26] Over the next few years, public lectures, Red Teahouses, political clubs, reading rooms, theater, and cinema presented the wisdom of the party and its decisions to the public. The ambitions were enormous, and they habitually outran the resources available.

Until the national delimitation, efforts at politprosvet produced only meager results, especially since many of the institutions had been foisted onto the budgets of local governments or trade unions or Qo'shchi. Red Teahouses were

---

23. "Zakrytoe pis'mo No. 2 (6) sekretaria TsK KPT tov. Epshteina za fevral' mesiats 1923 g.," in *TsK RKP(b)–VKP(b) i natsional'nyi vopros*, 102.

24. See, e.g., RGASPI, f. 62, op. 2, d. 535, ll. 73–75 (1926).

25. Bakhtiyar Babajanov and Sharifjon Islamov, "*Sharī'a* for the Bolsheviks? *Fatvās* on Land Reform in Early Soviet Central Asia," in *Islam, Society, and States across the Qazaq Steppe (18th-Early 20th Centuries)*, eds. Niccolò Pianciola and Paolo Sartori (Vienna, 2013), 233–263.

26. See E. Mezhenina, *Agitpoezd 'Krasnyi Vostok'* (Tashkent, 1962); Robert Argenbright, "Vanguard of 'Socialist Colonization'? The Krasnyi Vostok Expedition of 1920," *Central Asian Survey* 30 (2011): 437–454.

supposed to be hearths of political wisdom, where posters and newspapers would greet customers. Many, however, had become commercialized and indistinguishable from regular teahouses,[27] while reading rooms and libraries were in poor shape and lectures few and far between. Nevertheless, 1926 saw a massive outpouring of new material—plans of operation, curricula for political clubs and Komsomol courses, texts for use by agitators, and a large selection of revolutionary plays translated from Russian, Tatar, and Azerbaijani—that at least made such work possible, while conferences of politprosvet activists mobilized enthusiasm around the subject.[28] Politprosvet was twinned with a campaign for "the liquidation of illiteracy," without which "no cultural work is even conceivable."[29] As with state building at the grassroots level, none of these endeavors was a brilliant success, and yet the party's sense of a new beginning and of new possibilities was palpable. A new round of elections in 1926 was accompanied by an agitation campaign backed by new materials specifically created or translated for it. Agitators went around the countryside and held meetings, including separate ones for women.[30] They pointed to the Soviet regime's leadership in the struggle with the Basmachi, its role in economic reconstruction, the promise of land reform, and the development of cotton agriculture ("the most basic source for the wellbeing of peasants") as its main accomplishments.[31] The results were seldom satisfactory to the authorities, but such elections were a sign of a new presence of the state in the countryside.

The Limits of Korenizatsiia

Korenizatsiia was rooted in the Bolshevik need to differentiate Soviet rule in the Russian Empire's non-Russian borderlands from its Tsarist predecessor. "It is devilishly important," Lenin wrote in 1921, "to *conquer* the trust of the natives; to conquer it three or four times; *to show* that we are *not* imperialists, that we will *not* tolerate deviations in that direction."[32] The non-Russian peoples of the new

27. TsGARUz, f. 94, op. 1, d. 202, l. 196.

28. "Tezisy po dokladu formy i metody p-prosvet raboty v kishlake" (early 1926), TsGARUz, f. 94, op. 1, d. 223, ll. 114–120.

29. "Sostoianie politprosvetraboty v UzSSR za 1927/28 god," TsGARUz, f. 94, op. 5, d. 62, l. 10 (1928).

30. A. Cherniyayevskiy, *Saylovlar sayili* (Tashkent, 1927), 43, 99.

31. *Sho'rolarga qoytodon soylovlar to'g'risida tashviqotchi va ma'ruzachilar uchun materiyollar* (*sho'rolarning ishlari haqida qandoy hisob berish kerak*) (Samarqand, 1926).

32. V. I. Lenin, *Polnoe sobranie sochinenii*, 5th ed., vol. 53 (Moscow, 1965), 190; all emphases in the original.

Soviet state had to think of Soviet rule as their own. Soviet rule had to be "indigenized." Korenizatsiia provided a formal mandate to promote national elites and national languages in the non-Russian parts of the Soviet state. Its reception among Russians living in the national republics was, however, always problematic. This policy set up the theater of indigenous hope and European resistance on which the cultural politics of the early Soviet period was played out.[33]

In Turkestan, Muslim Communists moved enthusiastically to implement key features of this policy. "Turkic" had already been declared a state language in 1918. In January 1923, the Turkestan government made a concerted effort to switch official work to local languages. A circular from its sovnarkom over the signature of Sultanbek Qojanov directed all commissariats to conduct their correspondence in "local languages" (i.e., the predominant language of the place where a given office was located) while TurTsIK decreed that all offices from the uezd level up hire at least one person capable of conducting correspondence in the local language.[34] Korenizatsiia also underpinned the investment in the creation of new institutions of pedagogy and research in local languages. National Communists also saw in korenizatsiia the promise of economic development, jobs, social mobility, and a sense of national primacy. Ranking Muslim Communists set great store by korenizatsiia and were personally involved in seeking its implementation. They filled the vernacular press with reports of the nonfulfillment of the goals of the program and of instances of poor treatment of locals by European functionaries. Kolonizatorstvo could no longer be invoked, but there was plenty of scope still for complaining about the conduct of individuals and institutions.

The political goals of korenizatsiia often clashed with those of economic productivity. Korenizatsiia was expensive because it required hiring extra functionaries to provide translations, training natives in new jobs, and teaching Europeans indigenous languages. Korenizatsiia was introduced just as the advent of NEP transferred many expenses to local budgets. Members of indigenous nationalities were to be hired as apprentices (*praktikanty*) but there were precious few budgetary allocations for them. The argument for economic rationality—that apprentices brought down labor productivity—was easy to make against korenizatsiia. This was often made by European workers, who dominated the small industrial sector. In 1925, for instance, only 8.5 percent of the employees of Central Asian Railways were natives. A Russian author writing in the official journal of Sredazburo acknowledged that the dominance of transport gave Europeans a strategic

---

33. Terry Martin, *The Affirmative Action Empire: Nations and Nationalism in the Soviet Union, 1923–1939* (Ithaca, 2001).

34. TsGARUz, f. 25, op. 1, d. 923, ll. 12, 41, 48.

stranglehold on the region as well as a sense of ownership of the new order, which they were loathe to give up.[35] The state for its part was acutely aware that the region's Russian "proletariat" was, in the words of the 1920 Politburo decree, "the main support of the Republic" that could not be alienated. The Soviet state's measures at redistribution or equalization across ethnic lines met determined resistance from the region's European population. Running the whole gamut from foot dragging to vocal, public opposition, this resistance ensured that the basic parameters of Central Asia's dual society survived the revolution largely intact. The preferential hiring of natives created immense dissatisfaction among Russians and other Europeans in Central Asia. Ethnic conflict had been a defining feature of the politics of Central Asia since 1916, but preferential hiring provoked a new sense of outrage among the Europeans. It did not help that korenizatsiia came in the middle of rampant unemployment and provoked massive anxiety among the European proletariat of Central Asia.[36] Underneath the dissatisfaction there always lurked a racism that saw natives as inherently inferior. As a section chief on the Turksib construction site said, "Kazakhs are very poor workers from whom nothing will ever come. A proletariat will never arise from them."[37] It was question of ownership of the revolution, the regime, and the region. As a group of unemployed Russians shouted at a korenizatsiia commission in 1927, "Russians fought and won freedom for you devils, and now you say Uzbeks are the masters in Uzbekistan. There will come a time when we will show you. We'll beat the hell out of all of you."[38] Indeed, violence across ethnic lines, from individual fights to organized brawls (*draki*) between Russians and natives, were a common feature of life in the 1920s, and the largest ones of them—such as a riot at a silk factory in Margelan in 1931 or a fight between European and Kazakh workers on the Turksib line at Sergiopol'—could embroil hundreds of men on both sides and result in multiple casualties.

When it came to balancing the disgruntlement of the Europeans against those of native cadres, the Soviet state opted to not alienate its primary source of support in Central Asia. The OGPU, which itself remained immune to korenizatsiia, assiduously tracked this discontent (which is why we have such a rich trove of

35. N. Cheremukhin, "O korenizatsii transporta," *Krasnyi rubezh*, 1925, no. 1: 48.

36. In the BNSR, the situation with korenizatsiia was unusual. Linguistic korenizatsiia was not really an issue, since most internal correspondence was in Uzbek from the start, but there was concern with the number of Europeans in economic and military organs. Bukharan efforts to redress this balance were, however, not always appreciated by the Soviets. In 1923, we find the Soviet plenipotentiary Pozdnyshev accusing the whole Bukharan government of discriminating against Russians in hiring practices and calling for an end to them: TsGARUz, f. 56, op. 2, d. 4, l. 28 (circular, 06.11.1923).

37. Quoted by Matthew J. Payne, *Stalin's Railroad: Turksib and the Building of Socialism* (Pittsburgh, 2001), 138.

38. RGASPI, f. 62, op. 2, d. 881, l. 125; also quoted by Martin, *Affirmative Action Empire*, 149.

information about it), and it worried about its political consequences. Linguistic korenizatsiia was put on the backburner, while the recruitment of natives into industrial jobs and Soviet institutions, though never abandoned, proceeded with much less fanfare than had been the case in the mid-1920s. Indeed, by 1934, when Stalin declared that "local nationalism" posed as much a danger as "great power chauvinism," even the rhetorical possibility of arguing for korenizatsiia was greatly diminished.[39] In all this, indigenous activists walked a fine line. For the party and especially the OGPU, aggressive demands for korenizatsiia amounted to impermissible "nationalism." This in turn produced disgruntlement among indigenous cadres. A comment reported by the OGPU summed up their predicament: "Korenizatsiia is an extraordinarily important question but if you raise it, then you get accused of nationalism."[40] Ultimately, korenizatsiia was a gift for the party to bestow, not for the natives to demand.

But even the mere promise of that gift was significant. It constituted the framework in which cultural politics unfolded in the Soviet Union. The Soviet state could have chosen a different path, one in which it did not recognize the existence of different nationalities or in which it did not seek to intervene as forcefully in society or culture. Even if few of the elements of korenizatsiia were fully realized, the expectations it created defined the horizons of cultural change in the early Soviet period.

The Vanguard of the Revolution

The single most important institution of the revolutionary regime was the Communist Party. Unlike political parties in multiparty regimes, the Bolsheviks saw their party representing not just a constituency but History itself. It was supposed to be the vanguard of the revolution, the keeper of its ideological purity, and the maker of its policies. Membership of the party therefore was supposed to be limited to a select few, those who could prove their steadfastness to the cause. The Bolsheviks constantly worried about the social composition of their party and about the level of political consciousness and ideological purity of its members. At the same time, membership of the party brought with it access to power and resources and a chance to reshape society. The party's self-proclaimed monopoly on power made it the site of all politics in the country. Here, too, the Bolsheviks faced the choice between reliability and purity. They needed interlocutors in local

---

39. Adrienne Edgar, *Tribal Nation: The Making of Soviet Turkmenistan* (Princeton, 2004), 97–98.

40. "Svodka agenturno-dokumental'nykh dannykh o razvitii i roste shovinizma uzbekskoi intelligentsii" (31.05.1928), in *TsK RKP(b)-VKP(b) i natsional'nyi vopros*, 577.

society, but given the complete absence of any tradition of socialist politics in Central Asian society before 1917, most locals who joined the party in the early years had their own notions of what Communism, revolution, or Soviet power were all about. Bolshevik choices were further curtailed by the desperate shortage of people proficient in Russian and having enough of a modern education to function in the institutions the Bolsheviks hoped to build.

The KPT was founded only in June 1918, but its ranks grew rapidly, so that by early 1920, it counted no fewer than fifty-seven thousand members. Few of these members measured up to the criteria of political consciousness and ideological purity. The Turkkomissiia was profoundly suspicious of the Muslim Communists it encountered, most of whom it considered to be "bourgeois nationalists." In April 1920, the Turkomissiia had contemplated abolishing the KPT and restarting from a blank slate.[41] While the Politburo decrees of July 1920 stopped short of abolishing the KPT, they nevertheless led to radical changes. One of the first acts of the Turkburo was to launch a campaign to weed out "alien" or "politically unconscious elements" from the party. As a result, 42 percent of the party's membership was expelled. Another purge in early 1922 further reduced the ranks by 30 percent, so that the pan-Soviet census of the party on 1 August 1922 found only 15,273 full and candidate members in Turkestan.[42] The numbers hovered in this range until the autumn of 1924, when a large number of candidate members were inducted as part of the countrywide "Lenin levy," which brought the total number of members up to 24,166. The membership remained youthful. Of the 12,410 full members on 1 January 1924, 4,392 (35.4 percent) were under the age of thirty, and only 16 percent were over forty. Women numbered less than 3 percent in this period, and according to the party census of 1927, only 1.2 percent of the Uzbek members of the party were women at a time when women accounted for 8 percent of the party as a whole.[43] The party was a mechanism through which young males transformed society.

The party sought early to create ideologically trustworthy cadres in Turkestan. The first Soviet-Party School opened in Tashkent in 1920 and six such schools existed in Turkestan by 1923, including the Central Asian Communist University.[44] The term *university* was perhaps a bit misleading, because intake

---

41. RGASPI, f. 5, op. 1, d. 2920, ll. 64–64ob. The same was contemplated for Bukhara several times after the establishment of the BNSR.

42. The figures are from *Kommunisticheskaia partiia Turkestana i Uzbekistana v tsifrakh* (Tashent, 1968), 32–44. The figures are not always accurate and sometimes even contradictory, but the overall picture they paint is telling.

43. *Sotsial'nyi i natsional'nyi sostav VKP(b): itogi vsesoiuznoi perepisi 1927 goda* (Moscow, 1928), 126.

44. The academic program of the first party-soviet school is in TsGARUz, f. 34, op. 1, d. 567, l. 1; on the numbers in 1923, see "Obshchie usloviia raboty TsK KPT," TsGARUz, f. 25, op. 1, d. 1351, l. 306.

of students remained difficult, and of the 405 students enrolled in the 1923–24 academic year, 50 were illiterate and 172 barely literate (*kamsavodliq*).[45] From 1921 on, the party began sending promising young members to Russia for training. This cohort, which studied at institutions ranging from *rabfaks* through the Communist University for the Toilers of the East, the Sverdlov Communist University, to Moscow University, was to produce a new generation of communists in Turkestan with a different worldview. Their numbers remained small, however, and the main issue of the paucity of cadres remained a pressing concern.[46]

The party was far from homogenous. The most significant divide was between its native and European segments. Natives and Europeans joined separate party cells, which were divided by much more than just language. The secretary of the Tashkent *obkom* described his party organization as sharply divided between "its European part . . . and its local part, comprised of the local nationality," with the two parts having completely different levels of political awareness and, indeed, loyalty.[47] Here too lurked the same sense of ownership of the party and of the revolution that ordinary European workers had. The disdain went all the way up to the top and poisoned relationships even among the party elites. To be sure, ordinary indigenous members of the party, those in village or neighborhood cells, often knew little of the party or its goals and policies. "When we look at party organizations in Uzbekistan," an official publication noted in 1927, "we see that the majority of the members of the party are not acquainted with the program of the party. This is one of the fundamental shortcomings of the Communist Party in Uzbekistan."[48] A certain comrade Volkov recounted his experience of examining a Turkmen member of the Merv party organization in the winter of 1923–24. "We started asking [him] why he had entered the party, to which he answered that he himself did not know, and to the question whether he knew if a Communist is a good person or bad, he said that he knew nothing. And to the question of how he got into the party, he answered simply that a little while back a comrade came here who said, 'You are a poor man, you need help, and you should join the party; for this you will get clothing and matches and kerosene.'"[49] Many ordinary members of the party were "illiterate not only politically, but

45. A. Obiz, "O'rto Osiyo kommunistlor dorulfununi ta'rixi porchasi," in Ziyo Imodiy et al., eds., *Komunistlor maorifi ham uning tajribalari* (Tashkent, 1927), 42,

46. In April 1923, Turkompros knew of "about 600 students in Moscow and about 200 in Petrograd," who received varying degrees of financial support from it. This number, however, included Europeans as well as indigenous Central Asians. TsGARUz, f. 25, op. 2, d. 1028, l. 147 (14.04.1923).

47. RGASPI, f. 62, op. 2, d. 470, l. 72 (31.08.1926).

48. Usmonxon [Eshonxo'jayev], "Ikki og'iz so'z," preface to *Butun Ittifoq Kammunistlar Firqasining Prog'iromasi (o'rtoq Usmonxonning so'zboshi bilan)* (Tashkent, 1927), 4.

49. Verbatim record of plenum of CC KPT, March 1923, in RGASPI, f. 62, op. 3, d. 16, l. 43.

also technically."[50] Yet, for all that, the presence of party members altered power relationships in villages and neighborhoods. The rank and file may not have been very good Communists, but they recognized the access to power that their membership of the party provided. As we shall see in chapter 11, members of the party and the Komsomol were the foot soldiers in the assault on custom and tradition that was launched in 1927.

Muslims at the top of the party hierarchy had other concerns. From the Fifth Congress of the KPT in January 1920, Muslims had held leading positions in the Central Committee of the party in Turkestan and been admitted into the Turkburo from 1921. The first cohort led by Rïsqŭlov had, as we saw in chapter 3, seen the revolution through the prism of the nation and anticolonialism. The new leadership "elected" after its defeat differed little in its background or trajectory from the Rïsqŭlov group, except that it worked under stricter party discipline. Its members too were a modernizing elite impatient to force change in their society and saw in Soviet institutions the means to do so. They too hoped that the new organs of power would work to undo the colonial legacy in Turkestan and reshape its political landscape. They too came from prosperous urban families; they were mostly graduates of Russian-native schools and had been active in Muslim politics in 1917. Nazir Töreqŭlov (1892–1937), the new head of TurTsIK and first secretary of KPT, was a Kazakh from the Uzbek city of Kokand, where his father had been a wealthy merchant. Töreqŭlov had attended Russian schools from the beginning, and having graduated from the Kokand School of Commerce in 1913, studied commerce in Moscow in the years 1914–16. He entered public life in 1917 as an instructor for the All-Russian Zemstvo Union in Turgay oblast of the Steppe krai. He returned to Kokand and was working for the oblast soviet's education department and editing its Uzbek-language newspaper when Rïsqŭlov brought him to Tashkent in 1919 to work for the Musburo. He was elevated to the Central Committee and TurTsIK in July 1920 after Rïsqŭlov's ouster.[51] Abdulla Rahimboyev (1896–1938), who also served briefly as chairman of TurTsIK as well as secretary of the Central Committee of KPT, had attended a *gimnaziia* in Samarqand and continued to the Russian-language teachers' college in Tashkent. He had entered public life through soviet work in Samarqand and, having caught the eye of the Turkkomissiia, was rapidly elevated to the Central Committee in July 1920.[52] Sultanbek Qojanov (1894–1938), a Kazakh from

---

50. The archives are full of materials of this sort; this particular quote comes from a 1926 report on the inspection of village party cells in Tashkent oblast. RGASPI, f. 121, op. 1, d. 43, l. 2ob (29.08.26).

51. Rahmanqŭl Berdïbay, "Näzïrdïng jŭldïzï," preface to Näzir Töreqŭlov, *Shïgharmalar/ Sochineniia* (Almaty, 1997), 8–9.

52. Rahimboyev's life has received scant attention from historians; for a brief biographical note, see *O'zbekistonning yangi tarixi*, 3 vols. (Tashkent, 2000), 2:75–76.

the city of Turkestan, attended a Russo-native school before graduating from the Tashkent teacher's college. In 1917, he edited *Birlik tuï* (Banner of Unity), the liberal Kazakh newspaper published by Mustafa Cho'qoy in Tashkent. He was present at the founding of the Kokand Autonomy, but afterward turned to educational and food supply work in soviet organs, rising to the head of the Syr Darya oblast revkom appointed by the Turkkomissiia.[53] Inog'amjon Xidiraliyev (1891–1929) was yet another graduate of a Russo-native school. Born in a village near Namangan, Xidiraliyev was elected to the committee of public security in his village in March 1917 and in November 1917 to the administration of the Osh city duma (neither one of which was a revolutionary organ). He joined the party only in January 1919, when a cell was created in the old city of Margelan, but after that he was centrally involved in the struggle with the Basmachi for the control of the Ferghana Valley. In 1919 and 1920, he served in the Red Army and the Cheka, and was elected to the Ferghana oblast committee of the KPT, before being appointed to the Turkburo in 1922. He went on to become the commissar for land affairs in Turkestan and was also prominent at the All-Union level, serving on the central Military Revolutionary Committee from 1923 to 1925 and traveling to London in April 1924 as part of the Soviet delegation that negotiated the trade agreement with Britain.[54] The Turkmen Gaýgysyz Atabaýev (1887–1938) was born in a prominent family in Tejen uezd but orphaned at the age of six. He studied in Russo-native schools and graduated from the teachers' college in Tashkent. Before the revolution, he worked as a teacher and an interpreter, but entered the party through soviet work in 1919. He rose quickly through the ranks to be inducted into the Central Committee of the KPT in September 1920. He headed Turkestan's sovnarkom from 1920 to 1922.[55]

For the party, the fundamental problem was finding a cohort of native cadres that it could speak with and that would have some standing in the local population. Given the paucity of Muslims with modern educations and a command of Russian, party authorities had little choice but to look to the same kinds of individuals. Nor could the party afford to waste precious human resources. When indigenous Communists misstepped, they were only reprimanded. In September 1922, Töreqŭlov, Rahimboyev, and Atabaýev were accused of failing to arrest the qo'rboshi Bahrom when he was in the environs of Samarqand. The Sredazburo

53. Tleu Kul'baev, "Rasstrelian kak vrag naroda" (29.05.2006). Available at http://www.nomad.su/?a=15-200605290122.

54. I. Khidyr-Aliev, "Avtobiografiia" (22.02.1923), RGASPI, f. 62, op. 4, d. 633, ll. 73–77. A photograph of Xidiraliyev as part of the Soviet trade delegation appeared in *The Times* (London), 11.04.1924, 18.

55. K.A. Zalesskii, ed., *Imperiia Stalina: biograficheskii entsiklopedicheskii slovar'* (Moscow, 2000), 36–37; Edgar, *Tribal Nation*, 104.

found this neglect criminal, but instead of arresting or expelling them from the party, it sent them off to work at the Central Committee in Moscow.[56] Rahimboyev and Atabaýev were back in Turkestan the following year to resume their careers. Töreqŭlov worked at the Central Publishing House for the Peoples of the USSR in Moscow until 1928, when he was appointed Soviet consul to the Kingdom of Hejaz in Jeddah. In 1932, when diplomatic relations between the new-born Saudi state and the USSR were upgraded, Töreqŭlov became Soviet ambassador.[57] Rïsqŭlov himself returned to Turkestan in 1923 to head the republic's sovnarkom and sit on the Sredazburo, his return requested by Jānis Rudzutaks, chair of the Sredazburo who valued Rïsqŭlov's administrative and organizational capabilities.[58]

"Young Communists"

The first challenge to KPT leadership of the early 1920s came from a group of self-proclaimed "Young Communists," men of even younger age, and with some formal education in party institutions. They were also part of a general radicalization of youth among Central Asian elites as struggles raged within Muslim society. In 1924, members of this cohort launched a challenge to the existing Muslim leadership of the KPT, whom they accused of compromise, patriarchy, and careerism, and pushed for more rapid change, especially in the realm of culture. Yet their social origins were little different from those of their elders. The group was led by Usmonxon Eshonxo'jayev (1899–1937), yet another graduate of a Russo-native school and a gimnaziia in Andijon, who had entered public life through journalism and worked at the Commissariat of Education from 1921. In 1920, he was one of the first Turkestanis to attend Sverdlov Communist University; by 1922, he was appointed editor of *Turkiston*, the official organ of the KPT; in January 1924, he was elected to TurTsIK.[59] Rahimjon Inog'amov (1902–38), another "young Communist," had already spent three years at Sverdlov by 1924.[60] Hanifi Burnashev (1900–38) was born into a Tatar family in Namangon. Another

---

56. RGASPI, f. 62, op. 1, d. 4, l. 4 (Sredazburo minutes, 05.10.1922).

57. Tair Mansurov, *Polpred Nazir Tiuriakulov* (Moscow, 2005).

58. Xavier Hallez, "Communisme national et mouvement révolutionnaire en Orient: parcours croisés de trois leaders soviétiques orientaux (Mirsaid Sultan-Galiev, Turar Ryskulov et Elbekdorž Rinčino) dans la construction d'un nouvel espace géopolitique" (thèse de doctorat, EHESS, 2012), 650; Ordalï Qongïratbayev, *Tŭrar Rïsqŭlov: qoghamdïq-sayasi jäne memlekettïk qïzmetï* (Almaty, 1994), 306–307.

59. Rustambek Shamsutdinov, *Istiqlol yo'lida shahid ketganlar* (Tashkent, 2001), 338–375.

60. RGASPI, f. 62, op. 2, d. 88, l. 102.

graduate of a Russo-native school, he dropped out of the Tashkent gimnaziia to enter public life in 1917. He worked at *Ishtirokiyun* and joined the party in 1919. He rose quickly through the party hierarchy under the Turkburo, being elected to the party committees of the city of Tashkent and then Syr-Darya oblast, before becoming secretary of the Ferghana obkom in September 1921.[61] Akmal Ikromov (1898–1938) came from one of Tashkent's most respected families of Muslim scholars who had been active in public life before the revolution. One uncle had been involved with the official *Turkiston viloyatining gazeti*, while another had been elected to the Second Duma as Tashkent's sole "native" deputy.[62] Ikromov's early upbringing had been unexceptional for a young man of his rank. By 1917, he had been married off to the daughter of one of his father's business partners. But the revolution got him interested in public life along rather different lines than his family, and he followed the path from teaching to publishing to party membership usual for many early local Communists. He rose rapidly in the ranks and was sent off to the Sverdlov Communist University in 1922. He separated from his wife and eventually married Evgeniia Zel'kina, a Russian Jewish woman whom he met at university. The political rebellion was matched by a personal one.

In their statement of intent, the Young Communists declared themselves to be the most "Marxistically educated" among Muslim Communists, and for this reason "against all . . . factional-careerist, patriarchal-conservative demagogic influences" in the life of the party. Their "maximum program" involved "the total emancipation of the party from the past [which] had not yet been accomplished," but at the very least, they wanted to cleanse the KPT of all members with "patriarchal prejudices."[63] In the spring of 1924, they launched a major offensive, within and without the party, on the question of women's position in society, demanding that the party move to ban the heavy cloth and horsehair veil customarily worn by women in the sedentary societies of Central Asia. In the terminology of the RKP, the Young Communists were "Leftists," and it is easy to see them as part of a general pattern of Leftist Communists who were frozen out of the party in these years. Yet their quarrel with the old guard was primarily over cultural policy. Moreover, their impatience for change was underwritten by anticolonial sentiment and by concern for the nation, and for its rapid progress that they saw as impeded by careerism and insufficient devotion to revolution, and a similar

---

61. The only published biographical account of Burnashev's life is a generic late-Soviet biography in *Revoliutsiei prizvannye* (Tashkent, 1987), 290–292.

62. Kamil Ikramov, *Delo moego ottsa: roman–khronika* (Moscow, 1991), 15–20.

63. "K obshchei kharakteristike 'zdorovogo partiinogo techeniia' v Turkestane," sent to Stalin, 30.03.1924, RGASPI, f. 17, op. 84, d. 738, ll. 170–171.

critique of the local Russian leadership. As Eshonxo'jayev wrote in his first editorial upon becoming editor of the party newspaper, "Historically speaking, the last conquerors of Turkestan were the Slavs, and Turkestan was liberated from their oppression only after the great social revolution. But this liberation is only formal. Because the proletariat is from the ruling nation, the disease of colonialism has damaged its brain. This fact has had a great impact on the revolution in Turkestan."[64] His hope that Soviet rule would cure this disease of the mind *and* alter power relations in practice was little different from that of Rïsqŭlov.

The party leadership did not take kindly to such "Leftist excesses" in the national republics in those years.[65] The Central Committee had overseen the purge and exile of Leftists from the Bukharan Communist Party in 1922. In Turkestan, the reaction was more modulated. Eshonxo'jayev and Burnashev were sent off to the Sverdlov Communist University, but others, however, stayed in Turkestan and the following year acquired important positions in the newly formed Uzbekistan. The Central Committee had long been wary of the Tashkent old-city party organization. One of the first acts of Isaak Zelenskii upon his arrival in Tashkent as the new head of the Sredazburo was to oversee the ouster of the old guard and its replacement by a new crop of people. The Tashkent party committee was put under the direct supervision of the Central Committee in Moscow.[66] Akmal Ikromov was named secretary of the Central Committee of the new KPUz, and Rahimjon Inog'amov became the first commissar for education. The Young Communists were to play an important role in the cultural politics of the years that followed.

Yet, for all of Zelenskii's doctoring, the newly formed Communist Party of Uzbekistan proved a difficult beast to tame. Too many of its indigenous members, including those entrusted with leading it, saw matters their own way. For those in the party leadership, even the Young Communists, revolution still meant national uplift, the undoing of colonial legacies, the striving for "factual equality," and perhaps above all else, having a voice in setting the agenda for Soviet work in their republics. If the disease of colonialism had damaged the brain of the Russian proletariat, as Eshonxo'jayev had written, then Muslim Communists expected the Soviet regime to do something about it. None of this was on the party's agenda. The hopes of rapid change with local participation, therefore, were not requited, and Muslim Communists did not have the run of the land. The

---

64. Usmonxon, "Turkiston," *Turkiston*, 13.09.1922.

65. See Stalin's speech at the gathering of national Communists in June 1923: *Tainy natsional'noi politiki TsK RKP: Chetvertoe soveshchanie TsK RKP s otvetstvennymi rabotnikami natsional'nykh respublik i oblastei v Moskve 9–12 iiunia 1923 g. (stenograficheskii otchet)* (Moscow, 1992), 83–85.

66. RGASPI, f. 17, op. 67, d. 220, l. 1 (11.03.1925).

oversight of the center (through the appointed Sredazburo) was complemented by other appointments of Europeans, who exercised many powerful functions. Even in the Central Committee of the Communist Party of Uzbekistan, Uzbeks did not outnumber Europeans, and the responsible secretary remained Russian. Local Russians retained a sense of ownership not just of the party, but of the revolution and the Soviet order as a whole. More fundamentally, the party remained a European space in which even elite Uzbeks were outsiders. Tensions between Europeans and locals, therefore, were a pronounced feature of party life in the period. The inability of indigenous cadres to control the political agenda or even the pace of change led to considerable disgruntlement that came out in unapproved ways. At the second plenum of the Central Committee of the Communist Party of Uzbekistan in December 1925, eighteen indigenous members or candidate members of the committee signed a brief statement that read: "In view of the developing conditions not suitable for friendly and fruitful work, we ask to be freed from our work in Uzbekistan and to be put at the disposal of the Central Committee of the RKP(b) in Moscow."[67] Thus began the "Case of the 18." The underlying cause of the affair was dissatisfaction with heavy-handed interference in appointments by the Sredazburo and a general sense that European members of the party saw native cadres as untrustworthy and politically unreliable. The response of the party was instantaneous: it struck a commission to interrogate the eighteen even as the plenum continued. The commission expelled two of the signatories from the party and cautioned the rest, assigning some of them positions in hardship locations. But if the punishments were not drastic, the party launched a campaign of denunciation of the eighteen. In the weeks that followed, meeting after party meeting all over Uzbekistan issued lengthy resolutions condemning the one-sentence statement. The party leadership quickly divested the episode of its local specificity by interpreting the statement as the work of "bourgeois nationalists" who sought to undermine the forthcoming land reform. The statement was thus a form of Right deviation, a generic party phenomenon, and this was how the episode entered official party history.[68] A very similar "Case of the 30" had taken place in the newly established Kyrgyz Autonomous Oblast earlier in the year, and several other such cases were to come to light

---

67. RGASPI, f. 62, op. 2, d. 188, l. 1 (21.11.1925); see also Zh. A. Zaichenko, "Iz istorii odnogo zaiavleniia," *Chelovek i politika*, 1991, no. 1: 90–96.

68. The resolutions passed by various party organizations were duly deposited with the Sredazburo; many of them are found in RGASPI, f. 62, op. 2, d. 188. The first public notice of the statement of the Eighteen was through its critique as a form of factionalism: Mogun, "18larning chiqishi," *Qizil O'zbekiston*, 04.01.1926; for the standard account of the episode in late Soviet historiography, see *Ocherki istorii Kommunisticheskoi Partii Uzbekistana* (Tashkent, 1974), 210–213.

in the following several years in Central Asia.[69] The tension between national Communists' hopes for equalization and the party authorities' will to control the course of action was a defining feature of their awkward relationship. A decade later, it was to prove fatal to many in the Central Asian party elite.

And yet, in 1926, the mood in the party's leadership was optimistic. The national delimitation had given the Central Committee and the Sredazburo a sense of strength and confidence in their hold over Central Asia that they had not until then enjoyed. They were ready to assert control over the cultural field that had emerged in the years since the revolution. They also sought to straighten out the own ranks of the party itself by "Bolshevizing" it. This new assertiveness led to the opening of an "ideological front" in Central Asia that was to transform the cultural and political landscape of the region.

---

69. On the "Affair of the 30," see Benjamin Loring, "Building Socialism in Kyrgyzstan: Nation-Making, Rural Development, and Social Change, 1921–1932" (Ph.D. diss., Brandeis University, 2008), 115ff.

A REVOLUTION OF THE MIND

Miya o'zgarmaguncha boshqa o'zgarishlar negiz tutmas.
(No change can take hold until the mind is changed.)

—Motto of *Tong* (Dawn), journal of the Bukharan Communist Party in exile (1920), and *Bilim O'chog'i* (Hearth of Learning), published by Turkompros, 1922

The decade and a half after 1917 was a golden age of culture in Central Asia, a period of great creativity and incessant activity, as local intellectuals poured their energies into the creation of a self-consciously modern and "revolutionary" indigenous culture. Much of the modern culture of Central Asia has its roots in this brief period. During these fifteen years theater exploded with activity, the novel made its debut in Uzbek and Tajik, and a modern poetics displaced long-held conventions of poetry. The languages spoken and written in Central Asia today crystallized during this time, as did the national identities that underlie the claims of sovereignty of today's states in the region. The period witnessed nothing short of a cultural revolution.

For the small group of young men (and a few young women) involved in it, cultural revolution was intimately tied to a series of revolts—against the authority of the past, of aesthetic conventions, of their elders, of Islam itself. Political revolt was often also generational revolt, and both were directly connected to increasingly bitter conflicts within Muslim society that had come into the open in 1917. Their claim to leadership had been rejected at the ballot box (or, in the case of Bukhara, been met with violence and persecution). The nation, it turned out, did not care for their vision of change. This experience taught the Jadids not moderation, but further radicalization. "Many among us," Fitrat wrote in 1920,

> say, "Rapid change in methods of education, in language and orthography, or in the position of women, is against public opinion [*afkori umumiya*] and creates discord among Muslims. . . . We need to enter

into [such reforms] gradually." [The problem is that] the thing called "public opinion" does not exist among us. We have a "general" majority ["*umum*" *ko'pchilik*], but it has no opinion. . . . There is not a thought, not a word that emerges from their own minds. The thoughts that our majority has today are not its own, but are only the thoughts of some imam or *akhund*. [Given all this,] no good can come from gradualness.[1]

The nation had to be dragged into the modern world, kicking and screaming if need be. Change had to be radical, sudden, and imposed, and it was to be, above all, a revolution of the mind.

The main locus of responsibility and solidarity, the main beneficiary of reform, its raison d'être, was unquestionably the nation. Commenting on the news of the departure of a young Uzbek woman for Germany for higher education, Cho'lpon wrote in 1922:

The famous Pobedonostsev, champion of the Christianizing policies of Il'minskii—who [himself] was a Rustam in the matter of Christianizing the Muslims of inner Russia and the teacher of our own Ostroumov *to'ra*—once wrote, "Among the natives, the people most useful, or at any rate the most harmless, for us are those who can speak Russian with some embarrassment and write it with many mistakes, and who are therefore afraid not just of our governors but of any functionary sitting behind a desk." Now we are earning the right to answer back not just in Russian, but in the languages of the civilized nations of Europe. . . . If the free young men of the Uzbek [nation] and even its unfree young girls begin a revolt against the legacy of Il'minskii, . . . then we too can win our right to join the community of peoples without being beaten and humiliated [*turtki yemasdan, urilmasdan, so'qilmasdan*].[2]

The revolution made sense to Cho'lpon because it allowed the Uzbek nation to take its place in the world. The same went for Sadriddin Ayni. "Do we want freedom or not?" he asked rhetorically in 1920, when the indigenous population of Turkestan was first mobilized into the Red Army. "Do we want to be masters of our political, economic, and social rights? Do we want that our wives and children not be trampled? Do we want the liberation of the world of Islam from foreigners or not? Every Turkestani, every Muslim will answer yes to these questions."[3] Becoming the

---

1. Fitrat, "'Tadrij'ga qorshu," *Tong*, no. 3 (15.05.1920), 78–80.

2. Quoted by Naim Karimov, *XX asr adabiyoti manzaralari* (Tashkent, 2008), 190.

3. S.M., "'Askarī va islām," *Shu'la-yi inqilāb* (Samarqand), 01.03.1920, 3.

master of one's rights, taking one's place in the world required regeneration and self-transformation, which was possible only through a revolution of the mind.

The new ways of thinking this revolution would create had to be both national and modern. It was the promise of modernity that drew the Jadids to revolution. That modernity was not always coextensive with Communism or the Soviet state. Cho'lpon wanted to answer back not just in Russian but also "in the languages of the civilized nations of Europe." Shokir Sulaymon put the point more bluntly: "The current age has begun to demand specialists for Turkestan to administer itself. Seeing this, and knowing that our salvation lies in knowledge, and knowledge is to be found in Europe, the youth of Turkestan has begun looking toward Europe."[4] Indeed, the magazine published by Central Asian students in Berlin proclaimed on its masthead, "Bilim Ovrupodadir" (Knowledge Is to Be Found in Europe). Recall that Dr. Muhammad-Yor, Cho'lpon's character from 1914, had progressed all the way to Switzerland in his quest for knowledge that he would put to the nation's use (see chapter 1). That hope persisted. The founders of Turkestan National Unity had hoped to develop contemporary education and science, with direct access to "European civilization" (chapter 4), and the decision to send students to Germany was part of this project. Europe remained the benchmark for modernity and civilization, even if the models of progress came to Central Asia from the Ottoman Empire.

The Ottoman Empire was no more but the Turkish Republic that emerged in its place was very much informed by late Ottoman models as they were radicalized by war and upheaval. The early 1920s saw the beginning of a cultural revolution in Turkey too that shared many features in common with what is described below. There too, a radicalized intelligentsia experimented with language and literature, "purifying" and nationalizing the former and creating new genres in the latter, and came up with new conceptions of women's place in society. In Turkey, however, modernist elites controlled the state and used it to impose reform. In a series of sweeping acts of legislation, the Republic promulgated dress codes for both men and women, and brought the latter into the public space, introduced the Latin script for Turkish, bureaucratized Islamic institutions, and secularized education. "Raising the Turkish people to the level of contemporary civilization" was a major Kemalist goal, and European forms of culturedness and sociability were crucial to the mission of the republic.[5] Although sustained contact with

---

4. Shokir Sulaymon, "Ovrupada Turkiston o'quvchilari," *Turkiston*, 01.01.1923.

5. Hale Yılmaz, *Becoming Turkish: Nationalist Reforms and Cultural Negotiations in Early Republican Turkey, 1923–1945* (Syracuse, 2013); overviews of the Kemalist reforms can be found in Carter Vaughn Findley, *Turkey, Islam, Nationalism, and Modernity: A History* (New Haven, 2011), chap. 6, and Andrew Mango, *Atatürk* (London, 2000).

Turkey had ended by 1923, these reforms were reported in the Uzbek press and continued to be seen by many as models of reform in the Muslim world.[6]

None of this sat well with the Bolsheviks. They had their own agenda for cultural change and modernization, and from the outset they sought to remake not just economy and society, but humanity itself.[7] But the enlightenment they sought, the campaigns against illiteracy and for public health and for changing women's position in society, was geared to help with "Soviet work," to strengthen the new political order that was ostensibly internationalist. Indigenous elites' fascination with the nation had little place in it. The story, then, is of a contest between two visions of modernity that was fought out in new institutions being built by the revolutionary state. In the first decade of Soviet rule party authorities had little control over local cultural production. The only people in the regime who knew local languages were members of the intelligentsia themselves, and they could see the goals of Soviet power only through the prism of the nation. It was only in 1926 that the party felt powerful enough to seek to assert full control over the cultural field in Central Asia. That was when it opened the "ideological front" against the "old intelligentsia" and began actively to marginalize them.

Yet even this formulation is simplistic. The perspectives of European and indigenous Communists differed markedly. Overcoming backwardness and fighting sloth were, of course, central tenets of the Jadid project before the revolution and emerged with redoubled force after that. Indeed, this overlap between the worldview of colonialism and nationalism has been the point of departure for postcolonial critique, whose proponents have insistently reminded us of this similarity. The difference between indigenous elites' view of overcoming backwardness and the Europeans' was nevertheless fundamental. It was a question of politics: who would set the agenda, who would implement it, on whose terms, and for whose good. For Central Asians, the goal of social transformation was to put Central Asians into the modern world, and the nation occupied center stage. For the vast majority of Europeans, the uplift of the natives was a task for the Europeans, to be accomplished on their terms and in the interests of the Soviet state as a whole. The tensions between the two groups were palpable. I explore this Soviet Orientalism at the end of this chapter.

---

6. This was especially true of Turkish legislation on the question of women, where coverage of Turkish affairs continued late in the decade; see "Turk xonimlari ozodliq yo'lida," *Turkiston*, 13.06.1923; "Turkiyada ham paranjiga hujum," *Qizil O'zbekiston*, 21.02.1927; "Turklarda xotinlar kiyimi masalasi," *Qizil O'zbekiston*, 08.06.1927; and in Tajik in "Ḥarakat-i zanān dar sharq," *Rahbar-i dānish*, 1928, no. 3: 8–9 (with a portrait of the writer Halide Edib, described as "one of the famous leaders of women's liberation in Turkey").

7. This aspect of Soviet rule has attracted a substantial scholarly literature in recent years. I have been informed by Stephen Kotkin, *Magnetic Mountain: Stalinism as a Civilization* (Berkeley, 1995), and David Hoffman, *Stalinist Values: The Cultural Norms of Soviet Modernity, 1917–1941* (Ithaca, 2003).

Meanwhile, indigenous Muslim society was in turmoil. The old culture of Central Asia continued to exist, of course, and its carriers enjoyed much authority in society. However, the sites of its production were under threat, and it was excluded from the new ones built by the Soviet state. Nor did it remain entirely immune from the cataclysmic changes going on around it. The written culture was pushed back into the realm of the manuscript while the sociability of the ulama and eshons came to be attacked in the name of the nation and curtailed in the name of public order. The force of the new order was very much with the new culture.

A New Cultural Field

The seizure of power by the Bolsheviks transformed the public sphere radically and irredeemably altered the structures within which Muslim debates took place. Jadidism had emerged in a public space built around private publishing and a privately owned press, benevolent societies, the theater, and schools. The Tsarist state remained ever suspicious of private initiative and retained for itself the right to censor the press and all books and to require official permission for the organization of benevolent societies or the opening of schools or the staging of theater. Nevertheless, within those limits, there was considerable scope for unofficial activity. Things stood differently for the Bolsheviks. Their project was predicated on the conquest of the public sphere in order to mobilize the population for the thoroughgoing transformation they had in mind. The public was to be a space for the didactic practice of the party-state.

The fundamental trajectory was one of institutionalization and étatization of culture after the revolution. However, Soviet ambitions outran the resources available. In Central Asia, that also included human resources. The number of people who could participate in the building of a new culture was limited. The nationalization of printing presses by the Tashkent soviet in March 1918 caused the instant demise not just of the Muslim press that had flourished so remarkably in 1917, but also of the lithography-based trade in Uzbek and Persian books that was about thirty years old at the time.[8] The newspapers

---

8. This is all the more interesting because lithography was not affected by the poor quality of type and aging typesetting equipment. Rather, a combination of the proscription of private trade and the general economic collapse of the time seems to have put a sudden end to this trade. A small percentage of books published in the early Soviet period were produced by lithography, but the bread-and-butter genres of the lithographic trade (religious texts, popular literature, collections of poetry) simply disappeared. On the scope of prerevolutionary book publishing in the region, see Adeeb Khalid, "Printing, Publishing, and Reform in Tsarist Central Asia," *International Journal of Middle East Studies* 26 (1994): 187–200.

were replaced by an officially sanctioned "Red press," beginning with *Ishtiro-kiyun* (Communists), launched in June 1918,[9] and which by mid-decade had grown to include several newspapers and magazines, including illustrated periodicals.[10] The Soviet press was supposed to be funded through the budget of a sponsoring organization, but the funding often proved precarious, and even the most important newspapers struggled. As late as 1924, *Turkiston*, the official organ of the Central Committee of the KPT, was seeking donations to keep itself afloat.[11] Technical problems also remained: the machines were old, type was in short supply, paper was even scarcer. Samarqand had only two presses, where the available fonts were in such poor shape that, as Hoji Muin noted, "if the typesetter's attention wanders just a bit or if the paper is of poor quality, then even the author cannot read his own text."[12] Things did change after the territorial delimitation of 1924, when the Soviet press became quite solid and largely immune from the market pressures.

Moreover, party authorities had few means for enforcing political control over the content of the press, since censorship was not a real possibility as long as those entrusted with political oversight lacked linguistic competence. The Sredazburo's Agitational and Propaganda Section (Agitprop) compiled regular reports on the performance of the vernacular press, but it was always after the fact and served at best to keep tabs on the newspapers and their editors, rather than to preempt the publication of impermissible material. The vernacular press was edited by Muslim Communists and staffed by the local intelligentsia. Not surprisingly, then, the Soviet press of the 1920s bore striking continuities with the Jadid press of the prerevolutionary period. It did not aim to provide a record of the community it served (the "shipping news" function was almost entirely absent), but rather to enlighten and reshape it. It criticized, it named names, pointed fingers, and heaped ridicule on those it deemed obstacles to change. A major landmark in this regard was the appearance in 1923 of illustrated satirical magazines (as supplements to newspapers published by the party) in Tashkent and Samarqand that offered sardonic comment on many aspects of life. Particularly significant was their use of cartoons, often published in vivid color, since they overcame the barrier posed by the widespread illiteracy characteristic of the region. The press also functioned as a forum for cultural debate among the intelligentsia, both those who had joined the party and those who had not. It was in the columns of the

---

9. TsGARUz, f. 25, op. 1, d. 2, l. 92ob (07.06.1918).

10. The best guide to the Uzbek press of this period remains Ziyo Said, *O'zbek vaqtli matbuoti tarixiga materiallar* (Tashkent, 1927).

11. "'Turkiston' gazetasiga yordimga," *Turkiston*, 20.03.1924.

12. M., "Samarqandda bosmoxona va yerli matbuot ishlari," *Mehnatkashlar tovushi*, 03.03.1921.

vernacular press that the indigenous intelligentsia debated questions of education, language, and identity.[13] The political language used in the vernacular press tended to be more expansive than in its Russian counterpart or in internal party debates. Thus complaints about the behavior of Russians, dissatisfaction with the slow pace of korenizatsiia, and the unequal treatment of natives all featured prominently in the press. It was only in 1927 that the entrance of a new cohort of "cultural workers" into the fray allowed for greater compliance with party directives in the press.

Book publishing was transformed to a far greater extent. The first few years of Soviet rule saw very little book publishing in Turkestan. The booksellers of old were replaced by a state publishing house, which became functional only in 1921. In 1922, it published 223 titles in Uzbek, 103 in Kazakh, and 292 in Russian.[14] The Bukharan government sponsored the publication of a number of books, but it never managed to organize a state-run publishing house.[15] The new books looked different—they were all typeset—and had a markedly different content than the prerevolutionary book trade. The main genres of the old trade—poetry, religious works, popular history—were entirely absent and replaced by "useful texts," such as textbooks, political tracts, and in small numbers, self-consciously modern works of literature.

The revolution also transformed the geographical horizons of cultural production in Central Asia. The Ottoman connection receded. The Ottoman prisoners of war had left Turkestan by late 1920 and were evicted from Bukhara in 1922. The international borders that had become so porous in 1918 and 1919 were strengthened again and unauthorized travel halted. By 1923, Turkish publications were no longer available in Central Asia. Although Central Asian intellectuals avidly followed Turkish developments throughout the decade, no active engagement was possible across international borders.[16] However, a broader Turkic sphere continued to exist within the Soviet Union that encompassed the Tatar lands, Azerbaijan, and Crimea and in which texts and people circulated freely. Not only were many of the earliest staffers in the Uzbek Soviet

13. For an excellent account of the Turkmen Soviet press, see Adrienne Edgar, *Tribal Nation: The Making of Soviet Turkmenistan* (Princeton, 2004), chapter 3.

14. RGASPI, f. 62, op. 2, d. 16, l. 8; for a list of titles published in the first decade after the revolution, see *Sovet O'zbekistoni kitobi (1917–1927 yy.): bibliografik ko'rsatkich* (Tashkent, 1976).

15. Printing facilities in Bukhara remained scarce and some of these books were printed in Berlin. Plans for establishing a state publishing house were drawn up, but nothing seems to have come of them; see TsGARUz, f. 48, op. 1, d. 64, ll. 4–5.

16. Adeeb Khalid, "Central Asia between the Ottoman and the Soviet Worlds," *Kritika* 12 (2011), 468–470.

press Tatars, but translations of Tatar books accounted for a significant portion of new Soviet publishing in Central Asia in the 1920s. Many of the earliest
works of political literature in Uzbek were translated from or through Tatar,
while translations of Tatar and Azeri belles lettres provided a large portion of
modern prose in Uzbek. Tatar, Crimean, and Azerbaijani literatures witnessed
currents of cultural radicalism like the ones described here for Central Asia in
the decade after the revolution. These developments were interconnected and
informed each other. Orthographic reform and the advocacy of Latinization
(see chapter 8) were perhaps the most clear examples of this Turkic sphere
in operation, but it worked in other ways too. Fitrat, during his tenure as the
minister of education in the BNSR, corresponded with Muslim figures across
the Soviet Union.[17] Baku was an important destination for Uzbek students.
In 1926, Bekir Çobanzade, the Crimean Tatar linguist, lectured at the Higher
Pedagogical Institute in Samarqand where Fitrat also taught. Çobanzade knew
Fitrat from Istanbul, where he too had studied before completing his doctorate
in Budapest.[18]

Moscow was a new source of inspiration. Before 1917, only a very few
Central Asians had studied in Petersburg or Moscow. From 1921 on, Soviet
authorities began sending Turkestani students to Moscow in a systematic
fashion. Many went to rabfaks, and there was a sizable Turkestani contingent
at the Communist University for the Toilers of the East established in 1921.
The Bukharan government had established its own House of Learning in
Moscow as a staging ground for Bukharan students to enter Russian higher
education; it was inherited by Uzbekistan and continued to function late
into the decade. Others studied at regular universities and institutes, and
not just in technical fields. Nor was it just members of the Communist Party
who studied in Moscow. Abdulla Qodiriy attended the Briusov Institute of
Journalism during the 1924–25 academic year, while Cho'lpon spent three
years (1924–27) with the Uzbek Drama Studio in Moscow. Fitrat was in
Moscow for fourteen months of exile in 1923 and 1924. Botu spent six years
there, as he attended first a rabfak and then Moscow State University. Most
of those who went already knew Russian, but others learned Russian in this
fashion. These contacts brought new influences and new genres into Uzbek

17. This correspondence is gathered together in TsGARUz, f. 56, op. 1, d. 61.

18. Begali Qosimov, *Maslakdoshlar* (Tashkent, 1994), 133. On Çobanzade, see İsmail Otar,
Kırımlı Türk Şair ve Bilgini Bekir Sıdkı Çobanzade (Istanbul, 1999); "Choban-zade," *Liudi i sud'by*,
http://memory.pvost.org/pages /choban.html.

literature. The poet Oltoy (Bois Qoriyev) pioneered Futurist poetry in Uzbek.[19] Cho'lpon translated Shakespeare and Tagore, Chekhov and Gogol into Uzbek, while the drama studio brought new techniques to the Uzbek stage. It was not just new genres that came from Moscow, but new political attitudes and vocabularies.

New Forms, New Content

Theater had been a major locus of reform for the Jadids. In the words of Mahmudxo'ja Behbudiy, it was a "house of admonition" (*ibratxona*) where society could take stock of its ills,[20] its very presence a sign and a cause of progress. It was equally dear to the Soviets, who saw in traveling theater troupes an important way of spreading their message. Although private groups continued to stage theater in Turkestan until 1921, they could count on support from the Soviets. In 1918, the Tashkent old-city soviet requisitioned numerous properties on behalf of the Turon Fine Arts Union, the theater troupe established by Abdulla Avloniy in 1916,[21] and its ispolkom continued to support various groups through these lean years. In fact, the years between 1917 and 1921 saw a burst of activity in theater as numerous plays were staged in Tashkent and other cities. In 1921, Turkompros took over all theater production. The incomplete evidence of the periodical press would indicate that productivity of Tashkent's theater scene suffered in the immediate term, as the range of topics shrunk substantially, but in the medium to long term the takeover helped a great deal in professionalizing local theater. Theater had emerged in Turkestan through the efforts of enthusiasts, very few of whom had any training in theatrical technique. Although the first cohort produced such stalwarts as Hamza and Mannon Uyg'ur, local theater remained largely amateur. In 1924, however, Turkompros received funding to establish an Uzbek Drama Studio in Moscow, and over the next few years a number of actors and directors (Cho'lpon among them) studied in Moscow.

The press created a new kind of prose, using a language much closer to the spoken word and with a conscious avoidance of the various kinds of ornamentation (rhymed prose, complex metaphors, doubled adjectives) that earlier authors

---

19. Oltoy's poetry remains scattered in the pages of the press of the time and has never been republished. At the time, Oltoy faced considerable opposition and mockery. In a defiant rebuttal, Oltoy argued that all languages see new genres as they develop, and that opposition to novelty was futile, for "the epoch belongs to the youth." Oltoy, "Futurizm to'g'risida," *Turkiston*, 02.11.1924.

20. Mahmud Xo'ja [Behbudiy], "Tiyotir nedur?" *Oyina*, 10.05.1914, 550–53.

21. GAgT, f. 12, d. 12, ll. 7ob-8, 107, 113ob.

FIGURE 1. Abdulla Qodiriy in 1926. The picture bears an autograph dated 4 March 1926.

had routinely used to show their virtuosity. Out of this journalism arose the modern short story and eventually the novel, and no one was more important in the creation of modern prose literature than Abdulla Qodiriy in Uzbek and Sadriddin Ayni in Tajik. Qodiriy was a Tashkent native, the son of a man of modest means but high cultural capital, who had attended a Russian-native school. He had appeared in print (and one of his plays had been staged) before the revolution, but he really made his mark as a writer in the 1920s. He worked for various Tashkent newspapers and joined the satirical magazine *Mushtum* (The Fist) when it was launched in 1923. His satirical pieces, written under a variety of pseudonyms, broke new ground in the use of the Uzbek language. For the first time in Uzbek letters, he committed the living language of the street to paper and did more than most to turn literary Uzbek away from the models of the Persianate past to the Uzbek present. Satire was a potent form of criticism, and nothing and no one escaped the lash of Qodiriy's pen—mullahs, eshons, bureaucrats, fellow journalists, and even Communists, all suffered at his hands. All along, he was working on what would become his masterpiece, the novel *O'tkan kunlar* (Bygone Days), the first part of which appeared in 1926, and which was to be the founding document of modern Uzbek prose literature.

But if theater took off and a new prose made its presence felt, poetry retained its place through this tumultuous age. Every newspaper and every magazine carried poetry, and it was in verse that authors reminded readers of their opportunities and obligations in the new age. Like the prose, the poetry was new in its form as well as its content. A great deal of it was self-consciously a revolt against the conventions of Chaghatay poetry and its Persianate heritage; poets experimented with new rhymes and meters and imagery. The vocabulary was also remarkably new, with a conscious effort to eschew Persian and Arabic words, many long indigenized and some irreplaceable in Uzbek or Persian. Poetry was to be national, and it was nationalized by a cohort of young poets, of whom Fitrat and Cho'lpon were the acknowledged masters. The anthology, *Young Uzbek Poets*, edited by the two was both a manifesto and a showcase of the work of a new generation of poets.[22] We will discuss this poetry in chapter 8; suffice it to note here its novelty and its devotion to the nation.

New Faces

If the revolution saw the coming of age of writers who had been active before 1917, it also witnessed the entry into the world of letters of a new cohort of authors with similar outlooks. This early revolutionary cohort included figures such as G'ozi Yunus, Elbek, and Botu. The career of G'ozi Yunus (born in 1889) exhibits all the convolutions of the revolutionary era. In 1918, he had been deeply involved in the struggle against Soviet power and had traveled to Istanbul that summer in search of Ottoman help (see chapter 2). He recovered quickly from the collapse of those hopes, and upon his return to Turkestan joined the KPT and became an active member of the Musburo.[23] He was active in the press in 1920, when he wrote a number of scathing attacks on kolonizatorstvo. He also launched a private publishing venture, perhaps unique for the Soviet period, which put numerous literary works, including several of Fitrat's pieces, on the market. After 1920, he continued to publish in the press and was one of the founding figures at *Mushtum*. He also translated numerous works from Russian, Tatar, and Azerbaijani into Uzbek. By the middle of the decade, however, his past had caught up with him. He was pushed out of journalism and for the rest of his career worked quietly as a translator and a copyeditor, as well as doing historical work.[24] Elbek was born Mashriq Yunus o'g'li in 1898 and attended

---

22. *Yosh o'zbek shoirlari* (Tashkent, 1922).

23. GARF, f. 1235, op. 94, d. 587, l. 159.

24. There exists no adequate account of G'ozi Yunus's life; there is an overly schematic entry on him in the *O'zbekiston milliy entsiklopediyasi* (Tashkent, 2006), 11:235. The version presented here is based on materials encountered in the course of researching this book; a brief mention of him as a prominent Orientalist in the 1930s is found in Nicholas Poppe, *Reminiscences* (Bellingham, WA, 1983), 266.

the Namuna new-method school run by Munavvar qori. He entered public life in 1916 as a teacher and was part of the same circle as G'ozi Yunus. By 1922, he was prominent enough as a poet to be included in *Young Uzbek Poets*, the anthology edited by Fitrat. He went on to write numerous textbooks and primers, as well as being a poet of considerable talent. His repertoire also included numerous plays as well as scholarly work on the codification and orthography of the Uzbek language.[25]

Botu (Muhammad Hodiyev) was in many ways a transitional figure. Born in 1904, he was a prodigy who by the age of sixteen was making speeches on questions of language and orthography and who had appeared in print alongside Fitrat and Cho'lpon before he was eighteen. His trajectory until that point had differed little from that of any other Jadids. He had been a member of the Izchilar (Ottoman-style boy scouts) in 1918 and of Chig'atoy Gurungi in 1919. His pen name Botu referred, of course, to Chinggis Khan's grandson and evoked the Turko-Mongol legacy of Turkestan. In 1921, Botu was named editor of *Farg'ona* (Ferghana), the oblast newspaper, and later the same year he was sent off to Moscow. He continued to write poetry in the modernist style of the Young Uzbek Poets, but his politics drifted away from those of his mentors. His trajectory from then on had much more in common with a different cohort of writers whom we will encounter in chapter 10, and who were to denounce the prerevolutionary and the early-revolutionary intelligentsia. Nevertheless, the vitality of Botu's poetry was an integral feature of the cultural landscape of Uzbekistan of the 1920s.

Other names largely disappeared from literary life. The poet Tavallo joined the party and entered Soviet work in 1918. He went on to hold a number of important positions in the Tashkent city government and had a stint with the Cheka, but he hardly published anything after 1917.[26] Abdulla Avloniy, one of the most prominent Jadids before 1917, when he published poetry, textbooks, and plays, was a leading light in Tashkent's nascent theater scene and wrote very little after the revolution. Other than a few pieces in *Mushtum*, his public life revolved around teaching. Perhaps the most remarkable disappearance was that of Hamza, a very prominent Jadid figure before the revolution. The year 1917 was the apogee of his prominence, when he played a prominent role in politics in his native Kokand. The conflicts of the period cost him dear, however, and threats to his safety led to him to flee Kokand for the safety of the town of

---

25. In addition to Elbek's own publications, my main source for this sketch is an exculpatory autobiographical account he submitted to the Sredazburo in 1929, when he was faced with the first round of what would prove to be fatal denunciations: "Ariza," RGASPI, f. 62, op. 2, d. 1999, ll. 65–68 (27.04.1929). See also Haydarali Uzoqov, "Erk yo'lida erksiz ketgan fidoiy," in Elbek, *Tanlangan asarlar* (Tashkent, 1999), 5–20.

26. RGASPI, f. 121, op. 1, d. 514, l. 40 (autobiographical note by Tavallo); Begali Qosimov, *Milliy uyg'onish: jasorat, ma'rifat, fidoiylik* (Tashkent, 2002), 307–315.

Turkestan, where Saidnosir Mirjalilov provided him shelter. Hamza spent the crucial winter of 1917–18 tutoring Mirjalilov's daughters in music and poetry and flirting with one of them.[27] He returned to Ferghana in 1918 and threw his energies into the theater scene, undertaking a number of productions with the Karl Marx and Turk Kuchi troupes that were backed by the agitprop sections of the party and the Red Army. Yet, after 1920, Hamza's career went into a decline: his productivity dried up and he fell into grinding poverty. In 1922, he went to Xorazm People's Soviet Republic to write a commissioned play on the recent "revolution" there. He finished the project and stayed on for two years as the principal of a boarding school in Xo'jayli. There is every indication in Hamza's private papers that he hated the job, both its isolation and the bureaucratic work that it involved, but had to stay on for the sake of the salary. He managed to leave Xorazm in October 1924, only to end up unemployed and indebted and in poor health to boot. He lived out a couple of years in total obscurity in the village of Avvalkent in Ferghana, before an approach to Yo'ldosh Oxunboboyev, the head of Uzbekistan's government and a fellow Ferghana villager, netted Hamza a contract for a number of revolutionary plays and brought him back into public life. Although he wrote several plays after 1918, many of which were produced and found success, Hamza was barely visible in the press of the 1920s, and he did not publish a volume under his name in the Soviet period.

The Jadids did not command a monopoly on the new cultural field, however. The editorships of newspapers and magazines were political appointments made by TurTsIK and approved by the KPT. They brought into the cultural field young men of a rather different orientation, even if their attitudes about culture had much in common with those of the Jadids. Nazir Töreqŭlov (To'raqulov), who succeeded Turar Rïsqŭlov as head of TurTsIK, was very much a Jadid. He was working for the Kokand oblast soviet's Education Department and editing its Uzbek-language newspaper when Rïsqŭlov brought him to Tashkent in 1919 to work for the Musburo.[28] His elevation first to commissar of education in April 1920 and then to TurTsIK altered his circumstances. He could now make appointments to editorships (and indeed be editor himself—he edited *Inqilob* [Revolution], the "thick journal" published by the Uzbek Education Commission, as well as the Kazakh newspaper *Aq jol* [New Path]), but he found

---

27. Zarifa Saidnosirova, *Oybegim mening: xotiralar*, ed. Naim Karimov (Tashkent, 1994), 32–38.

28. Rahmanqŭl Berdïbay, "Näzïrdïng jŭldïzï," in Näzir Töreqŭlov, *Shïgharmalar/Sochineniia* (Almaty, 1997), 8–9.

FIGURE 2.   Members of the Uzbek intelligentsia on the eve of the ideological front. Seated from left to right: Sadriddin Ayni, Shokirjon Rahimiy, Rahimjon Inog'amov, Davlat Roziyev, Abdurauf Fitrat, Abdulahad Burhon; standing, Said Ahroriy, Abdulla Alaviy, G'ozi Yunus, Zafar Nasriy, Mahmud Suboy, Elbek, Vadud Mahmud, Qayum Ramazon. *Maorif va o'qutg'uvchi*, 1926, no. 5: 51.

himself subject to party discipline and accountable for their actions to political authorities. The younger men who took charge of the Soviet press belonged to the same social world as the Jadids and shared many of their concerns. Abdulhay Tojiyev, one of the Young Communists, was responsible for launching *Mushtum*. He had been Munavvar qori's student at Tashkent's Namuna school. Usmonxon Eshonxo'jayev, who found himself editing *Turkiston*, the mouthpiece of the Central Committee, at the age of twenty-two had been a schoolmate of Cho'lpon's. But they operated in different circumstances. Newspaper editors could lose their positions for permitting the publication of politically inadmissible materials. They therefore had to make an effort to "speak Bolshevik" and to couch their views in a vocabulary acceptable to the party. In many cases they created the Uzbek-language vocabulary of Bolshevism themselves. As we shall see, the relations between the Jadids and those who entered public life through the party were often fraught.

The Struggle over Muslim Education

It was in the realm of education that the revolution aroused the greatest enthusiasm among the intelligentsia, and the greatest opposition to it. In Tashkent in 1917, one of the first acts of the Shuroi Islomiya was to establish a schools commission with the goal of reforming and regulating Muslim schools.[29] In the ensuing months the Jadids organized numerous intensive courses for training new teachers and opened many new schools. As education reform became a point of contention, the madrasas emerged as bastions of the Ulamo Jamiyati. Education was therefore the area where the Jadids embraced Soviet institutions most thoroughly. The Tashkent old-city soviet, organized in March 1918, provided the first institutional base for the reform of education. Munavvar qori was the most important figure in this transition of the Jadids to Soviet institutions. In 1917, he took the lead in trying to reform schools, only to be snubbed by the ulama after their victory in Tashkent's municipal elections in July. The following spring, he turned to the old-city soviet, and in July 1918 was chair of a newly formed Teachers Union. In February 1919, he became head of the Turkic section of Turkompros and the chief of its waqf section.[30] These sections operated largely independently of the commissariat as a whole and, in conjunction with the ispolkoms of old-city soviets, provided the institutional mainstay of modern Muslim education. The network of Muslim schools that emerged was based on existing schools of the Jadids, the old Russo-native schools, as well as a number of new schools created in 1918 and 1919. For a decade and a half before the revolution, the Jadids had exhorted the wealthy in their community to provide benevolent support for new-method schools. Now, they used, via the soviets, "revolutionary" methods to requisition or confiscate property for new schools.[31] As many as seventy schools were opened in Tashkent between 1917 and 1920.[32] Kokand had twenty elementary schools and ten other educational institutions for its Muslim population in August 1919,[33] while in March of the same year, Samarqand uezd had nine functioning "Turkic" schools (and

29. Khalid, *Politics of Muslim Cultural Reform*, 253.

30. TsGARUz, f. 34, op. 1, d. 236, l. 6. Turkompros created the Turkic section in October 1918; see "Turk shu'basining xizmatlari," *Maorif*, no. 3 (27.12.1918), 1.

31. GAgT, f. 12, d. 9, ll. 64–66 (1918); d. 24, ll. 142, 302 (1919). The Tashkent old-city ispolkom had established a Commission for Finding Premises for Schools (*Maktabga joy topuv kamisiyasi*) in the autumn of 1918; ibid., d. 4, l. 141. For an example of confiscations from Andijon, see TsGARUz, f. 34, op. 1, d. 48, ll. 44, 45, 50 (Sept. 1918). Similar requisitions also took place on behalf of Turon Fine Arts Union, which acquired a building for use as a lecture hall and materials for its theater production through such means; GAgT, f. 12, d.. 12, ll. 7ob-8; d. 4, l. 107.

32. Mo'minjon Muhammadjon o'g'li, "Maktab va o'qituvchilarning ichki ko'rinishi," *Ishtiroki-yun*, 07.03.1920

33. TsGARUz, f. 34, op. 1, d. 222, ll. 72–72ob.

another thirty-five were planned for the coming year). As of 1 May 1919, Khujand uezd had thirty-seven schools, of which thirty-one had been opened in the previous year.[34] The issue of women's education received a great deal of attention, even if action lagged behind. Four girls' schools existed in Tashkent in 1919,[35] and courses for women teachers had been organized, the most important of them housed in the *hovli* of one Valixo'ja in Shayxontahur.[36]

The names chosen for the schools are indicative of the fact that they were seen as both national and revolutionary. In 1923, the old city of Tashkent had schools called Turon, Chig'atoy (Chaghatay), and Muxtoriyat (Autonomy). Others were named after poets of the Turkic canon such as Lutfi and Fuzuli (but also the Persian poet Sa'di); great scholars of the past from Turkestan such as Farabi and Ibn Sina; scions of the Timurid era such as Navoiy, Bobur, and Ulugh-bek; Uzbek poets of the recent past such as Nodira and Furqat; the Jadids Gasprinskiy and Behbudiy, and the Ottoman reformers Midhat Pasha and Namık Kemal. One school was named after Karl Marx.[37] Revolution and world-historical responsibilities were intertwined with the nation in the argument for the importance of education. As one enthusiast wrote, "The toilers of Turkestan have two historic duties [*vazifa*]: to call the whole East to rise up against imperialism and to spread the common task [*maslak*] to the whole East. But they are not aware of these duties. How can their duties be explained to such ignorant masses [*nodon avom*]?"[38]

The rapid expansion of new-method schools required new teachers. Turkompros funded intensive short-term courses for training teachers (one course in the spring of 1919 enrolled two hundred men),[39] but many of the jobs were taken up by Ottoman POWs (see chapter 2). They put their stamp on the schools they ran, which were characterized by an emphasis on physical education and martial music in the tradition of late Ottoman military academies. Ottoman officers also introduced scouting to Turkestan and formed the first troops of Izchilar (scouts) in Tashkent in late 1918.[40] This military focus produced quite a bit of criticism. Cho'lpon wrote that in such schools "nothing is heard other than the *boom boom* of cold, soulless martial music," and Elbek, while thanking "our brothers in blood and faith" for taking on the duty of teaching, criticized the amount of drill and

34. TsGARUz, f. 34, op. 1, d. 141, ll. 19, 36.
35. *Ishtirokiyun*, 06.02.1919.
36. TsGARUz, f. 34, op. 1, d. 235, l. 1.
37. GAgT, f. 12, d. 168 (late 1923).
38. A.H., "Umumiy ahvol va Turkiston mehnatkash avomi," *Ishtirokiyun*, 11.11.1919.
39. *Ishtirokiyun*, 19.02.1919; TsGARUz, f. 34, op. 1, d. 347, l. 5.
40. *Ishtirokiyun*, 23.10.1918, 15.02.1919.

music in their schools.[41] The Ottoman Turks disappeared from the scene by mid-1920, and the new vernacular schools went back to the Jadid model. Bolshevik innovations such as the comprehensive labor school (*edinaia trudovaia shkola*) seem to have been restricted to Russian schools only. Muslim schools were also exempted from the edict on the separation of church and school, one of the foundational decrees of Soviet power. "In view of the lack of consciousness of the Muslim popular masses and the comparatively low level of their culture," Turkompros permitted religious instruction in Muslim schools as long as it was not provided by a mullah.[42]

The enthusiasms of the early years soon ran into reality. The advent of NEP in 1921 brought a period of budget cuts and job slashing that led to a precipitous decline in the number of schools in Turkestan. The network of official schools contracted significantly even before Narkompros decided in 1923 to shunt elementary and middle schools off to local budgets. Turkestan's sovnarkom pointed out to Moscow that new budget allocations for education in Turkestan were much lower than those in the Tsarist period and warned of "complete disorder in educational affairs."[43] The number of schools shrank—Tashkent in 1923 had only thirty-eight elementary schools—and many schools resorted to the prerevolutionary practice of seeking donations or holding benefit concerts to support themselves.[44] The sovnarkom even contemplated making a virtue out of necessity and organizing a campaign "with an agitational goal" of raising funds for students and schools in the countryside.[45] State schools taught only 6 percent of school-age children, and their quality remained poor, especially in the countryside: hastily trained teachers, poor accommodations, and meager resources all combined to produce a miserable situation. "Parents don't want to send their children to Soviet schools," an inspector found in Samarqand oblast in 1922, "because the children never learn anything in a year and a half, whereas at a maktab they would."[46] In 1927, Uzbekistan's Commissariat of Education admitted

41. Cho'lpon, "Faryod!" *Ishtirokiyun*, 27.20.1920; Elbek, "Eski shahar maktablari to'g'risida bir kengash," *Ishtirokiyun*, 20.03.1920. These criticisms produced robust defenses of the schools by teachers and students alike: Osmanlı Türklerinden Nurî, "İlk ve son sözüm," *Ishtirokiyun*, 25.03.1920; O'rta Rishodiya hayron qolash talabalari, "O'rta maktabdan bir tovush," *Ishtirokiyun*, 07.04.1920; "Haqsizlik," *Ishtirokiyun*, 18.04.1920.

42. TsGARUz, f. 34, op. 1, d. 40, l. 37 (09.11.1918).

43. TsGARUz, f. 17, op. 1, d. 336, l. 182 (1923).

44. Such was the fate of the teacher training college in Samarkand, with an enrollment of 190 in 1922; see the report by its principal, Vadud Mahmud, in TsGARUz, f. 34, op. 1, d. 1011, l.64 (29.06.1922). A list of Tashkent's schools is in GAgT, f. 12, d. 168.

45. TsGARUz, f. 25, op. 1, d. 1414, l. 380 (27.10.1923).

46. TsGARUz, f. 21, op. 1, d. 168, l. 1 (31.12.1922).

that in many of its schools "children sit on the cold mud floor to study. It even happens that the condition of some of the maktabs is better than that of our labor schools."[47]

The situation was even worse in Bukhara. The BNSR government began with great enthusiasm, opening elementary schools and seeking to establish formal curricula in the city's famed madrasas.[48] In October 1920, the Ministry of Education even decreed school attendance compulsory for all children between the ages of seven and seventeen![49] Of course, neither financial, nor personnel resources at hand were remotely enough for such ambitious goals. The Ministry of Education routinely received a fraction of the funds it asked for.[50] It sent students to Tashkent and to Turkey to be trained as teachers and established two three-year teachers colleges (in Bukhara and Chorjuy), with teachers recruited from Azerbaijan and Tatarstan.[51] Textbooks were almost entirely lacking, and teachers used whichever materials they could lay their hands on, including prerevolutionary primers from Kazan, Baku, or even the Ottoman Empire.[52] But the biggest problem was attracting students to the new schools, for parents refused to send their children to them. The issues were the same as in the prerevolutionary period: the new school was widely seen as not providing the same kind of cultural capital as the maktab and many parents considered the new method of education to be outright *haram*, forbidden. Rumors flew that the emir would soon return and punish those who had sent their children to the new schools. In any case, physical conditions in the new schools were often so poor that they did not appear irresistible. The ministry resorted to using the police and even the Cheka to haul children off to school and to punish fathers who resisted. This seldom brought the desired results, for parents hid their children in trunks or cupboards if and when the police showed up.[53] By the winter of 1922–23, the ministry had reevaluated the situation and shut down two-thirds of the schools initially opened, but attendance still remained low.[54] Schooling clearly continued to be a site of cultural battles in Muslim society.

47. O'zbekiston Xalq Maorif Kamisarligi, *O'zbekistonda maorif ishlari* (Samarqand, 1927), 13–14.

48. TsGARUz, f. 56, op. 1, d. 10a, l. 23.

49. TsGARUz, f. 48, d. 20, l. 215.

50. In late 1923, Muso Saidjonov, the minister of education, told the Fourth Congress of Soviets of BNSR that his ministry received 815,000 gold rubles from the state and 63,000 from waqf revenues, when, in his estimation, 6–7 million rubles were needed to do what the ministry hoped to do. *Ozod Buxoro*, 28.10.1923.

51. TsGARUz, f. 48, d. 20, l. 293.

52. Ibid., l. 246–246ob.

53. TsGARUz, f. 47, d. 82, l. 25ob (01.12.1921); f. 56, op. 1, d. 24, ll. 3–6ob (21.11.1921)

54. Fitrat, "Maorif ishlari: Birinchi maorif qurultoyida Fitrat o'rtoqning ma'ruzasi," *Uchqun*, no. 2 (April 1923), 1–5.

In Turkestan too, the place of the old-style maktab remained secure in the esteem of the parents and its numbers did not decline. The Soviet school, said an official report in 1923, "is a tiny islet in a sea of confessional schools."[55] Local ispolkoms and their education sections struggled to regulate the maktab while new maktabs kept opening without permission.[56] There were modest successes for the Soviet side. In 1923, the Tashkent old-city soviet, armed with waqf funds, reportedly turned twenty-two maktabs over to the new method.[57] Two years later, it decreed the closure of all *qorixona* (schools devoted to the memorization of the Qur'an) in the city. There remained a deep well of hostility toward the new school and the methods used for its propagation, which sometimes turned violent. On 23 December 1923, the imam of the mosque in Hovuzlik mahalla in Tashkent led worshippers in an assault on a Soviet school, in which they sought to reclaim property that had been requisitioned in 1918.[58] The decision to close qorixonas provoked a demonstration and a statement in the name of "all inhabitants of Tashkent," asking the old-city education department what had happened to the religious liberty announced in 1917![59] Maktabs survived down to 1927.

Madrasas, however, suffered a precipitous decline, as students fled in the chaos of revolution, waqf property was embezzled, and the premises were often targets of requisitioning. In 1920, one of the first acts of the waqf section at Turkompros was to regulate the income of madrasas and hence to control them.[60] The hope was to modernize madrasas by forcing them to follow a graded curriculum, with exams marking passage through a clearly defined nine-year program that would also include nonreligious subjects.[61] In early 1923, the waqf administration was reported to have reformed four madrasas in Tashkent, introducing instruction in mathematics, natural science, geography, history, and Russian.[62] The following year,

---

55. TsGARUz, f. 25, op. 1, d. 1418, ll. 195–196.

56. On Majid qori, the muezzin of a mosque in Beshog'och quarter of Tashkent opening a maktab without permission, see *Turkiston*, 21.22.1923; on the Tashkent old-city education department closing 22 old-method schools in November 1923 and replacing them with new-method ones, *Turkiston*, 12.12.1923; on closures of schools in Andijon for infractions of the building code, *Qizil O'zbekiston*, 05.01.1925.

57. *Turkiston*, 12.12.1923. There were some reports of maktabs being closed by force in 1918 or 1919 and their pupils being carted off to Soviet schools (e.g., TsGARUz, f. 21, op. 1, d. 168, l. 3), but this was clearly not a common phenomenon.

58. "Maorifga qorshi 'yani jihod,'" *Turkiston*, 09.01.1924.

59. K. Aliyev, "Qorixona ig'vogarlari," *Qizil O'zbekiston*, 12.05.1925.

60. TsGARUz, f. 34, op. 1, d. 628, ll. 7, 18.

61. This was first mooted by a conference of Jadid teachers in August 1918 and articulated several times in the years that followed. A 1923 proposal by the Main Waqf Administration, "Kratkii proekt o reorganizatsii konfessional'nykh shkol (mektebov i medrese) i uchebnaia programma na 1923–1924 uchebnyi god," authored by Munavvar Qori, is in TsGARUz, f. 34, op. 1, d. 2302, ll. 140–142.

62. "Toshkentda," *Turkiston*, 20.02.1923.

the administration controlled eighteen madrasas, of which two had been turned into middle schools, one given gratis to a course in cotton cultivation, and one to Qo'shchi.[63] In 1925, the Tashkent ispolkom began requiring complete registration of all religious schools in the city. The move provoked a mass demonstration on madrasa students in early 1926, as a result of which the ispolkom closed all the madrasas in the city.[64] In Bukhara, many madrasas emptied out immediately after the invasion of Bukhara, as students, "believing all sorts of false and seditious rumors," fled the city, as did, no doubt, many of their teachers, and many of the famous madrasas of Bukhara lay vacant after 1920.[65] The state repaired five of them and reopened them with a reformed curriculum in 1922, while the premises of many others were requisitioned for various uses (barracks, elementary schools, etc.). The number of madrasas in the city declined sharply, so that only four still functioned in 1927.[66] With madrasa education abolished in Tashkent and contracted greatly in Bukhara and Samarqand, the center of gravity of Islamic learning had shifted to Ferghana, whose cities accounted for seventy-one of the eighty-four madrasas known to the OGPU in 1927.[67] This was the beginning of a long-term shift in the location of Muslim learning and Islamic conservatism in Central Asia, whose reverberations were felt in the late- and post-Soviet periods.

Debating Women, Imagining a New Life

The "women's question" was fundamental to the national project. It also provided a major arena for contestation between Jadid and Bolshevik visions of transformation. The Jadids' position on this question was rooted in modernist discourses common to much of the Muslim world. Before 1917, they had argued against many customary practices of family life (vast expenditures on life-cycle celebrations, polygamy, the seclusion of women, even veiling) by appealing to the authority of Islam, where they found no sanction for any of these practices. Their main concern, however, had been with women's education. Islam itself required that women receive education, they argued, because without education, women cannot be good Muslims or fully functional members of the nation, while uneducated women could not be good mothers. In their modernist interpretation of Islam, the Jadids banked on contemporary European medical science and reproduced whole cloth the sexual morality that underpinned it, citing the authority of science to

63. TsGARUz, f. 34, op. 1, d. 2318, l. 7 (27.02.1924).
64. RGASPI, f. 62, op. 1, d. 221, l. 201 (Xonsuvarov's report on Muslim clergy to Sredazburo).
65. TsGARUz, f. 48, d. 20, l. 154 (08.07.1922).
66. RGASPI, f. 62, op. 2, d. 1593, l. 6.
67. Bel'skii, "Po musul'manskomu dukhovenstvu v Sr. Azii," RGASPI, f. 62, op. 2, d. 1145, l. 39.

back their arguments for the shariat.[68] The question assumed practical shape in 1917 when the Provisional Government granted women the right to vote. Conservatives in Turkestan resolutely opposed allowing women to vote. For the Jadids, this was sheer madness, for all else aside, it meant disavowing half of the nation's votes and thereby ceding power to the Europeans. Indeed, debate over the role of women had been one of the key catalysts of the discord that marked Muslim politics in 1917. An article by a very young Abdulhay Tojiyev asserting the need for schools for girls had criticized the ulama for deeming women to be *noqisot ul-aql*, "of weak intellect." In response, a certain Mullo Sayyid Maqsudxon Maxdum thundered with indignation at Tojiyev's temerity in criticizing the phrase, for which the author found ample sanction in the Qur'an and hadith. Women's "deficiency in all respects is proven," he argued, "by divine verses and by the noble tradition of the Prophet. Writing vulgar and fictional words in periodicals without understanding their meaning is the height of ignorance" and bordering on infidelity, *kufr*.[69] The conservatives triumphed, and in many places Muslim women were not allowed to vote.[70] Making women useful members of the nation, therefore, became a key issue for the Jadids once they entered organs of Soviet power in 1918.

The debate that ensued remained, as in many other parts of the Muslim world, primarily a male discourse about national authenticity and progress.[71] For the Jadids, the nation remained the prism through which the question of women was viewed, and there was remarkable continuity of argument across the revolutionary divide, although the twists were often new. Times have changed, argued an author, and now men want educated wives; if we don't educate our girls, men will marry Russian women and thus harm the interests of the nation.[72] Women had to change if the nation was to progress. In this mode, women featured prominently in the poetry of the age, and poems about women or addressed to them were part of the repertoire of all (male) poets of the age.[73]

---

68. The key Central Asian text in this regard is Fitrat, 'Ā'ila, yākhūd vaẓā'if-i khānadārī (Bukhara, 1916); see also Khalid, *Politics of Muslim Cultural Reform*, 222–228, and Marianne Kamp, *The New Woman in Uzbekistan: Islam, Modernity, and Unveiling under Communism* (Seattle, 2007), 36–52.

69. Mudarris Mullo Sayyid Maqsudxon Maxsum, "Tanbih," al-Izoh, 16.06.1917, 10–11.

70. Khalid, *Politics of Muslim Cultural Reform*, 262–263.

71. E.g., Deniz Kandiyoti, "Women and the Turkish State: Political Actors or Symbolic Pawns?" in *Woman–Nation–State*, ed. Nira Yuval-Davis and Floya Anthias (London, 1988), 126–149.

72. "Xotin-qizlar tovushi," *Ishtirokiyun*, 22.02.1920. More conventional views of women's education being necessary for the nation's good were common in the press; see *Mehnatkashlar tovushi*, 23.10.1920, 25.11.1920.

73. Other poets who wrote about women included Hamza, Botu, and Shokir Sulaymon; see Ingeborg Baldauf, "Orient und Frau in der frühen uzbekischen Lyrik: Szenen vom Ausbruch aus Dichtungs- und Denktraditionen," in *Über Gereimtes und Ungereimtes diesseits und jenseits der Turcia: Festschrift für Sigrid Kleinmichel zum 70. Geburtstag*, ed. Helga Anetshofer, Ingeborg Baldauf, and Christa Ebert (Schöneiche bei Berlin, 2008), 175–198.

Seclusion and the lack of education were seen as the main causes of women's backwardness. Indeed, for Cho'lpon, women's seclusion was a form of imprisonment, and he likened women of the East to the colonized East itself:

Men bir sharq qizimen, Sharqning o'zidek	I am a daughter of the East, and like the East itself,
Butun tanim, jonim—xayol uyasi,	My body and soul are dens of fantasy.
Menim qora ko'zim kiyik ko'zidek	My dark eyes, like the eyes of a deer
Belgisiz ovchining o'qin ko'rguvsi.	Look at the hunter's arrow uncomprehendingly.
Aytalarkim, yozda har bir joni bor	They say that new life is afoot
Erkin nafas olar, shodlanar, yayrar.	We will breath freely, be happy, relax.
Aytmaylarkim, Sharqda bog'lik xotinlar	They don't say when the dependent women of the East
Ul yorug' dunyoga na zamon kirar?[74]	Will enter that free world.

Education remained the panacea. In April 1924, the Uzbek men's teacher training institute held a "literary trial" of "the Uzbek girl," and sentenced her to education for her crimes of "ignorance, of being a slave to the despotism of men, of rearing children without education, and for [her] inability to join in the currents of the new era."[75] However, a more systemic analysis of women's place in society that focused on their economic dependence had begun to be raised. In 1920, Muhammadjon Biserov, a member of the Musburo, saw relations between men and women in Turkestani society as no different from the relations between capitalists and workers, and that just as "workers cannot free themselves from the claws of the capitalists without shedding blood," women too will have to wage serious struggle.[76] Yet, even for him, the struggle would take the form of education and organization. Education would provide women a path to economic independence and allow them to overcome their seclusion. Indeed, opening up educational opportunities for women was one of the key initiatives in the first years of the revolution. Both male and female activists organized courses for

---

74. Cho'lpon, "Sharq qizi," *Ishtirokiyun*, 23.04.1920; also in *Yana oldim sozimni*, 388.
75. *Turkiston*, 19.04.1924.
76. M. Biserov, "Ish kerak," *Ishtirokiyun*, 31.03.1920.

women teachers, which were formalized into a teachers' institute (Xotin-qizlar Bilim Yurti) in 1919.[77] Over the first half of the 1920s, the Bilim Yurti produced a cohort of women graduates who took up teaching and made an entry into public life through the press. Some even appeared, unveiled, on the theatrical stage. The Bilim Yurti was accompanied by elementary schools for girls, and women were among the students sent to Moscow and Germany.[78]

The women's Bilim Yurti was funded by Turkompros but remained essentially a Jadid institution into the mid-1920s. During the 1921–22 academic year, it was headed by Shokirjon Rahimiy, a Jadid who had opened Turkestan's first new-method school for girls in 1912.[79] The teaching staff also included Shohid Eson, a Tashkent native who had studied for several years in Istanbul, and Usmonxon Eshonxo'jayev, the Young Communist.[80] Many of the first women teachers were Tatars, but the situation changed quickly. Such was the shortage of teachers that many students at the Bilim Yurti taught at elementary schools even before graduating. Still, the number of girls' schools remained small, while the Bilim Yurti graduated only a few of its students.[81] Nevertheless, these few graduates formed a small but vocal cadre of activists for women's rights. Many of them came from intelligentsia families. Xosiyat Tillaxonova was the sister of Salimxon Tillaxonov, a pedagogue and activist, and a member of Chig'atoy Gurungi. Manzura Sobirova who wrote under the pen name Oydin, came from an educated family, and went on to become a poet and short story writer of considerable renown. Robiya Nosirova had run a new-method school for girls in her home before the revolution.[82] Shohida Mahzumova, who went on to become a prominent actor on stage, likewise came from a learned family.

---

77. Xosiyat Rahim, "Xotin-qizlar Bilim yurtiga tarixiy bir qarash," *Yangi yo'l*, 1927, no. 5: 5–8; Kamp, *The New Woman*, 86–90.

78. Sherali Turdiyev, *Ular Germaniyada o'qigan edilar* (Tashkent, 2006), has biographies of some of the women who went to Germany. For group photographs of the contingent at the Bukharan Bilim Yurti in Moscow, see *Iubilennyi sbornik Bukharskogo Doma Prosveshcheniia imeni I.V. Stalina v Moskve/Moskovda Istolin ismida bo'lgan Buxoro Bilim Yurti yubeley majmaasi, moy 1923–1924* (Moscow, 1924).

79. TsGARUz, f. 34, op. 1, d. 1014, l. 1.

80. TsGARUz, f. 34, f. 1, d. 1333, l. 69ob; on Shohid Eson, see Sherali Turdiyev, "Ma'rifatparvarlardan biri. . . ," *Sharq yulduzi*, 2009, no. 2: 172–180.

81. In 1923, the institute enrolled 220 students, but graduated only 7 women. In 1926, there were 14 graduates and an enrollment of 600. Kamp, *The New Woman*, 89. A photograph of the graduating class of 1923 appeared in *Turkiston*, 20.10.1923.

82. Kamp, *The New Women*, 101–105, provides useful potted biographies of Oydin, Nosirova, and Tillaxonova; on Nosirova, see also Laziz Azizzoda, *Yangi hayot kurashchilari* (Tashkent, 1977), 116–118.

Her aunt, Bashorat Jalilova, was one of the most active proponents of unveiling in the early 1920s.[83] Zarifa Nosirova, who also graduated from the Bilim Yurti, was the daughter of Saidnosir Mirjalilov, the leader of the national movement. These were among the first women to appear in print in Central Asia and to articulate a vision of women's place in the new society being hoped for. They were to provide the core of the editorial staff for *Yangi yo'l* (New Path), the organ of the women's division of KPUz when it began publication in 1925.

Whether overcoming seclusion required unveiling—the casting off of the enormously cumbersome combination of *paranji* (a head-to-toe robe worn over clothing) and *chachvon* (a face veil made of horsehair) that defined modesty for urban (and many rural) women in the sedentary societies of Central Asia— remained an open question. This was partly because of the political sensitivity of the question, and partly because many authors made a distinction between unveiling and liberation. "How are we to liberate women?" Qayum Ramazon (O'ktam) once asked rhetorically in a newspaper. "Simply by casting off the paranji? Will women be thus liberated? No, their economic needs are still in the hands of men, meaning that men still hold the reins. . . . The paranji question is different from the question of women's rights." If women find economic independence, he argued, they will abandon the paranji of their own accord. On the other hand, "If we unveil women by force, we will see setbacks rather than any good, and we will even encounter bloody conflict."[84] A small number of women did unveil, some as a matter of course (when the need for employment made it necessary), others in more public acts. The wives of G'ozi Yunus and Elbek unveiled on International Women's Day (8 March) in 1924, and they visited the offices of the newspaper *Turkiston* "to share the joy and to convince others."[85] *Turkiston* carried several reports of women in the families of workers or Soviet functionaries casting off the paranji in 1924.[86]

Behind these debates lay new visions of society and of a new life that built on changing patterns of behavior among the urban elite across political lines. The private life of the youth was changing. An Ottoman officer who spent two years in Tashkent recalled being invited to a party at a Tatar home in the new city

---

83. Azizzoda, *Yangi hayot kurashchilari*, 199–120.

84. O'ktam, "Xotinlar masalasi," *Turkiston*, 14.02.1924.

85. "Ozodliq qaldirg'ochlari," *Turkiston*, 15.03.1924.

86. Several "government men" in raions around Tashkent had "cleansed their families of the paranji" in May: "Paranjiga qorshi," *Turkiston*, 14.05.1924; several women unveiled at the wedding of the tramway worker G'ofurxo'jayev in December: "Paranji tashlash," *Qizil O'zbekiston*, 29.12.1924. On unveiling before the hujum of 1927, see Kamp, *The New Woman*, chap. 6.

that featured mixed company and dancing.[87] Many men among the intelligentsia married European women while the ideal of companionate marriage gained
ground. By 1924, enough young people were enthused by the idea of a "new life"
to form a volunteer "Union of Friends of the New Life" (*Yangi turmush do'stlari
birligi*) in Tashkent. On 16 May 1924, they organized a day-long literary gathering
in the Qondirg'ach mahalla of old Tashkent in which unveiled women participated in equal numbers with men. We will tarry at this gathering, for we have
an unusually rich newspaper report on it that provides rare insight into cultural
dynamics in Turkestan of that time.[88]

The gathering was organized "at the initiative of those who had moved to
the new city," but "all the guests from the old city came with their wives, with
their faces uncovered." Ultimately, "sixty to seventy Uzbek women and girls and
about a hundred men filled a large hall, where they sat mixed together." "They all
smiled," enthused the reporter for *Turkiston*, "[and] every face had signs of happi-
ness." The gathering elected a presidium [*hay'at-i riyosat*] and elected Nadezhda
Krupskaia, Lenin's recently bereaved wife, as its honorary chair. But it was the
actual presidium whose composition is striking. It included Eshonxo'jayev; Nosirova, who in 1924 was married to Abdulhay Tojiyev, the Young Communist;
Shohid Eson, an Istanbul-educated Jadid and pedagogue who was often quite
skeptical of the Soviets (he was accused of not allowing the formation of Komsomol cells in schools he supervised); Komiljon Aliyev, another Young Communist who was also a member of the collegium of Turkompros; Mannon Romiz,
pedagogue, activist in Turkompros (and future commissar of education), and
at the time editor of *Turkiston*; and two women called To'rayeva and Rahimova
who are difficult to identify. Among those whose speeches were reported in the
newspaper account were Shokirjon Rahimiy, the director of the women's Bilim
Yurti; Ne'mat Hakim, a Tatar activist and a prolific author; Rahimjon Inog'amov,
another Young Communist and soon to become the first commissar of education
in Uzbekistan; Xosiyat Tillaxonova; Nizomiddin Xo'jayev, a central figure of the
Musburo who had been keeping a low profile since 1920; Zohida Burnasheva,
one of the founders of the women's Bilim Yurti; and the ubiquitous Laziz Azizzoda.[89] (Another participant was Qayum Ramazon, who wrote the newspaper
report.) This was a remarkable collection of individuals: they were all young,
most of them without a public presence before 1917, but they were all invested

---

87. Ziya Yergök, *Sarıkamış'tan Esarete (1915–1920)*, ed. Sami Önal (Istanbul, 2005), 238–239.

88. "O'zbek elining tarixida birinchi kunduz," *Turkiston*, 19.05.1924, 21.05.1924.

89. Azizzoda was only a few years away from arrest on changes of nationalism that landed him
in prison camps for a quarter of a century. He survived and worked him way back into publishing
in the Brezhnev years. In 1977, he published a collection of biographies titled *Fighters for the New
Life* that mentions, among other things, this gathering. Azizzoda, *Yangi hayot kurashchilari*, 118, 121.

in both the revolution and the nation, in politics as well as culture. Some were members of the party, others not. On the question of women, they could come together without any problem.

Eshonxo'jayev gave the longest speech. The shariat, he argued, does not command the use of the paranji. "Because, among us, women became the private property of men, they were forcibly veiled [*yopintirdilar*]. Veiling [*hijob*] is a way for the wealthy to distinguish themselves from the masses." The goal, he said, was not simply to unveil women but to explain to them that they were full human beings. He had in fact argued for more rapid and more forceful action on the part of the KPT at its Eighth Congress the previous month, even as he criticized the continuing hold of patriarchal relations (*patriarkhal'shchina*) in the party.[90] Rahimjon Inog'amov struck the harshest tone of the day when he argued that "the biggest cause of the paranji is religion. . . . The clerics [*ruhoniylar*] use religion as a weapon and allow all sorts of bad things in its name. The paranji was one such thing." The discussion that followed was largely amiable. Several speakers agreed with Eshonxo'jayev that both men and women were at fault in perpetrating the current situation. Tillaxonova, however, argued that "men are the cause of our slavery," and that they do not help women enough, "even those who call themselves intellectuals [*ziyoli*]." Nosirova argued for coeducation, which she argued people will learn "not to hate." What was striking about the debate is how little of it was cast in Bolshevik terms, despite the presence of several Young Communists. The main concern was still with locating the reform of the position of women in Muslim society and arguing with opponents within it. The fact that Young Communists here rubbed shoulders with the cultural intelligentsia is also important, for it shows that no hard and fast distinction may be made between those two groups.

Other than a few notices for meetings in the press,[91] the Friends of the New Life quickly disappeared from the record, but clearly new visions of society and of gender relations had captured the imaginations of many young intellectuals in Turkestan's society. In 1925, an author published a lengthy discourse on the family from a materialist point of view, which he nevertheless used to argue against free love and intermarriage with Russians.[92] What is remarkable here is not so much the analysis, but the mere fact that free love was being talked about among the young intelligentsia. That this piece was published only ten years after Fitrat had published his Muslim modernist tract on the family is an indication of the

---

90. Rustambek Sharafiddinov, *Istiqlol yo'lida shahid ketganlar* (Tashkent, 2001), 356–357.
91. *Turkiston*, 29.05.1924, 11.06.1924.
92. S. Ali, "Oila masalasi," *Maorif va o'qutg'vuchi,* 1925, no. 2: 25–32; no. 3: 25–29.

revolution of the mind that had swept the area. For those fascinated by the new life and its promises, women, public health, alphabet reform, theater, Futurist poetry all formed part of single whole, a vision of modernity that was the only guarantee of national survival.

The party, however, or rather its European leadership, had staked its own claim in the debate. Typically, it claimed to be the sole agent of change, the only guarantor of justice to women, providing them freedoms that "no self-proclaimed protector of the oppressed, no parliament in any 'civilized' state based on capitalism," could provide.[93] The radical revolutionary legislation on marriage and the family (which secularized marriage, recognized free union as equivalent to it, and made divorce available to both partners) did not apply to the Muslim population of Turkestan, where the Soviet state continued to recognize Islamic law. Nevertheless, in June 1921, TurTsIK outlawed the payment of bride wealth (*qalin*) and established a minimum age for marriage (eighteen for men, sixteen for women).[94] More significant than legislation (which could often go unimplemented), however, was the alternative discourse on women's issues introduced by the party. One of the first acts of the Turkkomissiia was to establish a branch of the Zhenotdel, the Women's Division of the Communist Party, in Turkestan.[95] Staffed largely by European women, the Zhenotdel entered the fray from a different direction than the local intelligentsia. It combined a concern with bringing women into economic production with ensuring legal equality, organization, and enlightenment. But the European women who staffed the Zhenotdel (most of whom were seconded from Moscow for the purpose) constructed the subject of their solicitude in a singularly condescending fashion. If women in "the East" were "slaves of slaves," those in Central Asia were the most oppressed of them all. "Dependent like slaves" from birth, they never saw the light of the sun and "until Great October, had not entered the ranks of humanity and [were] not considered human beings."[96] As the activist Rodchinskaia noted, in Central Asia "a woman is a machine. She is a machine that knows her place in the family; she is a production machine, a child-making machine. She is a nanny for rearing children, she is a cook.... She is the slave of her husband, a wordless donkey."[97] The liberation of Central Asian women was the work of the revolution and a gift of the party-state, but also the personal mission of the European women in the Zhenotdel. In the

---

93. Ozod xotin [pseud.], "O'ktobir inqilobi musulmon xotin-qizlarga nima berdi?" *Qizil bayroq*, 07.11.1921.

94. TsGARUz, f. 38, op. 2, d. 182, l. 192–192ob.

95. RGASPI, f. 62, op. 2, d. 427, l. 6.

96. [Sredazburo, Zhenotdel], *Besh yil* (Moscow, 1925), 5.

97. Ibid., 92.

words of O. Bulgova, "We are the liberators of Muslim women from this slavery, from the imprisonment of being married off before their youth is over. We will struggle on this path and we will achieve our goals."[98] Zhenotdel activists (and the party in general) sought to efface all other discourses of reform. To quote Rodchinskaia again, "Education among the indigenous women [of Central Asia] only began after October."[99]

The Zhenotdel introduced to Turkestan several types of initiatives it had used elsewhere in the Soviet state. It established women's clubs that served as a gathering place for women, but also sources for medical advice and literacy classes. It stationed delegates (*vakila*) in various locations throughout Turkestan who acted as its representatives, reporting abuses back to the center and trying to organize women locally. It provided legal help for women in trouble and worked to assure that women's cases received priority hearing in Soviet courts. The Zhenotdel also sought to organize women economically, creating labor cooperatives for women in need of work. As with all Soviet efforts to mobilize in the early years, the achievements were slender and the numbers of Muslim women reached by the Zhenotdel remained small: a couple of hundred members of trade unions, 1,668 in Qo'shchi, a few hundred in the organized cooperative sector.[100] (The Zhenotdel had much greater luck with European women in Central Asia.) Nevertheless, the upheavals experienced by Central Asia had shaken up society and left many women without the safety nets provided by family. The Zhenotdel looked to the margins of society—to women who had been widowed or cast out by their husbands, or those who escaped abusive relationships—and found a small but loyal constituency for itself.

There are many stories to be told here. Xayriniso Mahmudjonova refused to don the paranji when she turned fourteen or to agree to being married off; when her parents beat her, she escaped, unveiled and found employment at the women's Bilim Yurti.[101] During the famine in Ferghana, seven-year-old Zaynab Koribuva was given away in marriage in return for fifteen poods of grain. She ran away after being beaten senseless by her husband, made her way to Tashkent, and enrolled in the same Bilim Yurti as Mahmudjonova.[102] Zaynab Qosimova of Osh was married off at fifteen, but left her husband when her mother-in-law poisoned their relationship. Her father then gave her to a fifty-year-old man as his third

98. Ibid., 137.

99. Ibid., 91.

100. These are the figures proclaimed by the Zhenotdel itself in ibid., 19–24. Their accuracy is subject to doubt simply because of exceptionally poor typesetting of numbers in the text.

101. Ibid., 120, 241–242.

102. Ibid., 135–136.

wife. She had four children with him, but he turned them all out when she began attending women's meetings after the revolution.[103] Habiba was orphaned in her childhood and lived with her sister. Married off at the age of eleven, she found her mother-in-law "worse than a poisonous snake," and escaped to her brother, who then wanted to marry her off to another man. When Habiba refused, her brother threw her out of the house. She eventually found her way to Namangan and enrolled in a course for volost organizers.[104] Risolat Madraimboyeva of Namangan uezd was orphaned at five and widowed at nineteen. Her family married her off again, but her second husband beat her regularly and ultimately threw her out of the house. She found shelter at a Soviet school in Kokand and thus ended up at the Zhenotdel.[105] Sobira Rahmon-qizi escaped a husband who had taken a second wife.[106] No doubt, such instances were singled out in the press for "propaganda" purposes, but they were no less real for it. The Zhenotdel capitalized on existing cleavages in Turkestani society. To many women, it offered an alternative to the family or the courts of the qazis. And it was often such women who became the most loyal supporters of the Zhenotdel's mission in Turkestan.

Such women had a rather different understanding of the future than the intelligentsia women who passed through the Bilim Yurti. They had much less at stake in "culture" and were much more concerned with mobilizing in support of the party. Sobira Xoldarova worked as a housemaid from the age of thirteen before she was rescued and placed in the Bilim Yurti. She quickly rose to become editor of the institute's wall newspaper, and in 1925 was appointed the first editor of *Yangi yo'l*. She joined the party as a candidate and was sent to study in Moscow.[107] Tojixon Shodiyeva, who became editor of *Yangi yo'l* in 1928, had been married off as the second wife of a fifty-year-old man at the age of twelve. She was rescued by the Zhenotdel and brought to Tashkent, where she joined the Komsomol and eventually the party.[108] Activists like Xoldarova and Tojiyeva worked together with intelligentsia women in the Zhenotdel and on the editorial board of *Yangi yo'l*, but their life trajectories and their political instincts were different and produced different visions of the future.

---

103. Ibid., 238.
104. Ibid., 245.
105. RGASPI, f. 62, op. 2, d. 433, ll. 4–4ob.
106. S. R. Qizi, "Ular bo'lsam, o'lib bo'ldimku!" *Qizil O'zbekiston*, 03.01.1926. Similar cases were reported frequently in the press of the time; see, e.g., Bir kishi (pseud.), "Xotinboz erning zo'rliq va zulmi," *Qizil O'zbekiston*, 19.05.1925. The Zhenotdel also received many appeals for help from abused women or their families.
107. Kamp, *The New Woman*, 100–101.
108. Ibid., 105–106; Xolida Ahrorova, "Tojixon Shodiyeva," in *Qor quynida lolalar: Qatag'on etilgan ayollar haqida ocherklar* (Tashkent, 2001), 200–206.

They could be quite combative. In June 1924, when TurTsIK issued a new decree banning qalin and underage marriage, various party and soviet institutions were mobilized to explain the new legislation to the population. We read of a public meeting in the village of Qornoq (Turkiston uezd), organized by the heads of the local party and Komsomol cells as well as the ispolkom and representatives of the Zhenotdel. The meeting waited for the local ulama to arrive, who then listened to speakers tell the meeting, "The old Islamic shariat turns women and girls into slaves. In the land of the Soviets, there is no place for slavery or for a shariat that enslaves."[109] In Namangan, Valida Kuchukova, head of the uezd Zhenotdel, showed up unveiled at a *mazor* on the Feast of Sacrifice (*Qurbon hayiti*, the most important holiday of the Islamic calendar) and lectured women about the new legislation. Two days later, the local Zhenotdel, in conjunction with Qo'shchi and Komsomol organizations, held a concert at the mazor itself, even as worshippers went about their worship. The concert attracted 150 women, who saw a play about "the consequences of the forced marriage of an underage girl" and heard a lecture on how numerous practices current at the mazor (such as the kissing of the tombstone) were hazardous from the point of view of hygiene and caused the spread of syphilis and tuberculosis.[110] Such agitation engendered a great deal of conflict. Zhenotdel workers, especially in the countryside, faced immense hostility and were often the subjects of sexual violence.[111] Many women who enrolled in Soviet schools similarly aroused the opposition of their families or of the mahalla.[112]

The Zhenotdel faced its own problems with the party hierarchy. The party was suspicious of action in the name of women independent of notions of class.[113]

---

109. *Besh yil*, 88–89

110. Ibid., 138–139. The event passed without conflict, but a small earthquake struck the area the day after, which led to rumors that it was punishment for the desecration of the mazor.

111. Xodisa Ibrohimova, head of the Merv zhenotdel (Transcaspia), was kidnapped by three men and raped repeatedly for eight days. Ruqayya-bibi of Katartol village in Tashkent uezd had received death threats for her work, as did Taxtabibi Bekmuhammadova of Yo'l Tashkent village (Chinoz volost, Tashkent uezd). The latter had to flee to Tashkent after the head of the local Qo'shchi organization threatened her with murder for "teaching our women and dragging them off to [women's] clubs." A delegate who reported a man for taking a second wife without permission was threatened with a knife and barely escaped. Their petitions for help are in RGASPI, f. 62, op. 2, d. 433, ll. 13–15, 22.

112. Muazzama Maxzumova (b. 1904), a worker at the Tashkent oblast zhenotdel, went to school with the support of her husband but antagonized her own family as well as the entire mahalla by that act. RGASPI, f. 62, op. 2, d. 433, l. 1. Opponents routinely characterized female students in Soviet schools as immoral or lascivious, little better than prostitutes.

113. Elizabeth A. Wood, *The Baba and the Comrade: Gender and Politics in Revolutionary Russia* (Bloomington, 1997); Michelle V. Fuqua, *The Politics of the Domestic Sphere: The Zhenotdely, Women's Liberation, and the Search for a Novyi Byt in Early Soviet Russia* (Seattle, 1996).

In the conditions of Central Asia, the Sredazburo remained reluctant to act decisively on the question of women, despite pressure from both the Zhenotdel and the Young Communists. In the spring of 1924, Juozas Vareikis, the secretary of the Sredazburo, told the Central Committee of the KPT that "it is necessary to help the Zhenotdel but here there has to be maximal caution, for instances are not rare when manap-bai elements, making use of the darkness of the masses, conduct a struggle against us . . . under the slogan, 'Down with the Zhenotdel.' There is no need to hurry, we must begin with the political and cultural training of the masses."[114] The party did not see women, let alone unveiling, as a major issue. The *hujum*, the unveiling campaign in 1927, was to represent a major policy shift.

Soviet Orientalism

The era of the Russian revolution was, as we well know, a period of great enthusiasm and creativity, of experimentation and exploration.[115] The enthusiasms of the Uzbek intelligentsia were part of this broad phenomenon. Their relationship to the European population of the Soviet Union and with the Soviet state, however, was highly complex and worth consideration. Briefly put, the revolution did not lead to a significant rethinking of Central Asia's place in the cultural imagination of the European population of the Soviet state. We have already seen how the revolution could not dent the dual society in Central Asia. Similarly, almost no European intellectuals, whether in Central Asia or in the center, could move beyond the binaries that divided "Europe" from "Asia," West from East, progress from backwardness. At best, European intellectuals saw themselves as Kulturträgers, called upon to enlighten the natives, to raise them to civilization. At worst, they saw the natives as inherently alien and incapable of progress.

Few Europeans crossed the boundaries that divided them from native society. We know of Elena Sivitskaia, born in Poland, who came to Central Asia, converted to Islam in 1924, and took the name Lolaxon Arslanova. She became a prolific writer in Russian on Uzbek women. A collection of sketches she published in Moscow was much admired by Cho'lpon, who translated it into Uzbek.[116]

---

114. RGASPI, f. 62, op. 3, d. 16, l. 56 (Plenum of CC KPT, March 1924).

115. Richard Stites, *Revolutionary Dreams: Utopian Vision and Experimental Life in the Russian Revolution* (New York, 1988); René Fülöp-Miller, *The Mind and Face of Bolshevism: An Examination of Cultural Life in Soviet Russia*, trans. F. S. Flint and D. S. Tait (London, 1927).

116. L. Arslanova, *Uzbechki: p'esa* (Moscow, 1926); Lolaxon Sayfullina-Arslonova, *Ichkari: o'zbek xotin-qizlari turmushidan olingan sochmo she'rlar*, trans. Cho'lpon (Samarqand, 1926).

Lolaxon also wrote or co-wrote the scripts for six of the seven films made in Uzbekistan in 1927 and 1928.[117] The painter Aleksandr Nikolaev, a student of Malevich, similarly converted to Islam after he arrived in Turkestan at the invitation of TurTsIK to develop national art. He stayed in Uzbekistan to the end of his life, leaving a massive legacy of work under the name of Usto Mo'min.[118] Lidiia Sotserdotova, who spoke Uzbek flawlessly, became a close friend of Abdulla Qodiriy's and translated two of his novels into Russian.[119] But for the vast majority of European intellectuals, Central Asia, and "the East" in general, were to be beneficiaries of the gift of revolution and enlightenment. They did not have a place as equals in the utopias of the Soviet European imagination.[120] It was left for Central Asians to claim their place at the table.

In marked contrast to the Caucasus, Central Asia had produced barely a ripple in the Russian cultural imagination even after fifty years of imperial rule. This did not change after the revolution. Although Central Asia in the abstract featured in the writings of the Eurasianists and Scythianists, such imaginaries had little to do with the actual land and its people. The region is largely absent from the literary imagination of the Russian avant-garde of the 1920s. The one significant work of Russian literature to feature Central Asia was Aleksandr Neverov's novel, *Tashkent—City of Bread* (1923), which depicted Turkestan as a land of plenty where victims of the Volga famine could acquire bread cheaply. As twelve-year-old Mishka Dodonov's family starves in his village near Buzuluk, he hears "mujiks . . . talking about Tashkent" on the street. "Bread was very cheap there, only getting there was hard. Two thousand versts there, two thousand versts back."[121] Mishka decides to go to Tashkent to acquire bread for his family, and the book is the tale of his quest on which he embarks armed only with hope and ingenuity. It is a very Russian story, of *muzhik*s on the move. The trains on

117. Cloé Drieu, *Fictions nationales: Cinéma, empire et nation en Ouzbékistan (1919–1937)* (Paris, 2013), 186.

118. On the Central Asian artistic milieu of the 1920s, see Svetlana Gorshenina, "Une avant-garde stoppée en plein élan ou 'une logique de développement interne'?" *Missives: la Revue de la Société littéraire de La Poste et de France Télécom* (numéro spécial, 2001), 76–91.

119. Habibulla Qodiriy, *Otamdan xotira* (Tashkent, 2005), 330–331.

120. The one work of Soviet Russian literature to accord Central Asians a central place was Andrei Platonov's *dystopian* novella *Dzhan*, written in 1935, in the era of socialist realism, and published only three decades later (and then in a mangled form). In telling the story of the attempted Sovietization of the Dzhan people, a group of outcasts living in the Kara Kum desert in Turkmenistan, Platonov questions some of the collectivist ideals of the Stalinist dispensation.

121. A. Neverov, *Tashkent–gorod khlebnyi* (Moscow, 1923). The book was well received abroad and translated into a number of languages, including English, which I have used for the quotations here: Alexander Neweroff, *City of Bread*, trans. Theodore Nadejen (New York, 1927). The only analysis of this work seems to be in E. F. Shafranskaia, *Tashkentskii tekst v russkoi kul'ture* (Moscow, 2010), 45–51. Shafranskaia could not find anything else in Russian letters about Tashkent in the first two decades of Soviet rule.

which Mishka rides without a ticket, dodging the Cheka in the process but also benefitting from the kindness of fellow passengers, are all full of Russians, even as they pass through the Kazakh steppe. "The Kirghiz [i.e., Kazakhs] were not terrible at all, only queer," Mishka finds. That queerness lies in their strange bearing and language, and while they are not dumb (they do not part with their money easily), they remain hopelessly alien and exotic. Tashkent serves primarily as the object of Mishka's desire, which he finally does attain. Tashkent is a strange mixture of the exotic and the familiar: from the train, Mishka espies "the strangest men" riding horses, "unfamiliar carts on two high wheels," and women wearing paranji, but also "big black-bearded mujiks." Mishka found "all sorts of apples in baskets, and on little wooden trays, and then some kind of berry, black ones and green ones in clusters, and large white cakes," but also "all over the station lay [Russian] mujiks and peasant women, naked, half-naked, burnt by the Tashkent sun, sick, dying." Mishka is taken aback: "'Do they want for bread here too?'" But "he went on." And he was successful in the end. He found work "in the gardens of a rich Sart, then he met some Buzuluk mujiks, and went out with them on the steppe. He threshed wheat, cut weeds, earned two sacks of grain—four poods [65 kg] apiece." He used some of this grain to pay for his passage back home, and arrived with more than four poods of grain, which seemed to be enough to allow a fresh start for his remaining family. The novel depicts the misery of the Volga famine, but it renders Central Asia's own misery invisible. Central Asia appears as a land of plenty, of sunshine and rich Sarts. Tashkent ultimately is a Russian setting for a Russian quest.[122]

The nascent genre of film betrays this distance between Europeans and natives very clearly. The first films set in Central Asia were shot in 1925. Not surprisingly, given the lack of film professionals in Central Asia, they were made by Europeans, acted by Europeans, and ultimately intended for a European audience. As Cloé Drieu argues, these early films fit perfectly in the broader tradition of colonial film, from which they borrowed with ease. The exotic and the picturesque predominate, while the natives are primitive and often dangerous, and remain so. Unlike later Soviet film, the natives are not to be modernized.[123] This applied even to The Muslim Woman (Russ., Musul'manka; Uzb., Musulmon xotin), a consciousness-raising film commissioned by the Central Asian Zhenotdel. Proletkino, the Leningrad studio that made the film, transformed

---

122. The book produced an aura of plenty around the name Tashkent in the Soviet European imagination. In 1941, when the war created a massive evacuation from European Russia, Tashkent was a destination desired by many potential evacuees because of this association. See Rebecca Manley, To the Tashkent Station: Evacuation and Survival in the Soviet Union at War (Ithaca, 2009), 141–142.

123. Drieu, Fictions nationales, 90–95.

the original script quite drastically, adding several new developments largely out of commercial considerations, so that the mobilizational film became the tale of an adventure.[124] *The Minaret of Death* (Russ., *Minaret smerti*, Uzb., *Ajal minorasi*, 1925) told the story of a peasant revolt in eighteenth-century Bukhara, in which the son of the emir gets his comeuppance by being tossed from the Minor-i Kalon, Bukhara's "minaret of death." Yet the film, acted entirely by European actors, ends up being a love story set in an exoticized locale and the revolt becomes rather incidental to the plot. Even after film production came to Uzbekistan (the Sharq Yulduzi studio was established in 1926), filmmaking remained in European hands and representations of natives retained many continuities with colonial film all the way down to the early 1930s.[125]

Documentary film fared little better. All through the 1920s, Soviet filmmakers spent considerable energy documenting the "boundless space" of "land of the Soviets" in all its diversity. Along with fiction and illustrated journalism, this corpus created a new imaginary geography of the Soviet state, indeed, as Emma Widdis argues, of Sovietness.[126] This Sovietness, however, was vastly asymmetrical across the diversity of the Soviet state: Russians and natives had different stakes in it. For the former, a sense of ownership was fundamental. In fact, Russian-language cultural production of the period constituted the Soviet subject as European. It was the Europeans' job to get to know the boundless land, to discover it, and to conquer it; non-Europeans were there to be uplifted and civilized. The non-Russian spaces became sites for the heroic work of Europeans to tame, conquer, and civilize.

Viktor Turin's 1929 film about the Turksib railway charts the conquest of nature and primitiveness by "a new civilization" represented by technology. The bearers of this new civilization, the operators of the machinery are almost all visibly European, while the natives are clearly there to be uplifted. The first few scenes of the film depict the tyranny of nature in the Central Asian landscape, as humans and animals alike suffer terrible thirst, and a sandstorm leaves "the stillness of death" in its wake. Natives are routinely juxtaposed in these shots with animals. A key scene in the film depicts a Kazakh nomadic encampment at high noon, with its entire population along with all the animals fast asleep. "Life is asleep," says the intertitle, "and the tombs of the East stand sentry." There can have been few more transparent depictions of the somnolent Orient in the entire history of film than this scene. The East is awakened by the arrival of a team of

---

124. The film does not seem to be extant; this analysis is the result of Cloé Drieu's impressive detective work in the archives; ibid., 98–101.

125. Ibid., passim.

126. Emma Widdis, *Visions of a New Land: Soviet Film from the Revolution to the Second World War* (New Haven, 2004).

surveyors ("the advance guard of a new civilization"), who are all Europeans.[127] Technology awakens the East with its machines and "with the machines [comes] education." The new civilization declares "WAR . . . ON THE PRIMITIVE," as the intertitles scream in large capitals, but both civilization and primitiveness are nationally marked in *Turksib*. The Soviet civilizing mission was a European one. This message became ever more explicit over the next few years, so that Dziga Vertov's *Three Songs about Lenin* (1934) depicted unveiling as Lenin's gift to the women of the East. "My face was in a dark prison," state the intertitles on behalf of the women of the East. "I led a blind life. . . . But a ray of truth began to shine. . . . The dawn of Lenin's truth. . . . He is a father to us. No father ever did as much for his children as Lenin did for us."[128] Liberation and civilization were a gift bestowed on backward peoples by Lenin and the Soviet state.[129]

Turksib played to packed houses all over Europe and attracted critical acclaim from across the political spectrum.[130] Its evocation of a European civilizing mission and the suggestion that change could come to "Oriental" societies only from outside resonated with European audiences regardless of their political orientation. No surprise, then, to find that Rudyard Kipling was a popular poet in the Soviet Union in the 1920s, when his works began to be translated into Russian. Although his publications were prefaced by denunciations of his rather unapologetic imperialism, his celebration of selfless duty, his praise for progress and its carriers, and his taste for the exotic attracted Soviet Russian readers. "Kiplingism" enjoyed a considerable vogue in Russia at the time, for it spoke to the same combination of disdain for natives and sympathy for them that motivated many Soviet Europeans.[131] For them, civilizing the Soviet Union's backward masses was their burden.

The pattern held beyond the world of literature and film. Almost all technical experts (engineers, doctors, statisticians, agronomists, ethnographers) in Central Asia were Europeans, and the situation did not change over the course of the

127. *Turksib*, directed by Viktor Turin (Vostok Kino, 1929; VHS, Kino on Video, 1997).

128. *Tri pesni o Lenine*, directed by Dziga Vertov (1934), in *Kino-Eye / Three Songs about Lenin*, DVD (Kino International Corp., 2000).

129. Over the Soviet decades, the idea that the Russians had bestowed the gift of progress on the "Soviet East" came to be a fundamental part of Russian identity. On the broader underpinnings of this notion of gift, see Bruce Grant, *The Captive and the Gift: Cultural Histories of Sovereignty in Russia and the Caucasus* (Ithaca, 2009).

130. Matthew J. Payne, "Viktor Turin's *Turksib* (1929) and Soviet Orientalism," *Historical Journal of Film, Radio and Television* 21 (2001): 53–55.

131. Katherine Hodgson, "The Poetry of Rudyard Kipling in Soviet Russia," *Modern Language Review* 93 (1998): 1061–1062; Katharine A. Holt, "The Rise of Insider Iconography: Visions of Soviet Turkmenia in Russian-Language Literature and Film, 1921–1935" (Ph.D. diss., Columbia University, 2013), 79–81, 137–140.

decade (or, for that matter, until after the Second World War). Many of them were lukewarm at best toward the revolution, but they saw it as a moment when they could put their professional skills to unhindered use. The main task of the professionals was to productivize the land and make it more governable by the Russian state. As the charter of Tashkent's Oriental Institute stated, its main goal was the "easing, through teaching about the East, the service of persons who devote themselves to work in Turkestan and neighboring countries."[132] The professionals had a different stake in modernizing Central Asia than the natives, and few of them seem to have seen themselves as defenders of the local population or its friends. There were exceptions, to be sure. The polymath Vasilii Viatkin (1869–1932), from a Cossack family of Semirech'e, was already a distinguished scholar in 1917, having discovered the ruins of the fifteenth-century observatory built by Temur's grandson Ulugh-bek and published widely across disciplines. Unusually for a Russian scholar, he had always enjoyed close contacts with local scholars. After 1917, he worked for Turkomstaris, where he continued his archeological work. He also published primers in Uzbek and Tajik and was an accomplished translator. Upon his death, he was buried in the Registan, the Timurid square that marks the center of Samarqand, although two years later his remains were moved to the site of the observatory he had helped reconstruct.[133] Evgenii Polivanov spent several years in Tashkent and played a part in debates over the codification of Uzbek grammar and orthography. Viktor Uspenskii, invited by Fitrat to Bukhara to record and notate traditional music, emerged as a major figure in the creation of modern Uzbek music.

But it is easy to overstate the significance of such individuals.[134] For the vast majority of European professionals who supported the revolution, Central Asia and Central Asians remained the embodiments of backwardness and sloth, in need of improvement and tutelage. The region was a site for doing heroic work, conquering nature (and Oriental sloth), and building socialism against all odds. Thus the many thousands of European workers who flooded Central Asia in the decade, who came to work in factories and on railways newly being built, felt they were doing the region and its inhabitants a favor, for which the latter must

---

132. TsGARUz, f. 34, op. 1, d. 40, l. 20 (1918).

133. B. V. Lunin, *Istoriografiia obshchestvennykh nauk v Uzbekistane: bio-bibliograficheskie ocherki* (Tashkent, 1974), 138–143.

134. In a gratuitous case of such exaggeration, Vera Tolz, *Russia's Own Orient: The Politics of Identity and Oriental Studies in the Late Imperial and Early Soviet Period* (Oxford, 2011), argues that not only did Russian Orientalists prefigure the Saidian critique of Orientalism but that they were also instrumental in helping non-Russian nationalists imagine their communities. Here we are not very far from the idea of civilization as a gift of empire bequeathed by Lenin and Stalin.

be forever grateful.[135] Others, such as the Orientalist M. Sheverdin or the muckraking journalist El'-Registan (both of whom we will encounter again in chapter 12), identified closely with the center and saw themselves as watchdogs over errant natives. Max Penson was the bard of "Soviet construction" in Central Asia, his superb photographs showing the natives in heroic poses as they were transformed by the revolution and the party-state. For those who were lukewarm about the revolution, however, the natives represented something altogether different. While the party pushed the korenizatsiia, with its goal of incorporating the indigenous population into structures of power, medical research in Central Asia in the 1920s came to focus increasingly on innate differences between Europeans and Central Asians. Not only were native culture and way of life (*byt*) inherently backward and productive of disease, but the indigenous population also had distinctive physical traits that caused heightened susceptibility to disease (especially syphilis and tuberculosis) and lower capacities for mental and physical work.[136] Located in a long tradition of colonial medicine, this "racial pathology" directly challenged notions of equality that lay at the heart of the legitimacy claimed by the Soviet state.

Ultimately, it was a question of representation, of who would represent Central Asia and on whose terms, and it was not easily resolved. Most Europeans assumed that they, with their scientific knowledge and modern techniques, were best qualified to speak about Central Asia, whether in the realm of medicine or ethnography or film. Their claims were contested at many levels. Reviewing *Ravot qoshqirlari* (The Jackals of Ravot), the first film made in Uzbekistan, Abdulla Qodiriy wrote:

> It is safe to say that to this day, all films about Uzbek, or, more generally Central Asian, life have depicted our life in ways that are if not entirely, then in large part, fictional and fake. And this applies not just to cinema. We encounter the same horrible things based on fantasy and legend in pieces published about us in the press and the literature of the Europeans, even that which appears in Central Asia. Often, encountering such fakeries, an Uzbek naturally cannot keep himself from smiling. Faced with the insults of this "newly invented life," he goes around joking about it with his friends and comrades.

Qodiriy actually liked the film he was reviewing, but still found mistakes in its representation of Uzbek customs that "any Uzbek child would know."[137] The

---

135. Botakoz Kassymbekova, "Helpless Imperialists: European State Workers in Soviet Central Asia in the 1920s and 1930s," *Central Asian Survey* 30 (2011): 21–37.

136. Cassandra Cavanaugh, "Backwardness and Biology: Medicine and Power in Russian and Soviet Central Asia, 1868–1934" (Ph.D. diss., Columbia University, 2001), chap. 5.

137. Abdulla Qodiriy, "Ravot qoshqirlari," *Qizil O'zbekiston*, 28.04.1927.

previous year, the Uzbek directorate of political education (Glavpolitprosvet) had refused a suggestion from Anatolii Lunacharskii, the central Commissar for Education, to merge Uzbekgoskino, the Uzbek film studio, with the Moscow-based organization Vostokkino (Eastern Cinema). Not only did the merger not make budgetary sense (Uzbekgoskino had a capital of 300,000 rubles, while Vostokkino possessed only 550,000 rubles and was responsible for the entire Soviet Union), Vostokkino also could not address the basic task "of developing a national cinema in Uzbekistan." Located far away and "faced with the task of serving many different nationalities," Glavpolitprosvet resolved, Vostokkino "cannot, at the present moment, . . . satisfy the needs of our region, except for the release of films that distort the way of life of the Uzbek people, of which we were convinced by the films produced by central cinematic organizations, such as *The Minaret of Death*, *The Muslim Woman*, and many others."[138] Uzbekgoskino did retain its institutional independence until 1930, when all film production was centralized across the Soviet Union, but the struggle over representation was not so easily won. After ideological strictures began to tighten in 1926, Central Asia's recent history could only be recounted within the limits set by the party and in a vocabulary dictated by it. Class remained the only permissible vector, as nationality and kolonizatorstvo were delegitimized. The history of the revolution in Central Asia was to be only about class. It had no place for such inconveniences as the revolt of 1916 or the depredations of Russian settlers during the civil war.

Disenchantment

This chapter must end on a note of dissonance. For all the hopes invested in the revolution by the Jadids, it was increasingly clear to them that the Bolsheviks had little intention of changing their agenda to suit local conditions, let alone to accommodate alternative views of cultural change. The choking of the Bukharan republic in 1923 was a major landmark in this regard, for it showed that the Bolsheviks held most of the cards. Already by 1923, the rift was visible in Uzbek literary production.

For Fitrat, the expulsion from the government of Bukhara and the ensuing exile to Moscow in the summer 1923 were clearly a turning point. In a poem dated October 1923, Fitrat spoke of quiet, calm nights:

---

138. TsGARUz, f. 94, op. 1, d. 417, l. 4–4ob (13.05.1926).

Shunday kechalarni sevaman men,	I love such nights,
Bunda yugurush yo'q, surulush yo'q:	They have no running, no shoving;
Yurmoq-da, odoshmoq-da ko'rulmas;	No walking, no falling off the path;
Yolg'on ko'runush, soxta kulish yo'q.	There are no false sights, no fake smiles.
Yov shakli ko'zimdan ko'b uzoqda.	The enemy is far away.
Do'stlar esa undan-da yiroqda.	As for friends, they are even farther.
Shunday kechadan o'rgulaman	I am delighted by such nights!
men![139]	

Fitrat's preference for the quite of the night, without action and without fakeness, signified a disenchantment with the promises of the revolution. An even clearer example is that of Cho'lpon. He had attached great hopes of enlightenment and modernity and the overthrow of colonial inequalities to the revolution. The arrival of the agitation train *Krasnyi Vostok* in March 1920 was, for Cho'lpon, "one of the gifts of the new era." He hoped, "This train will give Turkestan and the whole East knowledge, education, enlightenment, [and] healthy ideas."[140] Similarly, he was sincere in his poetry celebrating the Comintern, for the liberation of the East was a matter close to his heart, yet the link with the nation and the land was absolutely fundamental for him. He continued to write about kolonizatorstvo, but his poetry failed to clothe its enthusiasm for the nation in acceptable Soviet garb. The patriotism of his numerous poems lamenting the destruction visited on Ferghana by Russian settlers and the Basmachi alike is striking. By 1923, his laments turned into a longing for retribution. As he wrote in a poem called "To the Despoiled Land":

O mighty land whose mountains salute the sky,
Why are there dark clouds over your head?

. . . .

Your beautiful green pastures have been trampled,
They have no cattle, no horses.
Which gallows have the shepherds been hanged from?
Why, instead of neighing and bleating,
There are only mournful cries?
Why is this?

. . . .

---

139. Fitrat, "Mening kecham," *Inqilob*, no. 13–14 (1924): 3–4.
140. Cho'lpon, "'Qizil sharq' poyezdi keldi," *Ishtirokiyun*, 17.03.1920.

Where are the beautiful girls, the youthful brides?
Is there no answer from heaven or earth?
Or from the despoiled land?!

. . . .

Why is the poisoned arrow
Of the plundered, heavy crown still in your breast?
Why don't you have the iron revenge
That once destroyed your enemies?
O, free land that has never put up with slavery,
Why does a shadow lie throttling you?[141]

Another poem published at about the same time, made the same point even more bluntly:

That's enough! There's finally a limit
To all these insults, this humiliation!
The edge that's arrived at bit by bit
Is only self-doubt and deprivation!

. . . .

This last stone that I hold in my hand
I long to fling at my nemesis.
This last tear that my eye contains,
I long to shed for my lifelong aims.[142]

Narrowly, these poems lamented the despoliation of Ferghana by Russian settlers, but there would have been no doubt in any reader's mind that Cho'lpon had a broader critique in mind. He made clear the identity of his "nemesis" in another poem called "Autumn" from the same year: "O you who come from cold places, clothed in ice / May that grating voice of yours be lost in the snow. / O you who pick the fruits of my garden, / May your dark heads be buried in the earth."[143] By the time Cho'lpon went off to Moscow, then, his reputation as a "nationalist" was in place. Dark clouds were building up over his head, but they broke only in early 1927.

---

141. Cho'lpon, "Buzulg'an o'lkaga (Sharq uchun)," *Bilim o'chog'i*, no. 2–3 (15.05.1923); also in *Asarlar*, 3 vols. (Tashkent, 1994), 1:33–34. Cho'lpon dated the poem to 1920, when the ethnic warfare of the civil war was at its height.

142. Cho'lpon, "Bas endi," *Inqilob*, no. 9–10 (Feb.–March 1923); in *Asarlar*, 1:55; translation by Timur Kocaoğlu, "Cho'lpon she'rlari ingliz tilida," *Jahon adabiyoti*, 1998, no. 4: 136.

143. Cho'lpon, "Xazon" (November 1923), in *Asarlar*, 1:156–157.

Yet, disenchantment with the Soviet regime did not mean the abandonment of the reform project. In fact, for Fitrat, the Moscow months were highly productive. Exile seemed only to have hardened his reformist convictions and given them a sharper edge. After his return to Central Asia in September 1924, Fitrat was constantly at odds with the party, yet he produced a vast array of scholarly works on Uzbek language, literature, and music in the years that followed. For others, too, disenchantment with the Soviet order did not mean reconciliation with "traditional" society. Disenchantment with the Soviet regime did not make the prerevolutionary intelligentsia give up its project of cultural transformation, but it did make its task much more difficult.

ISLAM BETWEEN REFORM
AND REVOLUTION

In March 1919, Hoji Muin ibn Shukrulla, the longtime Jadid activist, took to the pages of the newspaper *Mehnatkashlar tovushi* (Toilers' Voice) to discuss the prevalence of to'y, celebrations marking important life-cycle events, such as births, weddings, and deaths among the Muslims of Samarqand, as well as the fact that girls were married off without their consent. A critique of the to'y for its wastefulness and its nonconformance with the norms of "true Islam" had been a staple of Jadid critique, as was the question of women's position in society. Now Hoji Muin hoped that "the district and city soviets [of Samarqand] and our Muslim communists will discuss these customs and produce some good resolutions" to curb such un-Islamic customs.[1] A year earlier, the Soviet of Muslim Peasants' and Workers' Deputies in Samarqand had sought to establish reformed Islamic courts of qazis to deal with issues of personal and civil law for the Muslim population of the city.[2] At about the same time, the reformist ulama of the Fuqaho Jamiyati (Society of Jurists) had petitioned the Executive Committee of the Tashkent old-city soviet to ban various types of Sufi figures such as *maddoh* and *voiz* from the

---

1. Hoji Muin, "To'y va aza marosimi haqinda" (*Mehnatkashlar tovushi*, 22.03.1919), in *Tanlangan asarlar*, ed. N. Nozimova (Tashkent, 2005), 93.

2. TsGARUz, f. 38, op. 2, d. 24, ll. 76–98 (14.05.1918). A year later, a new qazi was inaugurated in Samarqand on 23 May 1919 at a ceremony involving both ulama and members of the government; see "Rasm-i kushād-i qażāvat-i Bāghishimāl," *Shu'la-yi inqilāb*, 29.05.1919, 8.

streets of Tashkent.[3] The Fuqaho accompanied the petition with a *rivoyat* (quotations from Islamic juridical literature) establishing the strength of their case.[4]

The early enthusiasm for the revolution included the hope that it would reform Islam itself. Just as local soviets helped finance new-method schools and theater, they also helped the Jadids in striking at their opponents. Local soviets routinely used the language of Islamic reform interchangeably with that of revolution and enacted the reform of Islamic practices. In 1918, it was the old-city soviet in Tashkent that had outlawed the Ulamo Jamiyati and confiscated its assets. In January 1923, the same soviet banned Sufi figures from the streets and outlawed the public performance of *zikr* as part of a wide-ranging decree that set forth new norms of public demeanor.[5] In Bukhara, of course, the state acted even more forthrightly, if not always successfully, to reform madrasas, nationalize waqfs, and control Sufi practice. Islam and the practices and institutions attached to it became a central site for the contestation for power in Muslim society.

However, reform and revolution were located in different discursive frameworks, even if they could converge on certain issues, such as the critique of customary practices of Islam. Jadidism had begun as a project of redefining "Islam" through appeal to Islamic sources of authority and from a discursive position located inside the Islamic tradition. Like their counterparts elsewhere in the Muslim world, the Jadids had long criticized customary practices such as shrine visitation, lavish feasts, and marriage at a young age as being impermissible in light of the scriptural sources of Islam.[6] They had also argued for the bureaucratization of Islamic authority. Revolution as understood by the party was something else entirely. It sought a transformation of Islam's position in society and politics wrought from a subject position entirely outside the Islamic tradition and indeed quite inimical to it. For the Bolsheviks, the extirpation of religion from society was an important goal. In Central Asia, they deferred it, in part because local Muslim Communists could not even begin to comprehend it. Customary practices denoted backwardness, superstition, or fanaticism. Antagonisms between reformers and their opponents transformed the contours of reform, which became ever more radical and the reformers' rhetoric ever harsher, while the

---

3. "Toshkand musulmon mehnatkash va dehqonlarining ijroiya komitetiga . . . Fuqaho Jamiyati idorasi tarafidan Arzihol," TsGARUz, f. 36, op. 1, d. 12, l. 174.

4. Ibid., ll. 172–173. The *rivoyat* was based on a fatwa from the *Fatāwā-yi 'Ālamgīriya*, an eighteenth-century collection of Hanafi jurisprudence widely accepted in Turkestan. These documents have now been published by Paolo Sartori, "Tashkent 1918: giurisperiti musulmani e autorità sovietiche contro i 'predicatori del bazar,'" *Annali di Ca' Foscari* 45:3 (2006): 113–139.

5. "Eski Toshkand ijroqo'mining majburiy qarori," *Turkiston*, 28.02.1923.

6. This attitude was most explicitly articulated by Fitrat on the eve of the revolution: Fiṭrat, *Rahbar-i nijāt* (Bukhara, 1916).

new cultural field shaped by the revolution provided new possibilities of critique. The boundaries between reform and revolution were difficult to demarcate, and there was constant slippage in practice between the two. Some Jadids, most notably Fitrat (whose trajectory we study in detail below), traversed a huge distance from religious reform to irreligion. In 1927, when the party finally launched a campaign against Islam and Islamic institutions, the shape of reform had been utterly transformed.

Nor was it a matter only of debate. Islamic institutions such as qazi courts and waqf (pious foundations) also became sites of intense contestation among Muslims. They also suffered grievously from the economic chaos of the period and from the new political order that sidelined them even if it did not outright abolish them. By 1927, the combination of reform and revolution had debilitated Islamic institutions in Uzbekistan to such an extent that their final abolition was less traumatic than might have been.

Religious Ferment

The revolution took place at a time of considerable religious debate in Central Asia and profoundly reshaped its contours. Jadidism was only one of the many movements that rejected the permissibility of customs and traditions (*urf-odatlar*) through which Muslims had known Islam and been Muslims. A different strand of reform, articulated by ulama mainly from Tashkent, also sought to anchor Islam in a rigorous scripturalism and "to cleanse the shariat of superstition [*xurofot*] and innovations [*bid'at*],"[7] but had little use for notions of progress or nation. The main vehicle of this reformist current was the journal *al-Isloh* (Reform), which began appearing in Tashkent in 1915. This current of reform bore a striking resemblance to that articulated by the ulama of Deoband in India and to Salafism in general.[8] It was out of the ranks of such ulama that the Fuqaho Jamiyati emerged in 1917.

A yet more rigorous strand of reform was the movement of the *Ahl-i hadith* ("Proponents of Hadith") who saw hadith as the supreme source of authority, overriding fiqh and other traditions. Although Ahl-i hadith influences can

---

7. "Islohmi, izohmi," *al-Isloh*, 15.01.1918, 22–25.

8. The lines connecting early twentieth-century Salafism to Central Asia remain to be investigated fully; for a preliminary assessment, see Stéphane A. Dudoignon, "Echoes of *al-Manār* among the Muslims of the Russian Empire: A Preliminary Research Note on Riza al-Din b. Fakhr al-Din and the *Šūrā* (1908–1918)," in *Intellectuals in the Modern Islamic World: Transmission, Transformation, Communication*, ed. Stéphane A. Dudoignon, Hisao Komatsu, and Yasushi Kosugi (London, 2006), 85–116.

be seen in *al-Isloh* before the revolution, the real growth in the popularity of Ahl-i hadith ideas in Turkestan seems to have taken place during the era of the revolution. It is usually tied to the arrival in Tashkent in 1919 of the somewhat mysterious figure of the Lebanese-born scholar Saʿid ibn Muhammad al-ʿAsali al-Tarablusi (ca. 1867–1932). Born in Tripoli, al-Tarablusi studied in Cairo. He was ostensibly exiled from the Ottoman Empire for his religious views and spent almost two decades in China, most of it in Kashgar, where he taught in local madrasas and acquired the epithet Shomiy Domla, the Syrian Professor. He was not a man of exceptional learning, but he seems to have acquired considerable personal influence in Chinese Turkestan, where his Arab origin and his Ottoman connection gave him great prestige.[9] For reasons not quite clear, he left Kashgar in early 1919 and came to Tashkent, where again he quickly acquired the respect of local ulama. From what little we know of his ideas, it is clear that Shomiy Domla was driven by a desire to restore, as he saw it, the authority of hadith, and particularly that of the *Ṣaḥīḥ* of Imam Bukhari, one of the canonical compilations of hadith he felt had been unjustly ignored. His arrival in Turkestan was part of a quest to visit Bukhari's homeland.[10] Once there, however, he became a vocal critic not just of local customs but of the whole tradition of teaching entrenched in the madrasas of Central Asia. During the first half of the 1920s, he was active in various initiatives to reform Islamic courts and to regulate waqf, both in Turkestan and Bukhara.

---

9. Shomiy Domla seems to have left a significant memory among the ulama of Tashkent who survived the Soviet assault on Islam of the 1930s. His name has been brought back into scholarly circulation by Ashirbek Muminov, "Shami-damulla i ego rol' v formirovanii 'sovetskogo islama,'" in *Islam, identichnost' i politika v postsovetskom prostranstve* (Kazan, 2005), 231–247. Yet much remains unknown about Shomiy Domla's life, his ideas, or his motives. David Brophy has found a few traces in Chinese archives, which make it clear that he spent close to ten years in Xinjiang before 1917; see David Brophy, "Tending to Unite? The Origins of Uyghur Nationalism" (Ph.D. diss., Harvard University, 2011), 177. He most likely left the Ottoman Empire because he did not agree with Unionist politics, but he nevertheless used his status as a subject of the caliph and an Arab to cultivate substantial influence in the region. He crops up in the memoirs of several Ottoman officers who encountered him in Xinjiang during or after the First World War, where his portrayal is uniformly negative, as a charlatan and a bigot who understood little of the modern world. Nevertheless, we also see Shomiy Domla enjoying great respect and influence locally and crossing the boundary between China and Russia seemingly at will. It was he who conducted Ziya Yergök from Siberia into Turkestan via Xinjiang, using his authority and connections to get him across the boundary twice. Ziya Yergök, *Sarıkamış'tan Esarete (1915–1920)*, ed. Sami Önal (Istanbul, 2005), 188–212; see also Adil Hikmet Bey, *Asya'da Beş Türk* (Istanbul, 1998), 238–240.

10. If Shomiy Domla was indeed a scholar, very little of his writing has survived. (His influence seems to have been conveyed largely dialogically.) My characterization of him is based on the one brief piece of his that has been published: Saʿīd b. Muḥammad b. ʿAbd al-Wāḥid b. ʿAlī al-ʿAsalī al-Ṭarābulusī al-Shāmī al-Dimashqī, "Al-jumal al-mufida fī sharḥ al-jawhara al-farīda," in B. M. Babadzhanov, A. K. Muminov, and A. fon-Kiugel'gen, eds., *Disputy musul'manskikh religioznykh avtoritetov v Tsentral'noi Azii v XX veke* (Almaty, 2007), 62–71 (text), 72–95 (trans.)

At the other end of the reformist spectrum stood the Baha'is, who took advantage of the liberties provided by 1917 to launch a campaign of proselytism with some zeal. The Baha'i faith had come to Turkestan through labor migration from Iran to Transcaspia, and a small Baha'i community had taken root in Ashkhabad by the turn of the century.[11] Before the Baha'i faith took on its universalist orientation in the West, it was an Islamic sect, and it appeared in Turkestan as such. In 1918, the Baha'i community began publishing a magazine called *Vahdat* (Unity) in Tashkent, and although that experience was short lived, the Baha'i presence was constant throughout the 1920s.[12] Traditionalist ulama often equated them with the Jadids as heretics. Like the Jadids, the Baha'is espoused a modernist approach to religion, and indeed the Baha'i faith seems to have appealed to many Jadids. At least one Jadid figure, Vadud Mahmud of Samarqand, formally became a Baha'i. His turn to Baha'ism came through his friendship with a certain Sayyid Fazluddin, an apothecary originally from Punjab who had arrived in Samarqand in 1914 from Afghanistan, where he had apparently become a Baha'i. He also counted Fitrat and Cho'lpon among his social circle.[13] The fact that an Indian Muslim was a major Baha'i figure in Samarqand is indicative both of the rise in Baha'i activity and of the persistence of transnational connections well after the revolution.

What all of these currents of reform had in common was a critique of traditional ways of knowing Islam, of customary practices (urf-odatlar) connected with them, and of their carriers, conservative ulama and Sufi figures (*eshon, maddoh, qalandar, voiz*). The challenge was both epistemological and political, fought out in the broader cultural field. Those who posed the challenge came from different positions—in the context of the 1920s in Central Asia, however, reformers found themselves making common cause with revolutionaries with a very different agenda.

Reform and Revolution

The critique of customary practices provided fertile ground for collaboration, and it is often difficult to determine where reformist critique melded into revolutionary condemnation of Islam. The decree of Tashkent's old-city soviet that banned Sufis from the streets of the city was both an instance of the reform of Islam and an exercise

---

11. For an "official" Baha'i account, see Moojan Momen, "The Baha'i Community of Ashkhabad: Its Social Basis and Importance in Baha'i History," in Shirin Akiner, ed., *Cultural Change and Continuity in Central Asia* (London, 1991), 278–305.

12. D. Iu. Arapov, "Musul'manskoe dukhovenstvo Srednei Azii v 1927 godu (po dokladu polnomochnogo predsedatelia OGPU v Srednei Azii)," in *Rasy i narody: ezhegodnik*, vyp. 32 (Moscow, 2006), 330–332.

13. Naim Karimov, *Istiqlolni uyg'otgan shoir* (Tashkent, 2000), 44.

FIGURE 3. Provocations at the destruction of the Shayxontahur mausoleum. *Mushtum*, no. 12 (25.06.1925), 24.

in new techniques of power.[14] It was on the question of shrines (mazor) that reformers of all stripes could find common cause most easily with the Soviets. Shrines dotted the landscape in Central Asia and rendered it Islamic. Visiting holy sites was a central feature of Islamic religious life in Central Asia as elsewhere. But it was also the custom that was most harshly criticized by reformers. Scripturalists saw the practice of seeking intercession from holy men as a form of idolatry that amounted to *shirk*, the sin of compromising God's unity. Modernists added to this critique another layer of disapproval, that made shrine visitation a sign of backwardness, of the ignorance of the people and their gullibility. Modernist critiques of shrines cast them as dens of pederasty and immorality, where unscrupulous eshons took advantage of simple folk and corrupted their morals. The eradication of shrines and shrine visitation was an important item on the reformist agenda. In 1924, Tashkent's mahkama-yi shar'iya (see below) issued a fatwa on the permissibility of destroying graves more than thirty years old, for "mazors take up too much space in the old city."[15] As a result, a number of graves in the Ko'kcha quarter were leveled and a school built in their place. Reformist Islamic practices, public health, and national education were all

---

14. "Eski Toshkand ijroqo'mning majburiy qarori," *Turkiston*, 28.02.1923.
15. *Turkiston*, 11.03.1924.

neatly intertwined in this episode. Such demolitions seem to have become common-place, mostly on the initiative of reformers. The Young Bukharan government began demolishing cemeteries inside the city of Bukhara in 1923.[16] Two years later, the mazor of Shayxontahur in Tashkent, one of the city's most prominent, was demolished. The event was noted in *Mushtum*, whose commentary was a striking example of the overlap between "reformist" and "revolutionary" critiques of customary practices. *Mushtum* ran a cartoon (figure 3) captioned, "Provocations at the Destruction of the Shayxontahur mazor," that showed the devil in two forms, Azazel and Iblis, both drawn according to European conventions (complete with horns and a tail), bemoaning the fact that "our house is being destroyed, the customs of our ancestors are being trampled." An accompanying article equated Azazel with vain pride and Iblis with cunning, and likened each to individual ulama who had opposed the destruction of the mazor.[17] Seeing mazors as Satan's houses was scarcely a Bolshevik tradition—the critique of mazors here is semantically located in the Islamic tradition even as its form is European and Bolshevik.

Mushtum was edited by Abdulla Qodiriy until 1926. Qodiriy was a man of solid Islamic credentials: he had studied at the Beglarbegi madrasa in Tashkent, knew not just Turkic and Persian, but also Arabic, which he used to follow both the modern secular work being produced in Arabic, as well as religious literature. We have reports of Qodiriy taking regular part in various discussion groups among the ulama of Tashkent at the same time as he edited *Mushtum* and contributed copiously to it. His depictions of traditionalist, conservative ulama make fun of their narrow-mindedness, their inability to understand the world they lived in, and above all their inability to understand Islam itself. But nowhere in his work does Qodiriy renounce Islam. Many of the pieces published in *Mushtum* when he was at the helm went further, of course, but there is little evidence that Qodiriy found them problematic. A clue to understanding this seeming paradox comes from a throwaway comment he made during his interrogation by the NKVD after his arrest in 1937. Statements made during interrogation are, of course, problematic sources, but one rings true: "I am a reformist, a proponent of renewal. In Islam, I only recognize faith in God the Munificent as the highest reality. As for the other innovations, most of them I consider to be the work of Muslim clerics."[18] This is a radically reformist position that many have espoused in the Muslim world in the modern age. In its sheer iconoclasm and rejection of traditional authority, however, it had much in common with the "revolutionary" position of the Soviet state, which stood self-consciously outside the Islamic tradition.

---

16. Cho'lpon celebrated the course of action, seeing in it a victory of life over death. Cho'lpon, "O'liklarga qorshi," *Buxoro axbori*, 07.05.1923.

17. "Azozil va Iblis," *Mushtum*, no. 12 (25.06.1925), 2.

18. Nabijon Boqiy, "Qatlnoma: hujjatli qissa," *Sharq yulduzi*, 1991, no. 5: 80.

Muslim Anticlericalism

The Jadids had long seen traditionalist ulama as the biggest obstacle to the reform of society and of Islam itself. Muslim reformers had at their disposal a long tradition of skepticism of piety indigenous to the Islamicate tradition, but in the decades before the revolution, this had been augmented by sources. By the turn of the twentieth century, Muslim critics of the ulama could also borrow from European anticlericalism. In the Ottoman Empire, both secularist and pious critics of the religious establishment began to brand Ottoman ulama as a clergy, associating them with the negative traits ascribed to Christian clergy in European anticlericalism.[19] In the Tatar lands, where the ulama were organized in the Orenburg Spiritual Assembly, they had begun to be referred to as *ruhanilar* ("spirituals"), a calque from the Russian term for clergy. In 1911, Fitrat incorporated French republican anticlericalism whole cloth in his critique of the state of affairs in Bukhara. In *The Tales of the Indian Traveler*, he quoted a long passage from "the great French professor" Charles Seignobos (whom he had read in Ottoman translation) about the glories of medieval Islamic civilization, before having the traveler tell his hosts:

> The activities of your self-proclaimed ulama are the reason for the extinction of your nation. But there's no need to grieve, brother, since your ulama aren't the only ones like this. The fact is, ulama all over the Muslim world in the last three centuries have committed similar crimes. Until yesterday, the majority of ulama among Turks and Tatars, and in Iran and India, just like yours, all drank the blood of oppressed people. But these nations scrutinized matters before you have done, and they overthrew the ulama from their pedestal. Quickly they distinguished real scholars from mullahs who only worshipped their own bellies; they placed crowns on the heads of the former and trampled the latter underfoot.[20]

The political confrontation of 1917 had raised the stakes—and the tone— considerably. As the conflict sharpened over the course of 1917, Jadid depictions of the ulama grew ever harsher and more sarcastic. In *Autonomy*, a short piece of comic theater, Hamza lampooned the ulama for being aggressively ignorant of the world around them and interested only in filling their own bellies. The play is set in the drawing room of a rich man's house, where a large group of ulama feast. They discuss the current political situation, which they do not understand at all (they think autonomy is a kind of automobile), but they can all agree in thinking

19. Amit Bein, *Ottoman Ulema, Turkish Republic: Agents of Change and Guardians of Tradition* (Stanford, 2011), 14–24.

20. Fiṭrat, *Bayānāt-i sayyāḥ-i hindī* (Istanbul, 1330/1912), 34–35, 40.

of the Jadids as infidels. Their main achievement is to pass a resolution to remove the table and to finish their feast on the floor in proper "Islamic" fashion.[21] In 1919, Fitrat quoted "a famous Turkish philosopher" to the effect "that the cause of the descent of the Muslim world into such dark days are the tyrannical kings, our poets who heaped false praise on them, and our eshons and mullahs who sold our faith."[22] Another author warned that in electing qazis in the new era, "we have to watch out for those who use the shariat as a tool for the satisfaction of their own personal desires, or those who calling themselves qazis, surround themselves with fatwa-mongering muftis without a conscience and completely ignorant of the shariat."[23] Sufi masters (eshon) came in for disdainful criticism for "going hunting for disciples" (murid ovlamoq) in order to line their own pockets.[24] The ulama became "religion-mongers" (dinfuro'shlar) who used religion as a source for private gain. Newspapers denounced eshons and other religious figures for various misdeeds, naming names and making public demands for punishment and retribution.[25] Few figures typify this critique of the ulama better than Qodiriy's character Kalvak Maxzum ("Friar Simple"), an unreconstructed mullah of the old stripe who combines conceit, bigotry, and ignorance in equal measure with cunning. "Pages from Kalvak Maxzum's Diary," which Qodiriy began publishing in Mushtum in 1923, contain the full catalogue of the criticisms of the ulama current at the time, but what sets this series of texts apart from the general run of the period's anticlericalism is its masterful use of language. Qodiriy very successfully used the argot of Tashkent ulama, with its ornate vocabulary larded with Perso-Arabic words and phrases, to poke fun at them.

Theater was another venue where the ulama could be ridiculed. The vibrant theater of these years was resolutely anticlerical, with no positive portrayals of the ulama. In fact, we find a reviewer criticizing an actor for not being able to convey "the duplicity characteristic of the clerics" in his portrayal of a character in Fitrat's Indian Revolutionaries.[26] But it was the cartoon that took the critique of the ulama and the eshons to new levels. The cartoon arrived in the Muslim world in the late nineteenth century and was quickly put to satirical use, for it could

---

21. Hamza, "Oftonomiya, yoki muxtoriyat," in To'la asarlar to'plami, 5 vols. (Tashkent, 1988–89), 3: 52–67.

22. [Fitrat], Insoniyat haqinda Navoiyning fikri (Tashkent, 1919), 2.

23. Abdulhamidzoda, "Shariat hukmi—vijdon hukmidur!" Ishtirokiyun, 18.01.1920.

24. Qilich So'fi (pseud.), "Murid ovlosh," Mashrab, no. 14 (11.01.1925), 7.

25. We read, thus, of one Said Ahmadxon to'ra Miyon Fathiyxon o'g'li who took a new wife, took her property, and promptly divorced her; Komil Aliyev, "Yana bir eshonning jinoyati," Turkiston, 15.12.1923. Abdulla Qodiriy wrote about a dynasty of eshons in Tashkent, describing with his usual sarcasm, their deep entanglement with the Tsarist order: Jiyan (pseud.), "Eshonlarimiz," Mushtum, no. 25 (08.04.1924), no. 2 (20.05.1924). See also Z. Nusrat, "Xurofotga qarshi: eshonlar kim?" Turkiston, 03.06.1924. There was much more in this vein than can be cited here.

26. Ishchi [G'ozi Yunus?], "Hind ixtilolchilari," Turkiston, 20.10.1923.

overcome the barrier posed by illiteracy. Central Asian readers had access to cartoons via the illustrated press that appeared in the Ottoman Empire after the Constitutional Revolution, but the most important channel was *Molla Nasreddin*, the Tiflis-based magazine that was read by Turkic language communities in both the Russian and the Ottoman empires, as well as in Iran.[27] Its cartoonists were almost all Europeans whose styles were rooted in contemporary Europe, but their work was tethered to an indigenous Muslim reformist critique. By 1917, *Molla Nasreddin* had created a substantial corpus of images and *topoi* that cast the ulama (and other worthies) in a caustic light. While *Molla Nasreddin* circulated in Central Asia (as did the illustrated press from the Ottoman Empire), a local illustrated press appeared only in 1923 as the result of a Soviet initiative. In that year, the party established a satirical press to act as a watchdog and as a spur for ensuring revolutionary zeal in Soviet institutions and society at large. The Moscow magazine *Krokodil* (Crocodile) acquired vernacular counterparts in other major languages across the Soviet state. In Turkestan, the most important magazine, *Mushtum* (Fist), published initially as a fortnightly supplement to *Turkiston*, was very much the counterpart of *Krokodil*, but it also carried the mantle of *Molla Nasreddin*. (That magazine had fallen victim to the war but made a comeback after the revolution and was published in Baku until 1931.) It featured not just prose and poetry poking often merciless fun at all aspects of society—its backwardness, its unwillingness to listen to ideas of progress and change, and attitudes toward women—but it also brutally lampooned the ulama and Sufi figures, both in text and in cartoons.

The main artist working for *Mushtum* was a European, a man by the name of Tulle, about whom we know unfortunately nothing. The cartoons use European conventions in their depictions, especially of religious figures (Jesus, even when he appears in purely Islamic contexts, Satan, God) and are often similar to what was appearing in *Krokodil* and other Russian magazines at the time. More radical than anything in the prerevolutionary *Molla Nasreddin*, these cartoons contributed to the transformation of the visual culture of urban Central Asia. Printed in large format in bright, if crude colors, these cartoons could be used as posters. They did much to displace the public authority of the ulama. It became possible to see the ulama caricatured and ridiculed as never before. To the extent

---

27. On Ottoman cartoons, see Palmira Brummett, *Image and Imperialism in the Ottoman Revolutionary Press, 1908–1911* (Albany, 2000). The entire run of *Molla Nasreddin* has been republished in Latin script in Azerbaijan, but neither the journal, nor its art have received the analytical attention they deserve. See Nazim Axundov, *"Molla Nəsrəddin" jurnalının nəşri tarixi* (Baku, 1959). (Many thanks to Bruce Grant for this reference.) The volume, *Molla Nasreddin: The Magazine that Would've Could've Should've*, edited by "Slavs and Tatars" (Zurich, 2010), is a curious mixture of analysis and misinformation.

FIGURE 4. The animals of Tashkent welcome Mahmudxon to'ra of Namangon. *Mushtum*, no. 16 (December 1923), 8.

that the dignity of proper comportment and personal gravitas were a large part of the cultural capital of the ulama, their portrayal as duplicitous, greedy, inebriated, or animalesque (see figure 4) was a major blow to the structures of value that underpinned the ulama's authority. In the same years, the nascent republican press in Turkey also used the cartoon to push back against the authority of the ulama, but Turkish cartoons, for all their radicalness, could not match their Uzbek counterparts in their vitriol.[28] The Soviet context made criticisms of the ulama much harsher.

The Ulama Besieged

What the traditionalist ulama—those who were not interested in any sort of "reform"—made of this is not always easy to discern. We are faced with the silence of the sources. After the Jadids used Soviet power to abolish the ulama's organizations in the spring of 1918, the ulama were excluded from the new public space.

---

28. Yasemin Gencer, "Pushing Out Islam: Cartoons of the Reform Period in Turkey (1923–1928)," in *Visual Culture in the Modern Middle East*, eds. Christiane Gruber and Sune Haugbolle (Bloomington, 2013), 189–213.

Their voices occasionally come through in the press (although almost always in the form of quotations used for hostile purposes) and the archives yield up a few gems. The records of the political police contain copious materials of surveillance and confession that are deeply problematic. Nevertheless, read against the grain, these materials allow us a certain sense of the ulama in this period.

The abolition of their organizations did not rob the ulama of their authority in society, which persisted and often took very tangible forms. Traditionalist ulama presented themselves as the upholders of order, of true Islam itself, in a time of chaos. During the short-lived Osipov uprising in January 1919, they sided with the insurgents and took over the old city of Tashkent for a day. They used their momentary ascendency to settle accounts with their Muslim enemies.[29] In areas held by the Basmachi too, the ulama exercised power as qazis, their authority subject only to the power of the warlords. In other instances, Sufi figures led the Basmachi, as was the case in Mastchoh (see chapter 2). The political police suspected some of the major figures of wanting to establish an Islamic state, and this was confirmed to the satisfaction of the NKVD in the self-incriminating confessions of many Tashkent ulama in 1938. The term used for this "Islamic state" was *Musulmonobod*, "Muslimland," and seems to have indicated a space under a Muslim sovereign in which the ulama would be able to administer the shariat by their own lights, unfettered by the restrictions placed on them by the Tsars or the Soviets.[30] Unfortunately, we have little direct evidence of these ambitions.

Other ulama sought to work within Soviet institutions. On a trip to rural parts of the Ferghana Valley in early 1923, the secretary of the Central Committee of the KPT, M. S. Epshtein was perturbed to find many ulama using their authority to appear before local ispolkoms as spokesmen for the population. They would even sing the "Internationale" at public meetings to assert their revolutionary credentials.[31] There are other accounts of such "Red Mullahs" from the period that have turned into a routinely cited myth, although the archival record is scanty. Most efforts by the ulama to use the language of the revolution came up short. In March 1923, a certain Mubashshirxon Sayyidxon o'g'li, qazi from Avliyo-ota, laid out a lengthy argument against the Soviet law on divorce, which gave women the right to initiate divorce. Islam, he argued, had rationalized divorce by taking it away from women, because "men lose the fruits of their labor when their wives

---

29. *Ishtirokiyun*, 19.02.1919.

30. Paolo Sartori, "The Tashkent 'Ulamā' and the Soviet State (1920–38): A Preliminary Research Note Based on NKVD Documents," in *Patterns of Transformation in and around Uzbekistan*, ed. Paolo Sartori and Tommaso Trevisani (Reggio Emilia, 2007), 175–176.

31. M. S. Epshtein, "Zakrytoe pis'mo No. 2 (6) sekretaria TsK KPT tov. Epshteina za fevral' mesiats 1923 g." (17.03.1923), in *TsK RKP(b)—VKP(b) i natsional'nyi vopros*, bk. 1 (Moscow, 2005), 102.

leave them"! Women like comforts and luxuries, our august qazi argued, and would leave the poor (*bechora kambag'allar*) for the wealthy (*boybachchalar*) in droves if divorce became possible. The new law oppressed the poor and allowed the wealthy to accumulate more wives; it thus increased inequalities. "If this continues for another ten years, only 10% of the poor in Russia will have wives left. Therefore, in the name of the entire poor oppressed male population of Avliyo-ota uezd [*butun Avliyo-ato uyozini kambag'al bechora ezilgan er kishilari tarafindan*], I ask you to resolve this matter quickly."[32] The document is remarkable for its combination of misogyny, customary Islam, and the language of class, but it produced little practical effect.

Most ulama seem to have been part of the grumbling majority of the population, but they occasionally were able to mobilize their authority in acts of resistance or violence. A year after Mubashshirxon wrote his memo on divorce, we hear of him as the leader of a group that was criticizing the government openly.[33] After the destruction of graves in the Ko'kcha district of Tashkent, anonymous proclamations appeared in mosques cursing the inhabitants of the mahalla for having destroyed the cemetery without having consulted "authoritative and trustworthy" ulama.[34] We have seen in chapter 6 other examples of mobilization led by the ulama in defense of qorixonas and madrasas in these years. The persistence of the authority of the ulama gave their opponents a certain desperation that drove them to more radical positions. For Epshtein, it was clear that "clerical elements, reflecting the mood of growing mercantile capital [during NEP], attempt to play the role of the organizer of the life of the popular masses, to become their leaders."[35] The OGPU constantly worried about conservative ulama infiltrating Soviet and party institutions.

Islamic Institutions in the Era of Revolution

The Bolsheviks, as true heirs of the materialist traditions of the radical Enlightenment, considered religion both an epistemological and a political challenge. Their first legislative acts separated the church from the state, banished religion from education, secularized marriage, and made divorce easily available. They also launched an assault on the Russian Orthodox church in the years of the civil war, expropriating its property and destroying its ability to organize in

---

32. TsGARUz, f. 38, op. 2, d. 396, ll. 53–54ob (13.03.1923).

33. "Ovliyo-otada eskilar harakati," *Turkiston*, 02.06.1924.

34. Turg'unboy, "Madaniyat va maorif aksilharakatchilari bosh kutarmakda," *Turkiston*, 28.05.1924.

35. Epshtein, "Zakrytoe pis'mo," 102.

opposition. Central Asia escaped most of these antireligious initiatives in the first years of Soviet rule from a combination of the thinness of Soviet rule and the Bolsheviks' fear of exacerbating existing opposition or ill will. Soviet legislation on religion applied only to the European spaces of Central Asia (i.e., the new cities and Russian settler villages), while in much of the rest of the region older practices continued.

In May 1919, TurTsIK issued a decree, modeled on pan-Soviet legislation, that abolished the legal pluralism of the Tsarist order and replaced Islamic courts with a unified people's court (*edinyi narodnyi sud*).[36] The decree provoked considerable opposition among the Muslim population, which took the form of demonstrations and petitions.[37] In February 1920, the Turkkomissiia received a petition with sixteen hundred signatures in which the petitioners threatened to emigrate en masse if the law on the unified people's court were not changed to accommodate the shariat.[38] Several Muslim Communists invoked all the usual arguments—the fanaticism of the population, the importance of Turkestan to world revolution, the backwardness of Turkestan—to plead with the Turkkomissiia for the retention of qazi courts and for attempting to reconcile the norms of the shariat and Soviet law.[39] None of this produced immediate effect, though a year later, after the Musburo was gone, TurTsIK established a commission to "harmonize shariat and adat with Soviet law" (*shariat va odatni shurolar qonuniga to'g'rilomoq*). The commission held a few meetings in 1921, but could achieve little beyond declaring that such harmonization was possible "only through culture being reformed among the Muslim people through education."[40] In practice, qazi courts continued to operate, as is clear from the number of exhortations to shut them down that emanated from the authorities.[41] This was particularly the case in Ferghana, where the local offices of Commissariat of Justice found it best not

---

36. Kh. S. Sulaimanova, *Sozdanie i razvitie sovetskogo suda v Turkestanskoi ASSR (1917–1924 gg.)* (Tashkent, 1954), 50–57.

37. Paolo Sartori, "What Went Wrong? The Failure of Soviet Policy on Sharīʿa Courts in Turkestan, 1917–1923," *Die Welt des Islams* 50 (2010), 405–406.

38. AAP RUz, f. 60, op. 1, d. 402, l. 63 (minutes of kraikom KPT, 12.02.1920).

39. Ibid., ll. 63ob-64ob.

40. TsGARUz, f. 38, op. 2, d. 195, l. 1. Sartori, "What Went Wrong?" has examined this episode in great detail, but he overstates its significance by seeing in it a serious attempt at indigenizing Soviet law, which failed because Soviet functionaries did not understand the niceties of Islamic law (i.e., they were not good enough Orientalists). Yet there is no reason to believe that the party leadership ever had any intention of compromising on a matter of principle and ceding Soviet law to the shariat.

41. E.g., Sovnarkom prikaz, TsGARUz, f. 38, op. 2, d. 98, l. 2–2ob (June 1920), or Musul'manskii Otdel Narkomiusta, "Plan blizhaishchei raboty (po ustroistvu musnarsudov)" (early 1921), TsGARUz, f. 38, op. 2, d. 195, ll. 8–8a.

even to publish the May 1919 decree. As the local section of the commissariat reported to Tashkent, "with the exception of the cities, the Basmachi strolled about the oblast without any restraint . . . and almost every single qazi, except in the cities, found himself in the hands of the Basmachi; therefore, the justice section considered publishing the order about the abolition of [the courts of] qazis and biys unnecessary saber-rattling. Indeed, publishing the order would only have given enemies of Soviet power the means to begin among the 2½ million-strong dark and fanatical Muslim population a provocation against Soviet power."[42] Instead, the section took measures to ensure that the unified people's court was given the possibility to bank on the shariat and adat in making its decisions, as long as they did not contradict socialist principles.[43] Shariat had crept into the unified people's court! Conditions continued to be bad enough for Soviet rule in Ferghana that in September 1921 TurTsIK formally allowed the reestablishment of qazi courts in that oblast. The terms of reference of the courts showed remarkable continuity with Tsarist legislation of qazi courts: they had jurisdiction over matters of marriage, divorce, and inheritance, as well as small-scale civil suits; they could impose modest fines; and sentence offenders to up to eighteen months of imprisonment.[44] One way or the other, qazi courts survived the early years of Soviet rule.

The same could be said of waqf. There is little evidence of systematic expropriation of waqf properties in these years, but it became a central point of contention between modernist and conservative Muslims. Tsarist authorities had tried to regulate waqf, but with only marginal success.[45] The Jadids, for their part, had long argued that waqf income should be regulated in the name of the community and made to serve communal goals.[46] Now they made the same point with greater insistence and urgency. In 1920, Munavvar qori told a conference of educators that waqfs were "founded not for serving religious and benevolent needs, but for the progress of culture and the enlightenment of the people." It was Russian colonial rule that had driven out all nonreligious learning from maktabs

---

42. Komissaru Iustitsii Turkestanskoi Respubliki ot Ferganskogo oblastnogo otdela Iustitsii (05.03.1920), TsGARUz, f. 38, op. 2, d. 53, ll. 145.

43. TsGARUz, f. 38, op. 2, d. 53, l. 141.

44. "Instruktsiia po uchrezhdeniiu v Ferganskoi oblasti sudei kaziev i biev," TsGARUz, f. 38, op. 2, d. 176, l. 17; *Farg'ona viloyatining qozi biylar ta'sisoti to'g'risida Ta'limot* (Tashkent, 1921).

45. For a useful overview, see Paolo Sartori, "Il *waqf* nel Turkestan russo tra legislazione e pratica amministrativa coloniale," *Quaderni Storici* 132 (2009): 797–826.

46. In 1906, Behbudiy, in his desiderata for Turkestan's constitutional future, had argued that all waqf income be given over to a religious administration that should use it on behalf of the community; see Necip Hablemitoğlu and Timur Kocaoğlu, "Behbudi'nin Türkistan Medeni Muhtariyeti Layıhası," in Timur Kocaoğlu, ed., *Türkistan'da Yenilik Hareketleri ve İhtilaller, 1900–1924: Osman Hoca Anısına İncelemeler* (Haarlem, 2001), 465.

and madrasas and turned them into hotbeds of fanaticism. Now, under the new conditions, waqf revenues, along with help from the government, could help "liberate the thousands of existing maktabs from their present pitiful condition and to transform them from religious institutions into sources of culture and enlightenment."[47] That argument was to be made ever more insistently over the next several years. Waqf had been reimagined by the Jadids.

A special commission on waqf affairs was established in Turkomnats in 1918, and over the next two years, the matter went back and forth between the commissariats of nationalities, internal affairs, and education. On 26 February 1920, at the height of the influence of Muslim Communists in Tashkent, TurTsIK transferred waqf affairs from the Commissariat of Internal Affairs to that of Education, which then resolved to establish a network of waqf sections in every branch of Narkompros.[48] A provisional statute created a Central Waqf Department in Tashkent, with branch offices in all areas with substantial amount of waqf property. The management of individual waqfs was left in the hands of the *mutavallis* (trustees), who formed part of a commission along with two other members, all elected from amongst teachers and students in a madrasas.[49] Matters seem to have rested there for the next couple of years, with the Communist Party of Turkestan affirming its disinclination to tamper with waqf properties at its Sixth Congress in 1921.[50]

Clearly, unlike in other Muslim regions of the country, in Turkestan waqfs were never systematically nationalized or confiscated. In general, the main damage to Islamic institutions in these years came more from the general upheaval of the period than from Soviet legislation. A number of waqfs passed into private property, while others no doubt became derelict, and in some cases, local revkoms and ispolkoms became involved in their fate. In Namangan, when a mosque burnt down in April 1919 during a Basmachi raid, the mutavalli took over the waqf property attached to it. The people who attended the mosque and those who received funds from the waqf petitioned the city revkom, the local Soviet people's court, and the local offices of Narkomnats for help with extracting the waqf property from the mutavalli, with permission to rebuild the mosque, and even for help with paying for the reconstruction.[51] A mutavalli in Tashkent

---

47. TsGARUz, f. 25, op. 1, d. 681, ll. 170–171ob (30.06.1920).

48. TsGARUz, f. 34, op. 1, d. 628, l. 18.

49. "Vremennoe polozhenie ob upravlenii vakufami Turkestanskoi Respubliki," TsGARUz, f. 25, op. 1, d. 681, ll. 172–176; see also Niccolò Pianciola and Paolo Sartori, "Waqf in Turkestan: The Colonial Legacy and the Fate of an Islamic Institution in Early Soviet Central Asia, 1917–1924," *Central Asian Survey* 26 (2007): 480–484.

50. *Kommunisticheskaia Partiia Turkestana v rezoliutsiiakh s"ezdov i konferentsii* (Tashkent, 1988), 151.

51. TsGARUz, f. 38, op. 2, d. 210.

sought help in action against a lessee who had sublet a shop to someone else and was pocketing the profit.[52] Numerous villages in Konibodom uezd had stopped paying the rent on waqf property they cultivated.[53] Madrasas shrunk in size as their waqf revenues dwindled, and even many rural mosques were destroyed or left desolate (*qavmsiz qoldi*).

In May 1922, as we have seen, the Politburo formally granted a "return" of waqf property to its beneficiaries and the reestablishment of Islamic courts. To a certain extent, the TurTsIK decrees that followed in July only recognized a situation that already existed on the ground, but they nevertheless inaugurated a brief period of relaxation in the state's attitude toward Islam in Central Asia. The qazi courts now operated officially and control of waqfs devolved to the uezd level. At the same time, shariat administrations (mahkama-yi shar'iya) also emerged into the open as organizations run by the ulama independently of the party. The autumn of 1922 also saw the brief appearance of the journal *Haqiqat* (Reality, or Truth), the only religious journal to be published in Central Asia in the Soviet period. The journal sought to give voice to a reformist vision of Islam that cohered with the revolution and the Soviet state's eastern policy, while also asserting a place for Islam in the Soviet order. Its masthead proclaimed, "There is no society without religion and no religion without society" (*Dinsiz jamiyat, jamiyatsiz din yo'qdir*).[54] For a brief while, reformist ulama had a place in the public space. In October 1922, the newspaper *Turkiston* had a regular page devoted to the mahkama-yi shar'iya and Zuhriddin A'lam, the editor of *Haqiqat* and chair of the Tashkent mahkama, appeared alongside members of the Sredazburo and TurTsIK at a public gathering to celebrate recent victories of Turkish nationalist forces at Bursa and Izmir.[55]

The qazi courts functioned under conditions very similar to those of the Tsarist era and those applied to Ferghana in 1921. Qazis were elected (although in practice, only people with the requisite learning and cultural capital won the elections) and had jurisdiction over civil affairs.[56] The "return" of waqf entailed little more than the abolition of the Central Waqf Department. In its place, each uezd acquired its own waqf commission, composed of two mudarrises, one qazi, one teacher from a Soviet school, and a representative of the local education department. The scope of

---

52. TsGARUz, f. 34, op. 1, d. 628, 16.

53. TsGARUz, f. 34, op. 1, d. 633, ll. 53–53ob.

54. See B.M. Babadzhanov, *Zhurnal 'Ḥaqīqat' kak zerkalo religioznogo aspekta v ideologii dzhadidov* (Tokyo, 2007), which also includes facsimiles of both issues of the journal.

55. "Turk qo'shinlarining so'nggi g'alabalari munosibati bilan ulug' nimoyish," *Turkiston*, 14.10.1922.

56. "Polozhenie o musul'manskikh sudakh Turkrespubliki," TsGARUz, f. 38, op. 4, d. 17, ll. 76–80ob.

the electoral principle was actually broadened, and elections had to be confirmed by local ispolkoms. Madrasas were to be managed by a council (*medresskii sovet*) composed of professors, the head of which appointed by the uezd commission. Mosques received control over their endowed property on similar terms, but madrasas had access only to nonagricultural land situated in cities. Rural property was to remain under the use of the peasants who occupied it and subject to normal Soviet law.[57]

The mahkama-i shar'iya had existed in unofficial or quasi-official form since 1918, although its early history remains only murkily visible in the archives. The creation of a bureaucratic body for the regulation of various Islamic practices was an important part of the Jadid program, dating back to well before the revolution and reasserted in 1917, when the term *mahkama-yi shar'iya* was commonly used. Those hopes foundered in the general chaos of the year, but a mahkama-i shar'iya existed in Samarqand in 1919 and another operated under the aegis of the old-city soviet in Tashkent in 1920.[58] We do not know with any certainty the scope of their activity, nor their legal position in the years before 1922 (although they seem to have comprised reform-minded ulama willing to work with the new order, and they cooperated closely with local soviets), but now they were formalized and made official. Reformist ulama saw the legalization of qazi courts and the establishment of shariat administrations as new possibilities of enforcing reform and they entered the fray with alacrity. The Tashkent mahkama claimed that, as the representative of the ulama, it had the right administer waqf property (since the June decree allowed for mudarrises and qazis to be elected to the various waqf departments).[59] Indeed, in several places, the local mahkamas succeeded in taking control of waqfs. In Konibodom, the local mahkama was founded in the summer of 1922, and already by September it had evicted the "waqf-eater" from a madrasa and converted it into a school in which "contemporary sciences" were taught alongside the usual madrasa subjects.[60] Such assertiveness worked in other directions as well. In June 1924, Abduvohid qori, the head of the Tashkent mahkama (and the uncle of Akmal Ikromov), gave permission of his own authority to eshons to resume zikr in the streets of Tashkent, which the old-city ispolkom had prohibited the previous year.[61] For some of the ulama involved, the ambitions extended further. They hoped to establish a single mahkama with jurisdiction over all of Turkestan and with functions extending beyond the oversight of waqf and Islamic education. The model in this regard was clearly the Central Spiritual

57. TurTsIK decree no. 75 (20.07.1922), TsGARUz, f. 25, op. 1, d. 1414, ll. 55–59.
58. GAgT, f. 12, d. 56.
59. Mahkama-i shar'iya Idorasi, "Ochiq xatga javob," *Haqiqat* (15.09.1922), inside front cover.
60. Ubaydulla Xon, "Biz ilgari ekanmiz," *Turkiston*, 16.02.1923.
61. PP OGPU to Sredazburo, 28.08.1924, RGASPI, f. 62, op. 2, d. 133, l. 28.

Administration based in Ufa, the descendent of the Orenburg Spiritual Assembly headed in those years by the renowned Jadid scholar Rizaätdin Fakhretdin.[62]

The party had little patience for such assertiveness. The return of qazi courts and waqfs was always intended to be tactical, "to create," as the Politburo put it, "a rupture [*perelom*] in the mood of the population,"[63] rather than a compromise in principle. The party was not pleased with how the first decrees on qazi courts and the waqf question turned out in practice, and it forced through new legislation in December that greatly curtailed the scope of both institutions. For Islamic courts, the new legislation proved fatal. It limited the authority of qazi courts in significant ways. Recourse to them was not mandatory; if one side wanted to take the case to a Soviet court, then the qazi court lost its jurisdiction.[64] Qazis' decisions could always be challenged in regular Soviet courts. Qazi courts also had to pay their own way through exactions on plaintiffs. Documents issued or notarized by qazis could not be used in Soviet courts, nor could qazis count on the police to enforce their verdicts.[65] It is impossible to estimate the percentage of eligible cases that were decided in qazi courts, but what we do know is that their numbers declined sharply, from 220 in 1922, to 85 the following year, to only 7 in all of Uzbekistan in 1927.[66] The assertiveness of the shariat administrations likewise aroused the suspicion of the OGPU and the party. The dream of a single mahkama for all of Uzbekistan never came to fruition before all local administrations were abolished in 1927, along with qazi courts (chapter 11).

The situation with waqf was similar. The party had hopes that the shariat administrations would lead to the strengthening of the reformers among the ulama, and the Commissariat of Justice was cautiously inclined to let the shariat administrations control waqf, but there was enough disquiet over this that the July statute was quickly revised and replaced by a new law in December. The new law brought back a central administration, now called the Main Waqf Administration (GVU, Glavnoe vakufnoe upravlenie, Bosh avqof idorasi), as part of the Commissariat of Education to be headed by an appointee of the Sovnarkom, and two other members appointed by the commissariats of internal affairs and

---

62. On the Ufa administration, see *Islam na territorii byvshei Rossiisskoi Imperii*, vyp. 2 (Moscow, 1999), 100–101, s.v. "TsDUM." The mahkama-yi shar'iya often referred to itself as *nazorat-i diniya* (religious directorate), the term used by the Ufa administration. See, e.g., Toshkand nazorat-i diniyasi, "Yoqin sharqdagi fitnalar munosibati bilan: butun musulmonlarg'a xitobnoma," *Qizil O'zbekiston*, 08.05.1925.

63. RGASPI, f. 17, op. 3, d. 293, ll. 9–10 (18.05.1922).

64. *O'zbekiston ijtimoiy sho'rolar jumhuriyatida sho'ro tuzulishi* (Samarqand, 1927), 44.

65. N. Fioletov, "Sudy kaziev v Sredne-Aziatskikh respublikakh," *Sovetskoe pravo* 1927, no. 1: 141–146.

66. AAP RUz, f. 58, op. 3, d. 514, l. 46 (Narkomiust figures from 1927).

justice.[67] At the local level, waqf departments were attached to ispolkoms; they were headed by the chief of the local education department and had as members one representative of the ispolkom and one elected representative of madrasas. Madrasas were to be run by mutavallis appointed by local waqf departments, which were to have oversight over both the financial and pedagogical sides of the institutions. Mutavallis for mosque-related waqfs were to be elected in an open election by inhabitants of the neighborhood. The new law left the ulama with only a token representation in the administration of waqfs in Turkestan and brought them under the purview of the state.

As a Soviet administrative organ staffed entirely by Muslims who sought to reconcile Soviet work with Muslim reform, GVU was a highly unusual organization. Munavvar qori was already under a cloud of OGPU suspicion, but he continued to work in GVU, for on this point he agreed with the Soviets.[68] GVU saw waqf property as "public-state property having a communal character" and channeled waqf revenue to cultural and educational causes.[69] At the same time, it battled attempts by the Commissariat of Finance to tax waqf properties.[70] Given that central subventions to Turkestan's education budget had been slashed with the advent of NEP, waqf revenues took on an ever more significant meaning for the education of the indigenous population. In 1923, according to figures of the Tashkent old-city ispolkom, forty-four of the city's forty-nine elementary schools were funded solely by waqf funds.[71] In the 1925–26 academic year, waqf revenues accounted for three-fifths of all expenditures on building new schools.[72] Waqf revenues also paid for scholarships for rural students to study in Tashkent and were an important source for the funding of students who were sent to Moscow or Germany in these years.[73] The channeling of waqf income to education was argued in the name of progress and the nation (figure 5), in direct line of descent from Munavvar qori's argument in 1920, although often with a "class" twist, which argued that because waqf was created from the labor of workers

67. Dekret Tsentral'nogo Ispolnitel'nogo Komiteta Sovetov TSSR no. 173, TsGARUz, f. 25, op. 1, d. 1414, l. 53.

68. In June 1923, he was director of GVU's Academic Department; TsGARUz, f. 34, op. 1, d. 2302a, l. 4.

69. TsGARUz, f. 34, op. 1, d. 2277, l. 91 (Xolmuhammad Oxundiy's memo, GVU to TsK KPT, 1923).

70. "Osoboe mnenie Glavnogo vakufnogo upravleniia ob osvobozhdenii vakufnykh imushchestv ot nalogi i sborov" (29.11.1923), TsGARUz, f. 34, op. 1, d. 2273, ll. 28–30.

71. "Godovoi otchet o deiatel'nosti starogorodskogo ispolkoma i ego otdelov s 1–go oktiabria 1923 goda po 1–go oktiabria 1924 goda," GAgT, f. 12, d. 221, l. 68ob-69.

72. O'zbekiston Xalq Maorif Kamisarligi, *O'zbekistonda maorif ishlari* (Tashkent, 1927), 12.

73. The Andijon waqf department paid fifteen thousand rubles in 1923 to support such students; TsGARUz, f. 34, op. 1, d. 2299, l. 22.

FIGURE 5. The Waqf question. In the top frame, the ulama struggle with education-ists over the control of waqf monies. (The choice on the road sign is between "degeneration" and "education.") Having lost the battle, they retreat to their bastions and denounce the times: "Faith has ended, Islam is gone! The legal right of the ulama is being spent on education! What horror!!" *Mushtum* no. 8 (17.05.1923), 5.

and peasants, it should be spent on their education.[74] This led to a distinction between "religious" and "cultural" waqfs. Formalized in the decree of December 1922, the distinction served to demarcate "religion" as a separate sphere of activity and to marginalize it in every way. In Turkestan, religious waqfs were supposed to be the sole source for paying the salaries of imams and muezzins in waqf-endowed mosques. The distinction also meant a progressive constriction of the role of the ulama in the administration of waqf and the channeling of waqf monies away for religious purposes. In January 1925, a conference of functionaries in the waqf administration voted to abolish the category of "religious" waqf altogether and to channel all waqf monies toward education.[75] It even argued that using waqf for paying religious functionaries not only contravened Soviet legislation on the separation of religion and state, but also the shariat itself.[76] Muslim anticlericalism had led to the reimagination of an old feature of Islamic law into something new.

If the enthusiasms of reformist Muslims chipped away at waqf from one direction, the Soviet state attacked it from the other. For all the talk of returning waqf to their beneficiaries, the December 1922 decree ushered in greater control of waqf properties by the state. That control gradually increased in the coming years while definitions of waqf-eligible activities shrank. The abolition of the category of "religious waqf" in 1925 transformed the meaning of waqf, for now it had little to do with pious deeds or ends. In December 1926, when all madrasas in Tashkent had been were shut down, TurTsIK took possession of the premises of the Eshonqul madrasa from GVU and gave them to Sharq Yulduzi film studio.[77] By 1927, then, when the final assault on it began, waqf property had already been brought under state control to a great extent. Combined with the diminution in the numbers of qazi courts, this meant that Islamic institutions had already been greatly weakened when they were finally abolished in 1927–28.

Fitrat's Revolt against God

The choking of Islamic courts and waqfs was accompanied by a shift in the religious mood of at least some Jadids. By 1923, the strident anticlericalism of the years since 1917 came to be joined by expressions of deep religious skepticism,

---

74. Z. Nosiriy, "Vaqf—ishchi dehqon sarmoyasi," *Maorif va o'qitg'uvchi* 1926, no. 2: 14–16.

75. TsGARUz, f. 34, op. 1, d. 2308a, l. 130.

76. X. O. Marg'iloniy, "Vaqf sarmoyasi va el tarbiyasi," *Maorif va o'qitg'uvchi* 1925, no. 1: 100.

77. Cloé Drieu, *Fictions nationales: Cinéma, empire et nation en Ouzbékistan (1919–1937)* (Paris, 2013), 84.

indeed of irreligion. This skepticism was expressed largely in an Islamicate idiom and while undoubtedly influenced by the revolution, it owed little directly to Soviet atheism. The main figure in this regard was Fitrat himself, whose journey to skepticism can be traced through a series of works that he published in these years. Fitrat's distinction between "real scholars," who served Islam and the nation, and "mullahs," who only worshipped their bellies, hardened once the urgency of political action began to press on him. In *Indian Revolutionaries* (1920), where patriotism and anticolonial struggle take center stage, the mullah type is represented by Maulana Nu'man, a scholar who has emigrated to India's mountainous frontier to wage a struggle against the British, but who balks at fighting alongside Hindus and Sikhs for the liberation of India and thus becomes an accomplice of the British. Fitrat's protagonist makes another speech reminiscent of the Indian Traveler of 1913:

> You mullahs always say this. For many years, you have filled India with disputes over tribes and nations. You have divided the people into 74 groups and set them against one another. You have filled our land with internal squabbles and thus brought the English upon our heads. After a hundred years, we have [finally] begun to unify in order to liberate ourselves. Again you want to block our path with squabbles over religions and sects! . . . We will struggle [for our freedom] hand in hand. Neither you, nor religion can keep us from this path.[78]

If here the ulama's petty squabbles stood in the way of national liberation, by 1923 Fitrat had carried his critique into new territory. A series of three works published in 1923 and 1924 mark a shift from anticlericalism to full blown irreligion for Fitrat.

This was a complex period of his life. He was ousted from the government of the BNSR and exiled from Bukhara in June 1923. Fitrat headed to Moscow where he was to spend the next fifteen months. Little is known for sure about his activities in Moscow, but the time he spent there was highly productive.[79] We know that upon his arrival in Moscow, Fitrat stayed at the Bukharan Bilim Yurti, but he was forced to leave the premises by the political police.[80] Fitrat's banishment

---

78. Fitrat, *Hind ixtilolchilari* (1920), in his *Tanlangan asarlar*, 5 vols. to date (Tashkent, 2000–), 3:63.

79. Contemporary Uzbek scholars claim that Fitrat in these years taught at the Lazarev Institute of Living Oriental Languages, Russia's premier institution of Oriental studies, and that he received the title of professor from Leningrad State University, but they proffer no documentary evidence, and I have found none. See Hamidulla Boltaboyev, *Abdurauf Fitratning hayoti va ijodi* (Tashkent, 1992), 22; Begali Qosimov, *Milliy uyg'onish: jasorat, ma'rifat, fidoiylik* (Tashkent, 2002), 360.

80. OGPU surveillance report, RGASPI, f. 17, op. 84, d. 507, l. 29 (28.07.1923).

was not total, for his plays continued to be staged in Turkestan while he was in Moscow. That city itself had become a hub of Uzbek cultural life at the time, for a concatenation of circumstances had put a number of major Uzbek intellectuals in the city. In 1924, Cho'lpon arrived there with the newly formed Uzbek drama studio and Abdulla Qodiriy to attend the Briusov Institute of Journalism. Nazir To'raqulov, whose own political disgrace had landed him the job of heading the publishing house of Narkomnats, was instrumental in having two of Fitrat's works published in Moscow. In fact, Fitrat's time in Moscow was a turning point in his intellectual development. In addition to the tragedy *Abulfayzxon*, he published three shorts work on questions of faith and doubt, obedience and authority.

Qiyomat (The Day of Judgment), a short story, operates at two levels of meaning. At one level, it is a satire of the Islamic understanding of afterlife. It recounts the adventures of Pochomir, an opium addict, through the grave and into afterlife.[81] Pochomir is a buffoon in the style of Molla Nasreddin, the proverbial character after which the satirical magazine was named, a man who through his artlessness casts a sarcastic light on all that is holy. The story begins with Pochomir down with an illness that keeps him from taking opium. The withdrawal is as bad as death for Pochomir. As his thoughts turn to the other world, he wonders whether there will be intoxication in afterlife. He duly dies and is buried in accordance with Islamic custom. As he lies in his grave, his sleep is disturbed by Munkar and Nakir, the two angels who according to Muslim belief examine the newly dead in the grave. Munkar and Nakir appear as officious bureaucrats who cannot, however, cow Pochomir. He asks them for their credentials, and his general defiance forces the angels to retreat in disarray. After that, "Pochomir slept somewhat more peacefully," we are told, and saw "nothing of the scorpions, the snakes, or the flames of Hell" that Islamic lore places in the grave (Q, 11). He is finally awakened by the trumpet that announces the arrival of the Day of Judgment. He emerges from his grave to witness total chaos, as all humanity mills around in a state of complete nakedness,[82] pushed and shoved by an army of angels who struggle to keep control as people wait for their sins and good deeds to weighed on a set of giant scales. After waiting for two and a half years, Pochomir manages to pass the test, and proceeds to the bridge of Sirat, the width of a hair, that every person has to cross on the back of an animal he or she has sacrificed in their life. Pochomir haggles with the angels over

---

81. Fitrat, *Qiyomat: xayoliy hikoya* (Moscow, 1923); subsequently cited as Q in the text.

82. The fact that humanity will be resurrected stark naked on the day of judgment is widely accepted but never thought about much in Islamicate descriptions of the afterlife. Fitrat's insistence in drawing the reader's attention to the fact is itself subversive.

which of the many sheep he had sacrificed during his lifetime he should ride and ultimately has his way. He badgers the angels into agreement and rides the sheep of his choice successfully across the bridge. Having finally arrived in paradise, he has to wander through the streets for a year and a half before he finds the little house made of precious stones that had been assigned to him. There he is welcomed by a host of houris and nubile young boys (*g'ilmon*), who are charged with looking after him. He enjoys the unlimited food and drink and sex for seven days but then gets bored. To escape the tedium, he goes exploring in the garden, where he is overjoyed to discover little canals flowing with milk, water, honey, and wine. "Tonight, let's get a little drunk," he says to his retinue, only to be told that heavenly wine does not lead to inebriation. He is stunned. "What's the point! Who drinks wine that doesn't even get one drunk?!" he exclaims. As he returns home in disgust, he catches sight of a bunch of poppies . . . and just then Pochomir wakes up in his own bed. "I ran into plenty of trouble," he says to his wife. "It's good that it was a dream!" He had tricked and bullied his way into paradise, only to realize that the rewards promised there were tedious and pointless.

At a second level, the story pokes fun at Soviet reality. Fitrat recounts Pochomir's journey as an encounter of a citizen with Soviet bureaucracy, using Russian words for comic effect. Pochomir addresses Munkar and Nakir as "comrades" and asks to see their credentials (*mandat*). The angels who manage the resurrected are angel police (*malak po'lislari*), while the register of each person's deeds and misdeeds is a booklet "that resembled the 'passports' [*paspo'rt*] of the era of Nicholas" (Q, 12). In the great field of Resurrection, "Pochomir waited for two and a half years but could not get near the giant scales [where his deeds were to be weighed]. For every step he took toward the scales, he had to take twenty steps back" (Q, 14). Pochomir hatches a plan [*plon*] for a disturbance, and begins to agitate: "What is this disorder?" he asks a person next to him. "Why do they have only one scale for weighing the deeds of so many people? Shouldn't they have ten or fifteen scales for starting such a huge affair? Shouldn't they have made preparations in advance?" Pochomir then suggests that the crowd make use of "a new system that has emerged recently in our Turkestan," called *ochirat* (<Russ. *ochered'*, queue), according to which people take a number as they wait for their turn in an orderly fashion. The process works and the crowd manages to have its deeds weighed efficiently. The satire on the Soviet order is impossible to miss, though much of the fun that Fitrat pokes at the realities of Soviet life does not go beyond what was commonplace in the satirical press of the time. Nevertheless, the implication drawn by him that the paradise promised by the Bolsheviks was not real was potentially deeply troubling.

Yet the satire on the Soviet system does not mean that the antireligious message completely vanishes.[83] Pochomir's sacrilegious account of his journey beyond the grave was perhaps just a fevered nightmare, but the fact of its very telling was important. Fitrat's story kept to the accepted Islamic version of life after death but subverted every step of it. If anything, the juxtaposition of images of the Soviet present with the story of the day of judgment furthers the desacralization of the Islamic narrative. The sacrilege lies in the words used, regardless of the intent of the author or the literary devices used. In this regard, very important is Pochomir's attitude of defiance: to death, to the angel-functionaries he meets along the way, and to paradise itself, which disappoints him greatly. The fundamental fact about the short story is its send up of the Islamic account of the Day of Judgment. Soviet publishers seemed to agree. The story was published in Moscow by the publishing house of Narkomnats, with a preface by Nazir To'raqulov, who lauded Fitrat for challenging the "superstition and bigotry" of Turkestan. "As for the practical value of this story, of course it will have great value for us and our affairs. By portraying in a funny and simple manner an edifice that appears so beautiful in a dream, the story extinguishes the passions of those inclined to the dream. *Qiyomat* will be an instructive story for educating young people in a materialist spirit" (Q, 3–4). In fact, *Qiyomat* was the only work of Fitrat's that was published during the later Soviet period. A second edition published in 1935 rewrote Pochomir as an exploited and therefore politically conscious worker and pushed the narrative firmly into the Tsarist period by removing the Soviet-era Russian terms used to great effect by Fitrat in 1923.[84] This sanitized version of the story was republished several times in the later Soviet period, in Uzbek as well as in Tajik and Russian translations.[85]

Fitrat followed up *Qiyomat* with a short one-act play in verse called *Shaytonning tangriga isyoni* (Satan's Revolt against God), which retold a crucial part of Islamic cosmogony. In the Islamic tradition, God's first creations were angels, made of light, and jinns, made of fire. Lacking knowledge or volition, these creatures occupied themselves solely with worshipping God. Then God decided to

---

83. Here I agree with Sigrid Kleinmichel, *Aufbruch aus orientalischen Dichtungstraditionen: Studien zur usbekischen Dramatik und Prosa zwischen 1910 und 1934* (Wiesbaden, 1993), 114–118; see also Sigrid Kleinmichel, "The Uzbek Short Story Writer Fiṭrat's Adaptation of Religious Traditions," in *Religious Perspectives in Modern Muslim and Jewish Literatures*, eds. Glenda Abramson and Hilary Kilpatrick (London, 2006), 138–139.

84. Prof. Fitrat, *Qiyomat: xayoliy hikoya* (Tashkent, 1935).

85. Fitrat, *Qijomat* (Stalinabad, 1936); Fitrat, *Strashnyi sud: satiricheskii rasskaz*, tr. L. Kandinov (Dushanbe, 1964); Fitrat, *Den' strashnogo suda: rasskaz-satira* (Moscow, 1965); an Uzbek edition was published in 1967.

make Adam from clay and asked all angels and jinns to prostrate themselves before his new creation. All angels obeyed, except for their teacher Azazel, who refused, saying, "I am better than him, for you created me from fire, and him you created from clay." For this he was cast out of heaven and became Iblis or Shaytan (Satan), the source of temptation for evil in the world.[86] While Iblis/ Shaytan represents evil, there is also a long tradition in Islamicate letters that sees him as a tragic figure, caught between God's will (to monotheism) and his command (to prostrate before someone other than God), and a few Sufis have even seen him as the ultimate monotheist, whose love for God led him to disobedience.[87] Fitrat however retells Satan's disobedience as a heroic act of defiance and liberation.[88] The play opens on a moonlit night with numerous angels in the act of prostrating themselves and endlessly repeating the formula, "Subhān Allah," praise be to God. As Azazel walks on stage, he looks at the worshippers with "a thoughtful, proud expression," and asks: "Why this baseness, this humiliation / this incomprehension, this lifelessness, this blindness?!" (*Nichun emish bu tubanlik, bu xo'rlik, / bu ongsizliq, bu jonsizliq, bu ko'rlik?!*) The disdain is both for the angels who do nothing but "petty, base, mindless, lifeless, blind" worship, and their creator who has made "millions upon millions" of angels, but allows them to do nothing but worship. Azazel's doubt has been brought forth by his having caught a glimpse of the Well Preserved Tablet (*lavh-i mahfuz*, the tablet on which God has inscribed his will) and seen on it God's plan to make a new creature from clay and to have all angels prostrate themselves before him. Azazel sees this as a betrayal ("this is the fruit of your obedience," he tells the prostrating angels [*Sh*, 14]) and is outraged; the outrage pushes him to revolt. "I spoke of your majesty / your beauty," Azazel says to God:

> I celebrated the wisdom of your every deed
> I closed my eyes and opened my mouth
> and spoke of your greatness, your power, your knowledge
> of your all-seeingness, your justness, your gentleness
> But today . . . this is what I say:
> I myself never believed those words
>
> (*Sh*, 4–5).

---

86. This story occurs in several places in the Qur'an (vii:11–18, xv:30–39, xvii:60–65) and provides one of the foundations of Islamicate discourses of good and evil, obedience and disobedience, and belief and disbelief.

87. Peter J. Awn, *Satan's Tragedy and Redemption: Iblīs in Sufi Psychology* (Leiden, 1983). For a compilation of references to Iblis/Satan in Sufi poetry, see Javad Nurbakhsh, *The Great Satan "Eblis"* (London, 1986).

88. Fitrat, *Shaytonning tangriga isyoni* (Tashkent, 1924); subsequently cited a *Sh* in the text.

The archangels Gabriel, Michael, and Azrael bring messages from God asking Azazel to return to obedience. Azazel in turn informs the messengers of God's new plan to create a new being from clay and to set it above the angels, "as a ruler over us and as his [God's] own deputy" (*Sh*, 11). There is a ripple of shock and surprise among the angels ("This can't be, God will not break our hearts like this" [*Sh*, 13]), and they decide to pray to God for guidance. God intervenes himself, calling down his displeasure at the disobedience from on high: "You do not know what I know / Do not stand against what I will. / This is your task" (*Sh*, 15). He then sends Gabriel to fetch Adam so that the angels may prostrate themselves before him. Azazel is outraged anew and tries to convince the angels to revolt. After some momentary commotion, the angels continue with their obedience, but Azazel is defiant: "We shall not bow down . . . send us to nonexistence, if you want!" A clap of thunder ensues and Azazel is divested of his accouterments and turned into Satan. His response is defiant still:

> From the bonds of this captivity you freed me
> God made me worship himself
> Without explaining, he made me follow his word
> He presented me with a filthy crown, a scepter
> Unknowingly I accepted them; it was a trap
> He wanted me to serve you too [he says to Adam]
> That is, so that once more I might snare myself to another abasement
> I opposed this meaningless order of his
> I became a mutineer today, against the Great God
>
> (*Sh*, 17).

Satan then turns to the newly created Adam and warns him to be wary of a similar trick: "By making me bow down to you, / He wished to deceive you too. / Deceiving, then very slowly tethering you / Think it over, does this have a darker meaning? / I have been liberated, I am going far away, / Be mindful, do not fall into the trap / Throw away the crown, do not fall for this scepter" (*Sh*, 18).

God's voice interrupts Satan's speech to warn God's creatures not to listen to "this rebel," and asks rhetorically, "Why does he [Satan] still reject my command?" At this, Satan makes his final speech:

> Because knowledge is your constant enemy
> Your hell, your flames, your torments,
> Your terrors are fantasies, your paradise is a falsehood.
> Your great book called the Eternal Tablet is filled with fictions, with lies
>
> . . . .

Freed from captivity, from servitude
My guide is science, my prophet is knowledge.
My aides are my brain and my tongue.

....

I shall not live without eternally inquiring about others (*points at Adam*)
I shall surely free even this man from your bonds
I shall rescue him from your incorrect path.

....

Get lost with your wisdom, your throne
With your power, your majesty, your world

(*Sh*, 19–20).

Expulsion as liberation, God as a trickster and the arch enemy of knowledge, and Satan telling him to get lost: a more complete inversion of the Islamic scheme of things is scarcely imaginable. God is a petty tyrant who creates angels only to worship him. Then he rewards the angels by making Adam and setting him above them. The angels are capable only of blind obedience and worship, but Satan sees through God's ways. Fitrat's Satan is not the perfect monotheist of the Sufis, but a rebel who disdains blind obedience and seeks freedom from God. Fitrat's account is inflected by post-Enlightenment concerns with human freedom and combined with faith in science and knowledge that differs radically from any treatment of Satan in the Islamicate tradition.[89]

A third work Fitrat published while in Moscow clarifies his trajectory.[90] *Bedil* is a short tract, somewhere between a short story and a play in terms of genre, in which Qutlug′, a young Bukharan recently returned from his studies in Moscow, uses the writings of Mirza Abdul Qadir Bedil (1644–1721), the Indian poet of Central Asian origin, to make a case for skepticism within the Central Asian tradition. Bedil was a canonical figure in the cultural life of Transoxiana, where his work was recited in formal gatherings called *bedilkhvoni* ("Bedil reading"). His work is marked both by a profound philosophical skepticism and an artfulness of language and imagery that clothes the skepticism in deliberate ambiguity. In *Bedil*, Qutlug′ subverts an evening's *bedilkhvoni* by challenging the audience's conventional understanding of the poetry and providing his own interpretation. "We always take Bedil at face value," says Qutlug′. "We yield to his mastery of the

---

89. Ingeborg Baldauf, "Abdurauf Fitrat: Der Aufstand Satans gegen Gott," in *Türkische Sprachen und Literaturen: Materialen der ersten deutschen Turkologen-Konferenz*, ed. Ingeborg Baldauf, Klaus Kreiser, and Semih Tezcan (Wiesbaden, 1991), 74, is quite right in suggesting that Fitrat's play stands out almost by itself in twentieth-century Islamicate letters.

90. Fitrat, *Bedil: bir majlisda* (Moscow, 1924); subsequently cited as *B* in the text.

word, his power, his skill, his play. All our *wows* and our *bravos* are only for his words. As for his real thought, either we do not understand it or do not want to understand it" (*B*, 12). Disregarding the artifice, the imagery, and cutting through the ambiguity to get to the literal meaning of Bedil's text, Fitrat presents a modernist reading of Bedil. Read thus, Bedil emerges as "a philosopher who is not content with the shape of the society of his time, who saw that most people were not happy, and who grieved about it" (*B*, 26), a humanist who is deeply skeptical of religion and other forms of authority. Bedil "raises humankind [*inson*], elevates it to great heights" (*B*, 15). Human ingenuity conquers nature but is constrained by conventions of imitation and obedience that serve the interests of the powerful. "Behind the veil of the idea of heaven and hell, Bedil finds shaykhs and ascetics who fill their bellies with the people's bread" (*B*, 28). Neither the Ka'aba, nor the temple of the polytheists (*dayr, butkhāna*) is for Bedil a house of truth, but merely a stopping place for those who have lost their way (*B*, 18–20). Indeed, God himself begins to vanish from Bedil's cosmology, as Fitrat finds elements of evolution in Bedil's poetry (*B*, 34–35), as well as a harsh critique of kingship and its pretentions. Kingship is based on merciless exploitation of peasants by the rich and the mighty. Bedil gives tidings of a revolution in which peasants, having gathered together and strengthened themselves, would topple their kings (*B*, 43–48).

Fitrat undertakes a dual move in this treatment of Bedil. He challenges many orthodoxies of Central Asia's tradition by confronting it with a highly skeptical worldview. He then locates support for the worldview in the very bosom of Central Asia's own cultural tradition, in the work of a canonical author that he argued had been willfully misunderstood until then. Fitrat's reading is not so much against the grain as perfectly along it: he insists on the literal meaning of Bedil's poetry. Read thus, Bedil shows religious skepticism, even irreligion, to be an authentically national phenomenon, not a European import. *Bedil* is intimately connected to all of Fitrat's preceding work. Like the *Munāzara*, this text is cast as a disputation. Qutlug' stands in the tradition of the Englishman and the Indian Traveler, but he is closest to the English-educated Indian patriot Karim Bakhsh from *Chin sevish* (see chapter 3). European education, whether in London or Moscow, does not compromise one's authenticity, but furthers it by giving one the skills to understand the world better and thus to serve the nation better. When Qutlug' arrives at the gathering, his hosts are inclined to be condescending to him on account of his Moscow education and his European dress and assume that he would not understand Bedil. Qutlug' surprises them with his mastery of Bedil's work, which he understands better than the audience, and proceeds to teach them the "real" meaning of it.

Indeed, Fitrat frames the whole debate in terms of a critique of imitation (*taqlid*) and obedience to tradition (*odatchilik*). "There is no public opinion among us," Fitrat has Qutlug' say, picking up a persistent theme of his writing of these years. "We just have the disposition to follow whatever our leaders say. The people believe whatever their leaders say. Even the ideas of heaven and hell are not their own. They too have been taken from the leaders" (*B*, 5).[91] Opposition to blind obedience, whether to God (as in *Sh*) or to tradition (as here) is therefore a good in itself. Qutlug' did that willfully: even when he was a madrasa student in Bukhara, we are told, he had "displayed a certain freedom, a certain independence not to be seen among his peers," and his education in Moscow had crystallized it further (*B*, 3–4). Now he finds in Bedil a thoroughly indigenous critique of *taqlid*, imitation. "Bedil is against imitation, of people copying those above them in every matter; he wants to attack this. He says, 'The imitation [*ergashmoq*] entrenched in human nature is a bandit on the path of truth'" (*B*, 13). "Bedil is the enemy of imitation [*taqlid*]; he trusts only his own conscience [*vijdon*]" (*B*, 16). Obedience limits human ingenuity and, more crucially perhaps, prevents the progress of the nation. This concern, so central throughout Fitrat's oeuvre, raises its head in the middle of *Bedil* too. Asked what importance Bedil's humanist vision had for Bukharans, Qutlug' replies, "Had you visited Europe and seen the miracles performed by His Highness the Human Being [*hazrat-i inson*], in the last two centuries, the results of his power, you would understand what Bedil means" (*B*, 22). He goes on to ask, "Is it necessary for us to subordinate the forces of nature to our will, to progress as the Europeans did, or not? If it is necessary, then is it possible? And if it is possible, then under what conditions? How can our society be saved?" (*B*, 23).[92] None of these questions, Qutlug' argues, can be answered through imitation of tradition. The good of the nation requires liberation from the constraints of tradition.

Taken together, these three works mark a major turning point in Fitrat's intellectual trajectory. Less than a decade earlier, between 1914 and 1916, Fitrat had written a short history of Islam, a panegyric to the Prophet, and a guide to conduct that saw the Qur'an as the guide to salvation. Those works featured squarely in the tradition of Muslim modernism. The works of the 1923–24 cycle are direct critiques of Islam. As Pochomir finds out (and Satan confirms), God is a trickster whose "terrors are fantasies, [his] paradise . . . a falsehood" (*Sh*, 19). Indeed, belief is the problem and *hazrat-i inson*, "his highness the human being," with its potential for knowledge, is the only measure of man. While *Bedil* shows stark continuities with concerns that had dominated Fitrat's writing from the outset, the tone

---

91. This is almost word for word the same statement that Fitrat made under his own name in 1920: Fitrat, "'Tadrij'ga qorshu," *Tong*, no. 3 (15.05.1920), 78–80 (discussed in chap. 6).

92. The continuity with Fitrat's concerns in his first published work (*Munāẓara*) from 1911 is blindingly obvious here.

is harsher and the concern with human will new. In the other pieces, Fitrat scouts out new territory, going well beyond anticlericalism to a critique of religion itself. Yet, this turn to irreligion had little to do with Bolshevik antireligious thinking. Fitrat's trajectory was affected no doubt by the radical new horizons made possible by the Russian revolution, but it was rooted ultimately in the radicalization of Muslim reformist thought more than in any direct borrowings from Soviet atheism. Fitrat's is in important ways an Islamicate critique of Islam.

Further evidence from Fitrat's oeuvre makes clear that his loss of faith cannot be explained away as simply an Aesopian critique of the Soviet order, as some scholars have sought to do.[93] In 1928, he wrote a short analysis of the poetry of Umar Khayyam, whom he described as an agnostic who had his own ideas about religion, but who could not properly maintain his agnosticism because of his position as a court poet.[94] By this time Fitrat was under great political pressure and his wooden use of Marxian categories is indicative of his attempt to deflect some of that pressure. Nevertheless, he reprises many themes from *Bedil*, such as the countertraditional readings of a canonical figure of Central Asian literature to assert an indigenous, if incomplete, source of religious skepticism. But it was several stories he wrote for *Xudosizlar* (The Godless), the newly founded magazine of the League of the Militant Godless (see chapter 10) that confirm Fitrat's irreligion, for they leave no possibility for an Aesopian reading.

---

93. In the only major English-language account of these works by Fitrat, Edward Allworth in *Evading Reality: The Devices of ʿAbdalrauf Fitrat, Modern Central Asian Reformist* (Leiden, 2002), insists on reading the texts solely as a critique of Soviet power that Fitrat smuggled into print despite Soviet censorship. While this reading is plausible to a certain extent, I do not find Allworth's analysis compelling. *Qiyomat* operates at two levels of meaning, but the satire on the Soviet order does not make the antireligious meaning disappear. *Satan's Revolt against God* can also be read as a comment on Bolshevik claims of infallibility—the party is God, the ever-worshipping angels the Communist faithful, and Satan the hero for refusing to accept the party's false claims to omniscience and omnipotence. Indeed, some in the party did see *Satan's Revolt* as an antiparty play; Akmal Ikromov stated as much at a Uzbek Central Committee plenum that discussed Fitrat and his work: RGASPI, f. 17, op. 27, d. 2, l. 102 (1926). Allworth, however, reads the play in yet a different way. For him, Satan represents the Bolsheviks' revolt against God, and he insists on seeing the revolt as a failure (on the basis of the cataclysmic last scene when thunder and lightning strike and everything vanishes from the stage). Such a reading simply does not square with the text itself. Even in *Bedil*, Allworth finds Fitrat's intent to be an argument "for the importance of a pure belief" (*Evading Reality*, 119) when little in the text supports such a reading. Allworth's method of reading these texts is better suited to the literature of the later Soviet period, when writers could slip dissent past censors by clever use of Aesopian prose, rather than for the tumultuous era of 1923 and 1924, when censorship was poorly institutionalized and sarcasm a commonplace. In his eagerness to read between the lines, Allworth forgets to pay enough attention to the lines themselves. His reading is also oblivious to the cultural radicalism of the period or to the historical realities of the time. Allworth also does not ask why a critique of Soviet power required blasphemy. Other scholars have indeed read the lines and see *Satan's Revolt* as an antireligious work; see Baldauf, "Abdurauf Fitrat," and Kleinmichel, *Aufbruch*, 119–122.

94. Fitrat, "Umar Xayyom: Fors adabiyotiga umumiy bir qarash," *Qizil qalam majmuasi*, no. 1 (1928), 20–52; Fitrat, *Fors shoiri Umar Xayyom* (Tashkent, 1929).

The first of these stories recapitulates many themes from *Qiyomat* in recount-ing the story of the *me'roj*, Muhammad's night-time ascension to heaven. The nar-rator falls asleep in a public bath and dreams that he is in Muhammad's presence when the archangel Gabriel arrives to escort him to heaven. The narrator manages to hide in Gabriel's wing and thus shares in the ascension as a stowaway. As Gabriel ascends into the heavens, he has to show his documents, in Soviet fashion, at each stage of the journey. Finally, they are summoned into the presence of God, who hides behind seventy-five thousand curtains. God offers Muhammad hospitality in the manner of a Central Asian merchant and the conversation between them is absolutely inane. When Muhammad asks God what his favorite food is, and God replies that it is rice pudding, the narrator cannot hold back, and reveals himself, exclaiming, "Sir, if that is the case, then what does your hiding out here behind so many curtains mean? Won't it be nice if you went out and showed your might to the people you like so much and had rice pudding with us?" The narrator is duly expelled from God's presence and wakes up in the bath.[95]

If Muhammad appears as a shallow petit bourgeois in the story of his ascen-sion, he emerges as a lascivious, deceitful eshon in "Zayd and Zaynab." Here, Fitrat retells the story of Muhammad's marriage to the divorced wife of his adop-tive son Zayd, an episode mentioned in the Qur'an itself.[96] Many early Muslim commentators had construed the passage to mean that Muhammad had been attracted to Zaynab while she was still married. Upon learning this, they argued, Zayd offered to divorce Zaynab, but Muhammad refused, thus keeping his temp-tation in control. The marriage ended in divorce anyway and ultimately Muham-mad married Zaynab, and the propriety of the proceedings was confirmed by revelations that abolished the practice of adoption in Islamic law. That view dis-appeared over the ages and modern Muslim commentators have tended only to emphasize the "legislative" function of the episode and to shy away from the story of Muhammad's temptation.[97] Fitrat, however, used this episode not only to put the focus on Muhammad's sexuality but on the nature of his prophethood. The story begins with a conversation among Muhammad's many wives, who are annoyed at him for producing revelations at will. "By God, Muhammad lies. . . . He misleads people," they say.[98] Zayd and Zaynab are in love, but Muhammad is clearly attracted to Zaynab and shows up one day at their house, "his eyes full of

95. Fitrat, "Me'roj," *Xudosizlar*, no. 1 (1928), 43–47.

96. Qur'an, iv: 23; xxxiii:37–38.

97. For an account of the shifting perceptions of this episode in the Muslim tradition (and its use by critics of Islam), see Ze'ev Maghen, *Virtues of the Flesh: Passion and Purity in Early Islamic Jurisprudence* (Leiden, 2005), chap. 3.

98. Fitrat, "Zayd va Zaynab," *Xudosizlar*, no. 4 (1928), 31.

lust." Zayd offers to divorce Zaynab, but Muhammad refuses, saying, "No, no, son, keep your wife. I don't need her." But, the narrator tells us, "These words were said with such mastery that it was not difficult for Zayd to understand that they consisted of hypocrisy." Zayd goes home, depressed, and dreams that he had died and was not admitted to paradise because of his marriage to a woman Muhammad desired. The next day, he divorces Zaynab, whom Muhammad marries right away, and a new revelation conveniently legalizes the situation. Muhammad's other wives are outraged: "Muhammad's God wasn't slow in coming to his defense and has sent down another verse," one of them says.[99] As if the story was not enough, Fitrat appended a note in his own name at the end: "Thus it was that God's 'best messenger,' going on sixty, managed to separate a young woman from his own son through deceit and to take her for himself."[100]

The story of Zayd and Zaynab had long been the stock in trade of missionary and secular critics of Islam and was widely used in anti-Islamic polemics. Fitrat's path to his retelling, however, passed through his own reading of early Islamic sources, rather than anti-Islamic polemics. In another piece in *Xudosizlar*, Fitrat quoted Tabari (d. 923) and Zamakhshari (d. 1143/44) at length in his retelling of the story of the angels Harut and Marut (who were sent down to tempt the people of Babylon) to show the irrationality and the internal contradictions of the stories treated with great seriousness in the Islamic tradition.[101] In fact, Fitrat is employing the same tactic here that he employed in *Bedil*—reading sources from the Islamicate tradition literally to subvert it. In "Zayd and Zaynab," of course, Fitrat embellishes a great deal, but the points that he makes are highly subversive, for it is not just that Muhammad comes across as a lecher, but his revelations (i.e., the Qur'an itself) are figments of his self-serving imagination.[102] There is not much left of Islam after this.

Unlike his cycle of works from 1923–24, Fitrat's writings in *Xudosizlar* cannot be explained away as anti-Soviet. The most that can be said is that he wrote these to burnish his revolutionary credentials and to ward off the attacks on him that were piling up then (see chapter 12). Publishing in *Xudosizlar* seems to have been a requirement for the old Jadids, a way for them to show loyalty to the new order, but not all those who published in its pages did so with such gusto. Sadriddin Ayni, for instance, published a couple of stories of the duplicity of local eshons

99. Ibid., no. 5 (1928), 26.

100. Ibid.

101. Fitrat, "Zahroning imoni," *Xudosizlar*, no. 2 (1928), 45–53.

102. In "Fitratning diniy mavzudagi asarlari," in *Milliy uyg'onish va o'zbek filologiyasi masalalari* (Tashkent, 1993), 51–64, the Uzbek scholar Boybo'ta Do'stqorayev has noted similarities between *Qiyomat* and Bertrand Russell's short story, "The Theologian's Nightmare" (1961). We might note resemblances between Fitrat's work and that of Salman Rushdie, whose *Satanic Verses* (1988) also uses Satan and Muhammad's wives as major topoi to subvert the Islamic narrative.

that would not have been out of place in the Jadid press before the revolution.[103] Fitrat seemed to relish the challenges he posed to conventional wisdom and to old patterns of belief. His undoubted mastery of Central Asia's Islamicate tradition also ensures that he knows where to turn the knife. Whether he is retelling the narrative of Muhammad's ascension to the heavens, mocking the procedure of weighing sins and good deeds on the Day of Judgment, reimagining Azazel's disobedience to God's will, or reinterpreting Bedil's oeuvre, there is never any question of his command of the material. Far from being a deracinated modernist, Fitrat was firmly rooted in his tradition, even as he rebelled against it.

The question of authorial intent and sincerity is there even under fully free circumstances. In the context of 1923–24, when Fitrat had just been squeezed out of office, it is all the more complicated. My reading of Fitrat's texts has been based on my sense of his intellectual trajectory and of the battles he was fighting within Uzbek Muslim society. A final piece of evidence about Fitrat's intellectual trajectory comes from a published biographical statement, one of the very few we have available, that Fitrat was allowed to make in 1929. Responding to Jalil Boybo'latov, who had accused him of being a Sufi, a pan-Islamist, and a pan-Turkist, Fitrat wrote, "I was once a proponent of religious reform, given over to the idea of separating religion from superstition. Precisely this path from religious reform brought me to irreligion [*dinsizliq*]. I saw that nothing remained of religion once it was separated from superstition. I came to believe that religion and science could never coexist and therefore I left religion and [began to] spread ideas against religion. My irreligion is well known to all Uzbeks and Tajiks. This fact cannot be denied."[104] Qodiriy's reformism led him to question the authority of the ulama; Fitrat's reformism led him to irreligion. To be sure, this is an "official" statement made at a time when attacks were mounting against Fitrat, and it was useful for Fitrat to stress his antireligious credentials. Yet, in the article quoted here, Fitrat does not make a great effort to prove his loyalty to the Soviet cause. The self-exculpation is there, but the evidence of Fitrat's own writings would suggest that we should take Fitrat at face value here.

From Muslim Irreligion to Soviet Atheism

How many others travelled the same path as Fitrat in these years? We have no evidence that *Satan's Revolt against God*, the most clearly theatrical piece of the three, was ever staged, and we should be hesitant to extrapolate too much from

---

103. Sadriddin Ayniy, "Buxoroda ruxoniylar harakati haqida ba'zi materiallar," *Xudosizlar*, no. 9–10 (1928): 27–33.

104. Fitrat, "Yopishmagan gajjaklar (O'rtoq Boybulatovga ochiq xat)," *Qizil O'zbekiston*, 16.09.1929.

these texts to the general mood of the Jadids in these years. Nevertheless, it is clear that anticlericalism and even irreligion, articulated in a Muslim idiom, pushed back against the authority of the ulama in Central Asia in the years after the revolution. By the mid-1920s, this anticlericalism was joined by a rather different discourse of atheism, unmoored from an Islamic critique of Muslim practices, and couched in peculiarly Soviet terms. The tone of the press became ever harsher and went beyond making fun of the ulama and the Sufis to ridiculing Islamic practices of worship and fasting. The advent of Ramadan in April 1924 saw a number of publications ridiculing the practice of fasting. Ne'mat Hakim expounded on the "scientific view of fasting," while *Mushtum* suggested that many ulama did not fast and that the only reason they had not invented a legal dodge (*hila-yi shar'iy*) to avoid fasting altogether was that fasting did not cost money.[105] Two years later, *Mushtum* published a cartoon captioned, "The Movement against Fasting Has Begun among Imams Too," that showed an imam eating in the privacy of his home but then ostentatiously breaking the fast in the company of others.[106]

Nazir To'raqulov had argued in 1921 that "religion today is a tool in the hands of governments. Ruling classes, i.e., capitalists, dress up their class interests in theology and, when needed, do not desist from any cunning and deception."[107] A new cohort of even more radical writers, many of them members of the party, began to stake out even more radical positions on the ulama and Islam. The subject of cultural critique shifted from *xurofot* (superstition) to *diniy xurofot* ("religious superstition"), and its object came to be defined not as *dinfurushlar* but simply as *dinchilar*, "the proponents of religion." The following poem by G'ayratiy (b. 1902) gives a taste of this new literary production:

Kim uchun

Qur'on,
machit,
ro'za,
mullolar,
eshonlar
manhuslar uchun.

---

105. N. H., "Fan qoroshida ro'za," *Turkiston*, 26.04.1924; Ayyor (pseud.), "Hila-i shar' (ramazon munosabatila)," *Mushtum*, no. 1 (24.04.1924). Making fun of Ramadan and fasting became a regular feature in the press; e.g., Yolg'onchi ro'zador (pseud.), "Ro'zachiliq," *Mashrab*, no. 20 (07.04.1925).

106. *Mushtum*, no. 5 (08.04.1926), 8.

107. "Islom va ko'mmunizm: Nazir To'raqulov tezislari," *Qizil bayroq*, 20.12.1921.

Din, eskilik,
mazhab, jonjol yo'li,
qiyomat, xoyol,
yong'lishqanlar uchun.
Zovud,
moshina,
cho'kich,
qoroqo'lli ishchilar uchun.
Yoqimli havo,
keng qirlar,
erkinlik bilan,
yer suruvchi
qo'shchilar uchun.
Taxt,
saltanat,
soroy
yirtqichlar,
xoqonlar uchun.

Din bilan kurash
mavhumot negizini bitirish,
dorulfunun,
qulub,
ishchi yoshlar uchun.[108]

For Whom?

Qur'an,
mosque,
fasting,
mullahs,
eshons—
they are for the ill-starred.

Religion, the old ways,
sects, the path of conflict,
the day of judgment, fantasy—
they are for the mistaken.
Factories,

---

108. G'ayratiy, *Erk tovushi* (Samarqand, 1927), 17.

machines,
tools—
they are for workers.
Pleasant breezes,
wide steppes—
they are for poor peasants
plowing their land
in freedom.
Thrones,
rulership,
palaces,
predation—
they are for emperors.

The struggle with religion,
the destruction of the basis for fantasy,
universities,
clubs—
they are for the toiling youth.

Here we are close to Soviet-style antireligious discourse, which arrived in Uzbek society only at the end of the 1920s, and which we will discuss in chapter 11. Poetry such as this was an indication of how radically the religious landscape of Central Asia had changed since 1917.

THE MAKING OF UZBEKISTAN

The nation, as we saw in chapter 6, was the central passion of the intelligentsia in the years after 1917. The limits, however, of the nation as imagined by the Jadids shifted substantially in these years. Most actors in the politics of 1917 had fought in the name of the "Muslims of Turkestan," and Turkestan remained the locus of the aspirations of most actors, both within and without the party, in the years that followed. Yet the rhetoric of Turkestan contained within it multiple understandings. Kazakh and Uzbek activists came to see things very differently. For the former, the idea of Turkestan carried less and less weight as they sought to unite with Kazakhs of the former Steppe krai, while for the latter, Turkestan came to be centered around the sedentary population of Transoxiana. The Jadids' celebration of Central Asia's Turko-Islamic tradition of statehood best embodied by Temur had little appeal to Kazakh intellectuals. The small Turkmen intelligentsia also had no investment in the discourses of Chaghatayism as they evolved in these years. The Chaghatayist project of the Jadids, far from being pan-Turkic, actually affirmed boundaries between various Turkic groups in Central Asia.

The distinction between the sedentary and nomadic populations, which in many ways had been constitutive of the social imaginary of the region since precolonial times, now reasserted itself in the language of nationhood. In 1924, the extension to Central Asia of a key tenet of Soviet nationalities policy—that national and administrative boundaries should coincide—territorialized this distinction. Presented with the opportunity of creating a territorial entity for the nation, Uzbek elites jumped at it with alacrity and created a territorial entity for the sedentary Muslim population of Central Asia, which they had come to imagine as Uzbeks. The Uzbekistan that emerged from the national-territorial delimitation of Central Asia in 1924 was thus not the artificial product of Soviet machinations, but the triumph of an indigenous national project. This chapter traces the unlikely success of the Chaghatayist project in Soviet conditions.

Imagining Uzbekness

In June 1916, in the middle of the Great War, the Third Conference of Nationalities met in Lausanne to discuss questions of self-determination of national groups in the empires of Europe. On the last day, a certain Muqimiddin Bekjon, a Bukharan student in Istanbul, spoke on behalf of a Chaghatay nation that inhabited "the khanates of Bukhara and Khiva and the province of Turkestan." His demands consisted of the return to Bukhara of the territory annexed by Russia during its conquest of Transoxiana in the nineteenth century.[1] Apart from this use, the term *Chaghatay* was seldom used for the nation. Rather, Chaghatay represented the cultural heritage claimed by a nation that was increasingly and insistently called Uzbek (*o'zbek*). Historically, the term *o'zbek* had referred to the nomadic confederation that displaced the Timurids from Transoxiana at the beginning of the sixteenth century and established the state order that prevailed in Central Asia until the Russian conquest. By the time of the revolution, however, Central Asian elites had begun to use "Uzbek" to denote the entire non-nomadic Muslim population of the region, its language, and its culture. The Chaghatayist project led to Uzbekness.

Chaghatayism was based on the assertion that Central Asia was the cradle of the Turkic peoples, that the entire population of the region was Turkic, and that only a reclamation of this national authenticity made progress possible. Uzbekness was defined in this broader Turkicness. The turn to Turkism was among other things a revolt against the Persianate tradition, a form of de-Persianization of identity. In the Chaghatayist view, Central Asians who spoke Persian did so under the cultural influence of morally corrupt royal courts. Fitrat, the main

---

1. *Compte rendu de la IIIme Conférence des nationalités réunie à Lausanne 27–29 juin 1916* (Lausanne, 1917), 198–199; see also A. Z. V. Togan, *Bugünkü Türkili (Türkistan) ve Yakın Tarihi*, 2nd ed. (Istanbul, 1981), 477–478. The conference was held by the Union des Nationalités, an organization that promoted the cause of national and political self-determination of nationalities in Europe. During the war, it acquired an increasingly pro-German outlook and the conference in Lausanne was primarily directed against Russia. See Artūras Svarauskas, "Union des Nationalités," in *1914–1918-Online: International Encyclopedia of the First World War*, ed. Ute Daniel et al. (Berlin, 2014); doi 10.15463/ie1418.10262.

theorist of Chaghatayism, had become convinced of this view during his stay in Istanbul.[2] So while he had published exclusively in Persian until 1916, even while he lived in Istanbul, he switched to Turkic in 1917 and wrote solely in Uzbek for the next decade. During this time, he also worked tirelessly to modernize the language and create a new vocabulary and orthography for it. Fitrat's first publication in Uzbek was a primer for elementary schools, in which Arabo-Persian grammatical forms were entirely absent and the vocabulary was so hyper-Turkic that Fitrat often found it necessary to explain some of the neologisms in footnotes.[3] As in many other national movements around the world, linguistic purity was an important measure of authenticity.[4]

Asserting the Turkicness of the population of Central Asia also meant disavowing other labels of identification. Already before the revolution, the Jadids had objected to the use of the term *Sart*, used in a number of ways to define the sedentary Muslim population of Turkestan. In everyday Russian and Kazakh usage, it carried the connotation of racial admixture of Turks and Persians, but for the Jadids, the main objection was that it did not reflect the "real" Turkicness of the groups so labeled.[5] The critique was passionate enough and politically relevant enough that the term disappeared from the political lexicon in 1917.[6]

---

2. Sohib Tabarov, *Munzim* (Dushanbe, 1991), 40. This was a fairly common position in the intensely Turkist attitudes gaining ground in the Ottoman Empire. In 1912, the journal *Türk Yurdu* had asserted that Bukhara's population was Turkic (Türk oğlu Türk), and that the dominance of Persian in it was abnormal. The situation, it predicted, "will change in the near future. The official language and the publications of [this] Turkic state will of course be Turkic, and the Persian language will be used, to an extent proportionate to their numbers, only for the few Tajiks who have immigrated from Iran." See "Turan Gazetesi," *Türk Yurdu*, 2 (1912), 631.

3. Fitrat, *O'qu!* (Bukhara, 1917).

4. Language purification is, of course, a common phenomenon of the nineteenth- and twentieth-century nationalisms and scarcely confined to the Muslim world. Turkism in both the (former) Russian and the Ottoman empires was deeply invested in purifying Turkic languages. On Ottoman, see Agâh Sırrı Levend, *Türk Dilinde Gelişme ve Sadeleşme Safhaları* (Ankara, 1949), and Geoffrey Lewis, *Turkish Language Reform: A Catastrophic Success* (Oxford, 1999). For modern Persian, see Ahmad Karimi-Hakkak, "Language Reform Movement and its Language: the Case of Persian," in *The Politics of Language Purism*, ed. Björn H. Jernudd and Michael J. Shapiro (Berlin, 1989), 81–104; John Perry, "Language Reform in Turkey and Iran," *International Journal of Middle East Studies* 17 (1985): 295–311. In Arabic, a reform movement challenged the hegemony of the classical tradition and led to the creation of Modern Standard Arabic. The literature on these developments is surprisingly slim, but see Kees Versteegh, *The Arabic Language* (Edinburgh, 1997), chap. 11, and Dagmar Glaß, "Creating a Modern Standard Language from Medieval Tradition: The Nahḍa and the Arabic Academies," in *The Semitic Languages: An International Handbook*, ed. Stefan Weninger (Berlin, 2011), 835–844.

5. See Adeeb Khalid, *The Politics of Muslim Cultural Reform: Jadidism in Central Asia* (Berkeley, 1998), chap. 6, for a more extended treatment of this question.

6. In the agricultural census conducted that year, census takers were told that "a separate Sart people [*narod*] does not exist and that this term should everywhere be replaced by 'Uzbek.'" I.I. Zarubin, *Spisok narodnostei Turkestanskogo kraia* (Leningrad, 1925), 15–16.

After that, its use provoked severe reactions from the nationalizing intelligentsia. When an article in the Kazakh newspaper *Aq jol* in 1922 used the term to denote the population of Tashkent, Abdulla Qodiriy went on the offensive. The term, he wrote, was reminiscent of "the times of Ostroumov *to'ra*," and clearly an insult to "us Uzbeks [who] have struggled with everyone who, for whatever reason, attaches the word 'Sart' to us."[7] Sart was banished from the political and ethnographic lexicon also because no group claimed it for itself. A few had spoken up in defense of the term, but after 1917 there seems to have been a total absence of any advocacy of it. The abolition of "Sart" as a label was driven by the passions of the local intelligentsia. As in so many of the national debates of the period, it was a question of which labels were recognized as legitimate (and "scientific"), and which were not. This was inherently a political question. National movements need not only to assert the boundaries of their nation but to have them recognized as legitimate, both by those on whose behalf they speak (the putative nation) and those in the world beyond. As Pierre Bourdieu put it, "[Just] as a constellation . . . begins to exist only when it is selected and designated as such, a group, class, 'gender,' region, or nation, begins to exist as such, for those who are part of it and for others too, only when it is distinguished, according to one principle or another, from other groups, that is via cognition and recognition."[8] Here "Uzbek" was recognized and "Sart" consigned to oblivion.

The main vehicle for Chaghatayism was Chig'atoy Gurungi (Chaghatay Conversation), a cultural organization formed in late 1918 by Fitrat and some colleagues with the aim of "collecting old and new Turkic works in Turkestan, of gathering materials for the rejuvenation of the Turkic language, and of enriching [its] vocabulary and literature."[9] Over the next two years, the organization held numerous discussions of literature and language and launched the question of the reform of orthography. The organization celebrated Turkicness and the heritage of the steppe. Its members wrote under pen names such as Botu, Uyghur, Chinggiz, and Temochin. A primer published by it contained the following remarkable reading passage for children just learning to read:

7. Julqunboy, "Sart og'a-inilarga," *Qizil bayroq*, 03.06.1922; Juboy, "Haqiqat–ochib so'zlashdadir," *Qizil bayroq*, 16.06.1922; also in Abdulla Qodiriy, *Diyori bakr: She'rlar, hikoyalar, sahna asarlari, hangoma, felyeton va maqolalar*, ed. Xondamir Qodiriy (Tashkent, 2007), 101, 105. Nazir Töreqülov (To'raqulov), then acting editor of *Aq jol*, had defended the use of the term *Sart* on the grounds of its long history and its continuing use: "Habit is stronger than man. It is natural that [the use of] this word will continue in Turkestan itself for a long time." Darvesh [Nazir To'raqulov], "O'zbek qarindoshlarimizning diqqatlariga," *Qizil bayroq*, 27.05.1922.

8. Pierre Bourdieu, "Social Space and Symbolic Power," in *In Other Words: Essays towards a Reflexive Sociology*, trans. Matthew Adamson (Stanford, 1990), 138.

9. "Chig'atoy gurungi," *Ishtirokiyun*, 04.02.1919.

O'g'uz Turklarning yolovuchidir (payg'ambar), Chingiz Turklarning xoqonidir, Temur Turklarning boturidir. Ulug'bek Turklarning bilgu-chisidir. (Oghuz is the prophet of the Turks, Genghis is the ruler of the Turks, Temur is the hero of the Turks. Ulughbek is the scholar of the Turks.)[10]

This unabashed pride in the Turkic heritage of Central Asia existed without explicit reference to Islam (indeed, the elevation of Oghuz Khan, the bringer of Islam to the Turks of Central Asia, to prophethood was mildly blasphemous), although Islam was never repudiated. Ethnic pride was backed by an unprec-edented interest in the Turkic past of the region. In both Turkestan and Bukhara, the 1920s were marked by an intense preoccupation with studying the past and the present of the region. Fitrat returned to Bukhara for the first time since 1917 in December 1920 with an "Uzbek scientific expedition" to survey the manu-script collections of the city.[11] Later, as a minister in the BNSR government, he organized a History and Archaeology Society (Tarix va osor-i atiqa anjumani) and a School of Eastern Music, both of which had the aim of studying and recording the heritage of the country.[12] Jadid figures traveled around the coun-tryside, gathering folklore and notating folk music and recording epics sung by baxshis around Central Asia. Scholarly journals carried articles on the archeology and ethnic history of Central Asia, a task later carried on by journals aimed at teachers.

A fundamental feature of the literature of this period was a relentless drive to assert the Turkicness of the written language, with a conscious attempt to spurn the vast storehouse of Arabic and Persian words that had entered Uzbek. The new poetry of the era was new not just in its subject matter, but also in its form, as new genres, new meters, and new systems of prosody redefined Uzbek poetry. Fitrat again was the main theorist here, even if Cho'lpon became its foremost practitio-ner. Chaghatay itself, of course, was a court language defined as much by its use of Arabic and Persian loanwords and its loyalty of Persianate literary forms and conventions as by its Turkicness. For Fitrat, the point was not to foist an archaic language on all of Central Asia (as his critics were to charge later), but to modern-ize that language. The Jadid project, like most nationalisms, saw the problem as a dialectic between modernity and authenticity: the nation had to be made more modern and more authentic at the same time. The modern had to be built on

10. Chig'atoy Gurungi, Bitim yo'llari (imlo) (Tashkent, 1919), 15.

11. "Buxoroga yuborilgan O'zbek bilim hay'atining ishlagan ishlari," Qizil boyroq, 23.02.1921.

12. Elif Kale-Lostuvalı, "Varieties of Musical Nationalism in Soviet Uzbekistan," Central Asian Survey 26 (2007): 539–558.

authentically national roots. Modern Uzbek was to derive its new vocabulary and the rules of its grammar from Turkic sources of Chaghatay, while disregarding its Perso-Arabic dimensions. In addition to purifying the vocabulary, Fitrat also argued that the *aruz* system of prosody, which had enjoyed canonical status in Chaghatay poetry since its inception, was not suited to "our language." Aruz is a metrical system that distinguishes between long and short vowels and open and closed syllables. It originated in Arabic poetry and was later nativized into Persian and became the paradigm for poetry throughout the Turco-Persian world. By the turn of the twentieth century, modernist poets throughout that world had begun to voice misgivings about the authority it continued to enjoy. While in Persian the critique centered on the rigidity of the form, Turkist poets in the Ottoman Empire and beyond argued that the system was inherently unsuited to Turkic languages, which do not distinguish between long and short vowels. The critique soon took on a national coloring, as Turkist poets counterpoised the Perso-Arabic aruz to the Turkish national syllabic meters.[13] This critique was at its peak in the years Fitrat spent in Istanbul. In 1918, he introduced it to Central Asia. For Fitrat, aruz worked for the "national" meters of the Arabs and the Persians, but its emphasis on vowel length meant that "even the most harmonious and playful aruz meter" produced clumsy results in Turkic poetry, so that "a village Turk who has not destroyed the harmony of his own language would, upon hearing [such poetry] smile at the way Turkic words had been dragged out and made vapid."[14] Poetry, Fitrat argued, should be written in the syllabic meter (*barmoq vazni*) that was the "national meter of the Turks," and appropriate to the phonetic structures of their languages.

The twin imperatives of modernization and authenticity also brought the question of the reform of the alphabet the fore. The question of reforming the orthography of Turkic languages had been around for several generations, but it had attracted little interest in Central Asia.[15] For the reformers, the Arabic script had three major problems. First, it indicated only long vowels (using characters that also serve as consonants); Turkic languages have numerous vowels but usually make no distinction between long and short vowels. Second, letters take

13. Hasan Kolcu, *Türk Edebiyatında Hece-Aruz Tartışmaları* (Ankara, 1993); I. V. Stebleva, *Tiurkskaia poetika: etapy razvitiia VIII–XX vv.* (Moscow, 2012).

14. Abdurauf Fitrat, *Adabiyot qoidalari: Adabiyot muallimlari ham adabiyot havaslilari uchun*, ed. Hamidulla Boltaboyev (Tashkent, 1995 [orig. 1926]), 39–40, 46–47. The incompatibility of aruz with Turkic poetry was a favorite theme of Fitrat's. The first time he made the point in print was in "She'r va shoirliq," *Ishtirokiyun*, 01.08.1919, and he repeated it on numerous occasions.

15. See Ingeborg Baldauf, *Schriftreform und Schriftwechsel bei den Muslimischen Russland- und Sowjettürken (1850–1937): Ein Symptom Ideengeschichtlicher und Kulturpolitischer Entwicklungen* (Budapest, 1993), 53–96; Bilâl N. Şimşir, *Türk Yazı Devrimi* (Ankara, 1992), 38–96; Hamid Algar, *Mīrzā Malkum Khān: A Study in the History of Iranian Modernism* (Berkeley, 1969), 82–95.

different forms depending of their place in a word; each letter has several shapes, which requires a mastery of a large number of ligatures for achieving functional literacy. Finally, the alphabet contained a number of letters indicating consonant sounds unique to Arabic. In Turkic languages, these letters were pronounced differently and their presence made teaching literacy difficult.[16] In addition, the conventions of orthography followed by Turkic languages paid scant attention to pronunciation and hewed much more closely to etymological principles. (Ironically, for precisely this reason, different Turkic languages were mutually intelligible in written form, because the script hid many of the differences of the spoken language.) The aspirations of language modernizers, that the written language should reflect the spoken, as should the orthography (the completely phonetic script being the ideal) ran directly against the established conventions of orthography in all Turkic languages.

It was largely the revolutionary enthusiasms of the 1917 era that put the agenda on the table in Central Asia, with Chig'atoy Gurungi playing the central role. A primer it published in 1919 modified the Arabic script to indicate all vowels and to separate the consonants specific to Arabic, putting them at the end of the alphabet, to be taught last.[17] This inaugurated a period of great ferment in which different individuals staked out a variety of positions, from a commitment to the old conventions and an aversion (or disdain) for reform, through the use of vowels throughout the text, to a full blown "Turkification" of the Arabic script that was fully vocalized and excluded Arabic-specific letters altogether. These issues came to a head at the First Conference on Uzbek Language and Orthography organized by the Chig'atoy Gurungi in January 1921. The debate proved to be quite sharp and continued in the press for the following year and a half. For Fitrat, the issue of the language was as important as that of mass literacy. "Our writing is without order, our spelling chaotic," he said in his opening remarks. "Now our government has started a campaign against illiteracy. That cannot be done without reforming the orthography."[18] Fitrat laid out the radical position at the conference: a fully phonetic orthography based on a six-vowel system; the abolition of Arabic-specific consonants; the spelling of words as they were pronounced, with every vowel indicated; and—most controversially—subjugating

---

16. Thus, in Persian and all Turkic languages (as well as in Urdu, Pashto, and many others), the letters ذ, ز, ض, and ظ were all pronounced as /z/; ث, س, and ص as /s/; and ح and ه as /h/. Words of Arabic origin continued to be written in their original forms in these languages, but their pronunciation was completely indigenized.

17. *Bitim yo'llari*, passim.

18. *1921 yil yanvarda bo'lgan birinchi o'lka o'zbek til va imlo qurultoyining chiqorgan qarorlari* (Tashkent, 1922), 13.

foreign words (i.e., those of Arabic origin) to these rules. Ashurali Zohiriy, an old Jadid from Ferghana, took the moderate position, arguing for sparing Arabic words from complete vocalization: "We will be cut off from the Muslim world. . . . [and] no one will be able to understand what we write and we will be unable to read books published until now."[19] There were no defenders of the status quo at the conference, but even so the debate was sharp. The exchange between Fitrat and Zohiriy got so heated that Zohiriy walked out during a vote and refused to give his presentation on grammar the following day. Fitrat, however, was out-flanked on the radical side by Botu, then all of seventeen years old, who advocated dropping the Arabic script altogether and opting for Latin. "The backwardness of a nation is the backwardness of its script," he argued. "If you are going to the railway station, you get there faster by car than on foot. The [Latin] script speeds up progress in the same way."[20] Latinization had been mooted in the wider Turkic world, but in January 1921 was nowhere a serious proposition. It was voted off the agenda, but the orthography ultimately approved by the conference was quite radical. It contained six vowels and twenty-three consonants. There were to be special letters for /ŋ/ and /v/, but /f/ was excluded on the argument that it was not used in Uzbek speech; it was assimilated to /p/. (Botu's proposition to exclude /h/ as well and thus to recognize the $h \rightarrow x$ shift in many dialects as standard was defeated.) All Arabic-specific letters were excluded, and Fitrat's arguments for spelling Arabic loanwords according to general rules won the day.[21] The reform was quite radical. Apart from everything else, it utterly transformed the visual character of Arabic script.

While orthographic reform was in the air throughout the Turkic-speaking world, and the years of revolution had produced similar activity among the Tatars, the Tashkent conference was not part of a broad organized effort.[22] Rather, it was a home-grown initiative, indicative of the urgency with which this matter was treated. Speeches at the conference make it quite clear that orthographic reform was seen as completely intertwined with broader cultural issues, as reports from the localities concentrated as much on theater and the press as on education. The most prominent figures at the conference (Fitrat, Ashurali Zohiriy, Shokir-jon Rahimiy, Vadud Mahmud) were all educators and cultural reformers of long standing. Even the passions aroused pertained to the nation. Mannon Romiz,

---

19. Ibid., 19–20.

20. Ibid., 22–23.

21. Ibid., 24–26. The verbatim record of the conference published the following year followed these rules. Fitrat's name was spelled "Pitrat" throughout.

22. On Tatar developments in this period, see Baldauf, *Schriftreform*, 186–196, and more gener-ally, Khälif Kurbatov, *Tatar ädäbi teleneng alfavit häm orfografiya tarikhï* (Kazan, 1999).

who represented the education section of the Tashkent old-city soviet, reported how the Ottoman teachers (who had mostly departed by the time of the conference) were opposed to the new orthography and that Efendiyev, the commissar for education, had threatened anyone teaching it with consequences. Now the tables were turned, and the reformers took on the mantle of revolution. Shahid Ahmadiyev, a Tatar delegate, had already argued that the ulama used the Arabic script to monopolize knowledge and to hold the common people back.[23] The circle of those assumed to benefit from the old orthography widened ever more, as reformers cast their opponents as "reactionaries who want to hold toilers back," religious [*dinchi*], or as counterrevolutionaries. Orthographic reform became the site of impassioned debate that sometimes even descended into violence. A conference of "teachers and writers" in Samarqand that resolved *against* the new orthography, finished its resolutions by "lamenting the fact that proponents of the new orthography, instead of using logical arguments in academic debates, used force and continuously exercised dictatorship in the name of Communism and the government."[24]

Debates over orthography were indicative of the nature of Central Asia's cultural revolution in the early Soviet years. It is tempting to see orthographic reform and Latinization as connected to "secularization" or "de-Islamization," and to lay them at the door of a malevolent Soviet regime. To do so would be to fail to understand the nature of the cultural radicalism of the 1920s. The proponents of the new orthography might have argued in the name of the revolution, and they certainly had support in the party and soviet apparatuses of the old cities, but the questions were debated in public, with input from literary figures and pedagogical or philological experts. These debates were a logical continuation of the reform of the language and orthography whose roots went back to prerevolutionary times and that were intimately connected to broader developments in the Turkic world. By 1926, when the first (and only) Turkological Congress met in Baku to deliberate on these questions, orthographic reform was also on the agenda in Kemalist Turkey. The nationalization of language and orthography, and the distancing of both from Arabic, were precisely the goals of the nationalizing intelligentsia, who saw in these moves the path to progress. Orthographic reform combined within it impulses for authenticity and efficiency, for modernity and progress, and for taking one's place in the world, and for that reason it had seized the imagination of the intelligentsias of many societies in the decades before the Russian revolution. For the Central Asia intelligentsia, the implementation

23. *1921 yil yanvarda*, 17.

24. M., "Imlo masalasi," *Kambag'allar tovushi*, 03.02.1922.

of orthographic reform became a central feature of the revolution. The reform was specific to Uzbek and served to differentiate it from other Turkic languages.

The Turkic Boundaries of Uzbekness

Uzbekness was defined against other Turkic groups. Much of the activity of Chig'atoy Gurungi was directed against the use of Ottoman in Tashkent's Muslim schools under the influence of Ottoman prisoners of war, who tended to see the local vernacular merely as a dialect of Ottoman Turkish. Indeed, the Tashkent education bureau headed by Munavvar qori wanted to institute a "common Turkic language" in Muslim schools after three years of instruction in "the mother tongue." Fitrat, who had actually spent four years in Istanbul, was opposed to such "insult and disrespect to our language," which he argued possessed "the most complete, the most numerous, the most valuable literature of all Turkic literatures."[25] Back in 1921, Fitrat and his colleagues in the Chig'atoy Gurungi had articulated a set of principles for the reform of the language: the standard for literary quality of Uzbek should be determined not by the degree of its "Arabicness"; its rules should come from itself, and not from Tatar or Ottoman; and the language should be cleansed of foreign words.[26] Uzbek had its own resources to create a modern language and had no use for tutelage to Ottoman or Tatar standards.

"Uzbek," then, was clearly not synonymous with the entire Turkic population of Central Asia, nor did it represent the unity of the region. Kazakh intellectuals never had any connection to Chaghatayism, nor any fondness for Temur. The Kazakh intelligentsia had developed along rather different lines in the years before the revolution. With Kazakh aristocratic elites sending their sons to Russian schools from the middle of the nineteenth century on, the Kazakh intelligentsia tended to be more comfortable with Russian, while the weakness of a group based in Islamic book learning (the ulama) meant that the intelligentsia's role in society was not questioned in quite the same way as it was in Turkestan. Already by 1917, the Kazakh intelligentsia had achieved considerable success in establishing Kazakh as a written language with its own distinctive orthography and established a literary community around periodicals such as *Ay qap* (Troitsk) and *Qazaq* (Orenburg), of which Kazakhs of Turkestan were also a part. In that year,

---

25. *1921 yil yanvarda*, 35–40. Fitrat was later to claim that this issue led to a serious conflict between him and Munavvar Qori, in which members of Chig'atoy Gurungi were subjected to physical threats and intimidation: "Yopishmagan gajjaklar," *Qizil O'zbekiston*, 15.09.1929, 16.09.1929.

26. *1921 yil yanvarda*, 40.

while the Kazakhs of Semirech'e and Syr Darya took part in the politics of Turkestan, the main locus of Kazakh activity lay to the north. Alash Orda, the Kazakh
national movement, sought autonomy for the Steppe krai and coexisted with the
Kokand Autonomy. Muhammadjan Tïnïshbayev was nominally the president of
the Kokand Autonomy, but he left before the sack of Kokand to focus his energies on Alash. Moreover, Kazakh literary production in Turkestan was entirely in
Kazakh and part of a separate conversation carried out in Kazakh newspapers.[27]
As Nazir Töreqŭlov (To'raqulov), the Ferghana-born bilingual Kazakh chair of
TurTsIK wrote in 1922, "A lot has happened in the past ten or fifteen years. Turkestanis have grown a great deal in this period. Everyone has recognized himself
and his companions. The Uzbek has found Amir Navoiy [and] the Kazakh has
caught hold of Abay."[28] In short, Uzbek and Kazakh intellectuals formed two different cultural communities.

The new political elite, those whose work lay primarily in the party or the
soviet apparatus, was equally invested in the nation, and they had no problem
assimilating it to their idea of the revolution. The party, far from being immune
to it, provided an essential arena in which national conflicts would be played
out. Rïsqŭlov had put together an alliance of Kazakh and Uzbek activists in the
Musburo, but that quickly frayed after his departure from the scene in 1920,
and relations among the leading Communists of Turkestan deteriorated along
national lines. "National relations here," Juozas Vareikis, the newly appointed
head of the Sredazburo, reported in early 1924, "are extraordinarily sharp for
the simple reason that there is a constant struggle between Uzbeks and Kazakhs
[in the party] for the right to be the ruling nation [in Turkestan]. . . . Conflicts
take place constantly between Kazakhs and Uzbeks in the struggle to acquire a
dominant position in the state."[29] Kyrgyz Communists had likewise mobilized
around nationality and in 1922 had organized a conference that passed resolutions seeking the formation of an autonomous Mountain Oblast for the Kyrgyz.[30]
In Bukhara, the few Turkmen members of the party began to organize as Turkmens and to demand national rights in the party and the state. The nation had
become the common currency in which political elites conducted their business.

---

27. G. K. Otarbayeva, "Tashkent qalasïnïng qazaq khalqïnïng sayasi-äleumettïk, ekonomikalïq
jäne rukhani ömïrïndegi mangïzï (XIX ghasïrdïng ekïnshï jartïsï–XX ghasïrdïng alghashqï shigerï)"
candidate's diss., M. Äuezov atïndaghï Ongtüstïk Qazaqstan memlekttïk universitetï, 2010).

28. Darvesh, "O'zbek qarindoshlarimizning diqqatlariga."

29. Vareikis to Stalin, 27.03.24, in TsK RKP(b)–VKP(b) i natsional'nyi vopros, vol. 1 (Moscow,
2005), 190.

30. Benjamin Loring, "Building Socialism in Kyrgyzstan: Nation-Making, Rural Development,
and Social Change, 1921–1932" (Ph.D. diss., Brandeis University, 2008), 75–88.

In fact, the conflict between Kazakh and Uzbek political elites had already in 1921 led to demands for altering the political boundaries of Turkestan. The question of changing the administrative structure of Turkestan to reflect the division between sedentary and nomadic populations had long been around. K.P. Kaufman, the first governor-general of Turkestan, had brought it up in 1881 and the idea reappeared in 1920, when during the dispute between TurTsIK and the Turkkomissiia, Lenin had suggested "the division of Turkestan in accordance with the territorial-ethnographic composition" so that "the national groups of Turkestan" could have "the possibility of organizing themselves in autonomous republics."[31] The creation of separate national oblasts for the three main nationalities was written into the Politburo resolution of June 1920 that defined Turkestan's place in the Soviet state as an important goal of Soviet power in Turkestan.[32] A different kind of pressure came from the demands, increasingly insistent, from Kazakh activists from outside Turkestan. Upon Alash Orda's defeat, the Kazakh lands of the former Steppe krai were turned into an autonomous Kazakh Republic with its capital at Omsk. In August 1920, the Kazakh-dominated Manghïshlaq Peninsula was transferred from Turkestan to the Kazakh Republic. In January 1921, the First Turkestan Congress of the Kazakh Poor, meeting in Avliyo Ota, asked for the oblasts of Semirech'e and Syr Darya to be united with the Kazakh republic since "the Kazakh people in both the republics are of one blood, one culture, one language, and at the same stage of economic development."[33] Since Syr Darya oblast included Tashkent, this became a major issue. In Tashkent, rumors flew that the city was going to be transferred to the Kazakh Republic. The situation was sufficiently grave for TurTsIK to ask Narkomnats for clarification and then to publish a rebuttal in the press.[34] Nevertheless, Aq jol, the Kazakh-language newspaper of the KPT, continued to publish articles on the issue and the leadership of the Kazakh Republic brought the matter up again at Narkomnats in 1922, asking for the transfer of the two oblasts on the grounds that allegedly 93 percent of the population of the two oblasts was Kazakh and that the concentration of all Kazakhs in one republic would make the work of

---

31. To this end, Lenin also suggested "creating maps (ethnographic and other) of the division of Turkestan into Uzbekia, Kirgizia, and Turkmenia." V.I. Lenin, "Zamechaniia na proekte Turkestan-skoi komissii" (13.06.1920), in *Polnoe sobranie sochinenii*, 5th ed., vol. 41 (Moscow, 1963), 435–436.

32. The Politburo resolution can be found in D.A. Amanzholova, ed., *Rossiia i Tsentral'naia Aziia, 1905–1925 gg.: sbornik dokumentov* (Karaganda, 2005), 279. The Turkkomissiia urged "caution against any such talk" and argued that such a project must come at the end of the process of reintegrating Turkestan into the Soviet state, "after all else is settled." Turkkomissiia to CC RKP(b), 05.06.1920, GARF, f. 130, op. 4, d. 786, l. 19.

33. GARF, f. 1318, op. 1, d. 12, ll. 143.

34. Rahimboyev to Stalin, 15.12.1921, in *Rossiia i Tsentral'naia Aziia*, 340; "Chegara o'zgarishi yo'qdur," *Qizil bayroq*, 20.12.1921.

"connecting Soviet principles to Kazakh reality" more efficient.[35] This argument played out against the background of a series of conflicts between the governments of Turkestan and the Kazakh Republic that ranged over issues of food supply, trade, and population movement. Turkestanis claimed that the absence of land reform in the Kazakh Republic allowed settlers to continue oppressing the Kazakhs who then fled to Turkestan and added to that republic's problems. The Kazakhs complained that the Turkestan government had stopped trains carrying food for the Kazakh Republic and searched "citizens of KSSR" as they traveled through Turkestan.[36] The situation was bad enough for the All-Union Central Executive Committee in Moscow to establish a special commission to resolve disputes between the two republics.[37] These conflicts were to cast a shadow over the negotiations for the national-territorial delimitation in 1924.

In short, by 1924, intellectuals in both Turkestan and Bukhara had come to imagine the sedentary Muslim population of Transoxiana as Uzbek (and quite different from their nomadic neighbors, the Kazakhs and the Turkmens). This marked a significant transformation in the political imagination. Its connection with the classificatory projects of Russian or Soviet ethnographers is, however, tenuous. Russian ethnographic discourses or classifications were not the most important impulse behind the nationalization of the discourse of Central Asian elites. The distinction between nomad and sedentary was of long standing in Central Asian discourses. It was now nationalized. For the Jadids, the path to nationalization lay through the prerevolutionary Turkist discourses popular in both the Russian and the Ottoman empires. As we saw in chapter 1, these discourses were informed by the work of European (including Russian) ethnographers, Orientalists, and historians, but they nevertheless retained their own distinctive parameters. Meanwhile, the Russian classificatory project remained mired in problems, and it would flatter the state to credit it with a significant role in defining the parameters of national debate among indigenous intellectuals. Central Asia had been subjected to ethnographic scrutiny since the Russian conquest, but the substantial corpus of literature that emerged had failed to create a stable nomenclature for describing, let alone analyzing, the region's population. The same applied to state practices. The decree that proclaimed Turkic the state language in 1918 stated, "the population of Turkestan is predominantly Turkic; half of it is *Kirgiz* [i.e., Kazakh and Kyrgyz], while the other half, with the exception of a very negligible quantity of the immigrant Russian element, is composed of Turkmens, Karakalpaks, Tajiks, along

35. GARF, f. 1318, op. 1, d. 12, ll. 144–144ob (21.03.1922).
36. GARF, f. 1235, op. 96, d. 755, ll. 28, 35 (1921).
37. GARF, f. 6987 (Komissiia VTsIK po uregulirovaniiu sporov mezhdu Turkestanskoi i Kirgizskoi respublikami).

with settled Uzbeks (Sarts) and others."[38] As late as 1924, even as the process of the national-territorial delimitation of Central Asia gathered pace, the ethnographer Vladimir Kun could write, "The academic literature on the ethnography of Turkestan, notwithstanding its abundance, still does not illuminate many aspects of native life. It is sufficient to say that the most basic object of study—the tribal composition of the population of Turkestan and its distribution—has been insufficiently studied."[39] The most tricky object of study had been the sedentary population of Central Asia, which had failed to yield its secrets to the positivist imaginations of ethnographers and statisticians during the fifty years of Russian rule.[40] The interconnections between the labels "Sart," "Turk," and "Uzbek" remained unclear, and these three were used simultaneously and interchangeably in the census of 1897. Turkestan's Statistical Administration did a lot of work in the years after 1917, but much of it was a matter of recording information, not analyzing it, and the same held true for institutions in Moscow or Leningrad. A Scientific Commission for the Study of the Way of Life of the Indigenous Population of Turkestan, supported by the republic's government, organized ethnographic expeditions in the summers of 1921 and 1922, but the Basmachi insurgency and a lack of funds meant that it never finished its work.[41] Similarly, all that the central Commission for the Study of the Tribal Composition of the Population of Russia managed to produce was a list of nationalities inhabiting Turkestan, hedged with all sorts of qualifications and protestations of incompleteness, and published only in 1925, after the delimitation had been carried out.[42] In 1924, then, when the process of delimiting Central Asia's boundaries on the national principle began, the classificatory grid of ethnography was extremely weak in Central Asia. The delimitation was therefore *not* the application of preexisting ethnographic knowledge (imperial or colonial) to state policy. Rather, the political process reshaped ethnographic knowledge to a certain extent. The opinions of experts played almost no role in the deliberations over the drawing of new boundaries in 1924.

From Bukhara to Uzbekistan

The decision by Moscow to extend to Central Asia the principle of ethnoterritorial delimitation practiced elsewhere in the USSR transformed the parameters of identity politics in Central Asia. The delimitation was decreed from above and

38. TsGARUz, f. 17, op. 1, d. 169, ll. 1–1ob (21.08.1918)
39. Vl. Kun, "Izuchenie etnograficheskogo sostava Turkestana," *Novyi Vostok*, no. 6 (1924), 350.
40. S. N. Abashin, *Natsionalizmy v Srednei Azii: v poiskakh identichnosti* (St. Petersburg, 2007).
41. Kun, "Izuchenie," 351–354.
42. Zarubin, *Spisok narodnostei.*

MAP 1. Central Asia on the eve of the national-territorial delimitation of 1924. Turkestan was an autonomous Soviet republic initially proclaimed in April 1918, while Khiva and Bukhara were "people's soviet republics" in a treaty relationship with the Soviet state. A Kazakh autonomous republic had been proclaimed in the lands of the former Steppe krai and had acquired territory in the Manghïshlaq from Turkestan. The Transcaspian oblast in Turkestan had been renamed the Turkmen oblast.

represented a sudden shift in the posture of central authorities, for the talk in 1923 had all been of the economic integration and harmonization of the three republics of Central Asia. Work was afoot to redraw Turkestan's internal boundaries to bring economic and administrative divisions in line. The commission charged with the "regionalization" (*raionirovanie*) of Turkestan had explicitly excluded the national dimension from its ambitions, "because the population is too mixed."[43] The commission had finished the work and presented its proposals to TurTsIK in January 1923. Yet, before any concrete measures could be taken, the Central Committee decided to go for the delimitation of boundaries on the national principle. The process began almost as an aside. In January 1924, the

43. D. P. Krasnovskii, ed., *Materialy po raionirovaniiu Turkestana*, vyp. 2, *Proekt administrativno-khoziaistvennogo deleniia TSSR* (Tashkent, 1924), 5. On the relationship between considerations of nationality and economic rationality in Soviet thinking of the period, see Francine Hirsch, *Empire of Nations: Ethnographic Knowledge and the Making of the Soviet Union* (Ithaca, 2005), chap. 2.

Organizational Bureau of the Central Committee sent Jānis Rudzutaks on a tour of inspection of Turkestan to deal with yet another political crisis in the ranks of the KPT. The last item on a list of tasks for him perform was to "organize a meeting of responsible workers of Bukhara, Khorezm (if possible), and Turkestan in order to initiate a preliminary discussion of the possibility and expediency of the delimitation of Kazakh, Uzbek, and Turkmen oblasts according to the national principle."[44] What began as an exploratory effort very quickly acquired serious momentum. The matter was discussed by the central committees of the parties of all three republics in February and March and the basic positions presented to Sredazburo in April. That body sent off a draft resolution to the Politburo which issued its decree on the matter on 4 June 1924. Over the summer, the Sredazburo established a Territorial Commission to work out the boundaries of the various republics, and the process was largely complete by 18 November 1924, when the central executive committees of the three republics met to dissolve themselves and to create the new republics. Yet, for all its haste, little about the process was foreseen, let alone foreordained, by Moscow. Rather, party organs acted as adjudicators and kept the right to make strategic decisions, but it was Central Asian Communists who carried the debate and in many crucial ways reshaped it.[45] The national delimitation was a high point for the political achievement of indigenous cadres in Central Asia as well as the moment when the national idea triumphed there.

The debate as it unfolded was remarkable for the absence of references to expert knowledge. Other than a few memoranda from the Central Statistical Administration, there was no input of expert knowledge into the process of delimitation. In any case, the territorial commission worked at breakneck pace—its deadlines involved weeks, not months—and it simply did not have the time to refer to ethnographic adjudication. Claims often took the form of assertion and counterassertion, rather than the use of ethnographic data. As we saw above, the Central Executive Committee of the Kazakh Republic in the RSFSR had asserted in 1922 that 93 percent of the population of Semirech'e and Syr Darya oblasts was Kazakh. In August 1924, Kazakh representatives brought up the question

---

44. RGASPI, f. 17, op. 163, d. 397, l. 33 (31.01.1924). By this time, the party leadership had much greater confidence in its grasp of power in Central Asia (the Basmachi insurgency seemed to be in its final stages while Bukhara had recently been tamed with the purge of the most obstreperous members of its government) as well as sense that something had to be done to curb factional struggles in the KPT that often took place along national lines.

45. Considerations of space preclude a fuller description of the process here; see, however, the thorough account in Arne Haugen, *Establishment of National Republics in Soviet Central Asia* (Basingstoke, 2003); see also Adrienne L. Edgar, *Tribal Nation: The Making of Soviet Turkmenistan* (Princeton, 2004), chap. 2.

of forming a separate autonomous oblast for the Kazakhs of the BNSR. Musa Saidjonov, the Uzbek-identifying Bukharan representative stated that there were 30,000 Kazakhs in Bukhara; the Kazakh delegate Narusbayev countered with a figure of 360,000! The two could not even agree on the number of Kazakh delegates at the last Bukharan Congress of Soviets.[46] Similarly, representatives of different sides cast aspersions of the accuracy of previous censuses (the imperial census of 1897 and incomplete agricultural censuses carried out in 1917 and 1920) and argued on the basis of the ones that supported their claims best.

The Uzbek position was articulated by the Bukharan Communist Party, not by its counterpart in Turkestan. The Central Committee of the BKP was the first to act on the initiative, meeting already in February and approving a document penned by Fayzulla Xo'jayev that proposed "the creation of Uzbekistan on the basis of Bukhara." Bukhara's enthusiasm for the delimitation contrasts with the position taken by Khorezm, whose government argued against the dissolution of the state on the grounds of economic and historical unity. Until the summer, the Khorezm government held out for entry into the Soviet Union as its own territorial republic.[47] Bukhara's enthusiasm for delimitation also contrasts with its own record of seeking to maximize its sovereignty against constant demands for "harmonization" of policies with those of Soviet Turkestan. A little over a year earlier, Fayzulla Xo'jayev had resisted attempts by the Sredazburo to impose a uniform economic system on all of Central Asia.[48] The delimitation, on the other hand, promised the demise of Bukhara as a state and the full incorporation of its territory into the USSR. The Bukharan government's enthusiasm for its own demise clearly requires explanation.

Fayzulla Xo'jayev's project for Uzbekistan provides the clues. "Bukhara will be the basis for the construction of the Uzbek republic," it states. "Uzbekistan will unite . . . Bukhara, except for the left bank of Amu Darya; Ferghana; Syr Darya oblast, excluding its Kazakh parts; Samarqand oblast; [and] Khorezm, except for regions inhabited by Turkmens and Kazakhs,"[49] that is, all territory inhabited by the sedentary population of Transoxiana. This territory would also incorporate all the historic cities of the region in one republic. This was the Chaghatayist vision of Uzbekness laid out in territorial terms. The document presents a narrative of "the nation of the Uzbeks" (narod uzbekov) and its travails in recent centuries: "The Uzbek people, earlier united in the state of Temur and his successors, disintegrated in recent centuries into various parts. Over the course of

---

46. RGASPI, f. 62, op. 2, d. 109, l. 73. In the end the Kazakh autonomous oblast did not materialize.
47. Edgar, Tribal Nation, 56.
48. RGASPI, f. 62, op. 1, d. 6, ll. 50–59.
49. "Osnovnye polozheniia po voprosu sozdaniia Uzbekistana," TsGARUz, f. 48, op. 1, d. 272, ll. 16–17ob.

centuries, this disintegration was characterized by the weakening of economic forces and of political structures, the final stage of which is the economic decomposition, the loss of state unity, and the physical destruction of the people under the domination of khanates, emirates, and Tsarism." This disunity meant that "the Turkic population could not historically resist its gradual disintegration or defend the unity of the people, the integrity and continuity of its culture." The "Uzbek people and its various states (Bukhara, Khiva) . . . were thrown off the basic historical path and became the object of struggle" between the British and the Russian empires. Xo'jayev asserted that the Timurid state was the national state of the Uzbeks—a key Chaghatayist point—and saw the loss of a unified state as the cause of decline, cultural backwardness, and even exploitation. This last then provides the link to Soviet considerations. The revolution, we read, has "put the Uzbek people at a new stage of historical development, lain the foundations for economic growth, . . . and simultaneously emphasized all aspects of the cultural-national order." Yet the continuation "of the old divisions imposed by force on Central Asia by conquerors," that is, the administrative boundaries created in the Tsarist era, produced national conflict between the sedentary population on the one hand and its nomadic and seminomadic neighbors on the other. It was necessary therefore to give "all peoples bearing a single name [*odnoimennye narod-nosti*]—on a national basis, according to the specificities of their way of life [*byt*] and economic habits—their own Soviet political units," which would be able to "undertake integral economic and cultural work." Xo'jayev had made reestablishing the national unity of the Uzbek people into a significant task of Soviet power!

It was on this basis that the Uzbek commission made its claims. "The Uzbek Republic," it argued, "should include in it Tajiks and those peoples of Turkestan, Bukhara, and Khorezm who speak Uzbek and consider themselves related to the Uzbeks, i.e., Uzbeks, Qurama, Kashgaris (the so-called Kashgar Sarts), Turks, Karakalpaks, and Qipchaqs."[50] The contention to these claims came not from the Tajiks (whose case we will discuss in detail in the next chapter), but from the Kazakhs, who claimed for their republic "that continuous space where the Kazakh population or cultural-national groups related to it, [i.e., those] of the Karakalpaks, Kyrgyz, Qurama, [and] Qipchaqs, form the absolute majority or plurality."[51] Both sides thus claimed the Qipchaqs and the Qurama, but the Kazakh delegation also repeated earlier demands for Semirech'e and Syr Darya oblasts, including the city of Tashkent.[52] The Uzbek side won out in its claim to the Qipchaqs and the Qurama

50. "Dokladnaia zapiska k proektu Uzbekskogo partiinogo biuro po organizatsii Uzbekskoi Respubliki," RGASPI, f. 62, op. 2, d. 115, ll. 3.

51. RGASPI, f. 62, op. 2, d. 101, l. 132 (14.05.1924).

52. Ibid., ll. 71–81.

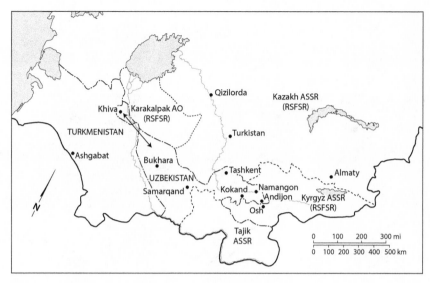

MAP 2. Central Asia after the national-territorial delimitation of 1924. Uzbekistan was considerably smaller than it later became. In 1936, when Kazakhstan became a union republic, the Karakalpak AO was raised to the level of ASSR, augmented with territory taken from Turkmenistan, and transferred to Uzbekistan. The Kyrgyz ASSR, which was originally created as an autonomous oblast, also became a union republic in 1936.

(it helped that no political actors claimed separate national status for these two groups, unlike the Karakalpaks and the Kyrgyz, who found their champions in the ranks of the local communist parties), as well as retaining Tashkent. In early June, the Sredazburo voted for the creation of Uzbekistan and Turkmenistan as republics that would enter the Soviet Union directly, and for the transfer of Semirech'e and most of Syr Darya oblast to the existing Kazakh Republic in the RSFSR. In addition, Tajik, Karakalpak, and Kyrgyz autonomous oblasts were to be carved out, the former in Uzbekistan, the latter two in RSFSR.[53] At the last minute, in October, the Tajik autonomous oblast was raised to the level of an autonomous republic and the Karakalpak autonomous oblast given to the Kazakh Republic. While disputes over the identity of individual villages continued for some time, the territorial extent of the various republics was largely set by the autumn after the Territorial Commission had rushed through its work. In November, the three existing republics dissolved themselves and the new territorial arrangements took effect (see map 2).

53. RGASPI, f. 62, op. 2, d. 100, ll. 29–30. The text of the Orgburo resolution on the question in *TsK RKP(b)–VKP(b) i natsional'nyi vopros*, 221–222.

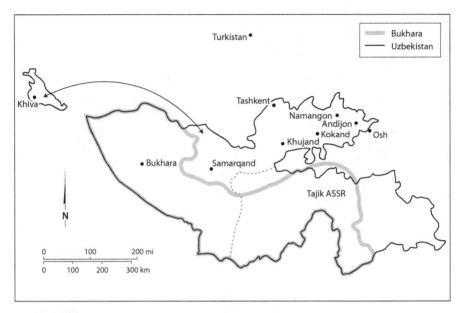

MAP 3.   Uzbekistan as Greater Bukhara.

The Uzbek project had largely succeeded: the final boundaries of the republic encompassed all of Central Asia's sedentary population and almost all its historic cities. Some cities were ceded to other republics on the principle, central to Soviet nationalities policy, that cities' role as economic centers for their hinterland overrode the concerns of nationality. Cities' fate was to be "nationalized" by the surrounding countryside. This strangely ruralist principle played an important role in the delimitation as it was carried out in Central Asia. The largely nomadic entities of Turkmenistan and the Kyrgyz autonomous oblast needed economic and administrative centers, and the cities of Toshhovuz/Daşoguz, O'sh/Osh, and Jalolobod/Jalalabat, their "Uzbek" population notwithstanding, were ceded to them. (The Kazakh claim to Tashkent was also based on this principle.)

Uzbekistan, as imagined by Fayzulla Xo'jayev, may also be seen as Greater Bukhara. The new republic provided for the restitution of historical losses suffered by Bukhara (to Russia in the nineteenth century and from the secession of Kokand in the eighteenth) and thus the fulfillment of Muqimiddin Bekjon's demands that we encountered at the beginning of this chapter.[54] Moreover, the

---

54. The point that Uzbekistan was Greater Bukhara was made two decades ago by Robert S. Carlisle: "Soviet Uzbekistan: State and Nation in Historical Perspective," in *Central Asia in Historical*

new republic was to be "independent," that is, independent of the RSFSR and a direct signatory to the Soviet Union. This was a higher status than either the BNSR or Turkestan enjoyed at that time. The founding congresses of Uzbekistan and its Communist Party were held in Bukhara and the capital of the new republic was in Samarqand, not Tashkent.[55] The creation of Uzbekistan was the fulfillment of the Chaghatayist project.

In practical terms, the creation of Uzbekistan meant combining areas from Turkestan, Bukhara, and Khorazm into a single republic. Soviet administrative institutions were much stronger in Turkestan than in the two people's republics, as was the transport infrastructure. Over the next decade, party authorities routinely conceptualized Uzbekistan as composed of advanced and backward regions, and calibrated the implementation of policies accordingly, so that both land reform and the campaign against unveiling were launched in the "advanced" regions before they were introduced to the "backward" regions. The Communist Party of Uzbekistan (KPUz) was similarly formed by combining cadres from the KPT, the BKP, and the Communist Party of Khorazm. Zelenskii had been deeply suspicious of the old Tashkent party organization and used the creation of KPUz to marginalize its members. He made sure that the Young Communists acquired leadership positions in the new party, with Akmal Ikromov being raised to the position of first secretary. The republican leadership was carefully balanced across regions. Fayzulla Xo'jayev from Bukhara became head of the sovnarkom (in effect, the prime minister), while the Central Executive Committee of the republic was to be headed by Yo'ldosh Oxunboboyev from Ferghana. Oxunboboyev was a peasant who had risen through the ranks of the Qo'shchi. His position was largely ceremonial, but Ikromov and Xo'jayev were responsible for policy decisions. They were both retained in their positions until 1937, even as they locked horns on a number of occasions.

Perspective, ed. Beatrice Forbes Manz (Boulder, 1994), 103–126. However, lacking archival access and being limited to Russian-language sources, Carlisle explained the Bukhara-Uzbekistan transition in terms of political rivalries between Bukharan and Turkestani cadres and presented it as a triumph of Xo'jayev over his rivals rather than that of the Chaghatayist project.

55. The main reason for moving the capital out of Tashkent was Moscow's deep distrust of the party organization of the old city of Tashkent. Stalin himself had decided that Tashkent was not "acceptable" as capital of Uzbekistan; Stalin to Zelenskii and Rudzutaks, 14.08.1924, RGASPI, f. 558, op. 11, d. 32, l. 94. Tashkent never ceded its importance as the center of power, however, for the Sredazburo stayed there. The Uzbek government returned to Tashkent in 1930.

Making Uzbekistan Uzbek

The enthusiasm unleashed by the creation of Uzbekistan was genuine and widely shared across the Uzbek intelligentsia. In March 1925, the young poet Oybek, then the editor of the wall newspaper of the party cell at the Tashkent old-city teacher training institute, celebrated the Uzbek nation thus:

Uzbek people, what have you not seen
　　In times just past.
Mourning, grieving, full of worries
　　you cried like a girl, your eyes full of tears . . . .
But now that age has passed—
The sun smiles in your mountains,
A singing *peri*
　　sings songs of freedom in your steppes
A red radiance spreads
　　on horizons far distant
Your banners are opening up paths for freedom
　　in the oppressed East.[56]

Revolution, nation, and anticolonialism remained deeply intertwined in this vision of Uzbekistan. For Rahimjon Inog'amov, Young Communist and Uzbekistan's first Commissar for Education, the creation of the republic was a fresh start when problems of backwardness could be tackled through national unity and revolutionary institutions.[57] Over the next few years, the passions for building Uzbekistan provided common ground for the intelligentsia across other political divides.

However, few outside the intelligentsia identified themselves as Uzbek at this time. We have rather few voices from below on the question of self-identification, but what evidence there is suggests that overarching, abstract forms of identification were highly uncommon even among the politically engaged urban population. A routine set of questionnaires filled out by members of the Tashkent old-city soviet in January 1922 is revealing in this regard. Respondents identified their "nationality" as follows: Uzbek, 43; Islam, 2; Muslim, 4; Sart, 2; Uzbek Turk, 1; Turk, 2; no answer, 33. (The large number of people who did not answer is partly explicable by the fact that nationality, *natsional'nost'*, was rendered incorrectly in Uzbek on the form as *firqa*, party.) The questionnaire also asked for languages spoken, and

---

56. Oybek, "O'zbek eli," *Tong yulduzi*, no. 1 (March 1925): 2.

57. See his speech at the First Congress of Soviets of the new republic: *Pervyi Vseuzbekskii s"ezd sovetov rabochikh, dekhkanskikh i krasnoarmeiskikh deputatov Uzbekskoi Sovetskoi Sotsialistisheskoi Respubliki: Stenograficheskii otchet* (Tashkent, 1925), 68–75.

respondents identified the Turkic language they spoke as follows: Uzbek, 53; Muslim [*musulmoncha*], 12; Sart, 1; Kashgari, 2; Turkic [*turkcha*], 9 (including two who reported "Tashkent Turkic" as their native language); 9 listed only Russian as a language spoken, forgetting to name their native language.[58] Another file of questionnaires, this time from Bukhara, provides similar evidence: different departments of the BNSR government used vastly different nomenclature to classify their staff, using Muslim, "local" (*yerli*), Turk, and Uzbek, along with a number of other designations.[59] Clearly there was no stable nomenclature for describing the "nationality" of Bukhara's population, although "Uzbek" was the most commonly used term. A different kind of evidence comes from Central Asians who emigrated in the early Soviet period. While members of the intelligentsia, who tended to go to Turkey or Europe, adopted surnames that evoked the Turkic past of Central Asia (Subuday, Çağatay) or the intellectual ferment of the early twentieth century (Öktem, Yarkın), other emigrants, especially those who went to Afghanistan or the Hejaz (present-day Saudi Arabia), came from different backgrounds and adopted surnames based on their place of origin (Turkistani, Bukhari, and so forth).[60] The Turkist enthusiasms of the intelligentsia had little appeal for them.

The establishment of a national territorial republic in itself was a mechanism for forging a national consciousness. Nationality became politically significant and more tangible at the same time. In common with the experience of many other state entities in the modern age, Uzbekistan came to acquire its own reality, as it acquired a host of national symbols and all sorts of common practices of being Uzbek.[61] The party's decision to establish national units in the Red Army fortuitously provided another institution that could be seen as national. These units were created not so much to increase the size of the Red Army but to mobilize citizens from the non-Russian parts of the USSR ("to allow small nationalities to participate in protecting the USSR"),[62] who would be led by officers who spoke their own language. Even before the national delimitation, the Uzbek press had described such units as a "national army."[63] After the delimitation, these units were widely seen in the press as an Uzbek national army. Fayzulla Xo'jayev himself

---

58. GAgT, f. 12, d. 63.

59. TsGARUz, f. 47, d. 474.

60. On this latter point, see Bayram Balci, "Les Ouzbeks d'Arabie Saoudite entre intégration et renouveau identitaire via le pèlerinage," *Central Asian Survey* 22 (2003): 23–44.

61. Marianne Kamp, "Pilgrimage and Performance: Uzbek Women and the Imagining of Uzbekistan in the 1920s," *International Journal of Middle East Studies* 34 (2002), 263–278.

62. From an Uzbek Komsomol brochure explaining the reasons for the creation of national units: V. Botmonov, *Qizil askarlar to'g'risida Komsomul muhosabasi* (Samarqand, 1926), 7; more generally, see I. Dubinskiy, *Milliy qo'shun nima*, trans. Usmon Mangushev (Tashkent, 1930).

63. Nurmat, "Milliy qizil urdumiz tuzamiz," *Turkiston*, 21.10.1923.

described the national units as "Uzbek national troops [that] are a fiery force that secures the independence of Uzbekistan."[64] As Marianne Kamp reminds us, for most Uzbeks, the experience of being Soviet was channeled through the experience of being Uzbek.[65] This was "banal nationalism" that took hold even as the content of a national identity was being debated.[66] That debate—over language, heritage, the very meaning of being Uzbek—took place in new institutions of culture built by the Soviet regime as part of its mission of transformation. The Committee for the Study of Uzbeks (O'zbeklarni o'rganish qo'mitasi), the Uzbek Committee for Museums and the Preservation of Ancient Monuments and Art (Uzkomstaris), the Uzbek Academic Committee (O'zbek Bilim Hay'ati) at the Commissariat for Education, and the enterprise of *kraevedenie* ("local study," rendered into Uzbek as *o'lkashunoslik*) provided venues where various aspects of Uzbekness could be studied and labeled as such.[67] The museum, the map, and the census were put to the work of building the Uzbek nation, but only *after* the Uzbek republic had been created.

The creation of Uzbekistan also fed the impulse to "Uzbekize" the republic. This position was validated by the policy of korenizatsiia. Korenizatsiia, we will recall, was meant to indigenize Soviet power in non-Russian areas by switching state and party institutions to indigenous languages and staffing them with members of the local population in order to distance Soviet power from its Tsarist predecessors. In practice, korenizatsiia only rarely challenged the position of Russians in the non-Russian parts of the Soviet state (and excessive enthusiasm for it could even arouse the ire of the OGPU), but across the USSR, it gave leaderships of union republics license to nationalize their republics and to assimilate populations that were now conceptualized as minorities.[68] Russians, however, were not considered a national minority in Uzbekistan (or any other national republic in the USSR). Fayzulla Xo'jayev had asserted this verity at the First Congress of Soviets of the republic, when he stated that the Russians' role in the establishment of Soviet power made them the equal of Uzbeks in all respects in

64. S. I., "Eski Toshkentda tarixiy majlis," *Qizil O'zbekiston*, 05.03.1926.

65. Marianne Kamp, *The New Woman in Uzbekistan: Islam, Modernity, and Unveiling under Communism* (Seattle, 2007), 64.

66. Michael Billig, *Banal Nationalism* (London, 1995).

67. Ingeborg Baldauf, "'Kraevedenie' and Uzbek National Consciousness," Papers on Central Asia, 20 (Bloomington, 1992).

68. The fundamental work on korenizatsiia remains Terry Martin, *The Affirmative Action Empire: Nations and Nationalism in the Soviet Union, 1923–1939* (Ithaca, 2001). The one success story of korenizatsiia was Ukraine, where briefly Russian was displaced in meaningful ways by Ukrainian; on it, see Elena Borisenok, *Fenomen sovetskoi ukrainizatsii: 1920–1930–e gody* (Moscow, 2006).

the republic.[69] The main target of korenizatsiia therefore turned out to be not the European population, but the "national minorities" of the republic, with the heaviest burden falling on its large Persian-speaking population. As we shall see in chapter 9, the attempted Uzbekization of the Persian-speaking population of the republic produced a Tajik nationalism that furthered the idea of nationalization of the region's population.

Making Uzbeks Uzbek

Here is a passage for second graders to read in one of the first textbooks of Uzbek to be published in Uzbekistan:

> Ziya Efendi, newly arrived from Istanbul, was appointed as teacher of native language at the Uzbek Bilim Yurti. . . . One day, he wanted to teach the present tense to the pupils of class 2.
>
> The pupils in class 2 were from various cities and villages. . . . After greetings, Ziya Efendi asked the students, "Ne yapiyorsunuz? What are you doing?" The Tashkent students replied, "Yozvotamiz, we're writing." Those from Samarqand said, "Yazaymiz," those from Kokand, "Yozyopmiz," and those from Namangan, "Yozutamiz." Some of the rural students replied, "Yozvotdimiz," while others said, "Yozyotimiz." There were also those who said, "Yozib o'turmiz," or "Yozib turibmiz."
>
> Hearing so many variations on the present tense from the mouths of the children of one state [*mamlakat*] and one nation [*millat*] surprised Ziya Efendi a great deal.[70]

This passage is fascinating simply because it features an Istanbul *efendi* as the central character a good six years after all Ottoman teachers had been banished from Turkestan and fears of foreigners and of pan-Turkism had come to define official thinking. (The textbook was attacked in the press for its "counterrevolutionary" and "narrow nationalist" content and the passage was excised from its next edition.) But it also represents in very clear form the dilemma facing the Uzbek nationalizing intelligentsia. They had Uzbekistan; now they had to make Uzbeks. The sedentary turcophone population of Central Asia was far from being a single speech community. It retained an enormous variety of dialects. The language planners' task of creating a single language out of this variety reflected

---

69. *Pervyi Vseuzbekskii s"ezd sovetov*, 30.
70. Qayyum Ramazon, ed., *O'zbekcha til saboqlig'i*, pt. 2, 3rd ed. (Tashkent, 1926), 103.

the broader problem of building a single nation out of the disparate sedentary groups that had found themselves classified as Uzbek at the time of the national delimitation. In many ways, the creation of a modern Uzbek literary language faced the same problems, if on a smaller and more local scale, as the creation of a common Turkic language that others had attempted.

Debates over language planning were indicative of broader uncertainties about the shape of national cultures in an era of revolution. The fundamental question was whether Soviet Uzbek national culture should be rooted in the masses or in the high tradition of the past. More broadly, what import was the past going to have in defining the Uzbek present in stirring times when new worlds were being built (or at least dreamed of)? For Fitrat, the answer was clear. The Uzbek present was rooted in a nationally authentic high tradition of the past, in a canon of greatness in which the Uzbeks of the present could take pride, even as the past stood in need of rectification. In a series of scholarly works (to which he was restricted after 1926), he imagined a genealogy for the Uzbek nation of the twentieth century that lay in the Islamicate Turkic past of the region. Music was one of Fitrat's main passions. In Bukhara, he had established a school of "eastern music" and invited Viktor Uspenskii to lead an expedition to collect and notate the Bukharan *maqom*. In 1927, he presented the maqom tradition, formed under "the influence of Arabs and Persians," as "Uzbek classical music." Modern Uzbek music was to have its basis in its own classical tradition, which had to be preserved through notation and study.[71] Similarly, in 1927 and 1928, Fitrat published two anthologies of Turkic literature from Central Asia that sought to establish a genealogy of contemporary Uzbek literature. "In tracing the history of the Uzbek language, we cannot stop with Chaghatay," he wrote, but need to go back to the Eastern Turkic that Mahmud Kashghari, the eleventh-century lexicographer, had called Khaqani (as opposed to Oghuz) Turkic.[72] The lineage of Uzbek literature was longer than the period of Uzbek rule. "Our region [*o'lka*] began to be called the Uzbek region only in the sixteenth century, but everyone knows that Turks have lived in Central Asia for a long time." The literature created by them had evolved into Chaghatay, which was the heritage that had come down to Jadidism.[73] The second anthology, *Examples of Uzbek Literature*, contained excerpts from Kashghari's *Divan lughāt at-turk* (Compendium of Turkic Languages), the Orkhon inscriptions (the eighth-century Göktürk text from

71. Fitrat, *O'zbek qilossiq musiqosi va uning tarixi* (Samarqand, 1927); see also Kale-Lostuvalı, "Varieties of Musical Nationalism in Soviet Uzbekistan."

72. Fitrat, *Eng eski turk adabiyoti namunalari: adabiyotimizning tarixi uchun materiallar* (Samarqand, 1927), iii–iv.

73. Fitrat, *O'zbek adabiyoti namunalari* (Samarqand, 1928), xi.

what is now Mongolia), the oral epics *Alpamish* (recorded from a *baxshi* by G'ozi Yunus in 1921) and *Dede Korkut*, the prose of Yusuf Khass Hajib and Rabghuzi, and the poetry of Yasavi, Otoiy ('Atā'ī), Husayn Bayqara, Navoiy (Navā'ī), and Bobur, the Timurid founder of the Mughal dynasty in India. Both volumes are solid works of textual scholarship, in conversation with Ottoman and Russian Turcological scholarship, and they serve to establish a canon of modern Uzbek literature, which emerges as the heir to the all Turkic literature created in Central Asia.

But this vision of language as the repository of the nation's self and a mirror of its achievements clashed with the impulse to bring the written language closer to the spoken, to make it more democratic and more comprehensible to the population (especially since the goal of mass education was an important one). The different dialects of "Uzbek" varied markedly from one another: some were vowel rich (having nine or ten vowels) and retained full vowel harmony (a key feature of Turkic languages), as well as a vocabulary "uncontaminated" by Perso-Arabic vocabulary, while others, especially those of urban areas, had acquired Persian phonetics (with only six vowels), lost vowel harmony, and assimilated a vast lexical trove of foreign origin. The most authentically Turkic dialects were also the most rural and the farthest away, linguistically, from Chaghatay. Many among the Jadids favored basing the literary language on the demotic dialects that retained vowel harmony, disagreeing with the position taken by Fitrat.

Nor could differences in pronunciation be brushed aside, since the goal of a phonetic orthography was accepted by all sides. The emergence of Latinization as a possibility brought matters to a head. The advocacy of the adoption of the Latin script for Turkic languages had become a popular movement in Azerbaijan in the immediate aftermath of the revolution, where the linguist and politician Səməd Ağa Ağamalı oğlu pushed it tirelessly as a panacea for overcoming not just illiteracy, but all forms of backwardness.[74] By 1923, at Ağamalı oğlu's insistence, the movement had spread well beyond Azerbaijan, and Narkomnats in Moscow had begun to consider Latinization.[75] This broader Turkic context proved crucial for Uzbekistan, even though Latinization had until then largely been absent in the impassioned debate on orthographic reform in Central Asia. Botu's advocacy of Latin characters in 1921 had been an unusual position that evoked little response at the time. Similarly, D. E. Polivanov, the Russian linguist

---

74. In 1928, he was to argue that women's liberation could not succeed without Latinization. Og'amoli o'g'li, "Madaniy inqilob va yangi alifbe," *Alanga*, no. 12 (Dec. 1928), 2–5.

75. The workings of the Commission for the Reform of the Arabic Alphabet at Narkomnats can be followed in GARF, f. 1318, op. 1, d. 1544.

at Turkompros, had worked out a Latin alphabet in 1922, but little had come of it. Things changed as Azerbaijani enthusiasts organized the First Turkological Congress at Baku in March 1926 to discuss the adoption of the Latin script for all Turkic languages of the Soviet Union. The Politburo was cautious in the beginning, but after the congress enthusiastically voted for the adoption of the Latin script and the creation of a unified alphabet for all Turkic languages of the Soviet Union, it threw its weight behind the movement.[76] Even before the Politburo's decision, however, Uzbek party authorities had adopted the cause as their own. In May, the Tashkent old-city Communist organization voted enthusiastic support for Latinization after hearing a report by Shokirjon Rahimiy, one of the Uzbek delegates to Baku.[77] Days later, an advisory commission had already met in Samarqand to begin drafting proposals. A more formal Central Latinization Committee (Markaziy lotinloshtirish qo'mitasi) was established by UzTsIK in July, which worked in conjunction with the Academic Center of Uzkompros, where Polivanov was in charge.[78] By October, a commission struck for the purpose had published its proposals, after which the momentum for Latinization only increased.[79] A five-year plan for the introduction of the script was worked out in 1927, but characteristically for the period, other resolutions brought forward the date for full implementation of Latinization to November 1930.[80] In the event, the shift was far more gradual, with many issues of newspapers between 1929 and 1931 carrying some articles in the Arabic script and some in Latin. Book publishing seems to have shifted entirely to Latin by 1930.

The party's decision to take control of this aspect of cultural policy was tied to the wider offensive on the "ideological front" that it began in 1926 (see chapter 10). On Latinization, the party faced remarkably little opposition or discontent. (The contrast with Tatarstan could not be greater, where many influential figures, such as Galimjan Ibrahimov, stoutly opposed Latinization.) The Latinization commission formed in July 1926 included many party figures (Inog'amov, Akmal Ikromov, Fayzulla Xo'jayev, Yo'ldosh Oxunboboyev), but it also included Fitrat, Elbek,

76. On the politics surrounding the Baku congress and its passage through the party hierarchy, see Martin, *The Affirmative Action Empire*, 186–190. The proceedings of the congress were published as *Pervyi vsesoiuznyi tiurkologicheskii s"ezd. 26 fevralia–5 marta 1926 g. Stenograficheskii otchet* (Moscow, 1926); see also Baldauf, *Schriftreform und Schriftwechsel*, chap. 18.

77. "Turkiyot qurilotyining yakuni," *Qizil O'zbekiston*, 14.05.1926.

78. O'zbekiston Xalq Maorif Kamisarligi, *O'zbekistonda maorif ishlari* (Samarqand, 1927), 85.

79. Rahim Inog'amov, "Lotin asosida tuzilgan yangi alifboga kuchamiz," *Qizil O'zbekiston*, 18.10.1926.

80. "Yangi o'zbek alifbesini amalga oshirish uchun 5 yilliq ish plani," TsGARUz, f. 94, op. 5, d. 64a, ll. 1–7. For an account of the various party and state resolutions in this regard, see William Fierman, *Language Planning and National Development: The Uzbek Experience* (Berlin, 1991), 106–110.

Shokirjon Rahimiy, and Hoji Muin, Jadids who had been involved in debates over language and orthography since before the revolution, but who had not favored Latinization before then.[81] Perhaps they had seen the writing on the wall and considered opposition to Latinization futile. But we also need to remember that while Latinization might have been made party policy in Uzbekistan, it was led by Azerbaijani figures who were greatly respected and admired by the Uzbek Jadids. The connection between Latinization and progress was widely drawn at the time, and not just in the Soviet Union. An advisory organization of the League of Nations even foresaw the universal adoption of Latin characters in the near future.[82] The Latin script had been adopted officially in Azerbaijan in 1924, and "Latinizers" had briefly even put the question of introducing the Latin script for Russian on the table.[83] It was no great coincidence that Atatürk also oversaw a transition to the Latin script in Turkey in 1928. In fact, the Turkish move was more directive and more abrupt—newspapers were given three months to switch to the new alphabet—than anything attempted in the Soviet Union.

Once it was decided to move to the Latin script, it became imperative to decide on the phonetic structure of the Uzbek language. The question of vowel harmony had not arisen before the national delimitation. The orthographic reform up until then had assumed a six-vowel system, which implied the absence of harmony. Polivanov had argued for the adoption of the harmony-free Tashkent dialect as the basis of the literary language, simply because it was the dialect of the most "advanced" region of Uzbekistan. Abdulla Alaviy, among others, argued the opposite: for Alaviy, most Uzbek poets already wrote in a literary form that assumed vowel harmony; modern Uzbek should be based on this "popular literature," and not on the "literature of the palace."[84] The battle raged on and the question was not decided until May 1929, when an Uzbek orthographic conference voted for a nine-vowel alphabet with full vowel harmony.[85] By that time, the debate among the intelligentsia had been joined by the party itself, and the vote on the script had been preceded by a volley of resolutions from various party entities in favor of full vocalization.

---

81. "Lotin harflarini qabul qilish to'g'risida to'rtinchi sessiyaning qarori," *Qizil O'zbekiston*, 04.07.1926.

82. International Institute of Intellectual Co-Operation, *L'adoption universelle des caractères latins* (Paris, 1934).

83. On this episode, see Martin, *Affirmative Action Empire*, 196–198.

84. Abdulla Alaviy, "Tilimiz to'g'risida bir ikki so'z," *Alanga*, no. 2 (1928): 9–10.

85. A sense of the openness of the debate can be gleaned from the materials collected in a volume prepared in advance of the 1929 conference: A. Yo'ldosh, ed., *Til-imlo masalalari* (*maqola va materiallar to'plami*) (Samarqand, 1929). For a succinct summary of the debate, see Andrei Vydrin, "Fitrat, Polivanov, Stalin i drugie," *Zvezda Vostoka*, 1994, no. 5–6: 150–172; see also Fierman, *Language Planning*, 69–81, 129–133.

A fully vocalized Uzbek language was deemed the language of the masses, hence more "proletarian" and more Soviet. The harmony-free urban dialects, on the other hand, represented the culture of the palace and of Islam, and by association, unhealthy bourgeois nationalism and pan-Turkism. It was not surprising, then, that the turn to full vocalization was accompanied by increasingly harsh attacks on Chaghatayism and on Fitrat personally (see chapter 12). Uzbekistan was there, but the Chaghatayist vision for it was under attack.

Uzbekistan in Comparative Perspective

We might pause at the end of this chapter to place the creation of Uzbekness and Uzbekistan in the context of nation making around the world. The Uzbek nation is not a "natural" phenomenon, nor is it simply the work of an imperial Soviet regime bent on dividing its subject populations the better to conquer them. Rather, it has been imagined and constructed in modern times through the complex interaction of intellectuals, state power, the classificatory grid of science, and much else. In this, it is like most other nations of the world. What is interesting about Uzbekistan is not that it was "constructed," but the conditions in which it came about. It was a prerevolutionary project of the national intelligentsia carried out in Soviet conditions and reshaped by them.

The making of Uzbekistan represented the triumph of the idea of the (ethnic) nation that came to Central Asia from multiple directions. As I have shown in this chapter, all parties involved—the Jadids, national Communists, European ethnographers, Soviet administrators—saw the population as composed of distinct nations that deserved (or required) territorial autonomy. For the Jadids (and the national Communists), the main inspiration was the rise of Turkism in the decades preceding the revolution, which resulted in the ethnicization of the confessional-territorial vision of the nation ("Muslims of Turkestan") that had underpinned the political imagination of the Jadids before 1917. Turkism, as we have seen, developed in a public space that encompassed both the Russian and Ottoman empires. The 1920s also saw the rise of Turkist national projects in Tatarstan, Azerbaijan, and, most spectacularly, Turkey. These various projects were intertwined in many ways (especially in the realm of language and orthographic reform) and there are many parallels to be discerned among them. The tired trope of "pan-Turkism," however, is of singularly little help in understanding the success of Turkism in these years. Turkism was always a polyphonic discourse. The Chaghatayist project was Turkist through and through, but defined itself against the Ottomans as much as against the Persian world. Nor did Turkism work in identical ways everywhere. In the Ottoman Empire, Turkism was a revolt against the Ottoman legacy. The dynasty and the high culture it had produced came to be seen as inauthentic, cosmopolitan, and corrupt. Turkism was profoundly subversive in that regard. In Central Asia, Turkism led to a valorization of a long lost empire, whose grandeur (and high culture) had to be reclaimed.

Soviets administrators and the European ethnographers who worked with them came to nationality out of an impulse to categorize as a technology of rule.[86] The national delimitation of Central Asia attempted to reduce complexity to clarity, to consolidate ethnic boundaries, and to unmix peoples, to replace complex locally rooted identities with broad abstract ones. It simplified the ethnic vocabulary of the region, imposing on the messy reality a single classificatory grid that could underlie the territorial constructions of nations. The delimitation resulted in the official recognition of eight groups among the indigenous population (the six that emerged as "titular" bearers of territorial autonomy, plus indigenous Jews and Uyghurs) and thus the simplification of the region's ethnic nomenclature. All other labels were relegated to "subethnic" (Qipchaq, Qurama) or informal status, while many designations simply disappeared. The delimitation marked the triumph of the idea of the nation as the fundamental node of cultural identity in Central Asia. In all of this, it was the implementation not just of a pan-Soviet policy but also the reflection of certain basic assumptions of modernity more generally. The unmixing of peoples, the crystallization of national classifications, and the homogenization of national space have all been the hallmarks of the modern age. The party abhorred comparisons with "bourgeois nationalism" elsewhere, but its understanding of the ontological reality of nations shared much with nationalists everywhere. The national delimitation of Central Asia was part of a pan-Soviet policy, but that policy had its most obvious counterpart in the boundary making that reshaped the lands of the Habsburg Empire in the same years. The transformation of Mitteleuropa, a place of intermixed populations with multiple levels of competing identities, into a nationalized Central Europe provides perhaps the most clear counterpart in the twentieth century to the remaking of Central Asia by Soviet nationalities policy. The disaggregation of "the Muslims of Central Asia" into Uzbeks and Tajiks was as big a transformation as the one that turned Budweisers into Czechs and Germans or the nationalization of the Polish-Ukrainian borderlands, the *kresy*.[87] The nationalization and unmixing of populations was driven both by national movements and by states, and it homogenized populations in many places across Eurasia. Such homogenization of populations was an essential part of modernity as it unfolded

---

86. This is a key point made by Hirsch, *Empire of Nations*.

87. Jeremy King, *Budweisers into Czechs and Germans: A Local History of Bohemian Politics, 1848–1948* (Princeton, 2002). On the *kresy*, see Kate Brown, *A Biography of No Place: From Ethnic Borderland to Soviet Heartland* (Cambridge, MA, 2004).

in Europe. Central Asia's experience under Soviet rule was depressingly normal in that regard.

The national delimitation in Central Asia, however, was primarily a *political* process in which expert knowledge was seldom called on.[88] While certainly initiated by Moscow, the delimitation was not simply a central imposition on indigenous reality. The insistent demands, dating back at least to 1920, for the transfer of Turkestan's Kazakh population to the Kazakh Republic in RSFSR offered clear evidence that notions of the desirability of ethnoterritorial homogeneity had taken root among Central Asian political actors. Nor were the decisions taken in 1924 based on the application of previously existing, uncontested ethnographic knowledge, which did not exist. Ethnographers played little role in the actual debates over classification (the question of how many nations were there in Central Asia) or over territorial claims in 1924. Once the new national republics had been formed, however, ethnographic expertise came to play an important role, to some extent in tweaking the boundaries that had been drawn in 1924, but more significantly in giving ethnographic sanction to claims of nationhood in the decades that followed. The folklorization of national identity in the USSR from the 1930s on owed much to ethnographers and ethnographic knowledge.

What had triumphed in 1924 were *national projects*, not nations. As we have seen, Uzbekistan and its inhabitants had yet to be made Uzbek. This process too is normal in the history of nation making, true as much of the so-called "historical nations" of Western Europe as of later upstarts. The French nation exists as a homogenous, self-conscious entity because the French state imposed a great deal of centralization over the territories it governed, destroying the heterogeneity of local identities, power structures, dialects, and so forth. Indeed, as Eugen Weber has famously argued, it was only developments of the late nineteenth century—military conscription, public schooling, railways, the telegraph—that finally turned peasants into Frenchmen.[89] The twentieth century is replete with cases of national projects using the agency of nationalizing states to mold their citizenry into national subjects.[90] The national project of turning "Muslims of Turkestan" into Uzbeks was similarly accomplished through a similar set of policies and practices.

A comparison with Turkey reveals striking parallels with the Uzbek case. The Anatolian resistance to Entente occupation had mobilized in the name of

---

88. Here I disagree with Hirsch.

89. Eugen Weber, *Peasants into Frenchmen: The Modernization of Rural France, 1870–1914* (Stanford, 1976).

90. On nationalizing states, see Rogers Brubaker, *Nationalism Reframed: Nationhood and the National Question in the New Europe* (Cambridge, 1996).

"Ottoman Muslims," and the rhetoric of Muslim nationalism had dominated the struggle while it lasted. It was the Turkish Republic that after its founding in 1923 turned "Ottoman Muslims" into Turks and Anatolia into the Turkish heartland.[91] In Atatürk's words, "the people of Turkey, who have established the Turkish state, are called the Turkish nation."[92] Especially in the 1930s, the Kemalist regime sponsored the elaboration of a new ethnic Turkish identity, complete with an official history and myths of origin.[93] This was accompanied by conscious policies of ethnic homogenization, squeezing out non-Muslims (through discrimination or outright expulsion), and forcibly assimilating non-Turkish-speaking Muslims. The primary victims of this process were, of course, the Kurds, who discovered that they were really "mountain Turks," but in some ways the disappearance of Bosnians, Albanians, Lazes, and Circassians into the common Turkishness of Anatolia is even more telling. The Republic also sponsored the creation of a canon of Turkish literature, pursued policies of language purification, and Latinized the orthography. All through the 1920s, a sustained campaign led to the purging of Arabic and Persian vocabulary and grammatical borrowings from Turkish and to the creation of new terms. In the early 1930s, under the auspices of the quasi-official Turkish Language Society, this process was taken to new extremes with the creation of pure Turkish (Öztürkçe) derived only from Turkic sources. Implemented under an explicitly national regime, these transformations mirror those in Uzbekistan in significant ways. Indeed, it is possible to think of Turkey and Uzbekistan as counterparts—as heirs to "western" (Ottoman) and "eastern" (Chaghatay) Turkic cultural and political traditions, each nationalized in the early twentieth century through intertwined but distinct discourses of Turkism. As noted above, Turkism in the Ottoman Empire proved to be anti-Ottoman and subversive of actually existing imperial realities; Turkism in Central Asia sought the resuscitation of a lost imperial unity. Nevertheless, there is a distinct similarity between the ways in which the Muslim inhabitants of Anatolia became Turks and those of Transoxiana became Uzbeks. Likewise, the transformation of literary languages is analogous between the two realms. Modern Uzbek has precisely the same relationship to Chaghatay that modern

91. Gülçiçek Günel Tekin, İttihat Terakki'den Günümüze Yek Tarz-ı Siyaset: Türkleştirme (Istanbul, 2006); Soner Çağaptay, Islam, Secularism, and Nationalism in Modern Turkey: Who is a Turk? (London, 2006); Uğur Ümit Üngör, The Making of Modern Turkey: Nation and State in Eastern Anatolia, 1913–1950 (Oxford, 2011); Hale Yılmaz, Becoming Turkish: Nationalist Reforms and Cultural Negotiations in Early Republican Turkey, 1923–1945 (Syracuse, 2013).

92. Quoted by Çağaptay, Islam, Secularism, and Nationalism, 14.

93. Büşra Ersanlı-Behar, İktidar ve Tarih: Türkiye'de "Resmi Tarih" Tezinin Oluşumu (1929–1937) (Istanbul, 1992); Etienne Copeaux, Espaces et temps de la nation turque: analyse d'une historiographie nationaliste, 1931–1993 (Paris, 1997).

Turkish has to Ottoman. They are the demotic, "simplified" versions of the literary standard of the eastern and western Turkic realms, respectively. Both have been Turkified and modernized since the turn of the twentieth century, though it is worth remembering that Uzbek today is closer to its predecessor, and less radically transformed, than Turkish. Contemporary Uzbeks can understand a text from, say, 1914 with greater ease than can contemporary Turks. Most late Ottoman and early Republican texts in Turkey, including the founding documents of the Turkish Republic, need to be translated into modern Turkish in order to be comprehensible to contemporary audiences. Such is not the case in Uzbekistan, the seven intervening decades of Soviet rule notwithstanding. Uzbekistan, of course, did not possess a national state like the one that Mustafa Kemal (Atatürk) commanded, but there were significant ways in which Soviet conditions made nationality politically and socially relevant to people's everyday life, while Soviet institutions such as schools, newspapers, museums, maps, and censuses nationalized populations that had been indifferent to the idea of the nation or who had identified themselves along axes of difference other than that of the nation.[94] Soviet republics acted as myriad other nationalizing states of the twentieth century in creating a sense of national identity among their citizens.

Yet much of this lay in the future. There was resistance, of course, and accommodation, too, but in the long run, the national projects succeeded. The short term was different. Defining Uzbekness in the immediate aftermath of the creation of Uzbekistan was a deeply fraught process in which Uzbek intellectuals had to contend with the requirements of the Soviet state and of the Communist Party. The last three chapters of this book will chart the fate of the prerevolutionary Uzbek intelligentsia. In the following chapter, however, we turn to the way "Tajik" came to be defined by the Soviet success of the Chaghatayist project.

---

94. The "passportization" of national identity in the USSR and its connection to some level of ethnic preferences is significant in this regard. See also Kamp, "Pilgrimage and Performance."

TAJIK AS A RESIDUAL CATEGORY

So far we have focused on the rise of Turkism and the triumph of the idea of an Uzbek nation that claimed for itself the mantle of Muslim statehood in Central Asia. In this chapter we turn to the fate of Central Asia's Persian-speaking population. Persian was the language of the madrasas of Samarqand and Bukhara and of the vast bulk of the cities' literary production. Down to the end of the old order in Bukhara in 1920, the emir's chancery functioned in Persian. What happened to that heritage? Why was the Tajikistan that emerged in 1924 so small and rural, and not a Persophone counterpart to a Turkic Uzbekistan?

These questions are very current today, as both Uzbekistan and Tajikistan seek legitimacy in the *longue durée* of the region's history. Tajik intellectuals, who see themselves as keepers of the Iranian (or "Aryan") flame in a sea of Turkicness, feel aggrieved that the ancient centers of Persian culture belong to Uzbekistan. They assign blame both to Tajik intellectuals of the 1920s who failed to defend the interests of their nation and to "Uzbek pan-Turkist chauvinists," who usurped Tajik rights, and argue that the delimitation was skewed against the Tajiks from the outset.[1] In this chapter, I provide a different set of answers to the question of the curious shape of Tajikistan that emerged in 1924. Tajikistan emerged the way it did because there

---

1. The Tajik position was perhaps best articulated by Rahim Masov in a series of works: *Istoriia topornogo razdeleniia* (Dushanbe, 1991); *Tadzhiki: istoriia s grifom 'sovershenno sekretno'* (Dushanbe, 1995); *Tadzhiki: vytesnenie i assimiliatsiia* (Dushanbe, 2003); see also Muhammadjoni Shakurii Bukhoroî, *Panturkizm va sarnavishti ta'rikhi tojikon* (Dushanbe, 2010).

was no Tajik nation in 1924. Persian-speaking intellectuals and political actors did not identify themselves as Tajiks and did not therefore seek rights for a Tajik nation. Most of them were committed to a Chaghatayist vision of Central Asia. The national delimitation froze in place all sorts of contingencies, one of which was the fascination felt for Turkism by all modernist intellectuals in Central Asia, regardless of the language they spoke. Tajiks were defined by others as the predominantly rural population of the mountain fastnesses of eastern Bukhara, the only place with a self-contained Persian-speaking population in Transoxiana. The creation of Tajikistan led to a number of defections from the Chaghatayist project, but these did not change the fundamental definition of Tajikness crystallized by the delimitation of 1924.

The Absence of the Tajiks

The most striking thing about the identity discourses of Central Asia in the early twentieth century is the almost complete absence of any mobilization or agitation on behalf of the Persian-speaking population of Transoxiana. While the Jadids were discovering the Turkic roots of Central Asia and an affinity with Turkic populations elsewhere, there was no parallel discovery of Iranian roots or of an affinity with Iran, and Persian never became a locus of national mobilization. This requires some explanation.

Transoxiana has long been a linguistic frontier between the Turkic and Persian language spheres. Centuries of migration and settlement by Turkic-speaking tribes had created a deep symbiosis between Turkic and Persian speakers that resulted in high rates of intermarriage and of bilingualism, so that separating "Uzbek" or "Turk" from "Tajik" or "Iranian" was not simply a matter of separating different colored marbles from a jar. Rather, Persian and Turkic speakers lived deeply interconnected lives, in which customs and practices were identical, bilingualism common, and *language never a node of identity*.[2] Other axes of difference overrode the linguistic one. The Persian-speaking population was divided along confessional and sectarian lines. Alongside the unmarked Sunni population, Persian speakers included the Eroni (Iranians), mostly Shiʻi descendants of Iranian

---

2. For Central Asia as a Turko-Persian frontier, see Scott Levi, "Turks and Tajiks in Central Asian History," in *Everyday life in Central Asia: Past and Present*, ed. Jeff Sahadeo and Russell Zanca (Bloomington, 2007), 15–31, or Maria Eva Subtelny, "The Symbiosis of Turk and Tajik," in *Central Asia in Historical Perspective*, ed. Beatrice Forbes Manz (Boulder, 1994), 45–61; on Turko-Persian bilingualism in Central Asia, see Aftandil S. Erkinov, *From Persian Poetic Classicism to Timurid Mannerism: Chaghatay (Turkic)-Persian Bilingualism in the Intellectual Circles of Central Asia (1475–1900)*, forthcoming; Gerhard Doerfer, "Central Asia, xiv. Turkish-Iranian Language Contacts," *Encyclopædia Iranica* (London, 1992), 5:226–235.

prisoners of war or slaves captured in Bukhara's wars with Iran in the eighteenth and early nineteenth centuries, and the sizable community of Bukharan Jews. Eronis were rendered synonymous with Shiʻism and deemed distinct from the Persian-speaking population of Transoxiana generally, which found more in common with sedentary Turkic-speaking neighbors than with their Shiʻi or Jewish neighbors of Persian speech.[3] Moreover, the Persian language spoken, let alone written, in Bukhara or Turkestan continued to be called *fārsī*, Persian, and the term *Tajik* was never used for it. Modernist writers did seek to write "in the idiom of Bukhara," as Fitrat did in his early works,[4] and when *Bukhārā-yi sharīf* (Bukhara the Noble), the first newspaper to be published in Bukhara, appeared, its Azerbaijani editor was criticized by many readers for using a language they considered too Iranian.[5] Such support for local usage, however, never turned into a claim for the distinctiveness of a Tajik language.

In fact, by the early twentieth century, Persian speech was in some sort of retreat in Central Asia. When the Orientalist Baron Rozen visited Samarqand in 1868, the language on the street was solidly Persian. By 1904, when V.V. Barthold (Bartol'd) saw the city, the situation was quite different.[6] The city had grown and attracted immigrants from the Turkic-speaking hinterland, while the Tsarist administration communicated with the native population largely through Turkic interpreters. The Jadid press that emerged in Samarqand was largely Uzbek, although Behbudiy's *Oyina* carried some articles in Persian. There was change even in Bukhara. Soon after its launch, *Bukhārā-yi sharīf* began to be replaced twice a week by a Turkic-language equivalent called *Turon*, since the Persian-language newspaper "left many people in Bukhara deprived" of its benefits.[7] The linguistic situation was changing.

---

3. In 1912, Munavvar qori had listed "Turk, Fors [and] Persiyon" as different groups of Muslims in Central Asia; Munavvar qori, *Adib-i avval* (Tashkent, 1912), 30. Fors (< *fārsī*) translates as Persian; Persiyon is borrowed from the Russian for "Persian"! Juxtaposed thus, the two terms were clearly meant to indicate sectarian, not linguistic, difference. In Russian usage, the term *pers*, "Persian," indicated Shiʻism as much as Persian speech. Thus we could have the following remarkable statement uttered at a meeting of Turkomnats in 1919: "Comrade Shokirov divided the Persian nationality into two peoples [*narodnosti*]: Comrade Efendiyev is a representative of the Caucasian-Tatar Persians [*persov-Kavkazskikh tatar*] who speak the Turkic language, but there are also Iranian Persians [*persy-farsy*], such as Persian Afghans and Tajiks who speak Persian [*po-farsidski*]. Therefore it is necessary to break them up into two sections, so that the Azerbaijani and Caucasian Turks form one section and the Persian-Afghans and Tajiks form another." TsGARUz, f. 34, op. 1, d. 327, l. 8ob (08.02.1919).

4. Fiṭrat Bukhārāyī, *Munāẓara-yi mudarris-i bukhārāyī bā yak nafar-i farangī dar Hindustān dar bārā-yi makātib-i jadīda* (Istanbul, 1327 m./1911), 2.

5. The debate that ensued centered on the choice between a single literary standard, which was also deemed pure and authoritative by its proponents, and proximity to the spoken language of the Bukhara; see *Bukhārā-yi sharīf*, 14.03.1912, 19.03.1912, 20.03.1912, 23.03.1912, 25.03.1912.

6. V.V. Bartol'd, "Tadzhiki: istoricheskii ocherk," in N. L. Korzhenevskii, ed., *Tadzhikistan: sbornik statei* (Tashkent, 1925), 111.

7. Jalol, "Vaqtimizga munosib," *Turon*, 11.07.1912.

The one attempt at articulating a language-based identity for the Persian-speaking population of Turkestan was the result of a Soviet initiative and was articulated by an Eroni. The category "Tajik" was largely absent from the view of nascent Soviet institutions. TurTsIK in 1918 declared Turkic to be a state language on par with Russian, and Soviet institutions tended to treat the unmarked sedentary Muslim population of Turkestan as synonymous with Uzbek. Similarly, the Politburo decree affirming Turkestan's autonomy in 1920 described the indigenous population of Turkestan as composed of Uzbeks, Kazakhs, and Turkmens, without any mention of the Tajiks.[8] However, in 1919, Turkomnats established a "Persian" section as one of a series aimed at various "national minorities" of Turkestan. It also funded the publication of a press organ in Persian.[9] *Shu'la-yi inqilāb* (The Spark of Revolution) was edited in Samarqand by Sayyid Rizo Alizoda, an Eroni with a long record in public life in the city: he had collaborated with Behbudiy on *Oyina* and was the author of several primers before the revolution. After 1917, he had enthusiastically participated in the Communist Party organization in the old city of Samarqand.[10] It was he who articulated the idea of a *millat-i fārs*, "the Persian nation," composed of all Persian speakers of Turkestan.[11] "Language," he argued, "is the great pillar of nationhood, for with the disappearance of the language, the whole nation speaking it is lost and obliterated."[12] Yet that Persian nation was firmly grounded in Turkestan, which was the supra-ethnic homeland, *vatan*, of the nation and the recipient of loyalty and adulation. "The homeland is our mother, our honor," Alizoda wrote. "Our flesh and our skins have grown on the land of Turan. Our bodies and our lives have been fostered by the air of Turkestan."[13] For contributors to *Shu'la-yi inqilāb*, there was little contradiction between their Persian speech, their loyalty to Turkestan-Turan, and their support for a Soviet regime they saw largely through the prism of "Eastern Policy." Indeed, the liberation of the Muslim world, especially of India and Afghanistan, the fortunes of the armies of Mustafa Kemal Pasha

---

8. GARF, f. 1235, op. 93, d. 582, ll. 173–173ob; *Izvestiia* (Moscow), 27.08.1920 (see chap. 3 above).

9. The issues discussed in the following paragraphs have been dealt with in greater detail by Lutz Rzehak, *Vom Persischen zum Tadschikischen: Sprachliches Handeln und Sprachplanung in Transoxanien zwischen Tradition, Moderne und Sowjetmacht (1900–1956)* (Wiesbaden, 2001), 88–113. Paul Bergne, *The Birth of Tajikistan: National Identity and the Origins of the Republic* (London, 2007), is largely derivative of Rzehak.

10. On Alizoda, see A'zamjon Azimov, "Saidrizo Alizoda va tashakkuli matbuoti tojik," in his *Publitsistika va zamoni muosir* (Dushanbe, 2004), 85–89; G'oibulloh as-Salom, *Fozil inson qissasi* (Samarqand, 2000).

11. "Khiṭāb bamillat-i fārs," *Shu'la-yi inqilāb*, 30.08.1919, 7.

12. Editorial announcement in *Shu'la-yi inqilāb*, 15.05.1919, 8; S. 'Alīzāda, "Shu'ba-yi fārs dar hużūr-i idāra-yi kārhā-yi millī," *Shu'la-yi inqilāb*, 10.07.1919, 1–2.

13. Sitamdīda, "Turkistān vaṭan-i māst," *Shu'la-yi inqilāb*, 22.05.1919, 1–2.

in Anatolia, and relentless criticism of British hegemony in the Muslim world dominated the pages of *Shu'la-yi inqilāb*, which differed not at all in this regard from the Turkic Muslim press of the time.

But the main passion of most politically active Persian-speaking intellectuals of Turkestan and Bukhara was reserved for Turkism. It was rooted in a fascination with the Ottoman Empire for its status as the most powerful Muslim state of the time and an exemplar of a Muslim modernity. For Bukharans in particular, Ottoman reforms became a model of to be emulated. Iran, on the other hand, was too small and embattled to provide the same kind of inspiration, while the sectarian divide that separated its Shi'i population from Sunni Bukhara was not irrelevant. It was no surprise, then, that Tarbiya-yi aṭfāl, the benevolent society organized by Bukharan philanthropists, sent students to Istanbul and not Tehran. The choice was fateful, for it was here that Bukharan students picked up a fascination for their Turkic origins and became invested in Turkism. Turkism was the path to progress and modernity, to an Islam rid of the corruption of the ages, and to a masculine, healthy future. The Persian heritage, on the other hand, came to represent the delicate poetry of the past, but also mysticism, religious corruption, weakness, and effeteness. Such a process of de-Persianization, which also took place in Transcaucasia, was a constitutive element of Turkism.[14]

The explosion of Turkism in 1917 therefore meant a disavowal of Persian and the heritage it represented. The period before 1917 saw a substantial amount of publishing in Persian in Central Asia, including Jadid literature. A number of textbooks and works of modernist poetry had appeared in Samarqand, as had the newspaper, *Bukhārā-yi sharīf*. Fitrat had pioneered a modern prose style devoid of the ornate vocabulary of the past. Mahmudxo'ja Behbudiy, the perfectly bilingual Samarqand Jadid, had argued for the significance of Persian "to us Turkestanis," because "it is the language of madrasas and litterateurs ... [and] is spoken in several cities and villages in the Samarqand and Ferghana provinces of Turkestan." He argued that in Turkestan, "every Turk should know Persian and every Persian speaker [*Fors*] Turkic," but went on to add that Turkestanis needed to master not two, but four languages, Arabic (in order to know Islam better) and Russian (to be aware of the world) being the other two.[15] Behbudiy's magazine *Oyina* (Mirror) was primarily in Uzbek, but it included a few pieces in

---

14. In Transcaucasia, in the late nineteenth century, a number of intellectuals came to emphasise their ethnic identity foremost and to deprecate the Persian connection. Tadeusz Swietochowski, *Russia and Azerbaijan: A Borderland in Transition* (New York, 1995), 30–35; Volker Adam, "Abdulla Sur (1883–1912) und seine 'Türkische Geschichte' als Quelle zur Erforschung nationaler Diskurse im vorrevolutionären Aserbaidschan," *Jahrbuch Aserbaidschanforschung*, no. 3 (Berlin, 2010), 112–141.

15. Behbudiy, "Ikki emas, to'rt til lozim," *Oyina*, 26.10.1913, 12–14.

Persian. The year 1917, however, marked a significant turning away from Persian in Turkestan. When Behbudiy launched the newspaper *Hurriyat* (Liberty), it was solely in Uzbek (and counted Fitrat as a regular contributor); Uzbek was the only language used by the Muslim cultural and political organizations that appeared in the aftermath of the revolution in Samarqand. Even in Bukhara, Uzbek was the language of modern politics. When the Young Bukharans staged their ill-fated demonstration in April 1917, the slogan, "Long Live Liberty," was shouted in Uzbek, not Persian.[16] The ulama continued to write in Persian, but they were not interested in the debates over identity and increasingly marginalized from public life after 1918. The modernists, however, published almost nothing in Persian after the revolution. Even the decision to publish *Shu'la-yi inqilāb* provoked opposition from some Muslim activists on the grounds that the official language of Turkestan was Turkic.[17]

In the Chaghatayist imagination, Turkestan had become simply the land of the Turks. Hoji Muin, a perfectly bilingual man of letters from Samarqand, could assert simply that "95 percent of the population of autonomous Turkestan is composed of us Turkic Muslims."[18] Many Persian speakers, in fact, had begun to see themselves as Turkic. Fitrat is, of course, the prime example. He had returned from Istanbul convinced that Bukharans were "really" of Turkic stock, but had forgotten their own language and adopted Persian under Iranian cultural influence.[19] This argument was central to the Turkism that burst forth in 1917, and many Persian speakers seem to have agreed with it. We know from critical references to *ūzbaknumāyī va tūrktarāshī*, literally "passing oneself as Uzbek and turning oneself into a Turk" (or, more loosely, "self-Uzbekization and self-Turkification"), in *Shu'la-yi inqilāb* that the phenomenon was quite common.[20] Even many of those who were to become the standard bearers of Tajik identity later in the decade thought of themselves as Uzbek until after the creation of

---

16. Muḥammad ʿAlī ibn Muḥammad Sayyid Baljuvānī, *Tārikh-i nāfiʿī*, ed. Ahror Mukhtor (Dushanbe, 1994), 43.

17. We know about this from a rebuttal of this position by Alizoda: "Yak sū-yi qaṣd-i gharżkārāna bamajalla-yi mā," *Shu'la-yi inqilāb*, 17.04.1919, 2–3. When the magazine folded for lack of funds, its editors asked the Uzbek-language Samarqand newspaper *Kambag'allar tovushi* to publish one issue every week or every fortnight in Persian to ensure that "the three million-strong Tajik and Persian nation[*tojik va fors millati*] is not completely deprived of publications." That request was turned down on the grounds that "all Tajiks and Persians can read Turkic and therefore there is no need to issue a separate newspaper or magazine in the Persian language." "'Shu'la-yi inqilāb' majallasining idorasi tarafindan," *Kambag'allar tovushi*, 17.01.1922.

18. Hoji Muin, "Til masalasi," *Mahnatkashlar tovushi*, 18.06.1918 (in his *Tanlangan asarlar*, ed. N. Nozimova [Tashkent, 2005], 81).

19. Sohib Tabarov, *Munzim* (Dushanbe, 1992), 40.

20. "Bamunāsibat-i anjuman-i imlā-yi ūzbakān," *Shu'la-yi inqilāb*, 20.02.1921, 2–4.

Tajikistan. In 1925, the Organizational Bureau (Orgburo) of the newly formed Tajikistan Communist Party bemoaned the fact that "the enormous majority of educated Tajiks, having received their education in Uzbek, speak it better than Tajik, and many of them even call themselves Uzbek."[21] The fascination of the Persian-speaking intelligentsia with Turkism was real and it defined the political future of the region.

The Chaghatayist view of the Persian-speaking population of the region was stated succinctly by Vadud Mahmud, another bilingual figure from Samarqand who was director of the women's teachers college, a literary critic, and a prolific writer. More pertinently, he was also a personal friend of both Fitrat and Cho'lpon and had been involved in Chig'atoy Gurungi.[22] The article in question was occasioned by its author's ire that "a student from Samarqand, one or two from Khujand, along with a Tajik teacher from the Pamirs have been raising the question [of Tajikness] in Tashkent in recent days." Vadud acknowledged that by Soviet law, all nations in the Soviet state enjoyed the right to self-determination and the use of their own language, but saw little applicability of it to the Tajik case. "The total number of Tajiks in Turkestan is not at all certain in terms of statistics. According to the count of the year 1920, there appear to be 1.2 million Tajiks across Turkestan. How was this count taken and who was given the name Tajik is a knotty question." Vadud also doubted that the cities of Samarqand and Khujand were predominantly Tajik. "There are many neighborhoods in Samarqand where the language of all families in Uzbek." Even Boghishamol, the Eroni-dominated neighborhood of Samarqand where *Shu'la-yi inqilāb* had been based, was inhabited by "Turkic tribes who have only recently migrated from Merv. Their family language is Turkic [*turkcha*]. . . . There are no [Tajiks] there except for a few 'sayyids' and 'aghas' from Iran who preside over the current of Tajik-ness and who for a while published journals in Persian." The same was true of Khujand and Bukhara.[23] Vadud acknowledged that there were Tajik populations in the countryside, but they all lived among Uzbeks and were bilingual to varying degrees. Language, however, was the crux of the matter for Vadud, and it was in this regard that he made the most striking assertions. "We know of many other peoples in the world who speak two languages, whose home language is different from their language of culture. These bilingual nations' cultural life [*madaniy turmishlari*] and literature is conducted in this official literary language." This

---

21. Tajik obkom to Stalin, July 1925, in *TsK RKP(b)—VKP(b) i natsional'nyi vopros* (Moscow, 2005), 291–292.

22. On Vadud, see Bahodir Karim, *Jadid munaqqidi Vadud Mahmud* (Tashkent, 2000); Sirojiddin Ahmad, "Vadud Mahmud." Available at www.ziyouz.com.

23. V. M., "Tojiklik atrofida," *Turkiston*, 30.12.1923, 04.01.1924.

should be the case with the Tajiks, who should confine their "home language" to the home and function in Uzbek in public life. Vadud's reasoning in worth quoting in full:

> Language is not simply a matter of acquiring literacy or reading the alphabet. . . . Language must be understood as the instrument of civilization. A language should have a literature and it should provide all the necessities of today's social life. . . . For [establishing such] a civilized life [*madaniy hayot*], the Tajik language or the Persian language of Iran do not suffice. To implement these languages is to prevent [us] from entering life [*tiriklikka kirmakdan uzoqloshmoq*], because both circumstance and history prohibit it. Second, to accept this language is to accept a useless, superfluous language. True, we love Persian for being an old literary language. It is a delicate, playful literary language. We benefit from its "classical Persian" literature. In this regard, Persian is a good language. But there is a difference between "good" and "useful," and we need the "useful" more than the "good."
>
> Precisely for this reason, we do not need a separate language for the Tajiks of the cities and their environs, but rather, the most rapid and direct introduction of Uzbek [among them].[24]

In arguing that Persian was a beautiful language but not suitable for modern life, Vadud was repeating here a central postulate of modernist Turkist thought. Turkic was more modern and more progressive because it had a greater store of modern knowledge. Vadud was willing to grant that Persian be taught in middle and high schools "in order to preserve this bilingualism" and "because I myself am among those who consider knowing Persian a great merit," but he saw no place for it in the public life of Turkestan.

There was one group of the Persian-speaking population that lived in compact groups with no contacts with Uzbeks and was exempt from these considerations. These were the "mountain Tajiks" of eastern Bukhara and the mountainous regions of Turkestan, the most rural and the most remote parts of Central Asia. "We need to pay attention to them and open schools for them, even if they do not so desire themselves," and given that they did not inhabit a bilingual zone, that education had to be in their own language. Thus it was these "mountain Tajiks"—unassimilable, distant, and different—who came to define Tajikness for the Uzbek-oriented intelligentsia, *including most Persian speakers*. It was they who were to be the beneficiaries of the territorial autonomy that came with the national delimi-

---

24. V. M., "Tojiklik atrofida," *Turkiston*, 04.01.1924.

tation in 1924, and it was they who were left to carry the burden of the Persian heritage of Central Asia.

The cultural policies of the Young Bukharans in government stemmed from these assumptions and were a crucial factor in determining the fate of Tajikness. As true scions of the emirate, most Young Bukharans were bilingual and being "Uzbek" or "Tajik" was a matter of choice for them. The vast majority opted for Uzbek. For them, Bukhara was the embodiment of the Chaghatay heritage of Central Asia, a Turkic state, the path to whose redemption lay through nationalization and Turkification. Once they found themselves in control of the Bukharan state, they proceeded to impose their understanding of Bukharan identity on the state. The new regime switched the language of the chancery to Uzbek and mandated that all the new schools that were opened in the first flush of revolutionary enthusiasm operated in Uzbek. The state allowed Persian-language schools for "our Iranian and Persian brothers [eroniy va forsiy birodarlarimiz]," but "Bukhara's own people [Buxoroning o'z xalqi]" were to be educated in Uzbek.[25] Inspectors from the Ministry of Education occasionally acknowledged that pupils in the Turkic-language schools did not understand their lessons because they spoke Tajik at home,[26] but that acknowledgment was politically inconvenient and disappeared into the archives. Fitrat again is indicative of broader passions. In 1923, he invited the musicologist Viktor Uspenskii to Bukhara to notate the Bukharan shashmaqom as a part of the program of gathering and formalizing the national heritage of the republic. The shashmaqom had always been sung in Persian, often by Jewish singers, and was thus testimony to the hybrid nature of Bukharan high culture. Fitrat wanted the heritage of Bukhara to be Chaghatayist, hence Turcophone, and the lyrics gathered by Uspenskii did not fit the desired pattern. The results of Uspenskii's efforts were eventually published, but the musical scores were not accompanied by the lyrics.[27] During his brief tenure as minister for education, Fitrat is said to have imposed fines on those who spoke Persian on the job.[28] One of his disciples, Sattor Jabbor, recounted with relish how during his time in office, Fitrat "made many Persianized mullahs Turks again [kaytadan Türk yapmıştır]" by forcing them, who "had forgotten their mother tongue," to speak only in Turkic with him.[29]

---

25. Maorif Nazorati, "Markaz ijroiya qo'mitasiga," TsGARUz, f. 47, d. 82, l. 25–25ob (01.12.1921).

26. "Turkiy ibtidoiy xalq maktablarining borishi to'g'risida Doklod," TsGARUz, f. 56, op. 1, d. 24, l. 4 (21.11.1921).

27. Aleksandr Dzhumaev, "Otkryvaia 'chernyi iashchik' proshlogo," Muzykal'naia akademiia, 2000, no. 1, 89–103.

28. Muhammadjon Shakuri Bukhoroi, Khuroson ast injo: ma'naviyat, zabon va ahyoi millii tojikon, 2nd ed. (Dushanbe, 1997), 146, citing an accusation aired in the Tajik press in 1930.

29. Settar Cabbar, Kurtuluş Yolunda: A Work on Central Asian Literature in a Turkish-Uzbek Mixed Language, ed. A. Sumru Özbay et al. (Stuttgart, 2000), 145. Cabbar/Jabbor was one of the students

Elsewhere in the practice of the BNSR government, too, Tajik barely existed as a category. The vocabulary of identity in the state's usage was unstable and (by ethnic criteria) quite confused. In early 1924, all government agencies in Bukhara were asked about the state of korenizatsiia in their ranks. The resulting paperwork makes for interesting reading. The process itself was called *musul'manizatsiia* ("Muslimization") in Russian-language correspondence and *milliylashtirish* ("nationalization") in Uzbek. In either case, the fundamental axis of difference was the one that distinguished Europeans from others. The Ministry of Finance divided its employees between Muslim, Tatar, and Russian. The Ministry of Agriculture used the simple categories of "local" (*yerli*) and "European" (*Ovrupoli*). The Bukhara provincial police administration classified its employees as Turk, Persian [*Fors*], Tajik, Russian, Jewish, and Tatar, while the provincial ispolkom used "Bukharan" [*Buxorolik*], Tatar, Russian, and Jewish.[30] The nomenclature was not standardized, but Tajik seems here to be used only for the inhabitants of eastern Bukhara; the population of the city of Bukhara and the republic's heartland was rendered as either Bukharan, Uzbek, or Turk. One set of statistics provided in 1922 by the Central Committee of the BKP to Sergo Orjonikidze put the number of Tajiks in Bukhara at 390,000, only 14 percent of the total population of 2.3 million.[31]

The Making of Tajikistan

Tajik voices were conspicuous by their almost complete absence in the debates over delimitation.[32] The establishment of a Tajik autonomous oblast within Uzbekistan was proposed by Fayzulla Xo'jayev, not by a Tajik committee, which did not exist. In May 1924, when Sredazburo entered the implementation phase of the delimitation process, it set up national subcommittees for all the nationalities that had been recognized territorially. The Tajiks were missing. Abdulla Rahimboyev was tasked with helping Tajik party members "if they wanted to hold their own conference on the question."[33] Nothing came of this offer and the process went ahead without a Tajik subcommittee and without even any Tajik-identifying

---

sent to Germany in 1922; the text quoted from here was composed in 1931 for a Turkish audience, and remained in typescript form until it was discovered by philologists in the 1990s and published with a linguistic analysis of its allegedly "mixed language" and a woefully poor translation.

30. TsGARUz, f. 47, op. 1, d. 474, passim.

31. RGASPI, f. 85, op. 23, d. 78, l. 12.

32. This point has been well made by Arne Haugen, *The Establishment of National Republics in Soviet Central Asia* (Basingstoke, 2003), 149–153.

33. RGASPI, f. 62, op. 2, d. 100, l. 2 (05.05.1924)

members in the Uzbek subcommittee.[34] When Sredazburo established a Territorial Commission to hammer out details of the new boundaries, there was still no Tajik subcommission, until Abdurahim Hojiboyev, Chinor Imomov, and Muso Saidjonov were appointed to one. Hojiboyev was born in Khujand in 1900 and attended a Russo-native school, before moving to Tashkent in 1918 to enroll at the newly founded People's University to study agronomy. As a student, he found himself sent off to Transcaspia to establish local soviets. He spent a year in Merv and Krasnovodsk, mostly teaching, before returning home. His exploits in Transcaspia brought him to the notice of Soviet authorities, and he was put to work in the agricultural department of Khujand uezd. He rose through the ranks to enter the Ferghana oblast ispolkom in 1923 and to be appointed deputy commissar for agriculture for Turkestan in December. None of his work had been specifically concerned with Tajiks, and there is little reason to believe that Hojiboyev identified as a Tajik before being appointed to the Territorial Commission as a Tajik delegate.[35] His trajectory differed little from that of many other party members who identified themselves as Uzbek. Imomov's career was very similar, except that he lived and worked mostly in Samarqand. Saidjonov came from an important Bukharan family and was a leading Young Bukharan figure. The Tajik subcommission was filled with appointees of the Uzbek delegation. No wonder, then, that the original proposal for a Tajik autonomous oblast passed into legislation without change or challenge.

That proposal exists in the archives in the form of an undated and unsigned document, but which clearly originated from the Uzbek side.[36] It replicates many of the assumptions that underlay Vadud Mahmud's view of the Tajiks quoted above. It begins by arguing that accurate statistics were unavailable but acknowledges the existence of 1,240,000 Tajiks across Central Asia. The one "continuous zone of Tajik predominance" was eastern Bukhara and the neighboring areas of Samarqand oblast, and it was to form the Tajik autonomous oblast. "As for the remaining Tajiks, it is for the moment inexpedient to attach them to the Tajik oblast," the document argued, because the bulk of that population lived in the cities of the Zarafshon Valley, where it even predominated, but since those cities were the centers of Uzbek districts, tightly connected to the surrounding Uzbek population through economic and trading interests and conditions of water

---

34. This observation was made by Usmonxon Eshonxo'jayev at the meeting on 10 May. Homutxonov, a member of the Uzbek subcommission from Samarqand, intervened to say that "when we met in Samarqand, we had resolved unanimously" to join the Uzbek subcommission. RGASPI, f. 62, op. 2, d. 100, l. 30.

35. This characterization is based on my against-the-grain reading of Hojiboyev's biography by his daughter, B.A. Khodzhibaeva, *Abdurakhim Khodzhibaev: stranitsy korotkoi zhizni* (Khujand, 2000).

36. "K voprosu ob organizatsii tadzhikskoi avtonomnoi oblasti," RGASPI, f. 62, op. 2, d. 102, ll. 8–19

supply, it "did not appear possible to separate these Tajik centers even in different autonomous okrugs or raions." Thus the bulk of the Tajik population was not to form part of the Tajik autonomy, which in turn was to comprise of the most rural, economically undeveloped, and isolated parts of Turkestan and Bukhara. The Tajiks of Tajikistan were thus rendered synonymous with "Mountain Tajiks," the embodiment of backwardness and oppression. In the words of the Uzbek proposal itself,

> The allocation of autonomy to this oblast has especially great significance, for no other people in the world has undergone such prolonged and heavy oppression as the mountain Tajiks. Driven by their Turkic conquerors into high and inaccessible mountainous ravines, they were obliged to lead a half-hungry existence, to suffer from a shortage of land, and to perpetually fight the severe mountainous landscape. Scattered into small and isolated groups, they were constantly subjugated to the despotic authority of petty khans of alien origin. Although belonging to one of the most cultured nationalities of Asia, with a centuries-old culture and rich literature, they themselves were exclusively ignorant. Literate men among them are a rarity or a lucky coincidence, while the women are almost universally illiterate.[37]

While this document acknowledged the existence of Tajiks in the cities of the Zarafshon Valley (i.e., Samarqand and Bukhara), it also began the process of their assimilation.

This basic proposal for the establishment of a Tajik autonomous oblast sailed through the entire process of delimitation largely unchanged. The only change came at the very end of the process from the center: the All-Union Central Executive Committee upgraded Tajikistan from an autonomous oblast to the level of an autonomous republic and attached the Pamir district to it as an autonomous oblast. The Tajikistan envisaged in 1924 was small, rural, and desperately poor. It had no cities of any kind; its capital was established in a small village named after the weekly market it hosted every Monday. The new republic could only be proclaimed after the new government had arrived in Dushanbe after a journey that resembled a colonial expedition. The First Congress of Soviets was held only in December 1926, until which time Tajikistan continued to be ruled by an appointed revkom with plenipotentiary powers. References to the exceptional cultural backwardness of "the Tajiks" were routine in the press of the time. In a stroke of political genius, the Tajiks, putative heirs to the urban civilization of

---

37. Ibid., l. 12.

Central Asia, had been turned into a rural, mountain-dwelling, isolated community defined by its "cultural backwardness."

This Tajikistan was, for all intents and purposes, eastern Bukhara redux. Eastern Bukhara was the home base of the archconservative ulama who had led opposition to reform in the emirate; it was also the bastion of the Basmachi who had fought the Young Bukharans and had ensured that central control over the region was still nominal in 1924. If Uzbekistan was to be based on Bukhara, then Tajikistan was conceived as the place not wanted in Uzbekistan. In fact, as we shall see anon, Tajikistan became the dumping ground for losers of political battles in Bukhara. The making of Tajikistan was thus the flip side of the creation of Uzbekistan. If Uzbekistan was the heir to Timurid statehood in Central Asia, Tajikistan represented little more than the least tamed parts of the Manghit order. Tajikistan's creation was an act of excision by the Uzbek leadership.

The number of Communists in the new republic was minuscule, and it proved difficult to find people to administer it. The first Tajik revkom was headed by Nusratulla Makhsum, a native of Gharm, and thus one of the very few Communists of any prominence actually from the territory of the new republic. Yet even he had grown up in Kokand before joining the Bukharan Communist Party after the revolution. In 1923, he had toured eastern Bukhara as the deputy head of a circuit court with plenipotentiary powers to establish the authority of the BNSR government.[38] In 1925, he arrived back in the region to establish the authority of a Tajik autonomous republic.[39] The new republic was staffed largely by outsiders, few of whom went there willingly. There were many Europeans in the institutions of the new republic, who brought with them a sense of mission but who were often disappointed with what they found.[40] The political leadership also included many "Tajiks" from Turkestan or Bukhara. Few of these individuals had claimed a Tajik identity before 1924, and most ended up in Tajikistan because they lost out in various factional struggles in Tashkent or Bukhara.[41] Abduqodir Muhiddinov, who became the chair of the Tajik sovnarkom after the First Congress of Soviets, had identified himself as an Uzbek throughout his career as a Young

---

38. TsGARUz, f. 48, d. 182, l. 30.

39. On Makhsum, see R. Masov, ed., *Fidoii millat* (Dushanbe, 2001). Biographical notices on him abound on the web; the best is, perhaps, R. Abdullo, "Nusartullo Makhsum: on stroil nezavisimyi sovetskii Tadzhikistan" (27.06.2011). Available at http://www.centrasia.ru/newsA.php?st=1309165380.

40. Botakoz Kassymbekova, "Helpless Imperialists: European State Workers in Soviet Central Asia in the 1920s and 1930s," *Central Asian Survey* 30 (2011): 21–37.

41. Gero Fedtke, "How Bukharans Turned into Uzbeks and Tajiks: Soviet Nationalities Policy in the Light of a Personal Rivalry," in *Patterns of Transformation in and around Uzbekistan*, eds. Paolo Sartori and Tommaso Trevisani (Reggio Emilia, 2007), 19–50.

Bukharan.[42] In 1924, he had participated in the delimitation debates as part of the Uzbek delegation and never uttered a word (at least not one caught by the stenographers) on the subject of the Tajiks. But he had a long running feud with Fayzulla Xo'jayev, and the creation of Tajikistan provided the opportunity for Xo'jayev to finally vanquish his rival. He used his membership of the Orgburo of the newly formed Communist Party of Uzbekistan to assign Muhiddinov to the Tajik revkom.[43] In Bukharan terms, this was administrative exile to eastern Bukhara. Political defeat had finally made Muhiddinov a Tajik.

There were many others who arrived in Tajikistan after losing political struggles in Tashkent. Abbos Aliyev, the first Tajik commissar for education, was born in Bukhara to a family of Iranian origin. His father was active in the Iranian Democratic Party. Aliyev himself studied in Russian and Iranian schools in Charjuy and Ashgabat before 1917, where he seems to have become involved in socialist organizations. His father was killed in 1917, and Aliyev joined the original Bukharan Communist Party when it was founded in 1918. Like many members of the BKP, Aliyev featured in the opposition to the Young Bukharans in the early years of the BNSR. He was disciplined and sent off to Moscow to attend the Communist University for the Toilers of the East in 1922. He returned when he was appointed to the Tajik revkom in 1925.[44] Abdulla Rahimboyev was, like Hojiboyev, from Khujand. He had risen high in the KPT as an Uzbek. A defeat in factional struggles, again at the hands of Fayzulla Xo'jayev, led to his departure for Moscow, where worked in a number of insignificant positions. He returned to Central Asia only in 1933, this time as a Tajik, to replace Hojiboyev as head of Tajikistan's sovnarkom. Many other party workers accused of factionalism and intrigue ended up in Tajikistan. In its early years, Tajikistan was run largely by people who had ended up there by chance.

Rahim Masov noted that reading the documents of the delimitation, one would not know that the Tajiks even existed. He is correct, but not for the reasons he believes, namely, the "unprincipled, or, more accurately, criminal, compromising, and treasonous (in relation to the Tajik people) position of the Tajik subcommission."[45] We may put the matter rather differently. In 1924, there were

---

42. See, for example, a questionnaire where Muhiddinov identified himself as Uzbek: "18-inchi fevrolda bo'lgan Nozirlar shurosining xodimlari isfiskasi," TsGARUz, f. 47, op. 1, d. 474, l. 9 (18.02.1924).

43. Fedtke, "How Bukharans Turned into Uzbeks and Tajiks," 33.

44. Most of the detail about Aliyev's early life comes from an autobiography he wrote for the party in 1923: RGASPI, f. 62, op. 4, d. 633, ll. 96–97 (Sept. 1923). Muhammadjoni Shakuri's modern biography, "Abbos Aliyev," in Muhammadjoni Shakurii Bukhoroî, *Fitnai inqilob dar Bukhoro/Abbos Aliyev* (Dushanbe, 2010), 103–139, omits Aliyev's political difficulties and presents him as a gallant battler against pan-Turkism.

45. Masov, *Istoriia topronogo razdeleniia*, 47.

many Persian speakers in Central Asia but no Tajik nation. More pertinently, there did not even exist a Tajik national movement that might have spoken on behalf of a potential Tajik nation, or made claims for it, and struggled for its recognition. In the absence of such recognition, the only thing that differentiated Persian speakers from their Turkic-speaking neighbors was language, and that simply never became a marker of identity or a node of mobilization for the Persian speakers of Turkestan. Tajiks indeed did not exist as a nation in 1924.

Building Tajik Culture

The original Uzbek proposal for the creation of a Tajik oblast had suggested that urban Tajiks from Uzbekistan would serve as a reserve for cadres in the "eastern Bukharan Tajik oblast."[46] Few of those cadres were keen to move to the rural wilds of Tajikistan, however. Samarqand remained the center of Tajik publishing for several years, in which the lead was taken by a number of exiles of different sorts. The most important figure in Tajik culture was Sadriddin Ayni. He was the leading Central Asian author writing in Persian (although he also wrote in Uzbek), and it was he who first used the term *Tajik* for the language, and set out to differentiate it from Persian. It was Ayni, too, who almost singlehandedly created a corpus of a Tajik literature, writing short stories, novels, and works of history in a life of extraordinary productivity. (It was also extraordinary in that it was not cut short in 1938.) He was recognized as the preeminent Tajik intellectual in his lifetime, yet he continued to live in Samarqand until almost the end of his life, moving to Dushanbe only a few months before his death in 1954. The second major actor in this period of Tajik cultural life was another exile, Abu'l Qasim Lahuti, a veteran of the political turmoil in Iran who fled to the Soviet Union after the failure of an audacious uprising in Tabriz in 1922.[47] Lahuti spent three years in Moscow, where he continued to write but also found a job at the Publishing House for the Peoples of the USSR, then headed by Nazir To'raqulov.

---

46. RGASPI, f. 62, op. 2, d. 102, l. 7.

47. Lahuti had been an important participant in the political turmoil of the years after the Iranian constitutional revolution. He fled Iran during the Great War, and spent several years in Istanbul during the First World War. He returned to Iran and threw himself back into the political struggle that culminated in the uprising in Tabriz. The best source on Lahuti's activities remains a short autobiographical piece he published in a very official venue, but which remains irreplaceable: Abdulkasim [*sic!*] Lahuti, "About Myself," *Soviet Literature*, 1954, no. 4: 138–144; on the broader Iranian context of Lahuti's life, see Stephanie Cronin, "Iran's Forgotten Revolutionary: Abulqasim Lahuti and the Tabriz insurrection of 1922," in *Reformers and Revolutionaries in Modern Iran: New Perspectives on the Iranian Left*, ed. Stephanie Cronin (London, 2004).

Lahuti quickly attained fame as a Soviet writer—a collection of his poetry celebrating the revolutionary era in the Soviet Union was published in Moscow and Cho'lpon translated it into Uzbek. In 1925, Lahuti was seconded to Dushanbe as the head of the agitprop section of the Tajik obkom, where he spent five years.[48] Yet another exile was Nisar Muhammad, an Indian revolutionary, who served as the republic's commissar for education.[49] Finally, no account of the early years of Tajik literature can be complete without mention of Fitrat himself, who returned to Tajik after a decade of disavowal.

Fitrat was the man who introduced modern prose writing to Persian letters in Central Asia. His Persian writings before 1917 were new not just in content but also in style.[50] Fitrat eschewed the often florid constructions favored by writers in the Persianate tradition and instead followed new conventions of simplicity, directness, and proximity to the spoken language that had also gained ground in modern Iranian letters. Yet he had foresworn Persian in 1917 and did not publish anything in it until 1927, when he wrote *Shŭrishi Vose'* (The Insurrection of Vose'), a play about a peasant uprising in Bukhara in the 1880s. The work parallels *Arslon*, his Uzbek-language play on the land reform that appeared the same year. What pushed Fitrat back into the realm of Persian was the severe criticism of him and his work for their alleged pan-Turkism. Writing in Tajik was a way for Fitrat to escape the harassment of new self-styled Soviet Uzbek "cultural workers" and to disprove the charges of pan-Turkism. Fitrat's literary output in the years after 1927 (when battles on the "ideological front" targeted the prerevolutionary intelligentsia with ever greater ferocity, as we shall see in the following chapter) focused on Persianate topics. This too was a form of exile, and Fitrat's case was in many ways analogous to Muhiddinov's. Political difficulties in Uzbekistan had led Fitrat back to the world of Persian letters, now christened Tajik.

Nevertheless, the creation of Tajikistan did lead to defections from the Chaghatayist project, as many Persian-speaking intellectuals came to identify themselves as Tajiks. Some were veteran men of letters, such as Ayni's old friend and colleague Abdulvohid Munzim and the redoubtable Sayyid Rizo Alizoda. Others had participated in Uzbek cultural life and seen themselves as Uzbek. Hoji Muin, who had chastised Fitrat for writing in Persian in 1917, emerged as a major Tajik figure, as did To'raqul Zehniy (1892–1983) of Samarqand, who had been a delegate at the Uzbek orthography conference in 1923.[51] Narzullo Bektosh

---

48. The circumstances of Lahuti's arrival in Dushanbe were quickly mythologized; for a post-Soviet appraisal, see Khudoinazar Asozoda, *Sarguzashti ustod Lohuti* (Dushanbe, 2009).

49. The details of Nisar Muhammad's life are scanty; he was known as Nisar Muhammad the Afghan, but Soviet sources also claimed that he was a British subject from Peshawar who had fled the country with a death sentence hanging over his head; see Rzehak, *Vom Persischen*, 148–149n.

50. Sadriddin 'Aynī, *Namūna-yi adabiyāt-i tājīk* (Moscow, 1926), 531.

51. "O'rta Osiyo o'zbeklarining imlo kanferensiyasi," *Turkiston*, 31.10.1923.

(1900–1938), born in Samarqand, had been an avid Chaghatayist until 1926. He took his nom de plume from the Anatolian Sufi of that name and even denied that any Tajiks existed in Samarqand. We do not know what led to his change of heart, but he moved to Dushanbe in 1928 and took up a number of important editorial positions.[52] Others entered literary life for the first time. The poet Payrav Sulaymoni (1899–1933) came from an affluent Bukharan family. He had studied at an Iranian school in Merv and was enrolled in the Russian Realschule in Kagan at the time of the revolution. He worked in Soviet institutions in Tashkent and Samarqand, where his short life ended. He never lived in Tajikistan.[53] Jalol Ikromi (1909–93) came from a prominent family of qazis in Bukhara who was dispossessed by the revolution. In 1927, he still thought of himself as an Uzbek, but he wrote in both languages. An encounter with Ayni got Ikromi's first story published in *Rāhbar-i dānish* while he was still a student in Bukhara. He moved to Dushanbe only in 1930.[54] These writers together constituted a self-consciously Tajik intelligentsia that did much to articulate the parameters of Tajikness.

They operated in a Tajik literary field that also emerged as a result of the creation of a Tajik republic. Central Asia had been without a Persian-language periodical since the closure of *Shu'la-yi inqilāb* at the end of 1921. The process of national delimitation led to the establishment of *Āvāz-i tājīk* (Voice of the Tajik) in Samarqand in August 1924. In December, it became the organ of the Tajik republican committee of the party but continued to be published from Samarqand for another two years and often did not reach Tajikistan. Eventually, help came from outside, as typographers and Arabic font were brought in from Kazan to set up a printing press in Dushanbe and to establish a Tajik publishing house (Nashri Tojik).[55] *Āvāz-i tājīk* was soon augmented by *Mullo Mushfiqī*, an illustrated satirical magazine named after a subversive cultural figure from the past, and by *Rāhbar-i dānish* (The Guide to Knowledge), a general-interest magazine aimed at teachers, but also a venue where questions of Tajik identity could be debated. These three publications, funded because the status of Tajikistan as an autonomous republic entitled it to them, played a fundamental role in the creation of a Tajik identity.[56] They attracted a number of writers from the Persian-speaking population of Central Asia.

---

52. Abdukholiq Nabiyev, *Narzulloi Bektosh va ilmu adabi tojiki solhoi 20–30 sadai XX* (Dushanbe, 2004).

53. Sohib Tabarov, *Payrav Sulaymoni: ocherki hayot va ejodiyot* (Dushanbe, 2013).

54. Dzhonon Ikromi, *Dzhalol Ikrami: neizvestnye stranitsy* (Dushanbe, 2010), 32–33.

55. I. K. Usmonov, "Stanovlenie i razvitie tadzhikskoi partiino-sovetskoi pechati 1917–1929 gg.," in I. K. Usmonov, *Zhurnalistika*, pt. 2 (Dushanbe, 2005), 66–67.

56. For a survey of the Tajik literary scene of this period, Jiří Bečka, "Tajik Literature from the 16th Century to the Present," in Jan Rypka et al., *History of Iranian Literature*, trans. P. van Popta-Hope (Dordrecht, 1968), 546–554, is still useful. On the early Tajik press, now see A'zamjon Azimov, *Voqeiyati zindagî va matbuoti tojik* (Dushanbe, 2000).

Yet, what Tajik culture was to be was not at all clear at the outset. In his earliest writings on the Tajik question, before Tajikistan had been established, Ayni used the word *Tajik* to mean "mountain Tajiks" only. "It is known to all that the Tajiks of Turkestan lag behind others in terms of knowledge and education," he wrote in September 1924. Education was therefore a "life-and-death question for the Tajik nation [*qavm*]."[57] That education should be given in "the language of the Tajiks of the mountains," and not the language of the cities, which was incomprehensible to the simple mountain folk. "The language of the Mountain Tajiks is a simple Persian language, devoid of Iranian formalities, free of the admixture of incomprehensible Arabic words, and in accordance with the morphology of Persian. True, the pronunciation seems sullied to urban Persians [*forsiyoni shahrî*]. Still, it is pure and according to rules. Such a language is understood from Folghar and Mastchoh to Qarotegin and Darvoz [i.e., throughout the Tajik republic]."[58] Tajik was to be a simple, ethnically pure language of the mountain Tajiks.

By the spring of the following year, Ayni had gone over to a much expansive definition of Tajikness, one which encompassed the entire Persian-speaking population of Central Asia and its "thousand-year-long" literary heritage. He laid out his vision of the Tajik heritage in an anthology of Tajik literature that was commissioned by the new government of Tajikistan. Ayni's preface to the anthology is worth quoting at length:

> From the first events recorded by history to today, a great nation called Tajik or Tazik has lived in the lands of Transoxiana and Turkestan. In the same manner, its language and literature have also developed. The development of Tajik language and literature has not been dependent on the ages or the occupation of the throne. Thus we see how highly Tajik literature developed in this land in the age of the Samanids, who were racially Persian speaking [*'irqan fārsīzabān hastand*], it developed the same way in the times of the Chinggisids, Temurids, Shaybanids, Astrakhanids, and Manghits, who were racially Mongol, Turk, and Uzbek. Thus it is clear that the development of Tajik language and literature in these places did not take place simply because of the dominion of the Samanids or the immigration of Iranians. Its real cause is the presence in these places of a large nation by the name of Tajik of the Aryan race.[59]

---

57. Ayni, "Dar borai maktab va maorifi tojik," *Ovozi tojik*, 01.09.1924, in Ayni, *Aknun navbati qalam ast*, 2 vols. (Dushanbe, 1977), 1:272–273.

58. Ayni, "Dar borai kitobhoi maktabii tojikon," *Ovozi tojik*, 12.09.1924, in Ayni, *Aknun*, 1:274.

59. 'Aynī, *Namūna-yi adabiyāt-i tājīk*, 3.

The Tajik nation had a continuous existence in Central Asia since time immemorial and its cultural development did not depend on political power or military conquest. If the Chaghatayist vision of the Uzbek nation centered on a tradition of statehood, Ayni's Tajik nation existed despite the lack of dominion; instead, it civilized its conquerors. Elsewhere, Ayni declared that "Tajiks have been in the forefront and the leaders of all cultural work" in the long history of "Tajikistan, Turkestan, and Transoxiana." The culture they created was adopted by those who conquered them, so that the "great conqueror Temur, despite the fact that he was a Turk, wrote his autobiography in Tajik." The culture of his court was expressed in Tajik, and Tajik culture continued in the courts of Central Asia down to the Russian conquest.[60] At the same time, Ayni's Tajik nation did not by definition include other Persian speakers, such as the Eroni, the Afghans, or for that matter, the inhabitants of Iran itself. Ayni here combined claims of longevity, historical primacy, and authenticity with those of cultural superiority on behalf of the Tajik nation. This was the first time in history that the Persian-speaking population of Central Asia had been conceptualized as a transhistorical community, a nation in its own right. Such a formulation was clearly a response to the claims of Chaghatayism, which saw state-building as a central pillar of the legitimacy of its claim to nationhood and thereby attempted to efface the existence of a Persian-speaking urban population in Central Asia.

Ayni was also appropriating themes from contemporary European Orientalism. Already in 1925, the Tajik government organized an Association for the Study of Tajikistan and Iranian Peoples Beyond, that brought together several Russian scholars to research the new republic's past and present. In a historical sketch of the Tajiks, V. V. Barthold, the renowned Orientalist, presented the Tajiks as "the original inhabitants of contemporary Turkestan" and sketched the history of the Persian-speaking population of the region as the history of the Tajiks.[61] Barthold's definition had much in common with Ayni's definition of the Tajiks as a continuously existing Persian-speaking nation and was to be quoted by Tajik representatives many times. Ayni's invocation of race, quite unprecedented in Persianate letters in Central Asia, can quite clearly be traced to the work of A. A. Semenov, who wrote about Aryan (not Persian or Tajik) culture in Central Asia.[62] The Aryan theme was to figure prominently in the Tajik press in the decade that followed.

---

60. Ayni, "Ba munosibati e'loni jumhuriyati mukhtori Tojikiston," in *Aknun*, 1:290–291. He also argued that eastern Bukhara had always been independent of the rule of the cities until emir Muzaffar subdued it with Russian help.

61. Bartol'd, "Tadzhiki," 93.

62. A.A. Semenov, "Material'nye pamiatniki ariiskoi kul'tury," in Korzhenevskii, ed., *Tadzhikistan*, 113–150.

It is also important to note that Ayni's formulation of Tajikness had nothing to do with Iran. The Tajik nation was indigenous to "Transoxiana and Turkestan," a community in its own right, with a culture and a literature all its own. *Samples of Tajik Literature*, Ayni's anthology, was also an exercise in canon building. It claimed for the Tajik nation all Persian literature composed in "Transoxiana and Turkestan," from Rudaki (d. ca. 941) to Fitrat and Ayni himself. From its focus on poetry to its use of the Islamic (*hijri*) calendar, the anthology is very much a traditional work in the *tazkira* genre, but through it Ayni staked out a claim for the Tajik nation to a large slice of the larger realm of Persian literature. Western observers have usually found the distinction between Tajik and Persian forced and artificial, another one of the divide-and-rule practices of the Soviets. Matters were a little more complex. Ayni's delineation of a separate Tajik tradition is part of the much larger phenomenon of the fracturing of the Persianate world that took place at this time. A Persianate world (*qalamrav-i zabān-i fārsī*), tied by common cultural norms and literary conventions, had always been larger than the state of Iran, and most of the contributors to this culture were not ethnically Iranian. Transoxiana's claim to a Persianate heritage was as old as that of Iran itself, and entirely independent of it. It is not just that New Persian arose in Bukhara, at the Samanid court, but much of the action in Firdawsi's *Shahnama*, the Persian book of kings, takes place in Transoxiana, in lands that have not been part of any state controlled from what is now Iran. Over the centuries, Bukhara was a major center of a Sunni *persophonie*, while more Persian poetry was produced in India in the ensuing centuries than in Iran itself. This Persianate world began to fragment in the nineteenth century in the face of more exclusivist national ideologies or colonialism. The role of the Persianate heritage diminished greatly in Indian cultural life as Persian was replaced by English as the language of government and by Urdu as the language of literature. Persianate elites in Bukhara, Turkestan, and Azerbaijan, as we have seen, also moved away from the heritage of Persian. In Iran, on the other hand, the rise of national sentiment led to the twin moves of denigrating Persian literature outside of the boundaries of Iran, with special derision reserved for the "Indian style" (*sabk-i hindī*), and of rendering Persian literature synonymous with Iranian. The late-nineteenth-century ideology of the literary return (*bāzgasht-i adabī*) denounced Indian poetry as derivative and inauthentic, while later modernists found it lacking in innovativeness. The effect was to nationalize the Persianate heritage on behalf of the modern Iranian nation-state. By the early twentieth century, at the same time as Ayni was composing his anthology of Tajik literature, Iranian nationalist historians were creating a canon of Iranian literature that claimed some figures as authentically Iranian (the celebration of Firdawsi's millennium in 1934 that turned Firdawsi into an *Iranian* poet was very much a part of this process) and excluded others.[63] Ayni's creation of a Tajik canon as distinct from an Iranian one is part of this greater phenomenon. Tajik had as much claim to the Persianate heritage as Iranian Persian.[64]

Ayni had conceptualized the indigenous Persian-speaking population of Central Asia a single nation with a transhistorical existence. In the long run, this view was to define Tajik national identity. In the short run, however, Ayni ran into a considerable amount of trouble. The poetry assembled in his anthology represented the literary tradition of the ages; it diverged a great deal from the language of the mountainous areas of eastern Bukhara. Was this language suitable for Soviet Tajiks building a new world? In the late 1920s, a fevered debate erupted on this question among Tajik intellectuals that paralleled in many way the debate over Chaghatay. The Tajik debate took place between "Internationalists," who believed that Tajik should be comprehensible beyond the borders of the USSR in order to fulfill its role as a revolutionary medium, and the "language inventors [*ejodchi*]" who wanted to create a written language from the speech of the rural (hence, linguistically and nationally authentic) population.[65] European scholars played a significant role in these debates, perhaps more significant than in the debates in Uzbekistan. A compromise emerged at the end, in which several features of rural Tajik speech were retained as part of the new literary standard, but the heritage of the centuries was not altogether dismissed. Tajikness was grounded both in its Persianate past, its specific geography, and its Soviet present.

The Emergence of Tajik National Consciousness

Lutz Rzehak is absolutely right when he notes that "the founding of Tajikistan was not the result of Tajik nationalism but the hour of its birth."[66] A Tajik national identity appeared only after a Tajik republic had been established. The

---

63. On canon building in Iran, see Farzin Vejdani, *Making History in Iran: Education, Nationalism, and Print Culture* (Stanford, 2014); on the nationalization of Firdawsi, see Afshin Marashi, *Nationalizing Iran: Culture, Power, and the State, 1870–1940* (Seattle, 2008), chap. 5.

64. In this regard, we might also heed the judgment of the Pakistani poet Faiz Ahmad Faiz (1911–84), practitioner and heir of the Persianate tradition and a frequent visitor to the Soviet Union. Introducing his Urdu-reading audience to Tajik, he had this to say: "The language of Tajikistan is Persian, but not the Persian of the Iranians, but ours. The people here do not call it Persian, but rather Tajik. This is just and correct. In fact, I think that the Iranian language of today should be called Iranian and not Persian, because its present vocabulary and pronunciation are very different from what was once the common scholarly and literary language of Central Asia." Faiż Aḥmad Faiż, *Mah o sāl-e āshnā'ī* (Karachi, 1981), 33.

65. Rzehak, *Vom Persischen zum Tadschikischen*, chapter 6, presents the most thorough discussion of these debates; see also B. S. Asimova, *Iazykovoe stroitel'stvo v Tadzhikistane, 1920–1940 gg.* (Dushanbe, 1982).

66. Rzehak, *Vom Persischen zum Tadschikischen*, 154.

most surprising feature of this transformation is the rapid pace at which a Tajik intelligentsia emerged and the vehemence with which its members pressed their claims. Initially, the claims centered on the language rights of Tajiks in Uzbekistan but very quickly escalated to territorial demands. Tajik claims took the form not just of demanding the elevation of Tajikistan's status to that of a full republic, but also of demanding additional territory from Uzbekistan. This second was highly unusual in the Soviet context, and potentially problematic, since it reeked of nationalism and irredentism. The cast of characters who pressed these claims included both new faces as well as men who in 1924 seen themselves as Uzbeks.

The policies pursued by Uzbekistan's authorities were a large part of the reason why Tajik national activism rose so rapidly. A fundamental feature of the Chaghatayist conception of Uzbekness was the disavowal of Central Asia's Persianate heritage and the concomitant denial of the presence of a large Persian-speaking population in the region. From the outset, Uzbek authorities sought to minimize the numbers of Tajiks in Uzbekistan. The All-Union census of 1926 reported a precipitous decline in the number of Tajiks in Uzbekistan over previous censuses. According to the Central Statistical Administration, there were 81,700 Tajiks in Samarqand out of a total population of 102,700 in 1923, but only 61,000 out of 138,800 in 1926.[67] The Central Statistical Administration offered the possibility that the national self-consciousness of many of the disappearing Tajiks had changed and they had now come to see themselves as Uzbeks.[68] Similarly, the Uzbek Commissariat of Education tried, by omission or commission, to restrict Tajik-language schooling. "The bulk of the population of the cities of Khujand, Bukhara, and Samarqand are Uzbeks," one of its resolutions asserted, "and even those who speak Tajik may not be Tajik, and Tajik may not be their native language, but simply a spoken one. Since 90 percent of Tajiks command Uzbek, the question of organizing Tajik schools is not important."[69] There were disputes even over the language children spoke at home, with Uzbek being taken as the default option for children of the sedentary indigenous population.

These policies created outrage among the nascent Tajik intelligentsia and led to the rapid radicalization of their positions. The main venue for the expression of this discontent was the Tajik press, whose pages are filled with reports about

---

67. GARF, f. 3316, op. 22, d. 127, ll. 148 (21.12.1929). The numbers were in fact lower in the published version of the census, which listed only 350,603 Tajiks in Uzbekistan outside the Tajik ASSR. Samarqand had only 10,716 Tajiks out of a total population of 104,444, while Bukhara had 3,977 out of 60,784. See *Vsesoiuznaia perepis' naseleniia 1926 goda*, vol. 15 (Moscow, 1928), 9, 19–20, 27–29.

68. GARF, f. 3316, op. 22, d. 127, ll. 148 (21.12.1929).

69. Quoted in "Svodka agenturno-dokumental'nykh dannykh o razvitii i roste shovinizma uzbekskoi intelligentsii" (31.05.1928), in *TsK RKP(b)-VKP(b) i natsional'nyi vopros*, 580.

Uzbek highhandedness. It reported many instances of people being told that if they declared themselves to be Tajiks, they will be forced to move to Tajikistan.[70] For Tajik representatives, this was incontrovertible proof that the census was rigged and that Tajiks had been registered as Uzbeks. Similarly, complaints about the lack of provision of Tajik-language schooling in Uzbekistan featured widely in Tajik newspapers.[71] These reports led to a rapid radicalization in the nature of Tajik demands. In 1929, when the Uzbek Commissariat of Education resolved to determine "by a true and objective approach" which language children spoke at home in order to shift instruction in minority schools to the language spoken by their pupils,[72] Tajik complaints had escalated into demands for secession from Uzbekistan.

Already in May 1926, the Tajik leadership had raised the matter with Stalin himself. In a memorandum, Shirinshoh Shohtemur, a member of the Tajik revkom, complained about the "Uzbekization . . . by means of savage administrative pressure and chauvinistic arbitrariness" of the 800,000 Tajiks in Uzbekistan that involved the denial of their language rights and their forced assimilation to Uzbekness. Shohtemur listed a series of abuses that went on it Uzbekistan. Tajik children were forced to attend Uzbek schools while "pan-Turkist chauvinists" denied the very existence of Tajiks as a nation. Tajik-language schools were in short supply, poorly funded, and in general not encouraged by the Uzbek administration. The Tajik Teachers Institute in Samarqand (which was also supposed to serve the needs of Tajikistan) was a miserable two-room affair while the teaching of Tajik was forbidden in most schools in Uzbekistan, even in areas of Tajik population. Speeches at the official celebrations marking the first anniversary of the establishment the Tajik autonomous republic were in Uzbek, which provoked a demonstration against Uzbekistan.[73] In the two years that followed, this catalogue of complaints was repeated in numerous petitions directed at different levels of the party and state hierarchies. Such complaints sought state intervention against Uzbek practices. In 1928, however, Muhiddinov put the matter on a different plane by demanding not just Tajikistan's separation from Uzbekistan but also the inclusion in it of the cities of Samarqand and Bukhara. The population of Bukhara, he argued, had since time immemorial been Persian-speaking and therefore Tajik. However, under the influence of pan-Islamism and

70. Mirzoalĭ Jŭrayev, *Az Samarqand to Bukhoro* (Dushanbe, 2013), 69.

71. See ibid., passim, for such reports in the press.

72. "O perevode prepodavaniia natsmenovskikh shkolakh UzSSR na rodnoi iazyk uchahshikhsia (Tezisy)," TsGARUz, f. 94, op. 5, d. 434, ll. 90–93.

73. Sh. Shotemor, "O kul'turnom i sotsial'no-ekonomicheskom polozhenii tadzhikov na territorii uzbekskoi repsubliki," GARF, f. 3316, op. 64, d. 224, ll. 1–5.

pan-Turkism, he wrote, the Young Bukharans had denied the existence of the Tajiks and sought to assimilate them forcefully to Uzbekness. Since the national delimitation, pan-Islamism and pan-Turkism had been replaced in part by a strident Uzbek nationalism that constituted a grave "political mistake," a perversion of nationalities policy, and had the potential to destabilize Soviet power in Central Asia.[74] The logical solution was to award the city to Tajikistan. It is also noteworthy that from the beginning, Tajik activists used the party's suspicions of pan-Islamism and pan-Turkism to criticize Uzbek policies and to cast them as harmful to the interests of the party, the state, and the revolution.[75] "Such a state of affairs," Shohtemur had asserted in his memorandum with emphasis, "completely corresponded and corresponds with the views of pan-Islamic, pan-Turkist, and pan-Uzbekist circles of the contemporary Uzbek intelligentsia and clergy." In complaining about the "perversion" of the party line by their opponents, Tajik activists thus positioned themselves as true Soviets. The accusations of pan-Islamism, pan-Turkism, and national chauvinism—the party's main phobias in Central Asia in the 1920s—continues to be the mainstay of Tajik complaints against Uzbek policies to this day.

Shohtemur, who emerged as the flag bearer of Tajik demands, was a new kind of Tajik. Born in Shugnan in the Pamirs, he came from an Ismaili family of Shugni speech. Orphaned in his childhood, he was adopted by a Russian officer, who took him to Tashkent, where he attended a Russian school. With the revolution, he followed many other young men with Russian educations into Soviet organs. He worked in Turkestan before being assigned in 1922 to a troika charged with establishing Soviet power in the Pamirs. He returned to Tashkent in 1924 just in time for the delimitation. He was thus neither Persian speaking, nor Sunni, but unlike most Tajiks who were, he had never been under the influence of the Jadids and their national idea.[76] Muhiddinov was quite the opposite, the scion of an important family in Bukhara who until 1924 had shown little interest in Tajikness. Now he used the critique of Jadidism, pan-Turkism, and pan-Islamism not just to position himself on the side of Soviet power and but also to discredit the

---

74. A. Muhiddinov, "Mardum-i shahr va aṭrāf-i Bukhārā tājīkand yā ūzbak," *Rahbar-i dānish*, 1928, no. 8–9, 15–18; a Russian version appeared in the organ of the Sredazburo: "Tadzhiki ili uzbeki naseliaiut gorod Bukharu i ego okrestnosti," *Za Partiiu*, 1929, no. 9.

75. In a different article, Muhiddinov attacked the Jadids directly, who by this time had come to denote bourgeois nationalism and counterrevolution, in party discourse. He incriminated himself to a certain extent in the counterrevolutionary conduct he denounced but claimed to have seen the light during a ten-month-long stay in Moscow as the republic's trade representative. A. Mukhitdinov, "Rol' dzhadidov v Bukharskoi revoliutsii," *Za Partiiu*, 1928, no. 9.

76. In post-Soviet Tajikistan, Shohtemur is seen as one of the founders of Tajikistan and his life has drawn considerable attention. The omnibus volume, *Shirinshoh Shohtemur*, ed. Q. Alamshoyev (Dushanbe, 2009), brings several different biographies together with a few documents.

Uzbek regime, headed by his nemesis, Fayzulla Xo'jayev. For Muhiddinov, clearly, the Tajik national issue was completely connected with his factional struggle with Xo'jayev. The only way for him to return to Bukhara was to claim it for the republic where he had ended up.[77]

Muhiddinov was backed by several other writers, including his fellow exile Aliyev. They made the issue one that the Sredazburo or the Central Committee could not ignore.[78] The OGPU, meanwhile, had long been gathering materials on "Uzbekism and the rise of chauvinism" among the Uzbek intelligentsia. As we shall in the following two chapters, those suspicions were to take a heavy toll on the Uzbek intelligentsia. Tajik complaints, couched in a language that conformed directly to that of the OGPU, meant that the issue of Uzbek-Tajik interethnic relations was very much on the agenda of the political police and the party. The discussion of Tajikistan's separation from Uzbekistan and of related territorial adjustments, launched in 1929, was directly tied to the state's suspicions of "Uzbek chauvinism." Those suspicions were in turn rooted in attempts to purify the ranks of the party and to assert central control over the direction of local cultural life that began with the opening in 1926 of an "ideological front."

---

77. Fedtke, "How Bukharans Turned into Uzbeks and Tajiks," 36–38.

78. Abbos Aliyov, "Mas'ala-yi millī dar Bukhārā va aṭrāf-i ān," *Rahbar-i dānish*, no. 11–12 (1928): 13–18; Sh. Dzhabbarov, "Protiv izvrashcheniia natsional'noi politiki," *Za Partiiu*, 1929, no. 3–4: 93–98. For other notices in the press and petitions in the archives, see Masov, *Istoriia*, 135–145, 163–169.

THE IDEOLOGICAL FRONT

In October 1924, at the moment of Uzbekistan's birth, Abdurahmon Sa'diy penned an overview of recent developments in the field of Uzbek literature. In this article, which appeared in *Revolutionary Youth*, the organ of the Komsomol, Sa'diy saw the main feature of current Uzbek literary life to be the emergence of a revolutionary literature, marked by romanticism, the simplification of language, and the use of symbolism. For Sa'diy, the main proponents of this revolutionary literature were Fitrat, Cho'lpon, Elbek, Botu, Shokir Sulaymon, and G'ulom Zaf-ariy, who together had closed the era of "the realism of Behbudiy and Avloniy" that had held sway before the revolution.[1] This mapping of the Uzbek literary field, where revolution had to do with the discovery of new aesthetic horizons rather than class conflict, was soon to be outlawed. In 1926, the party opened an "ideological front" against the "old intellectuals" and imposed a new vocabulary on cultural discourse in Uzbekistan, so that literary judgments could be made only on the basis of categories of analysis based on an authorized definition of revolution. The party inserted itself into the cultural life of Central Asia and the consequences were far reaching. As the parameters of the permissible shrunk, the pantheon of the new literature was drastically reshaped. Central Asia, its past and its present, had to be represented in universal Marxist categories as defined by the party. The names that had populated Sa'diy's article began to disappear from

---

1. A. Sa'diy, "O'zbek adabiy ijod maydonida harakatlar," *O'zgarishchi yoshlar*, no. 7 (1924), 49–50.

public use. Ironically enough, the last time the names of Fitrat and Cho'lpon appeared in print in a laudatory context was in a manual on *How to Write News, Articles, Verse, and Stories*, written by the young writer Anqaboy (Xudoyvohidov, 1905–38), for use by an emerging cohort of Soviet Uzbek writers. It was men like Anqaboy and the novices for whom he wrote who were the foot soldiers fighting on this front.[2] It was they who denounced the Jadids and knocked them off their pedestal.

Yet even if the party had mobilized a new cohort of enthusiasts, it never felt confident of their orthodoxy or loyalty. The Communist Party of Uzbekistan remained woefully divided along ethnic lines, and its early history was marked by a series of crises. The "Case of the 18" in 1925 was followed by several other scandals that made the party leadership deeply suspicious of local cadres, whom it considered ideologically unsound and susceptible to "nationalism." Nationalism in turn came to be defined in an ever more expansive fashion by party and the OGPU and became the main political sin of the period. The struggle against it, both within the party and without, was by far the most significant feature of political life in Uzbekistan in the second half of the 1920s. Combined with the party's newfound assertiveness in cultural policy, this struggle had profound consequences for the republic's intellectual and political elites. In asserting its presence in the cultural field, the party banked on a new cohort of intellectuals who were profoundly critical of their elders and willing to denounce them for their ideological sins. In the polemics that emerged, the Jadids ("proponents of the new") came to be castigated as "old intellectuals" (*eski ziyolilar*) whose time had passed. This transition from "new" to "old" within a decade was perhaps a sign of the rapidity of change in an age of revolution. But the cohort that replaced the newly old had its own problems: they too could never shake off the suspicion of nationalism and their fates were not always dissimilar to those of the Jadids.

Opening the Ideological Front

The timing of the opening of the ideological front in Uzbekistan is best explained by the party's increasing sense of strength in the aftermath of the national delimitation, which was routinely touted as the "second revolution" in Central Asia. Up until then, the party and its European leadership had been all too aware of the thinness of their support and of the paucity of personnel resources to impose their will on the region. This weakness had led to numerous tactical concessions and the uneasy collaboration with the prerevolutionary intelligentsia. Some

---

2. Anqaboy, *Xabar, maqola, she'r va hikoya yozish yo'llari* (Samarqand, 1927), 10, 49–60.

European Communists had felt that the tasks of enlightening the benighted Muslim population, reducing its "fanaticism," spreading literacy and education, required making use of all possible "intellectual forces" in Muslim society.[3] In 1920, Georgii Safarov, the political commissar of the *Krasnyi Vostok* agitational train, saw no problem with using the Turk Kuchi (Turkic Might) theater troupe to spread the Soviet message in Ferghana.[4] But such attitudes had always coexisted with a constant suspicion of alien ideologies and of the wandering imaginations of the local intelligentsia. Given that almost no European party members knew indigenous languages, the only people capable of exercising political control over local cultural life were indigenous cadres, many of whom were closely tied to the prerevolutionary intelligentsia, whose worldview they shared. The stronger the Bolsheviks felt in their control of Central Asia, the less tolerant they became of ideological unorthodoxy. Isaak Zelenskii, who arrived in Tashkent as the new head of the Sredazburo in December 1924, was particularly wary both of the national intelligentsia and of native Communists. For him, "the question of what to do with the nationally-minded intelligentsia" was one of the most pressing for the party in Central Asia.[5] The national delimitation created more homogenous republics and gave the party a sense of greater control over personnel. The confidence that came from this sense led the party to seek greater control over local cultural life. The opening of the ideological front in Uzbekistan was part of a pan-Soviet phenomenon, as the party sought everywhere to bring national intelligentsias to heel, but its timing in Uzbekistan had everything to do with local developments and the party's sense of its own strength.

The moving force behind the opening of the ideological front, however, was the political police. As the moral conscience of the regime and the keeper of its ideological purity, the OGPU was immune to indigenization. Although it had plenty of local informants (judging by the thickness of the materials gathered, their numbers must have been large indeed), its analytical staff in Central Asia was almost entirely European.[6] It made the struggle with nationalism a central

---

3. For a census of "Muslim intellectual forces" in Turkestan called by TurTsIK in October 1919, see TsGARUz, f. 17, op. 1, d. 244, l. 107.

4. *Hamza Hakimzoda Niyoziy arxivining katalogi*, 2 vols. (Tashkent, 1990–91), 1:346–348.

5. I. Zelenskii, "Chto nam nado dobit'sia?" *Krasnyi rubezh*, 1925, no. 1: 10.

6. I have not found figures for the 1920s, but during the Great Terror of 1937–38, the leadership of Uzbekistan's NKVD was composed entirely of Europeans—Russians, Jews, Georgians, and Armenians. See the list of the leading figures of the NKVD in *Repressiia 1937–1938 gg.: dokumenty i materialy*, vyp. 1 (Tashkent, 2005), 20–22. Complaints about the lack of indigenization in the political police were quite commonly picked up by the OGPU. See, for instance, RGASPI, f. 62, op. 2, d. 520, l. 101 (statement by Obidjon Mahmudov, Oct. 1926); "Svodka agenturno-dokumental'nykh dannykh o razvitii i roste shovinizma uzbekskoi intelligentsii" (31.05.1928), in *TsK RKP(b)-VKP(b) i natsional'nyi vopros* (Moscow, 2005), 577–578.

mission. (There was no analogous struggle with "great power chauvinism"; Central Asia's Europeans were only watched for nationally unmarked political sins of opposition to or deviation from the party line.) In January 1925, just as Uzbekistan was being established, the OGPU initiated the formation of a Commission for Working Out Questions on Attracting the Party's Attention to the Work of the OGPU in the Struggle with Bourgeois-Nationalist Groups and with Counter-Revolutionary Ideology that brought OGPU officers together with high-ranking party and government figures. According to Lev Nikolaevich Bel'skii, the long serving head of the OGPU in Central Asia, "it was no secret to anyone" that those who "fought us for five years . . . have not been beaten either physically, economically, or spiritually, and that their influence on the masses is still enormous." This situation was made worse for Bel'skii by the strivings of the "petit bourgeois governments" of the Muslim states bordering Central Asia, who "wanted to insure themselves against Soviet influence and the attraction of the model of Soviet rule in Central Asia." The internal and external forms of counterrevolution were especially intertwined in Central Asia. The tasks of Soviet power therefore included "a harsh struggle with the malicious national intelligentsia by way of revealing [to the masses] their pan-Islamic and their sell-out–anglophile essence."[7] All the bugbears were here: pan-Islamism, foreign intervention, and counterrevolution, embodied in the nationalism of the national intelligentsia. These themes featured large in the attacks on the intelligentsia that ensued.

As with many other Soviet categories, nationalism proved to be remarkably elastic. The OGPU's spies amassed a vast archive of material—reports of overheard conversations, perlustrated correspondence, secretly copied excerpts from personal diaries, denunciations—which their bosses used as evidence in their reports. "Nationalism" here covered everything from outright condemnation of the Soviet order (often ascribed to the Jadids) to expressions of discontent with the pace at which Soviet policies were being implemented. Thus the notice in the sarcastic magazine *Mushtum* of the paradox, "even though korenizatsiia is an extraordinary question, if you raise it, you are accused of nationalism," was proof for the OGPU of nationalism among the Uzbek intelligentsia.[8] In fact, korenizatsiia became a bête noir for the OGPU, which saw "conversations about korenizatsiia" as "a manifestation of the contemporary tactic of the anti-Soviet struggle of Uzbek nationalists: the infiltration of the Soviet apparat and the party, the preparation of youth, etc."[9] Given that many Uzbek Communists saw Communism

---

7. RGASPI, f. 62, op. 2, d. 194, ll. 8–17 (13.01.1925).

8. The passage was cited in "Svodka agenturno-dokumental'nykh dannykh," 577. I have been unable to locate the original. Available OGPU reports bear out the validity of this comment.

9. Ibid., 583.

through the prism of the nation and of anticolonialism, the OGPU definition of nationalism could prove quite dangerous even for party members. It is hardly surprising, then, that no one was spared the suspicion. The names of every single public figure appear in this vast archive. It was never difficult for the OGPU to come up with incriminating evidence on those who fell into its clutches.

In the spring of 1926, the OGPU made a number of arrests of people it characterized as "former leaders of armed struggle against Soviet power"—Saidnosir Mirjalilov, Obidjon Mahmudov, and Ubaydulla Xo'jayev.[10] These were figures associated with the Kokand Autonomy who had remained outside Soviet institutions. They had met Orjonikidze in 1922 and were suspected by the OGPU of being leaders of the local nationalist underground. Mirjalilov was sentenced to three years of forced labor in Solovetsky islands in the White Sea. Upon his release, he was exiled to Siberia, which soon claimed his life.[11] Xo'jayev was released and allowed to return to a quiet life in Tashkent until his final arrest in 1931.[12] Mahmudov underwent a lengthy interrogation at the hands of the OGPU in October, after which he was released. He remained the object of suspicion but died a natural death in 1936. At about the same time, Abdulla Qodiriy found himself under arrest. His crime was not in the past but the present: in a characteristic piece of satire published in February 1926, he had poked brutal fun at Ikromov in the pages of *Mushtum*.[13] The party had grown wary of the magazine as a whole and the previous year a complaint against the hostile depiction of the deputy chair of the Syr Daryo oblast ispolkom had gone all the way to Moscow.[14] Now, Qodiriy's infraction seems to have provided the opportunity to put him in his place. Qodiriy sat in jail for several months before he was tried. He was pardoned, but he never again worked in the press, making his living as a writer and a freelance translator for the rest of his days.[15]

These arrests were accompanied by a full frontal verbal assault on the Jadids led by stalwarts in the party. The attacks no doubt had Zelenskii's backing but they were led by Akmal Ikromov and his Young Communist friends who had been picked to lead the Communist Party of Uzbekistan. Their motivations were

10. RGASPI, f. 62, op. 2, d. 518, l. 167 (Sept. 1926).

11. Zarifa Saidnosirova, *Oybegim mening: xotiralar*, ed. Naim Karimov (Tashkent, 1994), 51, 70.

12. Kh. Sadykov, "Ubaidulla Khodzhaev: shtrikhi k politicheskomu portretu," *Chelovek i politika*, 1991, no. 11: 82; *Politicheskie deiateli Rossii 1917: biograficheskii slovar'* (Moscow, 1993), 335.

13. Ovsar (pseud.), "Yig'indi gaplar," *Mushtum*, no. 3 (25.02.1926), 2–3.

14. In August 1925, the Central Control Commission of the party had suggested that its Uzbek counterpart "ensure a radical transformation of the staff of the journal in the direction of the party line." RGASPI, f. 121, op. 2, d. 10, ll. 63–63ob. Another complaint from within the party about *Mushtum* can be found in RGASPI, f. 62, op. 2, d. 412, l. 106.

15. The best account of Qodiriy's life is in the memoir of his son, the most comprehensive (and uncensored) version of which is Habibulla Qodiriy, *Otamdan xotira*, ed. X. Qodiriy (Tashkent, 2005).

a mix of ideological radicalism, impatience with their elders, and the need to assert their orthodoxy in the eyes of party authorities. Factional struggles within the party were to be fought out by out-radicalizing one's opponents, although sometimes the immediate needs of factional conflict could even override the need to impress party higher-ups. The debate that ensued was carried out in Bolshevik vocabulary and centered on how well the Jadids and Jadidism fit the political categories of the new regime. The "political essence" of the Jadids and Jadidism was now to be judged retroactively by a set of criteria external to their own experience. Given that class was not a meaningful category to the Jadids and that there was no tradition of political organization along socialist lines among the indigenous population before 1917, it was no surprise that the Jadids were all found to be ideologically and politically suspect in the debate that followed. More crucially, the new critique of Jadidism seamlessly tied the cultural production of the Jadids to their short-lived political activity in 1917–18, which in turn it folded into a generic evolving narrative of the rise of Soviet power divested of the colonial dimension of Central Asia. The party's framing of the question in this manner effectively transformed the parameters of debate in Uzbekistan.

Matters came to a head on the eve of the first conference of Uzbek "cultural workers" in January 1926. This was meant to be a gathering of Uzbek intellectuals to discuss cultural policy in the newly created republic, but it also provided the party an opportunity to differentiate honest cultural workers from superfluous old intellectuals. In the period leading up to the conference, a number of critical analyses of the Jadids appeared in the press. The charge was led by Uzbeks. Abdulhay Tojiyev, then secretary of the Tashkent obkom of the party and a Young Communist, divided Uzbek intellectuals into two groups, those who had appeared on the scene before the revolution and were all "nationalists [*milliyatchi*] and representatives of mercantile capital," and those who were the product of Soviet rule, who were national [*milliy*] and served workers and peasants.[16] Ikromov was less forgiving. Speaking at the conference, he declared the Jadids to be the mouthpieces of the "national bourgeoisie" in the region. In the period of rule by "khans, beks, and the Russian monarchy," the Jadids had been revolutionary, but the revolution made them redundant. In 1917, they had struggled for a national state and fought against Soviet power on the basis of a nationalism composed of Turanism, Turkism, and Islamism, all ideologies inimical to workers. Ikromov accused the intellectuals of seeking support of the counterrevolutionary Russian bourgeoisie as well as of the Basmachi. The "national bourgeoisie" might have been progressive under the Tsars, but with the triumph of the Bolsheviks, it

---

16. Abdulhay Tojiy, "Milliy ziyolilar o'rtasida ishlash to'g'risida," *Qizil O'zbekiston*, 11.01.1926.

had become reactionary and had allegedly allied itself with English imperialism, the flag bearer of the interests of world capitalism.[17]

Ikromov's speech set the tone for the rest of the year and the attacks on the Jadids escalated. In April, the publication of an elementary school textbook for Uzbek language created a scandal. Published by a group of authors that included Munavvar qori, the book was attacked for its "counterrevolutionary" and "narrow nationalist" content. For Nazir Inoyatiy, the head of the Uzbek Academic Center at Uzbek Commissariat of Education, the publisher of the book, the ideological (*mafkuraviy*) stance of the book was unacceptable for Soviet schools. He objected to the inclusion in the book of such sentences as "Do not make your enemy angry," and "Do not fight with those who are powerful," both of which went against the intent of the Soviet school to produce heroic fighters for the interests of the workers. "To poison the immature minds of children with such harmful thoughts is a great crime," he thundered.[18] Munavvar qori had been under surveillance since 1921: he had been allowed to work in the waqf administration but was shut out of the press. This was to be his last pedagogical work. The book was withdrawn and pulped and a corrected version published quickly.

Not all agreed in the party with this drastic course. The "national intelligentsia" accounted for the vast bulk of those with modern educations and the skills necessary for making the regime function. Simple excision from public life was easier said than done. Tojiyev, in his comment on the intelligentsia, had left open the possibility that the old intellectuals could be put to Soviet work: "Of course, [the party] does not want to cast them aside or to have no dealings with them. It would be wrong to do so. Of course, we have to use those old intellectuals who can be used, to work those who can be worked."[19] Rahimjon Inog'amov, the Young Communist commissar for education, had offered a qualified defense of the Jadids. Uzbek intellectuals, he argued, had played a revolutionary role before the revolution, when the strongest current among the Uzbeks was an aspiration for independence. After the revolution, some intellectuals chose the path of counterrevolution, such as the "patriotic idealist White intellectuals [*vatanparvar xayolparast oq ziyolilar*]" arrested in 1921, but others still had a role to play because of their possession of culture. "Our task should be to turn intellectuals who are close to the ideals of the Soviets into true servants of the Soviet order." Russian analyses, he went on to argue, did not always fit Uzbek realities because of Uzbekistan's backwardness and its colonial context, which dictated

---

17. "O'zbekiston madaniy-maorif xodimlari quriltoyida," *Qizil O'zbekiston*, 28.01.1926.

18. Nazir Inoyatiy, "Tanqid va mulohaza: 'Til saboqlig'i' ismli o'quv kitobiga bir nazar," *Qizil O'zbekiston*, 28.04.1926.

19. Tojiy, "Milliy ziyolilar o'rtasida."

the maximal use of all intellectual forces.[20] Stalin himself intervened, declaring it impermissible "to see the Uzbek non-Communist intelligentsia as a general reactionary mass and to threaten it indiscriminately with arrest, as is done by some comrades among you."[21] But Ikromov and his backers had their compulsions that kept them from any compromise. Ikromov needed to consolidate his own position in the party, and he used the issue of the intelligentsia to attack his rivals. The first casualty was Inog'amov himself. His disagreement with Ikromov led to him being charged with nationalism and "providing support to the nationalist intelligentsia," as well as with a variety of infractions of party discipline (factional activity, "pessimism").[22] His dissent was considered serious enough to earn the dreaded -shchina suffix, and as "Inogamovshchina" entered party history as an expression of unhealthy nationalism within the party. Inog'amov himself was posted to a low-level position in rural Qashqa Daryo okrug and constantly persecuted afterward.

A more significant rival to Ikromov was Fayzulla Xo'jayev. The two sat on the opposite sides of several key divides. The merger of Turkestani and Bukharan territories in the formation of Uzbekistan had created considerable rivalries between Turkestani and Bukharan politicians, who came from different political situations. Xo'jayev's past as a Young Bukharan and his base in Bukhara gave him a distinctly different profile than Ikromov, the Tashkent Young Communist. The political differences between the two were capped by mutual personal disdain. All through 1925, Xo'jayev had complained to the Sredazburo about intrigue against him within the party and the government, although nothing was proved to the satisfaction of the Sredazburo.[23] In this situation, the fate of Fitrat became the lightning rod for a new conflict between the two men. Fitrat had returned from Moscow on the eve of the delimitation, but appears to have avoided serious involvement with the state after that.[24] He worked with the Academic Center of the Commissariat of Education, which recommended his books for publication,[25] but he did not attend the January 1926 conference of "culture workers" and is said to have declined an offer to teach at the Central Asian Communist University (SAKU) or to work permanently at the Commissariat of Education.[26]

20. Rahim In'om, "Ziyolilar to'g'risida," Qizil O'zbekiston, 10.01.1926.
21. Stalin to Sredazburo and CC KPUz, RGASPI, f. 558, op. 11, d. 34, l. 56 (22.04.1926).
22. RGASPI, f. 62, op. 2, d. 470, ll. 150–151ob.
23. The correspondence occasioned by Fayzulla's anxieties can be followed in RGASPI, f. 62, op. 2, d. 189, ll. 71–100.
24. "Fitrat afandi Toshkentda," Turkiston, 07.09.1924.
25. Fitrat's name appears in the minutes of the Academic Center a few times in 1925 and 1926, but he does not seem to have been a regular participant; see TsGARUz, f. 94, op. 1, d. 246, ll. 5, 59, 60.
26. RGASPI, f. 17, op. 27, d. 2, l. 102ob.

There were disagreements within the party's leadership over how to deal with him. In early 1926, the agitation and propaganda division of the Central Committee blocked the publication of a book by Fitrat. Xo'jayev publicly questioned the wisdom of the censorship. "Fitrat's books are the property of our culture and do not contradict our policy,"[27] he said, and argued for greater finesse in handling the question of the intelligentsia.[28] The question of the role of the intelligentsia, and of Fitrat in particular, was discussed at length at the second plenum of KPUz in May, where Xo'jayev defended Fitrat from the harsh attacks of Ikromov and other Young Communists such as Hanifi Burnashev. Xo'jayev's intervention was at least partly responsible for ensuring that Fitrat remained free and that his books continued to be published, even if he was largely shut out of the press.

Xo'jayev's support saved Fitrat but he himself was not entirely secure. As the son of a millionaire and a champion of reform, Xo'jayev was an "old intellectual." He felt the need to present the Jadids in the vocabulary of the new regime. In a series of works published in 1926, he argued that the old intelligentsia was not a class, but a "stratum" that expressed the interests of a class, but also of the society within which it grew. Jadidism was thus not solely a bourgeois movement but also represented many semiproletarian groups in society. Nor was it homogenous: after the revolution, different groups of Jadids had gone different ways, with some of them becoming Communists, while others acquired a more reactionary tinge.[29] Xo'jayev's invocation of Central Asia's specificity to argue for considering the Jadids in their context did not, however, go very far. He was immediately attacked in the party's own press, with the historian P.G. Galuzo taking him to task for not using proper Marxist categories in his analysis, turning Young Bukharans into revolutionaries, and equating them with Communists.[30] Galuzo was joined by Ikromov himself in January 1927, who castigated those members of the party who "attempt to prove that Jadidism was the predecessor of the Communist Party," and connected that attitude to the continuing presence of nationalism in the party's ranks.[31]

Xo'jayev survived the attack, ignoring Ikromov and accusing Galuzo rather haughtily of not understanding Bukharan realities,[32] but there was no question

---

27. Ibid., l. 65.

28. Ibid., ll. 112–119.

29. F. Khodzhaev, "Dzhadidy," in *Ocherki revoliutsionnogo dvizheniia v Srednei Azii* (Moscow, 1926), 7–12; idem., "O Mlado-bukhartsakh," *Istorik-Marksist*, no. 1 (1926), 123–141; idem., *K istorii revoliutsii v Bukhare* (Tashkent, 1926).

30. G. Turkestanskii [P.G. Galuzo], *Kto takie byli dzhadidy* (Tashkent, 1926). This pamphlet contained the text of two reviews by Galuzo, which were also published in Uzbek in the party's official theoretical organ: G. Turkistonskiy, "Bir ta'rixiy hujjat to'g'risida," *Kommunist*, 1926, no. 11: 8–25.

31. Akmal Ikromov, "Bor'ba za partiiu," *Pravda Vostoka*, 07.01.1927, and "Protiv izvrashchenii linii Partii," *Pravda Vostoka*, 24.01.1927.

32. Fayzulla Xo'jayev, "Izoh va javob," *Kommunist*, 1927, 1–2: 106–116.

that political force was with Ikromov. Xo'jayev could not prevail in the debate over the nature of the Jadids and indeed was compelled to revise his analysis, which he did in new editions of his history of the revolution in Bukhara.[33] The landscape had shifted. The party had begun to assert its monopoly on the representation of Central Asia's history, which had to fit into universal categories. It was the universalism of Marxism that had attracted many indigenous elites to the Soviets, but increasingly the Russian narrative of the Russian revolution came to stand in for universal categories. As the party canonized a single reading of "October," the events in Russia came to stand in for the universal.[34] Central Asians could at best contribute to a larger drama rooted somewhere else. The specificities of their own history—their colonial subjugation and their very different social and economic conjunctures—had to be subordinated to a generic narrative of the rise of the proletariat. "October" had arrived in Central Asia in the form of the seizure of power by the Tashkent soviet. The settler-colonial nature of that event, or the fact that the revolution had been turned upside down in the region, had no place in this authorized narrative. Instead, modernist intellectuals could be faulted for lacking proletarian credentials in a society that had no proletariat. Most Central Asian intellectuals had mapped the recent past of their society quite differently. Laziz Azizzoda had prepared a study of modern Central Asia as a doctoral dissertation at the Institute of the National and Ethnic Cultures of the Peoples of the East in Moscow. Titled *The History of the Awakening of Turkestan*, it traced the recent history of Turkestan as one of "awakening" through the cultural work of modernist intellectuals whose cultural ferment created political struggles within Turkestani society as well as with the colonial order. His text devoted a great deal of attention to the events of 1916, which for him represented the progression of intellectual ferment into the realm of politics, and then the political struggles of 1917 in Tashkent and Bukhara, but it barely mentioned the events of Petrograd.[35] Azizzoda was arrested on the day of his defense and charged with nationalism.[36] Several years later, Sulaymon Xo'jayev, one of the first Uzbek film directors, chose to make his first major film, *Tong oldidan* (Before the Dawn), on 1916. The focus

---

33. This episode has been examined in detail by Gero Fedtke, "Jadids, Young Bukharans, Communists, and the Bukharan Revolution: From an Ideological Debate in the Early Soviet Union," in *Muslim Culture in Russia and Central Asia from the 18th to the Early 20th Centuries*, ed. Anke von Kügelgen, Michael Kemper, and Allen J. Frank, vol. 2 (Berlin, 1998), 483–512.

34. On the canonization of a narrative of the October revolution, see Frederick Corney, *Telling October: Memory and the Making of the Bolshevik Revolution* (Ithaca, 2004), who unfortunately does not explore the implications of the canonization for the non-Russians of the USSR.

35. The actual text of the dissertation did not survive, but a recopied version is available at the Beruni Institute of Oriental Studies, where Azizzoda worked after his journey through the Gulag; see Laziz Azizzoda, "Turkistonning uyg'onish tarixi" (ms., 1968), O'zFAShI inv. 11895.

36. Laziz Azizzoda, "Avtobiografiia" (ms., 1975, in possession of the author), 6.

on colonial oppression rather than on class struggle marked the film as nationalist. It was made but never released. Xo'jayev was expelled from the party in 1931 and arrested a few years later.[37] Central Asia could only be represented on Soviet terms. A decade later, these historiographical conundrums were resolved by the proclaiming the Russian conquest to be "the lesser evil" that saved Central Asia from British imperialism and brought it in touch with "progressive Russian thought," but its logic lurked already in transformations of cultural politics of the mid-1920s.[38] No wonder, then, that Fayzulla Xo'jayev's pleading for local specificities of Central Asian history went only so far in 1926.

The opening of the ideological front turned the very term *ziyoli* into one of abuse. The play on words equating *ziyoli* ("enlightened") with *ziyonli* ("harmful") became commonplace, so that there was nothing new when Komiljon Alimov, another Young Communist, proclaimed at a meeting that "our older brothers the intellectuals [ziyoli] have become harmful [ziyonli]."[39] The new "culture workers" avoided the term and called themselves *madaniyatchi*. Over the course of 1926 and 1927, the attacks on the Jadids grew in intensity. By the time of the Second Uzbekistan Conference of Culture Workers in October 1927, the mood of their opponents was triumphant. A long diatribe against Cho'lpon by Shokir Sulaymon drew prolonged applause, but the apocalyptic moment of the conference came when Ikromov, in his keynote address, rounded on Vadud Mahmud for pointed criticism. Mahmud was present in the hall. All the madaniyatchi reportedly got to their feet and began to shout, "Enough! Away with such people!! Vadud, get lost!!!" They kept up the shouting until Mahmud left. Botu wrote gloatingly, "Red cultural workers of all Uzbekistan shamed an opponent of proletarian ideology and kicked him out of their midst."[40]

A Soviet Uzbek Intelligentsia

The young men who packed the conferences of culture workers in 1926 and 1927 were the first fruit of Soviet institutions. They included graduates of teachers training institutes and rabfaks, although the bulk of their numbers were made

37. Cloé Drieu, *Fictions nationales: Cinéma, empire et nation en Ouzbékistan (1919–1937)* (Paris, 2013), 256–282.

38. On the "lesser evil" and other aspects of the Soviet-era historiography of the nationalities, Lowell Tillett, *The Great Friendship: Soviet Historians on the Non-Russian Nationalities* (Chapel Hill, 1969), remains indispensable.

39. Komiljon Alimov, "Sho'ro madaniyatchilari va uning vazifalari," *Qizil O'zbekiston*, 06.06.1927.

40. Botu, "Qizil madaniyatchilar g'alabasi," *Qizil O'zbekiston*, 11.10.1927. Criticism of Cho'lpon continued beyond the podium; Komil Aliyev, "'Aqlli jinni," *Qizil O'zbekiston*, 12.10.1927, denounced Cho'lpon "who froths at the mouth about nation and homeland and as a result is ready to sell the homeland to the bourgeoisie and to English capital."

up of men with even more modest accomplishments: school teachers churned out by crash courses, rural correspondents for the press, literate activists in the village. Across the Soviet Union, the party had encouraged worker and peasant correspondents (*rabsel'kory*) to report on life in the factory, in the fields, and at home for the press. The party's hope was to mobilize support for its policies amongst the population, to attract ordinary people in Soviet work, but also to enable people to use the new press to challenge the established structures of authority.[41] In 1927, *Qizil O'zbekiston* boasted 610 correspondents, and all but 63 of whom were under the age of thirty.[42] In addition to contributing to the newspaper, they organized wall newspapers (of which there were 224). As with the Zhenotdel delegates, correspondents often faced the wrath of the population amongst whom they lived, and beatings and even murders of correspondents were common.[43] (For this reason, many writers used pseudonyms or initials, and indeed Soviet law forbade on pain of punishment the outing of writers who chose this path.)[44] This was a new group of Soviet intellectuals. Opposition from within society was an enduring bond in their sense of the self and the sense of mission that allowed them to attack their elders. It was they who terrorized the prerevolutionary and the early revolutionary intelligentsia, it was they who led the charge for a proletarian culture, even as an Uzbek proletariat failed to come into being. A report on party work in 1924 had referred to such people as a "petty intelligentsia."[45] A more apt term for them from within the Marxist lexicon might have been *lumpenintelligentsia*, for the group served the party well as a battering ram against the intelligentsia.

The Sredazburo also worked to "Bolshevize the press," even as it began to expand the number of periodicals being published. In April 1925, it invited all newspaper editors to a meeting to discuss the "creation of Bolshevik journalism in our national press" and to issue new directives.[46] In October, commissions at volost and oblast levels were looking through libraries and reading rooms to exclude "harmful books" from use.[47] The old-style maktab came under ever

---

41. See Jennifer Clibbon, "The Soviet Press and Grass-Roots Organization: The Rabkor Movement, NEP to the First Five-Year Plan" (Ph.D. diss., University of Toronto, 1993); Matthew Lenoe, *Closer to the Masses: Stalinist Culture, Social Revolution, and Soviet Newspapers* (Cambridge, MA, 2004), 105–108.

42. "'Qizil O'zbekiston' gazeta boshqormasi qoshidagi muxbirlar bo'limining ishlaridan hisobot," RGASPI, f. 62, op. 2, d. 1182, ll. 22–23.

43. Behlulzoda, "Shahrisabz muxbirlariga yana hujum," *Muxbirlar yo'ldoshi*, no. 2 (August 1929), 31; Sobir Abdulla, "O'tmas teshalar," *Muxbirlar yo'ldoshi*, no. 5–6 (July 1930), 31–34.

44. A., "Xotin-qiz muxbirlari ham ularning vazifalari," *Yangi yo'l*, 1927, no. 4: 18.

45. "Obshchie usloviia raboty TsK KPT," TsGARUz, f. 25, op. 1, d. 1351, l. 287.

46. RGASPI, f. 62, op. 2, d. 408, l. 40 (20.05.1925).

47. TsGARUz, f. 94, op. 1, d. 202, l. 26.

greater criticism, with Rahimjon Inog'amov, the commissar for education, describing it as an anti-Soviet institution and a bastion of counterrevolution,[48] and very quickly the discussion turned to the abolition of the maktab and its replacement by Soviet schools (see chapter 11). In general, the years 1925 and 1926 saw considerable investment and effort in strengthening the party's presence in the public space. The operations of all the periodicals funded by the Central Committee were consolidated in one agency, while a number of new titles appeared: *Kambag'al dehqon* (Poor Peasant), a "mass newspaper" for peasants; *Yer yuzi* (The World), an illustrated general interest magazine; *Yangi yo'l* (New Path), the illustrated organ of the Zhenotdel aimed at women; as well as *Kommunist* (Communist) and *Yosh leninchi* (Young Leninist), journals for the members of the party and the Komsomol respectively. For the press, 1927 was a turning point, as new appointments to editorial positions brought greater control over the political line. The Sredazburo and the Central Committee of KPUz both kept tabs on the "political trustworthiness" of those who worked in the press, even if reliable journalists remained in short supply. "As for comrades who are well developed and who can be transferred to more responsible work in the press," the Uzbek Central Committee admitted to Moscow in 1927, "they do not exist in [Uzbekistan's] editorial offices, since in general the quality of press workers in Uzbekistan is very limited."[49] Nevertheless, by 1929, almost all editorial positions in periodicals controlled by the party or the Uzbek government were in the hands of Uzbeks who were members of the party or the Komsomol. None of them had any experience of public life before 1922, let alone 1917.[50] The results of this tightening control were clear, as both tone and content changed in the press. Gone were the feuilletons that slipped into local national discourses, the small news items that provided unauthorized glimpses into everyday life, or poems or cartoons that conveyed ambiguous messages. They were replaced by much more solid party-speak, with its exhortations of eternal vigilance and barely concealed menace to a vast array of enemies, with an ever greater abundance of slogans, and, always, speeches.

The displacement of the Jadids was not simply the work of these anonymous figures. By the mid-1920s, a new cohort of accomplished writers had

48. Rahim Oxunjon o'g'li In'omov, "O'zbekiston xalq maorif kamisari o'rtoq Rahim Oxunjon o'g'li In'omovning Yoshlar Ittifoqi Markaziy qo'mitasining yalpi majlisda qilg'an ma'ruzasi," *Maorif va o'qitg'uvchi*, 1925, no. 7–8: 6–9.

49. RGASPI, f. 62, op. 4, d. 163, l. 155 (25.05.1927).

50. "Spisok sotrudnikov redaktsii...," RGASPI, f. 62, op. 2, d. 1996, ll. 84–87. The one editor who was not a party member was Shokir Sulaymon, who was responsible for both *Yer yuzi* and *Xudosizlar*. In terms of age and experience, however, he did not differ from the rest.

ياش ئەزبيلەرسزدەن غەفور غولام   ياش ئەزبيلەرسزدەن عەمەلە خانم   ئيمكى قەرغانە، گ زىتەمىسطلئ موخارىرمرى نو ئولنە عاليمى

FIGURE 6.   New Soviet Uzbek writers: left to right, G'afur G'ulom, Amala xonim, and Lutfulla Olimiy. *Yer yuzi* (15.12.1929), 5. Courtesy Library of Congress.

arrived on the scene, even younger than the Jadids, with an outlook that was not shaped by prerevolutionary struggles. This was effectively a new generation, the successors—and competitors—not just to the Jadids (Fitrat, Cho'lpon, Qodiriy) but also to the early-revolutionary intelligentsia (G'ozi Yunus, Elbek, Azizzoda). This new cohort "spoke Bolshevik" much better than their elders, although their command of the new language was seldom perfect.[51] Like the Young Communists in the party, members of this new cohort saw themselves as the real upholders of the new order, which they understood better than their elders. They were clearly enthused by the promises of the revolution and the path to the future that it opened up. They were comfortable in Soviet modernity in a way that the Jadids were not. G'afur G'ulom's portrait from 1929 (see figure 6), speaks a thousand words in this regard. A decade and a half earlier, Fitrat had scandalized Bukhara by returning from his travels dressed as an Istanbul dandy. Now, modern dress was taken for granted by all. Above all, perhaps, this was simply a generational revolt fueled by disdain for elders in an age of rapid change. Ideological and political posturing was deeply intertwined with personal rivalries and jealousies.

The new generation had mixed fortunes. Although their work appeared side by side in the pages of the Uzbek press of the 1920s, their fates were radically different. Some, such as Oybek (1905–58), G'afur G'ulom (1903–66), and Hamid

51. On "speaking Bolshevik," see Steve Kotkin, *Magnetic Mountain: Stalinism as a Civilization* (Berkeley, 1995), chap. 5.

Olimjon (1909–44), became the founding fathers of Soviet Uzbek literature. Once they had survived the terror of 1937–38, they were copiously awarded and praised; not only did they become household names, but their names were attached to streets, schools, publishing houses, and metro stations, and their visages adorned friezes and busts around Uzbekistan. Others, such as G'ayratiy (Abdurahim Abdullayev, 1902–76) and Mirtemir (1910–78), may not have found such enduring fame, but they too lived productive lives well into the Brezhnev years. Still others, such as Botu or Ziyo Said, were purged alongside those whom they criticized, but were remembered fondly, and their names and works were retrieved in the late Soviet era. But there are those, such as Qamchinbek, Anqaboy, or Amala-xonim, the first woman prose writer in Uzbek, have been almost entirely forgotten.

Some of them had backgrounds remarkably similar to those of the Jadids or had been their disciples. Indeed, some of those who became canonized as founding fathers of Uzbek Soviet literature were in many ways closer to the early revolutionary cohort of Elbek and Laziz Azizzoda than to this new cohort. Oybek (Muso Toshmuhammad o'g'li, 1905–68) began his studies at the Namuna new-method school in Tashkent in 1919, where he might have been taught by Munavvar qori, the school's founder.[52] In 1921, he matriculated at the teachers training institute in Tashkent, where he became editor of the wall newspaper. He joined the Komsomol and embarked on a bright educational career, entering the Central Asian Communist University in 1925 and being sent to the Plekhanov Institute of Economics in Leningrad in 1927. Ill health forced him to leave Leningrad in 1929. But during Oybek's time at the teachers training institute, the institute was headed by Shohid Eson, a Tashkent native who had studied in Istanbul, and who introduced Oybek to Cho'lpon and to Turkish poetry.[53] He was deeply impressed by Cho'lpon and on several occasions defended him from attacks of the madaniyatchi. At the teachers institute he also met Zarifa Saidnosirova, the daughter of Saidnosir Mirjalilov, and married her in 1929 while Mirjalilov was still serving time in the Solovetsky Islands! G'afur G'ulom was born in a Tashkent family of high cultural capital. One of his uncles was a published poet and his father regularly entertained literary figures at his house. He attended a maktab and a Russo-native school before becoming a teacher himself. Over the next decade, he worked in the interrelated worlds of education and

---

52. Naim Karimov, *Oybek va Zarifa: muhabbat va sadoqat dostoni* (Tashkent, 2005).

53. The institute had been founded in 1919 as a *rüşdiye* (middle) school by Talât Bey, an Ottoman POW. After the departure of the Turks, it was turned into a teachers' institute (technicum). A. X., "Maktabimizning qisqacha tarixi," *Tong yulduzi*, no. 1 (March 1925): 5.

the press and began writing. He was active in the Komsomol early on.[54] Two of the cohort's most prominent members, Botu and Romiz, had been members of Chig'atoy Gurungi and deeply involved in the cultural politics of the early Soviet years alongside the Jadids.

Others did have different trajectories. Many of them studied in Russia and found the experience transformative. They returned enthused by currents of cultural radicalism to which they were exposed. Those who attended the Communist University of the Toilers of the East in Moscow tended to be the most radical, with a well-articulated disdain for all others. A prime example was that of Qamchinbek (Abdulla Gaynullin), whose star shone briefly in the 1920s.[55] Others who returned as committed Bolsheviks and harsh critics of their elders included Young Communists such as Usmonxon Eshonxo'jayev, Rahimjon Inog'amov, and of course, Akmal Ikromov. But study in Moscow was not necessary. Hamid Olimjon was born and raised in Jizzax, where he finished middle school before attending the teachers institute in Samarqand. He began teaching and writing upon graduation in 1929.[56] He worked at many newspapers and magazines while being active in the Komsomol. G'ayratiy also studied at Munavvar qori's Namuna school in 1917–18 and went on to teach in a middle school from 1919 to 1923 before going to Baku for advanced studies in pedagogy. He returned to Tashkent in 1926, but he had already begun to appear in print in Turkestan in early 1924.[57] He was the self-proclaimed bard of the new order and a disdainful critic of his elders. Ziyo Said (1903–38) had attended only the party-soviet school in Tashkent but risen rapidly to become editor of Qizil O'zbekiston by 1927. He was also a prolific playwright. He had been in the party since 1919 and over the years had worked for the Cheka (most likely in Ferghana during the civil war).[58] Sotti Husayn (1906–42) went to Moscow only in 1934–35, well after he had made his name as a Komsomol purist and a harsh critic of nonproletarian trends in Uzbek literature. Born in 1906 in Kokand, he came to Tashkent and enrolled at the Central Asian Communist University. Because of his poor Russian, he asked to be put into "practical work" and was posted to the Yosh leninchi (Young Leninist),

54. XX asr o'zbek adabiyoti tarixi (Tashkent, 1999), 225–229.

55. Naim Karimov, XX asr adabiyoti manzaralari (Tashkent, 2008), 294–295.

56. XX asr o'zbek adabiyoti tarixi, 243.

57. On G'ayratiy, see O'zbekiston milliy entsiklopediyasi, 12 vols. (Tashkent, 2000–2006), 11:219; his first publication to my knowledge was the poem, "Ko'klam," Turkiston, 29.03.1924.

58. RGASPI, f. 62, op. 4, d. 163, l. 121 (personnel file, 03.03.1927).

FIGURE 7. The literary circle at *Yosh leninchi*: second row, seated from left to right, A'zam Ayub, Qayum Ramazon, Sotti Husayn, Abdulla Avloniy, Tiregulov, Olim Sharafiddinov, G'ayratiy. The most remarkable thing about this photograph is the presence in a place of honor of Abdulla Avloniy, a prominent Jadid before 1917, who had largely fallen silent after 1920. *Yer yuzi*, 1928, no. 10: 14. Courtesy Library of Congress.

where he organized a literary circle that produced many firebrands (see figure 7).[59] Husayn's radicalism came at a price to his personal life too. His father, who owned a shop in Kokand, was accused of being a wealthy haberdasher (although he himself claimed to be a simple grocer) and was deprived of his rights for that reason. Husayn cut off relations with his father and moved his mother and minor siblings to Tashkent under his care.[60]

But it was Mannon Romiz and Botu who carried the banner of Soviet authority in culture at the outset of the ideological front. Romiz had entered public life after the revolution with the usual combination of teaching and journalism. We find him heading the education department of the Tashkent old-city soviet in 1920, when he was also active in the Chig'atoy Gurungi. His involvement in the education department pitted him against the ulama in the struggle over waqf revenues

---

59. Husayn's autobiographical note from his party file is available now as "Avtobiografiia" (21.01.1940) in *Tarixning noma'lum sahifalari: hujjat va materiallar*, ed. Naim Karimov, bk. 1 (Tashkent, 2009), 150–162; see also Sirojiddin Ahmad, "Zafar va mag'lubiyat," *Sharq yulduzi*, 2007, no. 1: 149–156.

60. RGASPI, f. 121, op. 1, d. 543.

and he seems to have taken ever more radical positions in the years that followed.[61] He also negotiated a successful passage through the institutions of power, rising to become editor of a number of periodical publications, including *Turkiston* and *Qizil O'zbekiston*. In 1928 he was commissar for education and editor of *Alanga* (Flame), the magazine for the propagation of the Latin alphabet, and of *Xudosizlar* (The Godless), the journal for the dissemination of atheism published by the Central Committee of KPUz. Botu was the enfant terrible of Uzbek literature. His extreme youth and his cultural radicalism went hand in hand. He was a member of the Izchilar in 1918–19 and of the Chig'atoy Gurungi. He was publishing alongside Fitrat and Cho'lpon before he was out of his teens, taking part in the debates over language and culture, and arguing for Latinization in 1921, when the subject was not even on the agenda in Turkestan. He went off to Moscow in 1921, where he spent six years, returning to Uzbekistan in 1927 with a degree in economics and advanced credentials as a party ideologue. He was appointed instructor at the Central Committee of KPUz and embarked on short-lived career in the party, rising to commissar of education in early 1929. In Moscow, he had been on friendly terms with both Fitrat and Cho'lpon (who had apparently helped pick a name for Botu's son with his Russian wife).[62] But his views had diverged from them. In 1925, Botu broke with Cho'lpon publicly, proclaiming:

Sen o'zga banda, men o'zga bir kuch	You are a slave to yourself, I am my own force
Fikring, xoyaling yo'qlikda kezman.	I visit your thoughts, your dreams in nonexistence.
Nurlarga qarshi rejang, ishing puch	Your plan against light, your cause is hollow
G'oyamning amri g'oyangni kesmak.[63]	My cause commands fighting your cause.

After that, the tenor of his poetry grew ever more radical, as did his view on the legacy of his elders. In late 1928, he wrote that Jadidism could never get beyond the limits of "madrasa literature," and after the revolution, "continued to fill the minds of schoolchildren with the poison of homeland and nation."[64]

---

61. Little concrete is known about Romiz's life before he rose to prominence. An official autobiography (exceptionally sketchy and undated to boot) can be found in RGASPI, f. 62, op. 4, d. 633, l. 100–100ob. We do know that he took part in the 1921 conference on language and orthographic reform and was active in Turkestan's waqf administration (TsGARUz, f. 25, op. 1, d. 1029, l. 74).

62. Naim Karimov, "Shoirning fojiali taqdiri," preface to Botu, *Tanlangan asarlar*, ed. Naim Karimov and Sherali Turdiyev (Tashkent, 2004), 5–11.

63. Botu, "Javobim," quoted in Naim Karimov, *Istiqlolni uyg'otgan shoir* (Tashkent, 2000), 28.

64. Botu, "O'zbek adabiyotining o'ktabir inqilobi so'ng'i davriga bir qarash," *Alanga*, no. 10–11 (1928), 3–4.

This was a new language of criticism, completely alien to Abdurahmon Sa'diy, with whom we began this chapter. It had several key features. It ascribed a class position to each author, whose work was seen as transparently conveying the interests of that class. It carried boundless hope in the power of the internationalist Soviet project to bring goodness to Central Asia. And it criticized any special pleading as nationalism (*millatchilik*) and patriotism (*vatanparastlik*), both of which were irredeemably evil expressions of a class-specific (and anti-Soviet) ideology. Later Soviet critics were to call this "vulgar sociologism," but at the time this language served to make nationalism unequivocally evil, so evil indeed that it did not even have to be rhetorically paired with "great power chauvinism" in the critique.

We see the workings of this new language very clearly in the polemics around the figure of Cho'lpon. The first salvo was launched in February 1927 by the young writer Olim Sharafiddinov, another member of the Komsomol literary circle at *Yosh leninchi*. Acknowledging that "the Uzbek literary language of today is doubtless Cho'lpon's language," Sharafiddinov nevertheless went on to ask, "Who is Cho'lpon? Whose poet is he?" The answer was not pleasant: "Cho'lpon ... is a poet of the nationalist, patriotic, pessimist intelligentsia [*millatchi, vatanparast badbin ziyolilarning shoiridir*]. His ideology is the ideology of this group." Cho'lpon's nationalism led him to see all Russians as colonizers, to blame them, regardless of class, for "all the wretchedness afflicting Uzbekistan." Sharafiddinov's conclusion was perhaps not too far off the mark, but he could not pursue its implications to their logical conclusion, namely that "Cho'lpon is happy with the revolution, he is only not happy with the Russians and their staying behind in the 'homeland.'"[65]

Cho'lpon was defended in print by Oybek, who was about to set off for Leningrad. Oybek argued that it was foolish to expect Cho'lpon to be a poet of the proletariat, for proletarian ideology could be acquired only through struggle and life experience, and "not by reading a couple of books or listening to a few lectures." This was the reason why "to this day, proletarian poets have not emerged among us." Cho'lpon's lack of his proletarian ideology was not the most significant thing about him, however. Oybek's argument was aesthetic, and he played on Sharafiddinov's words to make it. Sharafiddinov had used the word *xayol-parast* to mean "idealist." The semantic range of the word *xayol* in Uzbek extends from *idea(l)* through *imagination* to *fantasy*, and Oybek played on that to argue that if "nationalism and imagination [*xayol*] were tied to one another, then all poets would be nationalist," for one cannot be a poet without imagination. Indeed, imagination was necessary even in mathematics (and Oybek brought the authority of Lenin himself to bear on this point). Cho'lpon's contribution was to create

---

65. Ayn [Olim Sharafiddinov], "O'zbek shoiri Cho'lpon," *Qizil O'zbekiston*, 14.02.1927.

a new poetics in accordance with the artistic tastes of the time, which was why "the young generation of today loves his simple language, his delicious style, his technique." Cho'lpon was like Pushkin, a poet who did not write for the poor, whose politics "does not accord with the today's ideology," but who was nevertheless loved by "our Russian brothers" regardless of class. "Pushkin remained Pushkin even after the revolution," Oybek stated, because "his works created the immortal richness of Russian literature."[66]

Oybek was criticized in turn by Usmonxon Eshonxo'jayev who took time off from his studies on Moscow to unleash the full arsenal of historical materialism and the dialectic (much of which he had to quote in the Russian original) on Oybek. For Eshonxo'jayev, Oybek was a fool to argue that one could separate the form and the aesthetics from the content of a piece of art. At a time "when, with the mercy of history, the culture of the Uzbek nation is being formed under the leadership of workers and peasants," it was impossible to stay neutral. Cho'lpon was a nationalist, and that made him an idealist and a utopian. "The defect and the harmfulness of Chol'pon's poetics lies in its ideology . . . which from the point of view of our time is reactionary. . . . The poet is an idealist and an individualist, and therefore sees every political and social event not from the side of the masses but from his own personal point of view."[67]

The sophomoric nature of this polemic immediately strikes the reader. Sharafiddinov, Oybek, and Eshonxo'jayev were all very young and experimenting with a genre that was brand new in Uzbek letters. The Uzbek vocabulary of Soviet criticism, not to mention Marxism in general, remained unsettled. While party resolutions and speeches of major Bolshevik figures were routinely published in Uzbek, theoretical works were only a trickle, while the works of Marx, Engels, and Lenin became available only from the 1930s on.[68] But it was more than a question of new vocabulary. The young firebrands of this era did not command the political language of the era with any confidence, least of all because that language also had an unsettling tendency to change without a moment's notice as the party line shifted constantly in these years.[69]

Eshonxo'jayev's intervention also sheds light on another dimension of the "ideological front." It was intrinsically connected to the new political game in

---

66. Oybek, "Cho'lpon: shoirni qanday tekshirish kerak," *Qizil O'zbekiston*, 17.05.1927.

67. [Usmonxon] Eshonxo'jayev, "Munaqqidning 'munaqqidi,'" *Qizil O'zbekiston*, 22.06.1927, 23.06.1927.

68. A. Guseinov, "Klassiki Marksizma-Leninzma na iazykakh narodov SSSR," *Revoliutsionnyi Vostok*, 1935, no. 3: 195–201; A. Akhmedov, "K istorii perevoda i izdaniia trudov klassikov Marksizma-Leninizma v Uzbekistane v 20-e gody," *Obshchestvennye nauki v Uzbekistane*, 1967, no. 6: 59–60.

69. Boybo'ta Do'stqorayev, "Bir munozara tarixidan," *Sharq yulduzi*, 1989, no. 6: 195. The same point was made at the time about a different polemic by the Orientalist A. Arsharuni, "Zametki o khudozhestvennoi literature Sr. Azii," *Novyi Vostok*, no. 26–27 (1929): 364–368.

town, one that required the constant assertion and reassertion of one's ideological purity and political steadfastness, which often came at the expense of
one's colleagues and competitors. Eshonxo'jayev was also from Andijon and
had known Cho'lpon since childhood. They had gone to similar schools and
their paths had crossed on many other occasions, and during his tenure at the
Commissariat of Education between 1922 and 1924, Eshonxo'jayev had helped
Cho'lpon find work.[70] His sudden attack on Cho'lpon perhaps had as much to do
with Eshonxo'jayev's struggle with Ikromov as with any animus toward the poet.
Eshonxo'jayev had been a fellow Young Communist with Ikromov, but the two
had fallen out after Ikromov's ascension to office. Eshonxo'jayev was in Moscow,
studying at the Institute of Red Professoriate, and mobilizing support among
Uzbek students in Moscow against Ikromov. Eshonxo'jayev's attack on Cho'lpon
was a way of asserting his own ideological steadfastness. Ikromov's enthusiasm
for the "ideological front" too cannot simply be explained by his cultural radicalism. He himself had shared the passions of the Jadids, having first appeared in
print in 1919 enthusing about the possibilities opened up by the Russian revolution to liberate the Hejaz and its holy places from British rule. But at a time
when the party's line was rapidly changing, constant reinvention of the self was
the order of the day. In all of this, the "old intelligentsia" made an easy target for
settling scores within the party. This was worse than cold comfort for the Jadids.
The younger generation's attack on the Jadids involved a degree of parricide and
many individual betrayals, the details of which we might never know in full.[71]

The Jadids Besieged

For the Jadids, the new situation was terrible, and they responded to it in different
fashions. Some avoided the spotlight, retreating into scholarly work, while others
sought to refashion themselves to stay in public life and to be able to contribute
to education and culture. Some made public expressions of loyalty or repentance.
Fitrat published an article in *Qizil O'zbekiston* in which he criticized the "old intellectuals" and suggested reform of the old-method school in a voice that pretended
to be that of the Soviet order.[72] He also published a play titled *Arslon* that depicted

---

70. Karimov, *Istiqlolni uyg'otgan shoir*, 40.

71. Both Romiz and Tojiy had been students of Munavvar qori's at the Namuna school; see
Munavvar qori Abdurashidxonov, *Xotiralar*, in *Tanlangan asarlar* (Tashkent, 2003), 239.

72. Fitrat, "Eski maktablarni nima qilish kerak," *Qizil O'zbekiston*, 06.03.1927. In chapter 8, I
argued against scholars who insist on reading Fitrat's antireligious works as coded critiques of the
Soviet order. In this case, however, the tone is so uncharacteristic of the rest of Fitrat's work that one
can safely assume that it was written as a way of signaling a sort of truce with the party.

the land reform then being carried out. Cho'lpon wrote an open letter to the presidium of the Second Congress of Culture Workers in which he admitted to having made "mistakes" and having expressed "nationalist and patriotic" views in the recent past. However, he also reminded the readers of his services to the revolution during the civil war and announced his resolve to rectify his mistakes and to work for the Soviet order.[73] Over the next two years, he wrote plays on land reform and unveiling.[74] Abdulla Qodiriy was sentenced to two years in prison but pardoned by the Central Executive Committee of Uzbekistan.[75] After that, he managed to get published but he was never employed in the press again. He used his unemployment to write. *O'tkan kunlar* (Bygone Days), the magisterial novel of Uzbek life before the Russian conquest, had just been published when Qodiriy was arrested. It was a stunning success. The press run of the first edition of its first volume was ten thousand copies, an astounding figure given the low rates of literacy, and it sold out in weeks. Qodiriy published a second novel, *Mehrobdan choyon* (Scorpion in the Altar), another historical work, in 1928 and continued to appear in the pages of *Mushtum* as a freelancer.[76] Yet this success was always overshadowed by political criticisms of his work. Writing in the pages of the Sredazburo's official organ, M. Sheverdin welcomed the appearance of the first novel in Uzbek and acknowledged that Qodiriy was "a master of the word," but nevertheless found that "the ideology of the novel is not ours." The novel fetishized the quotidian practices of the past, celebrated family life, was full of references to Islam, and contained "not the slightest representation of the lower classes of the population." As Sheverdin concluded in italics, *"Qodiriy has given us not a historical novel, not a picture of the epoch, but an idealized description of the rising merchant class."*[77] Sheverdin also expressed his surprise that the Uzbek press had published nothing on the subject and denied "the young author" the benefit of criticism. (As if to make up for the lapses of his peers, Sotti Husayn, much younger than Qodiriy, took up the challenge and unleashed a fusillade of articles aimed at the novel in the pages of *Sharq haqiqati*, the organ of the Tashkent obkom of the party, in which he attacked the "reactionary, romantic, nationalist essence" of the book.)

Others sought to gain acceptance through hard work on Soviet themes. G'ozi Yunus, who had held forth against the Bolsheviks in January 1918 and traveled to

---

73. "O'zbekiston ijtimoiy sho'rolar jumhuriyatining ikkinchi qurultoyi muhtaram riyosat hay'atiga Cho'lpon (Abdulhamid Sulaymon) tomonidan e'tiroz," *Maorif va o'qitg'uvchi*, 1927, no. 12.

74. The plays, *Mushtumzo'r* (Kulak) and *Zamona xotini* (Contemporary Woman), have apparently not survived; for plot summaries, see Salohiddin Mamajonov, "Cho'lponning nasriy va dramaturgik ijodi," in *Cho'lponning badiiy olami* (Tashkent, 1994), 66–67. They did not do him much good; *Mushtumzo'r* was harshly criticized not just for its political, but also its esthetic shortcomings by Sotti Husayn: S. Husayn, "Mushtumzo'r," *Qizil O'zbekiston*, 04.01.1929.

75. Boqiy, "Qatlnoma," *Sharq yulduzi*, 1991, no. 6: 125.

76. Habibulla Qodiriy, *Otamdan xotira*, 216.

77. M. Sheverdin, "Pervyi uzbekskii roman," *Za Partiiu*, 1928, no. 3: 88–96.

the Ottoman Empire in search of military assistance in the summer of that year, published a dozen plays in 1926 and 1927 for use in political education, many of them translated from Azerbaijani or Tatar. Elbek likewise did yeoman service in the realm of pedagogy and textbook production. Along with three Russian pedagogues, he worked with the students at the Karl Leibknecht Experimental School to create a set of textbooks for Uzbek elementary schools. In terms of their size, their organization, and their technical excellence, they were by far the most professional textbooks published to date for Uzbek schools. Munavvar qori made an effort at conciliation. By 1927, he was in the grip of the OGPU, with whom he had begun to negotiate. He was asked to provide a written testimony (*pokazanie*) of what he knew about non-Soviet actors, "Jadids" and "nationalists," in Uzbekistan. (This is the text that circulates as Munavvar qori's "memoirs" in Uzbekistan today.) Undoubtedly a part of the same strategy was his appearance at the Tashkent okrug conference of cultural workers in June 1927, where, in a sort of concession speech, he "admitted his mistakes" and offered his readiness to work with the party. (Indeed, the headline in *Qizil O'zbekiston* simply declared, "The Father of the Jadids Munavvar Qori Admits his Mistakes.") He argued that in the conditions of Turkestan of twenty years earlier, any struggle for modern education (and against the ulama) was "progressive" by its nature. He also reminded the audience, no doubt to its consternation, that Jadid schools had produced many people who were now held responsible positions in Soviet institutions. He readily accepted the superiority of the party: "Over the course of thirty years, we could not carry out land reform and unveiling. The Bolshevik party has accomplished these in ten years. . . . We are ready to support the revolution." He ended with a plea: "One or two Jadids have sinned, [but] it is not good to tar all of them with the same brush." None of this was enough. Sotti Husayn mocked Munavvar qori's claim that the Jadids were ready to join the revolution, and in his concluding address, Komiljon Alimov heaped condescension on Munavvar qori for claiming that the Jadids were not tied to a single class.[78] Munavvar qori never made a public appearance again.

The Wiles of the Nation

And yet, for all the venom heaped on "patriotism" and "nationalism" by the new critics, the nation would not leave the imaginations of the Uzbek intelligentsia alone. In the late 1920s, fascination with the nation cut across political lines among Uzbekistan's intellectuals. The new Soviet political and cultural elites might shout

---

78. "Toshkent o'krug' madaniyatchilar quriltoyida muzokiralar," *Qizil O'zbekiston*, 07.06.1927; "Tosho'krug' madaniyatchilar quriltoyida o'rtoq Komiljon Alimovning oxirgi so'zi," *Qizil O'zbekiston*, 08.06.1927.

the slogans of internationalism and class struggle, but they were nevertheless discomfited by the persistence of colonial inequalities and the ethnic division of labor. As we have seen over the last several chapters, the prime attraction of the revolutionary project for indigenous actors was its promise of the abolition of colonial inequality. Yet, as Soviet economic policy developed over the course of the 1920s, it became amply clear that the main role assigned to Central Asia in it was to grow cotton and to ensure the country's "cotton independence." Industrialization of the region was postponed indefinitely, while the little industry that existed continued to be dominated by Europeans. In fact, the 1920s saw a substantial influx, both planned and unplanned, of Europeans who came in search of jobs. Even as radical critics trumpeted the need for proletarian literature in Uzbek, an Uzbek proletariat steadfastly failed to materialize. All of this caused a great deal of discontent among Central Asian intellectuals, both within the party and without, all of which was construed by the OGPU as counterrevolutionary nationalism. In fact, by 1928, the OGPU was concerned with the rise of "pan-Uzbekism" and "chauvinism" among the Uzbek intelligentsia, party and nonparty alike.

There can be no question of the widespread fascination with the idea of Uzbekness among the Uzbek Soviet intelligentsia and party members. The drive to make Uzbekistan Uzbek, noted in chapter 8, was propelled as much by the Soviet intelligentsia as by the Jadids. But the cause of the nation also required equalization with the Europeans, economic development, and industrialization. The anticolonial rhetoric of the party produced hopes of some sort of decolonization. None of this had transpired. Europeans continued to dominate the party and the modern sectors of the economy (industry, such as there was, transport, mining). The party itself was beset with chronic ethnic strife. The petition of the Group of 18 in December 1925 was the result of deep dissatisfaction with the domineering role of Europeans in the party (see chapter 5). That dissatisfaction soon turned into something broader. OGPU agents compiled a vast archive of statements made by members of the Soviet intelligentsia expressing discontent with the unfulfilled promises of the new order. The party committee at the Kokand Teachers Institute confiscated an issue of the institute's journal that contained a piece on korenizatsiia: "Korenizatsiia—it's a travesty! When will the railway be indigenized? When will all the signs be in Uzbek? Complete indigenization has taken place only among watchmen and grooms."[79] There were many other examples:

> In Samarqand, the teacher KARIMOV stated, "The Russians are conducting a chauvinist policy. In Tashkent, all factories are packed with Russians; if an Uzbek ends up there, he is fired right away."[80]

---

79. "Svodka agenturno-dokumental'nykh dannykh," 575.
80. RGASPI, f. 62, op. 2, d. 882, l. 266 (OGPU report, 1927).

Sanjar (former editor of *Mushtum*), informing Tashkent's nationalist circles of a riot by imprisoned Basmachis in the Osh jail, said, "Nowhere is the world have prisoners in a jail been bombed."[81]

Inog'omov (party member): "Ferghana's peasantry is in a very difficult situation; colonists command everything. The situation is so catastrophic that one may expect an uprising. The line of the CC in regard to the intelligentsia is incorrect, [and] the struggle with kolonizatorstvo is conducted indecisively."[82]

In each case, the speaker's sin was to make the statement in question. The truth or otherwise, let alone the irony, of a given statement was irrelevant to the OGPU.

But the most incriminating whispers were those that questioned Uzbekistan's status within the Soviet state. OGPU agents began reporting whispered statements by party members (and others) that Uzbekistan, as a supplier of cotton, was merely a "red colony," no better (and perhaps worse) than Egypt or India under British rule. Many members of the "Soviet intelligentsia" of Samarqand saw the arrests of 1926 as an "ill-fated 'colonial' policy of Soviet power, its tendency to cleave the national intelligentsia for colonial goals."[83] Sho Rasul Zunnun, a teacher at the Tashkent district party school, told his students that Uzbekistan "is, in fact, a colony that exports cotton as a raw material."[84] A certain Mirza Rahimov tendered his resignation from the party in 1928 because he disagreed with key policies of the party. "Uzbekistan is a socialist colony," he stated, "and has no independence. It would be independent if it were like Egypt or Afghanistan. The chair of the TsIK [Central Executive Committee of Uzbekistan], comrade Oxunboboyev, is a puppet in the hands of Moscow."[85] Party authorities took this seriously enough to have such statements denounced in party meetings. Sometimes this concern even spilled out into the pages of the party press. An article in the organ of the Sredazburo criticizing nationalist deviations in Central Asia, for instance, mentioned with indignation a Tashkent student who asked at a party meeting, "What is the difference between the English colony of India and the administration of Kazakhstan by Goloshchekin?"[86]

---

81. "Svodka agenturno-dokumental'nykh dannykh," 585.

82. Ibid.

83. "O deiatel'nosti uzbeko-tadzhikskikh natskrugov" (Sept. 1926), RGASPI, f. 62, op. 2, d. 518, l. 180.

84. RGASPI, f. 62, op. 2, d. 882, l. 266.

85. "Nekotorye momenty raboty partorganizatsii Uzbekistana" (10.01.1929), RGASPI, f. 17, op. 67, d. 480, l. 27. Rahimov was expelled from the party for his pains.

86. Uraz Isaev, "O natsional'nostiakh i burzhuaznykh natsionalakh," *Za Partiiu*, 1928, no. 3: 23.

This was far beyond the critique of kolonizatorstvo that had flourished in 1920–22, and came very close to the ideas expressed by (or at least attributed by the OGPU to) the old Jadids or those being articulated abroad by the small Uzbek emigration. It is hard to discern how widespread this dissatisfaction was among Uzbek party members or the Uzbek Soviet intelligentsia, but it provoked a deep distrust of indigenous elites in the OGPU and the party higher-ups. In 1929, the distrust was to boil over in a full-blown purge of the national intelligentsia across party lines.

THE ASSAULT

In Central Asia has begun a great campaign of struggle for a new way of life, so that the initiative and leading role would be left in the hands of the party.

—Isaak Zelenskii, remarks at a party meeting, January 1927

The opening of the "ideological front" was accompanied by a full-blown assault on all forms of "backwardness" that transformed the cultural and political life of Central Asia in the years from 1927 to 1932.[1] The persecution of the old intelligentsia went hand in hand with the rapid abolition of Muslim education and of Islamic courts, the final confiscation of waqf property, the closing of mosques and shrines, and the campaign against veiling, all of which began in 1927. The name chosen for the unveiling campaign, *hujum*, "assault," encompassed the sense of the party's attitude toward its enemies and its own mission. Above all, these years saw the imposition of party control over the *meaning* of the cultural revolution as well as of the methods of its implementation. Other visions of culture, of modernity were finally delegitimized. These campaigns were part of pan-Soviet developments but in Central Asia they were tied also a final realization on the part of the party that it was strong enough to take on these challenges.

The attack on the Jadids was accompanied by attempts at tightening control over all forms of cultural production. There was heightened concern for ensuring the ideological purity of all "cultural workers," whether in the press or in education, for only then could mass work be successful. Education at all levels came under scrutiny. Schools had to be sovietized and the political rectitude of teachers ensured. The period after 1926 also saw an escalation in the rhetoric against Islam. Although anticlericalism, as we have seen, had been a staple in the

---

1. Epigraph, AAP RUz, f. 58, op. 3, d. 150, l. 51.

press since the revolution, full-blown "scientific atheism" now arrived in Uzbekistan. For the party, defeating its "class enemies" was intertwined with overcoming backwardness, and the campaigns of the years 1927–29 also targeted the latter. Alongside widespread illiteracy, the most obvious symbols of backwardness were "religious fanaticism" and the seclusion and veiling of women. All these phenomena were attacked with gusto. These campaigns melded into collectivization, the revolution from above that reshaped economic life in the countryside from 1929 on. The campaigns were more successful in destroying the old than building the new, but there can be no question that Uzbekistan was drastically reshaped in the process.

The Attack on Islamic Institutions

A decade after the revolution, according to official estimates, only 20.7 percent of children between the ages of eight and eleven were in school, and most of the schools they attended were not Soviet.[2] The continuing cultural authority of Muslim education, the poor quality of Soviet schools, and the limited resources of the latter, all combined to put the bulk of Muslim schooling beyond the purview of the state. In 1926, schooling had come under renewed attention from the government, with a joint commission of the commissariats of education and justice deliberating the fate of old-method schools, of which there were more than a thousand in Uzbekistan with an estimated thirty-five thousand pupils. Three options were on the table: to let the old schools die their own death, which many saw as imminent; to reform them and turn them into modern schools; or to abolish them forthwith by decree. The question was of a serious practical nature, and debate on it soon spilled onto the pages of the press. Nazir Inoyatiy, the head of the Uzbek Academic Center at the Uzbek Narkompros, laid out the reformist position, arguing that since Soviet schools would not be able to absorb the thirty-five thousand pupils rendered school-less if the maktabs were abolished, they should be reformed and put at the expense of the parents.[3] Otajon Hoshimov, then twenty-two and just returned from Institute of Red Professoriate, argued instead for abolition. Reforming the schools would put them in the hands of "our enemies," for mullahs and bais will take them over. Reformed schools would be better than Soviet schools and attract children of "the broad worker-peasant masses," and thus deliver the basic constituency of Soviet power

---

2. M. Romiz, *O'ktabir va xalq maorifi* (Samarqand, 1927), 83.
3. N. Inoyatiy, "Eski maktab va qorixonalar tevaragida," *Qizil O'zbekiston*, 10.02.1927.

into the hands of its enemies.[4] The party, however, had already decided on a radical course. Ishoq Xonsuvarov, then head of agitprop at Sredazburo, argued successfully for a "sharp break"[5] and by June 1927, the party had begun closing such schools, first in the Tashkent region, where their number was smaller, and then in the rest of the republic.[6] During the course of the following academic year, the abolition of old schools was largely accomplished. The directives of the Uzbek Narkompros that drove the closures were backed up by a decree from UzTsIK in October 1928.[7] The abolition of the maktabs was not accompanied by a growth in the numbers or capacity of Soviet schools enough to absorb the thirty-five thousand pupils of the maktabs. The party-state was more interested in destroying "survivals of the past" than in building the future.

Madrasas were a different story. They had suffered grievously in the years leading up to the opening of the ideological front, so that in 1927, Mannon Romiz could see no reason for their continued existence. "Madrasas might have been hearths of civilization in times past, but they fell under the influence of the clergy [*ruhoniylar*] and lost their old basis. . . . After the revolution, they remain only as historical buildings. They should be seen as such: just as their waqfs have been taken away, so their buildings must become monuments of the past [*osori atiqa*]. Just as the clerics cannot even begin to claim their rights to cultural waqfs, madrasas too have no right to claim their buildings."[8] This was already the case in practice. In March 1927, when the Andijon okrug education department decided to build a new school, the local waqf department, being short of funds, decided to obtain building materials by tearing down "unused" buildings from the Divonaboy madrasa complex. The municipal authorities approved the request, but as the work proceeded, its scope expanded, so that by the time the demolition was over, forty-three residence cells (*hujra*), a maktab, a mosque, and much else were gone.[9] The municipal authorities approved the application and used sanitary regulations to declare the buildings unfit for use, but it was the waqf department that initiated the project in the first place. By 1927, the waqf administration had turned into a parasite on madrasas, rather than their caretaker. Several madrasas managed to stay open during the 1927–28 academic year by fulfilling the sanitary requirements imposed on them by Soviet authorities, but were all shut down by late 1928. In Andijon, the closures took place on 28 October 1928,

4. Otajon, "Eski maktab," *Qizil O'zbekistan*, 21.02.1927.

5. RGASPI, f. 62, op. 1, d. 221, l. 115.

6. RGASPI, f. 62, op. 2, d. 1145, l. 72 (07.06.1927).

7. TsGARUz, f. 94, op. 1, d. 62, l. 41.

8. Romiz, *O'ktabir va xalq maorifi*, 82.

9. Shoshana Keller, *To Moscow, Not Mecca: The Soviet Campaign against Islam in Central Asia, 1917–1941* (Westport, CT, 2001), 142–145.

when a commission of the okrug education department went around the city accompanied by a doctor and found all madrasas and *qorixonas* to be in violation of sanitation codes.[10] By that time, there were no madrasas left in Samarqand.[11] The closure of madrasas spelled the end of a long tradition of Islamic learning in Central Asia and of an institution that had defined a certain understanding of Islam in the region and beyond for centuries.

The sudden change from reform to abolition in the party's position on maktabs was connected to a broader shift in its position on Islam in Central Asia in general. Earlier in the decade years, Soviet authorities were willing to align with "progressive" ulama and Muslim reformers, whom they saw as partners in a project of enlightenment. The height of this optimism came in August 1924, when Matvei Davydovich Berman, the deputy head of the OGPU for Central Asia, even suggested that the future Uzbek republic have a central religious administration (*mahkama-i shar'iya*) with control over all religious waqfs, as long as the leadership of "progressive" ulama could be ensured. The "progressive" ulama could not compete with the authority of their opponents, Berman reckoned, and therefore had no choice but to support Soviet power. The "progressive-loyal clergy" was the force that, "under our hidden leadership and support, can begin the struggle with religious fanaticism and the prejudices of custom . . . that will lead to the decay of the clergy."[12] The shariat administrations were to "cleanse Islam of the distortions of the conservatives and, in this case, the decisive negation of Sufism [*ishanizm*], of which nothing is known from the Qur'an." The OGPU could champion the scripturalist rigor of the progressive ulama in 1924, but this was a thing of the past by 1927. The previous year, the OGPU had become convinced that an organized "Muslim religious movement" was gaining strength and organizing in opposition to Soviet power all over the Soviet Union. The organization by the Tatar Central Spiritual Administration of a conference of ulama in Ufa in October 1926 was taken as proof of a movement that spanned Soviet space and connected with counterrevolutionary forces abroad.[13] The Anti-Religious Commission of the Central Committee had used this perceived threat to pursue a hardening of the party's line against Islam in the USSR. These concerns informed discussions in the Sredazburo and the Uzbek Central Committee, even though there were few ties between the ulama of the Volga region and those of

---

10. RGASPI, f. 62, op. 2, d. 1282, l. 43 (OGPU report, 25.12.1928).

11. RGASPI, f. 62, op. 2, d. 1593, l. 6 (July 1928).

12. RGASPI, f. 62, op. 2, d. 133, l. 17.

13. R.A. Nabiev, *Islam i gosudarstvo: kul'turno-istoricheskaia evoliutsiia musul'manskoi religii na Evropeiskom Vostoke* (Kazan, 2002), 85; D. Iu. Arapov and G.G. Kosach, *Islam i musul'mane po materialam Vostochnogo Otdela OGPU. 1926 god* (Nizhnii Novgorod, 2007).

Uzbekistan and conditions differed enormously between the two regions.[14] Emelian Iaroslavskii, the head of the Anti-Religious Commission, visited Uzbekistan himself and participated in meetings over the course of 1927 as the Uzbekistan Communist Party sharpened its "struggle with the clergy."

In Uzbekistan, the burden of suspicion fell on the shariat administrations. The OGPU and the party were wary that the shariat administrations took their public role too seriously and were using their authority to mediate between the government and the Muslim population.[15] "Today's clergy is not the clergy of five or ten years ago," the KPUz Central Committee declared in 1927, "it is a clergy that understands the *moment* of the struggle of labor with capital, of socialism with capitalism, going on in the country where socialism is being built, and adapts all its tactics to the current moment."[16] Now progressive ulama were *more* dangerous than the conservatives because they understood the present and were better organized. They were also deemed to be cunning, eager to hide their true colors by mouthing reformist views. The party consequently set out a plan to undermine their authority using a variety of overt and covert tactics: increasing oversight of schools and waqf incomes, subjecting waqf income to taxation, curtailing the leeway allowed the shariat administrations, but also attempting to use divisions among the ulama to engineer splits. The Central Committee of the KPUz considered it desirable to call for reelections in the shariat administrations of the major cities under the slogan of "purging them of merchant-bai and conservative elements," in order to remove the incumbent leaders, who were then to be exiled from Uzbekistan.[17] The meeting also resolved to explore the possibility of abolishing the administrations altogether. These decisions were rapidly implemented, and by the end of the year, the shariat administrations had indeed been abolished. Along with them went the courts of the qazis. Various measures over the past few years had already curtailed their competence and their numbers had shrunk precipitously, so that only seven of them remained in 1927.[18] A decision of UzTsIK abolished them outright later in the year.[19]

The campaign against Islamic institutions was accompanied by a heightening of the verbal attack on the ulama. The anticlericalism that had been around

---

14. The Uzbek Commission on the Clergy tried, somewhat timorously, to point this out, but went ahead in seconding the resolution; see AAP RUz, f. 58, op. 3, d. 1192, ll. 1–2 (19.06.1927). This archive was open to foreign scholars only for a brief period in 1991–92. All citations to materials from this archive in this chapter come courtesy of Shoshana Keller, who very generously shared her notes from this archive with me. I take this opportunity to express my gratitude again to her.

15. AAP RUz, f. 58, op. 3, d. 1192, l. 17–19 (09.05.1927).

16. AAP RUz, f. 58, op. 2, d. 955, l. 58 (07.08.1927).

17. AAP RUz, f. 58, op. 3, d. 152, ll. 5ob, 8.

18. AAP RUz, f. 58, op. 3, d. 614, l. 46.

19. Ibid., ll. 48–48ob.

for much of the decade now escalated into atheist propaganda in the authorized Soviet mode. Branches of the League of the Militant Godless began to be
established in Muslim spaces and the first Uzbekistan Congress of the Godless took place in November 1928.[20] The Uzbek-language journal *Xudosizlar*
(Godless), which had made its debut that spring, featured numerous translations from Russian that introduced the first theoretical arguments for atheism
into Uzbek. Fitrat had argued his irreligion from within the Islamicate tradition, but this new literature in Uzbek now found its moorings elsewhere, in
the direct oppositions between science and religion, myth and reality, freedom
and oppression. Mannon Romiz quoted Friedrich Engels to argue that religion
was the product of a primitive stage in human development when people, not
understanding nature, attributed all of its workings to supernatural beings.
Religion then became a tool in the hands of exploiting classes that used it to
maintain their power in society. But worse, religion "poisons a person's mind,
makes it believe in phantoms and suppositions, and exhausts his reason, filling it with unnatural notions, and gives rise to ideologies that stand in the
way of the struggle for socialism."[21] Furthermore, "the false poison" of Islam
was "a policy established by Muhammad to defend the class of the rich [*boylar
sinifi*] and to enable them to profit from the labor of the poor,"[22] and all of
Muhammad's closest companions were rich merchants and notables.[23] This
godless literature proffered scientific proofs for the absurdity or harmfulness
of Islamic rituals, such as fasting, ablution, and circumcision, and it sought to
expunge all sacrality from the Islamic narrative by providing a ruthlessly historical account of the rise and expansion of the religion. A certain Rashid Xon
read Islamic sources against the grain to argue that the writing and collation
of the Qur'an was the work of Muhammad and not of divine inspiration.[24]
This new literature was based on, and sometimes translated directly from, the
Russian-language anti-Islamic literature, which had begun to appear in the
early 1920s. That literature, in turn, reproduced many Orientalist and evolutionist tropes common to various strands of the European understanding
of Islam, from Orientalist tropes common to European scholarship, through

---

20. Hodiy Fayziy, ed., *Xudosizlar tugaraklari uchun darslik*, pt. 2 (Samarqand, 1929), 73.

21. Mannon Romiz, *Xoyoldon haqiqatga* (Tashkent, 1929), 19.

22. S. Aliullin, *Xotin-qizlar o'rtasida dinga qorshi tashviqot* (Samarqand, 1929).

23. Mustoqoy, "Din burjuvoziya madaniyatiga xizmat qiladir," *Xudosizlar*, 1928, no. 2: 9–12.

24. Rashid Xon, "Qur'onning yozilish ham to'planish tarixidan," *Xudosizlar*, 1928, no. 2: 21.
Another author added the charge of plagiarism to Muhammad, arguing that the illiterate Prophet
had put the Qur'an together from other earlier texts originating in an uncivilized age. S. Ali'ullin,
Xotin-qizlar o'rtasida dinga qarshi tashviqot (Samarqand, 1929), 37–43.

Tsarist-era missionary polemics, to evolutionist anthropology.[25] Islam was connected to specific stages in the rise of class relations, but it was also seen as hospitable to slavery and uniquely inimical to women.

The ulama now came to be depicted as tools in the hands of the bourgeoisie (*boylar*), but also as partners with the Basmachi, under whose rule they had taken much pleasure in hanging peasants and executing women and children.[26] (By shifting all responsibility for the bloodletting of the civil war years to the Basmachi and their reactionary allies, this shift in rhetoric also produced a complete amnesia about the violence of Russian settlers, which began to be written out of the history of the region at this time.) The OGPU reported rumors among the ulama in Andijon that, following the closure of the madrasas, they were all going to be arrested. Many had gone into hiding as a result.[27] Earlier in the decade, the strength of Islam had exempted Uzbekistan from antireligious legislation; now that very strength made anti-Islamic agitation an urgent task. As Abdulhay Tojiyev noted, "Uzbekistan is a place where the strength of religion is great" in comparison with other national republics of the USSR, which made it the duty "of every [politically] conscious individual to participate in the struggle against religion."[28] The duty could be quite onerous: Ikromov commanded fellow Communists that "if your family and your old life influence you in the old ways, then you have to cut off their relations with them."[29]

Closing Mosques and Shrines

Far more radical and intrusive than the closure of qazi courts and the nationalization of waqf properties was the campaign for the closure and destruction of mosques and shrines that also ran in these years. Mosques were more than mere places of worship—they provided the very fabric of social life and local

25. For preliminary analyses of early Soviet anti-Islamic discourse, see Michael Kemper, "The Soviet Discourse on the Origin and Class Character of Islam, 1923–1933," *Die Welt des Islams* 49 (2009): 1–48, and Vladimir Bobrovnikov, "The Contribution of Oriental Scholarship to the Soviet Anti-Islamic Discourse: From the Union of Militant Atheists to the Knowledge Society," in *The Heritage of Soviet Oriental Studies*, eds. Michael Kemper and Stephan Conermann (London, 2011), 66–85.

26. This is the main point of H. Bagayev, *Hozirgi musulmon ruhoniylarining basharasi* (Samarqand, 1929). Depictions of the ulama's alliances with politically regressive forces were legion in the press of the time; see Xudosiz, "'Taraqqiyparvar'–teskarichi–eshon," *Xudosizlar*, 1928, no. 9–10: 46–55; H. Fayziy, "O'ktabir inqilobi kunlarida ulamolar (bo'lg'on hodisalardan)," *Xudosizlar*, 1929, no. 10: 12–18; or Mullo Sobir o'g'li, "Saqlangan niqob...," *Xudosizlar*, 1930, no. 1: 84–88.

27. RGASPI, f. 62, op. 2, d. 1282, l. 25 (01.09.1928).

28. Abdulhay, "Dinga hujum," *Xudosizlar*, 1928, no. 1: 3.

29. Quoted in "Eski turmushga qorshi," *Xudosizlar*, 1928, no. 5: 4.

solidarities, while shrines symbolized the Muslim identity of the region in a very tangible sense, providing a link to the past and confirming the Muslimness of the present. In fact, their existence made the land itself Muslim. Unlike the closure of the courts and the confiscation of waqfs, however, the closure of mosques and mazors was not centrally contrived, but was carried out largely "from below" by stalwart enthusiasts from the Komsomol, the party, or local ispolkoms, often against the express wishes of the party hierarchy. For this reason, documentation on the campaign remains frustratingly elusive, with few records in the archives and the press largely silent. Nevertheless, we can discern the general tenor of the campaign from a few detailed accounts that we possess.

As we have seen, some shrines had been demolished before 1927, but it is difficult to ascertain when individual closures or demolitions turned into a sustained campaign and when mosques also began to be closed. Bukhara seems to have seen a big wave of closures in the late summer of 1928. On 16 September 1928, members of the soviet-party school in Bukhara organized a public meeting in Mir Do'stum mosque, which drew, according to the OGPU report, ninety-five people, including at least fifteen women, from three neighborhoods of the city. Participants of the meeting scattered the worshippers, tossed the imam's turban off his head, and threw him out of the *mihrab*, the niche from where he led the prayers. The meeting resolved to turn the mosque into a club and placed the building under lock and key. About the same time, the *aktiv* in the village soviet in nearby Hazrat-i Mir, comprised of Rajab Ashurov, Amin Mirzayev, Fayzi Nodirov, Jo'ra Saidov, and Nurulla Azizov, decided to use the rubble from three "nonfunctioning" (i.e., recently closed) mosques to build a club and a Red Teahouse.[30] The three-hundred-year-old Otoliq Xudoyor mosque in the center of the city was closed in October 1928 at the behest of the thirteen-member aktiv of the neighborhood committee, who auctioned off the mosque's property and used it to start a Red Reading Room. The reading room soon fell into disuse and the mosque was used as a warehouse until July 1929, when it was given over to the cavalry detachment of the local OGPU, which installed its stables in the mosque.[31] In Kokand in May 1929, six activists decided to shut down the Avda-boybachcha mosque and to turn it into a club. In Namangan, residents of four mahallas met and decided to close down the Xonaqoh mosque in June 1929.[32] In Izbaskent, a meeting of a hundred peasants authorized the village soviet to destroy a mosque to make way for a school.[33]

---

30. RGASPI, f. 62, op. 2, d. 1355, l. 9.
31. AAP RUz, f. 58, op. 5, d. 85, l. 5; Keller, *To Moscow, Not Mecca*, 181–187.
32. RGASPI, f. 62, op. 1, d. 562, l. 114.
33. AAP RUz, 58, op. 5, d. 613, l. 22.

Clearly, there were enthusiasts who wanted to destroy mosques and shrines, and they had ways of manufacturing votes at meetings of the population. In Tashkent, the inhabitants of a neighborhood voted to close down their mosque under fear of being deprived of their rights.[34] In G'ijduvon, the secretary of the party cell along with six other activists decided to shut down the local mosque. As they went around the village gathering signatures from the peasants for the closure, the activists threatened anyone who disagreed with expulsion from the village. Ashur-oqsaqqol, a former head of the village, gave his signature but was nevertheless forced to climb up the minaret and urinate into the courtyard at prayer time.[35] Once collectivization began, mosque closings often became part of the "bungling" (*golovotiapstvo*, as the Stalinist euphemism had it) that reigned in the process throughout the USSR, and many mosques were closed through "administrative means." In February 1930, Xudoynazar Xo'janazarov, a member of the party and director of the newly established kolkhoz in the village of Katta-Shirobod (Ferghana okrug) shut the village mosque and threatened the imam with arrest if he reopened it or conducted *namoz* (worship) close to it. In nearby Noyman-qishloq, the director of a sowing campaign forbade the performance of namoz, and in many places, those who prayed were threatened with expulsion from the kolkhoz.[36]

Closings of mazors followed a similar pattern. Of the many that were closed, we have records of only a few that caused major scandals. One such case took place in Vorukh in Tajikistan in the spring of 1929. In April, the local soviet offered a certain Qurbonov, head of the okrug fruit and grape producers' union, an old cemetery for establishing a procurement station for the harvest. The population of the village agreed to the deal on condition that it received funds for moving the bones of its ancestors to a newer graveyard nearby, which also contained a mazor. Qurbonov balked at the payment and asked the Vorukh soviet for an alternate arrangement. The Vorukh activists, led by one Sharif Saidov, were annoyed with the "obstinacy" of their own neighbors and, according to the OGPU, decided to show them that "power was still alive in Vorukh." On 11 July, they convened a plenum of the village soviet and signed over not just the old cemetery, but the mazor itself to the fruit producers' union. The following day, they flooded the mazor with water and began to dismantle it. When the villagers asked who had given permission for the destruction of the mazor, Saidov is said to have told them, "I bought your mazor and the dead for a sack of money." The villagers attacked him and other members of the aktiv and destroyed the Red

34. AAP RUz, f. 58, op. 5, d. 85, l. 10.

35. A. Mitrofanov, "K itogam partchistki v natsrespublikakh i oblastiakh," *Revoliutsiia i natsional'nosti*, 1930, no. 2, 37; Keller, *To Moscow, Not Mecca*, 205–206.

36. RGASPI, f. 62, op. 2, d. 2258, ll. 14–15 (OGPU reports, March 1930).

Teahouse in the village. Saidov fled to the district center in Isfara and sought police help.[37] Ultimately, okrug-level authorities from Khujand intervened and performed their own Solomonic justice. Saidov was arrested, but so were seven villagers, who were charged with the destruction of the Red Teahouse. Upon this, two hundred villagers, including women, set off for Isfara to protest the arrests. The raion soviet brought the situation under control, but could not find anyone to go to Vorukh for "explanatory work."

The best-known and best-remembered episode of violence in this campaign was one that came to acquire a significant place in the cultural mythology of Soviet Uzbekistan because it involved one of the main figures of Soviet-era pantheon of Uzbek culture. The episode took place in March 1929 in the mountain village of Shohimardon in the Ferghana Valley and involved a mazor attributed to Ali, Muhammad's son-in-law. Because of its attribution, Shohimardon had long been a major center of pilgrimage. The mazor's caretakers included dozens of families of sheikhs and Xo'jas who lived in a settlement around the shrine. In 1928, at the suggestion of Yo'ldosh Oxunboboyev himself, the local ispolkom decided to "liquidate" the mazor and to turn the village into a resort for poor peasants. In October 1928, the Uzbek Central Committee sent none other than Hamza Hakimzoda Niyoziy, the Jadid playwright, to oversee the implementation of this project. Hamza's motives were a mix of Jadid anticlericalism and a Soviet critique of economic exploitation. "Everyone knows that the King of Men [Shohimardon] Ali had never heard of Turkestan, let alone come here, and that his grave is in Medina," Hamza wrote in a newspaper article after his arrival in Shohimardon.

> The Xo'jas in the hamlet of Shohimardon have turned the fake grave of Ali into a resource and they rob the people with it. The sheikhs claim to have the key to paradise in their hands because of their descent from Hasan and Husain [Ali's sons]. They send those who do the proper sacrifice [and pay the sheikhs] to "paradise," and those who don't to "hell." These sheikhs of Shohimardon have to this day never worked, never labored, but, dressed in the garb of cunning, they have adopted the principles of Satan and, turning their rosaries, have fattened like the pigs of the Shohimardon steppe. . . . They have poisoned the minds of workers with superstition and [now] feed off their possessions.[38]

Upon his arrival, Hamza organized a Commission for the Struggle with Superstition (*Xurofot bilan kurash kamisiyasi*) and began mobilizing the landless peasants

37. RGASPI, f. 62, op. 2, d. 1815, l. 30 (OGPU report, 28.07.1929).

38. Nayza (pseud.), "Shohimardon po'nqorg'olari," *Yangi Farg'ona*, 11.12.1928, in Hamza Hakimzoda Niyoziy, *To'la asarlar to'plami*, 5 vols. (Tashkent, 1988–89), 4:303.

in the district against the mazor. In October, "hundreds" of them had marched on the mazor, placed a red flag on its cupola and a padlock on its door, and sent the key to the local ispolkom.[39] They also established a Red Teahouse and a kiln, and thirty-five families took up residence on the site, partly as a way of crowding out the Xo'jas.[40] The sheikhs fought back, writing to the local political police and petitioning the Uzbekistan TsIK itself against their treatment. Angered by such "provocation," according to the OGPU, Hamza demanded that the sheikhs publish a statement in the press acknowledging that their profession was criminal from the point of view of the shariat. He also threatened to call in the Red Army to arrest or exile the sheikhs.[41] The winter passed in this tense situation. In early March, on the eve of the holiday at the end of Ramadan (ro'za hayit), the secretary of the village soviet and head of the Komsomol cell Abdulla Xatam-o'g'li, with the help of some policemen, invaded the mosque on the premises, took down all the wall hangings, and arrested the muezzin. With matters at fever pitch, Hamza went to Kokand for a week, from where he returned on 17 March. The following day, the aktiv of the village soviet decided to bring the matter to its conclusion and to dismantle the mazor. As the destruction began, a crowd of three hundred gathered to defend the shrine. Matters turned violent—the mob disarmed the policemen, beat Xatam-o'g'li and other members of the aktiv, and when Hamza appeared on the scene, stoned him to death.[42]

This case is even more interesting than that of Vorukh, for here in addition to the exercise of power by a village aktiv is Hamza's use of the language of the shariat. His anticlericalism is inflected sharply with a critique of "leeches, free loaders and idlers" who lived off the labor of others, but it is nevertheless comprehensible from within an Islamic discourse. The defenders of the shrine, for their part, also destroyed the Red Teahouse and trampled on the literature and portraits found in it, and fulminated, according the OGPU, against Soviet power and the hujum. The OGPU was swift to act: it arrested fifty-four people and put them on a public trial in June, at which nine were executed, sixteen sentenced to prison, twenty-five exiled to other parts of the Soviet Union, and four acquitted.[43]

The party leadership and the OGPU seem to have been largely sidelined in the campaign against mosques and shrines. Local activists took the initiative, whether to assert their revolutionary credentials, out of fear of worse consequences, or as an

---

39. Ibid., 304.

40. Hamza, letter to an unidentified person (25.09.1928), in ibid., 5:107–110.

41. RGASPI, f. 62, op. 2, d. 1815, ll. 41–41ob (14.09.1929).

42. An OGPU report on the episode and its aftermath, though problematic, provides the closest (and quite candid) contemporary account of it: RGASPI, f. 62, op. 2, d. 1815, ll. 41–41ob (14.09.1929). The standard Soviet account asserted that Hamza had established a party cell and school at the mazor, as well as a kolkhoz and a music group; see Laziz Qayumov, *Hamza: esse* (Tashkent, 1989), 309–324.

43. RGASPI, f. 62, op. 2, d. 1815, l. 41ob

exercise in power over their neighbors. According to the secretary of the Bukhara okrug party committee, "mosques were closed by decisions of party cells, by decisions of Komsomol cells, by decisions of rural soviets, of meetings of the poor, or simply without any decision at all. Such an abominable situation continued from the beginning of 1927 to the end of 1928. . . . The closing of mosques took on the character of a competition."[44] The party leadership had in fact issued directives that places of worship could only be closed "with the sanction of UzTsIK," but they were routinely ignored as closures went on without number (attempts to collect information on the numbers of mosques and churches closed produced highly contradictory results). In July 1929, estimates for the number of mosques closed in Bukhara okrug ran from 200 to "at least 400."[45]

Mosques and shrines were turned into clubs, Red Reading Rooms, warehouses, schools, or as happened in Bukhara, stables for OGPU horses. Such desecration often produced anger and violence among the population, which discomfited the authorities. Curiously enough, as activists went about closing mosques, it was the OGPU, of all agencies, that fretted about the "administrative means" that were being used. The political police sought the Sredazburo's intervention to overturn a ban imposed by the Khujand city ispolkom on the old practice of beating drums before dawn during Ramadan to wake up inhabitants, because such measures fed the authority of "anti-Soviet elements" who could now argue that Soviet power was oppressing religion.[46] Elsewhere we find a certain Qodirov arguing that mosques could only be shut down by "the will of the people," and not by "administrative methods."[47] By the spring of 1929, the party had become wary of such scandals and the protests they provoked. Akmal Ikromov angrily noted, "As it is, nowhere does the population trust Soviet power. . . . If someone wants that there be an uprising in Uzbekistan, then a few more such abominable facts will be enough."[48] The Communist fraction at UzTsIK sent out a strongly worded circular to all ispolkoms reminding them of the impermissibility of unauthorized mosque closures.[49] Such expressions of alarm and annoyance reflect a situation common enough in the Soviet state during those years, of party-initiated campaigns running out of control and taking a life of their own in the lawless hands of enthusiastic activists. The party seldom retained control over the campaigns of social or cultural transformation that it unleashed. They all produced "bungling" and "dizziness" among the cadres and resulted in more

44. AAP RUz, f. 58, op. 5, d. 85, l. 4.
45. Ibid., l. 1.
46. RGASPI, f. 62, op. 2, d. 1355, l. 6 (10.03.1928).
47. AAP RUz, f. 58, op. 5, d. 641, l. 14 (06.04.1929).
48. AAP RUz, f. 58, op. 5, d. 85, l. 2–3 (08.08.1929).
49. AAP RUz, f. 58, op. 6, op. 206, l. 27.

destruction than construction. But they also mobilized people into the Soviet cause and made them Soviet citizens. The campaign against Islam in Uzbekistan was, in that sense, quite normal for the Soviet Union of the late 1920s.

Unveiling as Liberation

Finally, we come to the hujum, the campaign against the veil and female seclusion of women launched with great fanfare on 8 March 1927, International Women's Day. On that day, in hundreds of public meetings complete with revolutionary poetry and fiery oratory, in the old cities of Tashkent, Samarqand, Kokand, and Andijon, thousands of women tossed their paranjis and chachvons onto bonfires and proclaimed their entry into the "new life." Such meetings were repeated across Uzbekistan in the months to come. Public unveilings were a theatrical gesture, no doubt equally electrifying and terrifying to their participants, as they transgressed bounds of modesty and propriety that had been impressed on them through the intertwined sanctions of custom and religion. The hujum was a massive feat of mobilization that had been many months in the making. It marked a significant shift in party policy on women.

In the summer of 1926, the Zhenotdel had tied its cart to the horse of the ideological front and argued for ramping up work among women in Uzbekistan.[50] Spurred by a Central Committee directive to "strengthen" such work, the Sredazburo decided to move ahead. At a series of conferences, the goals of the party's "work among women" became ever more ambitious, moving from education and organization to an all-out assault on backward customs. The goal became nothing less that ending women's seclusion by bringing them fully into productive labor and battling customary cultural practices that underpinned the seclusion.[51] A conference of Zhenotdel workers in October decided to adopt hujum, "assault," as the slogan for the campaign, although the focus on unveiling was the subject of considerable debate within the party, and it did not emerge as the central feature of the campaign until early 1927.[52] (As a Sredazburo project, the hujum was to be implemented in all republics of Central Asia. In nomadic areas, where women customarily did not veil and where the specific form of paranji-chachvon were unknown, the hujum focused of other issues, such as bridewealth

50. S. Liubimova, "Bor'ba na ideologicheskom fronte," *Kommunistka*, 1926, no. 9: 74–75.

51. I. Zelenskiy, "Xotin-qizlar arasidagi ishlarda firqaning asosiy vazifalari," *Qizil O'zbekiston*, 15.10.1926.

52. B.P. Pal'vanova, *Emansipatsiia musul'manki: opyt raskreposhcheniia zhenshchiny sovetskogo Vostoka* (Moscow, 1982), 175; Marianne Kamp, *The New Woman in Uzbekistan: Islam, Modernity, and Unveiling under Communism* (Seattle, 2007), 162–165.

and underage marriage.)[53] The campaign thus became a hujum on the paranji itself, which came to be seen as the main instrument of women's seclusion and subjection. Conversely, unveiling meant casting off the paranji and opening up the face; it did not necessarily mean donning European garb. Most women who unveiled replaced the paranji with a shawl or a headscarf.

The initial unveilings were an impressive piece of mobilization that could not be sustained. As the campaign continued, the burden fell on male party members to liberate "their" women. The hujum became in many ways a site for the exercise of the power of men over women, often channeled through other men. In the village of Asaka, a meeting of the local union of cultural workers decided that whichever member unveiled his wife will have his name recorded on a board [krasnaia doska], while those who failed to do so will be expelled from the union (and from the party, if they were party members) and fired from their jobs.[54] The secretary of the party cell in Uychi village (Andijon okrug), Buzrukxonov, summoned fifteen imams from the area and asked them to sign a declaration mandating women to remove their paranjis. When the imams refused, Buzrukxonov had several of them arrested, and then proceeded to order all women of the village to attend a meeting the following day or else face the police.[55] An agitation commission in Samarqand threatened women with a tax if they did not unveil. At an unveiling meeting in the Ko'kmasjid neighborhood of Samarqand, on the other hand, the daughter of a certain Mufti Fayzulla snatched off the paranjis of many women who did not want to unveil.[56] Other men seemed to take the unveiling as sexual license. At a wedding in Axkachi village, the head of the mutual aid society, one Umarali Mirzaxonov, brought four unveiled women with him from Andijon, with whom he and a few friends "put together a drunken orgy," much to the consternation of the OGPU, which reported that the goings-on made villagers ask one another whether women who threw off their paranjis "will have to drink and pervert themselves." In Kasansoy, also in the Ferghana Valley, the head of the raion ispolkom forced an activist to divorce her husband and become his paramour.[57]

Unlike the other campaigns of this period, however, the hujum produced a massive, violent backlash. Most women did not want to unveil, either because their sense of modesty made the action unthinkable, or because they did not

---

53. See Adrienne Lynn Edgar, "Emancipation of the Unveiled: Turkmen Women under Soviet Rule, 1924–29," *Russian Review* 62 (2003): 132–149; Pal'vanova, *Emansipatsiia musul'manki*, 173.

54. RGASPI, f. 62, op. 2, d. 883, l. 50 (19.06.1927).

55. Ibid., l. 49.

56. Ibid., l. 42.

57. Ibid., ll. 51, 53. These examples of the reactions to the hujum, taken from a single archival file, are meant to convey a flavor of the evidence; a myriad other cases have been described and examined by Douglas Northrop, *Veiled Empire: Gender and Power in Stalinist Central Asia* (Ithaca, 2004).

want the social and moral opprobrium that came with such a drastic step. For most men, the assault on the paranji was an assault on their sense of a gendered moral order. Many people, men and women, dealt with the hujum by evasion or dissembling. Elsewhere, men protested, in mosques and on the streets. In Chust, a protest turned violent and resulted in the murder of a policeman by the mob, which then ransacked the City Soviet building.[58] In July, a speaker in a village near Kokand had to flee, accompanied by the policeman who guarded him, after the crowd turned menacing at a meeting.[59] But the real price for the hujum was paid by the women who unveiled. Very soon after the launch of the hujum, unveiled women became the target of terrifying violence. They were assaulted verbally, being called prostitutes; they were spat at and harassed in public; they were beaten, raped, and murdered. The numbers are difficult to establish with any degree of certitude, but over the three years of the campaign, they amounted to hundreds of deaths and many more rapes and injuries. The effect was to make unveiling dangerous and unpalatable, and many of the women who re-veiled did so out of desperate fear. The violence also produced high-profile victims, such as the young actresses Tursunoy Saidazimova and Nurxon Yo'ldoshxo'jayeva, who were both murdered by their relatives for dishonoring their families. They became the martyrs of the new life

Not everyone was cowed. The violence produced greater assertiveness among women activists and many of the newly unveiled. Pressure from the Zhenotdel forced Uzbekistan's government to tighten its prosecution of crimes against women. In October 1928, the state defined the murder of unveiled women as a terrorist act. Some murderers were given show trials that were covered prominently in the press. By 1930, the court systems of various okrugs had entered into "socialist competitions" on who could prosecute crimes against women faster.[60] The Soviet state presented itself as the protector of unveiled women and the patron of the new life. The Zhenotdel also demanded a decree banning the paranji, arguing that a law would make unveiling easier for women by putting the force of the state behind it. The question was debated for two years, and in April 1929, as the Third Congress of Soviets of Uzbekistan opened, women marched down the main avenue in Samarqand demanding such a decree. Saodat Shamsiyeva, as the representative of the Komsomol, brought the demand up in her

58. RGASPI, f. 62, op. 2, d. 883, ll. 31–32; this episode is examined in great detail by Northop, *Veiled Empire*, 139–163, who, however, greatly inflates its significance and the consternation it caused the party and the OGPU.

59. RGASPI, f. 62, op. 4, d, 112, l. 14.

60. See, for instance, "Dogovor po vypolneniiu sotsialisticheskogo sorevnovaniia po raskreposhcheniiu zhenshchin mezhdu Okrsudom Khorezma i vyzvavshego Okrsuda Kashka-dar'i," TsGARUz, f. 904, op. 1, d. 313, l. 23 (Jan. 1930).

speech at the congress. It was not to be, however. The congress refused to ban the paranji by decree, arguing instead that attracting women into Soviet institutions and into employment was the key issue without which liberation could not take place. Unveiling had to remain an act of will, not of legal compliance.[61]

The hujum thus became the most important site for the contestation over Uzbek culture and identity. The question of women's position in society had been debated since the revolution, and the Jadids had also argued for it. With the hujum, however, the party had hijacked the meaning of unveiling and the women's question in general. For the Jadids, unveiling was connected to education and the nation. The radical Friends of the New Life who had met in Tashkent in 1924 (see chapter 6) had been critical of the clergy, but they had still focused on education and women's participation in public life. On the day of the hujum was launched, Hamza framed a critique of the paranji in the anticlericalism of the decade, but combined it with the language of exploitation:

> **Today is March 8**
> Oh, you foreign thing called paranji, your hand is filthy; don't come
>   near Uzbek women and girls, get yourself out of here! . . .
> Oh you mullah, who for thirteen centuries has used the souls of women
>   as fodder for yourself, pack up this shroud with sleeves and put it on
>   your shoulder!
>
> . . . .
>
> Oh Domla!
> Bite your fingers in amazement, twist your beard until it looks like rice
>   straw. When you have tightened your turban, hang your head a bit.
>   If you're upset at why women are throwing off their paranjis, look at
>   yourself and cry
>
> . . . .
>
> Oh fanatic vermin!
> Smoke your opium sitting by the grate!
> Take pleasure, sip green tea,
> And gird your belt for the journey to the Other World!
> But I have some advice for you:

---

61. Kamp, *New Woman*, 207–210; on the broader debate over the law, see Northrop, *Veiled Empire*, 285–301; D.A. Alimova, *Zhenskii vopros v Srednei Azii: istoriia izucheniia i sovremennye problemy* (Tashkent, 1989), 21–24. The Soviets were not averse to the use of laws and decrees, of course; polygyny, child marriage, and bridewealth (*qalin*) had all been outlawed in Uzbekistan.

> Take the paranji and *chimmat* [chachvon], which you brought, away
> with you and go to your grave with it!
> Paranji and chimmat!
> Go back to where you came from,
> Make your way to Mecca,
> Find your place in Hell![62]

The hujum put unveiling firmly in the realm of "socialist construction." Uzbek
women activists distanced the hujum from previous debates about women
in Uzbek society. It is true, wrote Bashorat Jalol, "that some of our youth had
unveiled their wives and sisters after the revolution, but this legacy of our ancestors, the paranji, had never been really debated."[63] For European activists in the
Zhenotdel, the question was even more straightforward: the hujum had begun
the task "of bringing women out of the lazy and inactive life they have until now,
of including them in public life and production, and thus bringing them into
an active life, into the ranks of free, rights-bearing citizens."[64] It was to usher in
a new way of life and lead women to a Bright World, as the heroic image on the
front page of *Qizil O'zbekiston* announced on the day the hujum was launched
(see figure 8).

Women's liberation was now the party's gift to the oppressed women of the
East, and it was firmly tied to the struggle against Islam. The unveiled woman
in *Qizil O'zbekiston*, her head covered by a scarf, points to a bright future as she
bestrides a cityscape that contains all the trappings of the new life: school, artel,
cooperative store, an office of the Zhenotdel, and a soviet. A set of slogans in a
filler in the women's magazine *Yangi yo'l* (The New Path) described the new life:
"Down with the old life! Long live the new life! Long live toilers! Down with
idlers! Death to mullahs and eshons who spread religious superstition! Consciousness and knowledge to workers and toilers!"[65] There was no place for Islam
in the bright world for the future.

The party explicitly tied unveiling and the liberation of women to its struggle
against Islam and the ulama. Given that the party was gearing up then for a

---

62. Hamza Hakimzoda Niyoziy, "Bu kun—8 mart," *Yangi Farg'ona*, 08.03.1927, in Hamza, *To'la asarlar to'plami*, 2:199–200; partly based on Marianne Kamp's translation in *New Woman*, 174–175.

63. Bashorat Jalol, "8inchi martga bir sovg'o," *Yangi yo'l*, 1927, no. 3: 11. Sobira Xoldorova had already foreshadowed the hujum in the February issue of *Yangi yo'l*, the women's magazine, by asserting that "the question of women's liberation should be established on a Leninist footing," and not on the ideas of "narrowly nationalist counterrevolutionary intellectuals." S.X., "Xotin-qizlar ozodlig'ining leninincha qo'yilishi," *Yangi yo'l*, 1927, no. 2: 3–5.

64. Yelena G'ilozquvo [Elena Glazkova], "Ochilgan o'zbek xotin-qizlariga ko'makga," *Yangi yo'l*, 1927, no. 7: 5.

65. *Yangi yo'l*, 1927, no. 10: 31.

FIGURE 8. "New Life—Toward a Bright World," *Qizil O'zbekiston*, 07.03.1927.

"struggle with the clergy," it eschewed any help from the ulama in propagating its message. In fact, unveiling became the liberation of women *from* Islam, which came to be held accountable for women's oppression in Muslim societies. Godless authors highlighted numerous misogynist strands of the Islamicate tradition that describe women as the source of all trouble in the world, argued that Islamic marriage was the sale of the bride (because the Qur'an prescribes the payment of *mahr*, bridewealth, by the husband upon the solemnization of the marriage), and pointed to other aspects of Islamic law where women are treated unequally to men (in inheritance, as witnesses) or are legally subordinate to men.[66] The most daring arguments were based on the life of Muhammad himself and his multiple wives. In a story Fitrat wrote for *Xudosizlar*, Muhammad appeared as a lustful deceiver, no different from any eshon in Uzbekistan (see chapter 7), while for X. Obidov, Muhammad's eleven wives (including the child bride 'A'isha) and many concubines made him analogous to the emir of Bukhara, whose harem had become legendary.[67] But it was perhaps the filmmaker Oleg Frelikh who carried the connection between Islam and misogyny to its conclusion. His 1931 film *Doch' sviatogo* (Daughter of the Saint) about the sexual exploits of an eshon contains a striking scene that straightforwardly equates Sufi zikr with rape.[68]

This hijacking of the meaning of women's liberation by the party put the Jadids in an awkward position. They might have been opposed to the methods being pursued, but ultimately they favored the main goals of unveiling. Hamza was of course an enthusiastic supporter, but he had not been attacked in the press. Those who had been could use their support also to counter the attacks. Cho'lpon wrote a play, *Zamona xotini* (A Woman of the Times), on the subject of unveiling. He also mourned the murder of Tursunoy Saidazimova, whom he had taught at the Uzbek drama studio in Moscow and worked together on many plays, reading an eulogy at her funeral, and reportedly bringing the audience to tears.[69] Hamza also wrote a poem (*marsiya*) mourning her death.[70]

---

66. Kh. 'Ābidaf, *Dīn va āzādī-yi zanān*, trans. N. Erkayif (Dushanbe, 1930), 22–24; Ali'ullin, *Xotin-qizlar o'rtasida*, 19–20; Rashidxon, "Islom va xotin-qizlar," *Xudosizlar*, 1928, no. 6: 8–13 (mostly paraphrasing the Tatar work by Hadi Keldibek, *Islam häm khatïn-qïzlar* [Kazan, 1928]).

67. Fitrat, "Zayd va Zaynab," *Xudosizlar*, 1928, no. 4: 28–33; no. 5: 22–26; 'Ābidaf, *Dīn va āzādī-yi zanān*, 23–24. All of these tropes have been staples of anti-Islamic polemics in the West, but they have seldom appeared in Muslim societies themselves.

68. *Doch' sviatogo/Avliyo qizi*, Uzgoskino, 1931; many thanks to Cloé Drieu for sharing a digitized version of the film with me. For her own analysis of the scene, see her *Fictions nationales: Cinéma, empire et nation en Ouzbékistan (1919–1937)* (Paris, 2013), 174–175.

69. Cho'lpon, "Tursinoy sahnada," *Yer yuzi* (30.06.1928), 13–14; Naim Karimov, *Cho'lpon* (Tashkent, 1991), 25.

70. Hamza, "Tursunoy marsiyasi," in *To'la asarlar to'plami*, 2:216.

The hujum can only be understood in the context of the ideological front. Much like the campaign against the maktab, the hujum was to be a differentiated affair, to begin in the more "advanced" parts of the republic before encompassing the rest. Similarly, members of the party bore a special burden, for they were expected to set the example and unveil their wives and sisters. As with Latinization, the party took over and imposed its own meaning on an ongoing cultural project, and as with the campaign against mosques and shrines, the hujum too was imbricated in the exercise of power within Uzbek society. Yet much of the considerable interest it has generated among scholars has been misdirected. Students of the workings of the Soviet state, with access to Central Asia solely or primarily through Russian-language documentation, have tended to see to study the hujum in isolation from its context. For both Gregory Massell and Douglas Northrop, the hujum was the beginning of Soviet intervention in Central Asia society, rather than its culmination, born of a desperation at the regime's inability to effect change.[71] As a result, both scholars inflate the importance of the hujum and misread it as an encounter between "foreign, atheist, urban" Bolsheviks and "Uzbek Muslim society," as Northrop frames it. As this book has shown, "Soviet" and "Uzbek" were neither monolithic, nor mutually exclusive categories. It is absurd to speak of a single "Uzbek Muslim culture" in a society wracked by a decade and a half of conflict, a society that had experienced a murderous civil war and the dislocations of revolution and famine. Uzbek society was riven with conflict, with different visions of the future. What happened with the opening of the "ideological front" was the monopolization of the meaning of change by the party and the exclusion, first conceptual, then physical, of those who opposed it. But the party had launched this front not against "Uzbek Muslim culture," but against another modernizing elite. It was a conflict between two competing visions of modernity and transformation; both camps sought to overcome backwardness, neither had any patience with customs, traditions, or culture-as-it-was. Seeing the conflict as a Soviet-Uzbek encounter also denudes it of all sociological sense, for it does not explain how the hujum worked at the local level or what stake people such as Buzrukxonov or Saidov had in it. It also fails to explain the violence that the hujum engendered, which did not take place across the alleged Soviet-Uzbek divide, but was entirely gendered.

Nor did the hujum indicate a substitution of class with gender categories. Gender was not a category that the Soviets understood or used. The assault on the paranji was meant to get women into productive labor and to break the bonds

---

71. Gregory Massell, *The Surrogate Proletariat: Moslem Women and Revolutionary Strategies in Soviet Central Asia, 1919–1929* (Princeton, 1974); Northrop, *Veiled Empire*.

of tradition that defined backwardness, not necessarily to give them agency. It was not aimed at redefining gender relations and certainly women's liberation was not connected to any understanding of a sexual or a gender revolution. And the hujum was certainly not the central Soviet intervention in Central Asian society, but one of a constellation of initiatives launched by the party to assert its authority over the process of cultural change in Central Asia. The economic initiatives in the realm of land reform and the "cottonization" of the region's economy were far more important to the party than unveiling, while all the themes that emerge in the course of the hujum (distrust of native cadres, the visions of friends and enemies, the backwardness of Central Asia) can be seen in any number of other realms of policy.

The account of the Soviet assault on backwardness presented here should also make us rethink the balance of power in Uzbekistan in these years. Party and OGPU documents are replete with fears that indigenous party members themselves would prove unable or unwilling to tear themselves away from the influence of Islam. As Ishoq Xonsuvarov, head of the agitprop section of the Sredazburo lamented at a closed meeting, party members did not like antireligious work, and "sometimes are even afraid to do it. . . . There are many mahallas where there is not a single Communist, but a dozen eshons. Neither the GPU, nor the police can help them; no wonder they're afraid."[72] Public criticisms of the state of ideological commitment in the party were common. "Many in our own Communists have not got rid of the old way of life," ran a typical complaint. "They marry off their sisters, making them jump over the fire, and throwing a feast [to'y] in celebration."[73] Historians have taken these statements at face value and deduced from them the weakness of the Soviet presence in Central Asia.[74] Clearly, the party leadership and the OGPU thought very little of indigenous cadres, but to infer from this distrust the absolute incapability of the latter to act is unwarranted. Much of the work of the assault was done by Uzbeks. The three-member commissions that closed schools and confiscated their properties were composed of locals, even if the doctors that accompanied them were invariably Europeans. The experience of the campaign against mosques and shrines is evidence that indigenous cadres were not all that afraid of confrontation. Whether out of revolutionary enthusiasm or as an exercise in their own power, many of them had no compunction in taking on their neighbors and the customs and traditions of their society. Solidarities in indigenous society were not immune to the upheaval that had gripped it for over a decade.

---

72. AAP RUz, f. 58, op. 3, d. 1168, l. 27 (25.11.1927).
73. "Eski turmushga qorshi," 3.
74. Most notably, Northrop, *Veiled Empire*, chap. 6.

TOWARD A SOVIET ORDER

In a perverse way, Hamza was lucky to be killed by a mob. The murder turned him into a martyr and secured for him a reputation as a revolutionary and a literary giant that he did not quite deserve. A few weeks after his death, the campaign against "old intellectuals" took on a new intensity and culminated the following year in a major purge of the Uzbek intelligentsia. Had Hamza lived, he might very well have been among the victims. In other ways too, 1929 was a turning point that brought massive changes in the Soviet Union as a whole as the party launched a new revolution, this time from above, to reshape the revolutionary state. By November, when Stalin pronounced 1929 the "year of the Great Breakthrough," the era of the 1920s with its possibilities and its flux was over. In Uzbekistan, this transformation had particular local specificities. A few months after Hamza's murder, Tajikistan was raised to the status of a union republic, at par with Uzbekistan. The sedentary Muslim population of Central Asia had been disaggregated on the ethnic principle and come to be institutionalized as two different nations. The national principle had triumphed under Soviet auspices. But the national principle also had Soviet limits. The period between late 1929 and early 1931 saw a purge of Uzbekistan's national intelligentsia that left a swathe of destruction in its wake. It signaled the end of the cultural revolution of the previous decade, for it transformed the cultural field as it had existed for much of the 1920s and altered the parameters of cultural production. Combined with the destruction of Islamic institutions described in chapter 11, the purge meant that few alternatives to Soviet power remained in Central Asia. By 1931, Central Asia had been substantially transformed. This last chapter takes stock of these processes.

The Destruction of Alternatives

This was not a straightforward or orderly process. In the spring of 1929, the party worried that the assaults on mosques, shrines, and the paranji might lead to "uprisings." It pulled back the hujum and tried to curtail mosque closures, but the respite was momentary. By the autumn, collectivization had been unleashed across the Soviet Union. This new campaign sought to bring the countryside to heel and to extend the state's control to the rural economy. It produced much violence. The radical attempt to collectivize farmland and livestock tested social bonds. OGPU reports spoke of "terrorist acts" of bais and *lishentsy* aimed at farmhands and poor peasants as well as at representatives of Soviet power. Often, however, peasants of all strata came together in mass demonstrations to demand the reversal of new obligations and taxes, the release of those arrested, the end of the cotton program, and permission to "live according to the shariat."[1] The backlash often turned into armed insurgency in the countryside, for which the OGPU resurrected the term *Basmachi*.[2] By 1931, the Red Army and paramilitary units of the OGPU were engaged in full-blown operations to quell the unrest. In Turkmenistan, an uprising of several groups of Turkmen and Kazakh nomads, armed mostly with rifles, was countered by tanks, machine guns, and aerial bombardment.[3] The Afghan civil war of 1929 was a contributing factor, for it pushed many former Basmachi warlords who had escaped into Afghanistan earlier in the decade back into Soviet territory. There was a reverse movement as well, for the years of collectivization saw a mass exodus of nomads and peasants into Chinese Turkestan, Afghanistan, and Iran. The numbers, as always, remain difficult to ascertain, but tens of thousands were involved. And hunger returned. Prices of cotton relative to grain had fallen for several years before collectivization began. Now, in 1929 and 1930, bread disappeared from the stores. The OGPU was reporting lines of four hundred people or more at bread stores in Khorezm and Ferghana in the spring of 1929.[4] (In Kazakhstan, of course, collectivization,

1. "Svodka po voprosu massovykh vystuplenii dekhkanstva v sviazi s kollektivizatsiei," RGASPI, f. 62, op. 2, d. 2258, ll. 7–8 (March 1930). Many party and OGPU documents on this subject are now available in *Tragediia sredneaziatskogo kishlaka*, ed. R. Shamsutdinov and D. Alimova, 3 vols. (Tashkent, 2006), and *Sovetskaia derevnia glazami ChK-OGPU-NKVD*, 3 vols. in 4 (Moscow, 1996–2003).

2. For the OGPU, this wave of Basmachi was a "rural counterrevolution": Reinhard Eisener, ed. and trans., *"Konterrevolution auf dem Lande": zur inneren Sicherheitslage in Mittelasien 1929/30 aus Sicht der OGPU* (Berlin, 1999).

3. Turganbek Allaniiazov, *Krasnye Karakumy: ocherki istorii bor'by s antisovetskim povstancheskim dvizhenii v Turkmenistane (mart-oktiabr' 1931 goda)* (Jezkezgan, 2006); Adrienne L. Edgar, *Tribal Nation: The Making of Soviet Turkmenistan* (Princeton, 2004), chap. 6.

4. *"Sovershenno sekretno": Lubianka–Stalinu o polozhenii v strane (1922–1934gg.)*, 8 vols. in 13 (Moscow, 2001–2008), 7:209, 308, 349.

accompanied by the forced sedentarization of the nomads, brought about a full-scale famine that spelled demographic disaster for the Kazakh population.)[5] After half a dozen years of peace, Central Asia was in turmoil again.

Yet in this upheaval lay also the roots of a deeper transformation of the region. Collectivization reshaped the region in fundamental ways. Unveiling in the countryside proceeded alongside collectivization.[6] Mosques and mazors continued to be shut down throughout the decade, denuding the landscape of its markers of Muslimness and constricting the amount of Islamic knowledge in circulation. Collectivization also contributed directly to the solidification of cotton monoculture in the region. "Cotton independence" was a key goal of the first five-year plan, and it was Central Asia's lot to provide as much cotton as possible to the Soviet state. Cotton came to dominate all concerns of politics and culture in Uzbekistan. Already in 1928, the Komsomol had begun organizing "cotton days" as peasant holidays;[7] the party had declared cotton its honor;[8] and propagandists were declaring that the "struggle for cotton" was not just central to the five-year plan but also to the building of socialist culture and that it was even a part of the struggle against religion.[9] For the center, Sredazburo and KPUz had become procuring agents for cotton before everything else. In May 1930, Stalin commanded the two organizations to delay by a week the departure of their delegations to the forthcoming Sixteenth Party Congress until the backlog in the cotton sowing campaign could be remedied, since "the sowing of cotton is more important than punctual arrival at the congress."[10] By the middle of the decade, the cotton boll was firmly established as the symbol of the republic, and its chief identifying marker.[11]

Scholars have tended to emphasize the tenuousness of Soviet rule in Central Asia in the 1930s. I would argue that the triumph of cotton indicates

---

5. On collectivization and the resulting famine in Kazakhstan, see Isabelle Ohayon, *Le sedentarisation des Kazakhs dans l'URSS de Staline: Collectivisation et changement social (1928–1945)* (Paris, 2006); Niccolò Pianciola, *Stalinismo di frontiera: Colonizzazione agricola, sterminio dei nomadi e construzione statale in Asia centrale (1905–1936)* (Rome, 2009); Sarah I. Cameron, "The Hungry Steppe: Soviet Kazakhstan and the Kazakh Famine, 1921–1934" (Ph.D. diss., Yale University, 2010).

6. Marianne Kamp, "Where Did the Mullahs Go? Oral Histories from Rural Uzbekistan," *Die Welt des Islams* 50 (2010): 503–531, examines Uzbek peasants' memories of collectivization and the fate of mosques and mullahs in it.

7. H. Mirxo'jayev, *"Paxta kuni"—dehqonlar hayiti ("Paxta kuni"ni o'tkazish va hayitiga doir qo'llonmalar)* (Samarqand, 1929).

8. E.g., RGASPI, f. 62, op. 2, d. 2125, l. 5 (1930).

9. N. Qodirov, "Besh yilliq pilon ham xudosizlarning vazifasi," *Xudosizlar*, 1929, no. 9: 3–9.

10. RGASPI, f. 558, op. 11, d. 39, l. 9 (18.05.1930).

11. In Soviet parades and other celebrations of the 1930s, Uzbekistan was representationally reduced to a giant cotton boll; see Karen Petrone, *Life Has Become More Joyous, Comrades: Celebrations in the Time of Stalin* (Bloomington, 2000), 36–37.

otherwise. Cotton was an indication that the Soviet state had subjugated Central Asia to its control. To be sure, the subjugation was predicated more on the destruction of alternatives than the creation of stable institutions, but the destruction—of institutions, elites, and alternative political programs—cannot be gainsaid. Central Asia was a very different place in 1931 than it had been in 1917. And while the OGPU and the party continued to fear the malevolent influence of émigrés and foreign intelligence services, the reality was quite different. The Central Asian emigration was very small and without economic resources or political influence. Mustafa Cho'qoy had settled in the village of Nogent-sur-Marne outside Paris, from where he led a one-man campaign to keep the cause of Turkestan alive in Europe. He lectured and published widely, but his influence can easily be exaggerated. He had initially published in the Russian émigré press, but the Russian émigré community quickly soured on his "nationalism." In 1929, he began publishing *Yosh Turkiston* (Young Turkestan) from his home. Istanbul was another center of émigré organization and publishing, where *Yeni Türkistan* (New Turkestan) had appeared since 1927 under the editorship of Usmon Xo'ja o'g'li (Kocaoğlu). Yet the divisions almost inevitable in any émigré community quickly emerged, pitting Cho'qoy against Kocaoğlu and Togan, and leading to often ugly polemics.[12] Turkiston Milliy Birligi (TMB), the organization founded in Bukhara in 1921, continued to exist in emigration, but neither it, nor any of its leaders, had any contact with Central Asia itself, much less any influence on developments on the ground.[13] And while Polish intelligence had some contact with émigré leaders as part of its broad strategy to exacerbate national problems in the USSR, Central Asia had fallen off the radar of most foreign powers. British interest, such as it was, evaporated after the stabilization of the situation in Afghanistan in 1923, while in Turkey, Mustafa Kemal (Atatürk) had made disavowal of irredentist claims a central pillar of his policies and, in any case, was loath to sacrifice his good working relations with the Soviet state. By 1931, Central Asia had slipped into oblivion as far as the rest of the world was concerned. The Central Asian emigration was not a force of any consequence.

---

12. A dispassionate history of the Central Asian émigré community remains to be written; for a heroic version, see A. Ahat Andican, *Cedidizm'den Bağımsızlığa Hariçte Türkistan Mücadelesi* (Istanbul, 2003). A sense of the relationship between Cho'qoy and Ahmed Zeki Velidi (Togan) can be gleaned from S. Iskhakov, ed., *Iz istorii rossiiskoi emigratsii: pis'ma A.-Z. Validova i M. Chokaeva (1924–1932 gg.)* (Moscow, 1999); there is ample testimony to that rivalry in Cho'qoy's private papers.

13. Mustafa Cho'qoy's papers contain correspondence with Central Asian exiles around Eurasia, but only a few letters from Soviet Central Asia, and most of them date from before 1924.

A 1939 "plenary meeting" of TMB members resident in Europe consisted of five men meeting in a hotel room in Berlin.[14]

The Disaggregation of Uzbeks and Tajiks

The elevation of Tajikistan to union-republic status marked the final conceptual disaggregation of the urban Muslim population of Central Asia into two distinct nationalities. This was the triumph of the national idea that the Jadids had espoused and the Soviets made possible. In May 1929, the government of Tajikistan formally launched its case for separation from Uzbekistan and for the unification of the Tajik population of Uzbekistan with it.[15] The demand was based on the argument that Uzbek authorities were forcibly Uzbekizing the Tajik population of Uzbekistan. The concern was old, but it emerged as the cornerstone of the demand for separation in 1929. A petition with thirty signatures described the mechanisms of this Uzbekization: Uzbek authorities refused to establish Tajik schools, forced Tajiks to speak Uzbek, and registered Tajiks as Uzbeks in the 1926 census.[16] The petition also drew a straight line from the pan-Islamism and pan-Turkism of the revolutionary years to the "Uzbek chauvinism" of the present, between Jadidism and Uzbek nationalism.

Unlike the delimitation, which was carried out by party committees, the separation of Tajikistan from Uzbekistan was adjudicated by organs of the Soviet state. The All-Union TsIK established a Commission on the Separation of the Tajik ASSR from the Uzbek SSR, with representatives from both republics as well as from All-Union institutions.[17] The Tajik side relied largely on historical arguments and banked on the work of Orientalists and philologists, while the Uzbeks argued in terms of the present, in which they denied that Tajiks were numerous.

---

14. "'TMB' kengash majlisi mazbatasi (Berlin, 24/iii–2/iv 1939)," Archives Mustafa Chokay Bey, carton 5, dossier 2, ff. 184–193. With the outbreak of war in 1941, Central Asia acquired a certain significance for the Nazis, who sought to use all national grievances against the Soviet regime. With some trepidation, Cho'qoy collaborated in the establishment of the Turkestan Legion, recruited amongst Soviet POWs of Central Asian origin. This much-mystified episode is explored with documentary evidence by Bakhyt Sadykova, *Istoriia Turkestanskogo Legiona v dokumentakh* (Almaty, 2002).

15. GARF, f. 3316, op. 64, d. 768, ll. 2–11.

16. "Politicheskie obosnovaniia proiskhodiashchei uzbekizatsii tadzhikskogo naseleniia na territorii UzSSR," RGASPI, f. 62, op. 2, d. 1744, ll. 106–114.

17. These negotiations have been described by Francine Hirsch, *Empire of Nations: Ethnographic Knowledge and the Making of the Soviet Union* (Ithaca, 2005), 175–186; Paul Bergne, *The Birth of Tajikistan: National Identity and the Origins of the Republic* (London, 2007), 100–124; and R. Masov, *Istoriia topornogo razdeleniia* (Dushanbe, 1991).

At one point, Yo'ldosh Oxunboboyev, the head of Uzbekistan's TsIK, argued that although the emir of Bukhara was an Uzbek, he had pursued a policy of "Tajikization" that had made Uzbeks speak Tajik. Language, thus, was not an indication of ethnic origin.[18] This was the Turkist view of Central Asia at its most blatant. The Tajik side, for its part, laid claim to the cities of Bukhara, Samarqand, Khujand, their environs, as well as the Surxon Daryo okrug, which it argued had solidly Tajik populations that had been mistakenly given to Uzbekistan in 1924. These claims were hotly contested by the Uzbeks, who pointed to census data to argue that the population of the area was Uzbek. The Tajiks, in turn, cast doubt on the accuracy of the census and argued their point historically. Using Barthold's arguments, the Tajik side claimed the mantle of the region's original Iranian population "which later came to be called Tajik." The commission sought expert advice and gathered a large quantity of material from the Academy of Sciences, none of which proved decisive. In a short memo, Barthold questioned the very premise of the national delimitation, stating at the outset that "the national principle in the form that it was implemented in the national delimitation of Central Asia in 1924 was developed in the course of Western European history of the nineteenth century and was completely alien to local historical traditions."[19] Other arguments suggested recent change. Ilyas Alkin opined that while statistical data showed that historically Tajiks had predominated in the Surxon Daryo okrug, the present situation was different.[20] In analyzing the decline in the number of Tajiks recorded in Samarqand, the Central Statistical Administration suggested the possibility that "the national self-consciousness of the Tajiks themselves might have changed, who now have registered themselves as Uzbeks."[21]

Ultimately, the commission based its decisions on political, not ethnographic, considerations. At a meeting early in the process, Zelenskii declared that Tajik demands for annexing "continuous masses of Tajik population in cities" were to be rejected, and the question not be raised in any discussion. "The matter is clear: to separate the urban population of Tajiks from the rural masses is not possible.... If this is brought up in a discussion, there will be agitation for separation, and counteragitation, while nothing will be done about serving the population."[22] This position ultimately prevailed. Tajikistan received Khujand, but Tajik

---

18. GARF, f. 3316, op. 22, d. 129, l. 25.

19. GARF, f. 3316, op. 22, d. 127, ll. 164–165; see also Muzaffar Olimov, "V.V. Bartol'd o natsional'nom razmezhevanii v Srednei Azii." Available at http://www.ca-c.org/datarus/st_13_olimov.shtml. The memo was a short excursus on the long-term history of Central Asia with no practical recommendations; it was meant as much to sneer at the authorities as to help them out.

20. GARF, f. 3316, op. 22, d. 127, ll. 150–149ob (reverse pagination).

21. Ibid., l. 147ob (TsSU to VTsIK, 21.12.1929).

22. GARF, f. 3316, op. 64, d. 768, l. 81 (23.05.1929).

demands for Samarqand, Bukhara, and Surxon Darya were rejected.[23] The party leadership had long been wary of the factionalism of the Uzbek party elite and increasingly concerned with nationalism in its ranks, but at least a party elite existed among the Uzbeks. The same could not be said of the Tajiks. Moscow was loath to put a large republic in the hands of a nonexistent national party elite. At the same time, it perceived a foreign policy opportunity in a high-profile, Persian-speaking republic on the border of Afghanistan. Pieties about Tajikistan being "the vanguard not just of social and political revolution, but also of cultural revolution, in the Persian-speaking East"[24] were not entirely devoid of geopolitical reasoning. The outbreak of civil war in Afghanistan in 1929, which also meant a return of many exiled Basmachi to Tajikistan, heightened the significance of this far-off frontier of the Land of Soviets. The elevation of Tajikistan to the status of union republic was one answer, but such elevation required an urban center. Khujand was therefore annexed to Tajikistan, even as other Tajik demands remained unmet. The annexation was awkward, since the district was separated from the rest of Tajikistan by mountains not easily crossed. Yet, Khujand had a better-developed party organization than the rest of the republic, which dominated the republic for much of post–Second World War period.

Even the harshest critics of Soviet nationalities policy cannot ascribe the separation of Tajikistan from Uzbekistan and its elevation to the status of a union republic to a divide-and-rule policy. It was the result of demands from the Tajik leadership and, if anything, central authorities tried their best to moderate Tajik demands. Rather, the separation had to do with the way in which Tajik and Uzbek elites had internalized the categories of ethnic nationhood and had come to see the historically intertwined sedentary Muslim population of Central Asia as composed of two distinct national and racial groups, each with its own political rights. These conceptions were of prerevolutionary vintage, but they found resonance with classificatory schemes used by the Soviet state. The ethnic disaggregation of the Muslim population of Central Asia was thus the culminating feature of the age of revolution on Central Asia.

The disaggregation of the sedentary Muslims of Turkestan into Uzbeks and Tajiks has parallels in many parts of the world in the first half of the twentieth century. The ethnicization and subsequent unmixing of populations was a common phenomenon in a vast swathe of territory in Eurasia. The process was

---

23. Surxon Daryo was initially awarded to Tajikistan, but the decision was overturned, largely in the face of stiff opposition from the Uzbek side.

24. This quote comes from Tursunqul, "Sharqda inqilob omili," *Alanga*, no. 10–11 (Nov. 1928), 24–25.

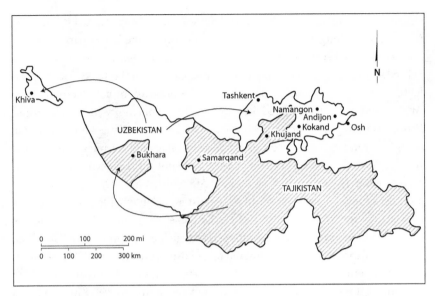

MAP 4. Uzbekistan as it would appear if Tajik demands had been upheld in 1929. It would have consisted of three exclaves unconnected to each other, while Tajikistan would contain the bulk of Transoxiana's population.

driven both by national movements and by states, and it produced the homogenization of populations in many places. We know of many examples from across Europe: Bohemians turned into Czechs and Germans, the Polish-Belarusian-Ukrainian borderland (the so-called *kresy*) was nationalized and its population classified into acceptable (or accepted) national categories, and Anatolia became the Turkish heartland—to cite just a few examples.[25] The unmixing and homogenization of populations was an essential part of modernity as it unfolded in Europe. Central Asia's experience under Soviet rule was depressingly normal in that regard.

At the same time, Soviet authorities' support for the Uzbek cause kept the Chaghatayist dream alive. Had all Tajik demands been fulfilled, the map of Central Asia would have looked very different (see map 4). Uzbekistan would have been reduced to three noncontiguous regions and the zone of sedentary

25. Jeremy King, *Budweisers into Czechs and Germans: A Local History of Bohemian Politics, 1848–1948* (Princeton, 2002); Kate Brown, *A Biography of No Place: From Ethnic Borderland to Soviet Heartland* (Cambridge, MA, 2004); Uğur Ümit Üngör, *The Making of Modern Turkey: Nation and State in Eastern Anatolia, 1913–1950* (Oxford, 2011).

population divided between two entities, with the major cities falling on both sides of the border. This would have been a total defeat for the Chaghatayist project that had sought to unite the zone of sedentary population under one political unit. The Tajiks' partial success meant that the fundamental claim of Uzbekistan as the heir to Islamicate statehood in sedentary Central Asia survived. Other than Khujand, ceded to Tajikistan, and Osh and Jalalabat, granted to Kyrgyzstan in 1924, Uzbekistan retained all the urban centers of Central Asia, while Tajikistan had only its picturesque mountains. The Tajiks who remained in Uzbekistan faced two choices: either to assume an Uzbek identity or to retain their status as Tajiks and to face the consequences of being part of a national minority. The idea that Uzbeks and Tajiks were two different peoples, divided by an essential ethnic difference, had won out. The national principle now made it possible to imagine the sedentary Muslim population of Central Asia population as composed of two distinct elements, speaking different languages and belonging to different racial groups. This was truly the triumph of the idea of the nation that was ushered in by a combination of native enthusiasms and Soviet institutional arrangements.

The First Purge and the Transformation of the Cultural Field

Six weeks after Hamza's murder, *Pravda Vostoka,* the Russian-language organ of the Central Committee of KPUz, published yet another scathing denunciation of nationalism and counterrevolution in the ranks of the Uzbek intelligentsia. Titled "The Bark of the Chained Dogs of the Khan of Kokand," the article was ostensibly a piece of investigative journalism that sought to uncover irregularities at the Uzbek State Publishing House (Uzgiz or O'zdavnashr), but behind financial irregularities it found nationalism, pan-Turkism, and Islamic reaction entrenched in the institution. Hadi Fayzi, the director, handed out appointments, publishing contracts, and honoraria to friends and colleagues, and approved the publication of ideologically unsound (hence "counterrevolutionary") books. A history of the Andijon uprising published by Uzgiz, for instance, glorified its leader Dukchi Eshon and turned him into a proletarian. But the author of the article reserved his thickest bile for Cho'lpon and Qodiriy, whose works had also been published by Uzgiz. Cho'lpon was "a prostitute of the pen ... [and] a stoker of chauvinism," whose patriotic anti-Soviet songs were sung "in chorus by Basmachis taken prisoner" years ago and now could be heard "all across Uzbekistan in any teahouse." His recent play *Mushtumzo'r,* commissioned by Uzgiz, had been sharply criticized by "worker Uzbeks" for its counterrevolutionary "poison."

Qodiriy, for his part, was "a homebred Cho'qoy," whose Kalvak Maxzum essays "heaped total abuse on Soviet power." Fayzi had been a member of the Kokand Autonomy, as was Bulat Saliyev, his brother-in-law, who was alleged to have received generous advances to publish an ideologically suspect history of Central Asia. The chain of guilt thus duly went back to that bête noir of the Soviet imagination, the short-lived and aborted experiment in autonomy at Kokand. The autonomists, however, were now not agents of British imperialism (which in fact did not rear its head in the article) or the bourgeoisie, but "lackeys of the khan of Kokand."[26] They had been orientalized and tied to Oriental despotism itself.

The article was the work of El'-Registan (1899–1945), the future author of the Soviet national anthem of 1943. Born Gabriel' Arkad'evich Ureklian to an Armenian family that had settled in Samarqand,[27] El'-Registan in 1929 was the special correspondent of *Izvestiia* in Tashkent and a "literary worker" at *Pravda Vostoka*, who had made a name for himself as a muck-raking journalist in Tashkent.[28] The article was noted by the Sredazburo, which requested (or received, at any rate) rebuttals to it. Cho'lpon wrote rather haughtily to deny that all the poems mentioned by El'-Registan belonged to him. As for criticisms of the play, "It is an old matter, for which I was abused plenty then. Now it's necessary to abuse [me] for new misdeeds, if there are any."[29] Among the others singled out by El'-Registan, Elbek wrote a more contrite letter, distancing himself from the Kokand Autonomy and his past connections with his teacher Munavvar qori.[30] Several of the Tatars accused by El'-Registan chose offense as the best form of defense. Ibrahim Tahiri accused El'-Registan of being a "paid servant of Uzbek chauvinism" and a dupe of Orifxonov, who had a shady past (his father was a qazi and he himself had been deprived of his rights), and who was denouncing Tatar employees of Uzgiz to assert his own rectitude. Behind Orifxonov, he argued, "stand the ultranationalists Ramziy and Botu, and they are directed by the former, but recent, counterrevolutionary, pan-Islamist, pan-Turkist–Chaghatayist Fitrat."[31] Fayzi repeated many of the same claims (without mentioning Fitrat), and concluded: "The company of tatarophobes and chauvinists

---

26. El'-Registan, "Lai tsepnykh sobak kokandskogo khana," *Pravda Vostoka*, 17.04.1929.

27. The pen name was composed of the last syllable of Ureklian's first name and the name of the famous square in Samarqand. However, "El" also evoked the Arabic definite article (not used in Uzbek, of course), and thus served an orientalizing function. The resulting combination was absurd: it was as if a Danish journalist working in Paris had assumed for himself the pen name of Die Bastille.

28. RGASPI, f. 62, op. 2, d. 1999, l. 80 (April 1929).

29. Ibid., l. 55ob (20.04.1929).

30. Ibid., ll. 65–69 (27.04.1929).

31. Ibid., l. 44 (20.04.1929).

headed by comrade Ramziy, embittered by my unmasking of their essence [*sushch-nost'*] and their activities, have decided to take me 'by hook or by crook.'"[32]

Such was the shape of political discourse in Uzbekistan in 1929: those accused of being pan-Islamic reactionaries in the service of the khan of Kokand could attack their accusers of being counterrevolutionary nationalists. Nationalism, it turned, was the most dangerous sin for national cadres to be accused of. Criticisms of "Uzbek chauvinism" therefore fell on fertile ground. As we have seen, the party leadership was worried about the rise of "Uzbek chauvinism" in the Uzbek intelligentsia at large and especially within its own ranks. In 1929, M. K. Ammosov, an instructor from the Moscow Central Committee, noted "the coarsest mistakes" in the implementation of nationalities policy in Uzbekistan, where national minorities (especially the Tajiks) had been coercively assimilated, so that "the indigenization of the apparat is replaced by its Uzbekization with a disregard of the interests of national minorities. The ideological expression of this practice appears in the preaching of the theory of the superiority of Uzbek culture over others (Uzbekism), the aspiration to subordinate and hold back the cultural growth of national minorities to the cultural level of the Uzbeks.... Similar theories, representing a throwback to pan-Turkism and Jadidism, or simply great-power Uzbek chauvinism have not until now been rebuffed within the party and are perceived by the masses as almost having become in practice the official ideology of the party."[33] But the malevolence of the national intelligentsia was also a useful scapegoat for explaining general discontent as new policies came in place. Early in 1930, the OGPU could write with assurance: "Materials in our possession indicate that 1929, especially its second half, was characterized not just by the general growth of anti-Soviet manifestations of the bais in the countryside, but also the growth in the activity of nationalist counterrevolutionary forces," including "a significant rearrangement of forces also among the national intelligentsia."[34] Nationalism was the biggest danger the party and the OGPU saw in Uzbekistan.

In the autumn of 1929, the OGPU moved into action. The arrests began on 6 November 1929, when OGPU agents arrested the alleged members of the Committee of National Independence, ostensibly "a counterrevolutionary organization of the national bourgeoisie" that sought independence for Uzbekistan. This marked the final arrest of Munavvar qori, who had been under surveillance for a long time. He was accused of "having preserved an irreconcilable enmity to

---

32. Ibid., l. 30ob.
33. Ammosov, "Materialy k dokladu TsK KP(b) Uzbekistana," RGASPI, f. 17, op. 67, d. 480, l. 149.
34. OGPU to Sredazburo, 06.02.1930, RGASPI, f. 62, op. 2, d. 2199, l. 2.

Soviet power," having "continued to group around himself the counterrevolutionary element of the bourgeois intelligentsia, conducted systematic anti-Soviet propaganda, in particular among the student youth, [and having] conducted espionage work on the instructions of Afghan diplomats."[35] Also arrested were Ubaydulla Xo'jayev (again), Salimxon Tillaxonov, Said Ahroriy, and Abduvahob Murodiy. Tillaxonov was the older brother of Xosiyat, a major figure at the women's magazine *Yangi yo'l* and a women's activist. Murodiy was one of the students sent to Germany, where he had studied agronomy. That alone made him suspect, but he had also been a student at Munavvar qori's Namuna school and a member of the Izchilar in 1918–19.[36] Next the OGPU uncovered a "National Committee" (Milliy Qo'mita) in Namangan.[37] In January 1930, the arrests reached the offices of the Kokand newspaper *Yangi Farg'ona* (New Ferghana), where Hamza had been a contributor. Several members of the staff had begun gathering with other local intellectuals in a regular *gap* in November 1929. Within weeks, they were arrested. The OGPU saw in the *gap* a secret counterrevolutionary organization called "Botir Gapchilar,"[38] with thirteen formal members. "During this short three-month period, it had strengthened organizationally, worked out programmatic and tactical arrangements, [and] determined its most immediate goals."[39] The *gap* brought together old Jadids with party members and students in Soviet institutions. Its most prominent member was Ashurali Zohiriy, the old Jadid who had worked on the newspaper until 1928, and was now characterized as "an active participant of the Kokand government [i.e., the Kokand Autonomy of 1917–18], nationalistically inclined."[40] All of them were arrested.

Even as these arrests were going on, a different case presented itself to the OGPU. In February 1930, Sa'dulla Qosimov, the head of the chief court of Uzbekistan, was arrested and put on trial on charges of corruption and "using Soviet institutions and his position in the interests of the enemy class."[41] The corruption trial very quickly became political as prosecutors discovered in Qosimov's motives not mere corruption but a careful nationalist plot. Not only was Qosimov in cahoots

---

35. Quoted by Sherali Turdiev, "Rol' Rossii v podavlenii dzhadidskogo dvizheniia (po materialam arkhiva SNB Uzbekistana)," *Tsentral'naia Aziia,* 1998, no. 1: 139

36. Abdulvahhob Murod, "Tarjima'i hol," *Qishloq xo'jalig'i turmushi,* 1927, no. 8: 23; Sherali Turdiyev, *Ular Germaniyada o'qigan edilar* (Tashkent, 2006), 42–59.

37. RGASPI, f. 62, op. 2, d. 2199, l. 11.

38. The term is absurd and OGPU materials leave it untranslated. It can be translated variously as "brave talkers" or "heroic feasters," although the OGPU would probably have favored a translation as "Heroic Debaters."

39. "O kontr-revoliutsionnoi organizatsii 'Batyr-gapchiliar,'" RGASPI, f. 62, op. 2, 2199, l. 3.

40. Ibid., l. 4.

41. *Pravda Vostoka,* 26.03.1930.

with the bais and the clergy, but also with a pan-Turkist organization in Tashkent, which counted many teachers in its ranks and was headed by none other than Munavvar qori. Qosimov had sought to plant the organization's agents in every Soviet institution with the aim of "wrecking" and infiltrating them.[42] From corruption to counterrevolution was a short path for Qosimov, who was sentenced to death in June.[43] Qosimov's name even acquired the dreaded suffix –shchina, and the case entered party history as "the Kasymovshchina," an episode in which "counterrevolutionary elements used our apparatus for their own uses in their struggle against Soviet power.... At the head of this counterrevolutionary organization stood one of the prominent members of old Jadidism... the well known Munavvar qori and his people."[44] Malfeasance in Soviet institutions was thus directly connected to counterrevolutionary nationalism.

The juggernaut rolled on. Two weeks after the conclusion of the Qosimov trial, Obid Saidov, the chief witness for the prosecution, fell ill after having dinner in company and died on 23 June 1930. The OGPU found traces of rat poison in his body and set in motion a full-blown investigation that very quickly led it to a counterrevolutionary nationalist organization. Saidov's death was a murder, it decided, the result of "a terrorist act of a counterrevolutionary organization" that sought revenge for Saidov's betrayal of nationalists.[45] The first to be arrested was Saidov's brother Nosir, who was the head of the Andijon okrug education department and a member of the collegium of Uzbekistan's Narkompros. In due course, he confessed to being party to the murder, which he told the OGPU had been ordered by none other than Botu himself. Botu, OGPU independently verified, had been deeply disturbed by the Qosimov trial. Now, Nosir Saidov's testimony revealed that Botu was a member of a secret nationalist organization called Milliy Istiqlol (National Independence). The goal of this organization, as allegedly articulated by Botu, was "the achievement of the independence of Uzbekistan in the form of a separate bourgeois-democratic republic. Not believing in the durability of the Soviet order, Botu [was supposed to have] said, 'It is necessary to think not only of the present, but

---

42. *Pravda Vostoka*, 03.04.1930.

43. This episode is often alluded to, but it has never been studied in detail; see the brief description in *O'zbekistonning yangi tarixi*, 3 vols. (Tashkent, 2000–2001), 2:322.

44. M. I. Kakhiani, "O Kasymovshchine," RGASPI, f. 62, op. 2, d. 2125, ll. 1–14. More publicly, the press proclaimed the "lessons of Kasymovshchina" to be the need for greater vigilance against masked enemies of the working class: "Uroki kasymovshchiny," *Pravda Vostoka*, 08.08.1930.

45. The above detail comes from the OGPU report on the case sent to Sredazburo: "Obzor sledstvennykh materialov po delu kontrrevoliutsionnoi natsionalisticheskoi organizatsii, raskrytoi PP OGPU v Srednei Azii v iiune 1930 goda (po sostoianiiu na 1 avgusta 1930 g.)," RGASPI, f. 62, op. 2, d. 2199, ll. 20–42 (August 1930).

also of the future.'" This required the preparation of cadres of specialists, which was to be achieved through the infiltration of Soviet institutions.[46] Already in the summer of 1929, he had allegedly told Nosir Saidov that "our Uzbek petty bourgeois [!] youth is in a very straitened condition, . . . excluded from schools and the Soviet apparat. In our thinking about education, we pay very little attention to the preservation in [the youth] of national feeling. Meanwhile, in the future [i.e., upon Uzbekistan's secession from the USSR] we will need cadres of nationalist youth. It is necessary to strengthen the nationalist reworking of the youth through the school and literature."[47] Further arrests yielded more confessions. It turned out that employees of Uzbekistan's Narkompros held a regular *gap*, which had led to the creation of a counterrevolutionary organization called G'ayratlilar Uyushmasi (Union of Enthusiasts) that functioned as a grassroots-level cell of Milliy Istiqlol. By the autumn, this was indeed the lesson being drawn from this series of investigations—that all Soviet institutions were had been infiltrated by nationalists and that the court and education systems in particular needed "renewal."[48]

Botu was arrested on 23 July 1930. His arrest triggered many others. Mannon Romiz was also arrested, as were Bois Qoriyev (Oltoy, the futurist poet), Qamchinbek, and many other young intellectuals, most of whom had enthusiastically denounced their elders in the preceding years. That the first blow struck the *Soviet* intelligentsia of Uzbekistan was deeply ironic, but not surprising in the context of the period. Corruption in Soviet institutions led to nationalism, and hence to the intelligentsia and the Uzbek Narkompros. The arrests did not go beyond Narkompros and the prerevolutionary intelligentsia was spared for the moment. Yet there could be no question that by early 1931 Uzbek cultural life had been shaken to its foundations.

None of those arrested in 1929–31 were given show trials. Rather, they were all shipped out to Moscow, where they underwent interrogation in the notorious Butyrka prison. The Milliy Istiqlol case involved eighty-seven accused, of whom fifteen were sentenced to death on 23 April 1931. Munavvar qori was executed immediately, but many of his codefendants were reprieved and sent off to labor camps.[49] Botu was shuttled between prisons in Moscow and

---

46. Ibid., l. 26.
47. Ibid., l. 25.
48. "Usilit' klassovuiu bditel'nost'," *Pravda Vostoka*, 07.08.1930.
49. The exact date of Munavvar qori's death remained unknown until after the collapse of the USSR; on his trial and execution, see Sotimjon Xolboyev, "Millatimizning ma'naviy otasi," in Munavvar qori Abdurashidxonov, *Xotiralarimdan (jadidchilik tarixidan lavhalar)*, ed. S. Xolboyev (Tashkent, 2001), 17–19.

Tashkent until 1933, when he and his codefendants were also sentenced to death. The sentences were then commuted to ten-year terms in labor camps. Botu spent five years in the Solovetsky Islands in the Arctic before he was summoned to Moscow and shot as part of the last wave of the Great Terror.[50] Romiz was sentenced to ten years' imprisonment, but released early and assigned to an inconsequential job in Rostov-on-the-Don, where he remained until his final arrest in 1937. Qamchinbek disappears from the published record. Oltoy spent years in camps but survived, and managed to return to scholarly work in the 1960s.

There was nothing original about the purge of the Uzbek intelligentsia. The OGPU had already played to this script in Ukraine in 1929, where it had uncovered a "Union for the Liberation of Ukraine" and used the ensuing show trial to purge Ukraine's Narkompros and the national intelligentsia. Over the decade that followed, the OGPU (and its successor, the NKVD) found similar plots in practically every republic—a Union of the East (Ittihodi Sharq) in Tajikistan, Turkmen Independence (Türkmen Azatlygy) in Turkmenistan, a Union for the Liberation of Belarus, and so forth—and used each one of them to purge the national intelligentsia of the republic involved. We have little reason, therefore, to believe in the actual existence of any of these organizations or of their goals. At the same time, there is no question that disaffection and disenchantment with party policies were rife among Uzbek intellectuals, including those who worked within Soviet institutions. The broad outlines of the critique of Soviet policies come to us from testimony recorded by the OGPU itself. The following passage from the testimony of Sobir Qodirov, one of the G'ayratlilar, is a case in point:

> The national policy of Soviet power in Uzbekistan we regard as a colonial [kolonizatorskaia] policy, as a continuation of the great power policies of Tsarism. Such a policy, in reality, provides for the wellbeing exclusively of the Russian nation at the expense of the exploitation of the indigenous population. Thus, for example, Europeans living in Uzbekistan find themselves in the most favorable situations, when the Uzbek part of the population is doomed to the most pitiable, beggarly existence.
>
> ... We consider that Uzbekistan has enough natural wealth and commodity production for it to be an independent economic unit, and consequently to have its own industry, both light and heavy.

50. Naim Karimov, "Shoirning fojiali taqdiri," in Botu, *Tanlangan asarlar*, ed. Naim Karimov and Sherali Turdiyev (Tashkent, 2004), 19–25.

We consider that Soviet power wittingly does not allow the development of independent industry in Uzbekistan exclusively because it seeks to keep Uzbekistan as a base for raw materials in order to extort its riches. In other words, Uzbekistan is a colony of inner Russia, supplying raw material for its industry.[51]

The Botir Gapchilar had a very similar critique of Soviet policies, and the OGPU reported Zohiriy as having said that "the current Red kolonizatorstvo . . . exceeds the kolonizatorstvo of Tsarist times."[52] Such grievances are to be found elsewhere in the archives too. In 1929, Yodgor Sodiqov, a party member from Khujand, took pen in hand to write directly to Stalin to report the dissatisfaction of Khujand's peasants at the shabby imbalance between the prices the state paid for cotton (and other cash crops) and what it charged for bread. "Peasants and artisans endure deprivation; they cannot complain, for they are afraid of arrest by the GPU. But the cup of the peasantry's patience is full to the brim. Waiting until it flows over is harmful. If the leadership of the party does not change and the people continue to be despised, then, without regard to my twelve years of work [for the party] and the loss of my health in this work, I will consider myself to have left the party."[53]

Uzbek Culture in the 1930s

The purge transformed the parameters of the cultural field as it had existed in the 1920s. Just as Tajikistan's case for elevation was being launched, a conference on language and orthography resolved to introduce a nine-vowel dialect with full vowel harmony as the basis of the modern Uzbek language. This triumph of the rural, more authentically Turkic dialects was in part a disavowal also of the literary heritage of Chaghatay. Over the next few months, shrill attacks on "Chaghatayism" appeared in the press. The lead was taken by Jalil Boybo'latov, who used the critique of Chaghatayism to attack Fitrat personally. Boybo'latov was a Chekist who had tracked Fitrat since the days of the BNSR.[54] Now he turned theorist and took to analyzing Fitrat's works on literary history. He found Fitrat's periodization of the history of Central Asia un-Marxist and his assertion of the link between Chaghatay and modern Uzbek problematic. "Chaghatay literature is alien to the contemporary Uzbek, both in content and in form. . . . Chaghatay

---

51. RGASPI, f. 62, op. 2, d. 2199, ll. 39–41.
52. Ibid., l. 4.
53. RGASPI, f. 62, op. 2, d. 1743, ll. 54–56 (1929).
54. Sherali Turdiyev, "Fitrat maxfiy siyosiy kuzatuvda," *Milliy tiklanish*, 17.12.1996, 3.

... is very distant from the contemporary literary language of the Uzbeks. Nine-tenths of Chaghatay is a mix of the Arabic and Persian languages. Therefore, not only does an ordinary literate Uzbek not understand it, but neither does an Uzbek intellectual who has emerged from a Soviet school or institute of education without additional training in the prerevolutionary religious 'university' of old Bukhara." Chagatayism was a thinly veiled form of pan-Turkism, pan-Islamism, and local nationalism, "the path of a breach with proletarian international ideology in the field of literature, the path to the breeding of literary chauvinists, the path of a return to the ideology of the 'golden age'—to mysticism."[55] Boybo'latov quoted Fitrat's earliest publications to claim that he was a Sufi, a pan-Islamist, a supporter of the emir (whom he had petitioned for reform in 1911), and so on. The article was republished several times, in both Uzbek and Russian, and eventually expanded into a book, and played a significant role in setting the tone for Uzbek Soviet literature of the 1930s. Fitrat was allowed to defend himself in the pages of the party's newspaper (it proved to be the last time Fitrat appeared in it) and Otajon Hoshimov, the director of the Uzbek Academic Center mounted a mild defense of Chaghatay heritage,[56] but "Chaghatayism" was effectively banished from the new literary landscape that emerged after the purge of 1929–30.

That landscape was fundamentally different from that of the 1920s. The institutionalization of cultural life that begun after the national delimitation allowed for far greater political control. Gone was the ability of indigenous intellectuals to carry out their own debates in the pages of the press or to use unauthorized or unorthodox formulations. The character of the press changed. *Maorif va o'qitg'uvchi* turned from a forum for the intelligentsia to a narrowly technical journal of pedagogy; *Yangi yo'l*, the women's magazine, became an agitprop organ for activists; and even *Xudosizlar* began carrying mostly advice for activists. Theater was ever more professionalized and ever more carefully monitored. The space for cultural experimentation shrunk and then closed. In English-language historiography, the transformations of the three years between 1929 and 1932, when the party-state asserted "proletarian" control over institutions of cultural and education, are known as the Cultural Revolution.[57] In Uzbekistan, as in many other non-Russian parts of the Soviet Union, the Cultural Revolution put paid to the cultural revolution—the blossoming of new forms of cultural expression,

---

55. Dzh. Baibulatov, "Uzbekskaia literatura i chagataizm," *Za Partiiu*, 1929, 3–4: 99–111; J. Boybo'latov, "O'zbek adabiyotida chig'atoychilik," *Qizil O'zbekiston*, 13.05.1929, 15.05.1929.

56. Otajon Hoshimov, "Adabiy meros va chig'atoy adabiyoti," *Qizil O'zbekiston*, 16.07.1929.

57. Sheila Fitzpatrick, ed., *Cultural Revolution in Russia, 1928–1931* (Bloomington, 1978).

the experimentation, and the autonomy—that had characterized the 1920s. This was not, however, simply the result of central interference, let alone of the assertion of the power of European cadres (although both did take place). The new form of Soviet power was staffed by indigenous cadres, but who labored under much stricter oversight in highly centralized institutions. In April 1932, the Sredazburo, following the resolutions of the All-Union Central Committee, established writers' unions in each republic under its oversight and resolved a greater role in providing party leadership for the "literary movement." Since "literature is one of the most powerful levers of cultural revolution among the backward, formerly oppressed nationalities of Central Asia," writers did important work. Under steadfast party control, they would engineer the human soul and contribute to the triumph of socialist construction.[58]

In its tone and its style, not to mention its content, the literature of the 1930s marked a drastic shift from the decade after the revolution. The polyphony of the first decade had been tamed already by 1929, but the purge at Narkompros inaugurated a period of homogenous obedience that would have been inconceivable earlier. The creation of a proletarian Uzbek literature became the foremost goal of the Soviet Uzbek intelligentsia, even as an Uzbek proletariat showed no signs of emerging. After 1934, when socialist realism was decreed to be the mandatory method of writing fiction, the possibilities of expression shrunk further. At the same time, the renunciation of the Persianate literary tradition, initiated by the Jadids themselves, went so far that Fitrat felt it necessary to write a manual "to acquaint our young poets and writers with aruz and to open a broad discussion of the question of prosody."[59] Fitrat was swimming against the tide here too. Uzbekness in the early 1930s was insistently contemporary, hence ruralist, with little use of the poetry of the past. The defeat of Chaghatayism seemed complete.

And yet the major Jadid figures—Fitrat, Cho'lpon, Qodiriy, Elbek—escaped arrest in 1929–30. To a certain extent, this is explicable by the political protection afforded them by Fayzulla Xo'jayev. No documentary proof of this has emerged (and such a proposition may inherently not be amenable to documentary proof), but Xo'jayev had defended Fitrat in 1926, and it is entirely plausible that he had something to do with the fact that the biggest names of Uzbek letters were spared

---

58. "O perestroike literaturno-khudozhestvennykh organizatsii v Srednei Azii: postanovlenie SrAzB TsK VKP(b)," *Sovetskaia literatura narodov Srednei Azii*, no. 1 (1932): 12.

59. Abdurauf Fitrat, *Aruz haqida*, ed. Hamidulla Boltaboyev (Tashkent, 1997 [orig. 1936]).

in this round.[60] They existed on sufferance, however, and the drumbeat of their vilification never ebbed. The dominant tone of the 1930s was one of constant and effusive thankfulness to the party and to Stalin himself for the gift of culture and liberation bestowed on Uzbekistan. "What belles lettres did we have in Uzbek before the revolution?" asked Akmal Ikromov rhetorically in 1934. "Prerevolutionary literature was the court poetry of khans and beks praising the eyes and waists of *bachchas*, or else works of a religious character."[61] Everything else had come with the revolution and was a gift of the party. This was combined with insistent denunciation of work that did not fit the limits of the permissible. Within these parameters, writers were obliged to take ideologically correct positions, to outflank each other, and to denounce those they thought were ideologically incorrect. The result was, as everywhere else in the Soviet Union, a culture of uncertainty in which denunciations became a way of asserting loyalty and belonging. There were enough generational and political conflicts among the Uzbek intelligentsia, but this new culture greatly heightened the stakes.

Joining the Writers' Union became all but mandatory for publishing authors after 1932. Membership had its benefits—by showing a willingness to bend to the Soviet order, members could hope to get published, or at least be left alone. They were made to eat a lot of crow, too. An anthology of Uzbek belles lettres published in Russian ("to acquaint the broad toiling masses of our Union with the Soviet literature of Uzbekistan") contained a short poem by Fitrat in praise of—of all things—cotton.[62] Other than this, Fitrat found himself shut out of the press and turned full time to scholarship, eventually acquiring the title of professor at the Institute of Language and Literature in Tashkent. Nicholas Poppe, a rising Turkologist in Leningrad, remembered

60. Begali Qosimov, *Maslakdoshlar: Behbudiy, Ajziy, Fitrat* (Tashkent, 1994), 145. The cultural memory of the late Soviet and post-Soviet Uzbek intelligentsia often sees Ikromov as a guardian angel in the 1930s. Rahmat Majidiy, head of the Uzbek Writers' Union in the 1930s, later recalled Ikromov telling him, "Be very careful in relation to authors [*ijodkorlar*]. For authors such as Abdulla Qodiriy, you will answer not just with your party ticket, but with your head." *Abdulla Qodiriy zamondoshlari xotirasida* (Tashkent, 1986), 9. Another story asserts that Cho'lpon succeeded in having his novel *Night* published in 1936 when he asked for Ikromov's intercession at a chance encounter in the Moscow metro; see Halim Kara, "Resisting Narratives: Reading Abdulhamid Suleymon Cholpan from a Postcolonial Perspective" (Ph.D. diss., Indiana University, 2000), 94n. This is partly the result of a will to remember both Ikromov and the "repressed" Uzbek literati as national heroes, but there is nevertheless a certain irony in the fact that this memory has turned the torchbearer of the ideological front into a miracle worker who looked out for the interests of the "old intellectuals."

61. Preface to *Literaturnyi Uzbekistan: al'manakh khudozhestvennoi literatury*, no. 1 (Tashkent, 1934), vii.

62. Fitrat, "Khlopok," in *Literaturnyi Uzbekistan*, 125.

receiving rare manuscripts from Central Asia courtesy of Fitrat.[63] Fitrat even published scholarly work in Russian: his last publication, which appeared in 1937, the year of his final arrest, was an analysis and translation into Russian of a collection of sixteenth-century qazi documents.[64]

Cho'lpon too remained under the gun. One of Oltoy's last published pieces before his arrest was an attack on Cho'lpon, and the poet continued to be attacked in both Uzbek and Russian.[65] In 1932, apparently on the advice of Fayzulla Xo'jayev, he left Tashkent for Moscow where he was less prominent. He worked as a translator and even married a Russian woman, possibly to counter his classification as a nationalist.[66] He had a few years of relative peace, in which he translated numerous works of Russian literature as well as *Hamlet* (via the Russian) into Uzbek. He also managed to publish a novel and what turned out to be his last collection of poetry. The novel *Kecha* (Night) is remarkable for its sensibility, which has nothing to do with the reigning orthodoxy of socialist realism. Yet the respite was not to last. In 1936, attacks on him picked up again in the press, accusing not just Cho'lpon but his editors and publishers of being counterrevolutionaries and "enemies of the people."[67] He was still defiant and sarcastic when he was hauled in front of a gathering of the Writers' Union to answer charges against himself in April 1937. "I have many mistakes, but I will correct them with your help. But what training have you given me in these years?" Pointing to the fact that his recent works had appeared without explanatory prefaces, he asked, "Abuse was required here, for the youth should not be allowed to read Cho'lpon's works without an intermediary. . . . Why did the work of this nationalist appear without a preface?"[68]

Qodiriy did better than the other two. He never had regular employment after his arrest in 1926, but he managed to find freelance work as editor and translator. Among other jobs, he compiled the section on the letter P in the first major Russian-Uzbek dictionary in 1934, translated a collection of antireligious essays, and was working on a film script based on Chekhov's *Cherry Orchard* at the time of his arrest.[69] And he continued to write. In 1932, he was admitted to the Uzbekistan Writers' Union and two years later elected as one of its delegates to the First

63. Nicholas Poppe, *Reminiscences*, ed. Henry Schwartz (Bellingham, WA, 1983), 119, 266.

64. R. R. Fitrat and K. S. Sergeev, *Kaziiskie dokumenty XVI veka* (Tashkent, 1937).

65. Oltoy, "Cho'lponchilik kayfiyotlari bilan kurashaylik," *Yosh leninchi*, 27.07.1930.

66. Murtazo Qorshiboyev, "Muhit erkidagi tutqinlik," *Sharq yulduzi*, 1990, no. 10: 196; Naim Karimov, *Cho'lpon* (Tashkent, 1991), 32.

67. For quotes from these denunciations, see Sherali Turdyev, "Sud'ba 'Utrennei zvezdy,'" *Zvezda Vostoka*, 1991, no. 10: 83–84.

68. Cho'lpon, "Nutq," in *Fitna san'ati*, 2 vols. (Tashkent, 1993), 2:189–194.

69. Habibulla Qodiriy, *Otamdan xotira* (Tashkent, 2005), 247–248, 276–279, 316–318, 332.

Congress of the All-Union organization. (There, in the company of Sadriddin Ayni, he met Maxim Gorky; a photograph of the three of them became iconic in later Soviet publications, which gave little indication of the dark shadows that hung over all three of them.) Qodiriy was asked, his son tells us, by Fayzulla Xo'jayev to write about Uzbek peasant life, "as Russian writers were doing" about Russian peasants. Qodiriy tramped around the Uzbek countryside for two years, researching a novel on peasant life during collectivization, which was serialized as *Obid ketmon* between 1932 and 1934. His novels were published with astonishingly large press runs (ten thousand copies for *O'tkan kunlar*, seven thousand for *Mehrobdan choyon*) and frequently reprinted, and Qodiriy had acquired the status of *the* outstanding Uzbek novelist—and the most beloved—that he never lost.[70] But in the spring of 1937, a campaign of vilification began against him too, with Olim Sharafiddinov and Jumaniyoz Sharifiy (Sharipov) criticizing *Obid ketmon* as anti-Soviet and Qodiriy himself as antisocial and apolitical.[71]

The protection of political leaders had its limits, of course, and they could not do anything about the general mood of the period which was extremely hostile to the Jadids and their nationalism and in which younger writers jockeyed to assert their credentials by criticizing their elders. Literary criticism (or what passed for it) of the decade is full of denunciations of the bourgeois nationalism that had contaminated Uzbek literature in the 1920s. Many of the critics were the young *madaniyatchi*. Ziyo Said had a particular animus toward Cho'lpon, and Hamid Olimjon and Olim Sharafiddinov penned many critical appraisals of "bourgeois Uzbek literature" in these years. A more unusual case was that of Miyon Buzruk Solihov, who wrote a number of scathing critiques of Jadid literature in the 1930s. These included histories of modern Uzbek literature and theater that, while providing invaluable firsthand information, were insistently denunciatory of bourgeois nationalism, pan-Islamism, and pan-Turkism.[72] Yet Solihov was not at all a madaniyatchi. Born in Tashkent, he had been active in the press in 1917–18 and had become involved in the secret societies of the period. At some point, most likely 1920, he went to Afghanistan as an agent of the national movement. In May 1921, we find the Bukharan ambassador in Afghanistan passing Fayzulla Xo'jayev's greetings to Solihov in Kabul.[73] In April 1923, Zeki Velidi

---

70. Qodiriy was one of the first victims of the 1930s to be rehabilitated during the Thaw. *O'tkan kunlar* was republished in 1958 with a print run of ninety thousand copies and bookshops had trouble keeping it in stock. Abdulaziz Muhammadkarimov, "Yuzimizni yorug' etgan kitob," in *Qodiriyni ko'msab: yodnoma* (Tashkent, 1994), 66.

71. H. Qodiriy, *Otamdan xotira*, 324–330.

72. M. Buzruk Solihov, *O'zbek adabiyotida millatchilik ko'rinishlari (qisqacha tarix)* (Tashkent, 1933); idem., *O'zbek teatr tarixi uchun materiallar* (Tashkent, 1935).

73. TsGARUz, f. 46, op. 1, d. 124, l. 2ob.

told the British attaché in Mashhad that Solihov was the Kabul representative of the TMB.[74] Solihov left Kabul in June 1923, travelling via Bombay to Jeddah on a pilgrim passport,[75] and eventually ending up in Turkey, where he was active in émigré circles as well as in the world of scholarship.[76] Then, for some reason, he returned, legally, to the Soviet Union in 1927. There might have been personal reasons for his return, or perhaps he was afraid for his family's safety. But clearly, the return came at a cost. He was an active agent for the OGPU until 1931, and many of his attacks on the Jadids—of whom he had been one—were clearly ways of distancing himself from them and of asserting his own loyalty and political steadfastness. It did not work, for he himself was also an easy target for attacks from others. Solihov spent some time in exile of sorts, teaching Tajik in Tajikistan, before ending up in Bukhara.[77]

The End

The end came in 1937 when the Great Terror arrived in Uzbekistan. Fayzulla Xo'jayev and Akmal Ikromov were both arrested in July 1937 after the Seventh Congress of KPUz. For all their differences over the years, they faced their ultimate fate together. They were duly discovered to have been part of a "bloc of Rights and Trotskyites" that had sought to dismember the Soviet Union on the instructions of the intelligence services of foreign states. They were accused of having belonged to conspiratorial organizations that engaged, among other things, in "wrecking, diversionist and terrorist activities, undermining the military power of the USSR, provoking a military attack . . . on the USSR, dismembering the USSR."[78] More specifically, Xo'jayev and Ikromov were accused of membership of Milliy Ittihod, whose goal was to separate Uzbekistan from the Soviet state and to place it under a British protectorate. They were executed on 15 March 1938.

---

74. IOR, L/P&S/10/950, f. 438.

75. Ibid., 441v.

76. When Zeki Velidi finally arrived in Istanbul in May 1925, he received help from Solihov, Usmon Xojao'g'li (Kocaoğlu), and Mehmed Emin Resulzade, the Azerbaijani émigré; A.Z.V. Togan, *Hâtıralar: Türkistan ve Diğer Müslüman Doğu Türklerinin Millî Varlık ve Kültür Mücadeleleri*, 2nd ed. (Ankara, 1999), 515.

77. Solihov's journey was complex and many of our questions about it might well be unanswerable; for a biography that still leaves a lot unexplained, see Burhon Abdulxayrov, *Miyon Buzruk— Jadid dramaturgiyasi va teatri tadqiqotchisi* (Tashkent, 2009), 16–36.

78. *Report of Court Proceedings in the Case of the Anti-Soviet "Bloc of Rights and Trotskyites," Heard Before the Military Collegium of the Supreme Court of the USSR . . . : Verbatim Report* (Moscow, 1938), 5 et passim.

Their removal opened the floodgates of arrests among Uzbekistan's intelligentsia. Cho'lpon was arrested on 13 July 1937, Fitrat nine days later. Abdulla Qodiriy survived until the last day of 1937, when he too was taken away. In the intervening months, the jails had filled with large numbers of writers and historians (as well as party and soviet functionaries). They were interrogated, made to sign confessions, and denounce their colleagues. As in the rest of the Soviet Union, the result was a tangled web of lies, half-truths, and dubious assertions, all intermixed with evidence of human frailty and desperation. The files pertaining to these cases survive, but have generally been made accessible to only a few select Uzbek scholars. This is partly because the ugliness they contain (especially in the denunciations, solicited or volunteered) leaves no one untainted.[79] The fate of those hauled in in these months was sealed. Between late 1936 and late 1938, various branches of the NKVD compiled lists of people to be arrested and tried by the Military Collegium of the Supreme Court of the Soviet Union, which were then sent for approval to the Politburo in Moscow; most of the 383 lists (with almost 44,000 names) were signed by Stalin himself, and the vast majority of those named in them executed. A list compiled on 28 March 1938 contained, among its 155 names, a directory of the Uzbek intelligentsia: in addition to Fitrat and Cho'lpon, it also carried the names of the old Jadids Go'zi Olim and Shokirjon Rahimiy (Elbek was in the supplementary list of those placed in Category 2, those destined for long imprisonments); early Soviet-era intellectuals such as Qayum Ramazon, Otajon Hoshimov, and Anqaboy Xudoyvohidov; the Young Communists Rahimjon Inog'amov, Usmonxon Eshonxo'jayev, and Abdulhay Tojiyev; the historian Ziyo Imodiy; Sattor Jabbor, who had studied in Germany; the madaniyatchi Ziyo Said; and even figures from the revolutionary era, such as Sa'dulla Tursunxo'jayev and Muhammadjon Biserov. Mannon Romiz was also there, as was Ikromov's wife, Evgeniia Zel'kina, and D. I. Manzhara, the longtime head of the republic's Central Control Commission.[80] A second list, dated 12 September 1938, added the names of Abdulla Qodiriy, Hadi Fayzi, Buzruk Solihov, and Shohid Eson to those of the condemned.

---

79. In the political turmoil of 1990–91, an Uzbek journalist gained access to Abdulla Qodiriy's files and published a "documentary novel" based on them in the journal of Uzbekistan's Writers' Union. The editorial board published it with a note expressing unease at the fact the files contained denunciations in the name of writers such as G'afur G'ulom, Oybek, and Abdulla Qahhor, all of them central figures in the pantheon of modern Uzbek literature, and trying to distance them from the implications. Tahririyat, "Qo'rquv saltanati qissasi," *Sharq yulduzi*, 1991, no. 5: 31–32.

80. These so-called "Stalin's Lists" have been published online by Memorial, the historical and civil rights organization in Russia. The list in question is in Arkhiv Prezidenta Rossiiskoi Federatsii, f. 3, op. 24, d. 415, ll. 220–228, and was signed by Stalin, Molotov, Kaganovich, Zhdanov, and Voroshilov; see http://stalin.memo.ru/regions/regi74.htm for all lists pertaining to Uzbekistan.

And yet, even though their deaths had been foretold, the accused continued to be interrogated and often confronted with one another. The charges were as fantastical as those against Xo'jayev and Ikromov. Fitrat "confessed" to having been a leading figure in Milliy Ittihod, into which he had been recruited by Fayzulla Xo'jayev and where he became the leading "ideologue of bourgeois nationalism and pan-Turkism." Along with Xo'jayev, Munavvar qori, and a host of others, he had organized the Basmachi to conduct armed struggle against Soviet power with the goal of establishing an independent, bourgeois nationalist state in Central Asia.[81] Qodiriy was accused of having been a member of a counterrevolutionary organization that collaborated with Trotskyites, of carrying out anti-Soviet work in the press, and of having direct relations with Xo'jayev and Ikromov.[82] Qodiriy admitted being a nationalist until 1932, but claimed to have mended his ways after that. After months of interrogation, he received the final resolution of the court. According to his son, the last page of Qodiriy's file contains a short, handwritten note in Qodiriy's handwriting (in the Arabic script) stating, "This resolution was announced to me (I read it); I do not agree to the charges contained in it and do not accept them."[83]

There were many other arrests and executions of people not on Stalin's lists. Botu, we will remember, was recalled from the Solovetsky islands in 1937 only to be rendered to Moscow and shot. Tŭrar Rïsqŭlov and Nazir To'raqulov were also arrested in 1937 and shot in 1938. Hoji Muin died in a prison camp in Solikamsk in the Urals in 1942,[84] Said Rizo Alizoda in prison in Vladimir in 1945.[85] Others survived, but spent many years in forced labor camps and political disgrace. Laziz Azizzoda, arrested in 1930, went from camp to camp until his release in 1954, as did Oltoy and many others. It is difficult to assign too much rationality to the choice of those who survived. While there is no question that the terror targeted anyone with a record of prerevolutionary activism, there was little to distinguish those of the younger generation who died from those of that generation who survived. Why Oybek survived and Ziyo Said did not, for instance, is not a matter of rational explication. The only major figure from the prerevolutionary period not to be touched by the madness was Sadriddin Ayni. He had his moments of difficulty, but he survived and died in his bed in 1954 at the age of 76, having outlived

---

81. The record of Fitrat's "cross examination" has now been published: "Protokol doprosa obviniaemogo FITRATA Rauf Rakhimovicha ot 25 oktiabria 1937 goda," in *Tarixning noma'lum sahifalari: hujjat va materiallar*, bk. 1 (Tashkent, 2009), 108–122.

82. Quoted by Nabijon Boqiy, "Qatlnoma," *Sharq yulduzi*, 1991, no. 5: 77.

83. H. Qodiriy, *Otamdan xotira*, 399.

84. Boybo'ta Do'stqorayev and Nilufar Namozova, "Behbudiyning munosib shogirdi," in Hoji Muin, *Tanlangan asarlar* (Tashkent, 2005), 17.

85. Sherali Turdiyev, "Maorif va matbuot fidoiysi," *Ma'rifat*, 07.05.2003.

Stalin. Other than luck, we can point to his being a Tajik living in Uzbekistan, and hence not connectable to nationalism or pan-Turkism, and to his low political profile, as explanations—to the extent explanations explain anything in the business of the Great Terror of 1936–38.

But to return to Stalin's lists: those on them awaited the arrival of a circuit session of the Supreme Military Court of the USSR in Tashkent, which apparently took place at the beginning of October 1938. On 5 October 1938, the court sentenced almost all the defendants to the "highest penalty." But the massacre had already taken place the night before. The night of 4–5 October 1938 saw the execution of two generations of the Uzbek intelligentsia, from the Jadids active before 1917 to real sons of the Soviet order such as Anqaboy (b. 1903) and Otajon Hoshimov (b. 1905). What brought them together before the firing squad was the Soviet state's fear of "nationalism"—a term whose definition had become desperately expansive by this time. Nationalism was clearly the biggest danger for the OGPU/NKVD and the party in the non-Russian regions of the USSR. Its rhetorical pairing with "great power chauvinism" in official discourse was deceptive. There were no trials, let alone any executions, for great power chauvinism anywhere in the USSR, but charges of nationalism proved fatal to the intelligentsias of many Soviet nationalities. Even in 1938, in the final act of the Great Terror, the charges against Fayzulla Xo'jayev and Akmal Ikromov were those of nationalism, not of right deviation or left. Xo'jayev was charged with establishing a nationalist organization that then *allied itself* with the right deviation in the party. He himself was not accused of a right deviation.[86] Natives could only be national; political deviation was the job of the Europeans.

This decapitation of the Uzbek intelligentsia—small as its ranks were—redefined the attitudes of the survivors. Both among the political elite and the intelligentsia, the response was one of fearful obedience. The new political leadership—what Donald Carlisle called the "Class of '38"—had learned the rules of the game the hard way.[87] Usmon Yusupov, the new first secretary of KPUz, had worked his way up through the ranks of the party and was a very different figure from Ikromov or Xo'jayev. Years of careful self-cultivation had taught him the virtues prized by the Stalinist leadership.[88] Similarly, the purge

---

86. See the record of his "interrogation" in *Report of Court Proceedings*, 212–243.

87. On "the class of '38," see Donald S. Carlisle, "The Uzbek Power Elite: Politburo and Secretariat (1938–83)," *Central Asian Survey* 5:3–4 (1986): 99.

88. On locating Yusupov in his context, see Christian Teichmann, "Cultivating the Periphery: Bolshevik Civilising Missions and 'Colonialism' in Soviet Central Asia," *Comparativ: Zeitschrift für Globalgeschichte und vergleichende Gesellschaftsforschung* 19:1 (2009): 49–51.

"imposed a devastating peace and conformity" in the ranks of the intelligentsia.[89] For the survivors, the task was to reorganize and to conserve what had not been lost. The generational and political battles of the previous fifteen years seemed irrelevant. It fell to Hamid Olimjon, the new head of Uzbekistan's Writers' Union, to undertake the effort once the terror ended in 1939. One key feature of this reconstruction of the literary establishment was the imposition of a complete amnesia about the past, especially about the first decade of Soviet rule. Even when the process of the political rehabilitation of the victims of the 1930s began, the cultural rehabilitation of the Jadids never really took place. Qodiriy's novels were back in print (and translated into numerous languages), but none of his other work saw the light of day. Fitrat and Cho'lpon remained anathematized until late into the era of glasnost, and the history of modern Uzbek literature continued to be written without them.

Coda

In 1941, the five hundredth anniversary of the birth of Alisher Navoiy was planned at the All-Union level. In connection with this jubilee, a special committee of Uzbekistan's sovnarkom commissioned the Russian historian and Orientalist A. Iu. Iakubovskii to prepare a work on the history of the Uzbek people. The resulting brochure, *On the Question of the Ethnogenesis of the Uzbek People*, was published only in Russian but it soon became the basic text of Uzbek national identity. In it, Iakubovskii argued against "the view, not extirpated to our days, that the Uzbek people derives all its existence from the Uzbek nomads who began to appear in Central Asia in the fifteenth century and conquered it under the leadership of Shaybani Khan only at the beginning of the sixteenth century." Instead, Iakubovskii laid out a much longer lineage for the Uzbeks: "The 'nomadic Uzbeks' entered the composition of the Uzbek people . . . as only the last essential ingredient. Its basis was not the nomads, but the entire Turkic population of Uzbekistan, which formed here in the course of many centuries in the complex process of ethnogenesis." The same applied to culture and language. "It is extraordinarily characteristic that the newcomer nomadic Uzbeks accepted in literature the language that had been dominant among the Turks of Transoxiana and which was called Chaghatay. . . . Philology and linguistics also give us the same unbroken line of development that passes from the language of Khoja

---

89. David C. Montgomery, "Career Patterns of Sixteen Uzbek Writers," *Central Asian Survey* 5:3–4 (1986): 214.

Ahmad Yasavi, through that of Lutfiy and Alisher Navoiy, to the contemporary Uzbek literary language."[90]

Fitrat would have wholeheartedly agreed had he not been lying in an unmarked grave by that time. This was the Chaghatayist view of Central Asian history dressed up in the garb of ethnogenesis, a concept just then beginning its rise to scholarly and political acceptability. Significant transformations in the nationalities policies in the 1930s demanded that Soviet nations all possess stable histories, well established claims to their territories, and ancient cultural pantheons. The proletarian enthusiasms of the 1920s and the early 1930s were a distant memory. It also helped that, by 1941, all prerevolutionary actors had been helped into their graves. In Uzbekistan, the rural, hyper-Turkic phonetics of the Uzbek literary language adopted in 1929 had already been abandoned in favor of a six-vowel standard without vowel harmony in 1934. Literary Uzbek as it developed after that was much closer to Chaghatay (which came to be called "old Uzbek") than the more radical reformers of the late 1920s had envisioned. The vision of the Uzbek heritage as encompassing the Turkic (and, implicitly, the entire Islamicate) heritage of Central Asia, with the Chaghatay epoch as its crowning glory, came to be accepted as official orthodoxy. Such luminaries of Chaghatay letters as Alisher Navoiy, Zahiruddin Muhammad Bobur, and Mirza Ulugh became the central heroes of the Uzbek pantheon, and Uzbek literature claimed the Turkic heritage of sedentary Central Asia. A four-volume anthology published in 1959–60 created a literary canon of "classical Uzbek literature" that scarcely differed from that of Fitrat's anthologies of 1927 and 1928, even though Fitrat's work could not be mentioned.[91] Temur remained off-limits, of course, but there was no question that the Soviet Uzbek nation laid claim to the Cha-ghatay heritage. The reemergence of Temur as a national symbol after the Soviet collapse is therefore scarcely surprising. All of this was, of course, cold comfort to the Jadids. They had paid for their enthusiasm for the nation with their lives.

---

90. A. Iu. Iakubovskii, *K voprosu ob etnogeneze uzbekskogo naroda* (Tashkent, 1941), 1, 12, 13, 18–19.

91. *O'zbek adabiyoti: to'rt tomlik* (Tashkent, 1959–60).

Epilogue

The massacre of the Uzbek intelligentsia in October 1938 marked the passing of an age. The flux and possibility of the 1920s had already been squashed by the purge of 1929–31, but the executions of 1938 put a final end to the enthusiasms of the era of the revolution. There were survivors, to be sure, but 1938 saw a changing of the guard in the realms of both politics and culture. The Jadid generation had come to an end. What are we to make of its experience?

The Fascination of Revolution

The Jadids were a modernizing elite that, fascinated by notions of progress and modernity, sought to transform its society. The nation was to them the obvious locus of solidarity, the only one that would allow society to unite, strengthen itself, and join the modern world on an equal footing with other modern nations. The world was reshaped in the twentieth century by numerous groups driven by similar passions for decolonization, nation building, economic development, modernization, and overcoming "backwardness." What made the Jadids of Central Asia (and their counterparts in many other nationalities of the Soviet state) different was their position vis-à-vis the state. In Turkey or Iran, to pick two relevant examples, modernizing elites controlled (or cooperated with) the state and put its apparatus to unprecedented use in implementing their agenda of cultural transformation. In Central Asia, on the other hand, the prerevolutionary intelligentsia could never control the state apparatus (the short-lived People's Republic of Bukhara was a partial exception) and instead fell victim to the Bolsheviks, a different kind of modernizing elite. The Bolsheviks' vanquishing of the Jadids should not make us forget how much the two projects had in common or the degree to which the Russian revolution radicalized the worldview of the Jadids.

The Jadids' relationship to their own society was highly fraught. Jadidism arose as a thoroughgoing critique of the state of Central Asian society, and the Jadids had little fondness for things as they were in their society. The modern future was legitimized by an appeal to authenticity, but recovering that authenticity required the rejection of the present and the recent past. Jadidism was in fact a series of revolts—against custom, against tradition, against the authority of the past, against the authority of their elders and of established elites in society, against the Persianate literary tradition, against Islam itself. The revolts spoke also to deep conflicts within Central Asia societies. In independent Uzbekistan, the Jadids have been anointed national heroes who acted on behalf of the nation and struggled for its rights against a despotic Soviet state. Outside of Uzbekistan, there remains a general hesitation to accentuate the radicalism of the Jadids, for fear, it seems, that it might dilute their resistance to the Bolsheviks or concede something to the Soviets. Yet viewing the Jadids as national heroes obscures the conflict within Central Asian society. It also downplays their cultural radicalism. Such moves only end up asserting the imperviousness of Muslim society to the world around and lead us to vastly underestimate the cultural ferment of the interwar period in the Muslim world at large.

A great deal of this cultural radicalism was borne of a sense of desperation as the Great War ended with the utter defeat of the Ottoman Empire. If the demise of the last remaining sovereign Muslim state called for desperate measures, then the Russian revolution provided hope and possible answers. The Russian revolution appeared to many in the colonial world (within and without the Russian Empire) as an anticolonial moment that might undermine the regnant imperial order. Herein lay the appeal of the Russian revolution for many colonial intellectuals. The Bolsheviks' civilizing mission, their promise of spreading enlightenment and progress to the colonial world, added to the appeal, which in some way or form survived until the end of the Soviet period. Unlike later Third World socialisms, however, Jadidism existed in the Soviet state and was subject to its policies. It had much less room for ideological heterodoxy. The Jadids' propensity to see the revolution through the prism of anticolonial national liberation got them into trouble as the party became less and less interested in polyvalent readings of its goals. And yet the Central Asian 1920s cannot be explained without acknowledging the fascination that the idea of revolution as a modality of change held for Muslim intellectuals. Nation, revolution, and anticolonialism fit perfectly together with a program for cultural transformation in the quest for modernity and progress.

The Fate of the Cultural Revolution

That era of revolutionary enthusiasms is very distant today. The cultural ferment of the 1920s had already been domesticated by 1938. Over the ensuing decades, many of its key features were reversed and even the memory of it largely disappeared. With a few notable exceptions (such as the novels of Abdulla Qodiriy), the literature of the 1920s was seldom republished, the theater forgotten. The Latin alphabet was replaced in 1940 by the Cyrillic. Unlike Latinization, which was based on enthusiasm for cultural transformation and widely debated, the switch to Cyrillic was decreed from on high and implemented without any debate. New histories of the region narrated a triumphant march of Soviet power in which the Russian proletariat shepherded all the fraternal peoples of the USSR to socialism. The bloody conflict between Russian settlers and natives had no place in this narrative, nor did the anticolonial passions of prerevolutionary intelligentsia. The cultural features that began to emerge in the 1930s conformed to demands of form and content dictated by cultural bureaucrats from Moscow. The models were all Soviet—and more concretely Russian—and access to modernity and world civilization possible only through Russian. Cotton never went away, moreover, and Uzbekistan and Tajikistan retained very high rates of rural population. Dual society survived in Soviet conditions, with Europeans dominating the technical sector and urban spaces. Nevertheless, the Soviet goal of universal public education came true and eventually produced almost universal literacy. The Second World War finally integrated Central Asia into the Soviet state, as Central Asian men fought in the war as conscript citizens. In the decades that followed, common practices and rituals of citizenship made Central Asians fully Soviet.

It was in these conditions that Uzbek culture—in its expressive forms, but also as customs and practices—developed in the twentieth century. Like all cultures, it was deeply affected by the socioeconomic and political conditions in which it took shape. All cultures are shaped by a host of forces—state policies, markets, intelligentsia projects, dissent, contestation—and they are never stable. All have been transformed by forces of modernity. The Soviet case had its peculiarities, such as the absence of a market and the preponderant presence of a state invested in cultivating ethnonational identities of its citizens, albeit on its own terms. Uzbek culture was all flux in the period studied here, contested from within and shaped and reshaped from without. Authenticity was simply out of the question.

Nevertheless, there remains a suspicion among many writers that Soviet trans-formations were somehow alien and inauthentic, that a "real" Uzbek (or Central Asian) culture exists somewhere in occultation. Both in the Soviet period and after, many national intellectuals were deeply concerned with the idea of authen-ticity. Historians of Central Asia need to see this search for authenticity as an object of study, rather than something to be taken for granted.

Uzbeks and Tajiks in the Twenty-First Century

The most enduring legacy of Jadidism, however, is the idea of the nation. As I have shown in this book, the nation was a central passion of the Central Asian Muslim intelligentsia in the early twentieth century. The Soviets, we have now come to recognize, were nation builders in their own way. The Jadids' national project—that of creating an Uzbek nation in a Chaghatayist key—succeeded in Soviet conditions. Refracted through the Soviet prism, it is very much alive today in independent Uzbekistan.

Yet the triumph of the Chaghatayist project was only partial. That project foresaw the assimilation of the Persian-speaking population into Uzbekness. However, as we saw, many Persian speakers defected from the Chaghatayist proj-ect and articulated an increasingly insistent Tajik counternarrative. The sepa-ration of Tajikistan from Uzbekistan and its elevation to the level of a union republic in 1929 had sanctified the notion of the Uzbeks and Tajiks as two com-pletely different nations. That notion was to acquire the status of incontrovertible truth over the decades that followed. The shifts in Soviet nationality policy in the mid-1930s mandated that each Soviet nation have a great past that could be celebrated with pride. The 1940s also saw the emergence of the concept of eth-nogenesis, which held that each nation had its own unique ethnic makeup that had crystallized over history. This deeply primordialist understanding of nation-hood came to underpin Soviet thinking both in the academic and policy realms. Moreover, each nation was tied to the territory on which its republic existed and that connection was pushed back into antiquity.[1] In Central Asia, imagining national histories based on the notion of ethnogenesis meant the division of the region's heritage into distinct national segments with current national and ter-ritorial arrangements projected into the ever more distant past. Thus Uzbekistan claimed the medieval Arabic-writing savants Avicenna and Abu Rayhan Beruni,

---

1. Marlène Laruelle, "The Concept of Ethnogenesis in Central Asia: Political Context and Insti-tutional Mediators (1940–50)," *Kritika* 9 (2008): 169–188.

while Kazakhstan acquired the rights to al-Farabi. All of this coexisted with other features of nationality policy as it evolved in the 1930s—that the nations of the USSR were knit together by a great friendship, that the Russians were the elder brothers to all Soviet nations, and that Russian conquest had been beneficial to its victims. This meant that the colonial past could not be invoked and grievances against the Russians had to be kept under wraps. The distant past, however, had few strictures, and it became fertile ground for national imaginings. The post-Stalin era, when increasingly self-confident indigenous political elites emerged in all the national republics, was the golden age of the articulation of national narratives, as historians and ethnographers working in national Academies of Sciences produced a vast corpus of national histories, while novelists and poets created glorious narratives that nationalized the past.

The Tajik national narrative was elaborated by Bobojon Ghafurov (1909–77), a historian and Orientalist trained in Moscow who also served as the first secretary of the Communist Party of Tajikistan before becoming the head of the Institute of Oriental Studies in Moscow in 1956. In a number of works, he created a narrative of Tajikness that encompassed the entire history of Central Asia from the emergence of "tribal society" (in the Marxist understanding of the term) on. For Ghafurov, the "process of the formation of the Tajik people" was completed in the ninth and tenth centuries with the achievement of national statehood under the Samanids.[2] The Uzbek case was a little more difficult. Temur remained unredeemable for the "feudal" character of his rule and "the unusual violence of his conquests," but other figures, including the Timurid princes Ulugh Bek and Bobur, became part of the Uzbek cultural pantheon. The Uzbek nation laid claim to the entire Turkic-language cultural heritage of Transoxiana. The canons of Uzbek literature and music from the later Soviet period were little different from what Fitrat had outlined in the 1920s, although his name could not be invoked.[3]

Thus it was that Central Asia came to independence in 1991. Despite highly developed national identities, there was little support for national independence and secession from the Soviet Union. As late as March 1991, Central Asians voted overwhelmingly to remain in the union. Once, however, events forced the issue, the republics of Central Asia all declared themselves independent. Their

---

2. The final form of Ghafurov's synthesis was presented in B. G. Gafurov, *Tadzhiki: drevneishaia, drevniaia i srednevekovaia istoriia* (Moscow, 1972); the book is now available in English as Bobojon Ghafurov, *Tajiks: Pre-Ancient, Ancient and Medieval History*, trans. P. Jamshedov, 2 vols. in one (Dushanbe, 2011).

3. For the canonization of the Uzbek literary heritage, see any history or anthology of Uzbek literature from the post-Stalin era. For the conceptualization of Uzbek musical heritage in the Soviet period, see Alexander Djumaev, "Musical Heritage and National Identity in Uzbekistan," *Ethnomusicology Forum* 14 (2005): 175.

leaders effortlessly reinvented themselves as national leaders. The crystallization of national identities in the Soviet period had made that all too easy. Now, however, national identities could be celebrated without the constraints of the Soviet era. Temur made a spectacular comeback after Uzbekistan's independence, as his statue replaced that of Karl Marx in Tashkent's central square, and his name became ubiquitous in public discourse. The Tajik state found its bearing in the deep Persianate history of the region. It renamed the province of Leninobod (Khujand) as Sughd (Sogdia) to evoke the Achaemenid Empire and thus stress the Tajik claim to antiquity and called its currency Somoni. The history of the region is, however, much too complex to yield to neat compartmentalization between Uzbek and Tajik. Rival claims to the past have clashed and given rise to disputes between Uzbek and Tajik historians, which, liberated from Soviet constraints, have taken ever harsher forms. Since many of these disputes now take place on the Internet, they are subject to neither political, nor normal academic etiquette (even if combatants are academics), and lead to an inflation of claims. The two sides engage in a race to the deepest points of antiquity, the Tajiks now claiming a lineage of eight thousand years of "Aryan civilization," and Uzbek writers responding with claims that the ancient Aryans were in fact Turkic speakers and thus the progenitors of the Uzbeks. Tajik writers carry a sense of grievance and are more concerned with denouncing and distancing themselves from Uzbeks and what they call "pan-Turkic imperialism."[4]

These controversies are not just games intellectuals play. Ordinary citizens in Central Asia do look at themselves and their neighbors through the prism of these national narratives. The idea that nations are organic communities and that everyone belongs to one is a fundamental building block in the worldviews of most Central Asians, whether Uzbek or Tajiks or Kazakhs or Kyrgyz. This is clearly a legacy of Soviet nationalities policies and the practices they underwrote.[5] Nevertheless, the content of many of these national imaginaries goes back to the Jadids. Especially in Uzbekistan, the national imaginary bears the seeds both of the Soviet order and of early twentieth-century Muslim discourses.

---

4. For a taste of these debates, see Slavomír Horák, "In Search of the History of Tajikistan: What Are Tajik and Uzbek Historians Arguing About?" *Russian Politics and Law* 48:5 (2010): 65–77. The debates generally take place in Russian on Internet sites such as Fergana.ru and Centrasia.ru. This competition over the past flows logically from the premises of Soviet nationalities policy and is to be found elsewhere in former Soviet space; see Victor A. Shnirelman, *Who Gets the Past? Competition for Ancestors among Non-Russian Intellectuals in Russia* (Washington, DC, 1996).

5. I have traced many of these processes in greater detail in *Islam after Communism: Religion and Politics in Central Asia* (Berkeley, 2007).

Glossary

aktiv core group of activists in an organization

AO Autonomous Oblast

ASSR Autonomous Soviet Socialist Republic

bai lit., wealthy (Uzb., *boy*); often used as equivalent of *bourgeois* in Soviet discourse on Central Asia

Bilim Yurti lit., "house of learning"; institutions of secondary education that also functioned as teacher training institutes

BKP Bukharan Communist Party

BNSR Bukharan People's Soviet Republic (1920–24)

Cheka Extraordinary Commission for Struggle with Counterrevolution; the first Soviet political police; succeeded by the GPU (q.v.)

eshon Sufi master

GPU State Political Administration; title borne by the Soviet political police between February 1922 and November 1923; succeeded by OGPU (q.v.)

ispolkom lit., executive committee; the executive organ of power at each level of Soviet government

kolonizatorstvo lit., "settlerism," the term was used in early Soviet times to denote the violent excesses of Russian settlers in Central Asia; colonialism

korenizatsiia indigenization, an official policy, launched in 1923, of basing Soviet power in the non-Russian parts of the Soviet state in local populations

KPT Communist Party of Turkestan

KPUz Communist Party of Uzbekistan

madaniyatchi "cultural worker," self-designation used by the first generation of radical Soviet Uzbek intellectuals

madrasa place of higher education in the Islamicate tradition

mahalla neighborhood

mazor shrine, usually built around the grave of a sacred figure

mudarris instructor in a madrasa

Musburo Bureau of Muslim Communist Organizations of KPT, 1919–20

mutavalli trustee and caretaker of a waqf (q.v.) property

Narkomnats Commissariat of Nationalities Affairs (in Moscow)

Narkompros Commissariat of Education

NKVD People's Commissariat of Internal Affairs, the successor to the OGPU (q.v.) from 1934

obkom oblast committee of the party

oblast administrative unit below the republic level

OGPU United State Political Administration, title borne by the Soviet political police between 1923 and 1934, when its functions were given over to the NKVD (q.v.)

qazi judge

qo'rboshi commander; titled used by leaders of armed bands during the Basmachi insurgency

rabfaks "workers' faculties," institutions meant to provide workers with preparatory instruction for higher education

revkom revolutionary committee, temporary organ of power established when a territory first came under Soviet rule; replaced by an elected ispolkom (q.v.)

RKP(b) Russian Communist Party (Bolsheviks), the official name of the Party from 1918 to 1925

Sovnarkom Council of People's Commissars; the main administrative authority at the republic and All-Union levels, equivalent of a cabinet

Sredazburo The Central Asia Bureau of the Central Committee of the Russian Communist Party, 1922–34; succeeded the Turkburo as the plenipotentiary organ of central power in Central Asia

Turkburo The Turkestan Bureau of the Central Committee of the Russian Communist Party, 1920–22; succeeded the Turkkomissiia as the plenipotentiary organ of central power in Central Asia

Turkkomissiia Turkestan Commission of the Central Committee of the Russian Communist Party, operated in 1919–20 as the plenipotentiary organ of central power in Turkestan

Turkomnats Turkestan's Commissariat of Nationalities Affairs

Turkompros Turkestan's Commissariat of Education

TurTsIK Central Executive Committee of Turkestan, the executive organ of power in Turkestan

ulama lit., "the learned"; scholars of Islam

waqf property endowed for specific purposes, usually pious

Zhenotdel women's section of the party

zikr ritual act of remembrance of God practiced by Sufis

ziyoli lit., "enlightened"; intellectual

Bibliography of Primary Sources

ARCHIVAL SOURCES

Archive Mustafa Chokai Bey. Institut des Langues et Civilisations Orientales, Paris

Arkhiv Apparata Prezidenta Respubliki Uzbekistan, Tashkent

    f. 58   Tsentral'nyi komitet KPUz

    f. 60   Tsentral'nyi komitet KPT

Gosudarstvennyi Arkhiv goroda Tashkent, Tashkent

    f. 12   Staro-Tashkentskii sovet rabochikh, dekhkanskikh i krasnoarmeiskikh deputatov

Gosudarstvennyi Arkhiv Rossiiskoi Federatsii, Moscow

    f. 130   Sovet narodnykh komissarov RSFSR

    f. 1235   VTsIK RSFSR

    f. 1318   Narkomnats RSFSR

    f. 3316   VTsIK SSSR

    f. 6987   Komissiia VTsIK po uregulirovaniiu sporov mezhdu Turkestanskoi i Kirgizskoi respublikami

Gosudarstvennyi Arkhiv Samarkandskoi Oblasti, Samarqand

    f. 65   Ispolkom ukoma soveta deputatov

    f. 89   Ispolkom musul'manskogo soveta raboche-dekhkanskikh deputatov

India Office Records, British Library, London

    L/P&S   Political and Secret Separate Files

National Archives (UK), Kew, London

    FO   Foreign Office series

    WO   War Office series

Rossiiskii Gosudarstvennyi Arkhiv Sotsial'no-Politisheskoi Istorii, Moscow

    f. 5   Kabinet V. I. Lenina

    f. 17   Tsentral'nyi komitet RKP(b)

    f. 61   Turkbiuro TsK RKP(b)

    f. 62   Sredazbiuro TsK RKP(b)

    f. 85   Lichnyi fond S. Ordzhonikidze

    f. 121   Upolnomochennyi TsKK VKP(b) v Srednei Azii

f. 122   Turkkomissiia TsK RKP(b) i VTsIK RSFSR
f. 544   Prevyi S″ezd Narodov Vostoka
f. 558   Lichnyi fond I. V. Stalina
f. 583   Tsentral'noe Biuro agitatsii i propagandy sredi tiurkskikh narodov pri
            TsK RKP(b)

Tsentral'nyi Gosudarstvennyi Arkhiv Respubliki Uzbekistan, Tashkent

f. 17   Turkestanskii tsentral'nyi ispolnitel'nyi komitet (TurTsIK)
f. 21   Tsentral'noe statisticheskoe upravlenie Turkestanskoi ASSR
f. 25   Sovet narodnykh komissarov Turkestanskoi ASSR
f. 34   Narodnyi komissariat prosveshcheniia Turkestanskoi ASSR
f. 35   Narodnyi komissariat truda Turkestanskoi ASSR
f. 36   Narodnyi komissariat po delam natsional'nostei Turkestanskoi ASSR
f. 38   Narodnyi komissariat iustitsii Turkestanskoi ASSR
f. 39   Narodnyi komissariat vnutrennykh del Turkestanskoi ASSR
f. 46   Revkom BNSR
f. 47   Tsentral'nyi ispolnitel'nyi komitet BNSR
f. 48   Sovet narodnykh nazirov BNSR
f. 56   Narodnyi komissariat prosveshcheniia BNSR
f. 57   Tsentral'noe vakufnoe upravlenie BNSR
f. 94   Narodnyi komissariat prosveshcheniia Uzbekskoi SSR
f. 904   Narodnyi komissariat iustitsii Uzbekskoi SSR
f. I-47   Upravlenie uchebnykh zavedenii Turkestanskogo kraia
f. I-461   Turkestanskoe raionnoe okhrannoe otdelenie
f. I-1044   Turkestanskii Komitet Vremennogo Pravitel'stva

PUBLISHED COLLECTIONS OF ARCHIVAL DOCUMENTS

Bol'shevistskoe rukovodstvo. Perepiska, 1912–1927. Moscow, 1996.
Ekonomicheskie otnosheniia sovetskoi Rossii s budushchimi soiuznymi respublikami, 1917–1922: dokumenty i materialy. Moscow, 1996.
Pobeda Oktiabr'skoi revoliutsii v Uzbekistane: sbornik dokumentov. 2 vols. Tashkent, 1963–72.
Rossiia i Tsentral'naia Aziia, 1905–1925 gg.: sbornik dokumentov. Edited by D. A. Amanzholova. Qaraghandï, 2005.
"Sovershenno sekretno": Lubianka–Stalinu o polozhenii v strane (1922–1934gg.). 8 vols. in 13. Moscow, 2001–8.
Tainy natsional'noi politiki TsK RKP: Chetvertoe soveshchanie TsK RKP s otvetstvennymi rabotnikami natsional'nykh respublik i oblastei v Moskve 9–12 iiunia 1923 g. (stenograficheskii otchet). Edited by B. F. Sultanbekov. Moscow, 1992.
TsK RKP(b)—VKP(b) i natsional'nyi vopros. Vol. 1. Edited by L. S. Gatagova, L. P. Kosheleva, and L. A. Rogovaia. Moscow, 2005.

PERIODICALS

Alanga. Tashkent, 1928–30.

Bilim o'chog'i. Tashkent, 1922–23.

Bukhārā-yi sharīf. New Bukhara, 1912–13.

Buxoro axbori. Bukhara, 1920–23.

Haqiqat. Tashkent, 1922.

Hurriyat. Samarqand, 1917–18.

Inqilob. Tashkent, 1922–24.

Ishchilar dunyosi. Tashkent, 1918.

Ishtirokiyun. Tashkent, 1918–20.

al-Isloh. Tashkent, 1915–17.

al-Izoh. Tashkent, 1917–18.

Kambag'allar tovushi. Samarqand, 1922.

Kengash. Tashkent, 1917.

Kommunist. Tashkent, 1925–31.

Krasnyi rubezh. Tashkent, 1925.

Mahnatkashlar tovushi. Samarqand, 1919–21.

Maorif va o'qitg'uvchi. Tashkent. 1925–31.

Mashrab. Samarqand, 1924–27.

Mushtum. Tashkent, 1923–29.

Muxbirlar yo'ldoshi. Samarqand, 1929–30.

Najot. Tashkent, 1917.

Nasha gazeta. Tashkent, 1917–18.

Oyina. Samarqand, 1913–15.

Ozod Buxoro. Bukhara, 1923–24.

Pravda Vostoka. Tashkent. 1925–32.

Qizil bayroq. Tashkent, 1920–22.

Qizil O'zbekiston. Tashkent, 1924–32.

Qizil qalam majmuasi. Tashkent, 1928–29.

Rahbar-i dānish. Samarqand, 1927–30.

Sadoi Farg'ona. Kokand, 1914–15.

Sadoi Turkiston. Tashkent, 1914–15.

Shu'la-yi inqilāb. Samarqand, 1919–21.

Taraqqiy—O'rta Azyaning umr guzorlig'i. Tashkent, 1906.

Tirik so'z. Kokand, 1917.

To'jjor. Tashkent. 1906.

Tong. Tashkent, 1920.

Tong yulduzi. Tashkent, 1925.

Turk eli. Tashkent, 1917.

Turkiston. Tashkent, 1922–24.

Turkiston viloyatining gazeti. Tashkent, 1910–17.

Turk so'zi. Tashkent, 1918.

Turon. Bukhara, 1912–13.

Turon. Tashkent, 1917.

Uchqun. Bukhara, 1923.

Ulug' Turkiston. Tashkent, 1917–18.

Vaqït. Orenburg, 1917–18.

Xudosizlar. Tashkent, 1927–30.

Xurshid. Tashkent, 1906.

Yangi yo'l. Tashkent, 1927–30.

Yer yuzi. Tashkent. 1927–30.

Za Partiiu. Tashkent, 1926–29.

Zarafshon. Samarqand, 1922–23.

Zhizn' natsional'nostei. Moscow, 1918–24.

SIGNIFICANT BIBLIOGRAPHIC GUIDES

Milliy matbuot sahifalarida: "Qizil O'zbekistan" gazetasida bosilgan asosiy maqolalar bibliografiyasi (1921–1926). Tashkent, 1999.

Qoriyev, Bois. "Adabiy taxalluslar haqida." *O'zbek tili va adabiyoti,* 1967, no. 1: 51–58.

Sovet O'zbekistoni kitobi (1917–1927 yy.): bibliografik ko'rsatkich. Tashkent, 1976.

Turdiyev, Sh., and B. Qoriyev (Oltoy). *O'zbek adabiyotshunosligi va tanqidchiligi bibliografiyasi (1900–1941 yillar matbuoti asosida).* 2nd ed. Tashkent, 2010.

Index

Italic page numbers indicate photographs. **Bold** page numbers indicate maps.